Pensions Law Handbook

Seventh Edition

Pensions Law Handbook

Seventh Edition

by the Pensions Department of Nabarro Nathanson

Head of Department: Geoffrey Preston LLB

Joint Editors

Jennifer Bell BA (Hons)
Partner

and

Douglas Sleziak BA (Hons)
Senior Legal Manager

Tottel
publishing

Tottel Publishing Ltd, Maxwelton House, 41–43 Boltro Road, Haywards Heath, West Sussex, RH16 1BJ

© Tottel Publishing Ltd 2006

A CIP Catalogue record for this book is available from the British Library.

ISBN 13   978 1 84592 176 7

ISBN 10   1 84592 176 3

Typeset by Kerrypress Ltd, Luton, Beds

Printed and bound in Great Britain by Antony Rowe Ltd, Chippenham, Wiltshire

Preface

I am delighted to introduce this seventh edition of the highly regarded Pensions Law Handbook. The book has been written and revised entirely by practising pension lawyers who are members of the Pensions Department at Nabarro Nathanson. The detailed work of editing the book has been undertaken by Jennifer Bell and Douglas Sleziak, and we are very grateful to them for that.

Nabarro Nathanson is one of the largest independent law practices in the UK. Its Pensions Department has for many years been one of its strengths. Our pension lawyers, both in London and in Sheffield, have a deep technical knowledge of their subject and advise an impressive range of clients on the areas that the book covers.

I am sure that readers will find this new edition valuable. The fact that it is now in its seventh edition reflects its popularity. It also reflects the constantly changing legal and economic environment within which trustees of pension schemes, sponsoring employers and their advisers operate. For instance, since the last edition, the Pensions Act 2004 has come into force, with more than 100 accompanying sets of regulations and codes of practice. The tax simplification sections of the Finance Act 2004 have also been brought in, replacing entirely the previous tax treatment of pension schemes which had developed, year by year, over decades. All of us in the Pensions Department have contributed to the book. My thanks to them all. The contributors are (in alphabetical order): Jennifer Bell, Alison Birkitt, Helen Butler, Amanda Day, Mike Draper, Lynne Flannaghan, Philip Goss, Alastair Govier, Ian Greenstreet, Dominic Harris, Sue Jones, Victoria Lee, John Murray, Geoffrey Preston, Kate Richards, Douglas Sleziak, Michal Stein, Mark Wellard, Janis Westley and Catrin Williams.

Our aim has been to state the law as at the end of November 2005, although we have tried to take into account later developments where we have been able to do so. I am confident that this new edition will be as useful to those working in the field of pensions law as the previous editions have been.

Geoffrey Preston
Head of Pensions Department
Nabarro Nathanson

Contents

Contents

Table of Cases

xiii

Table of Statutes

Table of Statutory Instruments

Table of European Legislation

Abbreviations and References

ABBREVIATIONS

APPS= Appropriate Personal Pension Scheme

APT= Association of Pensioneer Trustees

AVC= Additional Voluntary Contribution

Business Order = Financial Services and Markets Act 2000 (Carrying on Regulated Activities by way of Business) Order 2001 (SI 2001 No 1177)

CETV= Cost Equivalent Transfer Value

COMBS= Contracted-out mixed benefit scheme

Compensation Regulations = Pensions Compensation Board (Determinations and Review Procedure) Regulations 1997 (SI 1997 No 724)

Contracting-Out Regulations = Occupational Pension Schemes (Contracting-out) Regulations 1996 (SI 1996 No 1172)

CPR= Civil Procedure Rules

DSS= Department of Social Security

Deficiency Regulations = Occupational Pension Schemes (Deficiency on Winding up etc) Regulations 1996 (SI 1996 No 3128)

Disclosure Regulations= Occupational Pension Schemes (Disclosure of Information) Regulations 1996 (SI 1996 No 1655)

Dispute Regulations= Occupational Pension Schemes (Internal Dispute Regulation Procedures) Regulations 1996 (SI 1996 No 1270)

Divorce Regulations= Divorce etc (Pensions) Regulations 1996 (SI 1996 No 1676)

DWP= Department for Work and Pensions

EC= European Community

ECJ= Court of Justice of the European Communities

ECON= Employers Contracting-out Number

Equal Treatments Regulations= Occupational Pension Schemes (Equal Treatment) Regulations 1995 (SI 1995 no 3183)

ERA 1996= Employment Rights Acts 1996

Forfeiture Regulations= Occupational Pension Schemes (Assignment, Forfeiture, Bankruptcy etc) Regulations 1997 (SI 1997 No 785)

FSA= Financial Services Authority

FSAVC= Free Standing Additional Voluntary Contributions Scheme

FSMA 2000= Financial Services and Markets Act 2000

FURBS= Funded unapproved retirement benefits scheme

GMP= Guaranteed minimum pension

Goode Committee= The Pension Law Review Committee, chaired by Professor Goode, whose report was issued in September 1993 (CM 2342)

ICTA 1988= Income and Corporation Taxes Act 1988

DRP= Internal dispute resolution procedure

IFMA= Institutional Fund Managers Association

IMRO= Investment Management Regulatory Organisation

Independent Trustee Regulations= Occupational Pension Schemes (Independent Trustee) Regulations 1997 (SI 1997 No 252)

Investment Regulations= Occupational Pension Schemes (Investment Regulations 1996 SI 1996 No 3127)

IR SPSS= Inland Revenue Savings, Pension, Share Schemes Office

LEL= Lower Earnings Limit

LET= Low Earnings Threshold

LIBA= London Investment Bank Association

LPI= Limited price indexation

MCA= Matrimonial Causes Act 1973

MFR= Minimum funding requirement

MFR Regulations= Occupational Pension Schemes (minimum funding requirement and actuarial valuations) Regulations 1996 (SO 1996 No 1536)

MND's= Member-nominated director

MNT Regulations= Occupational Pension Schemes (Member-nominated Trustees and Directors) Regulations 1996 (SI 1996 No 1216)

MNT's= Member-nominated Trustees

Modification Regulations= Occupational Pension Schemes (Modification of Schemes) Regulations 1996 (SI 1996 No 2517)

NAPF= National Association of Pension Funds

NICO= National Insurance Contributions Office

NISPI= National Insurance Services to Pensions Industry

OEIC= Open-ended investment company

Ombudsman Regulations= Personal and Occupational Pension Schemes (Pension Ombudsman) Regulations 1996 (SI 1996 No 2475)

OPAS= Occupational Pensions Advisory Service

OPB= Occupational Pensions Board

Opra= Occupational Pensions Regulatory Authority

PA 1995= The Pensions Act 1995

PCB= Pensions Compensation Board

PMI= Pensions Management Institute

PPRP= Personal Pension Protected Rights Premium

PPSGN= Personal Pension Schemes Guidance Notes

Preservation Regulations= Occupational Pension Schemes (Preservation of Benefit) Regulations 1991 (SI 1991 No 167)

Protected Rights Regulations= Personal and Occupational Pension Schemes (Protected Rights) Regulations 1996 (SI 1996 No 1537)

PSA 1993= The Pensions Act 1993

PSO= Pensions Schemes Office of the Inland Revenue

QEF= Qualifying earnings factor

Registrar= Registrar of Occupational and Personal Pension Schemes

Regulated Activities Order = Financial Services and Markets Act 2000 (Regulated Activities) Order 2001 (SI 2001 No 544)

S2P= State Second Pension

Scheme Administration Regulations= Occupational Pension Schemes (Scheme Administration) Regulations (SI 1996 No 1715)

SCON= Scheme contracting-out number

SERPS= State Earnings-Related Pension Schemes

SIPP= Self-invested personal pension scheme

SMP= Statutory maternity pay

SSAS Regulations= Retirement Benefits Schemes (Restriction on Discretion to Approve) (Small Self Administered Schemes) Regulations 1991 (SI 1991 No 1614)

SSAS's= Small self-administered scheme

Surplus Regulations= Pension Scheme Surpluses (Valuation) Regulations 1987 (SI 1987 No 412)

TA 1925 = Trustee Act 1925

TCGA 1992= Taxation of Chargeable Gains Act 1992

TEP= Traded Endowment Policy

Transfer Regulations= Occupational Pension Schemes (Transfer Values) Regulations 1996 (SI 1996 No 1847)

TUPE= Transfer of Undertakings Protection of Employment Regulations 1981 (SI 1981 No 1794)

UCTA= Unfair Contract and Terms Act 1977

UURBS= Unfunded unapproved retirement benefits scheme

Voluntary Contributions Regulations= Pension Schemes (Voluntary Contributions Requirements and Voluntary and Compulsory Membership) Regulations 1987 (SI 1987 No 1108

Winding-up Regulations= Occupational Pension Schemes (Winding up) Regulations 1996 (SI 1996 No 3126)

WRPA= Welfare Reform and Pensions Act 1999

CASE REFERENCES

AC= Appeal Cases (Law Reports)

A11 ER= All England Law Reports

Ch= Chancery (Law Reports)

E & E= Ellis & Ellis Queen's Bench Report

ECR= European Court Reports

IRLR= Industrial Relations Law Reports
KB= King's Bench (Law Reports)
OPLR= Occupational Pensions Law Reports
PBLR= Pension Benefits Law Reports
PLR= Pensions Law Reports
TC= Tax Cases
TLR= Times Law Reports
WLR= Weekly Law Reports

Chapter 1

Pension provision in the UK – an introduction

Introduction

1.1   The word 'pension' is defined in the Oxford English Dictionary as 'an annuity or other periodical payment made, especially by a government, a company or an employer of labour in consideration of past services or of relinquishment of rights, claims or emoluments'.

A pension scheme is therefore a systematic arrangement for meeting these regular payments. As the definition suggests, pension schemes may be either State schemes or private arrangements. Where a scheme is established by the Government, it will often be a 'pay as you go' arrangement with no advance provision being made for funding of benefits. Private pension arrangements, whether established by an employer or by an individual, will usually be funded; contributions will be made by the individual and/or his employer during his working life to ensure that, when the individual retires, sufficient money is available to provide his pension and any other benefits which are payable.

Private pension arrangements are governed by a mixture of trust, employment, fiscal, social security and family law, which together provide the framework within which such schemes must operate. Pension provision for the public sector tends to be governed more rigidly by legislation. Many public sector schemes, including the Local Government Pension Scheme and the National Health Service scheme, are governed and administered almost exclusively by statutory instruments and are, to a degree, unaffected by other legislation. Such schemes are generally outside the scope of this book. The law relating to personal pension schemes and stakeholder pensions schemes is discussed in chapter 14.

A brief history of pension provision in the UK

1.2   The first arrangement to contain features which are recognisable in modern pension schemes was established in 1671 by HM Customs and Excise.

Originally the arrangement provided for a retiring employee to be paid a pension by his successor, but by 1686 employees were required to make advance provision for their own retirement by paying contributions towards a retirement fund.

Pension protection was gradually extended to a broader range of civil servants but it was not until the *Civil Service Superannuation Act 1834* (the first enactment devoted solely to pensions) that any formal legislative framework was established. During the early nineteenth century the concept of pension provision was extended so that other employees, both in the public and private sectors, became eligible for membership of pension schemes. Insurance and life assurance schemes became available and actuarial methods for assessing risk gradually developed.

The beginning of the twentieth century saw the introduction of the first State scheme. In 1908 the *Old Age Pension Act* was passed which gave those over 70 a non-contributory, but means tested, pension. General taxation paid for this early State scheme although that was changed following the passing of the *National Insurance Act 1911*. At the same time, there was a continuing increase in the establishment of pension funds by large private sector employers.

The growth in pension provision prompted pressure for change in the tax treatment of pension funds and in 1920 the Royal Commission on Income Tax recommended that investment income earned by pension funds should be tax-free. The *Finance Act 1921* provided a statutory right to tax relief on contributions made to pension funds by employers and employees and on the investment income of HMRC 'approved' pension funds. To gain HMRC approval, assets constituting pension funds had to be kept separate from an employer's other assets and consequently trust funds emerged as a natural vehicle for obtaining tax approved status.

The *Finance Act 1970* established a new system of approval for occupational pension schemes. Although the legislation has been consolidated and amended in the *Income and Corporation Taxes Act 1988*, the basic underlying taxation principles for UK occupational schemes remain the same today (although see 1.3 below in relation to forthcoming changes).

In addition to tax legislation, various pieces of social security legislation affecting pension schemes were passed during the 1970s which impacted on pension schemes, including the *Social Security Act 1973* which introduced provisions to protect early leavers and the *Social Security Pensions Act 1975*. The 1980s saw the introduction of further legislation; the *Social Security Acts 1985* and *1986* extended the protection offered to early leavers and, in particular, gave them the right to transfer their benefits to another pension scheme. The various Acts passed in the 1970s and 1980s, together with the relevant provisions of the *Social Security Act 1990*, are now consolidated in the *Pension Schemes Act 1993* (*PSA 1993*).

A major review of pensions provision in the UK was undertaken by the Pension Law Review Committee chaired by Professor Roy Goode following what has become known as 'the Maxwell scandal'. In their report, 'Pension Law Reform' (Cm 2342–1, September 1993), the Committee made many recommendations as to how the legislative framework for pension provision could be amended to provide greater protection for employees. Many of their recommendations were adopted in the *Pensions Act 1995* (*PA 1995*) which came into force on 6 April 1997. Two further significant Acts were passed by 2000, namely the *Welfare Reform and Pensions Act 1999* (*WRPA 1999*) and the *Child Support, Pensions and Social Security Act 2000*. The most notable changes introduced by these Acts were the introduction of new pension sharing on divorce provisions, the stakeholder pension requirements and the State Second Pension.

Pensions Act 2004 and Finance Act 2004

1.3   More recently, a number of consultations and reviews have been undertaken which have led to two new Acts – the *Finance Act 2004* and the *Pensions Act 2004*.

(*a*)   *The Finance Act 2004* (*FA 2004*)

The pensions tax simplification regime introduced by *FA 2004* follows, broadly, the proposals outlined in a consultation paper published in October 2002, 'Simplifying the taxation of pensions; increasing chance and flexibility for all'. From implementation on 6 April 2006 (known as 'A-Day'), the existing eight taxation regimes are replaced by a single set of rules, applicable to all 'registered schemes' (the equivalent of tax approved pension schemes under the previous regime), including defined benefit and defined contribution occupational pension schemes and personal pension schemes. The main features include:

- Removal of the pre-existing HMRC limits (including the earnings cap).

- The introduction of a single lifetime limit on the amount of pension saving that attracts favourable tax treatment (known as the 'lifetime allowance'). For the tax year 2006/2007 this will be set at £1.5 million per individual and will increase during the four tax years subsequently as follows:

  2007/2008 – £1.6 million

  2008/2009 – £1.65 million

  2009/2010 – £1.75 million

  2010/2011 – £1.8 million

The lifetime allowance will be reviewed quinquennially.

- The introduction of an annual limit on all inflows of value to an individual's pension fund (both in the form of contributions and growth) (known as the 'annual allowance') set at £215,000 for the tax year 2006/2007 and rising to £255,000 by the tax year 2010/2011.

- Subject to scheme rules, allowing members to draw pension benefits whilst continuing to work.

- The minimum age for taking early retirement benefits to be raised from 50 to 55 by 2010.

- The removal of the tax advantages for unapproved pension schemes.

- Increased flexibility in relation to the treatment of death benefits.

Transitional provisions give a level of protection to those who currently have rights which are inconsistent with the new regime. *FA 2004* is considered further in chapter 5.

(b)   *The Pensions Act 2004 (PA 2004)*

Key provisions of *PA 2004* (which is being introduced in stages) include:

From April 2005:

- The introduction of a new pensions regulator ('the Regulator') replacing OPRA, whose main objectives are to protect the benefits of members of occupational and personal pension schemes, to reduce the risk of situations arising which may lead to compensation being payable by the Pension Protection Fund (see below) and to promote and improve understanding of the good administration of occupational schemes. New powers to assist the Regulator in achieving those objectives include the power to issue contribution notices and financial support directions against employers and persons associated and connected with the employer; extended information gathering powers and extended whistleblowing requirements.

- The introduction of the Pension Protection Fund ('PPF') giving members of defined benefit schemes a measure of protection where their employers are in financial difficulty. The PPF will assume responsibility for eligible schemes where a relevant insolvency event has occurred in relation to the employer (or where the employer is unlikely to be able to continue as a going concern), the scheme is unable to secure its 'protected liabilities' and there is no possibility of a scheme rescue. Defined contribution schemes are not eligible to participate. Relevant insolvency events include entering administration and passing a resolution for voluntary winding up without a declaration of solvency.

For the first year of operation (April 2005 to March 2006) defined benefit schemes are required to pay an initial scheme-based levy. This is calculated on the basis of scheme membership and is not affected by the funding position of the scheme in question. In future years the PPF Board will introduce a risk-based levy whereby schemes with poor funding positions are likely to be required to pay more. [See chapter 12].

- A new statutory priority order is introduced for schemes that commenced winding up on or after 6 April 2005. The new priority order aligns the statutory winding-up priorities with the PPF provisions, the purpose being to afford those benefits which are guaranteed by the PPF priority over other benefits. [See chapter 12].

- The introduction of increased protection of pensions rights on business transfers. Where before the transfer, an employee is a member of an occupational pension scheme to which the employer contributes, or is entitled to be a member, or would be entitled to be a member if he had been employed for longer, the purchaser must ensure that after the transfer the employee becomes eligible to be a member of an occupational or stakeholder pension scheme. Where the previous scheme was money purchase, then the purchaser will have to match the employees' contributions up to 6 per cent of pensionable salary and where the previous scheme was final salary the new scheme must at least satisfy the current reference scheme test (or such other requirements as may be included in Regulations). Alternatively the employer may offer membership of a stakeholder scheme to which it must match employee contributions up to 6 per cent. [See chapter 15].

- The LPI requirement contained in *section 51 of PA 1995* for statutory increases to pensions in payment is, in relation to defined benefits, reduced from RPI capped at 5 per cent to RPI capped at 2.5 per cent. This applies to benefits accrued after 6 April 2005. In relation to defined contribution benefits, the requirement is removed altogether for any pension which comes into payment on or after 6 April 2005. This extends to pension attributable to contributions paid between 6 April 1997 and 5 April 2005 as well as contributions payable on or after 6 April 2005. [See 1.47 below].

From December 2005:

- Replacing the statutory minimum funding requirement with a new scheme-specific standard. [See chapter 11].

From April 2006:

- A requirement for all trustees to be conversant with their scheme documentation and to have an increased knowledge and understanding of pensions and trust law and of the principles underpinning investment and funding. [See chapter 3].

- A reduction in the level of prescription on selection processes for member-nominated trustees, but including a strict requirement for one third of the trustees to be member-nominated as the employer's ability to opt out is removed. There is also provision giving the Secretary of State the power to substitute the one-third member-nominated trustee require- ment with the requirement for at least half of the trustee board to be member-nominated trustees. [See chapter 3].

- *Section 67 of PA 1995* is amended in respect of the modification of occupational pension scheme rights, giving schemes greater freedom to amend their rules in order to adapt to changing circumstances an reduce administrative costs and complexity. [See chapter 12].

- Protection for early leavers with between three months and two years' pensionable service who will have the right to opt for either a cash transfer sum (cash equivalent) or a contribution refund. [See chapter 6].

- A requirement for employers to consult employees and/or their repre- sentatives before making certain prescribed changes to pension arrange- ments, including, for example, closing a scheme to future accrual, changing from a defined benefit scheme to a defined contribution scheme and reducing or removing the requirement for an employer to contribute to a defined contribution scheme. [See chapter 7].

Retirement provision by the State

Types of State pension

1.4   The provision of retirement pensions by the State is governed by the *Social Security Contributions and Benefits Act 1992* and the *Social Security Administration Act 1992*, as amended by *PSA 1993* and *PA 1995*. There are four categories of State retirement pensions, Category A, Category B, Category C and Category D.

Category A and Category B pensions are contributory and are made up of the basic State pension and any additional element payable from the State earnings-related pension scheme ('SERPS') or the State Second Pension ('SERPS/S2P') (see 1.9 and 1.10 below). The Category A pension payable to an individual is derived from his National Insurance contribution record. A Category B pension is payable by virtue of the contribution record of an individual's spouse and is only available to married women, widows and widowers.

Category C and Category D pensions are non-contributory and are payable only in very restricted circumstances. Category C pensions are payable to men and women who were over State pension age on 5 July 1948 and to the spouses of those men who qualified. Certain individuals who are over age 80 may receive a Category D pension if they are not entitled to any other category of State pension or if the pension they are entitled to is less than the Category D pension.

From 5 December 2005, in accordance with the *Civil Partnerships Act 2005* civil partners enjoy most of the same pension rights as husbands and wives and they will be treated the same as husbands and wives after 2010 when the treatment of men and women will be equalised (see 1.6 below).

Basic State pension

1.5   The basic State pension is payable to all individuals who have:

(*a*)   reached State pension age;

(*b*)   made sufficient National Insurance contributions; and

(*c*)   made a claim for a State retirement pension.

The rate of the basic State pension is increased each year. From 12 April 2005, the full rate of the basic State pension is £82.05 per week for an individual (this is the full Category A pension payable and the amount of Category B pension payable to a widow or widower). For a married couple, the full rate of the basic State pension is £131.20 per week which comprises a Category A pension of £82.05 plus a Category B pension payable to a spouse of £49.15.

In October 2003 the *State Pension Credit Act 2002* came into force. This introduced a new State Pension Credit for persons aged 60 and over. It provides for a minimum income guarantee (subsuming the minimum level of income support payable to such persons). It consists of two main elements:

● a guarantee credit, to ensure a minimum level of income; and

● a savings credit which from age 65 will provide an additional income for pensioners who have low or modest incomes in addition to the basic rate pension.

State pension age

1.6   A man reaches State pension age on his 65th birthday. A woman born before 6 April 1950 reaches State pension age on her 60th birthday. The State pension age for a woman born after 6 April 1950 will be equalised to age 65 progressively over the ten years between 2010 and 2020. The effect of this equalisation is that a woman born on or after 6 April 1955 will have a State pension age of 65. The date on which a woman born between 6 April 1950 and 6 April 1955 attains State pension age is determined in accordance with *paragraph 1* of *Schedule 4* to *PA 1995*.

The second report of the Pensions Commission chaired by Lord Turner, 'A New Pension Settlement for the twenty-first Century', was published on 30 November 2005. As widely expected, one of the key recommendations is for State pension age to be raised gradually to age 67 for both men and women. The Commission intends there to be staged increases of around one year per decade with State pension age starting to rise from 2020 (once the process of raising women's State pension age is completed). The issue is the subject of continued debate and it remains to be seen whether the Commission's recommendation will make it onto the statute books.

National Insurance contribution record

1.7   Generally, in order to qualify for a full Category A basic State pension, sufficient Class 1, Class 2 or Class 3 National Insurance contributions must have been paid or credited to the individual for approximately 90 per cent of his working life. An individual's working life starts on 16 April immediately preceding his 16th birthday and ends on 5 April immediately preceding his attaining State pension age. An individual's working life will therefore usually be 49 years in the case of a man and 44 years in the case of a woman (although this will increase to 49 years with the equalisation of State pension age and possibly further if the recommendation of the Pensions Commission is given legislative effect (see 1.6 above)). At the moment, to be eligible for the full basic State pension, National Insurance contributions must be paid by, or credited to, an individual for 44 years in the case of a man or 39 to 44 years (depending on her State pension age) in the case of a woman.

Where the individual's National Insurance contribution record falls short of these requirements, a reduced basic State pension may still be payable. To qualify the individual must have paid or been credited with National Insurance contributions for sufficient years to qualify for at least 25 per cent of the full rate of basic State pension.

Primary Class 1 National Insurance contributions at the rate of 11 per cent are payable by all employees whose earnings are in excess of the earnings threshold. They are paid on earnings up to the upper earnings limit. Those earning between the lower earnings limit and earnings threshold do not pay Class 1 contributions but are treated as having done so for contributory benefit purposes. The earnings threshold and upper and lower earnings limits are statutory limits which are prescribed each year. For the tax year 2005/2006, the lower earnings limit is £4,264 per annum, the earnings threshold is £4,888 and the upper earnings limit is £32,760. In addition those earning more than £32,760 will pay 1 per cent on earnings in excess of this amount. Secondary Class 1 contributions are payable by employers in respect of those employees whose earnings are in excess of the earnings threshold. There is no upper limit on secondary Class 1 contributions. Class 1 National Insurance contributions are collected through the PAYE system.

Class 2 National Insurance contributions are flat rate contributions payable by the self-employed. Class 3 contributions are voluntary contributions. They can be made by an individual to boost his contribution record so as to ensure that he has sufficient contributions to entitle him to a particular benefit. Class 4 contributions are paid by the self-employed on profits in excess of the lower profit limit. For the tax year 2005/2006 Class 4 contributions are payable at 8 per cent on profit between the lower profit limit (£4,895) and upper profit limit (£32,760) and at 1 per cent on profits in excess of the upper profit limit.

Application for a State retirement pension

1.8   An individual must apply for the State retirement pension. The Department for Work and Pensions sends the appropriate forms to those who are eligible shortly before they reach State pension age.

Additional State Pension scheme

1.9   The second element of a Category A or Category B pension is the additional earnings-related pension component previously known as SERPS (see 1.10 below). An individual will be entitled to this additional component if he has paid Class 1 National Insurance contributions on earnings between the lower earnings limit and upper earnings limit in any tax year since 1978/1979. As a consequence, those earning less than the lower earnings limit will not build up any entitlement to a pension under this earnings-related component. In order to receive an additional earnings-related pension the claimant must have reached State pension age.

An individual's additional pension is determined according to his 'surplus earnings' for each year which counts for additional pension (i e each year after 6 April 1978 in which he has paid Class 1 National Insurance contributions). To calculate 'surplus earnings' it is first necessary to determine an individual's earnings up to the upper earnings limit, for each relevant tax year. Then the earnings in any particular tax year are increased in line with the rise in national average earnings (as set out in the most recent Revaluation of Earnings Factors Order) to take account of inflation. Finally, an amount equal to the lower earnings limit in the last complete tax year before the one in which the individual attains State pension age is deducted. The resulting amount is the individual's surplus earnings for that tax year. The way in which an individual's additional pension is calculated then depends on whether he reached State pension age before or after 6 April 1999.

The annual rate of additional pension of an individual who reached State pension age before 6 April 1999 is calculated by multiplying the aggregate of his surplus earnings for all the years which count for additional pension by 1.25 per cent.

The annual rate of additional pension of an individual who reached State pension age on or after 6 April 1999 is:

(*a*)   the aggregate of his surplus earnings in the tax years from 6 April 1978 to 5 April 1988, multiplied by 25 per cent and then divided by the total number of years between 6 April 1978 (or 6 April immediately preceding his 16th birthday, if later) and 5 April immediately preceding his 65th birthday; plus

(*b*)   the aggregate of his surplus earnings in the tax years from 6 April 1988 to 5 April immediately preceding his attaining State pension age is multiplied by the relevant percentage (which varies between 20 and 25 per cent depending on the year in which the individual attains State pension age) and then divided by the total number of years between 6 April 1978 (or 6 April immediately preceding his 16th birthday, if later) and 5 April immediately preceding his 65th birthday.

If an individual is contracted out of this earnings-related pension component (see chapter 4), he will not be entitled to additional pension from the State for the period during which he is contracted out.

State second pension

1.10   From April 2002, SERPS has been replaced with a second tier State pension known as the State Second Pension, or 'S2P'. This was introduced by the *Child Support, Pensions and Social Security Act 2000* and is intended to provide a bigger pension than SERPS did by boosting the second tier pension of low and moderate earners, carers who are looking after young children or a disabled person and the long-term disabled with broken work records.

The S2P regime provides for a new low earnings threshold ('LET'), set at £12,100 for the tax year 2004/2005 (originally set at £9,500, and uprated in line with increases in national average earnings). In the case of low earners, individuals earning less than the LET, but in excess of the lower earnings limit ('LEL') (also called the qualifying earnings factor ('QEF')) (see 1.6 above), will be treated for S2P calculation purposes as if they had earnings equal to LET. Carers who have no earnings or earnings below the LEL will be treated for S2P purposes as if their earnings are at the LET if:

(*a*)   they receive Child Benefit for a child under six;

(*b*)   they are entitled to receive Invalid Care Allowance; or

(*c*)   they are given Home Responsibilities Protection because they are caring for a sick or disabled person.

Those entitled to long-term Incapacity Benefit or Severe Disablement Allowance throughout a tax year will also be treated as if they had an earnings factor of the LET in that year, provided that by the time they reach State pension age they have either worked and paid or are treated as having paid Class 1 National Insurance contributions for at least one tenth of their working life (see 1.6 above).

S2P will operate in two phases. During Phase 1 (to last for five years from April 2002), S2P accrual will be earnings-related, on the basis of three accrual bands:

Band	Earnings band	Accrual rate
1	earnings between LEL and LET	40%
2	earnings between LET and UET	10%
3	earnings between UET and UEL	20%

(The Upper Earnings Threshold ('UET') is equal to three times the LET, less two times the QEF, amounting to £27,800 for the tax year 2005/2006.)

During Phase 2, S2P will be calculated at a flat rate for individuals who are under 45 at the point of change, but will continue to be earnings-related for individuals who are over age 45 at the point of change. During Phase 2 the scheme will be aimed mainly at individuals earning less than the LET. It is intended that those who are aged under 45 but earning over the LET will not accrue benefits.

Occupational pension schemes

What is an occupational pension scheme?

1.11   The definition of occupational pension scheme as set out in *section 1* of *PSA 1993* has recently been amended by *PA 2004*. With effect from 22 September 2005, it is defined as a pension scheme:

11

'(a)   that—

(i)   for the purpose of providing benefits to, or in respect of, people with service in employments of a description, or

(ii)   for that purpose and also for the purpose of providing benefits to, or in respect of, other people, is established by, or by persons who include, a person to whom subsection (2) applies when the scheme is established or (as the case may be) to whom that subsection would have applied when the scheme was established had that subsection then been in force, and

(b)   that has its main administration in the United Kingdom or outside the member States;

or a pension scheme that is prescribed or is of a prescribed description; ...'

For the purposes of the definition, 'employment' means 'any trade, business, profession, office or vocation' and a person to whom *subsection* (2) applies means, broadly, the employer. The definition of an occupational pension scheme is therefore wide: it can be funded or unfunded; it can relate to an entire workforce, a specified group of employees or a single individual; it can be established and governed by a single clause in a contract of employment or by a complex trust deed.

The new integrated tax regime established by *FA 2004* applies to all 'registered' schemes (the equivalent of pre A-Day approved pension schemes). *FA 2004* separately defines 'occupational pension scheme' as meaning:

'... a pension scheme established by an employer or employers and having or capable of having effect so as to provide benefits to or in respect of any or all of the employees of—

(a)   that employer or those employers, or

(b)   any other employer,

(whether or not it also has or is capable of having effect so as to provide benefits to or in respect of other persons).'

During the passage of the Pensions Bill, the government justified the need for the amended *PSA 1993* definition of occupational pension scheme, on the basis that it was necessary in order to comply with the EU *Directive 2003/41/EC on the Activities and Supervision of Institutions for Occupational Retirement Provision* and also as a consequence of the new tax simplification provisions in the (then) Finance Bill. The main justification was that, in its previous form, the

PSA 1993 definition was very similar to the definition of personal pension scheme and as the new *FA 2004* regime does not distinguish between an occupational pension scheme and a personal pension scheme it was therefore necessary to create a legal distinction.

Traditionally, most occupational pension schemes have been able to benefit from tax privileges if correctly structured. Prior to 6 April 2006 (A-Day), schemes have been either approved by HMRC or unapproved. Those schemes approved by HMRC receive considerably more tax privileges than unapproved schemes but are, as would be expected, more heavily regulated.

On A-Day, these restrictions will be simplified, so that all types of registered pension schemes may pay members any type of payment and that where it is an authorised member payment under *FA 2004* the usual tax privileges will apply. Unauthorised payments will have adverse tax consequences, usually for both the member and the scheme.

Most occupational pension schemes, whatever their nature, are required to comply with the provisions of the *PSA 1993* and the regulations made under that Act. In particular, all schemes are required to comply with the provisions of the *PSA 1993* dealing with protection for early leavers. [See chapter 6]. Schemes which are contracted out of the State earnings-related pension component are also required to comply with the relevant provisions of *PSA 1993* relating to contracting out. [See chapter 4].

Occupational pension schemes are also regulated by *PA 1995* and *PA 2004* which aim to improve the administration of pension schemes and increase security for members. The effect of *PA 1995* and *PA 2004* is discussed throughout this book where relevant. Certain types of occupational schemes have been exempted from many of the provisions of *PA 1995* and *PA 2004* by regulations. Most notably, unapproved schemes are exempt from many, but not all, of the requirements [see chapter 5] as are most small self-administered schemes. [See chapter 13].

Why establish a pension scheme?

1.12   No occupational pension scheme (unless the benefits are particularly poor) is cheap to run. Understandably employers have to think carefully about the costs involved before establishing an occupational pension scheme. A scheme can often cost an employer as much as 15 per cent of payroll in contributions alone (and sometimes more, particularly where there is a past service deficit). On top of this there are often costs such as life assurance premiums and the general day-to-day expenses of running the scheme.

The most common reason for an employer to establish an occupational pension scheme is that it wishes to attract the right calibre of staff. Pension benefits often form a significant part of an employee's remuneration package and so having an appropriate scheme to offer can be important in attracting the right type of recruit. This is particularly so for employers in industries where pension provision is common, in which case the type of arrangement offered may sometimes be dependent upon the 'industry norm'. If an employer in a particular industry is thinking of establishing an occupational pension scheme, it is likely to undertake a survey of other schemes operated by employers in the same sector. If it discovers the vast majority of those employers operate a 'defined contribution arrangement' rather than a 'defined benefit arrangement' it is unlikely to establish a defined benefit scheme as defined benefit schemes are generally perceived to be more expensive (and can be particularly so in times of poor stock market performance).

A good pension scheme may also encourage an employee to remain with an employer, particularly if the scheme offers benefits which are more generous than those offered by similar employers. An employer may be able to encourage long and faithful service by providing employees with a good pension on their eventual retirement.

An HMRC 'exempt approved' scheme benefits from several tax advantages (as will registered schemes on and after A-Day [see chapter 5]) and so, although costly, provision of an occupational pension scheme remains a relatively tax efficient way of providing employee benefits.

From the employees' point of view membership of an occupational scheme can be very attractive. The pension provided by the State is unlikely to be adequate for many employees to maintain their standard of living during retirement; and although employees often have to contribute to an occupational pension scheme they will also obtain benefit from the contributions made by their employer in respect of them.

Types of benefits provided by occupational pension schemes

1.13   Occupational pension schemes are commonly described as either defined benefit schemes or defined contribution schemes, depending on the type of benefits they provide. Defined benefit schemes are also often referred to as 'final salary schemes' and defined contribution schemes as 'money purchase schemes'. In the former, the amount of pension which a member ultimately receives will be directly related to his remuneration, usually, at or around the date of his retirement (although schemes where benefits accrue on a 'career average' basis are becoming more popular). In the latter, the amount of pension a member receives will be related to the contributions made to the scheme by and in respect of him and the investment return on those contributions. The most important difference between the two types of schemes, other than the benefits they provide (see 1.35 to 1.46 below), is the way in which they are funded and the resulting implications, particularly in terms of burden of risk, for the employer and the member.

Defined benefit schemes

1.14   A member of a defined benefit scheme will generally be required to pay a specific proportion of his remuneration by way of contributions (although in some schemes this can fluctuate and in others the member may not be required to contribute) with the balance of the cost of providing the benefits under the scheme being met by the employer (hence these schemes are often also known as balance of cost schemes). The exact cost of providing the benefits will not be known until the last beneficiary under the scheme dies, so a defined benefit scheme represents a very open-ended risk to the employer. The way in which the contributions of the employer are calculated for the funding of such a scheme is considered further in chapter 11.

Defined contribution schemes

1.15   The rules of a defined contribution scheme will likewise usually specify the contributions a member is required to pay to the scheme and will also generally specify the contributions the member's employer is required to make to the scheme in respect of him. Usually the rules will provide for the member to have a notional 'individual account' which is credited with his contributions, the contributions his employer makes in respect of him and the investment growth attributable to those contributions. When the member retires, assets equal to the value of his account will be realised and the proceeds will often be used to purchase an annuity to provide him with an income.

The amount of pension the member receives from a defined contribution scheme will be wholly dependent on the contributions made and the investment growth achieved; it will not in any way be related to the member's earnings before retirement. For many employers a defined contribution scheme represents an attractive proposition as the cost of financing the scheme can be predicted with certainty. For an employee such schemes are often less attractive because if the investments perform poorly, it is the employee upon whom this will ultimately impact, rather than the employer.

Hybrid schemes

1.16   It is possible to have a hybrid scheme which provides pensions accrued on both a defined contribution basis and a defined benefit basis. A hybrid scheme can have a defined contribution section and a defined benefit section where a member will accrue benefits under one or other section, or possibly be able to switch between the two in certain circumstances, for example, on attaining a certain age or on having completed a specified number of years of service. Alternatively, a hybrid scheme can provide defined contribution benefits but with a defined benefit underpin (or vice versa) so that the member will receive the greater of the benefits that can be provided by his individual account and a pension calculated by reference to his salary before retirement.

As employers become more cost sensitive and wish to minimise scope for fluctuations in contribution rates for the future other variations are also becoming more prevalent.

KPMG case – the dividing line

1.17   Questions may arise as to whether a scheme is a defined benefit or a defined contribution arrangement, particularly where the benefit structure does not clearly fit into one category or another. In particular, for some schemes established many years ago, funding may not have been the key issue that it is today and therefore the question as to whether the scheme falls into one category or another may not have been directly addressed.

In *AON Trust Corpn Ltd v KPMG [2005] EWCA Civ 1004, [2005] All ER (D) 441 (Jul)* the question arose, in relation to the obligation of the employer to fund a deficit, as to whether the scheme was a defined benefit or defined contribution arrangement. The court looked in some detail at the meaning of 'money purchase scheme' and held that, although the scheme trustees had power to adjust the level of benefits in accordance with the assets available, the scheme in question was not, as the employer was asserting, a money purchase scheme. The court held that the requisite relationship between contributions and benefits was broken by the introduction of actuarial factors and because the scheme made provision for adjustments to be made there was a mismatch between assets and liabilities.

Application of legislation to different types of occupational pension schemes

1.18   The legislation relating to occupational pension schemes generally applies equally to schemes which provide defined contribution benefits as to those which provide defined benefits. However, there are exemptions for defined contribution schemes from some of the requirements of the legislation, as referred to in the table below.

Legislation relating to:	Applicability to:	
	Defined benefit schemes	Defined contribution schemes
Protection for early leavers, i e preservation, transfers and revaluation [see chapter 6]	All occupational pension schemes are required to comply with the legislation relating to the protection of early leavers although the time limits for the payment of transfer values and ways in which benefits are calculated will vary as between defined benefit and defined contribution schemes.	
Equal treatment [see chapter 9]	The equal treatment requirements set out in *sections 62* to *66* of *PA 1995* apply to both defined benefit and defined contribution schemes.	
Independent trustees [see chapter 3]	Under *sections 22–25* of *PA 1995* (as amended by *section 36* of *PA 2004*), the Regulator has power to appoint an independent trustee if the employer is insolvent, or if there is a Pension Protection Fund assessment period in relation to the scheme.	The independent trustee provisions in *PA 1995* apply to both defined benefit and defined contribution schemes.
Debt on the employer [see chapter 12]	Where a defined benefit scheme is being wound up, a 'relevant event' occurs or an employer ceases to participate (whilst at least one other continues) and the value of the assets of the scheme is less than the value of its liabilities, a debt may become due to the trustees of the scheme from the employer.	The legislation applies to defined contribution schemes only in limited circumstances where the general scheme levy has not been paid or assets of the scheme have been reduced due to criminal action. In both cases the employer becomes liable to the extent that it cannot be paid out of unallocated assets, (*Occupational Pension Schemes* (*Employer Debt*) *Regulations 2005* (*SI 2005 No 678*), *reg 10*).
Disclosure [see chapter 3 and appendix ii]	Trustees of all occupational pension schemes are required to comply with the requirements of the *Occupational Pension Schemes* (*Disclosure of Information*) *Regulations 1996* (*SI 1996 No 1655*) in so far as they relate to their scheme.	

17

Limited price indexation [see 1.47 below]	Limited Price Indexation (LPI) applies to all defined benefit occupational pension schemes.	With effect from 6 April 2005, there is no legal requirement for LPI increases for any pension coming into payment where the pension is attributable to contributions paid between 6 April 1997 and 5 April 2005 as well as pension attributable to contributions paid on and after 6 April 2005 (*section 51* of *PA 1995*, as amended).
Investments [see chapter 10]	All trustees must comply with the statutory requirements relating to investment, including the choice of investments, the appointment of fund managers, self-investment and the maintenance of a statement of investment principles (unless their scheme has an appropriate exemption under the relevant regulations).	
	The Myners principles (non-statutory) also apply to both defined benefit and defined contribution schemes, modified appropriately in each case.	
Contracting out [see chapter 4]	Contracting out is permissible on a reference scheme test basis or on a protected rights basis (but if a scheme, which before 6 April 1997 was contracted out on a guaranteed minimum pension (GMP) basis, wishes to contract out on a protected rights basis but does not wish to secure GMP liabilities outside of the scheme, it must have elected to do so by 31 January 1998).	Contracting out is permissible on a reference scheme test basis (if the scheme provides adequate benefits) or on a protected rights basis.
Voluntary membership [see 1.21 below]	Membership of any occupational pension scheme cannot be compulsory.	
Voluntary contributions [see 1.33 below]	Prior to 6 April 2006 members of occupational pension schemes must be permitted to pay voluntary contributions. *PA 2004* removes this requirement with effect from 6 April 2006.	

Registration and levy [see chapter 2]	Trustees are required to register their scheme with the Pension Schemes Registry and are required to pay a general levy. A separate PPF levy is also payable as from 6 April 2005.	
Dispute resolution [see chapter 3]	Trustees must put in place a dispute resolution procedure in accordance with *section 50* of *PA 1995*.	
Pensions Ombudsman [see chapter 2]	The Pensions Ombudsman has jurisdiction to investigate a wide range of complaints but cannot investigate a complaint that has not gone through the internal dispute resolution procedure unless he believes there is no prospect of a decision being made within a reasonable time.	
Appointment of professional advisers [see chapter 2]	Trustees of defined benefit schemes must appoint an individual as scheme actuary and an individual or firm as scheme auditor. An individual or firm must be appointed by or on behalf of the trustees as fund manager. Trustees should not rely on the advice of any professional adviser they did not appoint.	Trustees of defined contribution schemes must appoint an individual or firm as scheme auditor but do not need to appoint a scheme actuary (*Occupational Pension Schemes (Scheme Administration) Regulations 1996 (SI 1996 No 1715), reg 3*). An individual or firm must be appointed by or on behalf of the trustees as fund manager. Trustees should not rely on the advice of any professional adviser they did not appoint.
Member-nominated trustees [see chapter 3]	Trustees must arrange for the appointment of member-nominated trustees (or directors in the case of a trustee company) unless the scheme is exempt. At the time of writing, the employer is able to 'opt out' of the requirements. However, *PA 2004* removes the opt-out route with effect from 6 April 2006, although there are transitional arrangements proposed for schemes with an opt out in place at that date.	

Minimum funding requirement [see chapter 11]	Tax approved defined benefit schemes must comply with the minimum funding requirement (which includes maintaining a schedule of contributions) as set out in *sections 56* to *61* of *PA 1995*. *PA 2004* replaces the minimum funding requirement with a scheme specific funding requirement to be phased in with effect from 30 December 2005.	Neither the minimum funding requirement nor the scheme specific funding requirement apply to defined contribution schemes, but trustees are required to maintain a schedule of payments in accordance with *sections 87* to *90* of *PA 1995* (see 1.28 below).
Winding up [see chapter 12]	The order in which the liabilities of a tax approved defined benefit scheme must be secured in the event of a winding up is, to an extent, governed by *sections 73, 73A, 73B* and *74* of *PA 1995*.	The order in which the liabilities of a defined contribution scheme must be secured on a winding up is determined solely in accordance with the scheme's governing documentation.
Payment of surplus [see chapter 11]	With effect from 6 April 2006 *section 37* of *PA 1995* is replaced by *sections 250* and *251* of *PA 2004* which allow trustees to resolve to make a repayment of surplus to an employer (where the scheme rules permit) provided that certain conditions are satisfied, including the requirement for the trustees to have obtained a valuation from a 'prescribed person' and a certificate from that person setting out the maximum surplus that can be refunded.	In the case of a defined contribution scheme, a refund will only be permitted where assets are not required to meet the scheme's commitments.

How are occupational pension schemes established?

1.19   Before 6 April 2006, HMRC approval was only available to occupational pension schemes established under irrevocable trusts in accordance with the *Income and Corporation Taxes Act 1988, s 592*; therefore, the vast majority of such schemes were established by trust deed or a declaration of trust.

This has now been replaced by an equivalent requirement in *PA 2004*, whereby if an occupational pension scheme has its main administration in the UK, the trustees or managers of the scheme are unable to accept any payment to fund benefits unless the scheme is established under irrevocable trusts.

Schemes with HMRC exempt approved status prior to A-Day will be automatically registered by HMRC. Any new pension scheme established on or after A-Day will need to make an application to HMRC to be registered (*section* 153 of *FA 2004*). The application must contain any information reasonably requested by HMRC and must be accompanied by a prescribed declaration by the scheme administrator, and any other declarations reasonably required by HMRC (*sections 153(2)* and *270* of *FA 2004*). [See further chapter 5].

The documentation governing a scheme will usually consist of a definitive trust deed and one or more sets of rules. There is no particular agreed format as to what should be contained in the trust deed and what should be in the rules. It is quite common for the trust deed to contain the administrative provisions of the trust and for the rules to detail the benefits payable under the scheme, but there are many variations on this theme.

The first trust deed, whether interim or definitive, will generally appoint the first trustees of the scheme and set out the terms of the trust. In particular it will be necessary for the trust deed to include or make provision for a power of amendment so that the scheme can be amended for future changes in legislation and/or practice. The trustees will also need to be given sufficient powers in the trust deed to be able to administer the trust. For example, prior to the changes introduced by *PA 1995*, unless a trust deed contained a sufficiently wide investment power the trustees were restricted in the types of investments they could make to those set out in the *Trustee Investments Act 1961*.

When a scheme's documentation is first drafted, consideration needs to be given to the 'balance of power' between the trustees and the employer, ie it is necessary to decide which powers should be vested in the trustees, which powers should be vested in the employer and which powers should be vested jointly. As a general rule, if the exercise of the power could have a financial implication for the scheme, an employer will usually wish to be involved in exercising that power; the power could be vested in the employer or it could be vested in the trustees, subject to the consent of the employer. Legislation has, in some instances, overridden this 'balance of power' in the trust documentation. For example, under the statutory funding regime established by *section 222* of *PA 2004*, trustees have been given more power in the process of determining the level of the employer's contribution.

The rules of a scheme will generally detail the benefits which are payable under the scheme. They will usually also set out conditions for membership and specify the contributions (if any) which the members are required to pay. The exact details of the rules will, of course, depend on the benefit structure of the scheme. However, *section 164* of *FA 2004* defines the authorised payments that a registered pension scheme can make in respect of scheme members. These include pensions permitted under *sections 155* and *157*, lump sums permitted under *sections 156* and *158* and 'recognised transfers' as defined in *section 159*. Generally, any unauthorised payments made are likely to have adverse tax consequences and so the employers and administrators of both new and existing pension schemes are likely to need to review their scheme rules in advance of A-Day in order to check that they are *FA 2004* compliant.

The taxation of pension schemes is discussed further in chapter 5.

Centralised schemes

1.20   It may be possible for an employer to participate in a 'centralised' or 'multi-employer' occupational pension scheme, rather than establish its own scheme, thus benefiting from lower administration costs. Such schemes generally have a principal employer, which exercises those powers usually vested in the principal sponsoring employer, and a number of associated or participating employers, on whose behalf the principal employer will generally act.

Before A-Day, the general rule was that a non-sectionalised occupational pension scheme had to restrict membership to employers of 'associated' employers to obtain and retain HMRC exempt approved status. However, under the new *FA 2004* regime, a registered occupational pension scheme will now be able to include employees of other non-associated employers.

If an employer wishes to participate in a centralised scheme, it must agree to observe the rules of the scheme. This is usually achieved by the trustees, the principal employer and the associated employer executing a deed of adherence or participation setting out the terms on which the employer can participate in the scheme.

Membership of occupational pension schemes

Non-compulsory membership

1.21   Membership of an occupational pension scheme cannot currently be made compulsory and any term in a contract of employment or any rule in an occupational pension scheme to the effect that an employee must be a member of a particular pension scheme is void. Legislation relating to non-compulsory membership was first introduced by the *Social Security Act 1986* and first became effective on 6 April 1988; it is now contained in *section 160* of *PSA 1993*. The only exception to this is that membership may be compulsory for a death in service only benefit if that benefit is provided on a non-contributory basis. [*Pension Schemes* (*Voluntary Contributions Requirements and Voluntary and Compulsory Membership*) *Regulations 1987* (*SI 1987 No 1108*), *reg 3*]. In practice, it is, however, permissible (so long as the matter is correctly handled) for employees to be included automatically as members of their employer's scheme unless they specifically request to opt out. The Department for Work and Pensions' (DWP) consultation paper of February 2004 stated that the DWP is looking at ways to deliver increased pension saving in the UK, including the possibility of requiring automatic membership of an employer's scheme, but retaining an ability for members to opt out if they wish.

For the time being, however, the effect of current legislation is not only that a new employee has the option to choose whether or not to become a member of his employer's scheme, but also that an existing member may choose to opt out of membership whilst remaining employed by a participating employer.

HMRC requirements

1.22   Until 6 April 2006 (A-Day), membership of an approved occupational pension scheme is confined to employees of the employers participating in the scheme in order to obtain (and retain) exempt approved status. As from A-Day, a registered occupational pension scheme need not restrict membership to its own employees, though it need not be open to all employees, or to any particular category of them. However, discriminatory entry conditions which cannot be objectively justified should be avoided (see chapter 9).

In the past an employee could not be a member of an occupational pension scheme if he was also contributing to a personal pension scheme. The only situation where a person could be a member of both a personal pension scheme and an occupational pension scheme at the same time, and in respect of the same source of income, was where the occupational pension scheme provided only death benefits or where an 'appropriate' personal pension scheme was used for the purposes of contracting out of the State earnings-related pension scheme. The changes introduced by the stakeholder legislation provided employees with further flexibility and options. Employees with P60 earnings in 2004/2005 of less than £30,000 could also pay up to £3,600 to a personal pension or stakeholder pension, whilst at the same time continuing to be eligible for concurrent membership of their occupational pension scheme.

Under the new *FA 2004* regime, members' contributions to registered pension schemes are not subject to any limits as such. There is, however, an annual limit on the increase in the value of savings in registered pension schemes. This is known as the 'annual allowance'. The new regime also sets a personal lifetime allowance for all pension savings in registered schemes. There are tax penalties for sums saved in excess of the lifetime allowance and on any pension input above the annual allowance.

The taxation of registered schemes is discussed further in chapter 5.

Equal access

1.23   The terms on which employees may become members of an occupational pension scheme must be the same for both men and women (*section 62* of *PA 1995*).

A claim of discrimination in respect of the terms on which employees may become members of a scheme may be brought before a court or employment tribunal. Where discrimination is proven, the court or tribunal may declare that the employee has the right to be admitted on such a date on or after 8 April 1976 as it may specify and may also declare that the employer shall provide the resources necessary to provide the appropriate level of benefits for the employee (subject, in most cases, to the employee also making appropriate contributions).

The *Part Time Workers* (*Prevention of Less Favourable Treatment*) *Regulations 2000* (*SI 2000 No 1551*) and the *Fixed Term Employees* (*Prevention of Less Favourable Treatment*) *Regulations 2002* (*SI 2002 No 2034*) introduced measures to protect part-time and fixed term workers from unjustified exclusion from pension schemes (alongside more general employment protection).The issue of sex discrimination in relation to occupational pension schemes generally, and in particular the exclusion from membership of part-time and fixed term employees, is discussed further in chapter 9.

Disability discrimination

1.24   It is unlawful for an employer with 15 or more employees to discriminate, without justification, against disabled employees in terms of the benefits provided to those employees, including access to and benefits provided from, an occupational pension scheme. *Section 1* of the *Disability Discrimination Act 1995* provides that 'a person has a disability if he has a physical or mental impairment which has a substantial and long term adverse effect on his ability to carry out normal day-to-day activities'. An employer discriminates against a disabled person if it treats that person less favourably than it treats, or would treat, a person who is not disabled and it cannot show that the treatment was justified.

Section 4G of the *Disability Discrimination Act 1995* provides an overriding 'non-discrimination rule' into the rules of an occupational pension scheme, whereby trustees and managers may not discriminate against or harass a disabled person in relation to their admission and treatment. Trustees or managers must make 'reasonable adjustments' where practices or provisions (including scheme rules) put a disabled person at a substantial disadvantage.

No obligation is placed on trustees if they did not know and could not have reasonably known that a person is a disabled person for the purposes of the *Disability Discrimination Act 1995*, or that he has a disability and is likely to be disadvantaged.

Discrimination on the grounds of disability is discussed further in chapter 7.

Age discrimination

1.25   The introduction of age discrimination legislation derives from the EU *Equal Treatment Directive 2000/78/EC*. The basic principle is that direct and indirect discrimination on the grounds of age against employees will be unlawful unless it (a) can be objectively justified; (b) is a genuine and determining occupational requirement; (c) is to compensate for an existing age-related disadvantage; or (d) is exempt.

Article 6 of the Directive allows member states to exempt from the ambit of its domestic legislation certain aspects relating to occupational pension schemes, including the fixing of ages for admission or entitlement to occupational schemes and the use of age criteria in actuarial calculations.

The *Employment Equality (Age) Regulations 2006 (SI 2006 No 1031)* (which come into force on 1 October 2006) include the following exemptions (amongst others) for occupational pension schemes:

- Age-related employer contributions (subject to certain conditions).

- Age criteria in actuarial calculations.

- Setting benefit levels by reference to length of service.

- Adjustments to pension levels where there is more than a given number of years between member and spouse.

- Setting a minimum age before which unreduced benefits cannot be taken.

Discrimination on the grounds of age is discussed further in chapter 7.

Procedure for becoming a member

1.26   The rules of the scheme will often set out the procedure which an employee must follow if he wishes to become a member of the scheme. Often the rules will provide for a minimum and maximum entry age, thus allowing an employer to exclude the very young (who are likely to change jobs more frequently) and the very old (for whom the costs of benefits are particularly high). (See 1.25 above and chapter 7 in relation to age discrimination.)

It is not uncommon for the rules of a scheme to impose a 'waiting period' where an employee has to be employed for a certain period of time before being eligible to become a member (although this is becoming less common). A waiting period may correspond to an employee's 'probationary period' under his contract of employment; some rules will provide that an employee is only eligible once he is a 'permanent' employee. However, the *Fixed-Term Employees (Prevention of Less Favourable Treatment) Regulations 2002 (SI 2002 No 2034)* now provide that fixed term employees should be provided with benefits on a pro-rata basis equivalent to those provided to their permanent counterparts, unless their exclusion can be objectively justified (see chapter 7). There may also be difficulties for trustees under the age discrimination legislation in imposing a waiting period unless it can be justified.

An employee may be required to complete an application form for membership of an occupational pension scheme; in the case of a contributory scheme, this form will normally authorise the employer to deduct contributions from the employee's salary (see also 1.32 below). It is common for employers to ask employees who do not wish to join the scheme or who choose to opt out of the scheme to sign a waiver form confirming that they understand that they are giving up benefits.

Making contributions to occupational pension schemes

Employer's contributions

1.27   Before *PA 1995* came into force there was little in the way of statutory control over funding and the making of contributions (see chapter 11). *PA 1995* introduced provisions requiring trustees to maintain, in the case of defined benefit schemes, schedules of contributions and, in the case of defined contribution schemes, schedules of payment. With effect from 30 December 2005, *PA 2004* supersedes *PA 1995* in relation to defined benefit schemes.

Defined benefit schemes

1.28   The trustees of a defined benefit scheme which is subject to the statutory funding objective under *section 222* of *PA 2004* must produce, within

15 months after the effective date of the first actuarial valuation, a schedule of contributions which must be reviewed within 15 months after the effective date of subsequent valuations. The schedule must be signed by the trustees or manager of the scheme and must make provision for signature by the employer in order to signify its agreement to the matters included in it. The schedule must show:

(*a*)   the rates and due dates of all contributions (other than voluntary contributions) payable by or on behalf of the employer and active members of the scheme during the period of five years after the date on which the schedule is certified;

(*b*)   any contributions to cover expenses must be listed separately; and

(*c*)   additional contributions under a recovery plan must be shown separately.

The schedule must be certified by the scheme actuary, i e the actuary appointed under *section 47(1)(b)* of *PA 1995*. The schedule will not come into force until it has been so certified.

Where employer or employee contributions are not made on time in accordance with the schedule, reports to the Regulator are only required where there is reasonable cause to believe that the failure is likely to be of material significance in the exercise by the Regulator of any of its functions (*section 228* of *PA 2004*).

A Code of Practice has been issued by the Regulator, which states that the Regulator expects trustees to have a robust procedure for monitoring contributions and should investigate any employer failure whether there is a requirement to report or not. If the failure is likely to be of material significance to the Regulator, the report should be made within ten working days of the trustees becoming aware that a report is necessary. Members of the scheme must also be informed.

If there has been 'fraudulent evasion' in failing to pass employee contributions to the trustees or managers, criminal penalties may apply (*section 49(11)* and (*12*) of *PA 1995*)).

The statutory requirements relating to scheme funding and to schedules of contributions are discussed further in chapter 11.

Defined contribution schemes

1.29   The trustees of a defined contribution scheme must (unless the scheme is exempt, see below) ensure that a 'schedule of payments' is periodically prepared, maintained and revised in relation to the scheme. *Section 87* of *PA*

1995 and *regulations 18* and *19* of the *Scheme Administration Regulations* (*SI 1996 No 1715*) provide that the schedule must show, for the year to which it relates:

(*a*)   the rates of contributions payable towards the scheme by or on behalf of the employer (or in the case of multi-employer schemes, each employer) and the active members of the scheme;

(*b*)   the amounts payable towards the scheme by the (or each) employer in respect of expenses likely to be incurred during the year in question; and

(*c*)   the dates on or before which payments are to be made.

Where any amounts payable in accordance with a schedule of payments by or on behalf of the employer have not been paid on or before the due date, then a civil offence has been committed under *PA 1995*, punishable by fine (unless there has been 'fraudulent evasion' in failing to pass employee contributions to the trustees or managers, in which case criminal penalties may apply (*section 49(11)* and (*12*) of *PA 1995*)). The trustees or managers of the scheme must give notice to the Regulator of any non-payment within 30 days of the due date. The trustees must notify the members within 90 days of the due date.

Regulation 17 of the *Scheme Administration Regulations* provides that trustees of the following schemes do not have to maintain a schedule of payments:

●   unapproved occupational pension schemes;

●   certain public service pension schemes;

●   occupational pension schemes with less than two members;

●   schemes which provide only death benefits;

●   small self-administered schemes where all the members of the scheme are trustees and all decisions are made by the unanimous agreement of those trustees who are members;

●   *section 615* schemes; and

●   certain earmarked insured schemes (see *regulation 1(2)* of the *Scheme Administration Regulations*).

Any trustee who fails to comply with the requirement to maintain a schedule of payments may be fined (see also appendix I).

The Regulator has issued a Code of Practice on Reporting Late Payment of Contributions to Occupational Money Purchase Schemes. This sets out the Regulator's views on which late payments are likely to be material, and thus reportable. A reasonable period for a report would usually be within ten working days of the trustees having identified the late payment as material.

HMRC requirements

1.30   The tax treatment of contributions made by employers to registered occupational pension schemes is discussed in chapter 5.

Members' contributions

1.31   Most, but by no means all, occupational pension schemes require members to make contributions. These are discussed below.

Ordinary contributions

1.32   The level of the contributions which members are required to make is a matter of scheme design. Contributory schemes typically require a contribution of between 4 and 7 per cent of salary. Contributions will generally be deducted from a member's salary by his employer through the payroll. The employee must specifically consent to contributions being deducted for this purpose (*Employment Rights Act 1996, s 13*) and consequently membership application forms will generally include provision for the necessary consent to be given.

Contributions deducted by a member's employer must be passed to the trustees of the scheme within 19 days (or 14 days in the case of minimum payments made by virtue of the member being contracted out of SERPS/S2P) of the end of the month within which the contribution is deducted. [*PA 1995, s 49(8)* and the *Scheme Administration Regulations (SI 1996 No 1715), reg 16*]. Failure to do so is an offence for which the employer can be fined, imprisoned or both, depending on the circumstances. [See 1.28 and 1.29 above].

Voluntary contributions

1.33   A member may wish to enhance his pension benefits by making voluntary contributions in addition to any contributions he is required to make under the rules of the scheme. Prior to April 2006, the rules of an occupational pension scheme may not prohibit the payment of voluntary contributions, except to the extent necessary to comply with HMRC requirements. [*PSA 1993, s 111*]. However, the rules are able to provide that a member who has reached, or is within one year of reaching, normal pension age cannot make voluntary contributions. [*Pension Schemes (Voluntary Contributions Requirements and Voluntary and Compulsory Membership) Regulations 1987 (SI 1987 No 1108), reg 2(6)* ('the *Voluntary Contribution Regulations*')]. *Section 267* of PA 2004, which comes into force in April 2006, removes the requirement for schemes to provide an additional voluntary contribution ('AVC') facility. Trustees cannot, however, require members with existing AVCs to transfer out so will still have to administer the AVC facility for existing members even if the rules are changed.

The rules of a scheme may require that members who wish to make voluntary contributions have to make a certain minimum level, but any lower limit imposed cannot be higher than 0.5 per cent of the member's earnings in any tax year or, if greater, three times the weekly lower earnings limit. [*Voluntary Contribution Regulations, reg 2(8)*]. In practice, it is not common for schemes to restrict the payment of voluntary contributions in terms of the minimum amount that must be paid.

The rules of a scheme may also require a member to give notice of his intention to pay, or vary the rate at which he is paying, voluntary contributions. The maximum notice period that the rules can require is twelve months. [*Voluntary Contribution Regulations, reg 2(4)*]. It is not uncommon for a scheme to impose a notice period of one or two months so as to allow the employer sufficient time to make adjustments to the payroll.

The benefits deriving from voluntary contributions will generally be defined contribution benefits, irrespective of whether the scheme is defined contribution or defined benefit. Voluntary contributions may sometimes be used to purchase added years of service which count toward the member's defined benefits, but this is unusual. Any voluntary contributions paid by the member must be used to provide additional benefits for, or in respect of, that member. The amount of the additional benefits must be reasonable, having regard to the amount of the contributions paid and (if the benefits provided by the voluntary contributions are not defined contribution benefits) the value of the other benefits under the scheme.

Instead of making voluntary contributions 'in-house' through the employer's scheme, a member may choose to make contributions to a 'free standing additional voluntary contributions' ('FSAVC') arrangement. Legislation to provide for these arrangements was introduced in the *Finance (No 2) Act 1987*. An FSAVC arrangement has much in common with a personal pension scheme (see chapter 14), although regulations relating to the payment of voluntary contributions generally also apply. An FSAVC arrangement is established by a provider in exactly the same way as a personal pension scheme. Usually the provider is an insurance company, friendly society, bank or building society. The main disadvantage with an FSAVC arrangement is that the member is obliged to meet the fees associated with the administration and management of the arrangement whereas, if voluntary contributions are paid 'in-house', the employer will usually bear these costs.

HMRC restrictions

1.34   Prior to A-Day, the total amount of contributions (ordinary and voluntary) which could be made to a scheme by a member in any tax year was restricted by HMRC to 15 per cent of the member's remuneration in that year. [*ICTA 1988, s 592*].

Under the new *FA 2004* regime, contributions to registered pension schemes will not be subject to any limit as such. Employers can claim a deduction in profits chargeable to UK tax. Members are given relief on all employer contributions and the greater of £3,600 per annum or 100 per cent of UK earnings on their own contributions. There is, however, an annual limit on the increase in the value of savings in registered pension schemes. This is known as the 'annual allowance' and is set at £215,000 for the 2006/2007 tax year, rising to £255,000 for the 2010/2011 tax year. Individuals will be taxed at 40 per cent on any 'pension input' above the annual allowance.

Benefits payable from occupational pension schemes

HMRC requirements

1.35   Prior to 6 April 2006 (A-Day), the benefits payable from an approved occupational pension scheme, whether defined contribution or defined benefit, were limited by HMRC. To obtain HMRC approval, the rules of the scheme have to reflect these limits.

Under the new *FA 2004* regime, the types of 'authorised payments' that can be made are set out in *Part 4* of *FA 2004*. If a registered pension scheme makes 'unauthorised member payments' or 'unauthorised employer payments' there may be adverse tax consequences for the employer, the member and for the scheme administrator (which will usually be the trustees).

When are benefits payable?

1.36   Benefits will become payable under a scheme either on the death of a member or on the member's retirement, whichever is the earliest. Benefits are usually calculated on the basis of the member's 'normal retirement date' under the scheme, which will generally be between age 60 and 65. Under the Pension Rules set out in *section 165* of *FA 2004*, benefits cannot be paid before the 'normal minimum pension age' which will be increased from age 50 to age 55 from 2010, other than where the ill-health condition is met. However, members who have a prospective right under the rules of the pension scheme (as at

31

10 December 2003) to draw any benefit before age 55 may retain those rights and have a protected pension age (*Schedule 36* to *FA 2004*).

Normal retirement date may differ for different categories of members, for example, directors may have a normal retirement date of age 60 while all other members have a normal retirement date of age 65. In the past it was common to find schemes with a different retirement age for men and women (usually reflecting the State pension age) but following the decision in *Barber v GRE Insurance Group [1990] 1 ECR 1889*, this is no longer the case (see chapter 9 for a full discussion on the equalisation of normal retirement dates).

Benefits payable on early retirement are discussed further in 1.38 below. HMRC will not permit benefits to come into payment after age 75; benefits payable on late retirement are discussed in 1.39 below.

Final salary defined benefit schemes

Pension benefits at normal retirement

1.37   In the case of a final salary defined benefit scheme a member's pension is calculated by reference to the remuneration he is receiving at or shortly before he retires or leaves service. The level of remuneration by which benefits are calculated is often referred to as 'final pensionable salary' or some similar expression. The definition of final pensionable salary is a matter of scheme design; the wider the definition, the higher a member's final pensionable salary is likely to be and, consequently, the greater his resulting pension will be. A member's final pensionable salary may be his earnings at the date on which he retires, his total earnings during the previous year or his earnings averaged over a certain period, such as the previous three years; it may include fluctuating emoluments such as commissions or bonuses or it may simply be basic salary. There may be offsets against final pensionable salary; for example, it is not uncommon for a deduction equal to the lower earnings limit to be made.

Typically, a scheme's rules will contain a formula for calculating the pension payable. This will generally be expressed as a fraction or percentage of final pensionable salary for each year of pensionable service (i e service whilst an active member and any service deemed, under the rules of the scheme, to be pensionable service); $1/60$th or $1/80$th are the most common annual accrual rates. A formula such as this gives the member some reassurance that, assuming that he has been a member of a scheme for much of his working life, his pension will be a reasonable proportion of the salary he was earning at the time he retired. For example, a person who has been a member of a scheme offering a $1/60$th accrual rate for 30 years will receive a pension of $30/60$ths, or one half of his final pensionable salary.

32

Pension benefits on early retirement

1.38   The rules of the scheme may allow members to retire on pension at any time if retirement is due to incapacity, or at any time after age 50 for any other reason (this will rise to 55 in 2010). Generally the rules will specify that either employer or trustee consent is required for early retirement and, in the case of incapacity retirement, that satisfactory medical evidence is produced.

The level of benefits payable on early retirement will often depend on whether or not the member is retiring due to incapacity. A non-incapacity related early retirement pension will generally be calculated using the same formula as for normal retirement but taking account of actual pensionable service and final pensionable salary at the date of retirement. The resulting pension will often then be reduced to take account of early receipt. This is usually done by applying a percentage reduction, for example, a member's pension may be reduced by 3 per cent for each year that actual retirement precedes normal retirement date.

Sometimes rules may provide for a different level of benefit, depending on the circumstances of the retirement. In *AGCO v Massey Ferguson Works Pension Trust [2003] 57 PBLR*, the scheme rules provided more generous benefits on early retirement when it was at the request of the employer. The court was asked to consider the meaning of the words 'retires from Service at the request of the Employer' in the context of the terms of the particular scheme and, in particular, whether this included voluntary and/or compulsory redundancy.

The court held that 'retire' is intransitive (i e the employee elects to give up work rather than being required to leave) and that 'retire' covers situations different from dismissal and is distinct from 'leaving Service' which covers broader circumstances. The words 'retires from Service at the request of the Employer' did not include a case where the employer requests and subsequently enforces retirement – the natural meaning of 'request' is that the employee has a choice in the matter. There is a broad range of voluntary redundancy – from truly voluntary to a position where the employee has little choice in the matter. True 'voluntary' redundancy does fit within the wording as being 'retirement at the request of the employer'. Compulsory redundancy does not as it is a dismissal rather than a retirement.

Where the retirement is due to incapacity the benefits provided will often be more generous. They may, for example, be calculated without reduction for early receipt or possibly on the basis of the pensionable service the member would have completed had he remained a member until his normal retirement date. Such pensions are obviously more expensive than non-incapacity early retirement pensions and so are generally paid less frequently.

The definition of incapacity was contained in the glossary to the HMRC's Practice Notes and HMRC would not permit scheme rules to provide for an incapacity retirement pension to be paid unless the member concerned fell within this definition of incapacity. Rules of many schemes go further than the HMRC definition of incapacity. For example, self-induced incapacity (for example, self-inflicted injuries or drug addiction) may be excluded; employer and/or trustee consent will often be required; and the member may have to be incapacitated to the extent that he is incapable of any full-time employment, not just of working for his current employer.

Under the Pension Rules set out in *section 165* of *FA 2004*, the 'ill-health condition' is similar, but not identical, to the pre A-Day definition of 'incapacity' set out in the HMRC Practice Notes.

The 'ill-health condition' will be met if:

(*a*) the scheme administrator has received evidence from a registered medical practitioner that the member is (and will continue to be) incapable of carrying on the member's occupation because of physical or medical impairment; and

(*b*) the member has in fact ceased to carry on the member's occupation (*paragraph 1, Part 1* of *Schedule 28* to *FA 2004*).

The ill-health condition is discussed further in chapter 5.

The fact that there are often many conditions relating to the payment of an incapacity pension has given rise to a number of disputes between members and trustees as to whether such a pension should be paid. The decisions, to an extent, turn on the particular wording of the incapacity rule in question but generally an employer must act in good faith when considering any medical evidence provided in relation to an application for an incapacity pension. Trustees may be required to exercise a discretion in relation to the payment of benefits such as an incapacity pension. When exercising such a discretion, trustees should ensure that they ask themselves the proper questions, adopt a correct construction of the rules of the scheme and do not arrive at a perverse decision which no reasonable body of trustees could arrive at (taking into account all relevant, but no irrelevant, factors (*Lee v Showman's Guild (1952) 2 QB 329*; *Harris v Lord Shuttleworth and others (Trustees of the National Provincial Building Society Pension Fund) (1994) PLR 47;* and *Edge v Pensions Ombudsman (1999) 49 PBLR (37)*).

A distinction is sometimes drawn between voluntary and involuntary retirement. In *Brooks v National Westminster Bank plc*, an unreported decision of the Court of Appeal on 8 November 1993, the court decided that retirement was essentially a voluntary act as distinct from dismissal. In the case of a voluntary retirement, an ill-health early retirement pension was available and in the case of a dismissal, it was not. This decision was called into question by the Court of Appeal in *Harris v Lord Shuttleworth* which decided that it was possible to regard an individual who had been compulsorily retired by her employer as having retired by reason of incapacity.

Often an incapacity rule provides that the member must be 'permanently' incapacitated. The decision in *Harris v Lord Shuttleworth* suggests that being permanently incapacitated is synonymous with there being no reasonable prospect that the member will be able to work before normal retirement date either for the employer concerned or a similar employer.

Where a member receives his pension early he is effectively receiving benefits as an alternative to a preserved benefit and consequently the preservation legislation must be complied with. This is discussed further in chapter 6.

Pension benefits on late retirement

1.39   The rules of a scheme may permit a member to remain in service after his normal retirement date. Under the pre A-Day tax regime, where a member of an approved scheme postpones his retirement he is unable to take his benefits until he actually retires, but his benefits must be taken on or before the member's 75th birthday, even if he has not retired. However, if the member had joined (or was deemed to have joined) the scheme before 1 June 1989 he is able to take his benefits at any time after attaining normal retirement date even though he was continuing in service.

Post A-Day, under the new *FA 2004* regime there is nothing to prevent the member taking his benefits in tranches if the rules permit this. However, as under the pre A-Day regime, benefits must commence at age 75.

The benefits payable on late retirement will be greater than the benefits payable on normal retirement. A member may continue to accrue pensionable service after his normal retirement date or alternatively his benefits may be calculated as at his normal retirement date and then increased by actuarial factors to take account of late receipt. The age discrimination provisions may effectively require schemes to allow continued accrual.

As with early retirement benefits, the provision of late retirement benefits is considered to be an alternative to a preserved benefit and so the legislation relating to preservation of benefits must be complied with (see chapter 6).

Tax-free lump sum on retirement

1.40   A member may choose to take part of his retirement benefits in the form of a tax-free cash lump sum if the rules of the scheme allow for this option. Under the pre A-Day regime, the maximum lump sum that can be taken is restricted by HMRC and, to an extent, depends on the circumstances of the retirement.

Under the new *FA 2004* regime, there is generally more scope for a member to take tax-free cash. The general position s that up to 25 per cent of the value of an individual's fund or benefits crystallised on that date may be taken as tax-free cash.

If a higher amount is paid then it will be an unauthorised payment and adverse tax consequences will arise unless the individual is entitled to benefit from the automatic transitional protection provisions, available without registration, where the entitlement to maximum tax-free cash for service accrued up to 6 April 2006 exceeds the entitlement to tax-free cash under the new regime.

Under the pre A-Day regime, a member retiring due to serious ill-health may be able to commute the whole of his pension for a lump sum if the member has a very limited life expectancy, usually of less than one year.

Under the new *FA 2004* regime, a serious ill-health lump sum can be paid if:

(*a*)   before it is paid the scheme administrator has received evidence from a registered medical practitioner that the member is expected to live for less than a year;

(*b*)   it is paid when all or part of the member's lifetime allowance is available;

(*c*)   it is paid in respect of an uncrystallised arrangement;

(*d*)   it extinguishes the member's entitlement to benefits under the arrangement; and

(*e*)   it is paid when the member has not reached age 75 years.

There is no liability to income tax on a serious ill-health lump sum (*section 636A* of *ICTA 1998*, as amended by *PA 2004*).

Full commutation is also permissible where the benefits payable are classed as trivial (see chapter 5).

Lump sum death benefits

1.41   An occupational pension scheme will usually provide a life assurance benefit in the event of the death of an active member. This benefit is usually calculated by multiplying a member's salary (which can be pensionable salary, annual salary or final pensionable salary) by a specified figure, but occasionally it is a fixed sum. The maximum lump sum death benefit a scheme will usually provide is four times salary as under the current tax system, which is approximately the same as the maximum amount that HMRC will permit. From April 2006 this maximum amount will be changed to the Lifetime Allowance (see chapter 5 in relation to the new *FA 2004* taxation structure).

In the event of a member's death, the life assurance benefit will usually be payable under 'discretionary trust' in order to mitigate any potential inheritance tax liability. If a payment is made through a discretionary trust, it will not form part of the member's estate and consequently will not be taken into account when assessing liability for inheritance tax. A scheme's governing rules will therefore usually contain an appropriate discretionary trust provision. When a member joins the scheme he will be asked to complete a 'statement of wishes' form to indicate to the trustees who he would wish to receive a lump sum death benefit in the event of his death. This statement of wishes does not bind the trustees but simply acts as a guidance for them. Irrespective of whether the member has completed a statement of wishes form, the trustees should make proper inquiries to establish whether or not they are paying the benefits to the most appropriate person. This is particularly true where there has been a change in the member's personal circumstances, such as a remarriage or death in the family. The trustees should tread carefully as they will be exercising their discretion and so must ask themselves the proper questions, adopt a correct construction of the rules of the scheme and not arrive at a perverse decision which no reasonable body of trustees could arrive at (taking into account all relevant, but no irrelevant, factors). (See 1.38 above; and *Wild v Smith (1996) PLR 275*.)

Lump sum death benefits are usually insured with a life assurance company. Only the largest occupational schemes are inclined to pay death benefits directly out of the fund as such benefits can be very costly.

It is common for a refund of the member's contributions also to be paid in the event of his death, sometimes with interest, but often without.

Spouse's/dependant's pension

1.42   In addition to the lump sum life assurance benefit payable in the event of the death of a member, a pension is often payable to his surviving spouse. The amount of the benefit payable will generally vary depending on whether the member died before or after retirement.

If a member dies whilst an active member the amount payable will usually be a percentage (often 50 per cent) of the member's prospective pension. This will be calculated on the basis of either his actual pensionable service at the date of death or the pensionable service he would have completed had he remained an active member until his normal retirement date and had his pensionable salary remained static.

In the case of the death of a member following his retirement, the spouse's pension is often calculated as a percentage of the member's pension at the date of his death. A spouse's pension of 50 per cent of the pension the member was receiving at the date of his death is common. A lump sum death benefit may be payable if the member dies within five years of the date of his retirement (often known as a five-year guarantee). For example, if a member dies within two years of his retirement date a lump sum equal to three years' worth of pension instalments may be payable as a lump sum.

The rules of the scheme may also permit a child or dependant's pension to be paid and this may be either where the member dies leaving no spouse (or a spouse who subsequently dies) or in addition to any spouse's pension which is payable. Under the pre A-Day regime, in the case of an approved scheme, the HMRC will only allow such a pension to be paid to someone who is dependent on the member at the date of his death. Under *FA 2004*, the position has altered somewhat. For example, there are some minor differences to the definition of 'dependent' and there is no restriction on the amount of dependants' pensions that can be paid. (See chapter 5 for further details.)

Note that in accordance with the *Civil Partnership Act 2005*, with effect from 5 December 2005, the surviving civil partner of a member of a pension scheme is entitled to a spouse's pension based on the pension rights accrued by the deceased civil partner in respect of service from that date. Schemes that are contracted out are also required to pay a civil partner a pension in respect of contracted out employment from 6 April 1988. As the contracting-out require-ments are not overriding, rule amendments may need to be made to give effect to this, in which case *section 67* of *PA1995* must be complied with by trustees. Alternatively, *regulation 7* of the *Occupational Pension Schemes (Modification of Schemes) Regulations 2006 (SI 2006 No 759)* allows trustees to make appropriate modifications under *section 68* of *PA 1995*.

Benefits on leaving service other than on retirement

1.43   A member must be entitled to a preserved benefit within a scheme if his pensionable service under that scheme is terminated before his normal pension age and he has at least two years' qualifying service. If the member has transferred his rights under a personal pension scheme to his employer's occupational pension scheme he will be entitled to a preserved benefit from that scheme, even if he has not completed two years' qualifying service. Broadly speaking, qualifying service is pensionable service under the scheme, service in employment which was contracted out by reference to the scheme or service which is deemed to be qualifying service by virtue of a transfer payment received by the scheme in respect of the member. A member's normal pension age is the earliest date on which he has an unqualified right to retire on an unreduced pension, other than on special grounds, such as ill-health or redun-dancy. In most schemes it will be the same as his normal retirement date.

PSA 1993 sets out the minimum requirements with which schemes must comply and it is not uncommon for a scheme to grant a member a preserved benefit, even if he has not completed two years' of qualifying service. Such schemes are often described as having immediate vesting of benefits. If a member has a preserved benefit under a scheme he will generally have a statutory right to require that the 'cash equivalent' of his benefits be transferred to his new employer's scheme, a personal pension scheme or another suitable tax approved arrangement.

If a member does not qualify for a preserved benefit under the scheme, he will usually be entitled to a refund of any contributions he has made to the scheme. The refund will be net of tax and, if the scheme is contracted out of the State earnings-related pension scheme, will also be net of the cost of reinstating the member into SERPS/S2P. Contributions may be refunded with interest, but this is not a statutory requirement.

As from 6 April 2006, members who leave a scheme having completed at least three months' pensionable service will have the right to elect for a 'cash transfer sum' or a refund of their contributions paid into the scheme. The cash transfer sum is the cash equivalent value of the benefits that would have accrued for the member had there not been a rule requiring a minimum period of service before vesting of those rights. This means that early leavers will be able to benefit from the value of the employer's contributions after three months, rather than the current (pre-6 April 2006) period of two years.

The protection afforded to early leavers is discussed in detail in chapter 6.

Defined contribution schemes

Pension benefits

1.44   The benefits paid to a member of a defined contribution scheme are determined by two factors, namely:

(*a*)   the amount of money held by the trustees on behalf of the member at retirement; and

(*b*)   the annuity rates applicable at the time when the member's benefits become payable.

The amount of money held by the trustees under (*a*) will be determined by the level of contributions paid by the member's employer and the member himself, and the investment income realised in respect of those contributions. The total amount is generally referred to as the member's 'individual account' or, more colloquially, his 'pot'.

It is becoming increasingly common for members to be given some discretion over the way in which their individual account is invested. Often members will be given a choice of funds and are required to indicate to the trustees of the scheme what percentage of their individual account they wish to invest in each fund. The scheme must be carefully structured to ensure that the arrangements put in place, whilst offering the member choice, do not expose the trustees to potential claims from members whose investment choices do not perform as well as expected.

A member cannot have any claim to any particular asset, even if he is given some power in relation to how his account is invested. All the assets of the scheme will be invested together so that, although the member's account will be credited with interest and investment growth, no specific scheme asset will be attributable to his account.

On the member's retirement, whether at, before or after normal retirement date, assets equal in value to his individual account will be realised and the proceeds will be used to provide the member with a pension. Some defined contribution schemes provide additional benefits on the retirement of a member due to incapacity, but this will almost certainly be at the discretion of the employer.

Under the new tax regime, defined contribution schemes can pay a 'scheme pension', or a 'lifetime annuity' or an 'unsecured pension' to a member who has not yet reached age 75. However, a scheme pension can only be paid if the member has first been given the opportunity to select a lifetime annuity (*section 165* of *PA 2004*).

Scheme pensions are either pensions paid directly from the scheme out of its own resources, or by an insurance company selected by the scheme administrator (*paragraph 2* of *Schedule 28* to *FA 2004*). A lifetime annuity is an annuity payable by an insurance company which meets certain specified requirements (*paragraph 4* of *Schedule 28* to *FA 2004*). An 'unsecured pension' is, broadly, either a short-term annuity or income withdrawal arrangement (*paragraph 4* of *Schedule 28* to *FA 2004*).

The pension rules in relation to defined contribution schemes are considered further in chapter 5.

Death benefits

1.45   Most defined contribution schemes provide lump sum death-in-service benefits in much the same way as defined benefit schemes do (see 1.41 above).

The benefits provided to the spouse and/or dependants of a member of a defined contribution scheme may be a proportion of the member's salary or may be such level of pension as can be secured by the proceeds of the member's account. If the scheme provides a percentage of salary, there will usually be some form of insurance as it is possible (and in the case of young or new members, likely) that the member's account will be insufficient to provide the necessary funds to secure the benefit.

Benefits on leaving service

1.46 A member of a defined contribution scheme who terminates his pensionable service before his normal retirement date is entitled to benefits in much the same way as a member of a defined benefit scheme. The same statutory criteria determine whether the member has a right to preserved benefit or not, although the method of calculating the preserved benefit will, of course, be different.

A member of a defined contribution scheme who has a preserved benefit under the scheme will also generally have a statutory right to require that the 'cash equivalent' of his benefits be transferred to his new employer's scheme, a personal pension scheme or another suitable tax approved arrangement. However, the time limits within which the trustees must action his request differ from those applicable to defined benefit schemes (see chapter 6).

Increasing pensions in payment

1.47 *PA 2004* amended *section 51* of *PA 1995* with effect from 6 April 2005. A defined benefit occupational pension scheme which is approved by HMRC must increase pensions in payment attributable to:

(*a*) pensionable service completed on and after 6 April 1997, by a minimum of the lesser of 5 per cent per annum and the increase in the RPI for that period (known as limited price indexation or 'LP1'); and

(*b*) pensionable service completed on and after 6 April 2005, by a minimum of LP1 capped at 2.5 per cent.

In relation to defined contribution schemes, the requirement to increase pensions was removed altogether for any pension coming into payment on or after 6 April 2005. This extends to pension attributable to contributions paid between 6 April 1997 and 5 April 2005 as well as to pension attributable to contributions payable on and after 6 April 2005.

If an increase in excess of LPI is given, the excess may be offset against the following year's increase. [*PA 1995, s 53*]. LPI increases do not, however, have to be given in respect of pensions which derive from a member's voluntary contributions. [*PA 1995, s 51(6)*]. Nor do increases have to be given in respect of a pension paid to a member who has not attained the age of 55 at the time when the increase takes effect, unless he retired on account of incapacity. [*PA 1995, s 52*].

LPI increases do have to be given in respect of benefits derived from transfer payments but only to the extent that they are attributable to pensionable service completed on or after 6 April 1997. [*Occupational Pension Schemes (Indexation) Regulations 1996 (SI 1996 No 1679), reg 2*]. This requirement does not apply to transfer payments from a scheme which itself was not subject to the indexation requirement.

LPl increases do not have to be given in respect of benefits derived from a pension credit awarded as a result of a pension sharing order on the divorce of a member. [*PA 1995, s 51(6)*].

Forfeiture and suspension of benefits

1.48   Generally a member's entitlement or accrued right to a pension cannot be assigned, commuted, surrendered or charged. However, there are various exceptions to this general rule [*PA 1995, s 91*]. Furthermore, a court is not able to make an order (other than an attachment of earnings order, income payments order, pension sharing order or earmarking order) which would deprive a member of his entitlement (although unapproved schemes are excluded from this provision). An example of the extent of this principle is shown in the case of *Fisher v Harrison [2003] 49 PBLR, [2003] All ER (D) 484 (Jul)*. As part of the settlement of a dispute, Mr Harrison purported to assign all his pension benefits (past and future) to Mr Fisher by way of consent order. The scheme included a fairly standard forfeiture clause, providing that benefits purported to be assigned would be forfeited.

The court held that the forfeiture clause did not apply to the attempted assignment of the benefits to which Mr Harrison already had an absolute entitlement (i e those which had become due and payable between 1996 and the date of the consent order). It also held that *sections 91* and *92* of *PA 1995* did not prevent the assignment of the benefits already due. However, both the forfeiture clause in the scheme rules and *section 91* did apply to pension payments falling due after the date of the consent order.

In this case, the consent order could not be severed (to allow Mr Fisher to claim the payments already due) and therefore even the valid assignment of past pension payments could not be enforced. Mr Harrison was entitled to payment of the benefits due before the date of the consent order (although Mr Fisher could apply for a new order in relation to the freezing of those benefits). Those payable after that date were forfeit but Mr Harrison could ask the trustees to exercise their discretion under the forfeiture clause to make payments to him.

Exceptions to inalienability

Commutation of pension

1.49   The rules of an approved occupational pension scheme may, and generally do, allow a member to commute part or, in some circumstances, all of his pension for a lump sum at retirement (see 1.40 above). [*PA 1995, s 91(5)(c)*].

Surrender in favour of a spouse and/or dependant

1.50   The rules of a scheme may also allow a member to surrender part of his pension to provide a pension for his spouse and/or dependants in the event of his death after retirement. [*PA 1995, s 91(5)(a)* and *(b)*].

Charge, lien or set-off

1.51   *Section 91(5)(d)* and *(e)* of *PA 1995,* provide that the rules of a scheme may allow for a charge or lien on, or a set-off against, a member's pension benefits to be made for the purposes of:

(*a*)   enabling the member's employer to recover a monetary obligation arising out of a criminal, negligent or fraudulent act or omission by him;

(*b*)   discharging a monetary obligation due to the scheme arising out of:

    (i)   a criminal, negligent or fraudulent act or omission by him; or

    (ii)   where the individual is a trustee, arising out of a breach of trust by him (unless the court has relieved him, wholly or partly, from personal liability under *section 61* of the *Trustee Act 1925*). [*Occupational Pension Schemes (Assignment, Forfeiture, Bankruptcy etc) Regulations 1997 (SI 1997 No 785), reg 4* ('the *Forfeiture Regulations'*)].

A new *section 91(5)(f)* of *PA 1995* was inserted by *section 266* of *PA 2004* with effect from 6 April 2005, allowing trustees to reduce or suspend pensions in payment in order to recoup overpayments of benefits. There had previously been some debate as to whether *section 91* allowed trustees to do this. The Pensions Ombudsman had issued a number of determinations finding that the trustees could do so and the amendment to *section 91* confirms this position.

The amount of any charge, lien or set-off (including a suspension or reduction under *section 91(5)(f)*) is restricted to the amount of the monetary obligation due or, if less, the value of the member's entitlement (calculated on a cash equivalent basis (see chapter 6)). The member must be given a certificate showing the amount of the charge, lien or set-off and its effect on his benefits under the scheme. If the member disputes the amount, the charge, lien or set-off cannot be effected unless the obligation becomes enforceable by a court order or an arbitrator's award. It is questionable whether silence on the part of the member concerned amounts to consent to the amount of the charge, lien or set-off, even if the certificate specifies that any dispute must be raised within a certain time limit. In effect, unless the member agrees to the charge, lien or set-off being exercised, the safest course of action is to obtain a court order or arbitrator's award.

A charge, lien or set-off cannot be exercised against a member's protected rights or accrued right to a guaranteed minimum pension. Neither can a charge, lien or set-off be exercised against a transfer payment received by the scheme in respect of a member unless it is attributable to another scheme of the same or a financially associated employer, and the benefits transferred could have been subject to a charge, lien or set-off under the transferring scheme. [*Forfeiture Regulations, reg 3*].

Forfeiture

1.52   Under *section 92* of *PA 1995*, an entitlement, or accrued right, to a pension cannot be forfeited other than as a consequence of:

(*a*)   a purported assignment, commutation, surrender, charge, lien or set-off which is of no effect; or

(*b*)   the bankruptcy of a member which occurs prior to 6 April 2002; or

(*c*)   the member being convicted of certain offences such as treason; or

(*d*)   the failure of the member to make a claim within six years of the benefit becoming due; or

(*e*)   where a pension is payable to a person nominated by the member and that person is convicted of the murder, manslaughter or unlawful killing of the member.

Where a member's benefits are forfeited under the circumstances in (*a*) or (*b*) in accordance with the scheme's rules, the trustees have a discretion under *section 92(3)* of *PA 1995* to pay the pension or benefit to all or any of the following:

(*i*)   the member of the scheme to, or in respect of, whom the pension was, or would have become, payable;

(*ii*)   the spouse or any dependant of the member;

(*iii*)   any other person to whom, under the rules of the scheme, the pension was or could have been paid.

A member's benefits may also be forfeited if a charge, lien or set-off could be exercised against them. The same conditions apply to forfeiting benefits as apply when exercising a charge, lien or set-off. If a member's benefits are forfeited in these circumstances, the trustees have power to determine that the amount forfeited is paid to the employer. [*PA 1995, s 93(5)*].

Pension rights following a member's bankruptcy

1.53   When an individual is declared bankrupt the general rule is that his estate automatically vests in the trustee in bankruptcy. [*Insolvency Act 1986, s 306*]. The bankrupt's estate is defined as all property belonging to or vested in the bankrupt at the commencement of the bankruptcy, except for items for the bankrupt's personal use in his employment, and items for the basic domestic needs of the bankrupt and his family. [*Insolvency Act 1986, s 283*].

How does this affect an individual's pension rights? It was previously established that trustees in bankruptcy were entitled to claim the entire pension benefits of scheme members, not just pensions in payment (see *Re Landau [1997] 3 ALL ER 322*). In order to protect scheme members many pension schemes included forfeiture clauses – these will all be slightly different but the purpose of them was automatically to forfeit the member's entitlement to scheme benefits on his bankruptcy and for the trustees to have a discretion to distribute payments, up to the value of those benefits, to the member or his family (commonly known as 'protective trusts').

As a result of *WRPA 1999*, forfeiture clauses have become less significant. Indeed, for persons made bankrupt on or after 6 April 2002 forfeiture clauses are no longer effective (see 1.54 below).

However, while they still maintain some relevance in relation to bankruptcies prior to 6 April 2002, it is important to note that not all forfeiture clauses are automatically valid. The validity of forfeiture clauses has been scrutinised closely by the courts, most notably in *Kemble v Hicks [1998] 3 All ER 154*. This shows a difference between:

(*a*)   clauses which purport to forfeit an absolute life interest, which cannot be valid;

(*b*)   clauses which purport to forfeit determinable life interests (i e an interest that is valid until the happening of a certain event). These are only valid if the life interest is determinable in the same events that the forfeiture clause is expressed to operate; and

(*c*)   clauses which forfeit a contingent interest, which are generally acceptable (i e an interest that will only become payable on the happening of a future specified event).

The relevance of a valid forfeiture clause to an individual, depending on the time that the bankruptcy order was made, is shown more clearly in the table in 1.54 below.

The Welfare Reform and Pensions Act 1999

1.54 The law concerning the effect of bankruptcy on an individual's pension rights has changed dramatically under the *Welfare Reform and Pensions Act 1999* ('*WRPA 1999*'). This Act contains provisions on pensions and bankruptcy which apply to occupational, personal and stakeholder pension schemes, as well as retirement annuity contracts.

The treatment of a member's scheme benefits on bankruptcy will now depend on the date the bankruptcy order was made. The position, as it applies to benefits under all approved pension schemes only, is summarised below.

Date of bankruptcy order	Is there a valid forfeiture clause?	Treatment of bankrupt's benefit
Before 29 May 2000	No	Benefits vest in trustee in bankruptcy on his appointment.
Before 29 May 2000	Yes	Benefits are forfeit and may be applied by scheme trustees under 'protective trusts'.
On or after 29 May 2000 and up to and including 5 April 2002	No	Benefits do not vest in trustee in bankruptcy on his appointment and are payable from scheme under the provisions of the trust deed and rules.
On or after 29 May 2000 and up to and including 5 April 2002	Yes	Benefits do not vest in trustee in bankruptcy on his appointment but forfeiture clause will operate provided the clause is valid and benefits may be applied by scheme trustees under 'protective trusts'.
On or after 6 April 2002	All forfeiture clauses are void	Benefits do not vest in trustee in bankruptcy on his appointment and are payable from scheme under the provisions of the trust deed and rules.

Pensions in payment

1.55 If a member is in receipt of a pension during the period of his bankruptcy (between the date of bankruptcy order and the date of discharge) it is open to the trustee in bankruptcy to apply to the court for an income payments order under *section 310* of the *Insolvency Act 1986* requiring the pension to be paid to the trustee in bankruptcy rather than the member. This would equally apply if a lump sum payment was made from the scheme during the period of bankruptcy.

In most cases, income payments orders will be in force from the period of the commencement of the order until the bankrupt is discharged – it is currently one year until automatic discharge of the bankrupt. In certain limited circumstances, the duration of the order can be extended beyond the date of discharge of the bankrupt. It is important to remember that the trustee in bankruptcy can only exercise those rights under the pension scheme which the bankrupt himself can. Therefore, if there is a long period of time before a member reaches retirement age pension rights will be of little use to a trustee in bankruptcy. In addition it makes no difference if the bankrupt member is discharged before the pension comes into payment – if the benefits have vested in the trustee in bankruptcy, any future payments may still be made to the trustee in bankruptcy, until the bankruptcy itself, i e not the individual, is discharged.

The effect on unapproved schemes

1.56   The benefits provided by an unapproved pension scheme will vest automatically in the trustee in bankruptcy. However, the Secretary of State is able to make regulations that define what constitutes an unapproved pension scheme and how that might, in prescribed circumstances, be excluded from his estate. [*WRPA 1999, s 12*]. The member is now able to apply to the Court for an order excluding all or part of his entitlement under the scheme, or he may reach a formal agreement to that effect with the trustee in bankruptcy. [*Regulation 4* of the *Occupational and Personal Pension Schemes (Bankruptcy) (No 2) Regulations 2002 (SI 2002 No 836)*].

Excessive contributions

1.57   S*ection 15* of *WRPA 1999* amends s*ections 342A* to *342C* of the *Insolvency Act 1986*, so that the trustee in bankruptcy can seek an order from the court, where excessive contributions have been made to an approved pension scheme. If made, order will restore the position to what it would have been, had the excessive contributions not been made (and the trustees will be ordered to pay an amount to the trustee in bankruptcy). The court will look at whether the contributions:

(*a*)   have unfairly prejudiced individual creditors; and

(*b*)   have been made in an effort to keep them beyond the reach of creditors; and (*c*)   were excessive when looking at the individual's personal circumstances at the time.

Enterprise Act 2002

1.58   As a result of the *Enterprise Act 2002* ('*EA 2002*'), automatic discharge of the bankrupt now occurs after one year rather than the previous position where discharge occurred after three years. The bankrupt may be discharged prior to the expiry of one year where the official receiver files a notice at court that his investigations into the bankrupt's affairs are complete or if he believes that the period of one year until automatic discharge is unnecessary. [*Insolvency Act 1986, s 279*, as inserted by *section 256 of EA 2002*]. This means that the trustee in bankruptcy will have a shortened period of time in which to secure the bankrupt member's pension payments. This period may be extended, however, where the bankrupt member's level of income exceeds that which he reasonably requires for both his own and his family's needs. In these circumstances, the trustee in bankruptcy may secure an income payments order which will continue after the discharge of the bankrupt up to a maximum period of three years from the date of the bankruptcy order. [*Insolvency Act 1986, s 310(6)*, as inserted by *EA 2002, s 259*].

However, the official receiver and the trustee in bankruptcy can apply to the court for an order extending the period of discharge of the bankrupt beyond one year or until a specified condition is fulfilled by the bankrupt. An order will only be made by the court to extend the period of the bankruptcy in these circumstances where the bankrupt has failed or is failing to comply with his obligations under the bankruptcy. [*Insolvency Act 1986*, s *279(3)*, *(4)*, as inserted by *EA 2002, s 256*]. Further, in certain circumstances, the official receiver or Secretary of State may apply to the court for a bankruptcy restriction order after the discharge of the bankrupt. This allows the duration of the bankruptcy to be extended to between 2 and 15 years, if certain types of culpable behaviour by the bankrupt are identified. [*Insolvency Act 1986, s 281A*, as inserted by *EA 2002, s 257*]. *Schedule 4A* has been inserted in the *Insolvency Act 1986*, which outlines the type of conduct which will be taken into account when considering the culpability of the bankrupt. For example, this will include excessive pension contributions made by the bankrupt. [*Insolvency Act 1986, Sch 4A, s 2(2)(e)*].

Section 260 of *EA 2002* also introduces an 'income payment agreement'. An income payment agreement is similar to an income payments order and is a written agreement between the bankrupt and his trustee in bankruptcy (or official receiver) to pay an amount equal to a specified part of the bankrupt's income to his trustee or official receiver for a specified period. The income payment agreement can impact on third parties because under the terms of the income payment agreement a third party, which can include the trustees of a scheme, can be required to pay to the trustee in bankruptcy (or official receiver) a portion of the bankrupt's pension for a specified period.

Whilst, unlike an income payments order, an income payment agreement avoids the requirement of a court hearing, the terms of the income payment agreement can be enforced as if they were provisions of an income payments order. An income payment agreement must specify the period for which it is to have effect and it can continue in force past the date of the discharge of the bankrupt for up to a maximum period of three years from the date of the agreement. [*Insolvency Act 1996, s 310A*, as inserted by *EA 2002, s 260*].

Stakeholder pension schemes

Background

1.59   Stakeholder pensions were introduced by the government as a new way for individuals to make provision for their retirement. The stakeholder pension scheme was designed to be a low cost, easy to understand, defined contribution pension plan targeted at individuals earning between £9,000 and £18,000 per annum who were not making pension provision at the time of introduction. The original idea was first proposed in November 1997 with the issue of 'Stakeholder Pensions – A Consultation Document' by the (then) DSS. The ideas expressed in this document were carried forward in the December 1998 'Partnership in Pensions' Green Paper. Throughout 1999 several consultation papers seeking comment on the proposed workings of stakeholder pension schemes were issued until finally on 11 November 1999, with the publication of the *Welfare Reform and Pensions Act 1999,* the first statutory guidance on stakeholder pension schemes was published. The first stakeholder schemes became registrable from 1 October 2000 and were available to the public from April 2001. The primary regulations governing the operation of stakeholder schemes are the *Stakeholder Pension Schemes Regulations 2000 (SI 2000 No 1403).*

The basic elements of stakeholder

1.60   The following outlines the basic aspects of a stakeholder pension scheme.

(*a*)   *Legal structure*

Stakeholder schemes may be run either on the basis of a trust (i e similar to that of an occupational pension scheme) or on a contractual basis with the stakeholder scheme being run by a Financial Services Authority ('FSA') authorised 'stakeholder scheme manager'. If the scheme is to be trust based then one third of the trustees must be independent, but there is no requirement for there to be member-nominated trustees; where established on a contractual basis a contract between the manager and the scheme will set out the manager's responsibilities.

(b)   Regulation

All schemes must be registered with the Regulator in order to qualify as stakeholder schemes and the Regulator regulates their operation and management. (Before 6 April 2005, this was a function of Opra). Stakeholder scheme compliance broadly follows that of *PA 1995* requirements. The FSA regulates marketing and advice and supervises the firms responsible for managing the funds invested (stakeholders being 'investments' for the purposes of the *Financial Services and Markets Act 2000*). In addition, HMRC regulates the conditions for tax approval and stakeholder schemes will, from A-Day, come under the auspices of *FA 2004*. The Pensions Ombudsman has jurisdiction to hear complaints regarding maladministration.

(c)   Charging

Stakeholder schemes are intended to have a simpler and more transparent charging structure than is sometimes seen with personal pension contracts. An annual charge of 1 per cent per annum of the fund value held by an individual is currently the maximum that a stakeholder scheme provider can levy. This covers all costs associated with initial recruitment of members and the continuing costs of running the scheme. All other additional services (and attaching costs) are optional to the scheme member. Transfers in and out of the scheme do not attract charges. Investment choice options can be given, but with a default option for those who do not wish to choose.

(d)   Minimum contributions

To ensure that those of modest means are not precluded from joining stakeholder schemes, the minimum permissible level of contributions is £20, with members allowed to make contributions either on a regular or an infrequent basis, thereby catering for, amongst others, individuals who take a career break.

(e)   The duty on employers

Subject to the exemptions below, all employers are required to designate a stakeholder scheme, including at least one scheme which all employees can join. They are also required to pass details of that scheme to their employees, and to provide a facility for deduction of contributions from the pay of those employees who are a member of a scheme, if the employee wishes.

The requirement to provide access to stakeholder schemes applies to all employers, the current exemptions only applying to:

(*a*)   employers who already offer occupational schemes where the employee may join within a year of starting work and where the qualifying age is no older than 18 and no younger than five years before the scheme's normal retirement date;

(*b*)   employers with fewer than five employees;

(*c*)   employers whose employees all earn below the National Insurance lower earnings limit;

(*d*)   employers who offer a group personal pension to which they contribute at least 3 per cent per annum of their employees' earnings, and which levies no charges when an individual leaves the scheme to move to a new employer.

Further details relating to stakeholder pension schemes are set out in chapter 14.

Chapter 2

People involved with pensions

Introduction

2.1   This chapter considers the roles of the individuals and organisations involved in the administration, management and regulation of pension schemes. The people involved in pensions fall within four main categories:

(*a*)   those whose involvement is specific to the scheme in question; this group includes the trustees of the scheme and the professional advisers appointed by the trustees (i e the actuary, auditor and fund manager) to assist them in carrying out their functions;

(*b*)   those which can broadly be termed the regulatory bodies; this group includes the Audit and Pension Scheme Services ('APSS') of Her Majesty's Revenue and Customs ('HMRC') (formerly the Inland Revenue Savings, Pensions, Share Schemes ('IRSPSS')), the Pensions Regulator ('the Regulator') which has succeeded the Occupational Pensions Regulatory Authority ('Opra'), the National Insurance Services to Pensions Industry (formerly the Contracted-out Employments Group) of the National Insurance Services to the Pensions Industry ('NISPI') (which is an agency operated by HMRC) (previously the Contributions Agency of the DSS) and the Board of the Pension Protection Fund ('PPF').

(*c*)   the Pensions Advisory Service ('TPAS') (formerly OPAS) and the Pensions Ombudsman, both of whom may have a role to play when disputes arise; and

(*d*)   the various professional bodies, the most important of which are the Pensions Management Institute and the National Association of Pension Funds.

Trustees

2.2   Where a pension scheme is established by an employer under trust, the role of the trustees is to hold the scheme's assets separately from the employer's assets and to apply them for the benefit of scheme members in accordance with the trust documents, general trust law and overriding legislation. If the scheme's liabilities are funded in advance over a period of time by employers' and employees' contributions, the use of a trust creates a degree of security for scheme members by placing the scheme's assets beyond the reach of the employers' creditors. For schemes seeking the tax advantages of 'exempt approval' (see chapter 5), the existence of a trust is a Revenue requirement. With effect from 6 April 2006 the Revenue requirement will cease but any UK-based occupational pension scheme wishing to accept payments to the scheme to fund benefits must be established under trust (*section 252* of the *Pensions Act 2004* (*PA 2004*)).

The role of a pension scheme trustee is evolving. In the past, there were few restrictions as to who could be a pension scheme trustee: a trustee could be an individual, the scheme's principal employer, a company, an elected employee or a member representative. For practical reasons, however, a scheme's trustees would usually be either at least two individuals or a company, whose board of directors would take the relevant decisions. The *Pensions Act 1995* (*PA 1995*) imposed requirements as to who may and may not be a pension scheme trustee (see 3.2 below) and in broad terms, entitled scheme members to nominate at least one third of the trustees (unless the scheme members accept alternative arrangements proposed by the employers). The Government was concerned that many schemes do not have member-nominated trustees as a result of alternative employer arrangements. As a consequence, *PA 2004* introduces new require-ments for member-nominated trustees with effect from 6 April 2006. Most importantly schemes will no longer be able to opt out of the requirement to allow members to nominate at least one third of the trustees. Opt-out arrange-ments already in place will be allowed to continue until the earlier of the date on which the arrangement would have come to an end under the current legislation and 31 October 2007.

Trustees must act in the best interests of the beneficiaries (generally considered to mean their best financial interests) and in accordance with statute and the scheme's trust deed and rules. Chapter 3 takes a more detailed look at trustees' duties and responsibilities in light of recent developments.

In 2002, Paul Myners published his review of institutional investment in the UK setting out the 'blueprint' for change and recommendations for pensions schemes. The Government published consultation papers back in the beginning of 2002 focusing on three of the Myners' Report recommendations on which it intended to legislate. These included whether schemes should have independent custodians, encouraging shareholder activism and the need for trustees to be familiar with the issues concerned when reaching investment decisions. The Government's response to the Myners Report provided that March 2003 would see a public review to assess the effectiveness of the principles in bringing about the changes (which involved case studies using a small number of pensions schemes). Further information on the Myners Report and its impact is provided at 3.14 below.

PA 2004 introduces, with effect from 6 April 2006, a requirement for trustees to be conversant with key scheme documents (including the trust deed and rules) and to have knowledge and understanding of certain areas including the law relating to pensions and trusts and the principles relating to the funding and investment of occupational pension schemes. This is dealt with in more detail in 2.13 below.

PA 1995 introduced civil and criminal penalties for trustees in respect of breaches of certain sections of *PA 1995* (and *PSA 1993*, as amended) and the disqualification or suspension of trustees in certain circumstances (see 2.14 below). Certain breaches of *PA 2004* are also subject to penalties under *PA 1995*. Details of these appear throughout this book and are summarised in appendix I.

Actuaries

The role of the actuary

2.3   Actuaries assess financial problems, using mathematical and statistical methods, specialising, in particular, in problems concerning uncertain future events. In the context of pension schemes this most often involves predicting movements in the scheme (deaths, retirements and withdrawals) and estimating the costs of providing the benefits due and accruing in the future.

The actuary to a scheme will recommend the assumptions and methods to be used to value the scheme's assets and liabilities, will periodically value these (see chapter 11) and, where the scheme promises defined benefits, will recommend the rate of contribution which is necessary to provide those benefits. For valuations with effective dates from 22 September 2005 the actuary's role will be different. The trustees (in most cases with the consent of the employer) must choose the assumptions to be used in the valuation, adopt a statement of funding principles and set the contribution rate. The trustees are required by *PA 2004* to take advice from the actuary before making any decisions on these matters.

The actuary will also advise on a day-to-day basis on benefit issues, such as the calculation of cash equivalents and early retirement factors (for example, the extent to which an early retirement pension should be discounted to take account of early payment). An actuary may also advise the trustees on strategic investment decisions.

The appointment of the actuary under PA 1995

2.4   Under *section 47* of *PA 1995*, the trustees of most occupational pension schemes and stakeholder schemes (if registered in accordance with *section 2* of the *Welfare Reform and Pensions Act 1999 (WRPA 1999)*) must appoint an actuary. The actuary so appointed must be a named individual, even if working in a large actuarial firm *(section 47(1)(b))*. The individual actuary appointed under this provision ('the scheme actuary') has specific functions to perform under *PA 1995* and *PA 2004*. In particular, it is the scheme actuary who is responsible for signing valuations (see chapter 11).

Under *regulation 3(2)* of the *Scheme Administration Regulations (SI 1996 No 1715*, as amended), the requirement for a scheme actuary does not apply to:

(*a*)   defined contributions schemes;

(*b*)   public service schemes or schemes which are backed by a government guarantee;

(*c*)   unfunded schemes;

(*d*)   schemes with less than two members;

(*e*)   unapproved schemes with fewer than 100 members;

(*f*)   expatriate schemes under *section 615(6)* of the *Income and Corporation Taxes Act 1988* with fewer than 100 members; and

(g)   certain schemes established by statute.

With effect from 6 April 2006 there will be an additional exemption for schemes with fewer than twelve members where all the members are trustees and either all decisions must be made unanimously by the trustees, or a statutory independent trustee has been appointed.

Regulation 4(1)(b) of the *Scheme Administration Regulations (SI 1996 No 1715)* sets out the qualifications and experience or approval required for appointment as the scheme actuary. An actuary must be a Fellow of the Institute or Faculty of Actuaries or must be approved by the Secretary of State. Additionally, an actuary cannot be a trustee of the pension scheme nor must he be connected with or an associate of a trustee of that scheme (see 2.6 below).

Any actuary can perform functions which do not have to be performed by the scheme actuary, but if the trustees rely on the skill or judgement of an actuary not appointed by them, they will risk incurring civil penalties or removal. Consequently, whenever trustees of a pension scheme (even one that is exempt from having to appoint a scheme actuary) seek advice from an actuary, they should ensure that the actuary has been properly appointed in accordance with the requirements of *PA 1995*.

There are specific requirements for trustees to observe in making the necessary appointments (see *Scheme Administration Regulations (SI 1996 No 1715), reg 5* which includes stakeholder schemes and the actuarial guidance note, GN29, issued by the Institute and Faculty of Actuaries). The notice must be in writing, must specify the date of the appointment, and must set out to whom he shall report and take instructions from (*Scheme Administration Regulations, reg 5(1)*). The actuary must acknowledge the notice in writing within one month of its receipt. [*Scheme Administration Regulations reg 5(2)(a)*]. In addition, the actuary must confirm in writing that he will notify the trustees of any conflict of interest to which he is subject in relation to the scheme immediately on becoming aware of the existence of the conflict. [*Scheme Administration Regulations, reg 5(2)(b)(ii)*]. If the actuary resigns from the appointment or is removed by the trustees, he is required to certify whether the circumstances of the resignation or removal are likely to affect the members. [*Scheme Administration Regulations, reg 5(4)*]. Subject to these requirements, the trustees are free to determine the terms of the appointment and where an actuary resigns or is removed from the appointment, the trustees are required to appoint a replacement within three months. [*Scheme Administration Regulations, reg 5(8)*].

Whistleblowing

The scheme actuary is required by *section 70* of *PA 2004* to be a 'whistleblower' (see 2.14 below).

2.5   The actuary's professional obligations are set out in Guidance Note 29, 'Occupational Pension Schemes – Advisers to the Trustees or a Participating Employer' (GN 29). The Guidance Note is updated and the latest version (6.0) is effective from 6 April 2005. The Guidance Note applies principally to actuaries advising scheme trustees, but also contains guidance on advising an employer or the trustees (but not as the scheme actuary). The Guidance Note makes it clear that the scheme actuary is not expected to search for circumstances which would be reportable to the Regulator, but does have a duty to report circumstances which come to his or her attention (GN 29, para 6.2, version 6.0). The scheme actuary is expected to maintain a cumulative record containing details of any breach which does not itself fall to be reported to the Regulator but which may, when considered with other breaches, indicate a matter which must be reported (GN 29, para 6.3, version 6.0).

Ineligibility to act if a trustee

2.6   Under *section 27* of *PA 1995* a trustee of a pension scheme (including stakeholder schemes) (and any person 'connected' or 'associated' with such a trustee) may not be an actuary to the same scheme. (The terms 'connected' and 'associated' are defined in *section 123* of *PA 1995* by reference to *sections 249* and *435* of the *Insolvency Act 1986*.

However, a director, partner or employee of a firm of actuaries may act as a scheme's actuary even though another director, partner or employee of the firm is a trustee of that scheme (*PA 1995, s 27(2)*), and the firm may also provide trustee services to the scheme. [*Scheme Administration Regulations* (*SI 1996 No 1715), reg 7*].

Breach of *section 27* is a criminal offence (*PA 1995, s 28*) and may also lead to a prohibition order by the Regulator.

Auditors

2.7   An auditor is a person who is authorised by the Institute of Chartered Accountants of England and Wales or similarly recognised supervisory body (or, for the purposes of *PA 1995*, is approved by the Secretary of State) who receives, examines and officially verifies accounts of money in the hands of an individual or company.

Trustees of occupational pension schemes must appoint an individual or a firm as auditor under *section 47* of *PA 1995*. However, under *regulation 3(1)* of the *Schemes Administration Regulations*, this requirement does not apply to:

(*a*)   unapproved schemes (unregistered schemes after 6 April 2006);

(*b*)   unfunded schemes;

(*c*)   schemes with fewer than two members;

(*d*)   public service pension schemes, schemes backed by a Government guarantee and certain schemes established by statute;

(*e*)   defined contributions small self-administered schemes with fewer than twelve members in which all members are trustees and all trustee decisions are made by unanimous agreement;

(*f*)   expatriate schemes under *section 615(6)* of the *Income and Corporation Taxes Act 1988*;

(*g*)   schemes with fewer than twelve members providing defined contributions benefits where all benefits are by insurance or annuity contracts specifically allocated to members; and

(*h*)   certain schemes established by statute.

With effect from 6 April 2006 exemption (g) will be amended to exempt schemes with fewer than twelve members where all the members are trustees and either all decisions must be made unanimously by the trustees, or a statutory independent trustee has been appointed.

Rules similar to those applying to the appointment of actuaries apply to the appointment of auditors under *PA 1995* (see 2.4 above). However, the bar on a trustee (or anyone 'connected' or 'associated' with a trustee) acting as auditor (see 2.6 above) is arguably wider, in that there is no specific provision enabling a director, partner or employee of a firm of auditors to act as auditor where another director, partner or employee of that firm is a trustee of the scheme. The same sanctions as referred to in 2.6 above apply to any auditor who breaches the provisions of *section 27* of *PA 1995*. The auditor is also required to whistleblow in the circumstances set out in 2.5 above.

The *Occupational Pension Schemes* (*Requirement to obtain Audited Accounts and a Statement from the Auditor*) *Regulations 1996* (*SI 1996 No 1975*), as amended by the *Occupational Pension Schemes* (*Administration and Audited Accounts*) (*Amendment*) *Regulations 2005* (*SI 2005 No 2426*) which apply to all schemes except insured schemes which earmark insurance policies for each member, require:

(*i*)   the trustees in respect of scheme years ending on or after 6 April 1997 to obtain audited accounts and the auditor's statement regarding payment of contributions within seven months of the end of the scheme year;

(*ii*)   the trustees to make provision as to the form and content of the accounts; and

(*iii*) the accounts to contain a statement that they have been prepared and audited in accordance with the regulations.

In addition occupational pension schemes with 100 or more members which are unapproved or unregistered (after 6 April 2006) or expatriate schemes under *section 615(6)* of the *Income and Corporation Taxes Act 1988* are required to produce audited accounts (despite the fact they are exempt from the require-ments to appoint an auditor). This provision was introduced by the *Occupa-tional Pension Schemes* (*Administration and Audited Accounts*) (*Amendment*) *Regulations 2005* (*SI 2005 No 2426*) as a result of the European *Directive 2003/41/EC on the Activities and Supervision of Institutions for Occupational Retirement Provision*.

Further guidance for auditors can be found in the Auditing Practices Board's ('APB') Practice Note 15 – 'The Audit of Occupational Pension Schemes in the United Kingdom' which was revised in November 2004. Scheme auditors are advised to familiarise themselves with this publication before undertaking work in relation to pension schemes.

Investment managers

2.8   A scheme's trust deed and rules will usually give the trustees wide investment powers to enable the trustees to deal with trust assets as if they were the beneficial owners and to maximise their investment opportunities. In addition, *section 34* of *PA 1995* confers on occupational scheme trustees (including stakeholder scheme trustees registered in accordance with *section 2* of *WRPA 1999*) an investment power which is the same as if they were absolutely entitled to the scheme's assets themselves and which is subject only to any restrictions imposed by the scheme. *PA 2004* introduces amendments to *sections 34* and *36* of *PA 1995* which require trustees to exercise their powers of amendment in accordance with regulations. The *Occupational Pension Schemes (Investment) Regulations 2005 (SI 2005 No 3378)* require trustees to exercise their powers of investment in a manner calculated to ensure the security, liquidity and profitability of the portfolio as a whole and include some specific restrictions on investment and borrowing. These provisions are dealt with in more detail in chapter 10.

The Financial Services and Markets Act 2000 (FSMA 2000) prohibits a person from carrying on a regulated activity unless they are authorised or exempt. Trustees will generally delegate their investment power to a fund manager who is authorised rather than seek authorisation themselves. This is usually achieved by way of an investment management agreement ('IMA'). The IMA must contain certain information as prescribed by *PA 1995,* which includes dealing with any conflicts of interest that may arise.

Trustees are required under *section 47(2)* of *PA 1995* to appoint a fund manager if their scheme has 'investments', which include 'any asset right or interest' as defined in *section 22* of *FSMA 2000.* The regulated activities are described more fully under *Schedule 2* to *FSMA 2000* and separated into the following headings:

* dealing in investments;
* arranging deals in investments;
* deposit taking;
* safekeeping and administration of assets;
* managing investments;
* investment advice;
* establishing collective investment schemes; and
* using computer-based systems for giving investment instructions.

The *Scheme Administration Regulations (SI 1996 No 1715)* exempt (amongst others) unfunded schemes, schemes with less than two members, wholly insured schemes and small self-administered schemes in which all members are trustees and all investment decisions are made by all or a majority of the trustees (further exemptions are provided for under *regulation 3(3)* of the *Scheme Administration Regulations* and *para (4)* of *regulation 4* of the *Financial Services and Markets Act 2000 (Carrying on Regulated Activities by Way of Business) Order 2001) (SI 2001 No 1177),* as amended by the *Financial Services and Markets Act 2000 (Carrying on Regulated Activities by Way of Business) (Amendment) Order 2005 (SI 2005 No 922)).*

Audit and Pension Scheme Services of Her Majesty's Revenue and Customs (APSS)

2.9   In 2005 the Inland Revenue and Customs and Excise combined in a new department, Her Majesty's Revenue and Customs (HMRC). The pension scheme responsibility which was previously dealt with by the Inland Revenue Savings, Pensions, Share Schemes business stream of the Inland Revenue is now dealt with by Audit and Pension Scheme Services (APSS) of HMRC. APSS's main responsibility is to oversee the requirements placed on pension schemes claiming tax relief, as well as related implications for members, their employers and other parties.

The tax treatment of occupational pension schemes, including the new 'simplified' tax regime coming into force on 6 April 2006, is dealt with further in chapter 5 and of personal pension schemes in chapter 14.

HMRC's guidelines (relevant until 6 April 2006) are set out in its Practice Notes, IR12 (2001) (as updated from time to time) for occupational schemes and IR 76 (2000) for personal pension schemes (including stakeholder schemes), and a general inquiry service is available. From 6 April 2006 the relevant guidance will be the Registered Pension Schemes Manual. The APSS is located in Nottingham, and can be contacted at Audit and Pension Scheme Services, Yorke House, PO Box 62, Castle Meadow Road, Nottingham NG2 1BG. Tel: 0115 974 1600; fax: 0115 974 1480; website: www.hmrc.gov.uk.

National Insurance Services to Pensions Industry

2.10   The National Insurance Services to Pensions Industry (NISPI) (formerly the Contracted-Out Employments Group (COEG)) is a Directorate within the HMRC National Insurance Contributions Office and is responsible for ensuring that the pension rights of employees contracted out of the State Second Pension (S2P) (which replaced the State Earnings Related Pension Scheme (SERPS) with effect from 6 April 2002) are maintained and safeguarded (see chapter 4). In particular, NI Services to Pensions Industry is responsible for:

(*a*)   dealing with the termination of contracted-out employment, and all related matters;

(*b*)   approving and supervising schemes if they cease to be contracted out;

(*c*)   withdrawing approval of arrangements or refusing to approve them;

(*d*)   issuing certificates of non-approval and discharge of liabilities directives;

(*e*)   approval of arrangements for securing pension rights when a scheme ceases to contract out;

(*f*)   communicating with scheme authorities about the facility for checking National Insurance numbers, dates of birth etc for funding purposes; and

(*g*)   answering general queries regarding contracted-out arrangements (including personal pension arrangements).

NI Services to Pensions Industry can be contacted at the National Insurance Contributions Office, Service Development Group, Benton Park View, Newcastle upon Tyne NE98 1ZZ. Contracting-out pensions helpline: 0845 915 0150.

Occupational Pensions Board (OPB)

2.11   The OPB was dissolved by *section 150* of *PA 1995* with effect from 5 April 1997. Some of the OPB's overseeing functions were, following the OPB's dissolution, taken over by Opra (see 2.12 below) and subsequently the Regulator. The OPB's responsibilities for contracting out have been taken over by NISPI (see 2.10 above).

To place these matters in context it is worth mentioning the OPB's main functions before its dissolution on 5 April 1997, which were:

(*a*)   running the Pensions Registry (see 2.30 below, now a function of the Regulator);

(*b*)   making grants to approved bodies, for example, OPAS (see 2.43 below);

(*c*)   making modification orders, now a function of the Regulator (see 12.10 below);

(*d*)   monitoring and advising schemes on overriding legislation (for example, on preservation (see chapter 6) responsibility now rests with the trustees);

(*e*)   administering and dealing with the statutory disclosure requirements (see chapter 3, now a function of the Regulator); and

(*f*)   supervising schemes which have ceased to be contracted out (see chapter 4, now a function of the NISPI).

The Pensions Regulator (the Regulator)

Objectives and functions of the Regulator

2.12   The Pensions Regulator ('the Regulator') is the new authoritative body established under *Part 1* of *PA 2004*, effectively replacing with effect from April 2005 the previous regulatory body, the Occupational Pensions Regulatory Authority ('Opra'), which was established by *PA 1995*. The Chief Executive is Tony Hobman.

The Regulator has stated that it will be taking a more proactive and selective approach than Opra and is intended to be more flexible and responsive than Opra and thus more able to target its resources where it considers that members' benefits are at most risk. This approach recognises that Opra was restricted by the legislative framework, which often required it to take action in respect of fairly minor breaches of the law.

The role of the Regulator is defined by its objectives and functions as laid down by *PA 2004*. The objectives of the Regulator are wider than those of Opra and will not be solely concerned with occupational pension schemes. The four main objectives are as follows:

- to protect the benefits of scheme members under occupational pension schemes;

- to protect the benefits of scheme members under personal pension schemes;

- to reduce the risk of situations arising which may lead to compensation being payable from the Pension Protection Fund; and

- to promote, and improve understanding of, the good administration of 'work-based' pension schemes.

The Regulator operates in part through the Non-Executive Committee and the Determinations Panel, both of which the Regulator is under a duty to establish and maintain.

The *Non-Executive Committee* is essentially an internal regulatory body, established pursuant to *section 8* of *PA 2004* to monitor, assess and report on the functions carried out by the Regulator. Its role includes:

- reviewing the strategic direction of the Regulator;

- scrutinising the performance of the chief executive;

- monitoring the extent to which objectives and targets are being met;

- reviewing internal financial controls and statutory reporting; and

- setting the remuneration of the chief executive.

The *Determinations Panel* is the body established pursuant to *PA 2004, s 9* to determine and exercise the 'reserved regulatory functions' on behalf of the Regulator (which can be extended or modified by regulations). These functions are many and varied and are listed in *Schedule 2* to *PA 2004*. It is worth highlighting a few as follows:

Transferred from Opra (retained in relevant sections of *PA 1995*):

- trustee prohibition and suspension orders (*sections 3* and *4*);

- appointment of trustee (*section 7*);

- imposition of penalties (*section 10*);

- direct a winding up (*section 11*);

- give directions to trustees (*section 15*);

- authorise modifications to schemes (*section 69*).

Some of the new powers (as established by the relevant sections of *PA 2004*) include:

- to issue and extend freezing orders (*section 23*);

- to issue contribution notices and financial support directions (*sections 38* and *43*);

- to issue restoration orders where there has been a transaction at an undervalue (*section 52*);

- to issue notices requiring a report to be made to the Regulator (*section 71*); and

- to issue an order modifying a scheme, giving directions or imposing a schedule of contributions (*section 231*).

The Regulator may also delegate to the Determinations Panel other regulatory functions pursuant to *section 10* of *PA 2004*.

In addition to these and other specific functions the Regulator has supplementary powers under *section 6* of *PA 2004* to do anything, except borrow money, which '... is calculated to facilitate the exercise of its functions or which is incidental or conducive to their exercise'.

Codes of Practice (section 90)

2.13   The Regulator may issue practical guidance in relation to the exercise of its functions under pensions legislation and with regard to standards of conduct and practice in relation to the exercise of those functions.

The Regulator is also required to issue codes on a number of matters including what constitutes a 'reasonable period' for the purposes of any pensions legislation, the whistleblowing requirements under *PA 2004*, compliance with scheme specific funding requirements, member-nominated trustee requirements, knowledge and understanding requirements for trustees, requirements to report with regard to failure to pay contributions and other matters.

If any Code of Practice is not observed, this is not in itself a breach of a legal requirement. However, the Codes of Practice will be admissible in evidence in legal proceedings, including proceedings with the Pensions Ombudsman when, for example, consideration is given as to whether or not maladministration has occurred. *PA 2004* specifies a procedure to be followed for the issuing and publication of codes of guidance, including the publication of a draft and consultation on that draft.

The Regulator has issued a development schedule for the codes of practice it is required to issue.

Code of Practice	Summary of scope	Planned date for commencement of consultation on draft Code	Planned date for issue of Code	Expected 'in force' date
Code 1 Reporting breaches of the law	Reporting by statutory 'whistleblowers' of certain breaches of the law which affect pension schemes to the Regulator. (From April 2005 the requirement is extended to include trustees and their advisers and service providers, managers of schemes not set up under trust, and employers sponsoring or participating in work-based pension schemes.)	Consultation completed	Issued 6 April 2005	In force

Code 2 Notifiable events	Notifying the Regulator of prescribed events which occur in respect of pension schemes, and in respect of employers who sponsor pension schemes.	Consultation completed	Issued 30 June 2005	In force
Funding defined benefits	Implementation of the funding arrangements that apply to most private sector occupational pension schemes that provide defined benefits.	Consultation completed	Issued 15 February 2006	In force
Reporting late payment of contribu-tions to occupa-tional defined contribu-tions schemes	Trustees or managers of occupational defined contributions schemes to report late payments to the Regulator in certain circumstances.	Consultation completed	Early 2006	April 2006
Reporting late payment of contribu-tions to personal pension schemes	Managers of personal pension schemes to report late payments to the Regulator in certain circumstances.	Consultation completed	Early 2006	April 2006
Member-nominated trustees and directors	Implementation of arrangements to ensure that at least one third of the trustees or trustee directors are member-nominated. Definition of reasonable period within which specified steps must be taken.	Consultation completed	Early 2006	April 2006

Trustee knowledge and under-standing	Trustees of relevant schemes to have an appropriate body of knowledge and understanding of the law relating to pensions and trusts and the principles relating to the funding of occupational pension schemes and investment of scheme assets.	Consultation completed	Autumn 2005	April 2006
Reasonable periods for the purposes of the *Occupational Pensions Schemes* (*Disclosure of Information*) *Regulations 2006*	What constitutes a 'reasonable' period where mentioned in the Disclosure Regulations.	Consultation completed	Early 2006	April 2006
Early leavers – reasonable periods	Trustees' or managers' duty to provide members who leave schemes after a short period of membership with a statement of their entitlements. Definition of reasonable period within which specified steps must be taken.	Consultation completed	Early 2006	April 2006

Modifica-tion of subsisting rights	Exercise of new power to make limited modifications to subsisting rights to benefits under occupational pension schemes whilst protecting the accrued rights of members.	Consultation completed	Early 2006	April 2006
Internal controls	Implementation of the requirement for trustees and managers to have adequate internal controls to ensure that an occupational scheme is managed and administered correctly.	Consultation completed	Early 2006	Autumn 2005

Reporting breaches of the law

Who has a duty to report?

2.14   *Section 70* of *PA 2004* imposes on trustees, employers, advisors and anyone involved in the administration of a scheme a duty to report to the Regulator breaches of law in relation to the administration of the scheme which are likely to be of material significance to the Regulator.

A legal duty to report falls on:

- Trustees of trust-based pension schemes. The duty to report applies to each individually appointed trustee. If the trustee is a corporate body and the individuals concerned are trustee directors, the requirement to report falls on the trustee company.

- Managers of schemes not established under trust, i e managers of personal pension schemes, including stakeholder schemes.

- Persons otherwise involved in the administration of a scheme. This category covers all those who provide services for the trustees or managers that relate to the administration and management of occupational and personal pension schemes, including stakeholder schemes.

- Any employer participating in an occupational pension scheme.

- Professional advisers – scheme actuaries, scheme auditors, legal advisers, fund managers and custodians of scheme assets.

- Persons otherwise involved in advising a trustee (or manager of a scheme not established under trust) in relation to the scheme.

When does the duty to report arise?

2.15   The requirement to report breaches of the law arises when a duty which is:

- imposed by or by virtue of an enactment or rule of law; and
- relevant to the administration of a scheme

has not been or is not being complied with. Not every breach should be reported.

The decision to report

2.16   The decision to report requires two key judgments:

- Does the reporter have reasonable cause to believe there has been a breach of the law?
- If so, does the reporter believe the breach likely to be of material significance to the Regulator?

The Regulator has issued a Code of Practice and guidance on reporting breaches of law and some of the principal themes from those documents are described below.

Reasonable cause to believe

2.17   A reasonable cause to believe means more than a suspicion that cannot be sustained. The reporter is expected to make further inquiries if all the facts are not known. If, after further investigation, the reporter has reasonable cause to believe that a breach has occurred it is not necessary for them to gather all the evidence which the Regulator would require before taking legal action.

Likely to be of material significance

2.18   The legal requirement is that breaches likely to be of material significance to the Regulator in carrying out any of its functions must be reported. What is of material significance will depend on:

- the cause of the breach;
- the effect of the breach;
- the reaction to the breach; and
- the wider implications of the breach.

The cause of the breach

2.19   Where a contributory cause of the breach is:

- dishonesty;
- poor governance or inadequate controls resulting in deficient administration or slow or inappropriate decision-making practices; or
- incomplete or inaccurate advice; or
- acting (or failing to act) in deliberate contravention of the law,

then the breach is likely to be of material significance to the Regulator.

The effect of the breach

2.20   The Regulator considers the following to be particularly important elements which are likely to be of material significance to the Regulator in the context of its objective to protect members' benefits:

- substantially the right money is paid into the scheme at the right time;
- assets are appropriately safeguarded;
- payments out of the scheme are legitimate and timely;
- defined benefit schemes are complying with legal requirements on scheme funding;
- trustees of occupational pension schemes are properly considering their investment policy and investing in accordance with it; and
- contributions in respect of defined contributions members are correctly allocated and invested.

Making a report

2.21   All reporters should have effective arrangements in place to identify breaches that occur in areas relating to their functions. Reports must be submitted in writing and wherever practicable use the standard format available on the Regulator's website at www.thepensionsregulator.gov.uk. Each report should be dated and include as a minimum: the name of the scheme; description of the breach; any relevant dates; name of the employer; name, position and contact details of the reporter; and the role of the reporter. Additional information is required and can be reviewed on the website provided above.

Failure to comply with the obligation to report a breach is a civil offence.

The Regulator's response to a breach

2.22   The Regulator has a wide range of measures it can use in reacting to a report of a breach, including:

- assisting or instructing trustees and others to achieve compliance;

- providing education or guidance;

- appointing trustees to help run the scheme;

- removing trustees from office;

- freezing the scheme;

- imposing special measures where the scheme funding requirements of *PA 2004* are not complied with;

- ordering that the scheme's funding position be restored to the level before a breach or other detrimental events occurred; and

- imposing fines where appropriate.

Reporting notifiable events

Notifiable events duty

2.23   Trustees and employers of schemes eligible for the Pension Protection Fund (PPF) are required by *section 69* of *PA 2004* to notify certain events to the Regulator. We understand that the purpose of these provisions is to give the Regulator an early warning of problems which might give rise to a claim on the PPF. Details of events which are notifiable are set out in the *Pensions Regulator (Notifiable Events) Regulations 2005 (SI 2005 No 900)*, as amended by the *Occupational Pension Schemes (Miscellaneous Amendments) Regulations 2005 (SI 2005 No 2113)*. The Regulator has issued a Code of Practice and directions dealing with the notifiable events duty.

The duty to notify requires written notice to the Regulator of events:

- in respect of pension schemes (scheme-related events); and

- in respect of employers, in relation to their pension schemes (employer-related events).

The duty to notify falls on trustees (individually) and employers.

Timing of notification

2.24 An event must be notified in writing to the Regulator *as soon as reasonably practicable*. This will depend on the circumstances but in all cases it implies urgency. For example, where a trustee is made aware of a notifiable event on a Sunday, the Regulator should be notified on the Monday. It is not necessary to seek professional or expert advice on whether an event has occurred.

How to notify

2.25 All notifications must be in writing and, where practicable, use the standard form available on the Regulator's website at www.thepensionsregulator.gov.uk. Reports may be sent by post, e-mail or fax. The minimum information that should be included in a notification is the:

- description of the notifiable event;
- date of the event;
- name of the pension scheme;
- name of the employer; and
- name, position and contact details of the notifier.

Further additional information that the Regulator would find useful is also set out in the Code.

Events to be reported

2.26 The Regulations (which came into force on 6 April 2005) confirm which events which will need to be reported to the Regulator. The Directions (which also came into force on 6 April 2005) set down conditions excusing a report in certain circumstances.

Employer events

2.27   Employers must notify the following events:

- any decision by the employer to take action which will, or is intended to, result in a debt which is or may become due to the scheme not being paid in full;

- a decision by the employer to cease to carry on business in the UK, or cessation of business in the UK without a decision having been taken;

- receipt by the employer of advice that it is trading wrongfully or a director or former director of the company knows that there is no reasonable prospect that the company will avoid going into insolvent liquidation;

- any breach of a banking covenant by the employer *unless* the conditions in A and B below are satisfied;

- any change in the employer's credit rating or the employer ceasing to have a credit rating;

- a decision by a controlling company to relinquish control of the employer, or the controlling company relinquishing control without a decision to do so having been taken, *unless* the conditions in A and B below are satisfied;

- two or more changes in the holders of any key employer posts within the previous twelve months *unless* the conditions in A and B below are satisfied;

- the conviction of an individual for an offence involving dishonesty, if the offence was committed while the individual was a director or partner of the employer.

Trustee events

2.28   Trustees must report the following events:

- any decision by the trustees to take action which will, or is intended to, result in any debt which is or may become due to the scheme not being paid in full *unless* the conditions in A, B and C below are satisfied;

- two or more changes in the holders of any key scheme post within the previous twelve months *unless* conditions A and B below are satisfied;

- a decision by the trustees to make or accept a transfer value from another scheme, or making or accepting such a transfer where no decision is required, the value of which is more than the lower of 5 per cent of the value of the scheme assets or £1.5 million *unless* the conditions in A and B below are satisfied;

- a decision by the trustees to grant benefits on more favourable terms than those provided for by the scheme rules without either seeking advice from the actuary or securing additional funding where so advised;

- a decision by the trustees to grant benefits or rights to benefits to a member, or granting such benefits where no decision is required, the cost of which is more than the lower of 5 per cent of the scheme assets and £1.5 million *unless* the conditions of A and B below are satisfied.

The Conditions

2.29   *Condition A:* The value of the scheme's assets is equal to or greater than the value of the scheme's liabilities calculated on the relevant basis. The relevant basis is currently the most recent minimum funding requirement ('MFR') valuation. This will, in time, be replaced by the Pension Protection Fund risk-based levy valuation (*section 179* of *PA 2004* valuation).

Condition B: The trustees have not incurred a duty to make a report in the previous twelve months for:

- the employer's failure to make a payment to the scheme in accordance with the most recently agreed schedule of contributions; or

- the employer's failure to pay contributions due under the schedule of contributions on or before the due date.

Condition C: The decision by the trustees is in respect of a debt where the full amount is less than 0.5 per cent of the scheme's assets calculated on the relevant basis (see Condition A).

Condition D: The change in credit rating is other than from investment to sub-investment grade whether the credit rating is provided by a recognised credit agency.

The Registry

2.30   The office of the Registrar of Pension Schemes was established by the *Social Security Act 1990*. Opra took over the management of the Registry from the OPB on 6 April 1997. The office of Registrar was abolished on 6 April 2005 by *PA 2004* and the Regulator is now charged by *section 59* of *PA 2004* with maintaining a register of occupational and personal pension schemes.

The Regulator is required, in respect of each 'registrable scheme', to record in the register 'registrable information' and any notifications that a scheme has been wound up or transferred to the PPF.

Registrable schemes are prescribed in the *Register of Occupational and Personal Pension Schemes Regulations 2005* (*SI 2005 No 597*) and include all pension schemes with more than one member, other than those providing death benefits only, which were approved by the Inland Revenue before 6 April 2006 (or which are registered schemes with HMRC after that date) and public service pension schemes.

Registrable information is defined in *section 60* of *PA 2004* and includes:

- the name and address of the scheme;

- the names and addresses of each trustee or manager;

- the status of the scheme (for example, is it admitting new members and are benefits accruing);

- the categories of benefits; and

- the number of members (occupational schemes only).

The *Register of Occupational and Personal Pension Schemes Regulations 2005* require further additional information including the category of the scheme, the nature of the business of any relevant employer and whether the scheme has commenced winding up.

The Regulator may obtain the information required for the register by issuing scheme return notices under *section 63* of *PA 2004*. Where a new registrable scheme is established or a scheme becomes registrable the trustees or managers must notify the Regulator and provide the registrable information within three months. Where there is a change in registrable information or a scheme ceases to be registrable or is wound up, the trustees or managers must notify the Regulator as soon as reasonably practicable. Failure to do so could give rise to civil penalties under *section 10* of *PA 1995* (*section 62* of *PA 2004*).

The Department for Work and Pensions runs a pensions tracing service which allows individuals who think they are entitled to benefit under a scheme to make an application for information. The *Register of Occupational and Personal Pension Schemes Regulations 2005* allow the Secretary of State access to information from the register and the right to inspect the register for the purposes of operating the tracing service.

The Pensions Regulator Tribunal

2.31   The Pensions Regulator Tribunal was established with effect from 6 April 2005 by *section 102* of *PA 2004*. References may be made to the Tribunal by someone subject to or affected by a determination of the Regulator. Each tribunal is made up of individuals selected from a panel appointed by the

Lord Chancellor. There are currently eight legally qualified members of the 'panel of chairmen' (including the President, Stephen Oliver QC) and 18 lay members. When considering a reference the tribunal may consider any evidence relating to the subject matter of the reference, whether it was before the Regulator or not. On determining a reference the Tribunal must remit the matter to the Regulator with appropriate directions for giving effect to its determination. This may include directions to vary or revoke the Regulator's original determination or to substitute a different determination.

Matters should generally be referred to the Tribunal within 28 days of the determination or notice of the Regulator but an application to the Tribunal to make a late reference may be made (*rule 13* of the *Pensions Regulator Tribunal Rules 2005 (SI 2005 No 690)*). The *Rules* set out the procedures to be adopted by the Tribunal. Matters should usually be decided following an oral hearing but this may be dispensed with in certain circumstances including where the parties agree in writing, the Regulator does not oppose the reference, the Regulator does not properly respond to the reference or the reference is for directions only (*rules 20* and *21*). Appeals from the Tribunal may be made to the Court of Appeal (Court of Session in Scotland) with the permission of the Tribunal. Permission may be requested at the end of the hearing or in writing within 14 days of notification of the decision (*rule 28*).

A legal assistance scheme has been established (*Pensions Regulator Tribunal (Legal Assistance Scheme) Regulations 2005 (SI 2005 No 781)*) to provide funding for legal advice, assistance and representation for those referring matters to the Tribunal. Legal assistance may be granted where the Tribunal is satisfied that it is in the interests of justice to do so and that the applicant's financial resources are such that he requires assistance in meeting legal costs in relation to the proceedings before the Tribunal.

Cost of the Regulator

2.32   For the purposes of meeting the expenditure of the Regulator regulations under *section 175* of *PSA 1993* (as amended by *section 165* of *PA 1995* and *section 174* of *PA 2004*) make provision for imposing a levy. The levy is payable to the Secretary of State by or on behalf of the administrator of public service schemes or the trustees or managers of occupational or personal pension schemes.

The Regulator can be contacted at The Pensions Regulator, Napier House, Trafalgar Place, Brighton BN1 4DW. Tel: 0870 6063636; e-mail: customersupport@thepensionsregulator.gov.uk; website www.thepensionsregulator.gov.uk.

The Pension Protection Fund (PPF)

Establishment of the PPF

2.33

'The Pensions Act 2004 has established the Pension Protection Fund to protect members of private sector defined benefit schemes whose firms become insolvent with insufficient funds in their pension scheme.

We will make sure that in future individuals in final salary schemes will never again face the injustice of saving throughout their lives only to have their hard-earned pension slashed just before they retire. The Pension Protection Fund will allow individuals to save with confidence.'

Andrew Smith, the then Secretary of State for Work and Pensions,
12 February 2004.

The aim of the PPF

2.34   The main purpose of the PPF is to ensure that where a company with a UK-based defined benefit scheme becomes insolvent, and its pension fund is not sufficiently funded, members can be reassured that they will still receive the main benefits to which they are entitled. The PPF will, where it has assumed responsibility for the scheme, provide benefits in accordance with the *'pension compensation provisions'* which are:

- where a member has attained normal pension age, they will receive 100 per cent of their entitlement;

- for members who have yet to reach normal pension age, 90 per cent of their entitlement;

- dependants' pensions payable on the future death of the member are limited to 50 per cent of the member's pension;

- pensions in payment built up from April 1997 will increase in line with RPI capped at 2.5 per cent; and

- the amount of pension payable will be subject to an overall cap (£25,000 at age 65) – this cap will not apply to those over normal pension age or receiving an ill-health pension.

Eligibility for the PPF

2.35 Most private sector tax approved defined benefit or hybrid occupational pension schemes will be eligible for the PPF. Defined contributions schemes are not eligible (*section 126* of *PA 2004*). Any scheme which commenced winding up before 6 April 2005 will not be eligible (although some members of such schemes may be eligible for the Government's Financial Assistance Scheme). Schemes excluded from the PPF include those with fewer than two members and schemes with fewer than twelve members and all members are trustees and unanimous decisions are required or there is a statutory independent trustee. The *Pension Protection Fund (Entry Rules) Regulations 2005 (SI 2005 No 590), reg 2* (as amended) lists those schemes which are not eligible.

An otherwise eligible scheme will be rendered ineligible if the trustees compromise a *section 75* debt without actuarial advice or the consent of the Board (*regulation 2(2)*).

When will the PPF get involved?

2.36 In broad terms, the PPF will become involved in a scheme if an insolvency event (as defined in *section 121* of *PA 2004*) occurs in relation to the employer after 5 April 2005 or, where the employer is a non-corporate organisation such as a trade union or charity, it appears to the trustees or the Regulator that the employer is likely to cease to continue as a going concern (*section 129* of *PA 2004*).

Where a qualifying insolvency event occurs, there then follows an 'assessment period' during which the Board will determine whether the PPF will take responsibility for the scheme, which it must do if:

- the value of the assets of the scheme were less than the amount of the *protected liabilities*; and

- a 'scheme rescue' has been deemed impossible by the insolvency practitioner.

The protected liabilities are the liabilities for benefits up to the level of PPF compensation, plus scheme liabilities other than for benefits and the estimated winding-up expenses.

During this period of assessment, everything is frozen. No new members may be admitted to the scheme, contributions are suspended (other than those due to be paid before the beginning of the assessment period), no benefits accrue under the scheme in respect of the members and benefits in payment will be reduced to the PPF protection level. In addition, the Board may also give directions to ensure that the scheme's protected liabilities do not exceed its assets or keep the excess to a minimum.

In addition to the above, during an assessment period, the winding up of a scheme cannot begin, no transfers or transfer payments in respect of member's rights are to be made from the scheme and no other steps may be taken to discharge any liability to the scheme in respect of pensions or other benefits or such other liabilities as may be prescribed. For these purposes, the scheme, to a certain extent, ceases to function and civil penalties will apply to any trustee or manager who fails to take all reasonable steps to ensure compliance.

In order to assist with its assessment, the Board must obtain an actuarial valuation of the scheme. This is referred to as a *section 143* valuation. Regulations set out how the assets and protected liabilities are to be determined and the Board has issued guidance to assist actuaries undertaking *section 143* valuations.

If the valuation reveals a deficit of protected liabilities, the Board will issue to the trustees or the managers a 'transfer notice' and assume responsibility for the scheme. The effect of the Board assuming responsibility for a scheme is that:

- the property, rights and liabilities of the scheme are transferred to the Board without further assurance, with effect from the time the trustees or managers receive the transfer notice;

- the trustees or managers of the scheme are discharged from their pension obligations from that time;

- the Board assumes responsibility for securing that compensation is paid in accordance with the compensation provisions; and

- the scheme is to be treated as having been wound up immediately after that time.

If the Board determines that the valuation does not disclose a deficit, it must refuse responsibility for the scheme and issue a notice to that effect to the Regulator, the trustees/managers and to any insolvency practitioner (a 'withdrawal notice'). The trustees or manager can make an application to the Board asking them to reconsider their decision. Where the Board refuses responsibility the trustees will be required to wind up the scheme, unless a 'scheme rescue' has occurred and the scheme has been taken over by another employer.

The Board of the PPF

2.37   The role of the Board is to hold, manage and apply the PPF and the Fraud Compensation Fund (see below). Membership of the Board consists of a chairman (Lawrence Churchill was officially appointed by the Secretary of State on 1 July 2004), the chief executive of the Board (Myra Kinghorn was officially appointed on 1 September 2004) and at least five other people, who are described as 'ordinary members'. To ensure independence, the chairman cannot be appointed from the staff of the Board or be the chairman of the Regulator.

The Board has a Non-Executive Committee, consisting only of non-executive members of the Board. Its role is to keep under review the question of whether the Board's internal financial controls secure the proper conduct of its financial affairs; determining the terms and conditions as to remuneration of any chief executive and any member of the staff who is also to be an executive member of the Board. As part of its functions, the Board must submit an annual report and accounts to the Secretary of State who, in turn, will present them to Parliament.

Funding the PPF

2.38   The PPF will be funded by a levy for each financial year after the initial period (which will be funded by an initial levy) when the Board *must* impose both of the following:

- a risk-based levy; and
- a scheme-based levy.

A *risk-based* levy will be assessed by reference to the difference between the value of the scheme's assets and the amount of its protected liabilities, the likelihood of an insolvency event occurring in relation to an employer and other factors which the Board considers appropriate. These include, the risks associated with the nature of a scheme's investments when compared with the nature of its liabilities and other matters to be prescribed.

The *scheme-based* levy will be assessed by reference to various scheme factors, which include the amount of a scheme's liabilities to or in respect of members, the number of members, or category of members, the total annual amount of pensionable earnings of active members of a scheme and such other factors that will be prescribed in the regulations.

Before the beginning of each financial year, the Board must determine the factors with which to assess the levies, the timing of the assessments, the rate and when the levies will become payable. The levy imposed by the Board will be subject to a ceiling, which is set by the Secretary of State before the beginning of each financial year (to be increased annually in line with national average earnings), and the *risk-based* levy must amount to at least 80 per cent of the total amounts the Board estimates as being raised by both levies – the aim being that costs are minimised for 'good' employers with well-funded schemes.

The levy is payable by the trustees or managers of the scheme or such other person as prescribed in the regulations and is payable to the Board.

The 'initial levy' based on the scheme factors in respect of eligible schemes for the period which begins on 6 April 2005 and ends either on the following 31 March or potentially for an additional twelve months thereafter. In addition to the above levies, there is also an 'administration levy' which will be applied for the purpose of meeting the expenditure of the Secretary of State in establishing the Board and ongoing costs of the PPF.

The Board has undertaken consultation and proposes to introduce the risk-based levy from April 2006 (with 80 per cent risk-based levy and 20 per cent scheme-based). The current proposal for the first year is that scheme funding information may either be a full valuation undertaken for the purpose (this is referred to as a *section 179* of *PA 2004* valuation) or the most recent MFR valuation which will then be modified by the PPF to produce results consistent with the *section 179* valuations. The Board has engaged Dun and Bradstreet to provide insolvency risk scoring for employers, which will be ranked into one of ten grades. Each scheme's levy will be set based on a multiple of funding levels and insolvency risk. A cap on the levy of 3 per cent of each scheme's protected liabilities is proposed. The Board currently proposes that relevant information on scheme funding and details of employers should be provided by March 2006 but final proposals are awaited. During consultation the Board conceded that sums of money paid into schemes since the most recent valuation should be taken into account. It is going to consult further on whether contingent assets should also be taken into account.

Information to be provided to the Board

2.39   The Board may issue a notice to persons including the trustees or manager of the scheme, the employer, a professional adviser to the scheme and an insolvency practitioner, amongst others. When such a notice is received, the information must be provided in the form prescribed, at such a place and within timescales specified in the notice.

The Board's powers are such that it can enter premises at any reasonable time and whilst there, make inquiries as necessary, request any person on the premises to produce or secure the production of any relevant document, take copies of such documentation and may even remove them from the premises if it is necessary to prevent their interference.

Where a person (without reasonable excuse) neglects or refuses to provide information, he will be guilty of an offence and is liable on conviction to a fine not exceeding £5,000. If a person intentionally and without reasonable excuse alters, suppresses, conceals or destroys any document which is liable to be produced, a higher fine or a custodial sentence, not exceeding two years, could be imposed. The same penalties would be imposed on someone who knowingly or recklessly provides information which is false or misleading.

The Fraud Compensation Scheme

2.40   On 1 September 2005 the Board replaced the Pensions Compensation Board as the body responsible for fraud compensation. It may pay compensation to occupational pension scheme members where there has been a misappropriation of assets/funds or cases of fraud. This also covers some schemes that are not covered by the PPF, including defined contributions schemes. Compensation may be payable where:

- the value of the assets of an eligible scheme has been reduced as a consequence of an act or omission which constitutes an offence of dishonesty; and

- a qualifying insolvency event in relation to the employer has occurred and a scheme failure notice has been issued.

The Fraud Compensation Fund will be paid for by way of a levy. It will be determined by the Board, be payable at prescribed times, at a certain rate, and must be paid by the trustees or managers of a scheme. The Board will determine which schemes will be required to pay the levy, calculate the amount of the levy in relation to those schemes and notify any person liable to pay the levy in respect of the scheme as well as when it becomes payable. It is understood that no levy will be payable for the year 2006/2007.

PPF Ombudsman

2.41   The office of PPF Ombudsman was established with effect from 6 April 2006 by *section 209* of *PA 2004*. The first PPF Ombudsman is David Laverick, who is also the current Pensions Ombudsman. 'Reviewable matters' may be referred to the PPF Ombudsman following a reconsideration by the Board under *section 207* of *PA 2004*. Any person who is sent, or is required to be sent, a notice of the reconsideration decision is entitled to refer the matter to the PPF Ombudsman (*regulation 2* of the *Pension Protection Fund* (*Reference of Reviewable Matters to the PPF Ombudsman*) *Regulations 2005* (*SI 2005 No 2024*)).

Financial Assistance Scheme

2.42   The Financial Assistance Scheme (FAS) was introduced at a late stage of the Pensions Bill 2004 as a result of sustained lobbying by and on behalf of members of defined benefit pension schemes who had lost some or all of their benefits when their schemes wound up in deficit but would not be able to qualify for the PPF (because the winding up had commenced before 6 April 2005). The provisions of *section 286* of *PA 2004* allowed for the establishment of the FAS but provide very little detail. The *Financial Assistance Scheme Regulations 2005 (SI 2005 No 1986)* came into force for most purposes on 1 September 2005. The Regulations set out which members of which schemes will qualify for assistance. Schemes which qualify for the FAS will include most occupational pension schemes (other than defined contributions or public sector schemes) which commenced winding up between 1 January 1997 and 5 April 2005 where the employer suffers an insolvency event by 28 February 2006 at the latest (*regulation 9*). The scheme manager of the FAS has discretion to extend the period beyond 28 February 2006. Qualifying members are those members or former members whose benefits are unlikely to be (or have not been) satisfied in full and who will reach scheme normal retirement age by 14 May 2007. Assistance is also payable to those in receipt of survivor's benefits when the scheme commenced winding up and will reach scheme normal retirement age by 14 May 2007. Assistance is limited to 80 per cent of the expected pension capped at £12,000 per annum, with a spouse's (and surviving civil partner's) pension of 50 per cent of that sum on death (*Schedule 2* to *the Regulations*). Payments will usually not commence until the scheme has completed winding up. *Regulation 18* (as amended by the *Financial Assistance Scheme (Modifications and Miscellaneous Amendments) Regulations 2005 (SI 2005 No 3256)*) which allows interim payments of 60 per cent of the predicted capped pension to be made to qualifying members over 64 or in terminal ill health or to a survivor of a qualifying member during the winding up of a qualifying scheme.

The *Financial Assistance Scheme (Internal Review) Regulations 2005 (SI 2005 No 1994)* allow for those affected to apply for a review of a decision in relation to the FAS. The *Financial Assistance Scheme (Appeal) Regulations 2005 (SI 2005 No 3273)* came into force on 29 November 2005 and allow for the appeal to the PPF Ombudsman of a decision which had been subject to internal review (see 2.41 above).

The Pensions Advisory Service

2.43   The Pensions Advisory Service ('TPAS') (formerly 'OPAS'), is an independent, grant-aided, non-profit making company limited by guarantee with a network of local volunteer advisers, who are experienced pensions professionals. The aim of TPAS is to provide free assistance to members of the public with difficulties which they have failed to resolve with the trustees, administrators or pension provider of their pension scheme. The TPAS service is available to anyone who believes he has pension rights. This includes active members of pension schemes (including company, personal and stakeholder arrangements), pensioners, those with deferred pensions from previous employment, and dependants. TPAS can be contacted directly or via the Citizen's Advice Bureau.

TPAS's remit is to explain pension scheme benefits to members and liaise directly with trustees or administrators to provide further information to members or to assist a member in obtaining his correct legal entitlement from a pension scheme.

If TPAS is unable to resolve the problem but believe that the complaint is valid it will assist a member in making a formal complaint to the appropriate Ombudsman (the Pensions Ombudsman or the Financial Services Ombudsman). TPAS cannot:

(*a*)   initiate legal action on a member's behalf;

(*b*)   give financial advice;

(*c*)   deal with complaints from a group or body of pension scheme members;

(*d*)   act as a lobbying force for any improvement in pension scheme benefits;

(*e*)   act through intermediaries;

(*f*)   offer advice on State pension benefits; or

(*g*)   assist if legal proceedings have been initiated or if the Pensions Ombudsman (see 2.44 below) has already investigated a complaint.

TPAS can be contacted at 11 Belgrave Road, London SW1V 1RB. National telephone helpline: 0845 6012923; fax: 020 7233 8016. E-mail inquiries should be sent to: enquiries@opas.org.uk. Website: www.opas.org.uk.

Pensions Ombudsman

The role of the Pensions Ombudsman

2.44   The Pensions Ombudsman's office was established on 1 October 1990. The Ombudsman is appointed by the Secretary of State under *section 145* of *PSA 1993* which also sets out his role. Under *PA 1995* the Ombudsman has power to appoint his own staff (with the approval of the Secretary of State for Work and Pensions) and has taken advantage of this by seeking to appoint professional staff from the pensions industry and legally qualified pensions experts. The Ombudsman's budget is paid for out of the levy imposed on all occupational pension schemes.

The role of the Pensions Ombudsman is to investigate and decide complaints and disputes about the way that pension schemes are run. He is completely independent and acts as an impartial adjudicator.

The Pensions Ombudsman is dealing with more and more disputes; this is due to a number of factors including:

(*a*)   the extent of the Ombudsman's jurisdiction; and

(*b*)   a greater awareness of the existence of his office (particularly as all pension schemes are now required to notify their members of the existence of both TPAS and the Pensions Ombudsman).

In the light of this increased activity on the part of the Pensions Ombudsman's office it is more likely that, should a dispute not be resolved by the trustees under the internal dispute resolution procedure or by TPAS, a complaint will be made to the Pensions Ombudsman.

Section 274 of *PA 2004* inserted *section 145A* of *PSA 1993* which makes provision for the appointment of a Deputy Pensions Ombudsman from 6 April 2006. The Deputy Pensions Ombudsman is appointed by the Secretary of State and may perform the functions of the Pensions Ombudsman where there is a vacancy in that office, where the Pensions Ombudsman is for any reason unable to perform his duties or otherwise as allowed by the Secretary of State.

Jurisdiction

2.45   The complaints and disputes which the Ombudsman may investigate are described in *section 146* of *PSA 1993* (as amended by the *Child Support, Pensions and Social Security Act 2000*) and are summarised in the following table:

Type of scheme	Who may complain or refer a dispute to the Ombudsman	Parties against whom a complaint may be made or a dispute may be referred to the Ombudsman	Nature of complaint or dispute
'Complaints of maladministration'			
Occupational or personal	By or on behalf of any actual or potential beneficiary.	Trustees, managers, employers and/or administrators.	Complaint of injustice in consequence of maladministration of the scheme.

Occupational	By or on behalf of any trustee or, manager of a scheme.	Trustees, employers.	Complaint of maladministration of that scheme.
Occupational	An employer in relation to a scheme.	Trustees or managers of that scheme.	Complaint of maladministration of that scheme.
Occupational	By or on behalf of any trustee or manager of a scheme.	Trustees or managers of another scheme.	Complaint of maladministration of the other scheme.
Trust scheme	By or on behalf of an independent trustee.	Trustees or former trustees who are/were not independent trustees of that scheme.	Complaint of maladministration of that scheme.
'Disputes of fact or law'			
Occupational or personal	By any actual or potential beneficiary.	Trustees, managers and/or employers.	Dispute of fact or law.
Occupational	By or on behalf of any trustee or manager of a scheme.	Trustees, managers or employers of that scheme. (Note that trustees/managers cannot refer disputes with managers; and employers cannot refer disputes with other employers.)	Dispute of fact or law.
Occupational	An employer in relation to a scheme.	Trustees or managers of that scheme.	Dispute of fact or law.
Occupational	By or on behalf of any party to the dispute.	Trustees or managers of another scheme.	Dispute of fact or law in relation to the other scheme.
'Complaints or disputes'			
Occupational	By or on behalf of at least half the trustees of the scheme.	Different trustees of the same scheme.	Dispute of fact or law or maladministration of that scheme.

Occupational subject to insolvency procedures	By or on behalf of the independent trustee who is a party to the dispute.	Trustees or former trustees of the scheme who are not independent.	Any dispute (in relation to a time when *section 22* of *PA 1995* applies).
Occupational	By or on behalf of the sole trustee.		Any question relating to the carrying out of functions of that trustee.

The word 'maladministration' is not defined in the legislation, although the Pensions Ombudsman's booklet describes it as including bias, neglect, inattention, delay, incompetence and arbitrariness. The complaint must include behaviour which constitutes maladministration which in turn has lead to 'injustice'. Again, this is not defined but is described by the Pensions Ombudsman as not only including a financial loss, but incorporating distress, delay or inconvenience. In November 2005 the Pensions Ombudsman issued a guide 'How to Avoid the Pensions Ombudsman'. It contains guidance for those running pension schemes, based on actual cases which have been determined by the Pensions Ombudsman, on how they might operate schemes and manage disputes in order to avoid complaints being made. It is available on www.pensions-ombudsman.org.uk.

The *Personal and Occupational Pension Schemes* (*Pensions Ombudsman*) *Regulations 1996* (*SI 1996 No 2475*) ('the *Ombudsman Regulations*'), introduced under *PA 1995*, provide that the Ombudsman may not investigate or determine a complaint unless the internal dispute resolution procedure has first been followed (*Ombudsman Regulations, reg 3*). (The internal dispute resolution procedure is discussed in chapter 3.) The only exception to this is where a complaint has been referred to the internal dispute procedure and the Ombudsman is satisfied that there is no prospect of a decision being reached within a reasonable period (*regulation 3(2)* of the *Ombudsman Regulations*).

Regulation 5 of the *Ombudsman Regulations* covers the time limits for referring a dispute to the Ombudsman's office. The Ombudsman is not permitted to investigate a complaint if it is received by him more than three years after the date on which the act or omission complained of occurred, or three years after the date on which the complainant knew or ought to have known of its occurrence. However, this period can be extended where the Ombudsman believes it was reasonable for a complaint not to be made before the end of this period, in which case the time limit may be extended to such further period as he considers reasonable (*regulation 5(3)* of the *Ombudsman Regulations*).

Regulation 2 of the *Ombudsman Regulations* also confirms the extension of the Ombudsman's jurisdiction to administrators of pension schemes. The definition of 'administrator' includes 'any person concerned with the administration' of a scheme. It has been held that the jurisdiction of the Ombudsman extends to situations where an insurance company manages a scheme from day to day (*Century Life v The Pensions Ombudsman (1995) PLR 135*) even where there are separate trustees and that, in these circumstances, the insurance company can fall within the definition of a 'manager'. It may also extend to other advisers in some circumstances, as shown in the Pension Ombudsman's determination in the 2003 case of *McMann Interiors Limited [L00552]*, when the incorrect actuarial guidance produced by the insurance company's actuary was held to be maladministration. *Section 275* of *PA 2004* has clarified the jurisdiction in relation to administrators by inserting new *section 146(4A)* into *PSA 1993* which provides that a person is concerned with the administration of a scheme where he is responsible for carrying out 'an act' of administration concerned with the scheme. This effectively reverses the case of *Britannic Asset Management v Pensions Ombudsman (2002) 49 PBLR* where it was suggested that in order to be an administrator within the jurisdiction of the Pensions Ombudsman a person would have to be 'engaged to act, or advise, in or about the trustees' affairs in running the scheme' thus assuming some type of ongoing formal relationship.

Investigating a complaint

2.46 The procedure which the Ombudsman follows during his investigations is set out in the *Personal and Occupational Pension Schemes (Pensions Ombudsman) (Procedure) Rules 1995 (SI 1995 No 1053)* ('the *Procedure Regulations*' (as amended)); it is summarised in the booklet accompanying the complaint form, which is sent out, on request, to those wishing to bring a complaint. Upon receipt of the complaint form a caseworker at the Ombudsman's office will make an initial review of the case to decide whether it should be accepted for formal investigation. Then the complaint form and accompanying papers, if any, are copied to the respondent (ie the employer, trustees, managers or administrators) and any other person against whom allegations are made in order to allow them an opportunity to respond to the allegations (*regulation 5(2)* of the *Procedure Regulations*).

The Ombudsman has powers to demand papers from parties (*section 150(1)* of *Part X* of *PSA 1993*) who may hold them and can also hold oral hearings if he considers this necessary (although to date, these have been rare (*regulation 10(1)* of the *Procedure Regulations*)). Both the complainant and the respondent have an opportunity, with leave of the Ombudsman, to submit a supplementary statement and/or amend details of their original complaint/ response (*regulations 3* and *7* of the *Procedure Regulations*).

In conducting the investigation the Ombudsman must comply with the statutory rules to ensure fairness and must also comply with the principles of natural justice (*Duffield v Pensions Ombudsman (1996) PLR 285*). In particular, he must:

(a)   make clear to the respondent the specific allegation(s) to be investigated;

(b)   express the substance of the allegation(s) in plain and simple language; and

(c)   disclose to the respondent all potentially relevant information obtained by him (particularly all evidence and representations made by the complainant).

The Court of Appeal's 1999 decision in *Edge v Pensions Ombudsman (1999) PLR 215* emphasised this need for the Ombudsman to observe the principles of natural justice. In particular, it was decided that he could not consider complaints which could only be remedied by steps which would adversely affect someone who was not a party to the investigation. Turning this the other way, in the recent case of *Marsh Mercer Pension Scheme v Pensions Ombudsman [2001] 16 PBLR (28)* (the *Williamson Case*) heard in the High Court, the Ombudsman's decision that a pension scheme should equalise all GMP's between men and women was set aside. Principally, it was held that the Pension Ombudsman had affected all members of the scheme, not only the complainant. Accordingly, he should have either declined jurisdiction or made a decision which would only affect the complainant.

After receiving a copy of the complaint the respondent has 21 days within which to produce a written reply (*regulation 6(3)* of the *Procedure Regulations*), although time extensions can be requested (*regulation 16(1)* of the *Procedure Regulations*). The reply can include a reference to any other person (such as a manager or administrator of the scheme) who, in his opinion, has a direct interest in the subject matter of the complaint (*regulation 6(2)* of the *Procedure Regulations*). It is not, however, possible for the respondent to join a third party as a second respondent. The Ombudsman will then issue a written determination of his decision, which will initially be sent out to both the respondent and the complainant in draft form for their comments. At this stage, changes to the determination can still be made.

After investigating the complaint, and examining the comments of both parties, the Ombudsman will issue a final written determination. This determination will direct the trustees or managers of the scheme concerned 'to take or refrain from taking' such action as the Ombudsman considers appropriate (*section 151(2)* of *Part X* of *PSA 1993*). Following a number of conflicting authorities it is now thought that the Pensions Ombudsman can award compensation for distress and inconvenience to a complainant although this is not beyond doubt. In *Westminster City Council v Haywood and the Pensions Ombudsman (1996) PLR 161*, the Council appealed against the Ombudsman's directions for damages to be paid. The award was set aside by the High Court and an appeal was made to the Court of Appeal. The Court of Appeal did not rule on the matter as it held that the Ombudsman did not have the requisite power to hear the complaint at all.

However, the courts have made clear that if the Ombudsman does have power to award compensation he should consider not only the amount of compensation but also upon whom the ultimate liability for this will fall (for example, it may not be appropriate for a liability to fall on a scheme which is in deficit). The Ombudsman's determination is binding on the parties, subject only to an appeal to the High Court on a point of law, and can be enforced through the county court. Costs cannot be awarded against a complainant, even if the complaint is not upheld.

It is becoming increasingly common for the Ombudsman's determinations to be appealed to the High Court under the High Court's general jurisdiction to hear appeals from any court, tribunal or person. This is referred to in *Part 52* of the *Civil Procedure Rules*.

Notice of the appeal must be served and the appeal entered within 28 days after the date of the Ombudsman's determination. The appeal may only be made on a point of law and the Ombudsman himself will be a respondent to the Appeal (although in practice he may not appear), in addition to the original complainant. A High Court judge has discretion to remit matters on appeal to the Ombudsman for further consideration. The Ombudsman has stated that the number of appeals against his determinations may threaten his role as 'a provider of a cheap and informal service in relation to pension disputes'.

David Laverick (a solicitor who was Director for the North of England with the Office of the Local Government Ombudsman and, more recently, former Chief Executive of the Family Health Services Appeal Authority), took over the role of Pensions Ombudsman from Dr Julian Farrand on 1 September 2001.

The Pensions Ombudsman website can be found at www.pensions-ombudsman.org.uk and determinations issued from 1 April 2001 (and frequently requested determinations issued before 1 April 2000) are available for review. The Pensions Ombudsman can be contacted at 11 Belgrave Road, London SW1V 1RB. Tel: 020 7834 9144; fax: 020 7821 0065; e-mail: enquiries@pensions-ombudsman.org.uk.

Other bodies

Pensions Management Institute (PMI)

2.47   The PMI was established in 1976 to promote professionalism amongst those working in the field of pensions. It is an independent non-political organisation which establishes, maintains and improves professional standards in every aspect of pension scheme management and consultancy. There are four grades of membership: the first is student membership, which is the introductory level for those wishing to study the Institute's examinations. After student membership, there are a further three grades of qualified membership; Ordinary Member (someone who has passed one of the Institute's examinations), Associate Member (someone who has passed the Institute's examinations and has three years' experience in pensions management or administration) and Fellowship (an individual who was an Associate and has eight years' experience, five of which must have been spent in a position with 'substantial pensions accountability and responsibility'). The PMI is directed by a Council of 16 elected fellows, who are actively involved in pension schemes.

The PMI also offers examinations for trustees in basic pensions knowledge, a qualification in administration, a Diploma in international employee benefits and the retirement provision certificate to name a few.

The PMI can be contacted at PMI House, 4–10 Artillery Lane, London E1 7LS. Tel: 020 7247 1452; fax: 020 7375 0603; e-mail: enquiries@pension-pmi.org.uk; website: www.pensions-pmi.org.uk.

The National Association of Pension Funds (NAPF)

2.48   The NAPF describes itself as the 'principal UK body representing the interests of the employer sponsored pensions movement'. Among its members are large and small companies, local authority and public sector bodies which provide pensions for over ten million employees and five million people in retirement, accounting for more than £600 billion of pension funds. NAPF members also include corporate trustees and other organisations providing professional advice to schemes. The NAPF have also recently announced a new membership category which allows individual trustees, trustee directors and chairmen of trustee boards of NAPF member funds to join. The NAPF's principle aim is to encourage pension provision by employers by representing the interests of members to the UK Government, Europe, regulators and other professional bodies (including the media). It seeks to achieve this by:

(*a*)   influencing public opinion;

(*b*)   consulting government bodies;

(*c*)   collecting and disseminating information on best practice and trends involving schemes;

(*d*)   publishing guidelines and information; and

(*e*)   providing education in the form of seminars and conferences.

The NAPF can be contacted at NIOC House, 4 Victoria Street, London SW1H 0NX. Tel: 020 7808 1300; fax: 020 7222 7585; e-mail: mail@napf.co.uk; website: www.napf.co.uk.

Information Commissioner

2.49   Although not a pensions body as such, the Information Commission-er's Office regulates the holding, use and protection of personal information relating to living individuals by data controllers. The Information Commissioner enforces and oversees the *Data Protection Act 1998* and the *Freedom of Information Act 2000*. The Commissioner is a UK independent supervisory authority.

The Information Commissioner maintains a public register of data controllers. Each register entry contains the name and address of the data controller and a general description of the processing of personal data by a data controller. The public register is updated weekly, but new notifications, renewal and amendments may take several weeks to appear during busy periods. Under the *Data Protection Act 1998* the Information Commissioner can, in certain circumstances, serve an information notice and assess compliance with the Act and, where there has been a breach, serve an enforcement notice ordering compliance. The impact of the data protection legislation and in particular, the *Data Protection Act 1998* is considered further in chapter 3.

The Information Commissioner's Office can be contacted at:

Wycliffe House
Water Lane
Wilmslow
Cheshire
SK9 5AF

Information line: 01625 545 745;
website: www.informationcommissionergov.uk/.

The Department for Work and Pensions

2.50   The Department for Work and Pensions (DWP) is responsible for employment, equality, benefits, pensions and child support. It was formed in June 2001 from parts of the former Department of Social Security and the Department for Education and Employment.

The DWP's priorities include (amongst others) a new pension service to provide information and support to today's and tomorrow's pensioners. The Secretary of State for Work and Pensions is currently John Hutton MP and he has overall responsibility for all work and pension matters. Stephen Timms MP is the Minister for Pensions whose responsibilities include (but are not limited to): pensions overview, pensions legislation, the Pensions Service and regulatory reform.

2.50 *People involved with pensions*

To contact the DWP or any minister write to the Correspondence Unit, Room 540, The Adelphi, 1–11 John Adam Street, London WC2N 6HT or via their website: www.dwp.gov.uk. Tel: 020 7712 2171; fax: 020 7712 2386.

Chapter 3

Trustees

Introduction

3.1   The role of a pension scheme trustee is to apply the scheme assets for the benefit of scheme members and other beneficiaries, in accordance with the scheme's trust documents. This has long been a considerable responsibility and, under *PA 1995*, trustees' responsibilities increased further. Now *PA 2004* has made further changes to the role of trustees, raising the standard of care that they are expected to attain while altering the requirements and procedure for member-nominated trustees and internal dispute resolution.

PA 1995 introduced civil penalties (of up to £5,000 for individuals and £50,000 for companies) and criminal penalties (i e fines and/or imprisonment) for breaches of certain provisions of *PA 1995*. It also gave Opra (now superseded by the Regulator) power to suspend or prohibit a person from acting as a trustee of a particular scheme (most particularly, where he has been in serious or persistent breach of *PA 1995*) and disqualify a person from trusteeship of any scheme. Appendix I summarises the penalties which may be imposed by the Regulator under *PA 1995* and *PA 2004*.

Who can be a trustee?

3.2   Anyone who is legally capable of holding property can act as a trustee. In effect this means that anyone aged 18 or over can be appointed as a trustee. There are, however, circumstances where an individual may be disqualified from being a trustee. Under *section 29* of *PA 1995*, a person is disqualified from acting as a trustee if, for example:

(*a*)   he has been or is convicted of an offence involving dishonesty or deception;

(*b*)   he is an undischarged bankrupt;

(*c*)   he has made an arrangement with his creditors and has not been discharged in respect of it;

(*d*)   he is disqualified as a company director; or

(*e*)   in the case of a trustee which is a company, any director of the company is disqualified for any of the reasons set out above.

Additionally the Regulator has the power to disqualify a person from being a trustee if, in its opinion, it is not desirable for him to act as a trustee of a trust scheme and the person (or company) either:

(i)   has been prohibited from being a trustee by the Regulator; or

(ii)   has been removed as a trustee by the court on grounds of misconduct or mismanagement.

The Regulator may also disqualify a trustee from being a trustee of any trust scheme where:

(i)   in the case of an individual, he is incapable, in the opinion of the Regulator, of acting as a trustee by reason of mental disorder; or

(ii)   in the case of a company, it has gone into liquidation.

The consequences of disqualification are set out in *section 30* of *PA 1995*; see also chapter 2.

A trustee is prohibited from acting as actuary or auditor to the scheme of which he is trustee and so, in effect, the actuary and auditor will be prevented from acting as a trustee. This will not, however, prevent another person in the same firm of actuaries from acting as a trustee. [*PA 1995, s 27* and the *Scheme Administration Regulations (SI 1996 No 1715), reg 7*].

Type of trustee

Individual trustees and corporate trustees

3.3   A trustee will either be an individual, acting in a personal capacity, or a corporate body. A company will often be specifically formed to act as a trustee but any company may act as a trustee if its memorandum and articles of association contain the necessary powers. Although it is the company (not the directors) which is the trustee, in practical terms, the directors will take all the relevant trustee decisions. Whilst the exposure to liability of a director of a corporate trustee may be reduced (as compared with the position of an individual trustee), the director concerned may not escape all liability to the beneficiaries. For further discussion of this topic see 3.59 below.

A director (or other officer of a trustee company) is also subject to the same civil penalties as individual trustees under the *PA 1995* where it can be shown that a breach of the provisions of the *PA 1995* took place with his consent or connivance (*section 10(5)* of *PA 1995*).

Trust corporations

3.4   A trust corporation is a corporate trustee which is:

(*a*)   formed under the laws of the UK and has a place of business in the UK; and

(*b*)   empowered by its constitution to act as a trustee; and

(*c*)   either incorporated by a special Act of Parliament or Royal Charter or is a registered company with an issued share capital of at least £250,000, of which £100,000 is paid up. [See *Public Trustee (Custodian Trustee) Rules 1975* under *SI 1975 No 1189*].

A notable example of a trust corporation is the Public Trustee which was established by the *Public Trustee Act 1906*.

The main advantage of a trust corporation over a trustee company is that a trust corporation can give a valid receipt for the proceeds of a sale of land on its own. Otherwise at least two trustees will be necessary before a valid receipt can be given. [*Trustee Act 1925, s 14*].

Pensioneer trustees

3.5   This type of trustee has been required by HMRC for a small self-administered pension scheme and is considered further in chapter 13.

Independent trustees

Statutory appointments

3.6   In certain circumstances an independent trustee may be appointed. This legislation was first introduced by the *Social Security Act 1990* but, since 6 April 1997, such appointments have been governed by *sections 22* to *26* of *PA 1995* and the *Occupational Pension Schemes (Independent Trustee) Regulations 1997 (SI 1997 No 252)* ('the *Independent Trustee Regulations 1997*'). Under this legislation, if, in relation to an occupational pension scheme which is established under trust:

(*a*)   an insolvency practitioner was appointed in relation to an employer participating in the scheme; or

(*b*)   the official receiver became:

- the liquidator or provisional liquidator of a company which is an employer; or

- the receiver and the manager, or the trustee, of the estate of a bankrupt who is an employer;

then it was the duty of the insolvency practitioner or official receiver to satisfy himself that, at all times, at least one of the trustees of the scheme was an independent person. If the insolvency practitioner or official receiver was not satisfied that this was the case he had to appoint or secure the appointment of an independent person as a trustee of the scheme as soon as reasonably practicable. [*PA 1995, ss 22* and *23*].

The requirements did not apply to money purchase schemes, (including schemes which would be money purchase schemes except for the fact that they provide GMPs), unapproved schemes, schemes where all the members were trustees, schemes which provided only death benefits (and under the provisions of which no member had accrued rights), schemes under which all the benefits to be provided were secured by specifically allocated insurance policies or annuity contracts and '*section 615(6)* schemes' (a type of approved scheme for expatriates). [*Independent Trustee Regulations 1997, reg 5*].

Section 36 of *PA 2004* makes various amendments to *sections 22* to *25* of *PA 1995*. In general terms, the ability to appoint an independent trustee passes from the insolvency practitioner to the Regulator. The Regulator must maintain a register of trustees and may appoint an independent trustee from that register. The *Independent Trustee Regulations 1997* have been replaced by the *Occupational Pension Schemes (Independent Trustee) Regulations 2005 (SI 2005 No 703)* ('the *Independent Trustee Regulations 2005*') *Regulation 2* of those Regulations provides that the Regulator must compile and maintain a register of persons who satisfy various conditions set out in *regulation 3*. That regulation includes the requirements that the applicant must not be subject to a prohibition order or suspension order or be disqualified for being a trustee; the Regulator must be satisfied that the applicant has sufficient relevant experience of occupational pension schemes, is a fit and proper person to act as a trustee of an occupational pension scheme, the applicant operates sound administrative and accounting procedures, and the applicant has adequate indemnity insurance cover; the applicant must have premises in the UK from which he conducts his business as a trustee and he must disclose the address to the Regulator; the applicant must agree to have his fees and costs scrutinised by an independent adjudicator, must agree to the Regulator disclosing his name, address and area of trustee work on the version of the trustee register which is to be publicly available; the applicant must comply with the reasonable requests of the Regulator to provide information to the Regulator and must inform the Regulator as soon as is reasonably practicable if he becomes disqualified under *section 29* of *PA 1995*.

The *Independent Trustee Regulations 2005* also contain provisions regarding the refusal by the Regulator to register an applicant in the trustee register and the removal from the trustee register.

Where a trustee has been appointed under *section 7(1) or (3) of PA 1995* or *section 22* of *PA 1995* ('the appointed trustee'), it is the responsibility of such appointed trustee to supply in writing to every member (excluding deferred members whose address is not known to the trustees) or relevant trade union as of course within a reasonable period following his appointment the following information:

(i)   the name and address of the appointed trustee;

(ii)   the scale of fees that would be chargeable by the appointed trustee and payable by the scheme; and

(iii)   details of the amounts charged to the scheme by the appointed trustee in the past twelve months.

Section 25 of *PA 1995* has been amended by *section 36(4)* of *PA 2004* so that where an independent trustee having been appointed ceases to be an independent person, he must, as soon as reasonably practical, notify the Regulator in writing. Any failure to give such notice will result in civil penalties under *section 10* of *PA 1995*. The revised *section 25* provides that an order appointing an independent trustee may make provision for any expenses or fees of trustees to be paid either by the employer or out of the scheme's resources or by a combination of both. Where an appointed trustee's fees are to be met out of a scheme's resources, such fees will take priority over all other claims to be met by the scheme's resources.

Non-statutory appointments

3.7   An employer may still wish to appoint a trustee who is independent of the employer, even though there is no statutory requirement to make such an appointment. The main reason for doing so would be to demonstrate to the membership that the employer is not using its position as an employer to influence the trustee's decisions. Such an appointment would be made by exercising the scheme's power of appointment, as modified by *PA 1995* requirements in relation to member-nominated trustees (see 3.25 onwards below).

Member-nominated trustees

3.8   *PA 1995* provided for the appointment of member-nominated trustees and changes have been introduced by *PA 2004*. This is dealt with in 3.25 onwards below.

Constructive trustees

3.9   In certain circumstances, a person (although not formally appointed as such) may find that he is treated in law as being a trustee of a scheme. This will usually happen because the person has, by his conduct, assumed trustee-like responsibilities. For example, where a person has never validly been appointed as a trustee but has nevertheless acted as one, he could at law be regarded as a constructive trustee. Another example is where a scheme has a pensions committee whose role includes exercising discretionary functions which relate directly to members' interests.

Employment protection for trustees under the Employment Rights Act 1996

3.10   The *Employment Rights Act 1996* (*ERA 1996*) offers protection for employees who are trustees of their employer's occupational pension scheme (see also chapter 7). In particular the *ERA 1996*:

(*a*)   entitles employee trustees to time off to perform their trustee duties and undergo trustee training (*ERA 1996, s 58*);

(*b*)   entitles employee trustees to payment for time taken off due to his trustee role (*ERA 1996, s 59*);

(*c*)   permits employee trustees to complain to an employment tribunal if the employer has failed to comply with (*a*) or (*b*) above (*ERA 1996, s 60*) (generally, such a complaint must be made within three months (*ERA 1996, s 62(2)*));

(*d*)   provides that employee trustees are to be regarded as unfairly dismissed if the reason, or the principal reason for the dismissal is that they performed any functions as a trustee (*ERA 1996, s 102*).

Appointment, removal and discharge of trustees

3.11   Generally a scheme's documentation will contain a specific provision vesting the power to appoint and remove trustees, such power most frequently being vested in the principal employer. There are, in addition, statutory provisions governing the appointment and removal of trustees contained in the *Trustee Act 1925* and, in relation to member-nominated trustees, in *PA 1995* and *PA 2004* (see 3.33 to 3.49 below). In the majority of schemes, the power of appointment should be sufficiently widely drawn that reliance need not be placed on the *Trustee Act 1925*.

Section 36 of the *Trustee Act 1925* deals with the power of appointing new or additional trustees where a trustee:

(*a*)　is dead;

(*b*)　remains out of the UK for more than twelve months;

(*c*)　desires to be discharged;

(*d*)　refuses or is unfit to act;

(*e*)　is incapable of acting; or

(*f*)　is an infant.

In such a situation, the power of appointment is exercisable by the person as specified in the governing documentation. If there is no-one in whom such a power is vested (for example, because the employer has been liquidated) or no-one who is able and willing to act, then the surviving or continuing trustee or trustees or his or the personal representatives of the last surviving or continuing trustee may make the appointment. The court also has power to appoint trustees, either in addition to or in substitution for existing trustees, where it is otherwise difficult or impracticable to do so.

Section 39 of the *Trustee Act 1925* permits the retirement of a trustee without a new appointment being made, provided that, after the trustee's retirement, there remains either a trust corporation or at least two individuals appointed. In such circumstances, the retiring trustee is deemed to be discharged from the trust, provided a deed is executed by the retiring trustee, the remaining trustees and the person who has the power to appoint trustees. The appointment of a trustee who is also a member of the scheme does not automatically end on his leaving employment or ceasing to be a member of the scheme (but see 3.33 onwards below regarding member-nominated trustees).

The Regulator must be informed of changes of trustees (however they are appointed or removed) as soon as reasonably practicable after the change taking place. [*section 62(4)* of *PA 2004*].

An employer's power to remove or appoint trustees is generally regarded as a fiduciary power and so must be exercised in the interests of the scheme's beneficiaries. If an employer disregards those interests, his position will be similar to that of a trustee who has committed a breach of trust. Whenever there is a change in the trustees of a pension scheme, it is important to ensure that the ownership of the assets of the pension fund is transferred accordingly. Land and chattels (but not stocks and shares) vest automatically in a new trustee if the appointment is by way of a deed. [*Trustee Act 1925, s 40*].

In addition to the power to suspend, prohibit and disqualify trustees referred to in 3.2 above, the Regulator also has power to appoint a trustee or trustees to a scheme. [*Section 7* of *PA 1995*]. Such an appointment may be made following the prohibition or disqualification of a former trustee or may be where the Regulator is satisfied that an appointment is necessary:

(*a*)   to ensure that the trustees as a whole have the necessary knowledge and skill for the proper administration of the scheme;

(*b*)   to secure that the number of trustees is sufficient for the proper administration of the scheme; or

(*c*)   to secure the proper use or application of the assets of the scheme.

When making an order the Regulator may also determine the appropriate number of trustees for the proper administration of the scheme; require a trustee appointed by them to be paid fees and expenses out of the scheme's resources and provide for the removal or replacement of such a trustee. [*Section 7(5)*, of *PA 1995*]. Finally, in most cases, unlike a statutory independent trustee, a trustee appointed by the Regulator under *section 7* shall have the same powers and duties as the other trustees of the scheme, unless the order appointing the trustee restricts those powers and duties or provides that those powers and duties are to be exercised by the trustee so appointed to the exclusion of the other trustees. [*Section 8(3)* and *(4)* of *PA 1995*].

Trustees' duties

3.12   The following are some of the general duties with which trustees must comply. Except where those duties are stated as arising under a particular piece of legislation, they are general trust law duties and may, to some extent, overlap. Trust law duties are fiduciary; they must be exercised in the best interests of the scheme's beneficiaries.

Whilst there is argument as to what may or may not be in the best interests of the members, it is an established principle that the best interests of the beneficiaries of a scheme are usually the best financial interests of those beneficiaries. In *Cowan v Scargill [1984] 2 All ER 750* Megarry V-C stated: '... under a trust for the provision of financial benefits, the paramount duty of the trustees is to provide the greatest financial benefits for the present and future beneficiaries.'

The question as to how this duty may be modified by the duty of trustees to consider and to specify in their statement of investment principles their approach to 'socially responsible investment' remains to be seen.

Duty not to profit from position as a trustee

3.13   As a general principle, a trustee may not receive any benefit from the scheme (including benefits payable by virtue of his being a member of the scheme) or exercise his powers in a way which creates a conflict between his personal interest and his duties to the scheme's beneficiaries. However, *section 39* of *PA 1995* provides that this principle does not apply to a trustee who is also a member of the scheme, if on exercising his powers in any manner, he benefits merely because the exercise of a power in that manner benefits (or may benefit) him as a scheme member (for example, granting an augmentation to members' benefits). Despite this provision of *PA 1995*, a trustee may still not profit in other ways: for example, a trustee cannot buy assets from or sell assets to the scheme.

A trustee may, if the trust documents expressly permit it, be paid for acting as a trustee from out of the trust fund. An independent trustee appointed under *PA 1995* (see 3.6 above) may be paid his reasonable fees and expenses out of the trust fund regardless of whether this is permitted by the trust instrument. [*PA 1995, s 25(6)*]. Under *section 7(5)(b)* of *PA 1995*, the Regulator has the power to order that the fees and expenses of a trustee appointed by it are paid out of the scheme's resources.

Duty of prudence

3.14   Each trustee has an obligation to act as a prudent person would, not only in the conduct of his own affairs, but also in looking after the affairs of third parties. In doing so, trustees must also use any skills or expertise which they possess (so a higher standard will be required of professional trustees). (*Bartlett v Barclays Bank Trust Company Limited [1980] Ch 515* illustrates this point.)

The Government adopted Paul Myners' proposal in his report entitled 'Institutional investment in the United Kingdom: A Review' (6 March 2001) that trustees' duty of care in investment decision-making must be raised. The Government said that it would legislate to enforce the new standard, and *PA 2004* is an example of this intention. It has stated that where trustees are taking a decision, they should be able to take it with the care and skill of someone familiar with the issues concerned and that they should have appropriate training. If trustees do not wish to take investment decisions, they must delegate responsibility for these decisions to someone who does have the skills and resources to take them effectively. See 3.23 below for an outline of what issues trustees will have to be conversant with under *PA 2004*.

The *Trustee Act 2000* also introduced a new statutory duty of care for trustees, including trustees of occupational pension schemes (but they are excluded from the ambit of the duty as concerns the performance of their investment functions). The statutory duty of care is subject to the provisions of the trust documentation.

Duty to act in accordance with the trust deed and rules

3.15   Decisions and actions of trustees must be taken in accordance with the scheme's trust documents, and will be open to challenge if they are not. Trustees must therefore familiarise themselves with the scheme's documentation and if they are unsure as to the interpretation of any trust documentation (and any announcement which has not been incorporated into the trust documentation) suitable professional advice should be sought. Trustees should bear in mind that the effect of the trust deed and rules may be qualified or even contradicted by overriding legislation (a good example of this being *PA 1995, PA 2004* and regulations) and should, therefore, ensure that scheme documents are kept up to date. Opra recommended that amendments to the scheme be consolidated approximately every five years.

Duties relating to investment decisions

3.16   All trustees should familiarise themselves with their investment powers. This is one of the most fundamental duties of a trustee and must be exercised within the parameters of the trust deed, legislation and case law. *Section 34(1)* of *PA 1995* gives trustees of occupational pension schemes power 'to make an investment of any kind as if they were absolutely entitled to the assets of the scheme', subject only to any restrictions imposed by their scheme documents. If trustees disregard any such restrictions, they may find themselves liable for any resulting loss to the value of the fund.

The fact that trustees have power to make a particular investment does not necessarily mean that it is an appropriate investment for them to make; for instance, a high proportion of investment in property would be inappropriate in a fund where liquidity was required to pay pensions. Similarly, trustees should generally diversify their investments so as to maintain a balance between achieving good returns and protecting the fund against unnecessary risk.

PA 1995 contained specific provisions relating to the delegation by trustees of their investment discretions. *Section 244* of *PA 2004* makes various amendments to *sections 35* and *36* of *PA 1995*. (See chapter 10.) See also 3.14 above concerning the recommendations of the Myners Report.

Duty to act impartially between the different classes of beneficiaries

3.17 A trustee must act fairly between different classes of beneficiary (namely pensioners, active members, deferred pensioners, contingent beneficiaries and, in some cases, prospective members) and must also act fairly as between individuals. In some cases the employer may also be regarded as a beneficiary (see 3.70 below). This issue could arise where trustees are considering the allocation of surplus on the winding up of a scheme. The trustees must consider the interests of all beneficiaries (including, as appropriate, the employer as residual beneficiary) when deciding how to allocate any surplus.

That is not to say that all classes of beneficiary must be treated in an identical manner. In the case of *Edge v Pensions Ombudsman [1999] 49 PBLR (37)* Chadwick LJ summarised the current legal position when he confirmed that the duty to act impartially:

> '... is no more than the ordinary duty which the law imposes on a person who is entrusted with the exercise of a discretionary power: that he exercises the power for the purpose for which it is given, giving proper consideration to the matters which are relevant and excluding from consideration matters which are irrelevant. If pension fund trustees do that, they cannot be criticised if they reach a decision which appears to prefer the claims of one interest – whether that of employers, current employees or pensioners – over others. The preference will be the result of a proper exercise of the discretionary power.' (paragraph 50)

Duty to seek appropriate professional advice on matters which a trustee does not understand

3.18 This duty is self-explanatory and should be complied with in areas where a trustee is not an expert. A trustee's decisions will generally be harder to challenge if it can be shown to have been based on suitable professional advice. Specific requirements as to the use of professional advisers were introduced by *PA 1995* (see chapter 2).

Delegation

3.19 Trustees must not generally delegate their powers or discretions unless they are authorised to do so by the trust deed and rules (although there are some statutory powers of delegation, most notably the limited general power to delegate under *section 25* of the *Trustee Act 1925*, the narrow default powers contained by the *Trustee Act 2000* and the power to delegate investment discretions under *section 34* of *PA 1995* – see chapter 10).

It will generally be appropriate for the trustees (provided there is power under the scheme's documentation), to appoint a person (whether one of the trustees or an external person), as pensions manager to administer the scheme on a day-to-day basis. The person so appointed should be fully informed of the duties and responsibilities which the trustees have delegated to him. This person will usually be in the employment of the sponsoring company. The trustees may also appoint an outside party to provide other administration services such as payment of pensions, retention of their membership records and other services. There should be a written agreement between the trustees and the administrator not least because the trustees are required to ensure that the external administrator has appropriate systems in place to ensure the security and proper processing of membership data and the trustees should receive undertakings to that effect in the agreement. Some schemes use the employer's in-house staff to provide these services. The trustees are required to act prudently in choosing any person to whom they delegate any of their duties or responsibilities.

Duty to collect contributions

3.20   *PA 1995* introduced the requirement for trustees to arrange for a schedule of contributions (in the case of a final salary scheme – see *section 58*) or schedule of payments (in the case of a money purchase scheme – see *section 87*) to be prepared. In either case the schedule must show the rates of contributions payable and the dates on or before which such payments are due. *PA 1995* (and regulations made under it) set out the steps to be taken by the trustees if these contributions are not paid. Whilst *PA 2004* has maintained this requirement, trustees' duties generally in relation to scheme funding have increased very significantly with the introduction of the new overriding statutory funding requirement as set out in *section 222* of *PA 2004* (see also chapter 11).

Duty to keep receipts, payments and records

3.21   *Section 49* of *PA 1995* requires trustees to keep any money received by them in a separate bank account kept at an institution authorised under the *Banking Act 1987*. Trustees may arrange to keep money in a separate account operated by a third party if they have entered into a suitable arrangement or contract. Any such arrangement or contract must ensure that records (including details of the amount paid, date of payment, and from whom it was paid, the amount paid out, the date of withdrawal and to whom, and the interest earned) are kept for at least six years and that all interest is credited to the scheme. [*Scheme Administration Regulations 1996 (SI 1996 No 1715), reg 11*].

Trustees are required by *section 49* of *PA 1995* and *regulation 13* of the *Scheme Administration Regulations* to keep written records of their meetings (including meetings of any of their number, for example, sub-committees of the trustees) for at least six years from the end of the scheme year to which they relate, stating:

(*a*) the date, time and place of the meeting;

(*b*) the names of all the trustees invited to the meeting;

(*c*) the names of the trustees who attended the meeting and those who did not attend;

(*d*) the names of any professional advisers or other persons who attended the meeting;

(*e*) any decisions made at the meeting; and

(*f*) whether since the previous meeting there has been any occasion when a decision has been made by the trustees and if so the time, place and date of such a decision, and the names of the trustees who participated in the decision.

In addition, trustees are required by *section 49* of *PA 1995* and *regulation 12* of the *Scheme Administration Regulations (SI 1996 No 1715)* to keep, for at least six years from the end of the scheme year to which they relate, books and records relating to certain transactions including records of:

(i) any amount received in respect of any contribution payable in respect of an active member of the scheme;

(ii) the date on which a member joins the scheme;

(iii) payments of pensions and benefits;

(iv) payments made by or on behalf of the trustees to any person including a professional adviser, including the name and address of the person to whom the payment was made and the reason for that payment;

(v) any movement or transfer of assets from the trustees to any person including a professional adviser, including the name and address of the person to whom the assets were moved or transferred and the reason for that transaction;

(vi) the receipt or payment of money or assets in respect of the transfer of members into or out of the scheme along with certain prescribed details;

(vii) payments made to a member who leaves the scheme including the name of that member, the date of leaving, the member's entitlement at that date, the method used for calculating any entitlement under the scheme and how that entitlement was discharged;

(viii) payments made to the employer;

(ix) other payments to, and withdrawals from, the scheme, including the name and address of the person the payment was made to or from whom it was received; and

(x) generally where a scheme is wound up, details as to how protected rights were discharged (see chapter 4).

In addition, *regulation 18* of the *Registered Pension Schemes (Provision of Information) Regulations 2006 (SI 2006 No 567)* requires the scheme administrator (which will usually be the trustees) and the trustees to retain certain records for a period of six years from the end of the relevant tax year.

Disclosure of information to members

3.22   Trustees are obliged to disclose certain documents and information to scheme members, prospective members, beneficiaries and recognised trade unions under *section 41* of *PA 1995*, *section 113* of *PSA 1993* and the *Occupational Pension Schemes (Disclosure of Information) Regulations 1996 (SI 1996 No 1655)* ('the *Disclosure Regulations*'). The requirements do not apply to schemes with only one member nor to schemes which only provide death benefits.

The Government plans to replace the 1996 *Disclosure Regulations* with new Regulations (the draft *Occupational Pensions Schemes (Disclosure of Information) Regulations 2006*) which were issued with a consultation document for consultation on 9 September 2005. The consultation period was due to end on 2 December 2005.

The intention is from October 2006 to introduce:

- a more proportionate regulatory requirement; and

- a requirement that annual benefit information for non money-purchase benefits is provided automatically in respect of scheme years ending on or after 6 April 2007.

The consultation document states that the overall approach will shift the emphasis from the rigid timescales of the current disclosure regime to a simple requirement that information should be furnished within a 'reasonable period'. At the same time, the Regulator would also be consulting on a Code of Practice on the meaning of 'a reasonable time'.

The consultation document goes on to state that the draft *Regulations* strike a balance to allow trustees as much discretion as possible as to the form and content of non-critical information to be provided, but at the same time requiring that members have access to the information that they require.

Under the draft *Regulations*, as from 6 April 2007, schemes must furnish within 'a reasonable period' annual benefit information for non money-purchase benefits:

- automatically to:
    - all active members;
    - all active members who become deferred members on or after 6 April 2007;
    - anybody who becomes a pension credit member on or after 6 April 2007; and

- on request to any other deferred member or pension credit member, who will receive the information automatically thereafter.

The consultation document then states that the draft *Regulations* also introduce certain changes in relation to the information that has to be provided annually. In particular, active members:

- must be provided with both the amount of their own benefit and survivors' benefit if pensionable service were to terminate on normal scheme pension age;

and may

- optionally be provided with the amount of their own benefit and survivors' benefit payable from normal scheme pension age if pensionable service were to terminate within one month of the date of the annual benefit statement.

The revised nomination process for member-nominated trustees (see *sections 242* to *244* of *PA 2004*) will give legislative recognition to 'groups representing active members, and groups representing pensioner members'. The consultation document points out that the draft *Regulations* provide, in relation to trust schemes only, that basic scheme information and the annual report should be furnished to any group recognised by the trustees as representing active or pensioner members.

Currently, there are other regulations which also require disclosure of information to members in certain situations, for example, divorce. These are referred to in the context of the relevant chapter in this book and a general summary of the information which must be disclosed is given at appendix II.

Under the legislation, trustees are obliged to disclose, amongst other things, details of the scheme's governing documentation, basic scheme information (which is usually contained in the scheme's explanatory booklet), an annual report commenting on the accounts and funding of the scheme and details of benefits payable.

Most information need only be disclosed at the request of the member, prospective member, beneficiary or trade union although some information (most notably the basic scheme information) must be provided, as a matter of course, regardless of whether or not a request is made. The legislation does not entitle a person to receive information which is not relevant to his own rights or entitlements under the scheme.

Beneficiaries of a trust also have the right to compel trustees to disclose certain information so they can be satisfied that the trustees are performing their duties.

The right of a beneficiary to have access to certain trust documents was considered in the leading case of *Londonderry's Settlement re Peat v Walsh [1964] 3 All ER 855.* The Court of Appeal held that, whilst a beneficiary is entitled to see trust documents, this rule did not extend to requiring trustees to disclose documents recording the reasons behind the exercise of a discretion. Trust documents are documents in the possession of the trustees as trustees, which contains information about the trust which the beneficiaries are entitled to know and in which the beneficiaries have a proprietary interest.

The later case of *Wilson v Law Debenture Trust Corporation plc [1995] 2 All ER 337* applied the position in Londonderry more directly to the pension context. It showed that it is only in exceptional circumstances that trustees should be compelled to give reasons for the exercise of a discretion, for example, where there was evidence that the trustees had failed to take into account a relevant consideration when exercising that discretion. However, the general presumption was that 'in the absence of evidence to the contrary a trustee has exercised his discretion properly' (paragraph 29).

However, this long help position has come under attack recently both in the courts and in front of the Pensions Ombudsman. First, in the decision in *Allen v TKM Group Pension Trust Ltd [2002] PLR 333,* the current Pensions Ombudsman took a different view from the established position at law as concerns the disclosure of trustees' reasons. He decided in this case that it was maladministration for the trustees not to provide reasons for their decisions, not to have disclosed in full the minutes of their meetings and not to provide copies of the material they considered in taking their decision. This case illustrates the importance of trustees keeping clear records of decisions and it would appear that when making decisions, trustees will be expected by the Pensions Ombudsman to give their reasons or be at risk of a finding of maladministration.

Secondly, in *Schmidt v Rosewood Trust [2003] 2 WLR 1442, [2003] 3 All ER 76* a case before the Privy Council, the belief that a beneficiary's right to view trust documents was based on the sort of proprietary interest espoused in *Londonderry* was dismissed. Instead, the right was viewed as a part of the court's inherent powers of supervision over trusts. This is a difficult concept for a trustee to consider in practice, as it would seem to be at the court's discretion what documents ought to be disclosed to a beneficiary. However, trustees should seek to consider the competing interests of all different beneficiaries, the trustees and third parties when considering what ought to be disclosed.

The Pensions Act 2004

Trustee knowledge and understanding

3.23   Under *PA 2004*, trustees of occupational pension schemes (corporate or individual) must be 'conversant' with key documents including the trust deed and rules, any statement of investment principles, the most recent statement of funding principles (where appropriate) and any other document regarding the policy of the scheme's administration.

Trustees must also have knowledge and understanding of certain areas including the law relating to pensions and trusts, the principles relating to the funding of occupational pension schemes, the principles relating to the investment of assets and such other matters as are prescribed.

Sections 247 to 249 of PA 2004

3.24   The requirements for trustee knowledge and understanding are contained in *sections 247* to *249* of *PA 2004* and are stated to apply to 'every individual who is a trustee of an occupational pension scheme' and 'any company which is a trustee of an occupational pension scheme'.

Section 247 of *PA 2004* deals with individual trustees and *section 248* deals with corporate trustees. *Section 249* provides supplementary provisions in relation to both corporate and individual trustees.

Requirements

3.25   *Sections 247* and *248* state that trustees must be 'conversant' with the following scheme documents:

- The trust deed and rules.

- Any statement of investment principles (SIP).

- Any statement of funding principles (SFP).

- Any other document recording the policy adopted in relation to administration. This would include the scheme booklet, announcements, member communications, trustee minutes and the annual report.

The Regulator has stated in its consultation document that 'to be "conversant with" scheme documents is taken to mean to be familiar with and able to make use of them to carry out trustee functions'.

In addition to be 'conversant' with the above, trustees must have 'knowledge and understanding' of the following:

- the law relating to pensions and trusts;

- the principles relating to the funding of occupational pension schemes;

- the principles relating to the investment of assets; and

- such other matters as are prescribed.

Level of knowledge

3.26 In relation to individual trustees, *section 247(5)* states that the degree of knowledge and understanding is that appropriate for the purposes of enabling the individual properly to exercise his functions as a trustee.

In relation to corporate trustees, *section 248(6)* states that the degree of knowledge and understanding is that appropriate for the purposes of enabling the individual director properly to exercise his functions in relation to the trustee company.

Section 249 sets out supplementary provisions. It defines the functions of trustees and specifies that the new provisions do not affect any other rule of law relating to trustee knowledge or expertise.

The Regulator

3.27 Under *section 13* of *PA 2004*, the Regulator has the power to issue an improvement notice where it is of the opinion that a person is contravening pensions legislation or has contravened pensions legislation in circumstances that make it likely that the contravention will be continued or repeated.

Therefore, it is within the Regulator's power to issue an improvement notice where trustees have not complied with the knowledge and understanding requirements. Under *section 13*, where a trustee has failed to comply with an improvement notice then civil penalties may be applied.

The Regulator has stated in its consultation document that it will be routinely asking questions of trustees about their learning activities and, where appropriate, about their knowledge and understanding. The answers given to the Regulator may influence the Regulator's assessment of the risk profile of a scheme.

Code of Practice

3.28   The Regulator has laid before Parliament a Code of Practice on the trustee knowledge and understanding requirements.

The Code sets out the broad subject areas of knowledge and understanding that trustees must have to enable them to meet the legal requirements. These areas are set out under the following nine headings:

- The law relating to trusts.
- The law relating to pensions.
- Investment: defined benefit ('DB') and defined contribution ('DC') occupational arrangements (including AVCs).
- Funding: defined benefit (DB) occupational arrangements.
- Contributions: defined benefit (DB) occupational arrangements.
- Strategic asset allocation: defined benefit (DB) occupational arrangements.
- Funding: defined contribution (DC) occupational arrangements (including AVCs).
- Investment choices: defined contribution (DC) occupational arrangements (including AVCs).
- Fund management: occupational defined benefit (DB) and defined contribution (DC) scheme arrangements (including AVCs).

In addition, the proposed Code will be accompanied by guidance issued by the Regulator. The full guidance is available on the Regulator's website (www.pensionsregulator.gov.uk). The guidance consists of two 'scope' documents – one for trustees of DB/DC schemes and the other for trustees of DC schemes.

In both Scope documents the areas upon which trustees are required to have knowledge are divided into 'Units'. To give an idea of the breadth of the requirements, summarised below are some of the areas covered:

Scope Guidance – defined benefit schemes (with associated defined contribution arrangements)

3.29   **Unit 1 – The Law Relating to Trusts.** This unit includes the definition and nature of a pension trust, fiduciary duties, professional advice and decision–making, conflicts of interest, fitness and properness to act as trustees.

Unit 2 – The Law Relating to Pensions. This unit includes key provisions of *PA 1995*, *PA 2004*, the role of the Regulator, the Pensions Ombudsman, tax privileges and requirements for occupational pension schemes, and the relationship between an occupational pension scheme and the State pension scheme.

Unit 3 – Investment (DB and DC occupational arrangements). This unit includes the different types of assets available for investment, the major asset classes and their characteristics, valuation of assets (actuarial valuations and company balance sheets), and the implications of overseas investment.

Unit 4 – Funding (DB occupational arrangements). This unit includes how liabilities are valued, the nature and strength of the employer covenant, potential risks to the scheme, transfers and bulk transfers and the impact of trustee powers.

Unit 5 – Contributions (DB occupational arrangements). This unit includes the assumptions underlying the contribution calculation and funding deficits.

Unit 6 – Strategic Asset Allocation (DB occupational arrangements). This unit includes how to fund particular future benefits, reviewing asset allocation decisions and the process of strategic asset allocation.

Unit 7 – Funding (DC occupational arrangements). This unit includes how the funding for occupational DC arrangements works, the risks borne by members and the implications of contracting out.

Unit 8 – Investment Choices (DC occupational arrangements). This unit includes investment strategy and member investment choices, administration procedures specific to DC arrangements.

Unit 9 – Fund Management (DB and DC arrangements). This unit includes the statement of investment principles, measuring performance including the use of indices, the selection of fund managers and the structure of investment portfolios.

Unit 10 – Trust Deed and Rules. This unit includes the duties, powers and discretions of trustees, the balance of powers, benefits offered and classes of members in the scheme.

Unit 11 – Statement of Investment Principles. This unit includes investment objectives, socially responsible investment and corporate governance and the types of investments undertaken.

Unit 12 – Statement of Funding Principles. This unit includes responsibilities for preparing the SFP, contents of the SFP and review of the SFP.

Unit 13 – Other Scheme Documents. This unit includes the scheme booklet, announcements, actuarial valuations, annual reports and accounts, internal dispute resolution procedure, memorandum and articles of association of a trustee company and minutes of meetings.

New qualification

3.30   The Regulator is developing a free online modular course called the Trustee Toolkit which it hopes will help trustees to meet the required standards of knowledge and understanding. It is available at www.trusteetoolkit.com. In addition the Pensions Management Institute has developed a new certificate, the Award in Pension Trusteeship. There are no current plans for a mandatory qualification.

The Occupational Pension Scheme (Trustees' Knowledge and Understanding) Regulations 2006

3.31   These *Regulations* disapply the knowledge and understanding require-ments for individual trustees and directors of corporate trustees for six months from the date on which they are appointed. However, this six-month 'period of grace' does not apply to independent trustees or trustees or directors who hold themselves out as experts.

The Regulator states in its Code of Practice that although the legislative requirements do not apply immediately to newly appointed trustees, these new trustees remain responsible in law for any decisions that are taken during this period.

Trustees' meetings

3.32   Specific provisions relating to the conduct of trustees' meetings are sometimes specified in the trust documents (or, in the case of a corporate trustee, its articles of association) and will typically cover such matters as how notice of meetings is to be given, that notice must be given to all the trustees, the number of trustees that will constitute a quorum, how a chairman of the trustees is to be appointed and whether he has a casting vote. If not set out in the trust documents (or articles), there should be some written record of these details, perhaps in a minute or resolution passed at a trustees' meeting.

It is important to comply with these requirements. If, for example, notice has not been given to all of the trustees of a forthcoming meeting, then the validity of any resolutions passed at that meeting may subsequently be open to challenge.

Under *section 32* of *PA 1995*, unless the scheme provides otherwise, decisions of trustees may be made on the basis of a majority vote and trustees may set their own quorum for meetings at which majority decisions may be taken. In certain situations specific requirements apply (see *section 32(4)* of *PA 1995*), for example, the removal of a member-nominated trustee will require a unanimous vote (*section 16* of *PA 1995*). Notice of occasions where decisions may be taken by majority must be given to each trustee to whom it is reasonably practicable to give such notice.

Regulation 10 of the *Scheme Administration Regulations (SI 1996 No 1715)* specifies the way in which notice for trustees' meetings has to be given. The notice must state the date, time and place of the meeting and must be sent, at least ten business days before the meeting, to the last known address of each trustee entitled to attend the meeting or take part in the decision-making process. However, notice of a meeting does not have to be given where it is necessary, as a matter of urgency, for trustees to make a decision. [*Scheme Administration Regulations (SI 1996 No 1715), reg 9*].

Member-nominated trustees

The Pensions Act 1995

3.33   Under *PA 1995* and the *Occupational Pension Schemes (Member-nominated Trustees and Directors) Regulations 1996 (SI 1996 No 1216)* ('the *MNT Regulations 1996*') the trustees of occupational pension schemes were under a duty to secure arrangements for the selection of member-nominated trustees ('MNTs') and the implementation of the arrangements and the appropriate rules (*PA 1995, s 16(1)*) unless the employer 'opted out' of the MNT requirements or the scheme in question was exempt (see 3.34 below).

There was a parallel duty upon the directors of a corporate trustee to appoint member-nominated directors ('MNDs') where:

(*a*)   the employer is 'connected' to the trustee company; or (*b*)   the trustee company is:

- sole trustee of the scheme; or

- all the other trustees are also companies.

3.34   The trustees were required by *section 16(3)* to (*8*) (MNTs) and *section 18(3)* to (*7*) (MNDs) of *PA 1995* to put in place arrangements which ensured that:

(*a*)   persons were nominated and selected by 'qualifying members' under appropriate rules to become trustees;

(*b*)   the removal of an MNT/MND could only occur with the agreement of all the other trustees;

(*c*)   vacancies were filled where there were insufficient nominations (or alternatively the arrangements could specify that vacancies may remain until the expiry of the next nomination period);

(*d*)   the term of office was not less than three and no more than six years;

(*e*)   the minimum number of MNTs/MNDs was:

- two where the scheme had more than a hundred members (or one, where there were less than a hundred members) (members in this context including active, deferred and pensioner members); and

- one third of the total number of trustees.

If the trustees proposed a greater number of MNTs/MNDs the employer had to consent to the trustees' proposals;

(*f*)   the functions of an MNT are exactly the same as all the other trustees. This requirement did not apply to MNDs or to Opra-appointed trustees or to independent trustees appointed under statute;

(*g*)   where a member appointed as an MNT/MND ceased membership of the scheme, he had to resign from his post as MNT/MND.

3.35   The trustees had to decide whether to formulate their own rules for the selection of MNTs/MNDs which must be approved under the statutory consultation procedure, or to adopt the prescribed selection rules which are set out in the *MNT Regulations*.

Alternatively, the employer could opt out of the member-nomination requirements by proposing 'alternative arrangements'. The employer could propose a continuation of existing arrangements, or the adoption of new arrangements, for selecting the trustees of the scheme. [*PA 1995, s 17(1)(a)* (MNTs) and *s 19(1)(a)* (MNDs)]. In formulating its proposals, the employer was not constrained by any of the statutory requirements relating to MNTs/MNDs. An employer wishing to opt out would in some circumstances have to obtain the consent of the trustees and would always have had to gain the approval of the members through statutory consultation.

Modifications to the PA 1995 provisions

3.36   Originally the Government proposed to introduce changes which were contained in the *Child Support, Pensions and Social Security Act 2000*. However, following the publication of the Pickering Report into the simplification of pensions legislation entitled 'A Simpler Way to Better Pensions' (published in July 2002), the Government decided not to introduce the changes to the MNT regime which were proposed in that Act.

However, in view of the fact that schemes *PA 1995* provisions, the Government brought into force the *Occupational Pension Schemes (Member-nominated Trustees and Directors) Amendment Regulations 2002 (SI 2002 No 2327)* ('the *MNT Regulations 2002*') on 6 October 2002. The intention of these *Regulations* was to continue the status quo so as to allow the Government sufficient time to develop a more simplified regime.

The *MNT Regulations 2002*:

(*a*)   extended the validity of current approvals for existing arrangements from six years to ten years; and

(*b*)   allowed employers to propose new arrangements at any time, with the consent of the trustees, for a period of up to four years.

Employers and trustees of schemes where the existing member-nominated trustee arrangements were due to expire under the statutory six-year period needed to do nothing to extend the approval period for the existing arrangements. The *MNT Regulations 2002* automatically extended the approval period by a further four years. Express periods within existing arrangements for the appointment of trustees or directors were not affected by the *MNT Regulations 2002*. Nominations and elections would still have to be undertaken in accordance with the existing arrangements.

The Pensions Act 2004

3.37   The Government set out its long-term intention to simplify the member-nominated trustee regime in its Green Paper published in December 2003 (Cm 5677 'Simplicity, Security and Choice: Working and Saving for Retirement'), much of which has been subsequently carried through into *PA 2004*. The Government wanted schemes to have greater flexibility to manage themselves in a more efficient and effective way that reflects and supports the business of the sponsoring employer. It has reduced the level of prescription on selection processes for MNTs so that legislation focuses upon the outcome to be achieved – at least one-third of trustees should be member-nominated – and not on the detailed processes that schemes must follow to achieve that outcome (paragraph 61).

Main change under PA 2004

3.38   The principal change under *PA 2004* is the removal of the employer opt out, thereby making it mandatory for all affected schemes to have MNTs representing one-third of the trustee body.

Who has to comply with the new MNT provisions?

3.39   *Section 241(1)* of *PA 2004* provides that the trustees of an occupational trust scheme (other than those schemes exempted by the Regulations) must secure that the MNT requirements are complied with. An 'occupational trust scheme' is defined in *section 243* of *PA 2004* as 'an occupational pension scheme established under a trust'.

Section 241(8) of *PA 2004* (in relation to MNTs) provides the following exceptions:

● Where every member of the scheme is a trustee of the scheme and no other person is such a trustee.

● Where every trustee of the scheme is a company.

● Where the scheme is of a 'prescribed description'.

The prescribed exemptions in the *Occupational Pension Schemes (Member-nominated Trustees and Directors) Regulations 2006 (SI 2006 No 714)* (the *MNT Regulations 2006*) are broadly similar to those under the current MNT regime and include:

● a scheme with fewer than two members;

● a scheme to which *section 22* of *PA 1995* applies (conditions for a statutory independent trustee);

● a scheme which is not registered;

● a relevant small occupational pension scheme (fewer than twelve members and decisions must usually be unanimous);

117

- a relevant centralised scheme (non-associated employers);
- a stakeholder scheme;
- a small insured scheme (fewer than twelve members);
- the employer was dissolved or liquidated prior to 6 April 2006.

One important new exemption is for schemes where the sole trustee or all the trustees are independent of the employer (but not necessarily a statutory independent trustee). It has been suggested that for some schemes this will effectively allow the employer to opt out of the MNT provisions by appointing a sole professional trustee.

Time limit for compliance

3.40 *Section 241(1) of PA 20047* states that the new provisions must be implemented 'within a reasonable period of commencement date', i e 6 April 2006. The Regulator has issued a Code of Practice which proposes six months as the maximum 'reasonable period' but what is reasonable will depend on the circumstances of each scheme.

However, the *MNT Regulations 2006* provide that where an existing opt out is in force on 6 April 2006, the arrangements will be permitted to continue until their approval expires in accordance with the existing law, subject to an overall cut-off date of 31 October 2007. MNTs appointed under previous arrangements may remain until their term of office expires.

What are the new requirements?

Number of MNTs

3.41 Under *sections 241(1)* (MNTs) and *242(1)* (MNDs), trustees must secure that arrangements are in place and implemented which provide for at least one-third of the total number of trustees to be MNTs.

Nomination and selection

Who nominates and selects

3.42 Under *sections 241(2)* (MNTs) and *242(2)* (MNDs) the *nomination* process has to include all the active members of the scheme (or an organisation which adequately represents them) and all pensioner members of the scheme (or an organisation which adequately represents them). The representative organisations might be trades unions, staff committees, pensioner groups or any other organisation considered by the trustees adequately to represent the relevant members.

MNTs are to be *selected* as a result of a process which involves some or all of the members of the scheme.

The Code of Practice does not specify any particular processes which must be adopted for nomination or selection but does expect them to be 'proportionate, fair and transparent'.

Who may be nominated

3.43   *Sections 241(5)(c)* and *242(5)(c)* provide that the MNT arrangements must stipulate that where the employer so requires, a person who is not a member of the scheme must have the employer's approval to qualify for selection as a MNT.

Other provisions

Vacancies

3.44   *Sections 241(5)(b)* and *242(5)(b)* require that the MNT arrangements must provide that where a vacancy is not filled because insufficient nominations are received, then the nomination and selection process is to be repeated at reasonable intervals until the vacancy is filled. The Code of Practice suggests this period should be no longer than three years.

Removal of MNTs

3.45   *Sections 241(6)* and *242(6)* state that the MNT arrangements must provide that the removal of a MNT requires the agreement of all the other trustees or directors. Under the *MNT Regulations 1996* the right under *section 303* of the *Companies Act 1985* for shareholders to remove directors could be exercised in respect of an MND unless the corporate trustee was a wholly owned subsidiary of the employer. This provision has not been replicated in the *MNT Regulations 2006*.

Larger number of MNTs

3.46   *Sections 241(4)* and *242(4)* state that the MNT arrangements may provide for a greater number of MNTs than is required to satisfy the one-third minimum but only if the employer approves the greater number.

Functions of MNTs

3.47 *Sections 241(7)* and *242(7)* provide that the arrangements must not exclude MNTs from the exercise of any of the functions exercisable by the other trustees by reason only of the fact that they are MNTs.

Penalties for failure to comply

3.48 *Sections 241(9)* and *242(11)* provide for the imposition of civil penalties where the MNT requirements have not been complied with.

Scope for change

3.49 *Section 243* provides that the Secretary of State may, by order, amend *sections 241* and *242* to provide for a minimum of one-half MNTs. The consultation document issued with the draft Regulations proposed this will occur by 2009.

Internal dispute resolution

Introduction

3.50 *Section 50* of *PA 1995* requires trustees of occupational pension schemes to secure that arrangements are made and implemented for the resolution of disagreements about matters in relation to the scheme. Schemes of which all the members are trustees or which have only one member are exempt from the requirements. [*Occupational Pensions Schemes (Internal Dispute Resolution Procedures) Regulations 1996 (SI 1996 No 1270) ('the Dispute Regulations'), reg 8*].

The Act requires trustees to establish a two-stage procedure. The arrangements must provide for a specified person (which could be one of the trustees or a third party, for example, the administrator) to make an initial decision and for the trustees to reconsider the matter if the aggrieved individual so requests within six months of the initial decision.

Details of the internal dispute resolution procedure, including who to contact, must be set out in writing and must be given as part of the 'basic information about the scheme' under the *Disclosure Regulations (SI 1996 No 1655)* to:

(*a*) any prospective member or, if this is not practical, within two months of a person becoming a member;

(*b*)   all members who were members on 6 April 1997, by 5 April 1998 at the latest; and

(*c*)   any member, prospective member or beneficiary, the spouse of any member or prospective member and any independent trade union, within two months of them requesting the information. [*Disclosure Regulations (SI 1996 No 1655), reg 4* and *Sch 1*].

Ideally the internal dispute resolution procedure should be in addition to other efforts to resolve the matter and should be operated to provide an opportunity to resolve misunderstandings before they escalate. Bearing this in mind, it is useful to provide a simple form to assist individuals who have a complaint. Failing to help individuals with a grievance may, in some situations, amount to 'maladministration' and lead to criticism of the trustees.

The Government's Green Paper, 'Simplicity, Security and Choice: Working and Saving for Retirement' published in December 2002 included proposals to improve the procedures for dealing with internal disputes, in particular by giving scheme trustees more flexibility to adopt a procedure which best suits the scheme and its members and setting a shorter timescale for the process to be completed (paragraph 61). These proposals then formed the basis for parts of *PA 2004*, which are discussed at 3.58 below.

Who can make a complaint?

3.51   Under *PA 1995*, the internal dispute resolution procedure must cover disagreements between the trustees and:

(*a*)   members (i e active members, deferred pensioners and pensioners);

(*b*)   the spouse or dependants of a deceased member;

(*c*)   prospective members of the scheme. A 'prospective member' means any person who, under the terms of his contract or the scheme rules is:

   (i)   an individual who has satisfied the eligibility conditions of the scheme and could elect to become a member;

   (ii)   an individual who will satisfy the eligibility conditions providing he remains in employment for long enough;

   (iii)   an individual who will automatically become a member unless he elects otherwise;

   (iv)   an individual who may become a member if his employer consents;

(*d*)   any individual who was in one of the above categories within the six months prior to making a complaint;

(*e*)   any individual claiming to be within one of the above categories.

[*Dispute Regulations (SI 1996 No 1270), reg 2*].

A claimant can nominate a representative to make or continue the complaint on his behalf. If the claimant is incapable of acting for himself or is a minor, a family member or other appropriate person can bring or continue a claim. In the case of a deceased member, his personal representatives can bring or continue a claim. [*Dispute Regulations (SI 1996 No 1270), reg 3*].

The first stage of the procedure

The nominated person

3.52   The first stage of the procedure must provide for a person, on the application of a complainant, to give a decision on the disagreement. [*PA 1995, s 50(2)*]. *PA 1995* does not specify who the person should be; it could be one of the trustees, a committee of the trustees, the secretary to the trustees, the pensions manager, a representative of the employer (such as the personnel manager) or possibly an independent third party. When deciding who to appoint, trustees should consider factors such as:

(*a*)   whether the person they appoint will be able to deal with the disputes within the required time frame (see 3.54 below);

(*b*)   whether he will be, and be seen to be, impartial – it is unlikely that the procedure will be of any use in practice if members simply see it as a further hurdle to cross before being able to put a claim to OPAS or the Pensions Ombudsman;

(*c*)   whether he has sufficient knowledge of the scheme, and of pensions issues generally, to deal with complaints; and

(*d*)   if an independent third party is to be appointed, whether the scheme or the employer is able and willing to meet any cost involved.

It should be remembered that the person appointed has no special powers. His decisions are not binding on the trustees and he cannot exercise the trustees' powers. It is recommended formally to appoint the person chosen in writing, setting out parameters within which that person may operate.

Making an application

3.53   An application for a decision under the first stage must include:

(*a*)   the name, address, date of birth and National Insurance number of the complainant and, where the complaint is made by a spouse or dependant of a deceased member (or a person claiming to be a spouse or dependant), the relationship to the member and the member's full name, address, date of birth and National Insurance number must be stated;

(*b*)   the name and address of any representative acting on behalf of the complainant and whether that person's address is to be used for service of documents in relation to the complaint; and

(*c*)   a summary of the facts relating to the disagreement, with sufficient detail to show why the complainant is aggrieved.

The application must be signed by or on behalf of the complainant. [*Dispute Regulations (SI 1996 No 1270), reg 4*].

Giving a decision

3.54   The first stage decision, which will have to be given, in writing, within two months after receipt of the complaint, must include:

(*a*)   a statement of the decision;

(*b*)   a reference to any part of the scheme rules, trust deed or legislation which has formed the basis for the decision and where a discretion has been exercised, a reference to the relevant part of the scheme rules conferring it; and

(*c*)   a reference to the complainant's right to ask the trustees to consider the dispute within the appropriate time limit (see 3.55 below). [*Dispute Regulations (SI 1996 No 1270), reg 5(2)*].

If a decision is not given within two months, an interim reply must be sent immediately setting out the reasons for the delay and an expected date for the decision. [*Dispute Regulations (SI 1996 No 1270), reg 5(3)*].

Although the Regulations do not require an explanation for the decision to be given, it will usually be sensible to give one. An explanation should remove any misunderstandings and hopefully prevent the complainant proceeding to stage 2 of the process.

The second stage of the procedure

Making an application

3.55   The second stage of the procedure must oblige the trustees, on the application of a complainant, to reconsider the matter and give a decision or confirm a previous decision. [*PA 1995, s 50(2)(b)*]. Such an application will have to be made by the complainant within six months of the date on which the first stage decision was given. [*Dispute Regulations (SI 1996 No 1270), reg 6*]. The application must include:

(*a*) the name, address, date of birth and National Insurance number of the complainant and, where the complaint is made by a spouse or dependant of a deceased member (or a person claiming to be a spouse or dependant) the relationship to the member and the member's full name, address, date of birth and National Insurance number must be stated;

(*b*) the name and address of any representative acting on behalf of the complainant and whether that person's address is to be used for service of documents in relation to the complaint;

(*c*) a copy of the stage 1 decision;

(*d*) a statement of the reason why the complainant is dissatisfied with the first stage decision; and

(*e*) a statement that the complainant wishes the disagreement to be reconsidered by the trustees.

The application must be signed by or on behalf of the complainant.

Giving a decision

3.56 The trustees will then have to give a decision within two months of receipt of the complaint, or explain the reason for the delay. [*Regulation 7 of the Dispute Regulations (SI 1996 No 1270)*]. In addition to the information set out above, the second stage decision will have to include:

(*a*) a statement of the decision and an explanation as to whether and, if so, to what extent it either confirms or substitutes the previous decision;

(*b*) a reference to any part of the scheme rules, trust deed or legislation which has formed the basis for the decision and, where a discretion has been exercised, a reference to the relevant part of the scheme rules conferring it; and

(*c*) information about, and the address of, OPAS and the Pensions Ombudsman.

Although the legislation only requires a statement of the decision and an explanation as to whether and, if so, to what extent it confirms or substitutes the previous decision to be given, it will usually be sensible to give an explanation of the reasons for the decision.

Exempted disagreements and the Pensions Ombudsman

3.57   Under *regulation 9* of the *Dispute Regulations* (*SI 1996 No 1270*), internal dispute resolution procedure does not have to be used where proceedings have begun in a court or tribunal or where the Pensions Ombudsman has commenced an investigation into the same complaint. In addition, the Pensions Ombudsman will not be able to accept a complaint unless the complainant has first made full use of the internal dispute resolution procedure available to him unless he is satisfied that:

(*a*)   there is no real prospect of a notice of a decision under the procedure being issued within a reasonable period from the date on which he received a complaint; and

(*b*)   it is reasonable, in the circumstances that he should investigate and determine the complaint. [*Personal and Occupational Pension Schemes (Pensions Ombudsman) Regulations 1996 (SI 1996 No 2475), reg 3*].

The Pensions Act 2004

3.58   *Section 273* of *PA 2004* was due to make a number of key changes to how schemes will deal with dispute resolution from April 2006. In particular *section 50* of *PA 1995* was due to be replaced by new *sections 50A* and *50B,* to the effect that there would no longer be a requirement for a two-stage dispute resolution procedure, although it was intended that schemes could retain one if they wished to do so.

However, during the consultation period on the draft regulations and draft Code of Practice a question of interpretation and application of the new *section 50* requirements arose. On 17 January 2006 the DWP confirmed that it:

'… had reviewed the effect of the proposed change and now believes that it would not have the desired effect of simplifying procedures or introducing greater flexibility. In fact it could place additional burdens on schemes. It has therefore been decided not to bring in the new legislation. The existing *section 50* will therefore remain in force but will be amended at the first suitable opportunity in order to give schemes more flexibility.'

Protection from liability

General

3.59   Trustees who act outside of their powers, or who act in a way which is in breach of their trust law duties to scheme beneficiaries, may find themselves personally liable to the beneficiaries for breach of trust. Alternatively, where they are in breach of a statutory duty, they will usually be liable as stated in the relevant Act (see appendix I, for instance, in relation to breaches of *PA 1995*). In practice, directors of a trustee company may have more protection than they would if they were individual trustees, although the position is not straightforward. The extent to which directors of a trustee company can be held directly liable to scheme beneficiaries was considered in the case of *HR v JAPT [1997] PLR 99* where the court found that directors of a trustee company do not normally owe a direct fiduciary duty to beneficiaries of a trust. The exception to this principle is where a director is found guilty of 'accessory liability'. In order to be found liable as an 'accessory' to a breach of trust, the director must have acted dishonestly in the sense described in the case of *Royal Brunei Airlines v Tan [1995] 2 AC 378* and referred to in the case of *JAPT* as follows:

> 'It is Royal Brunei dishonest for a person, unless there is a very good and compelling reason, to participate in a transaction if he knows it involves a misapplication of trust assets to the detriment of the beneficiaries or if he deliberately closes his eyes and ears or chooses deliberately not to ask questions so as to avoid his learning something he would rather not know and for him then to proceed regardless.' (paragraph 61)

There are, however, some protections from liability available to trustees. These are considered below.

Exclusion clause in the trust deed

3.60   Most pension schemes' trust deeds will contain a provision under which the trustees (or directors of a trustee company) will not be liable except in limited circumstances. These circumstances will typically be conduct which involves some degree of bad faith or negligence on the part of the person sought to be made liable. 'Wilful neglect or default' is a phrase commonly used in exclusion clauses; 'deliberate and knowing breach of trust' is another. Clauses of this nature have been upheld by the courts in relation to trustees' liabilities to beneficiaries (for example, Walton J in *Re Imperial Foods Ltd Pension Scheme [1986] 2 All ER 802*), although such wording in a trust deed would not be sufficient to exclude liabilities to third parties (ie liabilities to persons with whom the trustees deal who are not beneficiaries or parties to the trust deed; such liability will most usually arise under the terms of a contract with that third party, rather than under the terms of the trust deed), or penalties imposed by statute, most particularly, those imposed under *PA 1995* (see appendix I) which cannot be met from the assets of the scheme.

Section 2(2) of the *Unfair Contract Terms Act 1977* restricts the validity of certain clauses which seek to exclude liability for negligence. However, this restriction applies only to business liability, and so (in the context of actions brought by beneficiaries) is likely only to apply to professional trustees who charge for acting as such; it is for this reason that some exclusion clauses in trust deeds specify that liability for the negligence of a professional trustee is not excluded.

Section 33(1) of *PA 1995* prohibits the exclusion or restriction of any liability for breach of an obligation under any rule of law to take care or exercise skill in the performance of any investment functions (where that function is exercisable by a trustee of the scheme or by a person to whom that function has been delegated under *section 34* of *PA 1995*). However, where the trustees have delegated to a fund manager under *section 34*, *section 34(4)* relieves of them of responsibility for any act or default of that fund manager in the exercise of any discretion delegated to him, so long as they (or anybody else making the delegation on their behalf) have taken all reasonable steps to satisfy themselves as to the fund manager's knowledge and experience and that he is carrying out his work competently and complying with the requirements of *section 36* of *PA 1995* (see Chapter 10).

It should be noted that the Law Commission in January 2003 issued a consultation paper (CP171) on exemption clauses, entitled 'Trustee Exemption Clauses'. The Law Commission's view is that increased regulation of trustee exemption clauses is necessary because their increased use in recent years has reduced the protection afforded to beneficiaries in the event of breach of trust. The Law Commission therefore proposes to draw a distinction between the professional and the lay trustee. The consultation paper suggests that professional trustees should no longer be able to rely on clauses which exclude their inability for breach of trust arising from negligence nor would professional trustees be able to be indemnified from the trust fund in respect of breaches of trust arising from negligence. Professional (and lay) trustees would however have the right to use trust assets to buy indemnity cover. Lay trustees would still be able to benefit from exemption/indemnity clauses. The closing date for comments upon the proposals in the consultation paper was 30 April 2003, and further proposals are awaited at the time of writing.

Indemnity clause in the trust deed

3.61   A scheme's trust deed will often provide for the trustees to be indemnified against liability. The clause may entitle them to be indemnified by the employers or from the trust fund or from the trust fund in the event of default on the indemnity by the employer. In any case, any kind of liability which is not covered by the trust deed's exclusion clause will typically also not be covered by the indemnity clause. *Section 256* of *PA 2004* prevents trustees from being indemnified out of the fund in respect of fines or civil penalties under the Act (see **APPENDIX I**).

There are particular concerns in relation to employer indemnities. Prior to 6 April 2005, *section 310(1)* of the *Companies Act 1985* threw some doubt over the validity of an indemnity from the scheme's principal employer. This section rendered void:

> '(1) ... any provision, whether contained in a company's articles or any contract with the company or otherwise, for exempting any officer of the company or any person (whether an officer or not) employed by the company as auditor from, or indemnifying him against, any liability which by virtue of any rule of law would otherwise attach to him in respect of any negligence, default, breach of duty or breach of trust of which he may be guilty in relation to the company.'

Where there is a corporate trustee with directors, or individual trustees, who are also officers of the company providing the indemnity (often the principal employer), it has been possible to argue that, they are not acting 'in relation to the company' and therefore the indemnity would remain valid. This has not been tested in the courts. These provisions continue to apply to indemnities in existence before 6 April 2005 (although may not apply to new directors or trustees appointed on or after 6 April 2005 even where an existing indemnity is in place: clarification from the DTI is awaited on this point).

Sections 309A to *309C* of the *Companies Act 1985* (inserted with effect from 6 April 2005 by the *Companies (Audit, Investigations and Community Enterprise) Act 2004*) replace *section 310*. *Section 309A* renders void any provision which purports to exempt a director of a company from any liability, or any provision which directly or indirectly provides an indemnity for a director of the company or an associated company:

> '... in connection with any negligence, default, breach of duty or breach of trust by him in relation to the company.'

The argument outlined above, that directors would not be acting 'in relation to the company' (but rather in relation to the corporate trustee or the pension scheme itself) would seem unlikely to succeed under these new provisions where the principal employer (and company providing the indemnity) and the corporate trustee are one and the same entity, or where the corporate trustee is a company associated with the principal employer (which will often be the case).

Section 309B provides an exemption for a 'qualifying third party indemnity'. In order for an indemnity to be a 'qualifying third party indemnity' three conditions must be satisfied. The provision must not provide any indemnity against any liability incurred by the director:

- to the company or any associated company;

- to pay a fine imposed in criminal proceedings or a sum payable to a regulatory authority; and

- in defending criminal proceedings in which he is convicted of defending civil proceedings brought by the company or an associated company in which judgment is given against him.

The qualifying third party indemnity exemption may be of little practical use to directors or corporate trustees caught by the provisions of *section 309A*. They prevent any indemnity covering fines imposed by the Regulator (neither can such fines be indemnified out of scheme assets) and they would also prevent any indemnity in relation to claims which a corporate trustee itself might bring against the trustee director in relation to losses to the scheme. These would be two of the most likely areas where trustee directors might be looking for an indemnity from the employer rather than from scheme assets. The Association of Pension Lawyers has expressed concern to the DTI that the provisions of *section 309A* (and in particular the way in which many corporate trustees may be caught as 'associated companies') may have unintended consequences for trustee directors. A reconsideration of these provisions, and a possible exemption for pension scheme trustees, has been requested. As far as we are aware the DTI has not responded positively to this request.

However, *section 309A* does allow a company, or associated company, to purchase an insurance against any such liability.

Section 256 of *PA 2004* prevents trustees from being indemnified out of the fund in respect of fines or civil penalties under the Act (see **APPENDIX I**).

Court's discretion

3.62   Under *section 61* of the *Trustee Act 1925*:

> 'If it appears to the court that a trustee ... is or may be personally liable for breach of trust ...but has acted honestly and reasonably, and ought fairly to be excused for the breach of trust ... the court may relieve him either wholly or partly from personal liability for the same.'

This is only a discretion of the court, and trustees should be reluctant to place too much reliance on it. In most situations the trustees are likely to rely on the indemnity in the trust deed and rules and only where none exists, would the trustees need to seek an order under the provisions of this section.

Insurance

3.63   Trustees may wish to take out insurance against liability, but should be mindful as to how far the terms of the policy restrict the circumstances in which they could make a claim. If it is intended that the premiums be paid from the trust fund, advice should be sought as to whether the circumstances and the terms of the scheme will permit this. In any event, *section 31(2)* of *PA 1995* prohibits the payment of premiums from a scheme's assets to insure against the imposition of fines or civil penalties under *PA 1995* (see APPENDIX I). More commonly insurance tends to be used to protect the trustees against claims by 'lost beneficiaries', rather than liabilities generally in relation to their actions.

It can therefore be seen that *PA 1995* does considerably more to introduce penalties and sanctions for trustees than it does to introduce protections for trustees from liability.

Data Protection Act 1998

3.64   Pension fund trustees will need to comply with the *Data Protection Act 1998 (DPA 1998)* which, despite its title, came into force on 1 March 2000. In most cases trustees will be 'data controllers' since they determine the purpose for which and the manner in which information is held and processed. The emphasis of *DPA 1998* is on compliance with the data protection principles and the rights of individuals in respect of whom information is held.

The data protection principles have been modified from previous legislation. In summary, the data protection principles require that information relating to individuals must be:

(*a*)   processed fairly and lawfully – in certain circumstances it will be necessary to obtain the consent of the data subject and provide certain information to him;

(*b*)   obtained and processed only for specified and lawful purposes;

(*c*)   adequate, relevant and not excessive;

(*d*)   accurate and kept up to date;

(*e*)   kept for no longer than necessary;

(*f*)   processed in accordance with the rights of data subjects;

(*g*)   kept secure, by ensuring appropriate technical and organisational measures are in place; and

(*h*)   not transferred outside the European Economic Area unless adequate data protection safeguards are in place.

The new law enhances the rights of data subjects by giving them:

(i)   stronger rights of access to information;

(ii)   express rights to prevent direct marketing;

(iii)   rights to rectify and erase inaccurate data;

(iv)   rights relating to decisions taken by computer;

(v)   certain rights to prevent processing of data; and

(vi)   greater rights to compensation.

Manual data

3.65   Paper records as well as computerised data are covered by *DPA 1998*. Paper records will be covered if they are part of a 'structured filing system' where specific information relating to a particular individual can be readily accessed. Manual files organised by reference to individual policy holders will, therefore, be caught.

Transitional relief

3.66   There was transitional relief from part (but not all) of *DPA 1998* for computerised records until October 2001. There is also relief from many provisions of *DPA 1998* for a further six years for manual data. These reliefs will only apply if the data is part of a collection which existed before 24 October 1998. Data added to such collections after that date will also benefit from this relief. However, data controllers will need to comply with the whole of *DPA 1998* straightaway in relation to new collections of data created after that date.

Registration of pension fund trustees

3.67   The registration procedure is being simplified although precise details are still awaited. Advice on registration can be sought from the Data Protection Office. It has indicated that it may be appropriate for pension fund trustees to register for the purpose of 'investment management' in addition to 'pensions administration' which is the main (if not sole) purpose for which pension fund trustees hold data.

Data processors

3.68   Under *DPA 1998*, data processors (known as computer bureaux under the *Data Protection Act 1984*) will no longer need to register. This means that pension fund administrators (who often act as agents on behalf of pension fund trustees in terms of processing data) will not need to register in that capacity.

A data controller will, however, need to ensure that its data processors comply with data protection legislation. A data controller will need to have a contract in writing with its data processors under which they agree only to act on the instructions of the data controller and to put in place sufficient technical and organisational measures to keep data secure. This is to comply with the seventh data protection principle referred to above. Processing is defined extremely widely and includes merely holding data on behalf of another and so would encompass data held by the likes of administrators and actuaries.

Practical steps to ensure compliance

3.69   Pension fund trustees would do well to take the following steps to show that they are complying with the new legislation:

(*a*)   appoint one person to take overall responsibility for data protection;

(*b*)   carry out an audit of current personal data activity;

(*c*)   update the forms used to collect personal data;

(*d*)   ensure that suitable agreements are in place with all data processors;

(*e*)   address security issues both technical and organisational;

(*f*)   establish procedures to deal with data subjects' requests; and

(*g*)   review how necessary it is to collect data, especially 'sensitive' data as defined under *DPA 1998*.

Of particular impact on pension fund trustees will be:

(i)   changes to data protection notices which need to be given to scheme members;

(ii)   the requirement to obtain express member consent for the use of 'sensitive' data;

(iii)   the security obligations, particularly with regard to data held by third parties; and

(iv)   restrictions on transferring data outside Europe.

Trustees' duties to the employer

3.70   Whilst it is true that trustees must act in the best interests (and that usually means best financial interests) of their members and other beneficiaries, case law requires trustees in certain circumstances to take into consideration the interests of the sponsoring employer. This follows on from the trustees' fundamental duty to give effect to the trust deed and rules which in turn is a reflection of the employer's contractual promise made to its employees to provide pension benefits. The trust deed and rules will confer a variety of powers, duties and discretions on the trustees to enable them to give effect to the contractual promises of the employer to the employees. How the trustees exercise their powers can have a significant impact on the ultimate costs borne by the employer.

An employer's interests in the occupational pension scheme which it sponsors are varied. One particular example of a trustee power which can significantly affect the interests of the employer is the trustee's power of investment. In a balance of cost scheme, any failure by the trustees to obtain reasonable returns on the investment of the pension fund will result in the employer having to make greater contributions to the scheme to fund the promised benefits. In support of this is *section 35(5)(b)* of *PA 1995* which obliges trustees to consult the employer when preparing or revising the statement of investment principles. Whilst the consultation process does not require the consent of the employer, the employer nevertheless may have rights against the trustees, should they cause loss to the employer by exercising their powers in an imprudent manner.

Another example where the employer's interests are evident is in the case of the distribution of a surplus, especially upon the winding up of a scheme. There is a significant body of case law on this subject, the most useful of which is the case of *Thrells Limited v Lomas [1993] 1 WLR 456*. In *Thrells* the scheme was winding up and was in surplus with an insolvent employer. The ultimate beneficiaries of any refund of surplus to the employer would be the creditors. The case set out factors that trustees should take into account in deciding how to exercise their discretion on allocation of surplus monies. The principal factors to consider are the scope of the discretion and its purpose, the source of the surplus (for example, is it due to excessive contributions from the employer?), the size of the surplus, the financial position of the employer and the needs of members of the scheme. The usual duties of trustees will also apply when exercising their powers and they should, therefore, give proper consideration to all matters relevant to the exercise of the power.

This duty to the employer was noted by the Court in *Edge v Pensions Ombudsman [1998] Ch 512* where the court stated:

> '... the proposition that the trustees were not entitled, when deciding how to reduce the £29.9 million surplus, to take any account of the position of the employers is one with which I emphatically disagree. The Employers play a critical part in this Pension Scheme. They have to pay contributions sufficient to keep the Scheme solvent.'

It is clear from the above that it would be wrong for the trustees blindly to ignore the interests of the employer when exercising their powers, especially in the often delicate situation of distributing a surplus. On those occasions when it is appropriate for the trustees to enter into negotiations with the employer for benefit improvements, the trustees should be mindful that any extra financial burden which they succeed in placing upon the employer could ultimately jeopardise the ability of the employer to continue sponsoring the scheme. The circumstances of each exercise of the trustees' powers should be carefully examined and the rights of the employer taken into consideration.

Reporting breaches of the law

3.71   From 6 April 2005 *PA 2004* imposed on trustees, employers, advisors and anyone involved in the administration of a scheme a duty to report to the Regulator breaches of law in relation to the administration of the scheme which are likely to be of material significance to the Regulator. [*PA 2004, s 70*]. The Regulator has issued a Code of Practice No 1 'Reporting breaches of the Law' setting out and amplifying on the new requirements.

Who has a duty to report?

3.72   A legal duty to report falls on:

- Trustees of trust-based pension schemes. The duty to report applies to each individually appointed trustee. If the trustee is a corporate body and the individuals concerned are trustee directors, the requirement to report falls on the trustee company.

- Managers of schemes not established under trust, i e managers of personal pension schemes, including stakeholders schemes.

- Persons otherwise involved in the administration of a scheme. This category covers all those who provide services for the trustees or managers that relate to the administration and management of occupational and personal pension schemes, including stakeholder schemes.

- Any employer participating in an occupational pension scheme.

- Professional advisers – scheme actuaries, scheme auditors, legal advisers, fund managers and custodians of scheme assets.

- Persons otherwise involved in advising a trustee (or manager of a scheme not established under trust) in relation to the scheme.

Whistleblowing protection and confidentiality

3.73   *PA 2004* makes clear that the duty to report overrides any other duties a reporter may have such as confidentiality and that any such duty is not breached by making a report. The Regulator expects reporters to act conscientiously and honestly and to take account of expert or professional advice where appropriate.

When does the duty to report arise?

3.74   The requirement to report breaches of the law arises when a duty which is:

- imposed by or by virtue of an enactment or rule of law; and
- relevant to the administration of a scheme,

has not been or is not being complied with. Not every breach should be reported.

The decision to report

3.75   The decision to report requires two key judgements:

(i)   Does the reporter have reasonable cause to believe there has been a breach of the law?

(ii) If so, does the reporter believe the breach likely to be of material significance to the Regulator?

Reasonable cause to believe

3.76   A reasonable cause to believe means more than a suspicion that cannot be sustained. The reporter is expected to make further inquiries if all the facts are not known. If, after further investigation, the reporter has reasonable cause to believe that a breach has occurred it is not necessary for them to gather all the evidence which the Regulator would require before taking legal action.

Likely to be of material significance

3.77   The legal requirement is that breaches likely to be of material significance to the Regulator in carrying out any of its functions must be reported. What is of material significance will depend on:

- the cause of the breach;
- the effect of the breach;

- the reaction to the breach; and
- the wider implications of the breach.

The cause of the breach

3.78 Where a contributory cause of the breach is:

- dishonesty;
- poor governance or inadequate controls resulting in deficient administration or slow or inappropriate decision-making practices; or
- incomplete or inaccurate advice; or
- acting (or failing to act) in deliberate contravention of the law,

then the breach is likely to be of material significance to the Regulator.

The effect of the breach

3.79 The Regulator considers the following to be particularly important elements which are likely to be of material significance to the Regulator in the context of its objective to protect members' benefits:

- substantially the right money is paid into the scheme at the right time;
- assets are appropriately safeguarded;
- payments out of the scheme are legitimate and timely;
- defined benefit schemes are complying with legal requirements on scheme funding;
- trustees of occupational pension schemes are properly considering their investment policy and investing in accordance with it; and
- contributions in respect of money purchase members are correctly allocated and invested.

The Regulator is also concerned with reducing the risk of compensation being payable from the PPF so is concerned that notifiable events are reported to it and that any PPF requirements are complied with during an assessment period.

Finally, the Regulator is concerned with promoting good administration of pension schemes so is concerned to hear that schemes are administered properly, appropriate records are maintained and members receive accurate, clear and impartial information without delay.

Making a report

3.80   All reporters should have effective arrangements in place to identify breaches that occur in areas relating to their functions. Reports must be submitted in writing and wherever practicable use the standard format available on the Pensions Regulator's website at www.thepensionsregulator.gov.uk. Each report should be dated and include as a minimum: the name of the scheme; description of the breach; any relevant dates; name of the employer; name, position and contact details of the reporter; and the role of the reporter. Additional information is required and can be reviewed on the website provided above.

Failure to comply with the obligation to report a breach is a civil offence.

The Regulator's response

3.81   The Regulator has a wide range of measures it can use in reacting to a report of a breach, including:

- assisting or instructing trustees and others to achieve compliance;

- providing education or guidance;

- appointing trustees to help run the scheme;

- removing trustees from office;

- freezing the scheme;

- imposing special measures where the scheme funding requirements of *PA 2004* are not complied with;

- ordering that the scheme's funding position be restored to the level before a breach or other detrimental events occurred; and

- imposing fines where appropriate.

Trustees must be aware of the new reporting requirements and should put in place a formal policy for identifying, investigating and reporting breaches. Any policy should include arrangements for liaising with other 'reporters' and ensuring that systems are in place to identify and, where appropriate, investigate suspected breaches at an early stage so that timely reports may be made where judged to be of material significance to the Regulator.

Reporting notifiable events

3.82   Trustees and employers of schemes eligible for the Pension Protection Fund (PPF) are required to notify certain events to the Regulator. The purpose of these new provisions is to give the Regulator an early warning of problems which might give rise to a claim on PPF. [*PA 2004, s 69* and the *Pensions Regulator (Notifiable Events) Regulations 2005 (SI 2005 No 900)* (as amended) ('the *Notifiable Events Regulations*')].

PA 2004 introduced, with effect from 6 April 2005, a new duty on the employer and the trustees to notify the Regulator of certain events (*section 69* of *PA 2004*). The notifiable events are laid out in the *Notifiable Events Regulations*. In addition the Regulator has issued Code of Practice No 2 'Notifiable Events' in June 2005 and Directions which provide exceptions to the duty to notify (broadly, fewer events need be notified if the scheme is funded above a certain level (see below)). The notifiable events regime applies to only those occupational pension schemes eligible for the PPF (for example, not money purchase schemes).

Notifiable events duty

3.83   The duty to notify requires written notice to the Regulator of events:

- in respect of pension schemes (scheme-related events); and
- in respect of employers, in relation to their pension schemes (employer-related events).

The duty to notify falls on trustees (individually) and employers.

Timing of notification

3.84   An event must be notified in writing to the Regulator *as soon as reasonably practicable*. This will depend on the circumstances but in all cases it implies urgency. For example, where a trustee is made aware of a notifiable event on a Sunday, the Regulator should be notified on the Monday. It is not necessary to seek professional or expert advice on whether an event has occurred.

How to notify

3.85   All notifications must be in writing and, where practicable, use the standard form available on the Regulator's website at www.thepensionsregulator.gov.uk. Reports may be sent by post, e-mail or fax. The minimum information that should be included in a notification is the:

- description of the notifiable event;
- date of the event;
- name of the pension scheme;
- name of the employer; and
- name, position and contact details of the notifier.

Further additional information that the Regulator would find useful is also set out in the Code.

Failure to notify

3.86   Trustees must take all reasonable steps to comply with the notifiable events duty and employers must comply unless they have a reasonable excuse for not doing so. In the event of a failure to notify, the Regulator will in the first instance seek an explanation. Following this it will have a range of actions it can take including requiring training or other assistance. Where appropriate, however, civil penalties can be imposed.

Events to be reported

3.87   The *Notifiable Events Regulations* (which came into force on 6 April 2005) confirm which events will need to be reported to the Regulator. The Directions (which also came into force on 6 April 2005) set down conditions excusing a report in certain circumstances.

Trustee events

3.88   Trustees must report the following events:

(*a*)   any decision by the trustees to take action which will, or is intended to, result in any debt which is or may become due to the scheme not being paid in full *unless* the conditions in A, B and C (set out below) are satisfied;

(*b*)   two or more changes in the holders of any key scheme post within the previous twelve months *unless* conditions A and B are satisfied;

(*c*)   a decision by the trustees to make or accept a transfer value from another scheme, or the making or acceptance of such a transfer value, the value of which is more than the lower of 5 per cent of the value of the scheme assets or £1.5 million *unless* the conditions in A and B are satisfied;

(*d*) a decision by the trustees to grant benefits on more favourable terms than those provided for by the scheme rules, without either seeking advice from the actuary or securing additional funding where the funding was so advised by the actuary;

(*e*) a decision by the trustees to grant benefits or rights to benefits to a member, or the granting of such benefits, the cost of which is more than the lower of 5 per cent of the scheme assets and £1.5 million *unless* the conditions of A and B are satisfied.

Employer events

3.89 Employers must notify the following events:

(*a*) any decision by the employer to take action which will or is intended to result in a debt which is or may become due to the scheme not being paid in full;

(*b*) a decision by the employer to cease to carry on business in the UK;

(*c*) receipt by the employer of advice that it is trading wrongfully or a director or former director of the company knows that there is no reasonable prospect that the company will avoid going into insolvent liquidation;

(*d*) any breach of a banking covenant by the employer *unless* the conditions in A and B are satisfied;

(*e*) any change in the employer's credit rating or the employer ceasing to have a credit rating;

(*f*) a decision by a controlling company to relinquish control of the employer *unless* the conditions in A and B are satisfied;

(*g*) two or more changes in the holders of any key employer posts within the previous twelve months *unless* the conditions in A and B are satisfied;

(*h*) the conviction of an individual for an offence involving dishonesty, if the offence was committed while the individual was a director or partner of the employer.

The Conditions

3.90 **Condition A:** The value of the scheme's assets is equal to or greater than the value of the scheme's liabilities calculated on the relevant basis. The relevant basis is currently the most recent MFR valuation. This will, in time, be replaced by the PPF risk-based levy valuation (*section* 179 valuation).

Condition B: The trustees have not incurred a duty to make a report in the previous twelve months for:

- the employer's failure to make a payment to the scheme in accordance with the most recently agreed schedule of contributions; or

- the employer's failure to pay contributions due under the schedule of contributions on or before the due date.

Condition C: The decision by the trustees is in respect of a debt where the full amount is less than 0.5 per cent of the scheme's assets calculated on the relevant basis (see Condition A).

Condition D: The change in credit rating is other than from investment to sub-investment grade where the credit rating is provided by a recognised credit agency.

Trustees should seek to enter into a dialogue with the employer with a view to agreeing a process for exchanging relevant information, on a confidential basis if required by the employer. They should also ensure that there is a system in place to identify relevant events or breaches at an early stage so that timely reports may be made. Trustees should also put in place a formal policy for identifying and reporting notifiable events.

Internal controls

Requirement for internal controls

3.91   *Article 14* of the EC *Directive on Institutions for Occupational Retirement Provision* requires that occupational pension schemes have adequate internal control mechanisms. The *Occupational Pension Schemes (Internal Controls) Regulations 2005 (SI 2005 No 3379)* came into force on 28 December 2005. These Regulations insert a new *section 249A* into *PA 2004* which requires trustees or managers of occupational pension schemes to establish and operate internal controls which are adequate for the scheme to be administered and managed in accordance with the scheme rules and in accordance with pensions and other relevant legislation. Internal controls are defined as arrangements and procedures for administering and managing the scheme, monitoring that administration and management and for the custody and security of assets.

Code of Practice

3.92   The Regulator has issued a draft Code of Practice relating to the requirement for internal controls. The draft Code sets out the Regulator's expectations of how occupational pension schemes might comply with the requirement to have adequate internal controls.

Chapter 4

Contracting out

Introduction

4.1 The combination of a 'pay as you go' arrangement, where the contributions of the workers pay for the pensions of the pensioners, and an ageing population has placed a heavy burden on the State. As a consequence, when the State earnings-related pension scheme ('SERPS') was introduced in 1978, the Government decided to allow employers to contract out of it if the contributions were instead paid to a suitable private arrangement. Initially, only defined benefit occupational pension schemes were permitted to contract out of SERPS but in 1988 the facility was made available to defined contributions arrangements.

Employers and employees who participate in a contracted-out scheme pay a reduced rate of National Insurance contributions. The reduction is known as the contracted-out rebate. The total contracted-out rebate for defined benefit schemes (5.1 per cent of band earnings, i e earnings between the lower and upper earning limits; the employee benefits from a 1.6 per cent reduction, and the employer from a 3.5 per cent reduction in the contributions paid) has remained the same for the tax year 2005/2006. The lower earnings limit for the tax year 2005/2006 is £4,264 and the upper earnings limit is £31,720. These limits are increased each year. The calculation of the contracted-out rebate for defined contributions schemes depends on the age of the member (see 4.23 below).

Commentators have criticised these rebates as not fully reflecting the cost of providing pensions due to increased life expectancy and lower interest rates. In addition, some believe it will be difficult to justify the use of an occupational defined contributions scheme for contracting out under new terms, since individuals may enjoy much higher rebates (at least 1 per cent of band earnings higher) under stakeholder/personal pension plans.

However, the Government has gone some way to addressing these concerns by replacing SERPS from April 2002 with the State Second Pension ('S2P'). The aim of S2P is to provide a bigger pension than SERPS.

The new State pension is described in more detail in chapter 1 and in 4.69 and 4.73 below. It is proposed that rebates remain earnings-related.

Further changes to simplify contracting-out legislation were introduced by the *Occupational and Personal Pension Schemes* (*Contracting-Out*) (*Miscellaneous Amendments*) *Regulations 2002* (*SI 2002 No 681*) which came into force from 6 April 2002.

This chapter examines the way in which occupational pension schemes can contract out. Contracting out by way of an appropriate personal pension scheme is dealt with in chapter 14. The requirements a scheme must fulfil in order to contract out of SERPS are set out in *Part III* of *PSA 1993* (as amended by *PA 1995* and the *Social Security Contributions* (*Transfer of Functions etc*) *Act 1999*), the *Occupational Pension Schemes* (*Contracting-Out*) *Regulations 1996* (*SI 1996 No 1172*) ('the *Contracting-Out Regulations*') (as amended by the *Personal and Occupational Pension Schemes* (*Miscellaneous Amendments*) *Regulations 1997* (*SI 1997 No 786*)) and, in the case of a defined contribution scheme, the *Personal and Occupational Pension Schemes* (*Protected Rights*) *Regulations 1996* (*SI 1996 No 1537*) ('the *Protected Rights Regulations*') and the *Social Security Contributions* (*Transfer of Functions etc*) *Act 1999*. In the case of both defined benefits and defined contributions schemes these *Regulations* have been amended by the *Occupational and Personal Pension Schemes* (*Contracting-Out*) (*Miscellaneous Amendments*) *Regulations 2002* (*SI 2002 No 681*).

A brief history of contracting out

Defined benefits schemes

4.2   Initially, defined benefits schemes could only contract out if they satisfied two tests:

(*a*)   a qualitative test, namely the requisite benefit test, which in simple terms meant providing ⅟₈₀th of pensionable salary for each year of pensionable service; and

(*b*)   a quantitative test, namely the provision of a guaranteed minimum pension ('GMP') broadly equivalent to the SERPS entitlement being given up.

The requisite benefit test was abolished in November 1986 and schemes only had to satisfy the GMP test in order to contract out. As from 6 April 1997 ('the appointed date'), defined benefit schemes wishing to contract out are once again required to pass a scheme quality test but for future service do not have to satisfy the GMP test. This new quality test, introduced by *PA 1995*, is based loosely on the requisite benefit test; it aims to ensure that a certain overall level of benefits will be provided for members of the scheme generally. Although members of defined benefit contracted-out schemes ceased accruing GMPs on 5 April 1997, GMPs are retained in respect of service completed before that date and so, in order to continue to be contracted out, schemes must continue to comply with the requirements relating to GMPs (see 4.11 to 4.16 below).

Defined contribution arrangements

4.3   In April 1988 it became possible for members of defined contributions arrangements, including personal pension schemes and freestanding additional voluntary contribution schemes, to contract out of SERPS. In the case of an employer-sponsored arrangement, generally a contracted-out defined contributions scheme, each member has to be provided with benefits based on contributions actually made and the investment return on those contributions. The employer's contributions must be at least equal to the contracted-out rebate to the contracted-out defined contributions scheme.

In order to promote contracting out for new arrangements, the Department of Social Security (now known as the Department of Work and Pensions ('DWP')) paid an 'incentive' of 2 per cent of earnings between the upper and lower earnings limit. This payment ceased in April 1993 but from 6 April 1997 age-related rebates are payable in addition to the flat rate contracted-out rebate. Irrespective of how an individual is contracted out, the same reduced S2P pension is paid to an individual by the State.

The contracting-out certificate

4.4   In order to deduct and pay National Insurance contributions at the reduced rate, an employer must have a valid contracting-out certificate.

A contracting-out certificate is issued by reference to the employments which are contracted out. The certificate generally has to relate to all employments with an employer but may exclude:

(*a*)   those employees who opt in writing not to join the part of the scheme which is contracted out, provided that this is allowed under the rules of the scheme; and

(*b*)   those employees who are within five years of normal pension age at the date of joining the scheme.

On 6 April 1997, the Secretary of State assumed responsibility (from the Occupational Pensions Board) for the issue, variation and withdrawal of contracting-out certificates. The Contributions Agency, an executive agency of the Department of Social Security (now the DWP), acted on behalf of the Secretary of State in this regard. The Contracted-Out Employment Group ('COEG') within the Contributions Agency had day-to-day responsibility for the monitoring of contracted-out schemes. In accordance with the provisions of the *Social Security Contributions (Transfer of Functions, etc) Act 1999*, from 1 April 1999, the Commissioners of Inland Revenue (through agency of the National Insurance Contributions Office ('NICO')), took over responsibility for matters related to contracted-out employment. Although COEG, now National Insurance Services to Pensions Industry, ('NISPI') remains as the sub-division of that office responsible for the day-to-day administration. The operational aspects of determining new elections to contract out and maintaining information on current contracted-out schemes were moved to the APSS in Nottingham from May 2003. Responsibility for policy will remain with the DWP and NISPI will continue to provide technical expertise on contracting out. NICO has updated its guidance manuals and forms to reflect the changes introduced by the *Occupational and Personal Pensions Schemes (Contracting-Out) (Miscellaneous Amendments) Regulations 2002 (SI 2002 No 681)*.

As a consequence of the changes introduced by *PA 1995*, all defined benefits schemes which were contracted out prior to 6 April 1997 were required to re-elect to contract out by 31 January 1998, at the latest, if they wished to continue to be contracted out after 6 April 1997. Failure to re-elect resulted in the cancellation of contracting-out certificates with retrospective effect to 6 April 1997.

Schemes contracting out for the first time after 6 April 1997 are required to comply with the election procedure set out in *regulations 2* to *12* of the *Contracting-Out Regulations (SI 1996 No 1172)* (see 4.43 to 4.48 below).

A contracting-out certificate shows both an employer's contracting-out number (ECON) and a scheme contracting-out number (SCON). An ECON is specific to a particular employer so even if an employer participates in several contracted-out schemes it will generally only have one ECON. Each scheme will have its own SCON. ECONs and SCONs are used by NISPI to monitor National Insurance contributions and liability to secure contracted-out rights.

Defined benefits schemes

Requirements for contracting out

4.5   A defined benefits scheme can be contracted out of the S2P after 6 April 1997 only if:

(*a*)   in relation to service completed before 6 April 1997:

    (i)   the scheme complies with the requirements of *PSA 1993* relating to the provision of GMPs (as set out in *PSA 1993, ss 13* to *23* and the *Contracting-Out Regulations (SI 1996 No 1172), regs 41* to *69*); and

    (ii)   the rules of the scheme applying to GMPs are framed so as to comply with any requirements relating to the form and content of contracted-out rules as may be prescribed in regulations or specified by NICO; and

(*b*)   in relation to service completed after 6 April 1997, NICO is satisfied that:

    (i)   the scheme satisfies the reference scheme test (see 4.6 to 4.10 below);

    (ii)   the scheme is subject to, and complies with, the provisions of *PA 1995* relating to employer-related investments (as set out in *PA 1995, s 40* and the *Occupational Pension Schemes (Investment) Regulations 1996 (SI 1996 No 3127)*, see 10.24 below);

    (iii)   the scheme satisfies the minimum funding requirement or, in the opinion of the actuary, will do so within the schedule period (which broadly speaking is the following five years) (and see 11.20 below);

    (iv)   the scheme does not permit the payment of a lump sum instead of a pension, unless the amount involved is trivial or the payment is permitted in accordance with APSS limits (see 5.8 below);

    (v)   the scheme provides for benefits to be payable by reference to an age which is equal for men and women and is permitted by the APSS (see 5.5 below); and

    (vi)   the rules of the scheme are framed so as to comply with any requirements relating to the form and content of contracted-out rules as may be prescribed in regulations or specified by NICO.

> [*PSA 1993, s 9* and the *Contracting-Out Regulations (SI 1996 No 1172)*].

Schemes which are not exempt approved by the APSS (see chapter 5) are not permitted to contract out. A small self-administered scheme cannot contract out if its rules are drafted so as to exempt it from the provisions of *PA 1995* relating to employer-related investments.

Post 6 April 1997 – the reference scheme test

The reference scheme

4.6   The reference scheme test is a statutory scheme quality test. It aims to ensure that the pensions to be provided for most members (which includes active members and deferred members) and their spouses, from a contracted-out scheme, are broadly equivalent to, or better than, the pensions which would be provided under the 'reference scheme'. Details of the reference scheme are set out in *section 12B* of *PSA 1993* and *regulations 25* and *26* of the *Contracting-Out Regulations* (*SI 1996 No 1172*). Essentially the reference scheme is an occupational pension scheme which:

(*a*)   has a normal pension age of 65 for both men and women;

(*b*)   provides a pension for life at normal pension age of ¹⁄₈₀th of average qualifying earnings in the last three tax years for each year of pensionable service, subject to a maximum of 40 years (qualifying earnings for the purpose of the reference test means 90 per cent of earnings between the lower and upper earnings limits for National Insurance contributions);

(*c*)   provides that, on the death of a member, a pension is payable to the member's spouse unless:

   •   the member marries his spouse after having received benefits under the scheme; or

   •   the spouse remarries or cohabits with another person after having received benefits under the scheme; or

   •   the spouse is cohabiting with another person at the time of the member's death;

(*d*)   provides that any spouse's pension payable on the death of a member before normal pension age is equal to 50 per cent of the pension the reference scheme would have been obliged to provide in respect of the member, based on the service he actually completed;

(*e*)   provides that any spouse's pension payable on the death of a member after normal pension age is equal to 50 per cent of the pension the reference scheme was obliged to provide for the member at the date of his death;

(*f*)   provides annual pension increases in accordance with *section 51* of *PA 1995* (see chapter 1);

(*g*)   revalues deferred pensions between the date of leaving and normal pension age in accordance with *PSA 1993* (see chapter 6).

The test – actuarial certification

4.7   A scheme meets the reference scheme test only if the scheme actuary (or an actuary appointed for this purpose if the trustees are not required to appoint a scheme actuary) certifies that the benefits of at least 90 per cent of the members and their spouses are broadly equivalent to, or better than, those payable under the reference scheme. Defined contributions benefits (such as additional voluntary contributions) and the pensions to be provided under the scheme in respect of members who are not contracted out under the scheme are ignored. In calculating the benefits payable to and in respect of members of a scheme, the actuary must follow the professional guidance note, 'Retirement Benefits Schemes – Adequacy of Benefits for Contracting-out on or after 6 April 1997' (GN 28), issued by the Institute of Actuaries and Faculty of Actuaries and approved by the Secretary of State.

A scheme does not have to match the benefit structure of the reference scheme in order to contract out but if it provides pensions equal to or better than the reference scheme in every respect, including spouse's pensions, the actuary can provide a certificate without further investigation (GN 28, para 4.1). If the benefit structure of a scheme does not match or better the benefit structure of the reference scheme, the actuary will have to determine whether the benefits are broadly equivalent to, or better than, the benefits payable under the reference scheme. Where benefits under a scheme are not directly comparable with the benefits provided for under the reference scheme, the actuary has to compare the actuarial value of the benefits.

For the purposes of providing the required certificate the benefits to be compared are those that members are expected to accrue during the three years following the effective date of certification, assuming that they leave service at the end of that period or on reaching normal pension age, if earlier. Spouses' pensions must be compared separately in respect of death in service, death in deferment (assuming in each case that the member in respect of whom the benefit is payable dies at the end of the three-year period) and death in retirement (assuming that the member in respect of whom the benefit is paid dies on the day after reaching the scheme's normal pension age). In the case of a scheme with a normal pension age of less than 65 the death in retirement benefit payable to a spouse will have to be compared with the reference scheme's death in service benefit.

To be able to certify that the benefits are broadly equivalent to or better than the benefits payable under the reference test, the actuary therefore has to make four separate comparisons, namely:

(*a*)   members' pensions;

(*b*)   spouses' pensions payable on death in service;

(*c*)   spouses' pensions payable on death in retirement; and

(*d*)   spouses' pensions payable on death in deferment.

For a scheme to be able to contract out, the actuary must be able to certify that at least 90 per cent of the persons within each group are entitled to benefits at least equal to the benefits they would receive from the reference scheme.

Schemes with more than one benefit structure

4.8   If a scheme has different sections which apply to different categories of employment or which offer different benefit structures, each section which is to be contracted out must satisfy the reference scheme test independently. [*Contracting-Out Regulations (SI 1996 No 1172), reg 22*]. If a scheme with two separate sections has one section which does not satisfy the reference scheme test that section cannot be contracted out, even if, overall, the scheme would satisfy the reference scheme test.

Schemes with more than one employer

4.9   Where there is more than one employer participating in a scheme each employer must either have its own contracting-out certificate or be included in a holding company certificate. If an employer wishes to have its own certificate in respect of its own employees, the reference scheme test must be complied with separately in respect of those employees. Where a holding company certificate is used, separate tests are not required unless different employers operate different benefit structures.

How stringent is the reference scheme test?

4.10   There are a number of reasons why a scheme may not satisfy the reference scheme test. The most obvious example is a scheme which has an accrual rate of less than 80ths, but the relationship between pensionable earnings and band earnings is equally significant, as shown in 4.6 above.

The reference scheme uses an average of 'qualifying earnings' in the last three tax years for calculating benefits. Qualifying earnings are defined as 90 per cent of earnings between the lower and upper earnings limits. If a scheme's benefits are based on a pensionable salary which is lower than a member's actual salary (for example, because it excludes commission, bonuses, overtime and other fluctuating emoluments or because there is an offset for the lower earning limit) there is a possibility that the benefits provided will not better those provided under the reference scheme. This is best illustrated by way of an example:

> 'A member's actual earnings during the tax year 2005/2006 are £24,500 comprising of £12,000 basic salary, £10,000 commission and bonuses and £2,500 overtime. The scheme's definition of pensionable salary for the purpose of calculating benefits is basic salary plus overtime (but excluding commission and bonuses) during the previous tax year. The member's pensionable salary is therefore £14,500. The average of 90 per cent of his band earnings (which will

take into account commission and bonuses) over the last three years (i e 2002/2003, 2003/2004 and 2004/2005) is £19,624.80. For the purposes of the reference scheme test, the member's scheme benefits, calculated on a salary of £14,500, will be tested against benefits based on a salary of £19,624.80.'

If a significant proportion of a scheme's membership receive much of their earnings in fluctuating emoluments which do not form part of pensionable salary, it is possible that the scheme will not satisfy the reference scheme test even if the accrual rate is greater than 80ths.

The other area where many schemes may need to re-examine their benefit structure is in relation to spouse's pensions on death in deferment. The reference scheme provides a 50 per cent spouse's pension on death in deferment whereas, in the past, many schemes have provided only a spouse's GMP. To meet the reference scheme test a scheme has to satisfy the test for all of the four categories referred to in 4.7 above separately, so a scheme which provided only a spouse's GMP on death in deferment is unlikely to pass the reference scheme test.

The reference scheme benefits do not form any kind of an underpin, they are simply a benchmark against which a scheme's benefits are measured. Once a scheme has met the contracting-out conditions, the scheme's normal benefit formula applies. A scheme could be designed so as to provide an underpin of the reference scheme benefits, with the rules being appropriately drafted to ensure that those benefits are provided as a minimum. This will clearly be more complicated to administer, and more costly to provide, as additional records will have to be maintained and checks made whenever a benefit becomes payable. However, an underpin may be attractive to employers, particularly if the scheme generally provides benefits greater than the reference scheme but has difficulty demonstrating that it meets the reference scheme test.

See 4.75 below in relation to the extension of spouse's reference scheme benefits to civil partners.

Pre 6 April 1997 – guaranteed minimum pensions

Conditions relating to GMPs

4.11   If a scheme was contracted out of SERPS (now S2P) on a salary related basis prior to 6 April 1997, or if a scheme wishes to be able to accept transfers of GMPs from a contracted-out salary related scheme, it must comply with the requirements of *PSA 1993* relating to the provision of GMPs. These requirements are contained in *sections 13* to *24* of *PSA 1993* and *regulations 55* to *69* of the *Contracting-Out Regulations (SI 1996 No 1172)*.

To be contracted out of SERPS (now S2P) on a salary related basis prior to 6 April 1997, the rules of the scheme had to provide for the member and, if applicable, the member's spouse to be entitled to a pension of not less than the guaranteed minimum. This guaranteed minimum pension or 'GMP' must be payable for life and must commence generally no later than State pension age. Although State pension age is being equalised (so that by April 2020 it will be 65 for both men and women), GMPs will continue to be payable on the appropriate State pension age when they ceased to accrue, i e 60 for women and 65 for men. A scheme can provide for the commencement of the GMP to be postponed for any period during which a member continues in employment after attaining State pension age. However, the consent of the member must be obtained if the period of postponement exceeds five years from State pension age or if the postponement relates to employment which is not contracted out by reference to the scheme. [*PSA 1993, s 13*]. Where payment of a GMP is postponed until after State pension age it must be increased to take account of late receipt. [*PSA 1993, s 15*].

All GMPs in payment which are attributable to service completed since 6 April 1988 must be increased each year by the lesser of the retail prices index and 3 per cent per annum. [*PSA 1993, s 109*].

Calculating the GMP

4.12 The original aim of the GMP legislation was to ensure that, on retirement, a member was entitled to a pension which was at least equal to that to which he would have been entitled had he remained contracted into SERPS (now S2P). A GMP does not, however, directly equate to the S2P entitlement being given up.

The GMP payable to a member is based on the level of his earnings whilst in contracted-out employment and is calculated according to the member's 'earnings factors' during the relevant period. A member's earnings factors are derived from his earnings between the lower earnings limit and upper earnings limit each year, revalued in accordance with the increase in the earnings index over the relevant period. The basis on which earnings factors are calculated changed in April 1987 so separate calculations must be made in respect of pre- and post-April 1987 service. The method of calculation also depends on the age of the member at 6 April 1978. Essentially the calculation is:

(*a*)   for a person within 20 years of State pension age on 6 April 1978 (i e a man born before 6 April 1933 and a woman born before 6 April 1938), 1.25 per cent of his revalued earnings factors for each year between 6 April 1978 and 5 April 1988 *plus* 1 per cent of his revalued earnings factor for each year between 6 April 1988 and 5 April 1997;

(*b*) for any other person (i e a man born after 6 April 1933 or a woman born after 6 April 1938), 25 per cent of his revalued earnings factors for each tax year between 6 April 1978 and 5 April 1988 divided by the number of complete tax years after 5 April 1978 (or the start of working life) up to State pension age *plus* 20 per cent of his revalued earnings factors between 6 April 1988 to 5 April 1997 divided by the number of complete tax years after 5 April (or the start of working life) up to State pension age.

A member is only entitled to a GMP from a scheme if he has been paid earnings in excess of the lower earnings limit from employment which is contracted out by reference to the scheme. The above calculations therefore only need to be made in respect of periods of contracted-out pensionable service where the member's earnings exceeded the lower earnings limit.

Spouse's GMPs

4.13 If a member of a contracted-out defined benefits scheme who is entitled to a GMP dies, leaving a widow or widower (whether before or after attaining State pension age), the widow or widower will be entitled to a GMP under the scheme. The GMP payable to a widow is one half of the GMP payable to the member. The GMP payable to a widower is one half of that part of the member's GMP which is attributable to her earnings factors for the period 6 April 1988 to 5 April 1997.

The scheme must provide for the widow or widower's pension to be payable to the widow or widower for the periods set out in the legislation. For example, the scheme must make provision for a widow's pension to be payable to her for any period for which a widowed mother's allowance or widow's pension is payable to her by virtue of the 'earner's' contributions (*PSA 1993, s 17*). See 4.75 below in relation to extension of spouse's GMPs to civil partners.

Trivial commutation

4.14 A member's GMP can only be commuted for a lump sum if the amount of all the benefits payable from the scheme to the member is trivial, i e less than £260 per annum (or such other amount as may be prescribed by regulations).

From 6 April 2002 the law changed to allow commutation of trivial amounts of GMP for members who have not reached State pension age ('SPA'). The conditions for this are:

(*a*) the total scheme benefits do not exceed £260 per annum;

(*b*) the scheme is winding up or a member retires before SPA;

(*c*)   the GMP is revalued at fixed or limited rate.

The future of GMPs

4.15   Although it is no longer possible to accrue GMPs in respect of service completed after 6 April 1997, schemes which were contracted out on a salary related basis prior to that date must continue to provide GMPs in accordance with the statutory requirements, some of which are detailed above.

Equalisation of GMPs

4.16   Julian Farrand, the then Ombudsman, ruled in 2000 that pensions that differ for men and women doing equal service violate EU law on equal treatment of pensions as 'pay'. On 23 February 2001, in the High Court of Justice, Rimer J decided that the Ombudsman did not have jurisdiction to direct that GMPs are to be equalised. (*Marsh Mercer Pensions Scheme v Pensions Ombudsman [2001] 16 PBLR 28*). The Ombudsman only had jurisdiction to make determinations affecting those directly party to the dispute. Rimer J left open the question of whether legislation requires GMPs to be equalised and if so how. Consequently, the detailed issue remains unresolved. Members could therefore still raise discriminatory issues on this point with trustees. Trustees and companies would then be left with uncertainty as how to address the point. However, they should be thinking about reserving costs to cover the issue if it is raised in the future and also about who is to bear the risk on a transfer-in, and in the context of share acquisitions, and transfers of past service rights. Sex equality of scheme benefits is dealt with in chapter 9.

Triennial re-certification

4.17   To ensure that contracted-out schemes continue to meet the necessary standard, schemes were required to re-certify at regular intervals. [*Contracting-Out Regulations (SI 1996 No 1172), reg 16*]. To re-certify a statement had to be submitted to NISPI (on form CA7322), at intervals of no more than three years, confirming that:

(*a*)   GMP requirements are met if the scheme was originally contracted out before 6 April 1997 or if any GMP liabilities have been transferred into the scheme;

(*b*)   the scheme is not one which is excluded from contracting out under the *Contracting-Out Regulations*;

(*c*)   the scheme is not exempt from and is complying with the *Occupational Pension Schemes (Investment) Regulations 1996 (SI 1996 No 3127)*;

(*d*)   a certified schedule of contributions is in place confirming that, in the opinion of the actuary, the rates of contributions are adequate for the purposes of securing that the scheme meets or will meet the minimum funding requirement during the period covered by the schedule (see 11.20 below).

When submitting the triennial statement a reference scheme test certificate was also required to be submitted. From 6 April 2002, schemes are no longer required to submit a Reference Scheme Test Certificate tri-annually and will instead rely on exception reporting. [*The requirement to re-certify every three years has also been dispensed with.*]

Defined contributions schemes

4.18   Since April 1988, when the relevant provisions of the *Social Security Act 1986* first came into force, it has been possible for employers and individuals to contract out of SERPS (now S2P) by way of defined contributions arrangements. Such arrangements are now governed by *sections 10* and *26 to 33* of *PSA 1993* (as amended by *PA 1995*), the *Contracting-Out Regulations* (*SI 1996 No 1172*) (as amended) and the *Personal and Occupational Pension Schemes (Protected Rights) Regulations 1996* (*SI 1996 No 1537*) ('the *Protected Rights Regulations*').

Requirements for contracting out

4.19   *Section 9(3)* of *PSA 1993* and *regulation 30* of the *Contracting-Out Regulations* (*SI 1996 No 1172*) provide that a defined contributions scheme can contract out of S2P only if:

(*a*)   it complies with the requirements of *PSA 1993* regarding the provision of protected rights (see 4.20 to 4.29 below);

(*b*)   it is subject to, and complies with, the provisions of *PSA 1993* relating to employer related investments (as set out in *section 40* of *PA 1995* and the *Occupational Pension Schemes (Investment) Regulations 1996* (*SI 1996 No 3127*), see 10.24 below);

(*c*)   its rules provide that contributions made by members are invested so as to provide defined contributions benefits;

(*d*)   its rules require 'minimum payments' to be invested on behalf of the member within one month of the end of the tax month to which they relate and age-related payments to be invested on behalf of the member within one month of the date of payment by the Secretary of State;

(*e*)   its rules are framed so as to comply with any requirements relating to the form and content of contracted-out rules as may be prescribed in regulations or specified by the Secretary of State.

A scheme which is not exempt approved by the APSS (see chapter 5) is not permitted to contract out unless it is a relevant statutory scheme as defined in *section 611A* of the *Income and Corporation Taxes Act 1988*. As with defined benefit schemes, a small self-administered scheme cannot contract out if its rules are drafted so as to exempt it from the provisions of *PA 1995* relating to employer-related investments.

Minimum payments and protected rights

4.20   A defined contributions scheme contracts out of S2P by providing 'protected rights'. These are the rights derived from the 'minimum payments' made to the scheme in respect of a member and certain other payments, including age-related rebates and transfers to the scheme of rights accrued in another contracted-out arrangement. [*PSA 1993, s 10* and the *Protected Rights Regulations (SI 1996 No 1537), reg 3*].

Identification and valuation of protected rights

4.21   Unless the rules of a scheme specify otherwise, a member's protected rights are his rights to defined contributions benefits under the scheme. However, protected rights exclude 'the appropriate percentage' of the rights which were his protected rights immediately before the day on which a 'pension debit' arose – for details on pension sharing on divorce, see chapter 8. Under *section 10* of *PSA 1993* the rules of the scheme may limit a member's protected rights to:

(*a*)   the rights derived from the payment of minimum payments (see 4.22 below), age-related rebates (see 4.23 below) and incentive payments (see 4.24 below) made in respect of the member; and

(*b*)   protected rights which have been transferred to the scheme from another arrangement (see 4.40 below); and

(*c*)   defined contributions benefits which represent a guaranteed minimum pension or post-1997 contracted-out rights deriving from a transfer made to the scheme from a contracted-out defined benefit scheme or an annuity contract (see 4.38 below).

If a scheme is seeking APSS approval (see chapter 5) its rules should limit the definition of protected rights (IR12 (2001) PN 7.30). If the rules of a scheme limit a member's protected rights they must also make provision for their identification. The value of protected rights must be calculated in a manner which is no less favourable than that in which the value of any other defined contributions benefits are calculated. [*PSA 1993, s 27*].

Minimum payments

4.22 To contract out of S2P through a contracted-out defined contribution scheme (commonly referred to as a 'COMPS') the employer must make minimum payments to the scheme for the benefit of each member who is contracted out by reference to the scheme. Minimum payments represent the contracted-out rebate, i e the difference between the full rate of National Insurance contribution and the reduced, contracted-out rate, payable on band earnings (i e earnings between the lower earnings limit and the upper earnings limit). This rebate, which is also known as the flat rate rebate, is set at 2.6 per cent of band earnings from 6 April 2005 (being 1.6 per cent for the employee and 1.0 per cent for the employer) for defined contributions schemes.

The Government Actuary has reviewed the technical issues underlying the calculation of rebates. Rebates must take account of benefits given up, life expectancy, investment returns to be achieved before and after retirement and expenses incurred in private pension arrangements.

The employer may recover the member's share of the rebate from the employee but this is not a requirement. [*Contracting-Out Regulations (SI 1996 No 1172), reg 31*]. If the member's share of the rebate is to be recovered, the scheme effectively becomes contributory for the members, even if no other contributions are payable, and the rules of the scheme should be framed accordingly so that the members receive tax relief on the contributions.

The employer must make the required minimum payments to the trustees of the scheme within 14 days of the end of the income tax month to which the payments relate, i e on or before the 19th of the following month. [*Contracting-Out Regulations (SI 1996 No 1172), reg 32*]. Minimum payments must be invested within one month of the end of the tax month to which they relate. [*Contracting-Out Regulations (SI 1996 No 1172), reg 30*].

Age-related rebates

4.23 The contracted-out rebate was originally intended to be equivalent to the cost of providing the S2P benefit being given up (which increases with the age of the person in respect of whom the benefit is provided). The contracted-out rebate has historically been based on the cost of providing the benefit for a person of 'average' age. As, prior to 6 April 1997, the same contracted-out rebate was available in respect of all members irrespective of age, it was financially advantageous for those younger than the average age to contract out of, and for those older than the average age to contract-in to, S2P.

PA 1995 changed the way in which the contracted-out rebate applies to defined contributions schemes by introducing age-related rebates. As from 6 April 1997 an age-related top-up became payable in addition to a flat rate rebate. From April 2002 age-related rates may range from 0 per cent to 7.9 per cent.

Age-related rebates are not payable in respect of a member for the tax year in which he reaches State pension age (or would have done but for his death) although the flat rate rebate is still available.

Once protected rights have been secured, no age-related rebate will be paid in respect of the member unless the amount due is at least ten times the weekly lower earnings limit. In such a case the payment will be made to the insurance company, if protected rights have been secured through the purchase of an annuity, or to the trustees if they are secured by the payment of a scheme pension. If effect has been given to protected rights by means of a transfer payment, the age-related rebate, up to the date on which the transfer payment was made, becomes payable to the trustees or managers of the scheme which accepted the transfer. If effect has been given to protected rights and the age-related rebate due is less than ten times the weekly lower earnings limit, the rebate may be paid to the member, the member's spouse or if the member dies unmarried, to any person at the discretion of the Secretary of State.

Age-related rebates are payable at the end of each tax year and must be invested by the trustees within one month of receipt. A member may be required to provide documentary evidence of his date of birth and that evidence may be disclosed by the authorities to the trustees or any person responsible for administering the scheme.

As the age-related rebate is effectively paid a year in arrears, the amount due will have to be taken into account on transfers and on the death or retirement of a member. The employer may choose to make arrangements actually to 'credit' the member on a month-by-month basis but the additional costs and cash flow implications will fall on the employer who would recover the expenditure at the end of the tax year.

Incentive payments

4.24   Prior to 6 April 1993 an 'incentive' payment of 2 per cent of band earnings was payable to those schemes which contracted out for the first time between 1 January 1986 and 5 April 1993. [*Social Security Act 1986, s 7*]. Although incentive payments are no longer payable, any made in the past still form part of a member's protected rights.

Giving effect to protected rights

Member's pension

4.25   The rules of a contracted-out defined contributions scheme must provide for a member's protected rights to be used to provide a pension from the scheme or be used to purchase an annuity. [*PSA 1993, ss 28* and *29* and the *Protected Rights Regulations (SI 1996 No 1537), reg 4*]. The pension or annuity must commence on or after the member's 60th birthday but before his 65th birthday, unless he agrees to a later date, and must continue for life. The rate of the pension or annuity must be calculated on a basis which does not discriminate on the basis of sex.

If the rules of the scheme do not provide for the payment of a pension from the scheme, or if the member requires that an annuity be purchased, the member must be given the opportunity to choose the insurance company which is to provide the annuity. The member must generally notify the trustees of his choice, in writing, at least one month, and not more than six months, before his normal retirement date. If the member does not notify the trustees of his choice, the trustees can decide from whom to purchase an annuity. A lump sum may be paid instead of a pension if the annual rate of pension is trivial (see 4.29 below).

In certain circumstances, effect may also be given to protected rights, by the making of a transfer payment in the case of an occupational pension scheme, to another occupational pension scheme, to a personal pension scheme or to an overseas arrangement. [*PSA 1993, s 28*].

Benefits payable on death after retirement

4.26   The rules of a contracted-out defined contributions scheme must provide for a member's protected rights to be used to provide a pension or annuity for the member's widow or widower on the death of the member after retirement. [*PSA 1993, s 29* and the *Protected Rights Regulations (SI 1996 No 1537), reg 5*]. The only exception to this is if the member is not married at the date of his retirement and specifically elects not to make provision for a spouse. The annuity or pension need only be paid to a qualifying spouse, i e a person who is the widow or widower of the member and who was at least age 45 when the member died, was entitled to child benefit in respect of a qualifying child under age 18 or was residing with a qualifying child under age 16. A qualifying child for this purpose is a child of the member and his widow or her widower or any child in respect of whom they were entitled to child benefit.

The rate of any qualifying spouse's pension or annuity must be one half of the amount that would have been payable to the member if he or she had survived. The rules of the scheme must provide for the pension or annuity to be payable:

(*a*)   for life, if the qualifying spouse was over 45 when the member died; or

(*b*)   until he or she ceases to be eligible for child benefit or ceases to reside with a qualifying child under the age of 16; or

(*c*)   until he or she remarries while under State pension age.

The rules of the scheme may provide for the pension or annuity to be payable for a longer period. They may, for example, provide for the benefit to be payable for life irrespective of whether or not the widow or widower remarries. Provision may also be made in the rules for benefits to be payable to a surviving spouse even if he or she does not fall within the definition of a qualifying spouse. They may, for example, provide for a pension to be payable to a spouse even though she has not reached age 45 and does not have any qualifying children.

Where a benefit is not payable, or ceases to be payable, to a surviving spouse the rules of the scheme may provide for a pension to be paid to or for the benefit of any qualifying children until they reach 18. The rate of the pension must not exceed one half of the amount of pension which would have been paid to the member had he survived.

The rules may provide for the pension or annuity attributable to protected rights to continue to be paid, at the full rate payable to the member, to any person for up to five years from the date on which the member's pension or annuity commenced.

See 4.75 below in relation to the extension of spouse's protected rights to civil partners.

Benefits payable on death before retirement

4.27   The rules of a contracted-out defined contributions scheme must provide that if a member dies before the benefits deriving from his protected rights come into payment, his protected rights will be used to provide a pension, an annuity, or, in certain circumstances, a lump sum. [*PSA 1993, s 28* and the *Protected Rights Regulations (SI 1996 No 1537), reg 12*]. The benefit must be payable to any qualifying spouse who is at least age 45 when the member dies or who is entitled to child benefit in respect of a qualifying child under age 18 or is residing with a qualifying child under age 16.

The annuity or pension must be paid to the qualifying spouse from a date which is as soon as practicable after the member's death and is payable until the surviving spouse either dies, remarries before State pension age or ceases to be a qualifying spouse.

The pension or annuity may contain a provision for the payment of a pension to qualifying children on the death of a qualifying spouse. It may also include a five-year guarantee period in the same manner as the pension payable on the death of a member after retirement.

Where the trustees of the scheme find that, after making reasonable inquiries, the member was not survived by a qualifying spouse, they must make provision for the cash equivalent of the member's protected rights to be paid to the member's estate or to or for the benefit of any person nominated, in writing, by the member.

See 4.75 below in relation to the extension of spouse's protected rights to civil partners.

Suspension and forfeiture

4.28 The rules of a contracted-out defined contributions scheme must not permit the suspension of a member's protected rights or of payments giving effect to them. [*PSA 1993, s 32* and the *Protected Rights Regulations (SI 1996 No 1537), reg 9*]. However, the rules may permit the benefits deriving from protected rights to be suspended where the person entitled to payment is, in the opinion of the trustees, unable to act for himself, for example, because he has a mental disorder. In such a situation, the trustees may pay the benefit to another person for the maintenance of the incapacitated person and/or his dependants. The rules may also permit the suspension of the pension when the recipient is in prison, in which case the benefit can be paid to his dependants.

Generally, the rules of the scheme must not permit forfeiture of a member's protected rights. However, the rules may permit forfeiture where the trustees of the scheme do not know the address of the person to whom the payment should be made and at least six years have elapsed since payment was due.

Lump sum

Trivial commutation

4.29 If the pension which could be provided by a member's protected rights, and all other benefits attributable to him under the scheme, is less than £260 per annum (or such other amount as may be prescribed by regulations), the member can elect to receive his benefits, including his protected rights, in the form of a lump sum. [*PSA 1993, s 28(4)* and the *Protected Rights Regulations (SI 1996 No 1537), reg 8*].

Other circumstances

4.30   A lump sum is also permitted to be paid in certain cases of terminal illness (*PSA 1993, s 28(4A)*).

Mixed benefit schemes

Governing legislation

4.31   Prior to 6 April 1997 a scheme could only be contracted out on either a defined benefits basis or a defined contributions basis. A scheme could not contract out by both methods simultaneously nor could it convert to a different method unless it ceased to contract out on the original basis and discharged its liability to pay either guaranteed minimum pensions or protected rights and then subsequently elected to contract out on the other basis.

From 6 April 1997 it became possible for schemes to contract out via both the defined contributions and defined benefits routes at the same time. These schemes are referred to as contracted-out mixed benefits schemes or 'COMBS'. Initially, only schemes which were contracting out for the first time and defined benefits schemes which were re-electing to contract out on or after 5 April 1997 were able to become COMBS. However, this flexibility has been extended to contracted-out defined contributions schemes from 6 April 1998.

COMBS are essentially treated as two different schemes so that the requirements relating to a defined benefits scheme apply to the salary related part and the requirements relating to a defined contributions scheme apply to the defined contributions part. Similarly, elections for contracting-out certificates must comply with all the requirements for both defined benefits and defined contributions schemes (see 4.43 to 4.49 below).

Electing to become a COMBS

4.32   A defined benefits scheme which was contracted out prior to 6 April 1997 and continued to be contracted out after that date can become a COMBS by opening up a defined contributions section. The rules of the scheme may permit members to move between the defined benefits and the defined contributions parts of the scheme or may restrict membership of each section depending on, for example, age or job description. Schemes contracting out for the first time on or after 6 April 1997 can elect to be a COMBS from the outset.

From 6 April 1998, existing defined contributions schemes have been able to become a COMBS by opening up a defined benefits part and then will be treated in much the same way as a defined benefit scheme which elected to become a COMBS.

All COMBS will be issued with a COMBS contracting-out certificate and two scheme contracting-out numbers or 'SCONs', one for the defined benefits part of the scheme and one for the defined contributions part.

Ceasing to become a COMBS

4.33   A COMBS can elect to become a pure defined contributions or defined benefits scheme by closing the defined benefits or defined contributions part, as appropriate, without discharging its liabilities in respect of existing contracted-out rights. NICO will treat the inactive part of the scheme as if it were a scheme which has ceased to contract out (see 4.65 below). Such a scheme will then be issued with a defined contributions or defined benefits contracting-out certificate, as appropriate.

Transitional provisions

4.34   During the period 6 April 1997 to 31 January 1998 an existing defined benefits scheme could switch to being a defined contributions contracted-out scheme for future service without first having to discharge its liability for GMPs. Such an election had to be made with effect from 6 April 1997. Future benefits accrue on a defined contributions basis although the scheme will continue to have liability for the accrued GMPs. The GMPs in such schemes will be supervised as if they were provided by a scheme which has ceased to contract out.

Such a scheme is technically not a COMBS as it does not have two separate active sections; it will be treated as a defined contributions scheme for contracting-out purposes although it will provide defined benefits. The rules of the scheme must state whether the member's contributions (in excess of minimum payments) will be used to provide defined contributions benefits or defined benefits. [*Contracting-Out Regulations (SI 1996 No 1172), reg 30*].

Transfers between contracted-out arrangements

4.35   Broadly speaking, a member who terminates pensionable service at least one year before his normal retirement date has a statutory right to require the trustees of the scheme to transfer the cash equivalent of his benefits to another pension arrangement and since 6 April 2002 both pre- and post-1997 protected rights can be transferred to an overseas arrangement as well as an overseas occupational pension scheme (see chapter 6 for details of conditions applying to such transfers). In certain circumstances, such as the sale of a business, a group or bulk transfer of the accrued rights of a group of members may be made to another scheme. In either case, where the transfer would include the accrued rights to which a member is entitled by virtue of his contracted-out employment, additional restrictions may apply.

A tabulated summary of 4.36 to 4.41 below is included at 4.42 below.

Transfers from a contracted-out defined benefits scheme to a contracted-in scheme

4.36   Before 6 April 1997, it was possible for a transfer to be made from a contracted-out defined benefits scheme to a contracted-in defined benefits scheme; the member's accrued rights in excess of his GMP could be transferred to the contracted-in scheme and his GMP could be secured by some other means. It is no longer possible to make such a transfer if the member has any post-1997 contracted-out salary related rights. A member's post-1997 contracted-out salary related rights are his rights to all benefits accrued after 6 April 1997 by virtue of contracted-out employment. Unlike an entitlement to a GMP, the member's rights under the scheme which are attributable to the fact that he is contracted out cannot be separately identified and so cannot be secured elsewhere.

Transfers from a contracted-out defined benefits scheme to another contracted-out defined benefits scheme

4.37   A transfer in respect of a member's GMP and post-1997 contracted-out salary related rights can be made from a contracted-out defined benefit scheme to another contracted-out defined benefits scheme if:

(*a*)   the member consents in writing; and

(*b*)   the member is either employed by an employer who contributes to the receiving scheme or has previously been a member of the receiving scheme;

(*c*)   the part of the transfer payment representing post-1997 contracted-out rights is applied to provide benefits for the member, in accordance with the rules of the receiving scheme relating to contracted-out employment, as if they had accrued in the receiving scheme; and (*d*)   if the transfer includes accrued rights to a GMP, the receiving scheme's rules provide for the conditions relating to the payment of GMPs accrued under the receiving scheme to apply equally to the transferred GMPs.

If the member does not enter contracted-out employment under the receiving scheme, the transfer can be made only if the receiving scheme provides for a GMP to be payable of at least the amount which would have been payable by the transferring scheme had the transfer not taken place. The receiving scheme must revalue GMPs for such members in accordance with the rules relating to the receiving scheme's own GMPs.

If the transfer includes liability for the payment of a GMP to or in respect of a person who has become entitled to it, the pension must commence from the date on which the receiving scheme assumes liability for the GMP. Any spouse's GMP must be calculated and paid in the same manner as under the transferring scheme.

Where the transferring scheme and the receiving scheme apply to employment with the same employer or the transfer is a bulk transfer as a consequence of a financial transaction between employers or between connected employers (i e where each of the employers is one of a group of companies consisting of a holding company and one or more subsidiaries, within the meaning of *section 736* of the *Companies Act 1985*) or associated employers (within the meaning of *section 590A(3)* and (*4*) of the *Income and Corporation Taxes Act 1988*) the first two conditions set out above do not apply. However, the transfer must be made in accordance with conditions set out in *regulation 12(3)* of the *Occupational Pension Schemes (Preservation of Benefit) Regulations 1991 (SI 1991 No 167)* ('the *Preservation Regulations*') (see chapter 12).

Transfers from a contracted-out defined benefits scheme to a contracted-out defined contributions scheme or a contracted-out personal pension scheme

4.38   A transfer in respect of a member's GMP and post-1997 contracted-out rights can be made from a contracted-out defined benefits scheme to a contracted-out defined contribution scheme if:

(*a*)   the member consents in writing; and

(*b*)   the member is employed by an employer who contributes to the receiving scheme or has previously been a member of the receiving scheme;

(*c*)   the transfer payment is applied so as to provide defined contributions benefits under the receiving scheme; and (*d*)   if the transfer includes a GMP, the amount of the transfer payment is at least equal to the cash equivalent of the GMP.

Again, the first two conditions do not apply where the transferring scheme and the receiving scheme apply to employment with the same employer or the transfer is a bulk transfer as a consequence of a financial transaction between employers or between connected or associated employers, provided the transfer is made in accordance with conditions set out in the *Preservation Regulations* (*SI 1991 No 167*).

Transfers from a contracted-out defined contributions scheme to a contracted-in defined contributions scheme or a contracted-in personal pension scheme

4.39   It is possible for a transfer to be made from a contracted-out defined contributions scheme to a contracted-in defined contribution scheme or a contracted-in personal pension scheme if the member's protected rights are separately identifiable. In this situation, the member's rights in excess of his protected rights can be transferred to the contracted-in scheme and his protected rights can be secured by some other means, such as a transfer to a suitable annuity contract or a contracted-out personal pension scheme.

Transfers from a contracted-out defined contributions scheme to another contracted-out defined contributions scheme or a contracted-out personal pension scheme

4.40   A transfer in respect of a member's protected rights can be made from a contracted-out defined contribution scheme to another contracted-out defined contributions scheme (or contracted-out part of a mixed benefit scheme) or contracted-out personal pension scheme if:

(*a*)   the member consents in writing; and

(*b*)   the member is either employed by an employer who contributes to the receiving scheme or has previously been a member of the receiving scheme;

(*c*)   the part of the transfer payment representing protected rights is of an amount which is at least equal to the cash equivalent of those rights, calculated in accordance with the requirements of *section 97* of *PSA 1993* (see 6.49 below);

(*d*)   the transfer payment is applied to provide defined contributions benefits for or in respect of the member.

From 28 November 2005 it was possible to make such a transfer without consent, if:

(i) conditions (*c*) and (*d*) are satisfied;

(ii) the transferring scheme is or was previously (and the receiving scheme is) a contracted-out defined contributions scheme (or a contracted-out part of a mixed benefit scheme);

(iii) the trustees have given three months' written notice (to the member's last known postal or e-mail address) and have not received any written objection; and

(iv) the employer in relation to both schemes is connected as required in *regulation 12(2)* of the *Preservation Regulations (SI 1991 No 167)*.

Alternatively, the requirement in (iii) can be dispensed with and replaced with just one month's notification (and no opportunity to object) if the actuary certifies to the trustees of the transferring scheme that the transfer credits in the receiving scheme are broadly no less favourable than the rights to be transferred. [*Protected Rights (Transfer Payment) Regulations 1996 (SI 1996/1461)* ('the *Protected Rights Transfer Regulations*'), *reg 3B*]. It is also possible to make transfers of protected rights without consent between stakeholder schemes where the transferring scheme is in winding-up and *regulation 6* of the *Stakeholder Pension Schemes Regulations 2000 (SI 2000 No 1403)* is complied with. *Regulation 3A* of the *Protected Rights (Transfer Payment) Regulations* also refers to transfers from stakeholder pension schemes without members' consent.

Transfers from a contracted-out defined contributions scheme to a contracted-out defined benefits scheme

4.41 A transfer in respect of a member's protected rights can be made from a contracted-out defined contributions scheme to a contracted-out defined benefits scheme if:

(*a*) the member consents in writing; and

(*b*) the member is either employed by an employer who contributes to the receiving scheme or has previously been a member of the receiving scheme;

(*c*) the part of the transfer payment representing protected rights is of an amount which is at least equal to the cash equivalent of those rights, calculated in accordance with the requirements of the *section 97* of *PSA 1993* (see chapter 6);

(*d*) any part of the transfer payment representing pre-1997 protected rights must be used to provide a GMP in accordance with the receiving scheme's rules;

(*e*) any part of the transfer payment representing post-1997 protected rights must be used to provide the member with contracted-out rights under the rules of the receiving scheme.

Transfers between contracted-out arrangements: tabulated summary

4.42

	Type of transfer	Is transfer permitted?		Conditions
		Pre-1997	Post-1997	
1.	*Contracted-out* defined benefits to *contracted-in* defined benefits	Rights over GMP could be transferred, and GMP secured separately	Not if rights to benefits after 6 April 1997 by virtue of contracted-out employment	Not applicable
2.	*Contracted-out* defined benefits to *contracted-out* defined benefits	Yes – subject to conditions	Yes – subject to conditions	Except in the case of employments with the same employer and bulk transfers (where (*a*) and (*b*) below will not apply, but conditions set out in the *Preservation Regulations* will): (*a*) member consents (*b*) member employed by employer who contributes to/or has previously been member of, receiving scheme (*c*) part of transfer representing post-1997 rights applied as if accrued in receiving scheme (*d*) receiving scheme's rules apply same conditions to transferred GMPs

3.	*Contracted-out* defined benefits to *contracted-out* defined contributions	Yes – subject to conditions	Yes – subject to conditions	Except in the case of employments with the same employer and bulk transfers (where (*a*) and (*b*) below will not apply, but conditions set out in the *Preservation Regulations* will): (*a*) member consents (*b*) member employed by employer who contributes to/or has previously been member of, receiving scheme (*c*) transfer payment applied to provide defined contributions benefits under receiving scheme (*d*) if transfer includes GMP, transfer payment is at least equal to cash equivalent of GMP
4.	*Contracted-out* defined benefits to *contracted-out* personal pension	Yes – subject to conditions	Yes – subject to conditions	See 3 above
5.	*Contracted-out* defined contributions to *contracted-in* defined contributions	If protected rights are separately identifiable, excess rights can be transferred, and protected rights secured separately		Not applicable
6.	*Contracted-out* defined contributions to *contracted-in* personal pension	If protected rights are separately identifiable, excess rights can be transferred, and protected rights secured separately		Not applicable

7.	*Contracted-out* defined contribu-tions to *contracted-out* defined contribu-tions	Yes – subject to conditions	(*a*)	Either:
				(i) member consents, and member employed by employer who contributes to/or has previously been member of, receiving scheme; or
				(ii) the notice and/or actuarial requirements in the Protected Rights Transfer Regulations are satisfied and the employers are connected
				(see 4.40 above)
			(*b*)	member employed by employer who contributes to/or has previously been member of, receiving scheme
			(*c*)	transfer payment representing protected rights is at least equal to cash equivalent of those rights
			(*d*)	transfer payment is applied to provide defined contributions benefits
8.	*Contracted-out* defined contribu-tions to *contracted-out* personal pension	Yes – subject to conditions	(*a*)	member consents
			(*b*)	member employed by employer who contributes to/or has previously been member of, receiving scheme
			(*c*)	transfer payment representing protected rights is at least equal to cash equivalent of those rights
			(*d*)	transfer payment is applied to provide defined contributions benefits

9.	Contracted-out defined contributions to contracted-out defined benefits	Yes – subject to conditions	(a)	member consents
			(b)	member employed by employer who contributes to/or has previously been member of, receiving scheme
			(c)	transfer payment representing protected rights is at least equal to cash equivalent of those rights
			(d)	transfer payment representing pre-1997 protected rights used to provide a GMP
			(e)	transfer payment representing post-1997 protected rights used to provide contracted-out rights

Electing for the issue, variation or surrender of a contracting-out certificate

4.43   Full details of the election procedures for obtaining, varying or surrendering a contracting-out certificate are given in the manuals 'Contracted-out Guidance for Salary Related Pension Schemes and Salary Related Overseas Scheme' (CA14C), 'Contracted-out Guidance for Money Purchase Pension Schemes and Money Purchase Overseas Schemes' (CA14D) and 'Contracted-out Guidance for Mixed Benefit Pension Schemes and Mixed Benefit Overseas Schemes' (CA14E), all of which are available from NISPI.

Notices of intention and notices of explanation

4.44   Before making an election for the issue, variation or surrender of a contracting-out certificate, the employer must give either a notice of intention or a notice of explanation. [*Contracting-Out Regulations (SI 1996 No 1172), regs 3 and 10*].

Notice of intention

4.45   A notice of intention must be issued in all cases unless the election to be made will not result in a change in contracted-out status for the employees involved (in which case a notice of explanation may be given (see 4.46 below)).

Notices of intention must be in writing and must contain the information specified in *regulation 3* of the *Contracting-Out Regulations (SI 1996 No 1172)*, which includes an explanation of the effect of making the election. Specimen notices of intention are given, for a defined benefits scheme, in the manual 'Contracted-out Guidance for Salary Related Pension Schemes and Salary Related Overseas Schemes' (CA14C) and, for a defined contributions scheme, in the manual 'Contracted-out Guidance for Money Purchase Pension Schemes and Money Purchase Overseas Schemes' (CA14D), copies of which are available from NISPI.

A notice of intention must be given to all employees in the employments which are to be covered by the certificate whether or not they are members of the scheme or can complete the minimum period of service before normal pension age. The notice must also be given to any appropriate independent trade unions, the trustees of the scheme, the scheme administrator and, if applicable, the insurance company. Notices can be given by sending or delivering them to all relevant parties or, in the case of employees, by exhibiting them conspicuously at the place of work and drawing each employee's attention to it.

A notice of intention must specify the notice period, which generally must be at least three months from the date on which the notice is given. If there are no independent trade unions involved or if all unions involved agree, the notice period can be shortened but it cannot be less than one month. During the notice period employees can raise objections with the employer or with the Commissioners of Inland Revenue.

An employer can amend his election at any time before the issue, variation or withdrawal of the contracting-out certificate but only if the amendment would not alter the categories or descriptions of the employees to which the election relates or the date from which it is intended that the certificate is to have effect. However, if incorrect information is shown in the original notice of intention the employer must issue fresh notices and the notice period will start to run again.

Notice of explanation

4.46   *Regulation 10* of the *Contracting-Out Regulations (SI 1996 No 1172)* permits a notice of explanation to be given (rather than a notice of intention) if:

(*a*)   the employees covered by the election will continue to qualify for either GMPs and post-April 1997 contracted-out salary related rights or protected rights, as the case may be, under the same scheme after the election takes effect;

(*b*)   the accrued rights of those employees to GMPs and post-April 1997 contracted-out salary related rights or protected rights, as the case may be, under the scheme will be unaffected; and (*c*)   the employment of those employees will continue to be contracted out by reference to the same scheme.

A notice of explanation will generally be used where changes occur within a group of companies. For example, if all the employees of a company are transferred to another company within the same group they may remain members of the same scheme, assuming that the new employer participates in the scheme. In such a situation, it would be appropriate to use a notice of explanation as the election would not result in any change of contracted-out status for any of the employees involved.

One notice of explanation can cover more than one election. For example, in the scenario referred to above, the notice would explain both the surrender of the certificate held by the original employer (or its removal from a holding company certificate) and the election for a contracting-out certificate by the new employer (or for its inclusion on a holding company certificate). A notice of explanation will have to be tailored to the exact requirements of the elections to be made but specimen notices of explanation are given in the appropriate manual issued by NISPI as referred to in 4.43 above.

Where a notice of explanation is used no notice period need be given and employees do not have to be allowed the opportunity to object to the election. Otherwise the requirements relating to how a notice is to be given are the same as for notices of intention.

Making an election to contract out

Timing of elections

4.47   An election to contract out must be made within three months of the expiry of the notice of intention or explanation. [*Contracting-Out Regulations (SI 1996 No 1172), reg 5*]. Elections made outside this period may be accepted if a satisfactory explanation can be given for the delay. Where possible, an election to contract out should be submitted before the date from which the contracting-out certificate is to have effect but back-dating may be permitted, at the discretion of NISPI, in some circumstances.

The election

4.48   The election must contain the information specified in *regulation 6* of the *Contracting-Out Regulations (SI 1996 No 1172)*. In particular, in the election to contract out the employer must confirm that:

(*a*)   the scheme is not exempt from and is complying with the *Occupational Pension Schemes (Investment) Regulations 2005 (SI 2005 No 3378)*;

(*b*)   that a notice of intention or explanation has been given and that, if appropriate, consultation requirements have been complied with.

If a scheme is contracting out on the defined contributions basis the employer must also confirm that it will comply with obligations concerning minimum payments as set out in *PSA 1993* and the *Contracting-Out Regulations*. In particular confirmation must be given that the rules of the scheme make provision for:

(*a*)   the investment of minimum payments within one month of the end of the tax month to which they relate;

(*b*)   the investment of age-related rebates made to the scheme within one month after payment;

(*c*)   employee's contributions to be used for defined contributions benefits unless those contributions are being used for salary related benefits payable in addition to the benefits accruing from minimum payments.

The election will generally be made by completing Form CA7300 in respect of a defined benefit scheme, Form C7301 in respect of a defined contributions scheme or Form C7302 in respect of a mixed benefit scheme (all of which are available from NISPI). The Form must be signed by both the employer and the trustees or by someone authorised to sign on behalf of either or both of these parties.

Supporting documents

4.49   When making an election in relation to a defined benefits scheme, until the minimum funding requirement is fully in place (ie 5 April 2007) an employer must provide a 'Certificate T' from the scheme actuary (*Contracting-Out Regulations (SI 1996 No 1172), reg 72*) confirming that:

(*a*)   the scheme complies with the funding requirements for contracting out;

(*b*)   the requirements of *PA 1995* relating to the minimum funding requirement (see 11.14 to 11.31 below) and employer-related investments (see 10.24 below) are complied with; and

(*c*)   if the scheme winds up it will be able to meet the liabilities specified in *section 73(4)* of *PA 1995* (as amended by the *Occupational Pension Schemes (Winding Up) Regulations 1996 (SI 1996 No 3126)* ('the *Winding-Up Regulations*')) (see 12.55 below) (currently valued on an MFR basis).

In order to complete a certificate, the actuary must carry out a full minimum funding requirement valuation and certify a schedule of contributions within twelve weeks of signing of the valuation (see chapter 11 for further details). The Certificate T must then be submitted within one month of the actuary certifying the schedule of contributions. Where a minimum funding requirement valuation is not available, the election package can contain a statement from the actuary confirming that an interim schedule of contributions is in place which, in his opinion, is adequate for the scheme to be able to meet its contracted-out liabilities and any prescribed liabilities with a higher priority on.

The employer must also submit a reference scheme test certificate signed by the scheme actuary confirming that the scheme satisfies the reference scheme test.

Variation of the contracting-out certificate

4.50 Minor variations to a contracting-out certificate may be made by notifying NISPI in writing or by submitting an appropriate form. Minor variations include the change of the name of an employer, an employer's address or the name of the scheme. Such changes must be notified within three months of the effective date of the change. Notice of such changes does not have to be given to employees or other interested parties.

Major variations require full election action including the issue of a notice of intention and consultation with independent trade unions or the issue of a notice of explanation, if appropriate. Specimen notices of intention are given in the appropriate manual issued by NISPI. Major changes include a change to the effective date of contracting out, the addition or deletion of a subsidiary to the schedule of the holding company's certificate or changes to the categories of employment covered by the contracting-out certificate. Major changes must be notified to NISPI on the appropriate form (Form CA7306) within three months of the effective date of change. [*Contracting-Out Regulations (SI 1996 No 1172), reg 9*].

Election to surrender a certificate

4.51 Before making an election to surrender a contracting-out certificate an employer must give a notice of intention and undertake consultation with any independent trade unions. Specimen notices of intention are given in the appropriate manual issued by NISPI. The notice period is the same as for the making of an election for a certificate, ie a minimum of one or three months depending on whether there are any independent trade unions involved and whether they agree to the shorter period. In order to surrender a contracting-out certificate a Form CA7313 must be submitted to the NISPI. [*Contracting-Out Regulations (SI 1996 No 1172), reg 9*].

Holding company certificates

4.52 An employer may hold a contracting-out certificate as a holding company whether or not it is itself contracted out by reference to the scheme. An employer can be a holding company if it is:

(*a*) one of a group of companies which consists of a holding company and subsidiaries (within the meaning of *section 736* of the *Companies Act 1985*); or

(*b*) an employer who controls associated employers (within the meaning of *section 590A(3)* and (*4*) of the *Income and Corporation Taxes Act 1988*); or

(*c*) an employer who is the principal employer in accordance with the rules of the scheme or who has power to act on behalf of all employers in the scheme in accordance with the rules.

A holding company may elect for a single contracting-out certificate which includes its associated or subsidiary companies on a schedule to the certificate. The requirements relating to the reference scheme test differ if a single contracting-out certificate is issued to a holding company rather than separate certificates being issued to each company (see 4.9 above). [*Contracting-Out Regulations (SI 1996 No 1172), reg 12*].

The periodic return system

4.53 In April 1993 the Occupational Pensions Board (now dissolved) introduced the periodic return system whereby notification of changes to holding company certificates were supplied on a six-monthly basis instead of as and when the changes occurred. Employers with holding company certificates participate in this system on a voluntary basis. The system has been continued by NICO but the periodic returns are now required to be made on an annual basis. The changes that may be notified on the periodic return Form CA7312 are:

(*a*) the addition or deletion of employers from the schedule to the contracting-out certificate held by the holding company;

(*b*) a change of scheme name;

(*c*) a change of name of the principal employer and/or any participating employer;

(*d*) the appointment of a new principal employer.

Termination of contracted-out employment

4.54 Full details of the procedures which must be adopted following the cessation of contracted-out employment are given in the manuals 'Termination of Contracted-out Employment – Manual for Salary Related Pension Schemes and Salary Related Parts of Mixed Benefit Schemes' (CA14), 'Termination of Contracted-out Employment – Manual for Money Purchase Pension Schemes and Money Purchase Parts of Mixed Benefits Schemes' (CA14A) and 'Cessation of Contracted-out Pension Scheme', (CA15), all of which are available from NISPI.

When does contracted-out employment cease?

4.55 A member will be treated as having terminated contracted-out employment if:

(*a*)   his contract of employment expires or is terminated; or

(*b*)   in the absence of a contract of employment, the employment itself has ended; or

(*c*)   he has ceased to be a member of a contracted-out scheme; or

(*d*)   the contracting-out certificate by virtue of which his employment was contracted out has been surrendered or cancelled; or

(*e*)   the contracting-out certificate by virtue of which his employment was contracted out has been varied in such a way that the certificate no longer applies to his employment; or

(*f*)   the earner's employer dies or disposes of the whole or part of his business so that the member ceases to be employed by that employer and the contracted-out employment is not, or cannot be, treated as continuing with any new employer.

When is a member's contracted-out employment treated as not having ceased?

4.56 A member's contracted-out employment is not treated as having ceased if he resumes membership of the same scheme within six months as a result of either employment with the same employer or employment with a new employer. However his contracted-out employment will be treated as having ceased if his protected rights or accrued GMP and post-1997 contracted-out salary related rights, as applicable, have been secured outside the scheme.

If the contracting-out certificate relating to the member's contracted-out employment has been varied, surrendered or cancelled so that it no longer applies to the member, the member's contracted-out employment will not be treated as having ceased if, within six months, he becomes a member of another contracted-out scheme of the same employer. The member's protected rights or accrued GMP and post-1997 contracted-out salary related rights, as applicable, must be transferred to the new scheme.

A member's contracted-out employment will not be treated as terminated if his employer's business is taken over by another employer provided the new employer accepts the liabilities and responsibilities of the old employer. The new employer must notify NISPI of the change within one month of the change taking place.

Securing contracted-out rights when a member leaves a scheme

4.57   Where a member's pensionable service terminates after he has completed two years of qualifying service he is entitled to a preserved benefit under the scheme (see chapter 6). In the case of a contracted-out scheme the member's protected rights or GMP and rights attributable to his post-6 April 1997 contracted-out employment, as appropriate, will form part of the preserved benefit and, as such, must be appropriately secured.

A member who leaves pensionable service before completing two years of qualifying service will usually only be entitled to a refund of his contributions. In this situation he will generally be reinstated into S2P.

The three options set out in 4.58 to 4.60 below are available for securing the contracted-out rights of early leavers.

Reinstatement into S2P

4.58   It may be possible to reinstate the member rights into the State scheme by a payment of a contributions equivalent premium. The consequence of paying such a premium is that the member is treated as if he had not contracted out for the period in respect of which the premium was paid. The member's protected rights or accrued GMP and post-1997 contracted-out salary related rights, as appropriate, are extinguished.

As from 6 April 1997 it is only possible to buy an employee back in to S2P if he had less than two years of qualifying service and took a refund of his contributions on leaving the scheme.

Retention of liability within the scheme

4.59   The second alternative is to retain the liability for the member's protected rights or accrued GMP and post-1997 contracted-out rights, as appropriate, within the scheme. Any such rights retained within the scheme must be revalued to take account of inflation (see 4.61 below).

Transfer to another arrangement

4.60   The third option is that liability for the member's protected rights or accrued GMP and post-1997 contracted-out rights, as appropriate, could be secured outside the scheme. This may be done by way of a transfer to another contracted-out scheme, such as the scheme of a new employer or a contracted-out personal pension scheme. Alternatively the liability could be bought out by the purchase of an insurance policy or an annuity contract (see 4.35 to 4.42 above for conditions relating to transfers).

Revaluation

Revaluing GMPs

4.61   To counter some of the effects of inflation and to allow for the fact that a GMP will be based on band earnings at the date of termination of pensionable service, *section 16* of *PSA 1993* provides that GMPs of early leavers must be revalued from the date of leaving up to State pension age. The two methods currently available to revalue GMPs are:

(*a*)   revaluation of earnings factors – this involves increasing the earnings factors used for calculating the GMP by the last earnings factor order made under *section 148* of the *Social Security Administration Act 1992* in the same way as for active members; or

(*b*)   fixed rate revaluation – in this case the rate of revaluation is fixed at a certain level depending on the date of the termination of contracted-out employment. Where contracted-out employment terminated before 6 April 1988 the rate is 8.5 per cent compound, for terminations during the period 6 April 1988 to 5 April 1993 the rate is 7.5 per cent compound, for terminations during the period 6 April 1993 to 5 April 1997 the rate is 7 per cent compound and for terminations on or after 6 April 1997 the rate is 6.25 per cent compound. The rate of revaluation for early leavers will be reduced to 4.5 per cent per year for leavers on or after 6 April 2002. The new fixed rate is reviewed every five years and this has consistently been reduced since its introductory level of 8.5 per cent per annum in 1978.

To a limited extent it is possible to revalue GMPs by what is known as limited rate revaluation. Using this method GMPs must be increased by the lesser of:

(i) five per cent compound for each complete tax year after that in which contracted-out service terminated; and

(ii) the increase which would apply using the last order made under *section 148* in the tax year before the member reaches State pension age.

From 6 April 2005, the figure for limited rated evaluation of GMPs by virtue of the *Guaranteed Minimum Pensions Increase Order 2005 (SI 2005 No 521)* is 3 per cent. If limited rate revaluation is used a limited rate revaluation premium has to be paid to NICO. Limited rate revaluation can only apply in respect of members for whom limited revaluation premiums were being paid prior to 6 April 1997. Otherwise the option is no longer available and schemes which previously adopted this method must adopt one of the other two methods available. The trustees and the employer must decide which method of revaluation is to be adopted and NISPI must be notified of any changes.

Post-1997 contracted-out salary related rights

4.62 The benefits payable to members in respect of post-6 April 1997 contracted-out employment are revalued in the same way as other benefits accruing under the scheme (see chapter 6).

Protected rights

4.63 The protected rights of a member must be revalued on the same basis as other defined contributions benefits (see chapter 6).

Anti-franking

4.64 The GMPs of early leavers are further protected by the principle of 'anti-franking'.

The legislation relating to anti-franking is contained in *sections 87* to *92* of *PSA 1993*.

The purpose of this legislation is to prevent the relevant pension benefits, broadly those in excess of GMP, from being eroded by financing the cost of providing for the revaluation of GMP rights out of the pensions being provided under the scheme in excess of GMP (i e by 'franking' that cost).

The principal circumstances in which the legislation applies are where the member ceases to be in contracted-out employment on or after 1 January 1985, and at that point the value of his deferred pension in accordance with the preservation requirements exceeds the value of his GMP rights at that time and the revalued GMP when it comes into payment is greater than it was when contracted-out employment ceased (which it generally will be).

Section 87(3) prescribes a minimum level of benefits (the sum of the following elements) which must be provided in these circumstances:

(*a*)   the pension on short service benefit payable to the member on the date on which pensionable service terminated in accordance with the preservation requirements;

(*b*)   the amount by which the GMP has increased between the date on which contracted-out employment terminated and the date of payment of GMP;

(*c*)   an additional amount in respect of any subsequent period of pensionable employment in the scheme on a contracted-in basis plus a later earnings addition where earnings at the date of termination of pensionable service are higher than at the date on which contracted-out service terminated.

The legislation provides equivalent protection in relation to spouses' and civil partners' GMPs.

Supervision of formerly contracted-out schemes

4.65   When a scheme ceases to be contracted out it must secure members' protected rights or accrued GMPs and post-1997 salary related contracted-out rights, as appropriate, in one of the ways mentioned in 4.57 to 4.60 above. The Secretary of State, acting through NICO and NISPI, has a duty to continue to supervise schemes which have lost their contracted-out status for whatever reason. [*PSA 1993, ss 52* and *53*]. The trustees of such a scheme can be directed to take such action as the Secretary of State may, in writing, specify. [*PSA 1993, s 53(1)*]. This will usually take the form of monitoring the funding of the scheme, by requiring actuarial certification, so as to ensure that the scheme has sufficient assets to meet its liabilities for protected rights or accrued GMPs and post-1997 salary related contracted-out rights, as appropriate.

Simplification of contracting out

4.66   The *Occupational Personal Pension Schemes (Contracting-out) (Miscellaneous Amendments) Regulations 2002 (SI 2002 No 681)* which came into force from 6 April 2002 introduced changes intended to simplify contracting out for both occupational and person pension schemes. A summary of these changes is contained in 4.73 below.

Contracted-out rights on divorce

4.67 The *Pension Sharing (Contracting-out) (Consequential Amendments) Regulations 2000 (SI 2000 No 2975)*, which came into force on 1 December 2000, amend the *Contracting-Out Regulations.* The aim is to ensure that those pension rights conferred under pension sharing arrangements, which are derived from the rights of a member protected under the contracting-out arrangements, receive similar protection to that accorded to contracted-out rights.

Stakeholder schemes

4.68 If an individual contracts out of S2P using a stakeholder pension plan, a rebate of National Insurance contributions is paid into their stakeholder plan.

There is a NICO manual explaining the procedures to be used from April 2001 where an individual uses a stakeholder pension to contract out of S2P. This is manual CA84 'Stakeholder Pension Scheme Manual'. The manual is available from HMRC (website www.inlandrevenue.gov.uk/stakepension).

Replacement for SERPS

4.69 SERPS was based on a standard target benefit of 20 per cent of average revalued earnings over a working lifetime restricted to earnings between the lower and upper earnings limits. This has been replaced with effect from 6 April 2002 by S2P which provides different accrual rates and target benefits depending on earnings.

Benefits under S2P

4.70 Different accrual rates apply depending on earnings:

(*a*)   accrual for a target benefit of 40 per cent for earnings between LEL (£4,264) and the new lower earnings threshold (LET) (£12,100);

(*b*)   accrual for a target benefit of 10 per cent between LET and new upper earnings threshold (UET) (£27,800);

(*c*)   accrual for a target benefit of 20 per cent between second threshold and UEL (£32,760);

(*d*)   everyone earning at least LEL will be treated as if earning LET.

It is intended that in 2006 all contracted-in employees will receive the same flat rate benefit based on LET.

Non-earners

4.71   S2P provides benefits for some non-earners, based on assumed earnings of LET. They are:

(*a*)   those receiving long-term incapacity benefits;

(*b*)   those caring for a disabled or sick person or a child under six.

Other non-earners remain excluded from S2P (as they were from SERPS) including:

(*a*)   self employed;

(*b*)   students;

(*c*)   unemployed;

(*d*)   early retired and short-term sick.

4.72   The main differences between SERPS and S2P are that the latter is intended to provide higher benefits to people on lower earnings and to provide assumed earnings equal to the LET in respect of non-earners such as those on long-term incapacity benefit.

Contracting out of S2P

4.73   Occupational schemes already contracted out under SERPS will continue to do so on a similar basis with the State providing pension top ups to the new S2P level for low and moderate earners. The NI rebate for COSRs is 3.5 per cent of band earnings (previously 3.0 per cent) and the employee rebate remains at 1.6 per cent. Age related rebates for COMPs are retained.

Personal pension schemes (see 15.30 below) will contract out at the S2P level of benefit with the State topping up to LET level for those earning between LEL and LET. Rebates will be calculated by reference both to age and to the different levels of accrual. It is intended that this will continue after the flat rate S2P is introduced.

Proposed legislative changes

4.74 In the Government's White Paper issued on 11 June 2003 entitled 'Action on Occupational Pensions', the Government indicated its intention to streamline the rules of contracting out. In particular, it stated its intention to find a 'workable and affordable solution to the problems created by the complexity of the Guaranteed Minimum Pension (GMP) element of contracted-out schemes'.

In a press release dated 17 October 2003 the then Secretary of State for Work and Pensions, Andrew Smith, announced measures that would enable occupational pension schemes which had contracted out of SERPS to convert the GMP element into their own scheme benefits, as long as the value of members' previously accrued rights are maintained. If schemes take up this option they will have to convert on the basis of actuarial equivalence with the proviso that any resulting changes will not affect the value of individual accrued rights.

However, neither the Pensions Bill nor *PA 2004* contained any of these proposed changes, and it is currently unclear when the government will be legislating to give effect to these proposals.

The one change that has occurred is to allow transfers of protected rights in some circumstances (see 4.40 above).

Civil partnerships

4.75 The *Civil Partnership Act 2004* came into force on 5 December 2005 (for a more general review of the provisions, see chapter 9). This will have implications for survivors' benefits in contracted-out schemes. Changes have been made to the contracting-out legislation by the *Civil Partnerships (Contracted-out Occupational and Appropriate Personal Pension Schemes) (Surviving Civil Partners) Order 2005 (SI 2005/2050)* ('*the Contracting-out Order*'). As discussed in chapter 9, the broad aim of the *Civil Partnership Act 2004* and associated legislation is to put people who enter into civil partnerships in the same position as married persons.

Most of the changes take effect in relation to service accrued on and after 5 December 2005. However, in relation to contracted-out benefits, following consultation, the Government decided to require contracted-out schemes to provide the same contracted-out benefits for civil partners as it did for spouses on the basis of contracted-out rights accrued from April 1988. Effectively, this put civil partners in the same position as widowers (see 4.13 above). However, the legislation is not overriding and this means that schemes wishing to continue to contract out will be required to amend their rules specifically. Schemes that do not wish to remain contracted out should arguably also do so to account for the backdating effect. However, if loss of contracted-out status is the only sanction, they may choose not to do so.

There may be *section 67* implications in relation to these retrospective amendments (particularly where the scheme provides that if there is no spouse the benefit is redirected to children or another dependant). There will also be the need for a *section 37* certificate from the actuary. (See 4.76 below).

Amendment of contracted-out schemes

4.76   *Section 37* of *PSA 1993* prohibits changes to the rules of contracted-out schemes unless the change is permitted by *regulation 42* of the *Contracting-Out Regulations (SI 1996 No 1172)*. In summary:

- changes that effect GMPs are prohibited;

- adverse changes cannot be made in relation to protected rights accrued before the change; and

- in relation to reference schemes test benefits, the scheme actuary will be required to provide a certificate that he is satisfied that the scheme will continue to meet the reference scheme test after the change.

Chapter 5

Taxation of registered schemes

Section A

Introduction

5.1   The existing eight pension taxation regimes are being replaced by a single integrated pension tax regime from 6 April 2006 ('A-Day'). The new integrated tax regime will apply to all 'registered pension schemes' (the equivalent of pre A-Day tax approved pension schemes). The new pension tax regime provisions are contained in *FA 2004* and follow the proposals outlined in the joint Treasury and Inland Revenue consultation paper, 'Simplifying the taxation of pensions; increasing choice and flexibility for all', published December 2002. The concept is simple. Tax relievable contributions can be made to build up benefits in a tax approved environment up to a lifetime allowance. There is nothing to stop tax relievable contributions being made to enable an individual to build up benefits with a value in excess of the lifetime allowance but, if the lifetime allowance is exceeded, there is an additional tax charge (the lifetime allowance charge) on any excess when the benefits come into payment. The restrictions that existed until A-Day on the form in which benefits can be taken in different types of pension schemes will be simplified. All types of registered pension schemes will be able to pay members any type of payment which is treated as an authorised member payment under *FA 2004*. If an unauthorised member payment is made by a registered pension scheme there can be penal tax charges.

This chapter is intended to give an outline of the tax treatment of registered pension schemes after A-Day including occupational and personal pension schemes. It will then consider the continued relevance of pre A-Day Revenue limits after A-Day to pension schemes as a result of the *Registered Pension Schemes (Modification of the Rules of Existing Schemes) Regulations 2006 (SI 2006 No 364)* ('the *Modification Regulations*'). Unless steps are taken to disapply the *Modification Regulations*, pension schemes will not be able to pay out benefits in excess of pre A-Day Revenue limits for a period of five years (or possibly longer) after A-Day. For the reasons discussed in this chapter many occupational pension schemes may choose not to disapply all or some of existing pre A-Day Revenue limits or will write similar requirements into their rules as scheme limits. Pre A-Day Revenue limits may therefore still be applicable after A-Day. Under the *Modification Regulations* the scheme administrator will also have discretion not to pay out any payment which could have been paid by a tax approved scheme before A-Day but which counts as an unauthorised payment on and after A-Day.

The pre A-Day treatment of personal pension schemes and stakeholder pension schemes and the requirements that apply to stakeholder pension schemes generally are considered in chapter 14 (Personal pension and stakeholder schemes). From A-Day the same tax treatment will apply to those schemes as apply to all other types of registered schemes.

The tax treatment of unapproved pension schemes established before A-Day and non-registered pension schemes established on and after A-Day is considered in section C of this chapter at 5.122 below.

Treatment of existing tax approved schemes

5.2   Pension schemes which are already tax approved before A-Day will automatically become registered schemes under the new regime from A-Day unless they take action to opt out (*paragraphs 1* and *2* of *Schedule 36* to *FA 2004*). This will include:

(a)   Private sector defined benefits and defined contributions retirement benefit schemes that were previously approved on a discretionary basis under *Chapter 1* of *Part XIV* of the *Income* and *Corporation Taxes Act 1988* (*ICTA 1988*) – this will include free-standing AVC schemes.

(b)   Relevant statutory schemes (more commonly known as public sector schemes) defined in *section 611A* of *ICTA 1988*, for example, the Local Government Pension Scheme.

(c)   Certain deferred annuity contracts used to secure pension benefits under (a) and (b) that do not provide for the immediate payment of benefits. These deferred annuity contracts were not previously approved before A-Day (note this category does not cover most annuities used to secure benefits under an occupational pension scheme which come into payment immediately, for example, on a scheme wind up).

(d)   A retirement annuity contract or retirement annuity trust scheme previously approved under *section 620* or *621* of *ICTA 1988* or a substituted contract within the meaning of *section 622(3)* of *ICTA 1988*. These were the only type of policy that could be taken out by the self-employed and individuals without access to an occupational pension scheme before personal pension schemes were introduced with effect from 1 July 1988.

(*e*)   Personal pension schemes previously approved under *Chapter IV* of *Part XIV* of *ICTA 1988* (*paragraph 1* of *Schedule 36* to *FA 2004*) which will include most stakeholder pension schemes and 'group personal pension schemes'.

(*f*)   Former approved schemes (often referred to as 'old code schemes'). These schemes were schemes approved before 1970 but have not been re-approved as new code occupational pension schemes.

Existing approved schemes do not need to fill in any forms to register as registered pension schemes, this will happen automatically.

There are transitional provisions in *paragraph 4* of *Schedule 36* to *FA 2004* which will determine who will be the scheme administrator where a pre-existing approved scheme is treated as becoming a registered pension scheme on A-Day. In the case of:

(i)   retirement benefit schemes referred to in (*a*) above, relevant statutory schemes referred to in (*b*) above and a former approved superannuation fund referred to in (*f*) above, the person who was administrator of the scheme immediately before A-Day will become the administrator on A-Day. In the case of a retirement benefits scheme under (*a*) this will generally be the trustees;

(ii)   deferred annuity contracts under (*c*) or retirement annuity contracts under (*d*) above, the trustees of the pension scheme or the insurance company that is party to the contract in which the pension scheme is comprised will become the scheme administrator at A Day;

(iii)   personal pension schemes referred to in (*e*) above, the person who is referred to in *section 638(1)* of *ICTA 1988* will become the scheme administrator.

The responsibilities of the scheme administrator are discussed later in this chapter.

Application to become a registered scheme on or after A-Day

5.3   Any new pension scheme established on or after A-Day will have to make an application to HMRC to be registered (*section 153* of *FA 2004*). The application is made by the person who will become the scheme administrator.

An application to register must contain any information reasonably required by HMRC and must be accompanied by the required declaration by the scheme administrator (see below) and any other declarations reasonably required by

5.3 *Taxation of registered schemes*

HMRC (*sections 153(2)* and *270* of *FA 2004*). The declarations that HMRC may require to accompany an application to register may include a declaration that the pension scheme's constitutional documentation do not entitle any person to unauthorised payments (see 5.24 below).

At the date of writing, the declarations required are that:

(*a*)   the scheme meets all the conditions to be a registered pension scheme; and

(*b*)   information supplied in the application is correct and complete; and

(*c*)   the scheme administrator understands that false statements may lead to a penalty and/or prosecution under the Registered Pension Schemes Manual ('RPSM') (*RPSM02101010*).

Registration will be made online by the completion of a form by the person agreeing to be the scheme administrator.

An application to register a pension scheme may be made only if the pension scheme is an occupational pension scheme or has been established by:

(i) an insurance company;

(ii) a unit trust scheme manager;

(iii) an operator, trustee or depositary of a recognised European Economic Area ('EEA') collective investment scheme;

(iv) an authorised open-ended investment company;

(v) a building society;

(vi) a bank; or

(vii) an EEA investment portfolio manager (*section 154* of *FA 2004*).

This is similar to the position under the pre A-Day regime, i e only certain financial institutions can establish non-employer sponsored trust-based tax approved pension schemes.

There is no longer a requirement in the tax legislation that the only type of occupational pension scheme that can be registered as a registered pension scheme must be set up under irrevocable trusts. However, this has been replaced by an equivalent requirement in *PA 2004* that if an occupational pension scheme has its main administration in the UK, the trustees or managers of the scheme cannot accept any payment to fund benefits for or in respect of its members unless the scheme is established under irrevocable trusts (*section 252* of *PA 2004*). The trustees or managers can be liable to penalties if they make a funding payment to an occupational pension scheme in breach of this requirement.

An occupational pension scheme that does not restrict membership to its own employees can now be a registered pension scheme and can include employees of other non-associated employers. Before A-Day the general rule was that a non-sectionalised occupational pension scheme (i e not a multi-employer scheme for non associated employers) had to restrict membership to employees of associated employers to obtain and retain exempt approved status. *RPSM02102010* confirms that employees of any employer can be included. If the rules of an occupational pension scheme for associated employers were changed after A-Day to allow employees of non-associated employers to join, consideration would need to be given as to whether this is consistent with the main purpose of the scheme which will often be to provide pension benefits for employees working in the undertaking of the sponsoring employer establishing the scheme and associated employers. However, the cases do suggest that the main purpose of a trust can change over time.

The scheme administrator of a pension scheme that is registered on or after A-Day is the person who is, or persons who are, appointed in accordance with the rules of the pension scheme to be responsible for the discharge of the functions conferred or imposed on the scheme administrator of the pension scheme under *Part 4* of *FA 2004* (*section 270* of *FA 2004*). A person or persons can only become the scheme administrator if the person or one of the persons is resident in the UK or another State which is an EEA Member State or a non-Member EEA State and has made the required declaration to HMRC. The required declaration is a declaration that the person:

(*a*)   understands that the person will be responsible for discharging the functions conferred or imposed on the scheme administrator of the pension scheme under *Part 4* of *FA 2004*; and

(*b*)   intends to discharge those functions at all times, whether resident in the UK or another State that is a Member State or a non-Member EEA State.

Responsibilities of the administrator

5.4   The administrator is responsible for the discharge of certain functions under *FA 2004* (see 5.83 to 5.94 below on scheme administration) and is liable to pay certain tax charges (*sections 270* to *274* of *FA 2004*). In certain circumstances the trustees of the registered pension scheme or, failing that, certain other persons who fall next down a statutory priority order set out in *section 272* of *FA 2004* (including the sponsoring employer of an occupational pension scheme) can be liable as scheme administrator if:

(*a*)   there is no scheme administrator; or

(*b*)   the person who is the scheme administrator cannot be traced; or (*c*)   the person who is the scheme administrator is in serious default.

There are further default provisions under *section 273* of *FA 2004* which can make members of the pension scheme liable as scheme administrator in certain circumstances to pay the tax that was due under *section 239* (scheme sanction charge) or *section 242* (de-registration charge) where the tax has not been paid.

Finding your way round FA 2004

5.5   Finding the relevant provision in *FA 2004* can sometimes be difficult. *FA 2004* was amended before it came into force by *FA 2005* and is expected to be amended again by *FA 2006*.

The main provisions relating to pensions in *Part 4* of *FA 2004* are as follows:

(*a*)   *Chapter 1* (Introduction) – defines some key concepts used in *FA 2004* some of which are discussed below – *sections 149* to *152*;

(*b*)   *Chapter 2* (Registration of Pension Schemes) – is about the registration and deregistration of pension schemes – *sections 153* to *159*;

(*c*)   *Chapter 3* (Payments by Registered Schemes) – is about the payments that may be made by registered pension schemes and related matters – *sections 160* to *185*;

(*d*)   *Chapter 4* (Registered Payments: Tax Reliefs and Exemptions) – deals with tax reliefs and exemptions in connection with registered pension schemes – *sections 186* to *203*;

(*e*)   *Chapter 5* (Registered Pension Schemes: Tax Charges) – imposes tax charges in connection with registered pension schemes – *sections 204* to *242*;

(*f*)   *Chapter 6* (Schemes that are not Registered Schemes) – is about some schemes that are not registered schemes – *sections 243* to *249*;

(*g*)   *Chapter 7* (Compliance) – makes provisions about compliance – *sections 250* to *274A*;

(*h*)   *Chapter 8* (Supplementary) – contains interpretation and other supplementary provisions – *sections 275* to *284*.

The schedules relating to the tax treatment of registered pension schemes are as follows:

(i) *Schedule 28* – Registered pension schemes: authorised pensions – supplementary:

   •   *Part I* – Pension Rules;

- *Part 2* – Pension Death Benefit Rules;

(ii) *Schedule 29* – Registered pension schemes: authorised pensions – supplementary:

- *Part 1* – Lump Sum Rule;

- *Part 2* – Lump Sum Death Benefit Rule;

(iii) *Schedule 30* –Registered pension schemes: employer loans;

(iv) *Schedule 31* – Taxation of benefits under registered pension schemes;

(v) *Schedule 32* – Registered pension schemes: benefit crystallisation events – supplementary;

(vi) *Schedule 33* – Overseas pension schemes: migrant member relief;

(vii) *Schedule 34* – Non-UK schemes: application of certain charges;

(viii) *Schedule 35* – Pension schemes etc: minor and consequential changes;

(ix) *Schedule 36* – Pension schemes etc: transitional provisions and savings:

- *Part 1* – Pre-commencement pension schemes;

- *Part 2* – Pre-commencement rights: lifetime allowance charge;

- *Part 3* – Pre-commencement benefit rights;

- *Part 4* – Other provisions.

Key definitions

5.6   *FA 2004* makes use of certain key definitions set out in *section 154* of *FA 2004* that are, in the main, borrowed or adapted from pre A-Day requirements. Some key definitions are set out below. The other important *FA 2004* definitions can be found in *sections 275* to *280* of *FA 2004* and are discussed later in the chapter.

'**Arrangement**' in relation to a member of a pension scheme, means an arrangement relating to the member under the pension scheme (*section 152* of *FA 2004*). Arrangement is a concept borrowed from the regime that applied to personal pension schemes before A-Day and is now applied generally to all types of registered pension schemes. Typically personal pension schemes were set up before A-Day so that the funds invested on behalf of the member were divided into 1,000 or multiple arrangements so that the member could just vest part of his benefits at any one time. Under the new regime it is possible to have multiple arrangements under an occupational pension scheme that vest at different times. There are different types of arrangement under the new regime, namely: 'defined contributions arrangements'; 'cash balance arrangements'; 'defined benefit arrangements'; and 'hybrid arrangements' which provide benefits of the type corresponding to their name. Where not all of the benefits provided under an arrangement are of the same one of the above varieties, the arrangement is treated for *FA 2004* purposes as separate arrangements one of which relates to each of the two or three varieties of benefits that can be provided (*section 152(9) of FA 2004*). However, there is nothing to stop an occupational pension scheme that wants to offer phased vesting of benefits providing for members' defined benefits or defined contributions benefits to be provided under multiple arrangements.

'**Occupational pension scheme**' means a pension scheme established by an employer or employers and having or capable of having effect so as to provide benefits to or in respect of any or all of the employees of:

(*a*)   that employer or those employers;

(*b*)   any other employer,

whether or not it also has or is capable of having effect so as to provide benefits to or in respect of other persons (*section 150(5) of FA 2004*).

'**Pension Scheme**' means a scheme or other 'arrangements', comprised in one or more instruments or agreements, having or capable of having effect so as to provide benefits to or in respect of persons:

(*a*)   on retirement;

(*b*)   on death;

(*c*)   having reached a particular age;

(*d*)   on the onset of serious ill-health or incapacity; or

(*e*)   in similar circumstances (*section 150(1) of FA 2004*).

A pension scheme is a 'registered pension scheme' at any time if it is registered under *Chapter 2* of *Part 4* of *FA 2004* (*section 150(2) of FA 2004*).

'**Personal pension scheme**' is not defined in *FA 2004* as the definition is not used as the provisions relating to registered pension schemes apply at an arrangement level (see below). However, the definition of 'personal pension scheme' under *PSA 1993* is being amended by *section 239* of *PA 2004* from 6 April 2006 so that it means a pension scheme that:

(*a*)   is not an occupational pension scheme; and

(*b*)   is established by a person within any of the paragraphs of *section 154(1)* of *FA 2004*.

Effectively this means if a registered pension scheme is not a trust based occupational pension scheme established by an employer and is established by:

    (i) an insurance company;

    (ii) a unit trust scheme manager;

  (iii) an operator, trustee or depositary of a recognised EEA collective investment scheme;

  (iv) an authorised open-ended investment company;

   (v) a building society;

  (vi) a bank; or

 (vii) an EEA investment portfolio manager,

it will be a personal pension scheme for *PA 1995* and *PA 2004* purposes.

The lifetime allowance and benefit crystallisation events

5.7   The new post A-Day tax regime sets a personal lifetime allowance for all pension savings in registered pension schemes. For the tax year 2006/2007, the standard lifetime allowance will be set at £1.5 million (*section 218* of *FA 2004*). The original proposal was that the lifetime allowance would increase in line with inflation. However, the Government changed its mind and it announced that the annual allowance will be increased by Treasury Order in the subsequent four tax years after 2005/2006 as follows:

Tax year	Standard lifetime allowance (£ millions)
2006/2007	1.50
2007/2008	1.60
2008/2009	1.65
2009/2010	1.75
2010/2011	1.80

The lifetime allowance available to an individual can be increased in certain circumstances by multiplying the standard lifetime allowance by a lifetime allowance enhancement factor (see below).

The amount of the individual's lifetime allowance available is tested on 'benefit crystallisation' events occurring in relation to an individual such as a pension coming into payment or a lump sum death benefit being paid or on the commencement of income withdrawal (see below). For defined contributions arrangements the amount applied under a pension policy or under the member's account to provide pension or other benefits on a benefit crystallisation event will be tested against the individual's lifetime allowance (Benefit Crystallisation Event 4 – *section 216* of *FA 2004*). For defined benefits schemes, a pension coming into payment is valued using a standard valuation factor of 20:1 (Benefit Crystallisation Event 2 – *section 216* of *FA 2004* and *section 276* of *FA 2004*). For example, when a defined benefits pension of £25,000 comes into payment it will be valued at £500,000 for the purpose of assessing how much of the lifetime allowance is available. This factor is based on certain assumptions with regard to the benefits the scheme will offer. Schemes offering more generous benefits can negotiate a higher factor with HMRC (*section 276(2)* of *FA 2004*). On a benefit crystallisation event occurring the member's lifetime allowance is then reduced by the percentage of the lifetime allowance used up. So in the previous example if the pension of £25,000 per annum came into payment in the tax year 2006/2007 when a standard lifetime allowance of £1.5 million was available this will have used up one-third of a member's standard lifetime allowance. Two-thirds of the lifetime allowance will still be available on future benefit crystallisation events.

When pension benefits come into payment under a scheme after A-Day, the member will need to be informed of the percentage of the lifetime allowance that is being used up by the pension. The member will then need to confirm whether he has sufficient lifetime allowance remaining after taking into account other pension benefits that have already come into payment. To do the calculations the scheme administrator may need details of the percentages of the lifetime allowance used up by previous benefit crystallisation events. If the pension provided by the scheme takes the member over the lifetime allowance (or if the lifetime allowance has already been used up), then the benefits will be subject to a lifetime allowance charge (*section 214* of *FA 2004*). The lifetime allowance charge for sums in excess of the lifetime allowance will be 25 per cent, or 55 per cent if the excess funds are taken as a lump sum (*section 215* of *FA 2004*).

The scheme administrator and the member will generally be jointly and severally liable to pay the lifetime allowance charge (*section 217(1)* of *FA 2004*). However, when a benefit paid on the death of a member gives rise to a lifetime allowance charge, the person to whom the benefit is paid is liable to pay the lifetime allowance charge (*section 217(2)* of *FA 2004*).

In practice (other than in death benefit cases) the scheme administrator of registered pension schemes (assuming their governing documentation permits them to do so) should deduct the recovery charge and make net payments to the member or other recipient. The scheme administrator should account to HMRC for the tax due in the next quarterly return (see 5.85 below) and pay the tax within 45 days of the end of the quarter in which the charge arose (see *RPSM11105390*). The scheme administrator then gives details of the lifetime allowance due, how the amount was calculated and whether the amount due has been accounted by them within three months of the benefit crystallisation event (see *RPSM11105390*).

The scheme administrator can, in certain circumstances, apply to HMRC to be absolved from any liability to meet the lifetime allowance charge where:

(*a*)   the scheme administrator reasonably believed that there was no liability to the lifetime allowance charge in respect of the benefit crystallisation event; and

(*b*)   in all the circumstances of the case, it would not be just and reasonable for the scheme administrator to be liable to the lifetime allowance charge (*section 267(2)* of *FA 2004* and RPSM11105330).

It is therefore important to keep documentary evidence of the information requests made to the member and the responses.

Lifetime allowance – transitional provisions

5.8   Three main options will be allowed to protect rights accrued prior to A-Day from the recovery charge (see Chapter 3 of RPSM).

(*a*)   *Primary protection*

Primary protection will be available to individuals with pension benefits in excess of £1.5 million at 6 April 2006 (*paragraphs 7 to 11* of *Schedule 36 to FA 2004*). Individuals claiming primary protection can continue to make tax relieved contributions to accrue further benefits under registered pension schemes after A-Day. The value of their rights will be the individual's individual lifetime allowance, expressed as a percentage of the standard lifetime allowance. This will then be indexed in line with the lifetime allowance. For example, a member with accrued benefits valued at £3 million on A-Day could register a figure of 200 per cent. If, when that member came to draw his benefits, the standard lifetime allowance had increased to £2 million, his personal lifetime allowance would be £4 million (see *RPSM03100050*).

To claim primary protection the individual must notify HMRC of his intention to rely on this protection. Notification must be made on the 'Protection of Existing Rights' form and must reach HMRC on or before 5 April 2009.

(*b*)   *Enhanced protection*

As an alternative to primary protection, an individual (whether above or below the lifetime allowance at A-Day) can opt for enhanced protection (*paragraphs 12 to 17A* of *Schedule 36* to *FA 2004*). Enhanced protection fully protects the value of the individual's pension rights on A-Day. Such rights will not be subject to the lifetime allowance charge when they are brought into payment. Effectively this means that if the value of the rights increases faster than the increase in the standard lifetime allowance, the individual will still be protected from the lifetime allowance charge (see *RPSM03100040*).

To take advantage of this option there can be no further accrual of defined benefit or cash balance rights above a specified level of indexation, and no contributions can be paid to increase pension rights in defined contributions arrangements. No benefits can be taken as a lifetime allowance excess lump sum while a claim to enhanced protection is in place.

Once an individual has made a valid notification of his intention to rely on enhanced protection, it will remain in force until they lose it because they fail to comply with the conditions for enhanced protection. If enhanced protection is lost the individual will revert to primary protection if they have claimed this as well (see below) or the standard lifetime allowance if they have not claimed primary protection.

To claim enhanced protection, an individual must notify HMRC of their intention to rely on this protection. Notification must be made on the 'Protection of Existing Rights' form which must reach HMRC on or before 5 April 2009. In practice, to ensure that the conditions for enhanced protection are met, individuals will have to cease accrual before A-Day so decisions on whether to rely on this type of protection need to be made before A-Day.

(c)   Enhanced protection with primary protection

Individuals with pension rights valued at more than £1.5 million at A-Day may notify HMRC that they wish to claim both enhanced protection and primary protection. If they do so the claim for enhanced protection will take precedence. The protection will operate on an enhanced protection basis until it is lost (see *RPSM03100050*).

When enhanced protection ceases, the protection will default to primary protection for benefit crystallisation events after enhanced protection is lost. In some circumstances primary protection will apply to the benefit crystallisation event which causes enhanced protection to be lost.

Valuing pension rights when claiming primary protection

5.9   To claim primary protection it is necessary to value the member's rights as at A-Day (see *RPSM03101020* and onwards – Technical Pages: Protecting pension rights from tax charges: Valuing pension rights as at 6 April

2006 for detailed guidance on the valuation of member's rights). The value of the individual's rights is the aggregate of:

(*a*)   crystallised pension rights from 'relevant existing pensions'; and

(*b*)   uncrystallised pension rights from 'relevant pension arrangements'.

Rights are uncrystallised where the member has not become entitled to the present payment of benefits in respect of those rights. Where income withdrawal/drawdown under a personal pension scheme has begun, or a small self-administered scheme or a retirement benefits scheme is paying a drawdown pension, the rights have crystallised (see *RPSM0301010*).

Crystallised pension rights from any 'relevant pension arrangements' have to be valued. Broadly the expression 'relevant pension arrangement' will include most types of pension or income withdrawal from a scheme that was tax approved before A-Day other than entitlement which arises on the death of another individual (for example, a spouse's or dependant's pension).

The value of any crystallised rights is broadly 25 times the annual rate of the 'relevant existing pension' (lump sums paid at commencement of benefits are ignored). For pensions under income withdrawal/drawdown the maximum annual pension is 25 times the maximum annual pension permitted at A-Day (*paragraph 10* of *Schedule 36* to *FA 2004*).

Uncrystallised pension rights under 'relevant pension arrangements' are valued using the same method as is used for valuing surchargeable unauthorised employer payments under *section 212* of *FA 2004* (*paragraph 8* of *Schedule 36* to *FA 2004*). Different methods are specified for cash balance arrangements; defined contributions arrangements (other than cash balance arrangements); defined benefits arrangements and hybrid arrangements. Defined benefits arrangements are valued as at 5 April 2006 by multiplying the aggregate of the gross annual pension by 20 and adding the value of any separate lump sum under the arrangement. The value is calculated on the standard valuation assumption that, where the benefit would otherwise be reduced because the individual has not reached a specified age, that the individual has reached age 60 (or the earliest age which no reduction will apply) and the individual is in good health (*paragraph 8(6)* of *Schedule 36* to *FA 2004* and *section 277* of *FA 2004*). Defined contributions arrangements are valued by taking the value of the cash held under the arrangement and the market value of any assets held under the arrangement to provide the individual's benefits as at 5 April 2006.

The value of any pension rights that can be protected cannot generally be greater than the maximum approvable pension that could be paid to the individual under HMRC limits for approval (*paragraph 9(4)* of *Schedule 36* to *FA 2004*). So even if a greater amount could be paid under preservation requirements before A-Day the excess cannot be taken into account.

Enhanced lifetime allowance when an individual acquires pension credit rights that relate to pensions that came into payment on or after 6 April 2006

5.10 If an ex-spouse acquires pension credit rights that are derived from a pension of a scheme member already in payment that relate to a pension that came into payment on or after 6 April 2006, that pension will have already been tested against the lifetime allowance. To avoid the same pension being tested again for lifetime allowance purposes the ex-spouse who has acquired the pension credit rights is entitled to a lifetime allowance enhancement factor (*section 220* of *FA 2004*). Notice has to be given to HMRC of intention to claim the lifetime allowance enhancement factor.

Enhanced lifetime allowance where the member acquired pension credit rights before 6 April 2006

5.11 The individual may also be able to increase the standard lifetime allowance by a 'pre-commencement pension credit factor' where he has acquired pension credit rights under the pension scheme as a result of a pension sharing order being made before 6 April 2006 (*paragraph 18* of *Schedule 36* to *FA 2004*). Notice has to be given to HMRC in accordance with regulations made by HMRC to claim this enhancement to the lifetime allowance. An enhancement cannot be claimed where the member has claimed primary protection. Details of the procedure to be followed to claim an enhancement to the lifetime allowance to reflect the value of the credit will be set out in regulations.

Enhanced lifetime allowance where member is a relevant overseas individual

5.12 The individual may also be able to increase the standard lifetime allowance by a 'lifetime allowance enhancement factor' on a benefit crystallisation event occurring in relation to the individual if, during any 'active membership period' of a registered scheme, the individual is a 'relevant overseas individual' (see *section 221* of *FA 2004* and 5.82 below). Broadly this means that, if the individual did not receive tax relief on any contributions made to a UK registered scheme while the individual was accruing benefits in the scheme (other than tax relief on contributions of up to £3,600 where the individual has been resident in the previous five years – see below), his lifetime allowance can be enhanced.

Reduction in lifetime allowance to reflect the value of pensions in payment before 6 April 2006

5.13 Pre-6 April 2006 pensions are only considered for lifetime allowance purposes if there is a benefit crystallisation event on or after 6 April 2006. If there is no benefit crystallisation event they do not need to be considered. Broadly, on the first benefit crystallisation event occurring on or after 6 April 2006, it is assumed that a benefit crystallisation event occurred immediately before that date in relation to all the individual's pre-commencement pensions. The amount crystallised is the value of the individual's pre-commencement pension rights. Generally this will be 25 times the annual rate or rates at which the relevant pension or pensions is payable to the individual at that time. In the case of unsecured pension or alternatively secured pension (see below) the value is the maximum amount that may be paid in the unsecured pension year or alternatively secured pension year calculated in accordance with the Pension Rules (*paragraph 20* of *Schedule 36* to *FA 2004*).

Reduction to lifetime allowance where member has a protected normal minimum pension age

5.14   If a member has a protected normal minimum pension age of below age 50 (or age 55 from 2010) (see 5.30 below) the amount of the member's lifetime allowance is generally reduced by 2.5 per cent for each complete year falling between the date of the benefit crystallisation event and the date the individual will reach his normal minimum pension age (*paragraph 19* of *Schedule 36* to *FA 2004*).

Benefit crystallisation events in more detail

5.15   The different types of 'benefit crystallisation events' are set out in a table contained in *section 216* of *FA 2004*. The table refers to various types of 'authorised payments' under the new regime which are described in more detail later in this chapter (see 5.22 to 5.64 below). The expressions used in the table are defined in *Schedule 31* to *FA 2004* which sets out details of how the amounts crystallised should be calculated. Reference should be made to *Chapter 11* of *RPSM* for a comprehensive treatment of the subject.

	Benefit crystallisation event	Amount crystallised
1.	The designation of sums or assets held for the purposes of a defined contributions arrangement under any of the relevant pension schemes as available for the payment of *unsecured pension* to the individual Where a member with defined contributions arrangements still has any uncrystallised funds at age 75 the individual is treated as having designated the funds under the arrangement for the payment of unsecured pension immediately before the member reached age 75 (*paragraph 8* of *Schedule 28* and *paragraph 14* of *Schedule 32* to *FA 2004*) Uncrystallised funds held under 'hybrid arrangements' immediately before age 75 are dealt with in the same way so there is a deemed crystallisation event immediately before age 75 (*paragraph 8(2)* of *Schedule 28* and *paragraph 5* of *Schedule 32* to *FA 2004*)	The aggregate of the amount of the sum and market value of the assets designated
2.	The individual becoming entitled to a *scheme pension* under any of the relevant pension schemes	RVF x P 'RVF' or the 'Relevant Valuation Factor' will generally be 20 but in certain circumstances a higher RVF can be agreed 'P' is broadly the amount of pension which will be payable to an individual in the twelve months from the date the individual becomes entitled to it

3.	The individual having become so *entitled*, becoming *entitled* to payment of the *scheme pension,* otherwise than in excepted circumstances, at an increased rate which exceeds by more than the permitted margin the rate at which it was payable on the day on which the individual became *entitled* to it The 'permitted margin' will generally be 5% per annum but if a Relevant Valuation Factor of more than 20 is agreed with HMRC the permitted margin can be increased thus avoiding a benefit crystallisation event every time a pension increase is granted of more than 5%	Relevant Valuation Factor x XP 'Relevant Valuation Factor' will generally be 20 but a higher factor can be agreed with HMRC by the scheme administrator (see opposite) 'XP' will be broadly the amount by which the increase in the pension exceeds the 'permitted margin'
4.	The individual becoming entitled to a *lifetime annuity* purchased under a *defined contributions arrangement* under any of the relevant pension schemes	The aggregate of the amount of such of the sums, and the *market value* of such of the assets, representing the individual's rights under the *arrangement* as are applied to purchase the *lifetime annuity* and any *relevant dependant's annuity*
5.	The individual reaching the age of 75 when prospectively entitled to a *scheme pension* or a lump sum (or both) under a *defined benefits arrangement* under any of the relevant pension schemes	(RVF x DP) + DSLS 'DP' is broadly the annual rate of the scheme pension to which the individual would have been entitled if, at the date the individual reached age 75, the individual acquired an actual right to receive it 'DSLS' is the amount of free-standing lump sum (i e not a commutation lump sum) the individual would have been entitled to at age 75 if the individual had taken the lump sum
6.	The individual becoming entitled to a *relevant lump sum* under any of the relevant pension schemes	The amount of the lump sum paid to the individual

7.	A person being paid a *relevant lump sum death benefit* in respect of the individual under any of the relevant pension schemes A *relevant lump sum death benefit* is a defined benefits lump sum death benefit or an uncrystallised funds lump sum death benefit (see below)	The amount of the *relevant lump sum death benefit*
8.	The transfer of sums or assets held for the purposes of, or representing accrued rights under, any of the relevant pension schemes so as to become held for the purposes of or to represent rights under a *qualifying recognised overseas pension scheme* (see 5.81 below) in connection with the individual's membership of that pension scheme	The aggregate of the amount of any sum transferred and the market value of any assets transferred

If an unauthorised member payment is made this will not count as a benefit crystallisation event but there will be various adverse tax consequences (see 5.25 to 5.28 below).

Contributions and the annual allowance

Tax relief on employee contributions

5.16   Tax relief on employer and employee contributions is dealt with in *Chapter 5* of *RPSM*. Broadly any member of a pension scheme may make unlimited contributions to a registered pension scheme during a tax year. However, to qualify for tax relief on a contribution to a registered pension scheme the contribution must be a 'relievable pension contribution' made by a 'relevant UK individual' (see *section 188(1)* of *FA 2004* and *RPSM 5100030*).

A 'relievable pension contribution' is broadly any contribution paid by or on behalf of a member of the pension scheme other than any contributions made after age 75; contributions made by employers (these are not taxable as a benefit in kind on the employee but do not qualify for tax relief by the member) and age related or minimum payments under the contracting-out requirements (see *section 188(2)* of *FA 2004*). Transfers in and pension credits granted under a registered pension scheme do not count as relievable pension contributions (*section 188(4)* and *(5)* of *FA 2004*).

An individual is a 'relevant UK individual' (*section 189* of *FA 2004*) if they:

(*a*)   have relevant UK earnings chargeable to income tax for that tax year;

(*b*)   are resident in the UK at some time during that tax year;

(*c*)   were resident in the UK both at some time during the five tax years immediately before the tax year in question and when they became a member of the pension scheme; or

(*d*)   have for that tax year general earnings from overseas Crown employment subject to UK tax (as defined by *section 28* of the *Income Tax (Earnings and Pensions) Act 2003 (ITEPA 2003)*;

(*e*)   are the spouse of an individual who has for the tax year general earnings from overseas Crown employment subject to UK tax (as defined by *section 28* of *ITEPA 2003*).

'Relevant UK earnings' are:

(i)   employment income such as salary, wages, bonus, overtime, commission providing it is chargeable to tax under *section 7(2)* of *ITEPA 2003*;

(ii)   income chargeable under *Part 2* of the *Income Tax (Trading and Other Income) Act 2005 (ITTOIA 2005)*, that is income derived from the carrying on or exercise of a trade, profession or vocation (whether individually or as a partner acting personally in a partnership);

(iii)   income arising from patent rights and treated as earned income under *section 833(5B)* of *ICTA 1988*;

(iv)   general earnings from an overseas Crown employment which are subject to tax in accordance with *section 28* of *ITEPA 2003* (*section 189(2)* of *FA 2004*).

Members will generally be given tax relief on the greater of £3,600 per annum or 100 per cent of their relevant UK earnings that are chargeable to income tax for the tax year on the individual's own contributions (*sections 188* and *190* of *FA 2004*).

If relevant UK earnings are not taxable in the UK due to *section 788* of *ICTA 1988* (double taxation agreements), those earnings are not regarded as chargeable to income tax and will not count towards the annual limit for relief (*section 189(3)* of *FA 2004*).

A relevant UK individual under (*c*) who has no *relevant UK earnings* in a tax year may still qualify for tax relief on contributions to a registered pension scheme up to the basic amount in any tax year (initially £3,600) (see *section 190(2)* of *FA 2004*). However, the individual will only be able to claim this if the arrangement operates the 'relief at source' system – tax relief cannot be given where the scheme operates the 'net pay system' (*section 191(7)* of *FA 2004*).

A transfer by an individual of shares that have been acquired under an SAYE option scheme or appropriated to the individual under a share incentive plan to a registered pension scheme can count as a tax deductible contribution in certain circumstances (*section 195* of *FA 2004*).

Tax relief on employer contributions

5.17   Employers will generally be able to claim a deduction in profits chargeable to UK tax in the year the contributions are made. Relief is not automatic; it will be considered in accordance with the normal rules in relation to deductibility of business expenses (see *section 74(1)(a)* of *ICTA 1988*). The pensions legislation amends the normal rules applying to allowable deductions (*section 196* of *FA 2004*). In particular:

(*a*)   a pension payment is not treated as a capital payment if it otherwise would have been; and

(*b*)   a deduction can only be given for the period in which the contribution is paid.

Spreading of tax relief may occur on contributions in excess of £500,000 if the contribution to a registered scheme exceeds 210 per cent of the contribution paid in the previous chargeable period. The spread is generally as follows:

(i)   £500,000 or over and less than £1 million – two years;

(ii)   £1 million or over and less than £2 million – three years;

(iii)   £2 million or over – four years (*section 197* of *FA 2004*).

If a contribution is made to discharge any liability of the employer under the debt on employer requirements of *section 75* of *PA 2004* (see *Chapter II*) this will be treated for tax purposes as if it were the payment of a contribution by an employer under a registered pension scheme (*section 199* of *FA 2004*).

As was the case before A-Day, employees will not be taxed as a benefit in kind on any employer contributions (*sections 188(3)(b)* and *201* of *FA 2004* and *sections 307* and *308* of *ITEPA 2003*).

As a general rule contributions made by persons other than employers or members will be treated as member contributions and will not be tax deductible but there are exceptions (see *RPSM05100030*).

Employees may in certain circumstances be able to obtain tax relief on contributions to certain foreign pension schemes under the new 'migrant member relief' provisions of *FA 2004* (see 5.82 below).

Annual allowance tax charge if contributions exceed the annual allowance

5.18 As explained above there are no limits on the maximum amount of employee or employer contributions that can be made under a registered pension scheme but tax relief will not be granted above the annual limit for relief. There will also be a 40 per cent tax charge (annual allowance charge) on the member if the combined member and employer contributions or the value of benefits that accrue, in any year exceeds the annual allowance for that tax year (*section 227* of *FA 2004*).

The 'annual allowance' will be £215,000 for the 2006/2007 tax year (*section 228(1)* and (*2*) of *FA 2004*) and it has been announced that it will be increased by Treasury order in the five tax years from April 2006 as follows:

Tax year	Annual allowance
2006/2007	£215,000
2007/2008	£225,000
2008/2009	£235,000
2009/2010	£245,000
2010/2011	£255,000

If the aggregate of the *pension input amounts* to all registered pension schemes of the individual exceeds the annual allowance in a *pension input period* the individual will be taxed on the excess at 40 per cent whether or not the individual and the scheme administrator are resident, ordinarily resident or domiciled in the UK (*sections 227* and *229* of *FA 2004*). There will be no test, however, against the annual limit in the pension input period in which the individual dies or becomes entitled to benefits under the arrangement (*section 229(3)* of *FA 2004*). If the individual has multiple arrangements and has not crystallised the benefits under the other arrangements the test will still apply to any pension input amounts in respect of the other arrangements.

The initial 'pension input period' will be the twelve month-period from the date of commencement of accrual in a defined benefits or cash balance arrangement or the date of commencement of contributions in a defined contributions arrangement or the date nominated by the administrator (or individual or administrator in a defined contributions scheme) for this purpose, if earlier. Subsequent 'pension input' periods generally will run for twelve-month periods until the member becomes entitled to all benefits under the arrangement (see *section 238* of *FA 2004*). There is therefore flexibility to set a pension input period for all members over the same twelve-month period. If required a pension input period could therefore be aligned with the tax year.

In a defined benefits scheme (other than a cash balance scheme) the 'pension input amount' is the increase in the adjusted capital value of the individual's rights under the scheme during the pension input period (*sections 234, 235, 236* and *238* of *FA 2004*). The value of the pension that accrues is generally calculated by multiplying the gross annual value of the pension at the beginning and the end of the pension input period by 10 (*section 234(4)* and *(5)* of *FA 2004*). Any free-standing tax-free cash is then added on.

In a defined contributions scheme the 'pension input' is the amount of any employer and employee contributions paid in the pension input period that ends in the pension input period (*section 233* of *FA 2004*). Any protected rights contributions are ignored (*sections 233(2)* and *238* of *FA 2004*).

In a cash balance scheme the 'pension input amount' is the adjusted amount of increase in the value of the individual's rights under the pension input period of the arrangement that ends in the tax year (*sections 230, 231, 232* and *238* of *FA 2004*).

It is the responsibility of the individual, not the administrator, to declare on his tax return if his 'pension input' exceeds the lifetime allowance (*section 227(2)* of *FA 2004* and see *RPSM06100120*). The individual (not the scheme administrator) is responsible for paying this tax (see *section 227* of *FA 2004*). However, administrators of defined benefits occupational pension schemes may want to put systems in place to provide high earners with information to ensure that the pension input figure does not exceed the annual allowance.

Different methods of obtaining tax relief

5.19   There are three methods of obtaining tax relief. The method that applies will depend on the type of pension scheme (*sections 192* to *194* of *FA 2004* – see also *RPSM05101310*).

Personal pension schemes must operate the 'relief at source' arrangement (as is presently the case) under which the individual makes his relievable pension contribution, after deducting a sum equivalent to basic rate tax, and the scheme administrator then claims back a sum equal to the basic rate of tax from HMRC. So a member who wishes to contribute £100 to a scheme would pay £78 and the administrator would then claim back the remaining £22 from HMRC. A higher rate taxpayer can also obtain tax relief at the higher rate by making a claim when he fills in his tax return or by way of adjustment to his PAYE code. Relief at source enables individuals who have earnings below £3,600 or no relevant UK earnings to claim tax back on contributions of up to £3,600 (*section 192* of *FA 2004*).

Occupational pension schemes can continue to use a 'net pay arrangement' instead of 'relief at source' as long as the member is an employee of a sponsoring employer of the pension scheme and all the other contributing scheme members who are employees of the same employer are also receiving tax relief under the net pay arrangement (*section 191(3)* of *FA 2004*). A net pay arrangement allows the employer to give relief at source so employees are only taxed on their net pay after the pension contributions are deducted. So, where a member wishes to make a relievable pension contribution of £100, the employer will deduct £100 from the member's employment income and pay £100 to the pension scheme (*section 193* of *FA 2004*).

The third type of arrangement for obtaining tax relief on contributions is 'relief on making a claim' (*section 194* of *FA 2004*). Broadly the member makes the contribution to the pension scheme and then claims tax relief from HMRC on their relievable pension contributions.

Authorised and unauthorised payments under the new regime

Move from a discretionary to a mandatory tax regime

5.20   The majority of UK occupational pension schemes were approved before A-Day on a discretionary basis under *Chapter I* of *Part XIV* of *ICTA 1988*. The types of benefits that can be provided without jeopardising HMRC approval were set out in the Occupational Pension Scheme Practice Notes on Approval of Occupational Pension Schemes (IR12 (2001)), as amended. The types of benefits that could be provided under personal pension schemes before A-Day were set out (on a non-discretionary basis) in *Chapter IV* of *Part XIV* of *ICTA 1988*.

Under the new integrated tax regime the types of 'authorised payments' that can be made by all registered schemes are set out in *Part 4* of *FA 2004*. If a registered pension scheme makes 'unauthorised member payments' or 'unauthorised employer payments' there can be adverse tax consequences for both the member and the scheme administrator (see below). In an extreme case if:

(*a*)   in any twelve-month period the *scheme chargeable payment percentage* (broadly most unauthorised payments) exceeds 25 per cent of the market value of the scheme's assets;

(*b*)   the scheme administrator fails to pay a substantial amount of tax (or interest on tax) due from the scheme administrator by virtue of *Part 4* of *FA 2004;*

(*c*)   the scheme administrator fails to provide information required to be provided to HMRC by virtue of *Part 4* of *FA 2004* and the failure is significant;

(*d*)   any information contained in the application to register the pension scheme or otherwise provided to HMRC is incorrect in a material particular;

(*e*)   any declaration accompanying that application or the provision of other information to HMRC is false in a material particular; or

(*f*)   there is no scheme administrator,

HMRC has power (but is not required to) to withdraw registration of the pension scheme (*sections 157* and *158* of *FA 2004*). These are the only grounds on which deregistration can occur. There is an appeals procedure against deregistration (*section 159* of *FA 2004*).

HMRC only has power to withdraw registration from an entire pension scheme and not from an arrangement or arrangements in a pension scheme (see *RPSM04105020* and onwards for further commentary). It does, however, have power to treat registered schemes as separate schemes in certain circumstances (*section 274A* of *FA 2004*). In practice de-registration is unlikely to happen in a large occupational pension scheme and HMRC is likely to enforce compliance through the tax charges that will fall on the administrator and the member if unauthorised payments are made. The trustees of occupational pension schemes and administrators of other registered pension schemes may, however, want to ensure that their existing rules or other scheme documentation do not provide for the payment of unauthorised payments. There are certain benefits or payments that are currently permitted under existing HMRC requirements that may be unauthorised under the new *FA 2004* tax regime.

Activities of registered pension schemes to be restricted to retirement-benefit activities

5.21   Currently, for an occupational pension scheme to retain its status as an exempt approved scheme, it must meet the 'sole purpose' test, i e in exercising its discretion to approve schemes HMRC required them to be bona fide established for the sole purpose of providing 'relevant benefits', and continued approval was dependent on the sole purpose being maintained. There is no longer a requirement under *FA 2004* to meet the sole purpose test. However, under *PA 2004*, the trustees or managers of occupational pension schemes with their main administration in the UK will, from A-Day, have an obligation to secure that the activities of the scheme are restricted to 'retirement benefit activities' (*section 255 of PA 2004*). Broadly 'retirement benefit activities' are operations relating to retirement benefits and activities arising from operations relating to retirement benefits. 'Retirement benefits' are defined as:

(*a*)   benefits payable by reference to reaching, or expecting to reach, retirement; and

(*b*)   benefits that are supplementary to benefits within (*a*) and that are provided on an ancillary basis in the form of payments on death, disability or termination of employment and in the form of support payments or services in the case of sickness, poverty or need, or death.

Trustees of registered schemes can be fined by the new Regulator if the scheme has activities that are not retirement-benefit activities and the trustee or manager has failed to take all reasonable steps to secure that the activities of the scheme are limited to retirement-benefit activities (*section 255(3) of PA 2004*).

Authorised member payments

5.22   The only authorised payments a registered scheme can make to or in respect of a member are:

(*a*)   pensions permitted under the 'pension rules';

(*b*)   pensions permitted under the 'pension death benefit rules';

(*c*)   lump sums permitted by the 'lump sum rule';

(*d*)   lump sums permitted by the 'lump sum death benefit rules';

(*e*)   recognised transfers;

(*f*)   scheme administration member payments (i e payments made for the purposes of the management or administration of the scheme such as the payment of wages or salary or fees to persons engaged in administering the scheme);

(*g*)   payments made under a pension sharing order or provision; and

(*h*)   other payments permitted under HMRC regulations (*sections 164 to 174* and *Schedules 28* and *29* to *FA 2004*).

Payments include a transfer of assets and any transfer of money's worth. A payment made by a registered pension scheme to or in respect of a person who is connected with a member or sponsoring employer (or was connected with a member at the date of the member's death) and is not a member or sponsoring employer is treated as if it were made in respect of the member or sponsoring employer. Any increase in the value of an asset held by, or reduction in the liability of, a person connected with a member or sponsoring employer (or who was connected with a member at the date of the member's death) is treated as an increase or reduction for the benefit of the member or sponsoring employer (*section 161* of *FA 2004*).

Authorised employer payments

5.23   The only payments which a registered scheme that is a private sector occupational pension scheme is authorised to make to or in respect of a sponsoring employer are:

(*a*)   authorised surplus payments;

(*b*)   compensation payments (i e payments made to an employer in respect of a member's liability to the employer in respect of a criminal, fraudulent or negligent act or omission by the member);

(*c*)   authorised employer loans; and

(*d*)   other payments permitted under HMRC regulations (*sections 175* to *184* of *FA 2004*).

Unauthorised member payments

5.24   Any payment made to or in respect of a member that is not an authorised member payment will be an unauthorised payment with the various tax consequences discussed below (*section 160(2)* of *FA 2004*). There are also various provisions which may deem a payment to be an unauthorised member payment including where:

(*a*)   value shifting of assets occurs (*section 174* of *FA 2004*);

(*b*)   a member of a pension scheme assigns or agrees to assign any benefit they have a right to under a registered scheme other than in certain permitted circumstances, including the making of a pension sharing order (*section 172A* of *FA 2004*);

(*c*)   there is an increase in rights on death of a connected person (*section 172B* of *FA 2004*) (a transfer lump sum death benefit paid when a member has alternatively secured income after the age of 75 (see below) will not be treated as an unauthorised payment under this provision – see *section 172B(5)* of *FA 2004*);

(*d*)   an asset held for the purposes of a registered pension scheme is used to provide a benefit other than a payment to a member, or a member of the member's family or household;

(*e*)   if unallocated contributions are allocated to a member who is connected with the employer or any other person connected with the employer above a certain permitted level (*section 172C* of *FA 2004*);

(*f*)   if the contributions made in respect of a member, or the capital value of the benefits that accrue in a pension input period in respect of a defined benefits arrangement, a cash balance arrangement or a hybrid arrangement relating to a member, exceed a certain amount where the member is connected with the employer or a person connected with a sponsoring employer (*section 172D* of *FA 2004*);

(*g*)   direct or indirect investment in prohibited assets (for example, residential property or fine wines or vintage cars) by a self-directed pension scheme (see 5.71 below and chapter 14).

Tax consequences of making unauthorised payments – unauthorised payments charge

5.25   If unauthorised payments are made, this can give rise to punitive tax charges and, in an extreme case, deregistration of the scheme (see above).

If an unauthorised member payment is made, generally the member will be liable to an 'unauthorised payments charge' of 40 per cent of the value of the unauthorised member payment (*section 208(2)(a)* of *FA 2004*).

If the unauthorised member payment is made, after the member's death (for example, an unauthorised death benefit) the recipient of the unauthorised benefit is subject to an 'unauthorised payment charge' of 40 per cent of the value of the unauthorised member payment (*section 208(2)(b)* of *FA 2004*).

If an unauthorised employer payment is made the sponsoring employer in respect of whom the payment is made is subject to an unauthorised payment charge of 40 per cent of the value of the unauthorised employer payment (*section 208(2)(c)* of *FA 2004*).

Tax consequences of making unauthorised payments – unauthorised payment surcharge

5.26   An unauthorised member payment surcharge may also be payable if the unauthorised payment percentage in respect of an arrangement relating to a member exceeds 25 per cent in a twelve-month reference period (*section 210* of *FA 2004*). The unauthorised payments percentage is the total of the percentages that each unauthorised member payment represents in relation to the value of the arrangement when these payments are made on or after a reference date.

An unauthorised employer payment surcharge may also be payable of an extra 15 per cent broadly if the unauthorised payments percentage exceeds 25 per cent in a twelve-month reference period (*section 213* of *FA 2004*). The unauthorised payments percentage is the total of the pension fund used up by each unauthorised employer payment made on or after a reference date by the scheme to or in respect of an employer.

Tax consequences of making unauthorised payments – scheme sanction charge

5.27 In addition to the liability for the 'unauthorised payment charge' the scheme administrator will be subject to a 'scheme sanction charge' in respect of any unauthorised payment which qualifies as a 'scheme chargeable payment' (*sections 239* to *241* of *FA 2004*). An unauthorised payment is exempt from being a scheme chargeable payment in certain circumstances including where a payment is made to the employer in respect of a member's liability to a sponsoring employer in respect of a criminal, fraudulent or negligent act or omission by the member and where the payment is made to comply with an order of a court or of a person or a body with power to order the payment or it is made on the ground that a court or any such person or body is likely to order such a payment (for example, compensation for maladministration that might be ordered by the Ombudsman) (*section 242(2)* of *FA 2004*).

Potentially the scheme administrator could have to pay up to 40 per cent of the amount of the unauthorised payment that counts as a 'scheme chargeable payment'. However, there is a complicated formula which allows the scheme administrator to reduce its liability by part of any tax paid by the member or recipient to meet the unauthorised payments charge. As long as the 40 per cent tax is paid by the member or recipient this should result in the scheme paying an extra 15 per cent (*section 239* of *FA 2004*).

Tax consequences of deregistration – deregistration charge

5.28 If in any twelve-month period unauthorised payments of more than 25 per cent of the market value of the scheme's assets are made HMRC can de-register a scheme. If the registration of the scheme is withdrawn, a deregistration charge is payable of 40 per cent of the value of any sums held by the pension scheme immediately before deregistration and the market value of any assets held at that time for the purposes of the pension scheme (*section 241* of *FA 2004*).

The Pension Rules (section 165 of FA 2004)

5.29   The new regime governing the form in which pensions have to be paid is an amalgam, with certain modifications, of the regimes that applied to occupational and personal pensions, giving greater flexibility as to the form in which the benefits can be taken.

Normal minimum pension age

5.30   Under Pension Rule 1, broadly benefits cannot be paid before the 'normal minimum pension age,' other than where the ill-health condition is met (see below). The normal minimum pension age will initially be age 50 but will increase to age 55 from 2010. However, members who have an existing actual or prospective right under the rules of the pension scheme (as at 10 December 2003) to draw any benefit before age 55 may retain those rights and have a 'protected pension age' (*paragraphs 21* and *23* of *Schedule 36* to *FA 2004*). The Explanatory Notes issued at the time the Pensions Bill was going through Parliament indicated that someone would not have a right to take their benefits if it required trustee and/or employer consent to exercise that right. At the date of writing there was some uncertainty whether, if a member of an occupational pension scheme had a *contractual right* to take benefits from say age 50 but there was still an employer consent requirement under the rules, the member will have a protected pension age.

The right to a protected pension age under an occupational pension scheme is lost if all the member's benefits payable under arrangements under the pension scheme (to which a member did not have an actual entitlement before 6 April 2006) are not paid at the same time and the member remains employed by the sponsoring employer after becoming entitled to any benefit under the pension scheme (*paragraph 22(7)* of *Schedule 36* to *FA 2004*). This issue therefore needs to be considered if flexible benefit commencement provisions are introduced post A-Day. The right to a protected pension age can be preserved in certain circumstances on block transfers (*paragraph 22(6)* of *Schedule 36* to *FA 2004*).

Personal pension scheme members with a right to retire before age 50 where the member's occupation was one prescribed by regulations made by the Board of HMRC (*paragraphs 21* and *22* of *Schedule 36* to *FA 2004*) will also be able to protect this right to take benefits before the normal minimum pension age. Again the right to a protected pension age under a personal pension scheme can be lost if not all benefits payable under the arrangements under the pension scheme are payable at the same time (*paragraph 22(7)* of *Schedule 36* to *FA 2004*).

If a pension is paid to a member before the normal minimum pension age other than when the 'ill-health condition' is met (see 5.31 below), or the member has an earlier protected pension age, it will be an unauthorised member payment.

Incapacity retirement

5.31   The ill-health condition is met if:

(*a*)   the scheme administrator has received evidence from a registered medical practitioner that the member is (and will continue to be) incapable of carrying on the member's occupation because of physical or mental impairment; and

(*b*)   the member has in fact ceased to carry on the member's occupation (*paragraph 1* of *Part 1* of *Schedule 28* to *FA 2004*).

A registered medical practitioner is expected to be defined as a fully registered person within the meaning of the *Medical Act 1983* (*RPSM09104610*). HMRC expects this evidence to be in writing and appropriate records should be kept to demonstrate that it has been received.

It is permissible (as was the case before A-Day) to stop an ill-health pension if the member recovers (*paragraph 2(3)* and (*4*) of *Part I* of *Schedule 28*).

The new ill-health condition is similar, but unfortunately not identical, to the pre A-Day definition of 'Incapacity' in IR12 (2001) (see 5.113 below). Therefore, care will need to be taken to ensure that operation of pre A-Day ill-health retirement rules do not result in the making of unauthorised member payments.

Flexible retirement

5.32   Under the pre A-Day taxation regime, it was a requirement in occupational pension schemes that, to take benefits, a member must retire from service. Benefits could not generally be taken in tranches unless the member transferred out his benefits to a personal pension scheme or, if the scheme rules permitted, took advantage of the opportunity to delay taking his AVC fund until a later date.

Under the new regime there is nothing to prevent the member taking benefits from any type of registered pension scheme in tranches if the scheme rules permit it. In certain circumstances, however, this can lead to the loss of transitional relief. For example, if a member has a protected pension age below age 55 this protected minimum pension age may be lost (see 5.30 above). Any protection relating to the maximum amount of tax-free lump sum relating to pre A-Day rights where this exceeds the normal 25 per cent limit, can be lost if not all pensions are taken at the same time.

Pensions payable by defined benefits arrangements

5.33 Defined benefits arrangements can only pay 'scheme pensions' (Pension Rule 3). Scheme pensions are either pensions paid directly by the scheme out of its own resources or by an insurance company selected by the scheme administrator (*paragraph 2* of *Part 1* of *Schedule 28* to *FA 2004*).

Generally scheme pensions must be payable (at least annually) until the date of the member's death or until the later of the member's death and the end of a fixed term of up to ten years.

FA 2004 does permit the pension to be reduced in certain circumstances. These circumstances include the situation when all scheme pensions payable to or in respect of the members are reduced or in relation to the payment of bridging pensions in certain circumstances.

If a scheme pension is reduced in circumstances other than those permitted under the Pension Rules this will result in all subsequent pension payments being treated as unauthorised payments with the tax consequences discussed above.

Pensions payable by defined contributions arrangements

5.34 Defined contributions arrangements can pay a 'scheme pension', a 'lifetime annuity' or an 'unsecured pension' to a member who has not yet reached age 75. However, a scheme pension can only be paid if the member has first been given the opportunity to select a lifetime annuity (Pension Rule 4 – *section 165* of *FA 2004*).

'Unsecured pension fund'

5.35 There is also a concept of 'unsecured pension fund' which is used in various places in *FA 2004* and broadly means any sums or assets held for the purposes of the arrangement as are member designated funds. Sums or assets will be member designated funds if they:

(*a*) have been designated at any time under the arrangement as available for the payment of unsecured pension, and (*b*)   arise or (directly or indirectly) derive, from sums or assets which have been so designated or which so arise or derive, and

(*c*)   have not been applied towards the provision of a scheme pension (*paragraph 8* of *Part I* of *Schedule 28* to *FA 2004*).

In practice this means any funds that the member is entitled to after he has crystallised his entitlement to benefits under the scheme and is in income drawdown but which have not yet been applied to secure a pension or annuity. If a member reaches age 75 and still has any relevant uncrystallised funds, such funds are then treated as having been designated under the arrangement for the payment of unsecured pension.

'Lifetime annuity'

5.36   A 'lifetime annuity' is an annuity payable by an insurance company which meets certain specified requirements. Broadly:

(*a*)   the member has to have an opportunity to select the insurance company;

(*b*)   it is payable until the member's death or for up a term certain of up to ten years after the member's death;

(*c*)   its amount can either decrease or falls to be determined in a manner prescribed in regulations made by the Board of the Inland Revenue (*paragraph 3* of *Schedule 28* to *FA 2004*).

'Unsecured pension'

5.37   An 'unsecured pension' is broadly either a short-term annuity or income withdrawal (*paragraph 4* of *Schedule 28* to *FA 2004*).

'Short-term annuity'

5.38   An annuity is a 'short-term annuity' if:

(*a*)   it is purchased by the application of sums or assets representing the whole or any part of the member's unsecured pension fund in respect of an arrangement;

(*b*)   it is payable by an insurance company;

(*c*)   the member has an opportunity to select the insurance company;

(*d*)   it is payable for a term that does not exceed five years and ends before the member reaches the age of 75; and (*e*)   its amount either cannot decrease or falls to be determined in any manner prescribed by regulations made by HMRC (*paragraph 6 of Part 1 to Schedule 28 to FA 2004*).

The idea of short-term annuities was thought up by the Treasury when it was under pressure to relax the requirement that pension funds had to be applied at age 75 to purchase an annuity. It is designed to give members greater flexibility as to how they apply assets in retirement under income drawdown arrangements.

Income withdrawal works in a similar way to income withdrawal in a personal pension scheme before A-Day (see chapter 14 and *paragraphs 7* to *9 of Part 1* of *Schedule 28* to *FA 2004*). Under an income withdrawal arrangement the assets in the member's arrangement can remain invested and he can withdraw up to 120 per cent of the basic amount in the unsecured pension year (Pension Rule 5 – *section 165* of *FA 2004*).

Alternatively secured pension

5.39   Once a member of a defined contributions arrangement reaches age 75 a scheme pension, a lifetime annuity or alternatively secured pension must be provided. Again, a scheme pension may only be provided if the member has first been given the opportunity to select a lifetime annuity instead. In practice this means that, when the member reaches age 75, the member must use his pension pot to provide a pension unless he wants to take advantage of the new alternatively secured pension option.

The alternatively secured pension is a type of income draw-down which can continue on and after age 75 to age 85 under which the amount withdrawn each year cannot exceed 70 per cent of the basic amount for the alternatively secured pension year (Pension Rule 7 – s*ection 165* of *FA 2004*). There are complicated rules relating to the calculation of the amount that can be withdrawn (*paragraph 12 of Part 1* of *Schedule 28* to *FA 2004*). The reason why members may wish to take advantage of this option is that it avoids having to purchase an annuity at 75 and on their death. If they do not have any dependants at the date of death it may then be possible to apply any remaining assets for the benefit of other members of the scheme by paying a 'transfer lump sum death benefit' (the family pension fund that is being much talked about) or by paying a charity lump sum death benefit (see below). If a 'transfer lump sum death benefit' is paid there are likely to be inheritance tax implications (see 5.81 below).

Ten-year guarantee

5.40   Like the pre A-Day regime, if the member dies before the end of the period of ten years beginning with the day on which the member became entitled to a scheme pension, an annuity or alternatively secured pension, payment of the scheme pension, annuity or alternatively secured pension may continue to be made (to any person) until the end of that period (Pension rule 2 – *section 165* of *FA 2004*).

It is permissible, however, for a scheme pension or a lifetime annuity with a ten-year guarantee to cease after the date of the member's death and before the end of the ten-year term if the annuitant marries, reaches the age of 18 or ceases to be in full-time education (*paragraphs 2(6)* and *3(6)* of *Schedule 28* to *FA 2004*).

The lump sum rule (section 166 of FA 2004)

5.41   Under the lump sum rule no lump sum may be paid other than:

(*a*)   a pension commencement lump sum;

(*b*)   a serious ill-health lump sum;

(*c*)   a short service refund lump sum;

(*d*)   a trivial commutation lump sum;

(*e*)   a winding-up lump sum; or

(*f*)   a lifetime allowance excess lump sum (*section 166* of *FA 2004*).

If it is, it will count as an unauthorised payment unless it is covered by any of the transitional saving provisions which can apply in certain circumstances, for example to funeral payments.

Pension commencement lump sums

5.42   A person becomes entitled to a pension commencement lump sum immediately before a person becomes entitled to a pension in connection with which it is paid (*section 166(2)* of *FA 2004*).

A person is entitled to a pension commencement lump sum if:

(*a*)   the member becomes entitled to it in connection with the member becoming entitled to a relevant pension;

(*b*)   it is paid when all or part of the member's lifetime allowance is available;

(*c*)   it is paid within the period of three months beginning with the day on which the member becomes entitled to it;

(*d*) it is paid when the member has reached normal minimum pension age (or the ill-health condition is satisfied);

(*e*) it is paid when the member has not reached the age of 75; and

(*f*) it is not an excluded lump sum (*paragraph 1* of *Part 1* of *Schedule 29* to *FA 2004*).

Generally, when a member becomes entitled to a scheme pension, a lump sum can be paid of up one quarter of the total lifetime allowance crystallisation value of the pension and lump sum entitlements arising at a particular time under an arrangement or arrangements under a registered scheme. Any lump sum paid in excess of the permitted maximum lump sum will count as an unauthorised payment.

The pension commencement lump sum is paid tax free (*section 636A(1)(a)* of *ICTA 1988*, as inserted by *paragraph 11* of *Schedule 31* to *FA 2004*).

The pension entitlement giving rise to the pension commencement lump sum does not have to arise under the same arrangement paying the lump sum but may be calculated on a scheme wide basis. For example, as long as all benefits are taken at the same time as the scheme pension comes into payment, in a defined benefits scheme the member's additional voluntary contribution fund could be applied to provide all the lump sum rather than commuting scheme pension to provide the lump sum. The pre A-Day restrictions preventing additional voluntary contributions to be used in occupational pension schemes to provide the lump sum where the additional voluntary contributions commenced on or after 8 April 1987 no longer apply. The existing requirement under *PSA 1993* that occupational pension schemes have to make an AVC facility available to members will, however, also no longer apply. Some occupational pension schemes may therefore withdraw the AVC facility, at least for post A-Day contributions.

The pension commencement lump sum is similar to the tax-free cash sum which could be paid under a retirement benefits scheme approved under *Chapter I* of *Part XIV* of *ICTA 1988* before A-Day.

Pension commencement lump sum – transitional relief

5.43 A pension commencement lump sum in excess of the normal 25 per cent limit may be paid in certain circumstances where the member was entitled or prospectively entitled to a higher lump sum benefit on 5 April 2006.

In the case of a member who has primary protection and lump sum rights of more than £375,000 on 5 April 2006, the permitted maximum lump sum will be replaced by a different higher figure. The manner in which this works is complicated and is explained in *RPSM03105140*.

In the case of a member with enhanced protection and lump sum rights of more than £375,000 on 5 April 2006, the permitted maximum will broadly be the proportion of the fund which could have been taken as a lump sum benefit on 5 April 2006.

Members who do not have primary or enhanced protection and whose uncrystallised lump sum is less than £375,000 on 5 April 2006 may also be able to take a larger lump sum if the percentage of their benefits that could be taken as a lump sum as at 5 April 2006 under pre A-Day HMRC requirements exceeded 25 per cent (*paragraph 31* of *Schedule 36* to *FA 2004*). There is no need to register with HMRC to benefit for this protection but scheme administrators will need to calculate and keep a record of the maximum permitted percentage tax-free cash that could be taken immediately before A-Day. This transitional protection is only available if the individual becomes entitled to all pensions payable to the individual under the arrangements under the pension scheme (to which the individual did not have an actual entitlement before 5 April 2006) on the same date (*paragraph 31(3)* of *Schedule 36* to *FA 2004*).

Broadly, in respect of pensionable service up to and including 5 April 2006, a member who could have taken more than 25 per cent of the value of his rights as a lump sum at 5 April 2006 will be able to take the value of his lump sum rights as at 5 April 2006, uprated by the percentage increase in the lifetime allowance, plus a quarter of the value of any rights accrued on or after 6 April 2006.

Pension commencement lump sums – recycling of lump sums

5.44   The Government announced in its 'Pension Tax Simplification – Pre Budget Report Technical Note' that it would take action to stop potential abuse of the pension tax simplification rules by boosting the amount in the pension scheme through artificially generated tax reliefs. In particular, where the member withdraws a tax-free lump sum and then reinvests it back into a registered pension scheme, generating further tax relief on the amount reinvested. This allows a further lump sum to be paid out, which is then recycled again. Anti-avoidance provisions will be inserted into *FA 2004* to target cases where lump sums are taken with the sole or main purpose of reinvesting them through the pension scheme to create additional savings through the additional relief granted. The report states that the legislation will not affect cases where a person withdraws a tax-free lump sum as part of the normal course of taking pension benefits. At the date of writing the detailed statutory amendments to *FA 2004* had not been drafted.

Serious ill-health lump sum

5.45   Under pre A-Day Revenue requirements, an exempt approved occupational pension scheme could permit a member who was in exceptional circumstances of serious ill health to commute the whole of his own pension (other than, in respect of a contracted-out scheme, any guaranteed minimum pension, post April 1997 statutory reference scheme rights and, where the member was married, at least half of any protected rights) at the time his benefits become payable (paragraphs 8.17 to 8.22 of IR12 (2001)). Any contingent spouses/ dependant's pension could not be commuted at the same time.

The term 'exceptional circumstances of serious ill health' was interpreted strictly before A-Day. It was not intended to refer to the kind of ill health which prevented someone from working, but to cases where the expectation of life was measured in months rather than years and so short pensions were not a reasonable proposition, i e expectation of life must have been unquestionably less than a year (paragraphs 8.17 to 8.21 of IR12 (2001)).

Under the new regime, a serious ill-health lump sum can be paid if:

(a)   before it is paid the scheme administrator has received evidence from a registered medical practitioner that the member is expected to live for less than a year;

(b)   it is paid when all or part of the member's lifetime allowance is available;

(c)   it is paid in respect of an uncrystallised arrangement;

(d)   it extinguishes the member's entitlement to benefits under the arrangement, and

(e)   it is paid when the member has not reached the age of 75 (*paragraph 4 of Part 1 of Schedule 29 to FA 2004*).

An uncrystallised arrangement is an arrangement in respect of which there has been no previous benefit crystallisation event (*paragraph 4(2) of Schedule 29 to FA 2004*).

There is no liability to income tax on a serious ill-health lump sum (*section 636A of ICTA 1988*, as inserted by *paragraph 11 of Schedule 31 to FA 2004*).

At the date of writing details of the contracting-out requirements relating to the commutation of contracted-out rights on grounds of exceptional circumstances of serious ill health were not finalised. It is expected that commutation of contracted-out rights on these grounds will be permitted.

A short service refund lump sum

5.46   A short service refund lump sum is the old return of employee contributions (paragraphs 10.52 to 10.54 of IR12 (2001)) for an individual who is a member of an occupational pension scheme and his pensionable service is terminated in circumstances where he is not entitled to a short-service benefit (*paragraph 5* of *Part 1* of *Schedule 29* to *FA 2004*).

The scheme administrator is liable to tax on the short-service refund lump sum. Tax is paid from A-Day at the rate of 20 per cent on short service refund lump sums up to £10,800 and 40% on any excess above this amount (*section 205* of *FA 2004*). The Treasury has power, by order, to increase or decrease these rates, or the £10,800 limit. Tax should be deducted from any payment by the administrator where the rules of the scheme so permit. Before A-Day, tax was paid at 20 per cent on a return of contributions.

Where interest is paid on a short service refund lump sum it is treated as a scheme administration member payment. Payments must be made on an arm's length commercial basis. If the interest paid exceeds a reasonable commercial rate of return, any excess will be treated as an unauthorised member payment and will be taxed in the manner described above (*RPSM09104740*).

Under the preservation requirements of *PSA 1993* members of occupational pension schemes with less than two years' qualifying service who are not entitled to preserved benefits in the scheme are entitled to a return of contributions. From 6 April 2006 a deferred member of an occupational pension scheme whose pensionable service terminates before he attains normal pension age with between three months' and two years' pensionable service in a scheme will have a right either to a cash transfer sum to another registered scheme or a return of contributions (*PSA 1993* and the *Occupational Pension Schemes* (*Early Leavers: Cash Transfer Sums and Contribution Refunds*) *Regulations 2006*) (*SI 2006 No 33*) – see chapter 6).

Refund of excess contributions lump sum

5.47   A refund of excess contributions can be made where the member has paid relievable pension contributions in any tax year which are more than the maximum amount that can receive tax relief. Given that the maximum relievable employee contributions in any year is normally equal to his salary capped at £215,000 (with no limit in the final year he takes the benefit), it is unlikely that there will be many cases where this lump sum is paid (*paragraph 6* of *Part 1* of *Schedule 29* to *FA 2004*). The rules of a registered scheme would need to be amended to permit this payment to be made. Any repayment must be made before the end of six years following the end of the tax year in which the excess contributions are paid. A refund of excess contributions is not subject to income tax (*paragraph 11* of *Schedule 31* to *FA 2004* and *section 636A* of *ITEPA 2003*). If interest is paid it will count as a scheme administration member payment and, if the interest is not calculated at a reasonable commercial rate, the excess may be treated as an unauthorised member payment with the resulting tax consequences discussed above.

Trivial commutation lump sum

5.48   A lump sum is a trivial commutation lump sum if:

(*a*)   it is paid when no trivial commutation lump sum has previously been paid to the member (by any registered pension scheme) or, if such a lump sum has previously been paid, before the end of the commutation period;

(*b*)   on the nominated date, the value of the member's pension rights does not exceed the commutation limit;

(*c*)   it is paid when all or part of the member's lifetime allowance is available;

(*d*)   it extinguishes the member's entitlement to benefits under the pension scheme;

(*e*)   it is paid when the member has reached the age of 60 but has not reached the age of 75 (*paragraphs 7* to *9* of *Part 1* of *Schedule 29* to *FA 2004*).

The commutation limit is 1 per cent of the standard lifetime allowance on the nominated date. The member's pension rights on the nominated date are all the member's crystallised and uncrystallised pension rights on that date under all registered arrangements. The benefits from the registered pension schemes that are going to be commuted have to be commuted within the trivial commutation period which is the twelve-month period beginning with the day on which a trivial lump sum is first paid to the member.

If a member receives a trivial commutation lump sum he is treated as having taxable pension income for the tax year in which the payment is made equal to the amount of the lump sum. However, if the member has not become entitled to any benefits under the pension scheme, the taxable pension income is 75 per cent of the lump sum (*section 636B* of *ITEPA 2003*, as inserted by *paragraph 11* of *Schedule 31* to *FA 2004*).

At first sight the new trivial commutation requirements appear more generous than the pre A-Day requirements that applied to retirement benefit schemes approved under *Chapter I* of *Part IV* of *ICTA 1988*, but in certain respects they are more restrictive post A-Day. Under the pre A-Day requirements a trivial commutation lump sum payment could be made when the aggregate of total benefits payable to the employee under all schemes providing benefits in respect of the employment did not exceed the value of a pension of £260 per annum (i e account did not have to be taken of arrangements unrelated to the employment). Under pre A-Day requirements, commutation also normally had to take place at the time the pension became payable (which is no longer the case, so the new regime is more flexible) and could also occur before age 60 (so the old regime was more flexible). Under pre A-Day requirements there was generally a tax charge of 20 per cent on the trivial commutation lump sum payment under *section 599* of *ICTA 1988*.

Post A-Day, care must be taken only to pay trivial commutation payments in accordance with the new requirements, otherwise the payment will count as an unauthorised payment with the tax consequences described above.

Before A-Day there were detailed requirements setting out when guaranteed minimum pensions and statutory reference scheme rights and protected rights could be commuted on grounds of triviality (*section 12(1)(c)* of *PSA 1993* and *regulation 20* of the *Occupational Pension Schemes (Contracting-out) Regulations 1996 (SI 1996 No 1172)* and *section 28(4)* of *PSA 1993* and *regulation 8* of the *Personal and Occupational Pension Schemes (Protected Rights) Regulations 1996 (SI 1996 No 1537)*). At the date of writing details of the new requirements relating to commutation of GMPs, statutory reference scheme rights and protected rights are still awaited.

Winding-up lump sum

5.49   This is similar to a trivial commutation lump sum that was paid on the winding up of a retirement benefits scheme approved under *Chapter I* of *Part XIV* of *ICTA 1988*. Before A-Day it was possible to commute a pension and any contingent spouse's pension on grounds of triviality when the scheme was winding up. Contracted-out rights could generally be commuted at the same time as long as the aggregate value of the commuted benefit did not exceed the £260 per annum triviality limit.

Under the new requirements a lump sum is a winding-up lump sum if:

(*a*)   the pension scheme is an occupational pension scheme;

(*b*)   the pension scheme is being wound up;

(*c*)   the member's employment meets certain conditions;

(*d*)   it is paid when all or part of a member's lifetime allowance is available;

(*e*)   it extinguishes the member's entitlement to benefits under the pension scheme; and

(*f*)   it is paid when the member has not reached age 75 (*paragraph 10* of *Part 1* to *Schedule 29* to *FA 2004*).

There is no lower age limit for payment of the benefit and again the commutation limit is 1 per cent of the standard lifetime allowance when the lump sum is paid.

The employment conditions are that the employer (which for this purpose includes former employer):

(i)   has made contributions under the pension scheme in respect of a member;

(ii) is not making contributions under any registered pension scheme in respect of the member; and

(iii) undertakes to HMRC not to make such contributions during the period of one year beginning with the day on which the lump sum is paid (*paragraph 10(3)* of *Part I* to *Schedule 29* to *FA 2004*).

If a member receives a winding-up lump sum he is treated as having taxable pension income for the tax year in which the payment is made equal to the amount of the lump sum. However, if the member has not become entitled to any benefits under the pension scheme, the taxable pension income is 75 per cent of the lump sum (*section 636B* of *ICTA 1988*, as inserted by *paragraph 11* of *Schedule 31* to *FA 2004*).

Lifetime allowance excess lump sum

5.50   This is the lump sum which is paid when none of the member's lifetime allowance is available. A lifetime allowance excess lump sum is subject to the 55 per cent lifetime allowance tax charge described above. It cannot be paid before the member reaches normal minimum pension age (unless the ill-health condition is met) (*paragraph 11* of *Part 1* of *Schedule 29* to *FA 2004*). The payment has to be made before age 75 or it will count as an unauthorised payment.

Scheme rules will generally need to be amended to permit this payment to be made after A-Day.

Pension death benefit rules (section 167 of FA 2004)

Dependants' and children's pensions

5.51   Under the pension death benefit rules, pension death benefits can only be made to 'dependants' (Pension Death Benefit Rule 1 – *section 167* of *FA 2004*).

Under pre A-Day HMRC practice as set out in IR12 (2001) 'dependant' meant a person who was financially dependent on the employee or ex-spouse or dependent on the employee or ex-spouse because of disability or who was so dependent at the time of the employee's death or retirement or at the time of the ex-spouse's death or when the ex-spouse's pension credit commenced payment. A spouse of an employee who was in receipt of payments from an employee up to his death in respect of, for example, a provision under the *Matrimonial Causes Act 1973*, could be regarded as financially dependent on the employee. An adult relative who is or was not supported by the employee or ex-spouse is not the employee's or ex-spouse's dependant. However, subject to certain conditions, a pension payable to an adult dependant who qualified on grounds of financial dependency or disability could continue indefinitely.

It was not necessary to show financial dependency for a person dependent on the employee because of disability. But an unmarried partner, whether of the same or opposite sex (other than a civil partner post 5 December 2005 when the provisions of the *Civil Partnership Act 2004* came into force) could not qualify for a survivor's pension without showing financial dependence. Financial interdependence was also an acceptable criterion: for example, a partner relied on a second income to maintain a standard of living.

Under pre A-Day HMRC practice a children's pension could be paid to children of the employee or ex-spouse if at the time of death they were:

(*a*)   under age 18;

(*b*)   over 18 but continuing to receive full-time education or vocational training; or

(*c*)   dependent on the employee or ex-spouse because of disability.

Other children (i e neither natural nor adopted children of the employee) could only qualify as dependants if they were financially dependent. Any pension paid to such children on grounds of financial dependence had to cease when they reached age 18 or full-time education or vocational training ceased, whichever was later. A pension paid because of dependency by reason of disability could continue indefinitely.

The new *FA 2004* definition of 'dependant' broadly follows the pre A-Day definition but there are some minor differences. 'Dependant' is now defined as follows:

(i)   A person who was married to the member at the date of the member's death is a dependant of the member.

(ii)   If the rules of the scheme so provide, a person who was married to the member when the member first became entitled to a pension under the pension scheme is a dependant of this member.

(iii)   A child of the member is a dependant of the member if the child:

- has not reached the age of 23; or

- has reached that age and, in the opinion of the scheme administrator, was at the date of the member's death dependent on the member because of physical or mental impairment.

(iv)   A person who was not married to the member at the date of the member's death and is not a child of the member is a dependant of the member if, in the opinion of the scheme's administrator, at the date of the member's death:

- the person was financially dependent on the member;

- the person's financial relationship with the member was one of mutual dependence; or

- the person was dependent on the member because of physical or mental impairment (*paragraph 15* of *Schedule 28* to *FA 2004*).

In certain respects, however, the new definition is more restrictive than the existing definition in IR12 (2001), including a requirement that a child's pension must cease by age 23 whether or not the child is in full-time education. This means that if such a pension continues to be paid post 5 April 2006 it is potentially an unauthorised payment with the tax consequences that entails. In response to lobbying, transitional provisions are being introduced under the draft *Finance Act (Transitional Provisions) Order* (not yet laid at the date of writing) which will enable certain children's pensions to continue beyond age 23 in limited circumstances.

Defined benefits dependants' pensions

5.52   The only type of dependants' pensions that can be paid in respect of a defined benefits arrangement is a dependant's scheme pension (Pension Death Benefit Rule 2 – *section 167* of *FA 2004*).

A dependant's scheme pension is either a pension paid directly by the scheme out of its own resources or by an insurance company selected by the scheme administrator (*paragraph 16* of *Part 2* of *Schedule 28* to *FA 2004*).

Defined contributions dependants' pensions

5.53   Defined contributions arrangements can pay a 'dependant's scheme pension' (see 5.52 above), a 'dependant's lifetime annuity' or a 'dependant's unsecured pension' to a member who has not yet reached age 75. However, a dependant's scheme pension can only be paid if the member has first been given the opportunity to select a dependant's lifetime annuity (Pension Death Benefit Rule 3 – *section 167* of *FA 2004*).

A dependant's unsecured pension means:

(*a*)   a dependant's short-term annuity; or

(*b*)   a dependant's income withdrawal.

Again *FA 2004* uses a concept of a dependant's unsecured fund where a crystallisation event has occurred but the funds in the dependant's account have not yet been applied to provide a dependant's scheme pension, a dependant's annuity or a dependant's short-term annuity or paid as dependant's income withdrawal.

A dependant's short-term annuity is similar to a member's short-term annuity so is secured with an annuity using unsecured funds and can last for a period of up to five years.

Income withdrawal is also possible up to age 75 and again the total amount of dependants' unsecured pension paid to a dependant in respect of a defined contributions arrangement must not exceed 120 per cent of the basis amount for the unsecured pension year (Pension Death Benefit Rule 4 – *section 167* of *FA 2004*).

Once the dependant reaches age 75, again it is possible to have a dependant's alternatively secured pension fund. The total amount of dependant's alternatively secured pension paid to the dependant in each alternatively secured pension year must not exceed 70 per cent of the basis amount for the alternatively secured year (Pension Death Benefit Rule 6 – *section 167* of *FA 2004*).

Lump sum death benefit rule (section 168 of FA 2004)

Death benefits (before and after benefit crystallisation)

5.54   Under the lump sum death benefit rule, no lump sum death benefits can be paid other than:

(*a*)   a defined benefits lump sum death benefit;

(*b*)   a pension protection lump sum death benefit;

(*c*)   an uncrystallised funds lump sum death benefit;

(*d*)   an annuity protection lump sum death benefit;

(*e*)   an unsecured pension fund lump sum death benefit;

(*f*)   a charity lump sum death benefit;

(*g*)   a transfer lump sum death benefit;

(*h*)   a trivial commutation lump sum death benefit; or

(*i*)   a winding-up lump sum death benefit.

For this purpose 'lump sum death benefit' means a lump sum payable on the death of the member.

A defined benefits lump sum death benefit

5.55   A lump sum death benefit is a 'defined benefits lump sum death benefit' if:

(*a*)   the member has not reached the age of 75 at the date of the member's death;

(*b*)   it is paid in respect of a defined benefits arrangement;

(*c*)   it is paid before the end of the period of two years beginning with the day on which the member died; and

(*d*)   it is not a pension protection lump sum death benefit, a trivial commutation lump sum death benefit or a winding-up lump sum death benefit.

The pre A-Day restriction limiting the maximum tax-free lump sum death benefit payable under a retirement benefits scheme approved under *Chapter I* of *Part XIV* of *ICTA 1988* to (normally) four times final remuneration plus a return of employee contributions (see 5.117 below) no longer applies. All of the member's benefits can be paid out as a tax-free lump sum death benefit on death in service or death in deferment after A-Day up to the available lifetime allowance applicable to the member.

A defined benefits lump sum death benefit is free of income tax (*section 636A* of *ICTA 1988*, as inserted by *paragraph 11* of *Schedule 31* to *FA 2004*).

A pension protection lump sum death benefit

5.56   This is a different type of death benefit that can be paid on death before age 75 in respect of a scheme pension under a defined benefits arrangement to which the member was entitled to at the date of the member's death and the member has specified that it is to be treated as a pension protection lump sum death benefit (instead of a defined benefits lump sum death benefit).

A lump sum death benefit is a pension protection lump sum death benefit if:

(*a*)   the member has not reached the age of 75 at the date of the member's death;

(*b*)   it is paid in respect of a defined benefits arrangement;

(*c*)   it is paid in respect of a scheme pension to which the member was entitled at the date of the member's death; and

(*d*)   the member has specified that it is to be treated as a pension protection lump sum death benefit (instead of a defined benefits lump sum death benefit).

To count as a pension protection death benefit the lump sum must also not exceed the pension protection limit.

The maximum lump sum that can be paid under the pension protection limit is broadly the amount crystallised by reason of the member becoming entitled to a pension, less the amount of pension paid before the date of death and less the amount of pension protection lump sum death benefit previously paid in respect of the pension (*paragraph 14* of *Part 2* of *Schedule 29* to *FA 2004*).

An administrator is subject to tax on the payment of a pension protection lump sum death benefit at the rate of 35 per cent (*section 206* of *FA 2004* and *section 636A* of *ITEPA 2003*, as inserted by *paragraph 11* of *Schedule 31* to *FA 2004*).

In the run up to A-Day there has been considerable uncertainty about whether an existing five-year guarantee lump sum payable on death after retirement under a defined benefits arrangement would be an unauthorised payment, a defined benefit lump sum death benefit or a pension protection fund lump sum death benefit. It would appear that, in most cases, the payment will be treated as a 'defined benefit lump sum death benefit' and can still be paid tax free (as was the position pre A-Day) as long as the member is below age 75 at date of death and the member has not specified that the payment should be treated as a pension protection lump sum death benefit, in relation to a defined benefits arrangement. The position in relation to defined contribution arrangements is set out at 5.58 below. There is transitional protection for five-year guarantee payments where the pension is in payment before A-Day and the member dies after age 75 where the member has specified that the payment should be treated as a pension protection lump sum death benefit (*paragraph 36* of *Schedule 36* to *FA 2004*). There will, however, be a 35 per cent tax charge.

Uncrystallised funds lump sum death benefit

5.57   An uncrystallised funds lump sum death benefit is a lump sum death benefit paid from a defined contributions arrangement out of relevant uncrystallised funds before the end of a period of two years beginning on the day the member died (*paragraph 15* of *Schedule 29* to *FA 2004*). It cannot exceed the sums and market value of the assets that constitute the relevant uncrystallised funds immediately before the payment is made.

An uncrystallised funds lump sum death benefit is free of income tax (*section 636A* of *ITEPA 2003*, as inserted by *paragraph 11* of *Schedule 31* to *FA 2004*).

Annuity protection lump sum death benefit

5.58   This is the equivalent of the pension protection lump sum death benefit but paid from a defined contributions arrangement in respect of a scheme pension or lifetime annuity to which the member was entitled at the date of the member's death if the member has not reached the age of 75 at the date of death (*paragraph 16* of *Part 2* of *Schedule 29* to *FA 2004*).

Again, a scheme administrator is subject to tax on the payment of an annuity pension protection lump sum death benefit at the rate of 35 per cent (*section 206* of *FA 2004* and *section 636A* of *ITEPA 2003*, as inserted by *paragraph 11* of *Schedule 31* to *FA 2004*).

It would appear that a payment under a five-year guarantee paid from a defined contributions arrangement will count as an annuity protection lump sum death benefit and be subject to a 35 per cent tax charge.

There may be inheritance tax consequences on the payment of an annuity protection lump sum death benefit (see 5.81 below).

Unsecured pension fund lump sum death benefit

5.59   If a member is below age 75 and is entitled to income withdrawal from the arrangement at the date of death or if a dependant is below age 75 and is entitled to income withdrawal at date of death, the member's or dependant's unsecured pension fund can be used to provide an unsecured pension fund lump sum death benefit.

An administrator is subject to tax on the payment of an unsecured pension fund lump sum death benefit at the rate of 35 per cent (*section 206* of *FA 2004* and *section 636A* of *ITEPA 2003*, as inserted by *paragraph 11* of *Schedule 31* to *FA 2004*).

There may be inheritance tax consequences on the payment of an unsecured pension fund lump sum death benefit (see 5.81 below).

A charity lump sum death benefit

5.60 A charity lump sum death benefit can be paid if the member has reached the age of 75; there are no dependants of the member; it is paid in respect of income withdrawal to which the member was entitled at the date of death and it is paid to a charity nominated by the member (*paragraph 18* of *Part 2* of *Schedule 29* to *FA 2004*). A charity lump sum death benefit can also be paid on the death of a dependant of a member in similar circumstances. The charity lump sum death benefit cannot exceed the amount of the member's or dependant's alternatively secured pension fund before the payment is made. There does not appear to be any tax charge in relation to this type of payment.

Transfer lump sum death benefit

5.61 A transfer lump sum death benefit is the benefit that caused considerable excitement amongst the pensions industry in relation to 'family pension schemes'.

It can be paid if:

(*a*)   the member has reached the age of 75 at the date of the member's death;

(*b*)   there are no dependants of the member;

(*c*)   it is paid in respect of income withdrawal to which the member was entitled in respect of an arrangement at the date of the member's death;

(*d*)   it is paid so as to become held for the purposes of, or to represent accrued rights under, arrangements under the pension scheme relating to one or more members of the pension scheme nominated by the relevant person (or if the relevant person made no nomination by the administrator) (*paragraph 19* of *Part 2* of *Schedule 29* to *FA 2004*).

A transfer lump sum death benefit can be paid in similar circumstances on the death of a dependant of a member with an alternatively secured pension.

At the date of writing a transfer lump sum death benefit is free of tax (*section 636A* of *ITEPA 2003*, as inserted by *paragraph 11* of *Schedule 31* to *FA 2004*).

There will usually be inheritance tax consequences if a transfer lump sum death benefit is paid (see 5.81 below).

Trivial commutation lump sum death benefit

5.62 A trivial commutation lump sum death benefit can be paid to a dependant where the member dies before age 75 to extinguish his entitlement to a dependant's pension as long as the amount of the lump sum does not exceed 1 per cent of the standard lifetime allowance on the date the lump sum is paid (*paragraph 20* of *Part 2* of *Schedule 29* to *FA 2004*).

If a trivial commutation lump sum death benefit is paid, the person who receives it is treated as having taxable income for the tax year in which the payment is made equal to the amount of the lump sum (*section 636C* of *ITEPA 2003*, as inserted by *paragraph 11* of *Schedule 31* to *FA 2004*).

Winding-up lump sum death benefit

5.63   A winding-up lump sum death benefit can be paid to a dependant on the winding up of a pension scheme to extinguish his entitlement to pension death benefit and lump sum death benefit in respect of the member. Again the amount of the lump sum paid cannot exceed 1 per cent of the standard lifetime allowance on the date the lump sum is paid (*paragraph 21* of *Part 2* of *Schedule 29* to *FA 2004*).

If a winding-up lump sum death benefit is paid, the person who receives it is treated as having taxable income for the tax year in which the payment is made equal to the amount of the lump sum (*section 636C* of *ITEPA 2003*, as inserted by *paragraph 11* of *Schedule 31* to *FA 2004*).

Life assurance only members in occupational pension schemes

5.64   There is still some uncertainty at the date of writing whether it is possible to retain life assurance only members in occupational pension schemes after A-Day of whether it will be necessary to establish a separate scheme to deliver this benefit. As explained in 5.21 above the trustees or managers of occupational pension schemes with their main administration in the UK will from A-Day have an obligation to secure that the activities of the scheme are restricted to 'retirement benefit activities' (*section 255* of *PA 2004*). Broadly 'retirement benefit activities' are operations *related to* [our emphasis] retirement benefits and activities *arising from* operations *related to* retirement benefits.

There is uncertainty whether the provision of life assurance benefits for members who are included in a scheme solely for such benefits fall within the definition of 'retirement benefits'. This will depend on what is meant by 'related to', as highlighted above. It would appear from the parliamentary debates that the relevant provisions in *PA 2004* were inserted to mirror the EU *Directive 2003/41/EC on the Activities and Supervision of Institutions for Occupational Retirement Provisions* ('*IORP Directive*') and were not intended to restrict existing activities of occupational pension schemes. However, on a narrow interpretation of *PA 2004* provisions only members with full scheme benefits could have death benefits 'arising from' or 'supplementary to' them. But on a wider view the death benefits would be sufficiently 'related to' the retirement benefits provided to other members to be allowed.

Transfers

Transfers-out

5.65   If the rules of the scheme permit, or the member has a statutory right to transfer the cash equivalent of all or part of his rights under *PSA 1993*, the member will, generally, be able to transfer their benefits under the new *FA 2004* regime without adverse tax consequences, subject to certain conditions (see *RPSM, Chapter 14*). Broadly a transfer can be made without adverse tax consequences if it counts as a 'recognised transfer' – a type of authorised payment (*sections 164(c)* and *169* of *FA 2004*). A 'recognised transfer' is a transfer of sums or assets held for the purposes of, or representing accrued rights under, a registered pension scheme so as to be held for the purposes of, or to represent rights under:

(*a*)   another registered pension scheme; or

(*b*)   a qualifying recognised overseas pension scheme (see below),

in connection with a member of that pension scheme (*section 169* of *FA 2004*). Transfers from a registered pension scheme to an insurance company will also generally count as recognised transfers if the sums transferred are applied to provide a scheme pension or dependant's scheme pension (*section 169(1A), (1B)* and *(1C)* of *FA 2004*).

The transfer will not be treated as a benefit crystallisation event for lifetime allowance purposes. A transfer will also not be treated as a contribution (*section 188(5)* of *FA 2004*). For the purpose of calculating the member's annual allowance for contribution purposes in a defined benefits scheme or a cash balance arrangement where the member has a defined benefits arrangement, the market value of the assets transferred out of an arrangement during a pension input period has to be included in the member's closing value in the arrangement (i e they are added back) and where there has been a transfer-in they should be subtracted from the member's closing value in the pension input period in a receiving defined benefits scheme (*section 236(4), (5), (6)* and *(7)* of *FA 2004*).

If a transfer is made which is not a recognised transfer it will count as an unauthorised payment with the tax consequences discussed previously. The transferring scheme should also ensure that any transfer is made directly to the administrator or the insurance company which issues policies under the receiving scheme. Failure to do so can result in a fine of £3,000 (see *section 266* of *FA 2004* and the commentary in *RPSM 14107010*).

Partial transfers

5.66   Under pre A-Day HMRC requirements applicable to retirement benefit schemes approved under *Chapter I* of *Part XIV* of *ICTA 1988* generally it was not possible to make a partial transfer from a retirement benefits scheme other than where the transfer was coupled with the retention of certain residual benefits in the scheme:

(*a*)   GMP or statutory reference scheme rights or protected rights were retained where the rest of the benefits were transferred;

(*b*)   pension credit rights were transferred but not employee benefit rights (or vice versa);

(*c*)   a two-stage transfer was made on winding up or in the circumstances set out in paragraph 10.41g of IR12 (2001).

Personal pension schemes approved under *Chapter IV* of *Part XIV* of *ICTA 1988* were able to make partial transfers before A-Day (see chapter 14) as they could transfer the benefits held under some of the arrangements under the scheme. Most personal pension schemes have historically been set up as multiple arrangements.

Under the new *FA 2004* regime it is possible to make a partial transfer from any type of registered pension scheme (including a retirement benefits scheme that used to be approved under *Chapter I*) as long as the rights under the arrangement being transferred are uncrystallised. Any transfer is also subject to relevant contracting-out transfer requirements and the cash equivalent transfer ('CETV') requirements under *PSA 1993* (see chapter 6). Generally if a member exercises his right to take a CETV under an occupational pension scheme he can transfer his contracted-out and non-contracted-out rights separately but cannot make a partial transfer of part of his contracted-out or non-contracted out rights while leaving the remainder of those rights behind.

So, if a partial transfer is to be made from an occupational pension scheme, a specific power will need to be inserted in the scheme's rules (independently of any CETV transfer right) with an appropriate discharge for trustees when a partial transfer is made. In practice most defined benefits occupational pension schemes that adopt a partial transfer rule will only want to use it to permit members to transfer their defined contributions AVC funds. Defined contributions schemes approved before A-Day under *Chapter I* of *Part XIV* of *ICTA 1988* may want greater flexibility.

Care also needs to be taken to avoid any loss of transitional protection on making a partial transfer. For example, an individual with enhanced protection will lose that enhanced protection if they make a partial transfer as it will not count as a 'permitted transfer' (see *paragraph 12(7)* of *Schedule 36* to *FA 2004*).

Transfers to recognised qualifying overseas pension schemes

5.67 A transfer-out can also be made without adverse tax consequences to a recognised qualifying overseas pension scheme. A recognised qualifying overseas pension scheme is a pension scheme which:

(*a*) meets the conditions enabling it to be treated as an overseas pension scheme under *section 150(7)* of *FA 2004*;

(*b*) meets the additional conditions enabling it to be treated as a recognised overseas pension scheme under *section 150(8)* of *FA 2004*; and

(*c*) meets certain other conditions laid down in *section 169* of *FA 2004*.

An overseas pension scheme is broadly a pension scheme (other than a registered scheme) which:

(*a*) is established in a country or territory outside the UK; and

(*b*) must be regulated as a pension scheme in the country in which it is established;

(*c*) must be 'recognised for tax purposes' by the country or territory in which it is established; and

(*d*) must satisfy either of the following conditions:

    (i) the scheme must be approved or recognised by, or registered with the relevant taxation authorities in the country or territory in which it was established (if such approval or registration system exists); or

    (ii) if there is no system in that country or territory for approving, recognising or registering pension schemes, the scheme must be resident there (*section 169* of *FA 2004* and *regulation 2* of the *Pension Schemes* (*Categories of Country and Requirements for Overseas Pension Schemes and Recognised Overseas Pension Schemes*) *Regulations 2006* (*SI 2006 No 206*) and see also *RPSM14101030*).

An overseas pension scheme will count as a recognised overseas pension scheme broadly if it is established:

(*a*) in the EEA, i e EU Member States and Norway, Lichtenstein and Iceland; or (*b*)   a country or territory with which the UK has a double taxation agreement that contains exchange of information and non-discrimination provisions; or

(*c*)   any other country or territory if, at the time of the recognised transfer:

(i)   at least 70 per cent of the funds transferred would be used by the receiving scheme to provide an income for life of the member (subject to reaching minimum pension age);

(ii)   the benefits payable under the scheme are not payable earlier than would be permitted under a UK registered pension scheme; and

(iii)   membership of the scheme is open to persons resident in the country or territory in which it is established (*section 150(8)* and *regulation 3* of the *Pension Schemes* (*Categories of Country and Requirements for Overseas Pension Schemes and Recognised Overseas Pension Schemes*) *Regulations 2006* (*SI 2006 No 206*)).

For a recognised overseas pension scheme to count as a 'qualifying recognised overseas pension scheme' the scheme manager of the scheme to which the transfer will be made must:

(*a*)   have notified HMRC that the scheme is a recognised overseas pension scheme and provide any such evidence that it is an overseas pension scheme as HMRC may require;

(*b*)   have informed HMRC of the name of the country in which the scheme is established, providing evidence, if the scheme is not a scheme in the EU economic area or in a country with a double taxation treaty, that the scheme meets the other requirements for a recognised overseas pension scheme (see above);

(*c*)   have undertaken to notify HMRC if the scheme ceases to be a recognised overseas pension scheme;

(*d*)   have undertaken to provide HMRC with certain information on benefit crystallisation events in respect of certain scheme members (*section 169(2)* of *FA 2004* and *regulation 4* of the *Pension Schemes* (*Information Requirements – Qualifying Overseas Pension Schemes, Qualifying Recognised Overseas Pensions Schemes and Corresponding Relief*) *Regulations 2006* (*SI 2006 No 208*) and *RPSM 14101050*).

HMRC has power to exclude a scheme from being a recognised qualifying pension scheme in certain circumstances where there has been a failure to comply with the prescribed information requirements and, broadly, by reason of the failure, it is inappropriate that a transfer from a registered scheme should be a recognised transfer (see *section 169(5)* of *FA 2004* and see *RPSM 14101050* for commentary). There is an appeal procedure against such a decision under *section 170* of *FA 2004*.

If a transfer is made to a qualifying recognised overseas pension scheme, the transfer will be a benefit crystallisation event for the purposes of the member's lifetime allowance (Benefit Crystallisation Event 8 – *section 216* of *FA 2004* and see *RPSM14101060*). Accordingly, if the amount crystallised exceeds the individual's remaining lifetime allowance, tax is chargeable at 25 per cent not the 55 per cent lump sum rate. The administrator will also have to report to HMRC that a transfer has been made to a qualifying recognised overseas pension scheme (*regulation 3* – Reportable Event 9 of the *Registered Pension Schemes* (*Provision of Information*) *Regulations 2006* (*SI 2006 No 567*).

Retention of pre A-Day rights transitional protection post transfer

5.68   If a member is entitled to a protected low pension age they may be able to retain their low protected pension age following the transfer if certain conditions are met (*paragraphs 21* and *23(5)* of *Schedule 36* to *FA 2004*).

If a member is entitled to a normal minimum pension age of below 55 (see 5.30 above) they may still be able to retain that low normal minimum pension age following a transfer if they meet certain conditions (*paragraphs 21* and *22(5)* of *Schedule 36* to *FA 2004*).

The requirements for the continued application of:

(*a*)   primary protection;

(*b*)   enhanced protection (*paragraph 12* of *Schedule 36* to *FA 2004);*

(*c*)   lump sum protection in transferring a scheme where the member has primary protection;

(*d*)   lump sum protection where the member is entitled to a lump sum of more than 25 per cent of rights;

(*e*)   a protected low pension age (*paragraphs 21* and *23* of *Schedule 36* to *FA 2004*); and

(*f*)   a low normal minimum pension age (*paragraphs 21* and *22* of *Schedule 36* to *FA 2004*),

following a transfer are described in *RPSM14105000*. Careful consideration needs to be given before making a transfer as to whether any of these protections could be lost as a result of the transfer.

Transfers of pensions in payment or rights where there is already an entitlement to benefits

5.69   Generally under the pre A-Day tax regimes, transfers could not be made once the member had reached normal retirement age (see, for example, paragraph 10.22 of IR12 (2001)).

New provisions have been introduced by *FA 2004* which will permit the transfer of pensions in payment or rights where there is an entitlement to benefits (for example, income withdrawal or drawdown) subject to certain conditions being met.

The conditions relating to such transfers are described in *RPSM14106000*. Failure to meet the required conditions will result in the payment being an unauthorised payment with the tax consequences discussed previously. To make such a transfer, generally the rules or governing documentation of the registered scheme will need to be amended.

Transfers-in

5.70   A transfer-in can be accepted post A-Day from:

(*a*)   a registered scheme; or

(*b*)   a recognised overseas pension scheme; or

(*c*)   an unregistered pension scheme which does not count as a recognised overseas pension scheme (for example, an employer financed retirement benefits scheme or a non-UK pension scheme that does not satisfy the requirements to count as a recognised overseas pension scheme).

A transfer-in from any of these sources will not count as an unauthorised payment. Under the pre A-Day regime the only transfers permitted were between tax-approved arrangements (see paragraph 10.21 of IR12 (2001)). Transfers-in also do not count as a contribution to the scheme so are not tax relievable (see *section 188(5)* of *FA 2004*). There will also be no benefit crystallisation event on a transfer-in.

Contracting-out requirements relating to transfers-in also have to be complied with (see chapter 4).

As, generally, no UK tax relief will have been received on benefits transferred in from a recognised overseas pension scheme, special treatment is given in relation to the lifetime allowance. Generally the individual's lifetime allowance can be enhanced by the amount of the transfer-in if an application is made to HMRC to claim this enhancement (see *sections 224 to 226* of *FA 2004* and *RPSM14103020* and onwards). The enhancement will not apply in relation to any part of the transfer payment which is derived from tax relieved contributions to a qualifying overseas pension scheme.

On a transfer from a non-registered scheme that is not a recognised overseas pension scheme again there is no tax relief on the transfer-in but the investment funds derived from the transfer will be free of income and capital gains tax (see

RPSM14104010). There will again be no benefit crystallisation event on the transfer-in but when the member takes their benefits the amount crystallised that is derived from the transfer-in will count towards the lifetime allowance.

Investment and scheme borrowing

5.71 It was originally proposed that from A-Day, there would be a single investment regime for all types of registered pension schemes. Under the original proposals registered pension schemes were to be given the right to invest in residential property and other tangible assets. This rule was to extend to self-directed pension schemes which were, under the pre A-Day rules, prohibited from investing in certain assets. Details of the pre A-Day rules are set out in section B of this chapter at 5.96 below.

It was announced in the 'Pensions Tax Simplification – Pre-Budget Report Technical Note' published in December 2005 that, to prevent abuse of the proposed new investment rules by people directing the scheme to acquire assets from which a personal benefit is derived, rather than acquiring assets for the purpose of building a fund for retirement, the Government had decided to tighten the rules governing allowable investments by certain types of registered pension schemes, notably those where investment could be member directed. The amended legislation will apply to all registered pension schemes where the member can direct member investment. Although the legislation had not been drafted at the time of writing, it is understood that it will apply to direct and indirect investment in residential property and most forms of tangible moveable property which will be collectively referred to as 'prohibited assets' (see chapter 14 for a more detailed discussion of this subject).

Broadly if a self-directed pension scheme, directly or indirectly, purchases a prohibited asset, the purchase will be subject to an unauthorised payment charge with the various tax consequences discussed above.

Scheme borrowing will be limited to 50 per cent of scheme assets at the time the loan is taken out. Any borrowing above those limits will count as an unauthorised payment with the tax consequences discussed above (*section 189* of and *Schedule 30* to *FA 2004*). In practice, only trust based occupational schemes with fewer than 100 members or certain categories of 'small schemes' will be able to take advantage of this flexibility as, generally, trust based schemes are not permitted to borrow money or act as a guarantor, other than for the purpose of providing temporary liquidity for the scheme and on a temporary basis (*regulation 5* of the *Occupational Pension Scheme (Investment) Regulations 2005 (SI 2005 No 3378)* – see chapter 10).

Restrictions on investment in the sponsoring employer and associated employers will continue to be limited to 5 per cent of the fund value (see chapter 10).

Fund income

General

5.72   Investment income derived from investments or deposits held for the purposes of a registered pension scheme is exempt from income tax (*section 186* of *FA 2004*). This exemption does not apply, however, to investments or deposits held as a member of a property investment LLP (*section 186(2)* of *FA 2004*).

Income from a trading activity of a registered pension scheme does not fall within the above exemption (see below and chapter 10 for a discussion of what is meant by 'trading').

Underwriting fees are included within the definition of 'investments' under the above exemption, so will qualify for tax relief in relation to investments held by a registered pension scheme (*section 186(3)* of *FA 2004*). Stock lending fees received by a registered pension scheme from any investment held by a registered pension scheme will, generally, also be exempt unless they derive from investments in a property investment LLP (*section 186* of *FA 2004* and *section 129B* of *ICTA 1988*).

Underwriting commissions applied for the purposes of a registered pension scheme which are not relevant foreign income and which would otherwise be chargeable to income tax under *Chapter 8* of *Part 5* of *ITTOIA 2005* (income not otherwise charged) are also exempt from income tax (*section 186(2)* of *FA 2004*).

Futures and options contracts involving registered pension schemes are also defined as falling within the definition of investments and therefore fall within the exemption for income tax (*section 186(3)* of *FA 2004*).

Any gains realised by a person on a disposal of investments held for the purposes of a registered pension scheme are not chargeable to capital gains tax (*section 271* of *TCGA 1992*, as amended by *section 187* of *FA 2004*). However, a gain arising from the acquisition or disposal of assets held as a member of a property investment LLP will be a chargeable gain liable to capital gains tax (*section 271(12)* of *TCGA*, as amended by *section 187(7)* of *FA 2004*).

Capital gains derived from dealing in financial futures or options are also exempt from capital gains tax (*s 271(10)* of the *Taxation of Chargeable Gains Act 1992* (*TCGA 1992*)).

Trading

5.73   Certain activities undertaken by pension scheme trustees may be classed as trading by HMRC. This does not prevent a pension scheme being a registered scheme. However, tax is payable on the income derived from such activities.

The question as to whether the trustees are trading or not is a matter for the inspector of taxes to decide, not HMRC. The relevant considerations in deciding whether a transaction involves trading or not are usually described as the six 'badges of trade' (1954 Royal Commission (Cmd 9474), paragraph 116). These are discussed in chapter 10.

Tax treatment of payments to employers

Authorised surplus payments

5.74   The pre A-Day requirement that exempt approved occupational pension schemes would partially lose full tax exempt status if they overfunded their benefits, unless they put forward proposals to reduce the surplus below 105 per cent funding on the Government Actuary's Basis in accordance with the various permitted methods, no longer applies after A-Day (old *section 603* of and *Schedule 22* to *ICTA 1988*). However, if a repayment of surplus is made to an employer this must be made in accordance with the requirements of *section 37* of *PA 1995* (see chapter 11). An authorised surplus payment will be an authorised employer payment if it meets the requirements prescribed under *section 177* of *FA 2004* (at the date of writing the relevant regulations had not yet been published). There will generally be a free-standing 35 per cent tax charge on any authorised surplus payments to the employer. The scheme administrator is liable to pay the tax and should account for it by using the accounting for tax return (see 5.85 below and *RPSM04102030*).

Tax treatment of benefits paid out to members

Pension benefits

5.75   Pensions paid under a registered pension scheme (other than any pension which gives rise to an unauthorised payments charge) will be taxable as pension income (*section 566(4)* and *sections 579A* and *579B* of *ITEPA 2003*). The taxable pension income for the year is the full amount of the pension under the registered pension scheme that accrues in the year irrespective of when any amount is actually paid (*section 579B* of *ITEPA 2003*). The person liable for the income tax is the person receiving or entitled to the pension under the registered pension scheme (*section 579C* of *ITEPA 2003*). The above taxation treatment applies to all types of pensions paid under a registered scheme including:

(*a*)   an annuity under, or purchased with sums or assets held for the purposes of, or representing acquired rights under, a registered pension scheme; and (*b*)   income withdrawal or dependant's income withdrawal under a registered pension scheme (*section 579D* of *ITEPA 2003*).

Any unauthorised pension paid under a registered pension scheme will also be chargeable to income tax as pension income unless the unauthorised pension has been assessed to income tax as an unauthorised payment.

PAYE will apply to all pensions from registered pension schemes. The payer of the pension must deduct PAYE in accordance with PAYE rules before paying the pension. There are transitional provisions for:

  (i)   retirement annuity contracts;

 (ii)   pensions that were taxed before 6 April 2006 but accrued after 6 April 2006; and

(iii)   annuities that were paid from a scheme that was formerly an approved scheme that does not become a registered scheme (see *RPSM 4101020* for details).

Lump sums free of income tax

5.76   No liability to income tax arises on a lump sum paid under a registered pension scheme if the lump sum is:

(*a*)   a pension commencement lump sum;

(*b*)   a serious ill-health lump sum;

(*c*)   a refund of excess contributions lump sum;

(*d*)   a defined benefits lump sum death benefit;

(*e*)   an uncrystallised funds lump sum death benefit; or

(*f*)   a transfer lump sum death benefit (*section 636A* of *ITEPA 2003*).

A lifetime allowance charge can still arise, however, if the benefits crystallised on a benefit crystallisation exceed the remaining available lifetime allowance.

Lump sums subject to 35 per cent tax under section 206 of FA 2004

5.77   A lump sum under a registered pension scheme which is:

(*a*)   a pension protection lump sum death benefit;

(*b*)   an annuity protection lump sum death benefit; or

(*c*)   an unsecured pension fund lump sum death benefit,

is subject to income tax under *section 206* of *FA 2004* (charge to tax on scheme administrator in respect of such lump sum death benefit but not otherwise). The rate of tax is 35 per cent in respect of the lump sum death benefit, but the rate of tax charged may be decreased or increased by Treasury order. The person liable to the tax is the scheme administrator. Tax is charged on the amount of lump sum paid, or, if the rules of the scheme permit the scheme administrator to deduct the tax before payment, the amount of the lump sum before deduction of tax (*section 206* of *FA 2004*).

The accounting for tax return is used to account for the special lump sum death benefit charge (see 5.100 below).

Tax treatment of short service refund lump sums

5.78   A short service refund lump sum under a registered pension scheme (see 5.46 above) is subject to income tax in accordance with *section 205* of *FA 2004* (charge to tax on scheme administrator in respect of such a lump sum) but not otherwise.

Tax treatment of trivial commutation and winding-up lump sums

5.79   If a trivial commutation lump or winding-up lump sum is paid to a member of a registered pension scheme they are treated as if they have received taxable pension income for the tax year in which the payment is made equal to the amount of the lump sum.

If a trivial commutation lump sum death benefit or a winding-up lump sum death benefit is paid to a person under a registered pension scheme the person is treated as having taxable pension income for the tax year in which the payment is made equal to the amount of the lump sum.

Scheme administration member charge

5.80   A scheme administration member payment is a payment by a registered pension scheme to or in respect of a member of a pension scheme that is made for the purposes of the administration or management of the pension scheme (*section 171* of *FA 2004*). This might include payment of wages to a person administering the scheme or payments made to purchase a pension scheme asset or a payment of interest on a short service refund lump sum payment (see 5.78 above).

As long as the payment does not exceed the amount that would be expected to be paid to a person who was at arm's length, the excess will count as a scheme administration payment. If a scheme administration payment is made normal tax rules would apply to each type of payment (see *RPSM04101150*).

Inheritance tax

5.81   There is no general inheritance tax exemption for registered pension schemes (see *RPSM04100060*).

Most occupational pension schemes that are registered pension schemes will be set up under trust. Trusts are a kind of settled property for inheritance tax ('IHT') purposes and this could potentially have a number of consequences for registered pension schemes. There are, however, a number of specific exemptions which take registered pension schemes outside the usual charges on this type of settlement for IHT purposes (as was the position before A-Day). As explained in *RPSM04100060* this means that:

(*a*)   contributions by individuals under registered pension schemes are not treated as chargeable transfers and not subject to IHT (*section 12(2)* of the *Inheritance Tax Act 1984 (IHTA 1984)*);

(*b*)   property held for the purposes of a registered pension scheme are not subject to an IHT charge which would otherwise be levied on a discretionary trust every ten years (*section 58(1)(d)* of *IHTA 1984*);

(*c*)   IHT charges do not generally arise on a distribution of capital from a registered pension scheme such as a payment of a lump sum on death or retirement (*section 58(1)(d)* of *IHTA 1984*);

(*d*)   the value of the IHT estates on death will not include any value representing a proportion of the value of the scheme funds (*sections 4* and *151* of *IHTA 1984*).

If a lump sum death benefit is paid under discretionary trusts, so the trustees or employer have discretion to determine who it should be paid to, an IHT charge should also not arise. However, if it is paid automatically to the deceased's personal representatives, it will form part of the deceased's estate and will be subject to IHT if the size of the deceased's estate exceeds the nil rate band. No IHT charge will arise to the extent the estate passes to the deceased member's spouse, civil partner or to a charity.

There may, however, still be inheritance implications for a member if he does not opt to take his benefits at the earliest opportunity. At the date of writing, HMRC was still consulting on the application of the existing inheritance tax regime to pension choices post A-Day on the subsequent death of the member ('Discussion paper on Inheritance Tax (IHT) and Pension Simplification' issued by HMRC on 21 July 2005).

The consultation paper notes that under *IHTA 1984* IHT is charged on 'transfers of value', arising either:

(i)   on death (where *section 151* of *IHTA 1984* will prevent a charge arising – see above); or

(ii)   by virtue of lifetime dispositions that reduce the value of the person's estate (*section 3(1)* of *IHTA 1984* where a charge is more likely to arise under the post A-Day regime).

The normal meaning of estate is extended by *section 3(3)* of *IHTA 1984*, to include cases where a person omits to exercise a right, with the consequence that their estate is diminished and that of another person (or the value of property in trust) is increased. In such a case, the person in question is treated as making a disposition at the time, or at the latest time, at which they could have exercised the right unless it is shown that the omission was not deliberate. There is also a general exemption for dispositions not intended to confer gratuitous benefit on another person and is made in a transaction either at arm's length or on arm's length terms (*section 10* of *IHTA 1984*).

HMRC's conclusions in the paper were that:

(*a*)   if a member draws a regular pension before age 75 (even though there is choice about timing of commencement) and dies within seven years of committing to the pension, there is, in principle, a possibility of a charge arising. But, in practice, this is looking at things with hindsight and HMRC accepts that, in most cases, the *section 10* non-gratuitous exemption will apply;

(*b*)   where the member dies after the earliest age an individual can draw the pension (50 in some schemes and age 55 from 2010) not yet having drawn a pension HMRC considers the position more uncertain and distinguishes between members above and below age 75:

　　(i)   for members aged 75 plus who have taken an alternatively secured pension, HMRC consider that it will be very difficult to rely on the *section 10* non-gratuitous benefit exemption as the effect of the decision will be to increase the estate. Accordingly HMRC consider that the member's estate immediately before death would be boosted by a chargeable transfer under *section 3(3)* of *IHTA 1984* roughly equal to the value of his fund;

(ii) for members who are entitled to draw a pension but have not yet reached age 75 the position would depend on why the member made a decision to defer taking the pension. If, initially, the decision to defer was made while the member was in good health but they then became ill, a charge under *section 3(3)* may arise in principle at the latest time at which the member could have exercised a right to annuitise. There may also be cases where the decision was made for estate planning reasons. In its consultation paper HMRC considers that, in this situation, the onus will be on the member's estate to demonstrate that the member's decision not to commit to a regular pension is exempt by virtue of *section 10*. HMRC recognises that this will give rise to some sensitive issues because it will require disclosure of intimate personal details of the deceased.

HMRC concludes that it will not, post A-Day, be able to operate its practice with the same light touch as before. In its consultation paper HMRC is therefore seeking suggestions about how it might modify its approach in a manner that is consistent with the current law but also to give IHT certainty to scheme members. It does seem, however, that if the approach outlined in the paper is followed, there will be many more cases where a member's pension choices may now impact on the IHT position following his death.

If a registered scheme invests directly in assets the income and gain from that investment will benefit from tax relief. Registered pension schemes can also pay premiums to invest indirectly in assets through an insurance policy where the underlying assets are owned by the insurance company. These underlying investments do not benefit from the same tax exemptions.

The insurance company can, however, apply the premiums it receives from tax registered schemes to its 'pension business fund' which will enable them to benefit from a similar tax treatment to that which would apply if they were directly invested. The tax treatment of an insurance company's pension business fund is set out in *Chapter I, Part XII* of *ICTA 1988*. The definition of 'pensions business fund' in *section 431B* of *ICTA 1988* has been amended to remove the existing pre A-Day 'correspondence' requirements that used to apply for investments made by occupational pension schemes approved under *Chapter I* of *Part XIV* of *ICTA 1988* (*paragraph 20* of *Schedule 35* to *FA 2004*). Under the new definition, broadly, 'pensions business' is so much of a company's life assurance business as is referable to contracts entered into for the purposes of a registered pension scheme or the reinsurance of that business. If, immediately before A-Day, an annuity policy was treated as falling within the definition of pensions business it will be treated as having been entered into for the purposes of a registered pension scheme for the purposes of the definition of pensions business (amended *section 431B(3)* of *ICTA 1988*). When a pension scheme ceases to be a registered scheme any of the insurance company's business that was pension business when the registered scheme ceased to be a registered scheme ceases to be pensions business (amended *section 431B(2)* of *ICTA 1988*).

International benefit issues

The new regime

5.82   The post-A-Day *FA 2004* regime relating to international benefits set out in *Schedules 33* and *34* of *FA 2004* is complicated and can only be described in outline in this chapter. Reference should be made to *Chapter 13* of the *RPSM* which contains a detailed description of the new regime. The main elements of the regime are as follows:

(*a*)   a member of a registered pension scheme who is a 'relevant overseas individual' can apply to receive an enhancement to their lifetime allowance in respect of non-UK tax relieved contributions;

(*b*)   a member of a registered pension scheme who receives a transfer from a recognised overseas pension scheme can apply for an enhancement to their lifetime allowance in respect of the transfer to the extent that it relates to non-UK tax relieved benefits;

(*c*)   migrant member tax relief can be obtained from UK tax on contributions to a qualifying overseas pension scheme in certain circumstances;

(*d*)   members of a qualifying overseas pension scheme may be subject to UK tax charges in certain circumstances even when they have ceased to be tax resident in the UK; and

(*e*)   overseas members of a registered pension scheme receiving payments from a registered pension scheme can be subject to UK income tax unless exempted by virtue of a double tax agreement.

Administration

General

5.83   Detailed guidance on the administration of registered pension schemes on and after A-Day for tax purposes will be contained in *Chapter 13* of the *RPSM* (still in draft at the date of writing). Broadly, most of the obligations to comply with these requirements will fall on the administrator, who can be subject to penalties for non compliance. Members and associated employers of registered pension schemes, qualifying overseas pension schemes and qualifying recognised overseas pension schemes may also be obliged to provide information in certain circumstances. Certain information must be submitted electronically and the administrators have the option of submitting other information electronically. (See *section 255A* (Electronic Payment) of *FA 2004* and *Schedules 1* and 2 to the draft *Registered Pension Schemes and Overseas Pension Schemes* (*Electronic Communication of Returns and Information*) *Regulations 2006* (*SI 2006 No 570*).

Administration expenses

5.84   If a pension scheme bears the costs of its administration itself, it will not be able to obtain tax relief on those costs as its income is not taxable (unless it is trading and the costs relate to the trading activity). Whilst a pension scheme's rules may provide for administration costs to be paid either by the employers or from the scheme's resources, it is advisable for the employer and trustees to have a clear idea of which costs will be borne by each party. The employer may obtain tax relief in respect of the costs of establishing and operating a pension scheme if the expenses concerned are wholly and exclusively incurred in running the employer's business (*section 74(1)(a)* of *ICTA 1988*). However, if the employer pays costs which are attributable to the trustees, for example, a valuer's fees incurred on property valuations, tax relief will not be given.

At the date of writing it is understood that regulations will be made giving power to grant tax relief for the payment of statutory levies such as those to the pension protection fund (see *RPSM05102050* and *section 102* of *FA 2004*).

If the trustees employ someone (as opposed to appointing an agent) to carry out duties in connection with the pension scheme then they will be responsible, as the employer of that person, for deducting income tax via the PAYE system on the remuneration paid.

Value Added Tax ('VAT') incurred by the trustees is an expense of the pension scheme and may be recoverable in certain circumstances. HMRC has published useful guidance on VAT and pension schemes covering registration and VAT costs which can and cannot be recovered by the trustees. ('Value Added Tax Funded Pension Schemes: VAT Notice 700/17', March 2002 version).

Annual returns by scheme administrator

5.85   A scheme administrator is required to complete and submit an annual return in relation to any tax year if HMRC have served notice on him requiring him to file one (*section 250* of *FA 2004*). The return must be filed by 31 January next following the end of the tax year to which it relates. The return has to be submitted online (see 5.83 above).

The notice from HMRC will specify the period to be covered by the annual return, which can be the whole or part of any tax year or, where audited accounts have been prepared which end in that tax year, the period or periods covered by those accounts.

Accounting for tax returns

5.86   The scheme administrator of a registered pension scheme must make returns to HMRC of the income tax to which the scheme administrator is liable for each period of three months ending 31 March, 30 June, 30 September or 31 December (*section 254* of *FA 2004*). A return is only required if tax has been charged on the administrator during this period. Nil returns are not required (confirmed in draft *Chapter 13* but administrators should check this point when the final draft is published because of the potential penalties).

An accounting for tax form is provided in electronic format and the return must be delivered electronically (see 5.83 above). The return must be delivered within 45 days of the end of the relevant three-month period. The income tax has to be paid within the same period without the need for an assessment to tax (*section 254(5)* of *FA 2004*).

Notices under section 252 of FA 2004 requiring production of documents or particulars

5.87   HMRC has wide powers to serve notices requiring any person of a description set out in regulations made by the Board of HMRC to produce, or make available for inspection, documents within the person's possession or power relating to the matters set out below which HMRC may reasonably require and to provide HMRC with any particulars relating to those matters which HMRC may reasonably require (*section 252* of *FA 2004*).

There is an appeals procedure to the General Commissioners allowing an individual to appeal against any requirement under a *section 252* notice (see *section 253* of *FA 2004*).

Events reports to HMRC

5.88   The scheme administrator of a registered pension scheme has to provide the following information to HMRC in respect of such of the reportable events in column (1) of the following table as have occurred in the scheme year to which the report relates containing the information set out in column (2) of the table (*regulation 3* of the *Registered Pension Schemes (Provision of Information) Regulations 2006 (SI 2006 No 567)*).

Reportable event	Information
1. Unauthorised payments	
The scheme makes an unauthorised member payment or an unauthorised employer payment.	The name, date of birth (if applicable), address and National Insurance or company registration number of the person to whom the payment was made, together with the nature, amount and date of payment.
2. Payments exceeding 50% of the standard lifetime allowance	
The scheme makes a lump sum death benefit payment to a person in respect of the death of a member, and that payment, either alone or when aggregated with other such payments from that scheme, amounts to more than 50% of the standard lifetime allowance applicable at the time of the member's death.	The name, date of birth, last known address and National Insurance number of the deceased member, together with the name and address of the person to whom the payment was made, and the amount and date of the payment.
3. Early provision of benefits	
The scheme provides benefits to a member of the scheme who is under the normal minimum pension age and before the benefits were provided the member was, either in the year in which they were provided or any of the preceding six years: (*a*) in relation to the sponsoring employer, or an associated company of that employer, a director or a person connected with a director; (*b*) whether alone or with others, the sponsoring employer; or (*c*) a person connected with the sponsoring employer.	The name, address, date of birth and National Insurance number of the member, the nature, date and amount of the benefits provided, and reasons for those benefits having been provided under normal minimum pension age.

4. Serious ill-health lump sum	
A scheme pays a member of the scheme a serious ill-health lump sum and before the payment was made the member was, either in the year in which they were provided or any of the preceding six years:	The name, address, date of birth and National Insurance number of the member, and the date and amount of the payment.
(*a*) in relation to the sponsoring employer, or an associated company of that employer, a director or a person connected with a director; or	
(*b*) whether alone or with others, the sponsoring employer; or	
(*c*) a person connected with the sponsoring employer.	
5. Suspension of ill-health pension	
An ill-health pension which has been paid pursuant to Pension Rule 1 in *section 165(1)* of *FA 2004*, is not paid because the ill-health condition is no longer met.	The name, address, date of birth and National Insurance number of the member to whom the pension had been paid, the date on which the period of non-payment began and the annual rate of the pension, to which the member was entitled, immediately before that period began.
6. Benefit crystallisation events and enhanced lifetime allowance or enhanced protection	
A benefit crystallisation event occurs in relation to a member in respect of the scheme and:	The name, address, date of birth and National Insurance number of the member, the amount crystallised by the event, the date of the event and the reference number given by the Commissioners for HMRC under the *Registered Pension Schemes (Enhanced Lifetime Allowance) Regulations 2006 (SI 2006 No 131)*.
(*a*) the amount crystallised by the event:	
(i) exceeds the standard lifetime allowance, or	
(ii) together with amounts crystallised by other events in relation to that member, exceeds the standard lifetime allowance,	
for the year in which the event occurs; and	
(*b*) the member relies on entitlement to either an enhanced lifetime allowance or enhanced protection in order to reduce or eliminate liability to the lifetime allowance charge.	

7. Pension commencement lump sum	
The scheme makes a pension commencement lump sum payment to a member which:	The name, address, date of birth and National Insurance number of the member, together with:
(*a*) when added to the amount crystallised, by reason of the member becoming entitled to the pension with which the lump sum payment is associated, exceeds 25% of the total so found; and	(a) the amount and date of payment of the lump sum; and
(*b*) is more than 7.5%, but less than 25%, of the standard lifetime allowance for the tax year in which the sum is paid.	(b) the amount crystallised on the member becoming entitled to the pension, with which the lump sum is associated.
8. Pension commencement lump sum: primary and enhanced protection provisions of *Schedule 36*	
The scheme makes a pension commencement lump sum payment to a member and the amount of the payment is an authorised payment by reason only of the application of *paragraphs 24* to *30* of *Schedule 36*.	The name, address, date of birth and National Insurance number of the member, the amount and date of the payment, and the reference number given to the member by the Commissioners [for HMRC] under the *Registered Pension Schemes (Enhanced Lifetime Allowance) Regulations 2006 (SI 2006 No 131)*.
9. Transfers to qualifying recognised overseas pension schemes	
The scheme makes a recognised transfer to a qualifying recognised overseas pension scheme which is not a registered pension scheme.	The name, address, date of birth and National Insurance number of the member, the amount of the sums or assets transferred, the date of the transfer together with the name of the qualifying recognised overseas pension scheme and the country or territory under the law of which it is established and regulated.

10. Member able to control scheme assets	
A member of the scheme, whether alone or with others, gains or loses the ability to control the way in which scheme assets are used to provide pension benefits.	The dates on which: (*a*) at least one member becomes able to exercise control where none had been able to do so immediately before; and (*b*) no member is able to exercise control, where at least one had been able to do so immediately before.
11. Changes in scheme rules	
The scheme changes its rules to permit: (*a*) the making of unauthorised member payments; (*b*) the making of unauthorised employer payments; or (*c*) investment other than in policies of insurance.	The fact of the change and the date on which the change takes effect.
12. Changes to rules of pre-commencement scheme treated as more than one scheme	
The scheme, being one which immediately before 6 April 2006 was treated in accordance with *section 611* of *ICTA 1988* as two or more separate schemes, changes its rules in any way.	The fact of the change and the date on which the change takes effect.
13. Change in legal structure of scheme	
The legal structure of the scheme changes from one of the following categories to another. The categories are:	The date on which the change took effect, together with: (a) the new category listed in column 1 which applies to the scheme; and

(a) a single trust under which all of the assets are held for the benefit of all members of the scheme; (b) an overall trust within which there are individual trusts applying for the benefit of each member; (c) an overall trust within which specific assets are held as, or within, sub-funds for each member; (d) an annuity contract; (e) a body corporate; and (f) other.	(b) in the case of a change falling within category (*f*), a brief description of the nature of the new category of legal structure of the scheme.
14. Change in number of members The number of scheme members falls in a different band at the end of a tax year from that in which it fell at the end of the previous tax year. The bands are: (a) 0 members; (b) 1 to 10 members; (c) 11 to 50 members; (d) 51 to 10,000 members; and (e) more than 10,000 members.	The new band applicable to the number of scheme members.
15. Alternatively secured pension Sums or assets in respect of at least one member of the scheme meets Condition A or Condition B in *paragraph 11* of *Schedule 28* for the first time during the reporting year.	The number of members who, having met Condition A or Condition B in *paragraph 11* of *Schedule 28* for the first time during the reporting year, fall within each of the following bands in respect of the funds or assets held. The bands are: (a) £1 to £50,000; (b) £50,001 to £100,000; (c) £100,001 to £250,000; (d) £250,001 to £500,000; and (e) more than £500,000.

16. Transfer lump sum death benefit	
At least one transfer lump sum death benefit is paid during the reporting year.	The number of transfer lump sum death benefits paid during the reporting year, the value of which falls in each of the following bands: (*a*) £1 to £50,000; (*b*) £50,001 to £100,000; (*c*) £100,001 to £250,000; (*d*) £250,001 to £500,000; and (*e*) more than £500,000.
17. Lump sum payment after the death of a member aged 75 or over A lump sum payment is made in respect of a member after the member has died after reaching the age of 75.	The name, date of birth, last known address and National Insurance number of the deceased member, together with the name and address of the person to whom the lump sum payment was made, and the amount, nature and date of the payment.

Where a registered pension scheme is wound up, notice that the winding up has been completed must be given to HMRC by the person who, immediately before the scheme was wound up, was the scheme administrator (*regulation 4* of the *Registered Pension Schemes* (*Provision of Information*) *Regulations 2006* (*SI 2006 No 567*)).

A person who has been, or has ceased to be, the scheme administrator must notify HMRC of the termination of his appointment, together with the date the termination took effect, within 30 days (*regulation 6* of the *Registered Pension Schemes* (*Provision of Information*) *Regulations 2006* (*SI 2006 No 567*)).

5.89   A scheme administrator who makes a payment of a relevant lump sum death benefit must, also on request from HMRC, provide the following information within two months of the date of request:

(*a*)   the name and last known address of the person to whom the payment was made;

(*b*)   the recipient's date of birth, and National Insurance number, if known to the scheme administrator;

(*c*)   the amount of the payment; and

(*d*)   the date on which the payment was made (*regulation 10* of the *Registered Pension Schemes* (*Provision of Information*) *Regulations 2006* (*SI 2006 No 567*)).

Information to be provided to the member or his personal representatives by the scheme administrator

5.90   Certain information must also be provided by the scheme administrator to the member or the member's personal representatives, including:

(*a*)   If a registered pension scheme has made an unauthorised payment to a member of the scheme, the scheme administrator is required to provide to the member who has received the payment details of the nature of the benefit provided; the amount of the unauthorised payment which is treated as being made by the provision of the benefit and the date on which the benefit was provided. This information must be provided no later than the 7 July following the tax year in which the payment was made (*regulation 13* of the *Registered Pension Schemes* (*Provision of Information*) *Regulations 2006* (*SI 2006 No 567*)).

(*b*)   Generally the scheme administrator has to provide to each member:

　　(i)   to whom a pension is being paid, at least once in each tax year; or

　　(ii)   in respect of whom a benefit crystallisation has occurred, within three months of that event,

a statement of the cumulative total percentage of standard lifetime allowance crystallised, at the date of the statement by benefit crystallisation events in respect of the scheme, by whose administrator the statement is given and any scheme from which that scheme has received (whether directly or indirectly) a transfer payment in respect of the member. The information does not have to be provided if the scheme administrator is aware that the same information has been provided to the member by an insurance company (*regulation 14* of the *Registered Pension Schemes* (*Provision of Information*) *Regulations 2006* (*SI 2006 No 567*)).

(*c*)   The scheme administrator must also provide the personal representatives of a deceased member of the scheme with information regarding the percentage of the lifetime allowance crystallised by and the amount and date of payment of a relevant lump sum death benefit in relation to the member. This information must be provided within three months beginning with the date of the final payment of the benefit. Additionally, the personal representatives may request a statement of the cumulative total percentage crystallised, at the date of the statement, by benefit crystallisation events in respect of the deceased member under the scheme, or any scheme from which assets have been transferred to the scheme (whether directly or indirectly), in respect of the deceased member's pension rights, but excluding from that percentage any amount in respect of any relevant lump sum death benefit payment in respect of the deceased member. Where the personal representatives request this information, the scheme administrator must provide it within two months of the date on which the request is received (*regulation 8* of the *Registered Pension Schemes (Provision of Information) Regulations 2006 (SI 2006 No 567)*).

(*d*) If the scheme administrator has made or intends to make a payment on account of his liability to tax in respect of the lifetime allowance charge on a benefit crystallisation event, he must provide the member with a notice giving details of the chargeable amount in respect of the benefit crystallisation event, how the chargeable amount has been calculated and the amount of the resulting tax charge and stating whether the administrator has accounted for the tax or intends to do so. The notice must be provided within three months after the benefit crystallisation event (*regulation 12* of the *Registered Pension Schemes (Provision of Information) Regulations 2006 (SI 2006 No 567)*).

Information to be provided by the member and his personal representatives

5.91 If a member of a registered pension scheme wants to rely on entitlement to an enhanced lifetime allowance he must give the scheme administrator the reference number issued by HMRC in respect of that entitlement (*regulation 11* of the *Registered Pension Schemes (Provision of Information) Regulations 2006 (SI 2006 No 567)*).

If a relevant lump sum death benefit has been paid in respect of a deceased member of a registered pension scheme and the payment, together with any other relevant lump sum death benefits, results in a lifetime allowance charge, the personal representatives of the deceased member (who will be liable for any tax due) have to provide HMRC with certain specified information about the deceased member and the payment (*regulation 10* of the *Registered Pension Schemes (Provision of Information) Regulations 2006 (SI 2006 No 567)*).

Information to be provided to and by annuity providers

5.92 If a registered pension scheme has provided an insurance company with funds to secure the payment of a lifetime annuity for the member or a related dependant's annuity within the meaning of *paragraph 3(4A)* of *Schedule 29* to *FA 2004* the scheme administrator is required to provide the insurance company with a statement containing details of the cumulative total percentage of standard lifetime allowance crystallised, at the date of the statement, by benefit crystallisation events in respect of the scheme, by whose administrator the statement is given, and any scheme from which that member has received (whether directly or indirectly) or transfer payment in respect of the member. This information must be provided within three months of the purchase of the annuity. The insurance company must then provide the annuitant, at least once in each tax year, with a statement of the percentage of the standard lifetime allowance crystallised at the date of the statement in respect of that annuity (*regulation 16* of the *Registered Pension Schemes* (*Provision of Information*) *Regulations 2006* (*SI 2006 No 567*)).

Where an insurance company or other person has paid to a member of a registered pension scheme an annuity purchased with sums held for the purposes of that scheme and the member to whom the annuity is paid has died, the insurance company or other person is required to, on request and within two months of that request, provide to the personal representatives of the deceased member details of the cumulative total percentage of the standard lifetime allowance crystallised, at the date of the statement, by benefit crystallisation events in respect of the deceased member under the scheme or any scheme from which assets have been transferred to the scheme (whether directly or indirectly) in respect of the deceased member's pension rights (*regulation 9* of the *Registered Pension Schemes* (*Provision of Information*) *Regulations 2006* (*SI 2006 No 567*)).

Retention of records

5.93   Any of the following documents that are in the possession or control of the persons listed below relating to any of the following matters have to be preserved in relation to a registered pension scheme, namely:

(*a*)   any monies received by or owing to the scheme;

(*b*)   any investments or assets held by the scheme;

(*c*)   any payments made by the scheme;

(*d*)   any contracts to purchase a lifetime annuity in respect of the member of the scheme; and

(*e*)   the administration of the scheme.

> (*regulation 17(1)* of the *Registered Pension Schemes* (*Provision of Information*) *Regulations 2006* (*SI 2006 No 567*))

The persons subject to this record keeping obligation are:

(i)   any person who is or has been the scheme administrator;

(ii)   any person who is or has been a trustee of the scheme;

(iii)   any person who provides or has provided administrative services to the scheme; and

(iv) if the scheme is an occupational pension scheme, any person who is or has been a sponsoring employer or a director of an employing company.

> (*regulation 17(2)* of the *Registered Pension Schemes (Provision of Information) Regulations 2006 (SI 2006 No 567)*)

The obligation to preserve the documents does not apply to a person who has ceased to act in relation to a scheme or ceased to provide administrative services in relation to a scheme if he has transferred all documents to another person who has succeeded him in acting in relation to the scheme or providing administrative services to the scheme (*regulation 17(3)* of the *Registered Pension Schemes (Provision of Information) Regulations 2006 (SI 2006 No 567)*).

The obligation to preserve the documents applies for the tax year to which they relate and the following six tax years (*regulation 17(4)* of the *Registered Pension Schemes (Provision of Information) Regulations 2006 (SI 2006 No 567)*).

Information requirements in relation to qualifying overseas pension schemes and qualifying recognised overseas pension schemes

5.94 The information requirements in relation to qualifying overseas pension schemes and qualifying recognised overseas pension schemes (see 5.82 above) are not detailed in this chapter.

Penalties

5.95 Penalties that can be levied include the following:

(*a*) Failure to provide the registered pension scheme return in relation to any tax year where notice has been served requiring one to be submitted can give rise to a penalty of £100 on the scheme administrator. A further penalty not exceeding £60 a day for each day on which the failure continues can also be levied (*sections 250* and *257(1)* of *FA 2004*).

(*b*) If the scheme administrator of a registered pension scheme fraudulently or negligently makes an incorrect registered scheme return in response to a notice from HMRC to provide one or delivers any incorrect accounts, statements or other documents with such a return the scheme administrator is liable to a penalty not exceeding £3,000 (*section 257(4)* of *FA 2004*).

(*c*) Failure by the administrator of a registered pension scheme to provide an accounting return can give rise to a fine of £100 for each quarter or part quarter for which the failure continues up to the fourth quarter where the number of people covered by the return is ten or less. Where the number of persons whose particulars should have been included in the return is more than ten the penalty rises to £100 for each ten persons or part thereof (so for 25 persons there will be a £300 penalty) for each quarter or part quarter from which failure continues up to and including the fourth (see *section 260* of *FA 2004*).

(*d*)   If the scheme administrator fraudulently or negligently makes an incorrect accounting return the scheme administrator is liable to a penalty not exceeding the difference in the amount of tax shown in the form and the amount that should have been due (*section 260(6)* of *FA 2004*).

(*e*)   Any person who fraudulently or negligently makes a false statement or representation is liable to a penalty not exceeding £3,000 if the person or any person obtains relief from or repayment of tax chargeable under *Part 4* of *FA 2004* as a result or a registered scheme makes a payment which is an unauthorised payment (*section 264(1)* of *FA 2004*).

(*f*)   Any person who assists in or induces the preparation of any document which the person knows is incorrect and will or is likely to cause a registered pension scheme to make an unauthorised payment is liable to a penalty not exceeding £3,000 (*section 264(2)* of *FA 2004*).

(*g*)   A failure in accordance with *section 98* of the *Taxes Management Act 1970* (penalties for failure to provide information and providing false information) can give rise to a penalty not exceeding £300. Where the failure continues, a further penalty not exceeding £60 a day can be levied.

(*h*)   A failure to produce a document required by a notice served under *section 252* of *FA 2004* can give rise to a penalty not exceeding £300. Where the failure continues, a further penalty not exceeding £60 a day can be levied (*section 259(1)* and (*2*) of *FA 2004*).

(*i*)   A person who fraudulently or negligently produces or makes available for inspection any incorrect documents or provides incorrect particulars in response to a notice under *section 252* of *FA 2004* can be liable to a penalty not exceeding £3,000 (*section 259(4)* of *FA 2004*).

(*j*)   Failure to provide or make available any document or information required under the enhanced lifetime allowance regulations can result on a penalty not exceeding £3,000 on the individual (*section 262* of *FA 2004*).

(*k*)   Where an individual has claimed enhanced protection failure to notify HMRC that relevant benefit accrual has occurred resulting in loss of protection within 90 days of it occurring can result in a penalty on the individual of up to £3,000.

(*l*)   If HMRC considers that a scheme is being wound up wholly or mainly to facilitate the payment of winding-up lump sums or winding-up lump sum death benefits (or both) the scheme administrator is liable to a penalty of up to £3,000 in respect of each member to or in respect of whom such payments are made (*section 265* of *FA 2004*).

Section B

Pre A-Day revenue limits

5.96 As mentioned at the beginning of this chapter (see 5.1 above), many tax approved occupational pension schemes may choose not to disapply all or some of the existing pre A-Day Revenue limits or will write similar requirements into their rules as scheme limits. Consequently, for a number of occupational pension schemes, the limits (or some of them) will have continued application. For reference purposes, this part of the chapter outlines the key features of pre A-Day Revenue limits on benefits provided under tax approved occupational pension schemes.

Transitional arrangements

5.97 Under *paragraph 3* of *Schedule 36* to *FA 2004*, the Commissioners of HMRC have the power, by regulations, to modify the rules of pension schemes if such modifications appear to be appropriate as a consequence of the introduction of the new taxation regime. HMRC intend to exercise this power in accordance with the *Registered Pension Schemes (Modification of the Rules of Existing Schemes) Regulations 2006 (SI 2006 No 364)* ('the *Modification Regulations*'). Their main effect is to provide schemes with a transitional period of five years from A-Day (originally three years) in which to modify their scheme rules to comply with the requirements of the new legislation.

During the transitional period, the Regulations are intended to have the following effects:

(*a*) any rule *requiring* trustees to make an unauthorised payment (see 5.24 above) will be construed as conferring a *discretion* to make that payment;

(*b*) if the scheme rules limit any benefit by reference to the permitted maximum (see 5.100 below), the permitted maximum will continue to apply;

(*c*) if the scheme rules provide for the payment of a specified sum or rate of pension and refer to the possibility of that sum or rate of pension being a greater amount which would not prejudice approval of the scheme by

HMRC, the rules will be construed as authorising the trustees to make only those payments they could have made prior to A-Day;

(*d*) if the scheme rules provide for benefits to be limited to those which would not prejudice approval of the scheme by HMRC, the rules will be construed as prohibiting the trustees from making payments that they would not have been authorised to make prior to A-Day;

(*e*) scheme rules are modified to permit the trustees to reduce a member's benefits in respect of the administrator's liability for the lifetime charge (see 5.1 and 5.50 above).

With regard to limits on benefits provided by occupational pension schemes, the net effect of the *Modification Regulations* is that, until the scheme rules are amended (and the provisions of the Regulations are expressly disapplied), no additional liabilities will be imposed on schemes as a result of the introduction of the A-Day taxation regime. In particular, the limits imposed or benefits in order for a scheme to obtain tax approved status under the pre A-Day regime will continue to apply to a registered pension scheme during the transitional period. This will, of course, be of most relevance to defined benefit occupational pension schemes. At the time of writing, there is some doubt as to whether the provisions of the *Modification Regulations* may be *partially* disapplied, i e whether an amendment may be made to scheme rules in order to take advantage of some of the relaxations offered by the A-Day regime, whilst otherwise retaining the protection of the *Modification Regulations*. If this cannot be achieved, it will be necessary, from the effective date of the A-Day amendments, for the scheme rules to fully reflect the desired position with regard to any limits on benefits to be provided.

Limits applicable to exempt approved schemes

5.98 Prior to A-Day, pension schemes which were 'exempt approved schemes' under *section 592* of *ICTA 1988* gained certain tax advantages, including tax relief on employers' and employees' contributions and some relief from income tax and capital gains tax on the investment income of the fund. The HMRC exercised its discretion under *section 591* of *ICTA 1988* to approve schemes in accordance with guidelines set out in an office manual which was summarised in Practice Notes, the last version of which was IR12 (2001).

The requirements which a scheme had to meet in order to obtain approval related primarily to the maximum benefits which could be paid from the scheme. There were also limits on the contributions members could pay to the scheme, although these limits are superseded from A-Day by the provisions of *FA 2004* relating to contributions and the 'annual allowance' (see 5.16 to 5.19 above). Further details of the limits on benefits are summarised in 5.103 to 5.121 below.

It is important to note that HMRC's Practice Notes set out the maximum benefits that could be paid. Pension schemes were not obliged to pay maximum benefits and, in the vast majority of final salary schemes, the rules effectively limited the benefits payable to lesser amounts.

Remuneration and final remuneration

5.99 The maximum benefits a member could receive from an exempt approved occupational pension scheme and the maximum contributions he could make to such a scheme were calculated by reference to his 'final remuneration'. As the expression suggests, final remuneration was itself calculated by reference to 'remuneration'.

Remuneration

5.100 Remuneration included any emoluments chargeable to tax under *sections 15* or *21* of *ITEPA 2003* except:

(*a*) sums arising from the acquisition or disposal of shares or from a right to acquire shares; and

(*b*) payments on the termination of office (for example, redundancy payments and golden handshakes).

[*Chapter 3* of *Part 6* of *ITEPA 2003*]

(Glossary to IR12 (2001) and *ICTA 1988, s 612*)

Remuneration was limited in certain circumstances by legislation.

For members joining pension schemes on or after 17 March 1987, but before 1 June 1989, generally known as 'high earners', the amount of remuneration which could be used to determine cash lump sum benefits could not exceed £100,000. [*ICTA 1988, Sch 23, para 6(2)*].

The level of remuneration which may be taken into account for the purposes of determining the maximum benefits payable was restricted to the 'permitted maximum' or, as it is colloquially known, the 'earnings cap' imposed by *section 590C* of *ICTA 1988*.

The earnings cap was first introduced in 1989 and was set at £60,000 per annum for the tax year 1989/1990. The legislation contained provision for the earnings cap to be increased annually in line with the retail prices index rounded up to the nearest multiple of £600. [*ICTA 1988, s 590C(5)*]. The earnings cap for the tax year 2005/2006 was £105,600.

The earnings cap generally applied to all members of schemes established on or after 14 March 1989. It also applied to members of schemes established before 14 March 1989 who became members on or after 1 June 1989. However, it did not apply where employees were considered to have continuity of membership from before 1 June 1989. [*Retirement Benefits Schemes (Continuation of Rights of Members of Approved Schemes) Regulations 1990 (SI 1990 No 2101)*]. For example, if a member moved from one pension scheme of an employer to another scheme of the same employer he could be treated as if he had always been a member of the second scheme and so would not necessarily become subject to the earnings cap.

Pensions Update 110 reported amendments to recognise participation in employee share ownership plans and restrictive undertakings.

Amounts deducted from pay to purchase 'Partnership Shares' (which are not subject to tax under *section 15* or *21* of *ITEPA 2003*) as part of a share incentive plan could be included in the calculation of remuneration (and final remuneration – see 5.101 below) (*Finance Act 2000, Sch 8, para 83*). Pensions Update 110 also confirmed that payments made to employees on leaving in consideration for them agreeing (for example) not to work for a competitor, could not be included in remuneration as they are not a reward for working for the employer.

Final remuneration

5.101   The definition of final remuneration is set out in HMRC's IR12 (2001) Appendix I. There are two basic definitions of final remuneration depending upon the category of member involved. Broadly these definitions are:

(*a*)   the highest remuneration liable to income tax under *section 15* or *21* of *ITEPA 2003* for any one of the five years preceding a member's date of retirement, leaving pensionable service or death (whichever is earlier), being the total of:

    (i)   the basic pay for the year in question ('the basic pay year'); and

    (ii)   the yearly average over three or more consecutive years ending with the expiry of the corresponding basic pay year of any fluctuating emoluments; or

(*b*)   the yearly average of the total remuneration liable to income tax under *section 15* or *21* of *ITEPA 2003* for any three or more consecutive years ending not earlier than ten years before the date of retirement, leaving pensionable service or death (whichever is earlier).

Whichever formulae gave the best results could be used for most members but only the second formula could be used for controlling directors or other members whose remuneration after 5 April 1987 exceeded £100,000 per annum. The restriction was introduced because the directors of private companies are able to control the remuneration paid to them. Their ability to increase their remuneration just before they retire was therefore restricted by the imposition of the three year averaging. The three-year averaging also applied to any member who was a controlling director at any time in the last ten years before retirement. These restrictions prevented a director who had relinquished control just before retirement from using the best year in the last five for final remuneration purposes. A controlling director was any member who, at any time after 16 March 1987 and within ten years of retirement or leaving pensionable service, had been a director and, either on his own or with one or more associates, had beneficially owned or been able to control directly, indirectly or through other companies, 20 per cent or more of the ordinary share capital of the company. ('Controlling director' is defined, in *paragraph 5(5)* of *Schedule 23* to *ICTA 1988*, as a person who is a director (as defined in *section 612*) and is within *paragraph (b)* of *section 417(5)* in relation to the employer company).

Fluctuating emoluments include any remuneration other than basic salary which fluctuates from year to year, for example, bonuses and profit related pay (IR12 (2001) Appendix I). If only one year's fluctuating emoluments were used to arrive at the figure for final remuneration it could distort the final figures considerably or could be manipulated. There was therefore a requirement that this type of remuneration be averaged over a period of three years. If fluctuating emoluments were only paid in a single year and were to be included when calculating final remuneration, the agreement of HMRC had to be sought beforehand.

The 'basic pay year' used for calculating final remuneration would not necessarily end at the date of retirement or leaving service or death. In some cases it could be several years before then. To allow for inflation, remuneration paid in earlier years could be increased in line with the Retail Prices Index up to the last day of the basic pay year.

The date of the particular year's end that was used for calculating final remuneration was flexible provided it fell in the relevant period prior to the date of retirement, leaving service or death (as the case may be). It could, for example, be convenient to use the company's accounting year, the tax year, or the year ending on retirement.

Pension Update 110 reported modifications to recognise absences on paid maternity leave and participation in employee share ownership plans and restrictive undertakings.

Where an employee left service during a year which included paid maternity leave or within twelve months of the end of paid maternity leave, then final remuneration could include a notional amount based on the greater of the remuneration the employer would have been obliged to pay under the contract in force prior to the start of the paid maternity leave and the actual remuneration received in the twelve months immediately prior to the commencement of paid maternity leave.

As mentioned in 5.100 above, amounts deducted from pay to purchase 'Partnership Shares' (which are not subject to tax under *section 15* or *21* of *ITEPA 2003*) as part of a share incentive plan could be included in the calculation of final remuneration (*Finance Act 2000, Sch 8, para 83*).

Normal retirement date

5.102   There was a requirement that the normal retirement date of any member must be specified in the rules of the scheme (IR12 (2001) PN 6.5 to 6.11). It could differ for different categories of member but had to be between the ages of 60 to 75. Lower ages were permitted in some employments, for example, for sportsmen or those with hazardous occupations. However, HMRC pointed out in Pension Update 120 that lack of success as a result of waning popularity or the deterioration of a solo singer's or pop group's technique were not arguments that prove sufficient grounds for agreeing a low normal retirement date. Female members of occupational pension schemes who joined before 1 June 1989 were permitted to have a normal retirement date of 55. This HMRC distinction did not, however, override the requirements for equal treatment of men and women.

Maximum benefits

The three regimes

5.103   The maximum benefits in respect of a member were partly governed by his date of admission to membership of the pension scheme. There were three regimes in this respect:

(*a*)   admission to membership before 17 March 1987;

(*b*)   admission to membership of a scheme established before 14 March 1989, between 17 March 1987 and 31 May 1989 (inclusive); and

(*c*)   admission to membership from 1 June 1989.

In some circumstances a member who would otherwise have fallen within categories (*b*) and (*c*) could be treated for these purposes as if he had joined the scheme on an earlier date. [*Occupational Pension Schemes (Transitional Provisions) Regulations 1988 (SI 1988 No 1436); Retirement Benefits Schemes (Continuation of Rights of Members of Approved Schemes) Regulations 1990*

267

(*SI 1990 No 2101*)]. One example of this was where a member moved between schemes following the sale of his employer. Another was where a member was reinstated to membership following a successful claim relating to mis-selling of personal pensions.

Members who fell within categories (*a*) and (*b*) were said to have 'continued rights' (IR12 (2001) Appendix III). Such a member could elect to be treated as if he had been admitted to membership on or after 1 June 1989. An election could be made at any time before benefits commenced, were bought out or transferred, or attainment of age 75, whichever occurred first. Following such an election the member's benefits would be based on HMRC's permitted maxima for members joining pension schemes on or after 1 June 1989, but they became subject to the earnings cap (see 5.100 above).

Pension at normal retirement date

Maximum total benefits

5.104 The maximum total benefits that could be provided on retirement under an approved scheme were calculated by reference to an employee's length of service with the employer and his final remuneration. Total benefits were measured in terms of an annual pension for the member payable for life being the aggregate of any pension payable (including, where the member did not fall within the administrative easement described in 5.105 below (IR12 (2001) PN 7.7), any pension debit) and the pension equivalent of any non-pension benefits (IR12 (2001) PN 7.2). The maximum aggregate benefit payable without taking account of 'retained benefits' (see 5.121 below) was a pension (of which part could be taken in lump sum form as described in 5.108 below) of $\frac{1}{60}$th of final remuneration for each year of service (up to 40 years) (IR12 (2001) PN 7.3). However, this was subject to special provisions relating to controlling directors (IR12 (2001) PN 7.10) and the aggregation of benefits with other approved schemes (IR12 (2001) PN 7.25 and 7.26).

Pension sharing easement

5.105 Under an administrative easement, pension debits could be ignored in calculating the member's maximum permissible total benefits, both pension and lump sum, under IR12 (2001) PN 7.2. With two important exceptions, the easement applied to members of schemes other than simplified defined contribution schemes. The first exception was a controlling director (within the meaning in *regulation 5(5)* of the *Retirement Benefits Schemes (Sharing of Pensions on Divorce or Annulment) Regulations 2000* (*SI 2000 No 1085*). The second exception related to members whose earnings exceeded one quarter of the permitted maximum determined at its level for the year of assessment in which the marriage was dissolved. For this purpose, earnings meant those in respect of pensionable service to which the scheme related, and which were received during the year of assessment immediately preceding the year of assessment in which the dissolution or annulment of the marriage occurred, and from which tax was deducted under PAYE.

The test was applied as at the date of divorce and once it was satisfied, the pension debit could be permanently ignored, that is irrespective of subsequent employment changes (IR12 (2001) PN 7.7).

Pre-17 March 1987 member

5.106   For a member who became, or was treated as having become, a member prior to 17 March 1987, the maximum permissible pension of two-thirds of final remuneration could be accrued over a period of ten years' service, in accordance with the following table:

Years of service to normal retirement date	Maximum pension (before any commutation and including the annuity value of any lump sum entitlement) expressed as 60ths of final remuneration
1–5	1 for each year
6	8
7	16
8	24
9	32
10 or more	40

Regardless of the date on which the member joined the scheme, the pension (unless it did not exceed ⅟₆₀th of final remuneration for each year of service) could not, when aggregated with any 'retained benefits' (see 5.121 below), exceed two-thirds of final remuneration.

Post-17 March 1987 member

5.107   The maximum pension payable to a member on retirement at normal retirement date was, as indicated in 5.104 above, two-thirds of his final remuneration (IR12 (2001) Part 7). For a person who became, or was treated as having become, a member on or after 17 March 1987 (that is a person who was within either category (*b*) or (*c*) as described in 5.103 above) this was restricted to ⅟₃₀th of final remuneration for each year of service subject to a maximum of 20 years.

Cash lump sum at normal retirement date

5.108   Members were allowed to commute some or all of their pension for a tax-free cash lump sum (IR12 (2001) Part 8). Pensions Update 135 issued on 20 December 2002 clarified how the Inland Revenue expected approved schemes to administer tax-free lump sum retirement benefits. The lump sum was limited to no more than ⅜₀ths of final remuneration for each year of service up to a maximum of 40 years. This allowed a cash lump sum of one and a half times final remuneration to be paid after 40 years of service. A higher accrual rate was permitted if the member had continued rights (see 5.103 above).

The actual accrual rate depended on when the member was treated as having joined the scheme and was calculated in accordance with 5.109 to 5.111 below as appropriate.

Pre-17 March 1987 member

5.109   If the member was treated as having joined the scheme before 17 March 1987, the following table applied:

Years of service to normal retirement date	Maximum lump sum expressed as 80ths of final remuneration
1–8	3 for each year
9	30
10	36
11	42
12	48
13	54
14	63
15	72
16	81
17	90
18	99
19	108
20 or more	120

The limits described in this paragraph did not apply where a member's benefit entitlement in a scheme was permanently reduced following a pension sharing order and the member did not fall within the pension sharing administrative easement described in 5.105 above. The calculation of the maximum lump sum benefit, in these circumstances, depended on whether the lump sum is obtained by commutation of pension or whether the scheme rules provided for a pension and a separate lump sum rather than a commutable pension. In the former case the maximum lump sum benefit was the greater of:

(*a*)   2.25 times the initial annual rate of pension after reduction to take account of the pension debit; or

(*b*)   an amount determined in accordance with the scheme rules as if there had been no pension share, then reduced by 2.25 times the amount of pension from the pension debit calculated at the member's normal retirement date.

Where scheme rules provided for a pension and a separate lump sum as opposed to a commutable pension, the maximum lump sum benefit was the greater of:

(*a*)   three times the initial annual rate of the separate pension after reduction to take account of the pension debit; or

(*b*)   an amount determined in accordance with the scheme rules as if there had been no pension share, but then reduced by three times the amount of pension from the pension debit calculated at the member's normal retirement date (IR12 (2001) PN 8.26).

Post-17 March 1987 but pre-31 May 1989 member

5.110   If the member was treated as having joined the scheme during the period from 17 March 1987 to 31 May 1989 (inclusive) then (except for schemes commencing on or after 14 March 1989 (see 5.111 below)) a more complex formula applied. The member could use the higher accrual rate set out in the table in 5.109 above, but only to the same proportionate extent that his pension from the scheme (before any part of it had been exchanged for a lump sum or given up to provide further pensions for dependants) fell within the range between ⅟₆₀th and ⅟₈₀th of final remuneration for each year.

These limits did not apply where a member's benefit entitlement in a scheme had been permanently reduced following a pension sharing order and the member did not fall within the administrative easement. In such circumstances, the maximum lump sum benefit was calculated in accordance with 5.109 above.

Post-1 June 1989 member

5.111   If the member was treated as having joined the scheme on or after 1 June 1989 (or before then if the scheme itself commenced on or after 14 March 1989), and his pension (before any part of it had been exchanged for a lump sum or given up to provide further pensions for dependants) exceeded

⅟₆₀th of final remuneration for each year of service, his lump sum could be increased to 2.25 times the annual amount of that pension.

However, in any of the above cases, the lump sum plus any 'retained benefits' (see 5.121 below) could not exceed one and a half times final remuneration.

For the purpose of calculating Revenue limits, commutation factors were set by the Inland Revenue to determine the cash value provided for each £1.00 of pension given up (IR12 (2001) Part 7). A commutation factor of 12:1 had to be used irrespective of age, sex or escalation rate for current members and those members with continued rights who opted for the post-1 June 1989 regime. For members with continued rights, commutation factors differed according to age. At age 60 a commutation factor of between 10.2 and 11.0 could be used; at age 65 the range was 9.0 to 9.8 (IR12 (2001) PN 7.59). It was possible to agree enhanced commutation factors with HMRC outside these ranges.

Early retirement and leaving service before normal retirement date

5.112   The rules of approved occupational pension schemes could permit members to draw early retirement benefits at any age after 50 (or earlier on grounds of incapacity) provided they actually retired or ceased pensionable service with the employer concerned (IR12 (2001) PN 10.8). A female member with continued rights could receive early retirement benefits from age 45 if she retired within ten years of her normal retirement date as such members were permitted to have a normal retirement date of 55.

The receipt of an early retirement pension did not preclude a member from taking up employment elsewhere although the early retirement benefits may have had to be taken into account as 'retained benefits' (see 5.121 below) if the member joined the subsequent employer's pension scheme. If a member was subsequently re-employed by the employer from whose scheme early retirement benefits had been, or were being, paid the rules of the scheme could permit the suspension of the early retirement pension (IR12 (2001) PN 7.32); if the member was to accrue further benefits under the scheme the early retirement benefits had to be suspended (IR12 (2001) Appendix IV).

Early retirement on grounds of incapacity

5.113   If a member retired early at any age on grounds of incapacity, his benefits could be calculated in the same manner as if he had retired at normal retirement date. Both his actual service and potential service (i e the service he would have completed had he remained a member up to his normal retirement date) could count towards the calculation. Final remuneration was calculated as at his date of actual retirement.

'Incapacity' is defined in the Glossary to IR12 (2001) as 'physical or mental deterioration which is sufficiently serious to prevent the individual from following his or her normal employment, or which seriously impairs his or her earning capacity. It does not mean simply a decline in energy or ability'.

Early retirement other than on grounds of incapacity

5.114 The maximum pension payable from an approved scheme on early retirement, other than on grounds of incapacity (IR12 (2001) PN 10.9 to 10.14), for a member without continued rights was the greater of:

(*a*)   ¹⁄₆₀th of final remuneration for each year of service up to a maximum of 40 years; and

(*b*)   the lesser of:

(i)   ¹⁄₃₀th of final remuneration for each year of service up to a maximum of 20 years; and

(ii)   ²⁄₃rds of final remuneration less 'retained benefits' (see 5.121 below).

Where the member had a pension debit in relation to the scheme and did not fall within the administrative easement described in 5.105 above, the maximum benefits were calculated in accordance with the requirements set out above but had to be reduced by the pension debit.

The maximum cash lump sum payable in such circumstances (IR12 (2001) PN 10.15 to 10.18) was ³⁄₈₀ths of final remuneration for each year of service up to a maximum of 40 years or, if greater, an amount equal to 2.25 times the initial annual rate of pension to be paid (before any part of that pension had been commuted for the lump sum or given up to provide further pensions for dependants). However, (unless the lump sum did not exceed ³⁄₈₀th of final remuneration for each year of service) the lump sum could not, when aggregated with any 'retained benefits' (see 5.121 below), exceed one and a half times final remuneration.

For members with continued rights (see 5.103 above), the maximum pension on early retirement was either ¹⁄₆₀th of final remuneration for each year of service up to a maximum of 40 years or, if more favourable, the amount calculated by the formula:

N / NS x P;

where:

N is the number of actual years of service up to a maximum of 40 years;

NS is the number of actual years of service plus years of potential service to normal retirement date; and

P is the maximum pension the member could have received had he remained in service until normal retirement date calculated by reference to final remuneration as at the date of termination of pensionable service.

For members with continued rights (see 5.103 above) the maximum cash lump sum available on early retirement was either ⅜₀ths of final remuneration for each year of service up to a maximum of 40 years or, if more favourable, the amount calculated by the formula:

N / NS x LS;

where:

N is the number of actual years of service with a maximum of 40 years;

NS is the number of actual years of service plus years of potential service to normal retirement date; and

LS is the maximum lump sum the member could have received had he remained in pensionable service until normal retirement date calculated by reference to final remuneration at the date of termination of pensionable service.

Leaving service benefits

5.115   If a member leaves service before reaching normal retirement date, several options were available regarding his accrued benefits (IR12 (2001) Part 10). If the member was at least age 50, retirement benefits could be paid immediately if the scheme's rules permitted it. If the member had not reached age 50, benefits could be left in the scheme and paid after age 50 as early retirement benefits or at normal retirement date. The maximum benefits payable on leaving service in respect of pensions and cash lump sums were, broadly, the same as those payable on early retirement.

Alternatively a deferred annuity could be purchased or a transfer value paid to another occupational or personal pension scheme. In these circumstances, it is important to remember that the amount used to purchase the annuity or the amount of the transfer value could not exceed HMRC's maximum amount for early retirement benefits. In particular, there were limitations on making transfer payments to personal pension schemes for controlling directors and other members whose remuneration exceeded the earnings cap. [*Personal Pension Schemes (Transfer Payments) Regulations 2001 (SI 2001 No 119)*].

Retirement after normal retirement date

5.116   In certain circumstances, a member could be permitted to postpone receipt of his benefits until after normal retirement date (IR12 (2001) PN 7.43 to 7.46). The calculation of the maximum pension permissible by HMRC on late retirement depended on whether the member had continued rights.

If the member had continued rights (see 5.103 above), his maximum pension was the greatest of:

(*a*)   his maximum pension at normal retirement date, but substituting the date of actual retirement for normal retirement date;

(*b*)   his maximum pension at normal retirement date plus ⅟₆₀th (up to a maximum of ⅝₀th) for each further year of service over 40 years after normal retirement date; and

(*c*)   his maximum pension at normal retirement date increased by increases in the Retail Price Index or by actuarial increases (whichever produces the greater result) since normal retirement date,

except that the first two options were not available to controlling directors other than in respect of service after age 70.

If the member did not have continued rights (see 5.103 above), the maximum pension was the maximum pension he could have received if his date of actual retirement had been substituted for his normal retirement date.

Death benefits

Lump sums payable on death in service before normal retirement date

5.117   On a member's death in service before reaching normal retirement date (IR12 (2001) Part 11), a lump sum could be paid equal to the greater of:

(*a*)   £5,000; and

(*b*)   four times final remuneration less 'retained benefits' (see 5.121 below).

In addition, a refund of the member's own contributions could be paid with or without interest. As a member's death cannot be foreseen, the definition of final remuneration was more generous than at normal retirement date. Final remuneration on death could be:

(i) the annual basic salary immediately before death; or

(ii) the annual basic salary immediately before death plus the average of fluctuating emoluments during the three years up to the date of death; or

(iii) the total remuneration, fixed and fluctuating, paid during any period of 12 months falling within the three years prior to death.

If a scheme's rules provided for a lump sum benefit on death that did not exceed twice the member's final remuneration, 'retained benefits' (see 5.121 below) did not need to be taken into account.

Spouses' and dependants' benefits

5.118 Following the death of a member in service or after retirement, a spouse's and/or dependant's pension could be provided. The maximum level of all such pensions could not exceed two-thirds of the maximum pension that could have been provided for the deceased member had he retired due to incapacity immediately before death, calculated on the basis of there being no lump sum commutation at retirement and as if the deceased had no 'retained benefits' (see 5.121 below) from earlier occupations.

Death of an early leaver

5.119 If a former member died before age 50, having deferred benefits in the scheme, a cash lump sum could be paid. Spouse's and dependant's pensions could also be provided, calculated by reference to the deceased member's maximum approvable deferred pension.

Death in service after normal retirement date

5.120 Where a member died in service after normal retirement date, maximum benefits could be provided on the basis of death in service (see 5.117 and 5.118 above). In the case of a member with continued rights, benefits could be provided on the basis that the member died in retirement having retired the day before the date of death.

Retained benefits

5.121   Retained benefits *(IR12 (2001) Appendix I)* generally were retained rights to relevant benefits and, where appropriate, pension debits built up in previous employments or periods of self-employment from schemes or contractual arrangements which have benefited from tax privileges. These included:

(*a*)   retirement benefit schemes approved by HMRC or seeking approval;

(*b*)   retirement annuity contracts and personal pension schemes; and

(*c*)   certain overseas schemes.

Retained benefits could be ignored in any of the following circumstances:

(i)   in the case of pensions benefits, if they did not exceed £260 in total from all sources;

(ii)   in the case of lump sum retirement benefits, if they did not exceed £2,500 in total from all sources;

(iii)   in the case of death benefits, if they did not exceed £2,500 in total from all sources;

(iv)   refund of a member's personal contributions.

Appendix 1 to IR12 (2001) describes 'relevant benefits' as follows:

'Relevant Benefits are defined in *section 612 (1)* of *ICTA 1988* in very wide terms, and broadly cover any type of financial benefit given by an employer on retirement or death or by virtue of a pension sharing order but excluding benefits given in connection with genuine redundancy (as opposed to retirement). The definition does not include benefits receivable only in the event of death by accident or disablement by accident during service'.

Appendix 1 to IR12 (2001) describes 'retirement benefits scheme' as follows:

'Retirement Benefits Scheme is defined in *section 611* as a scheme for the provision of *relevant benefits* for one or more employees but does not include any national scheme (such as the State Earnings Related Pension Scheme) providing such benefits. In this context "scheme" needs to be interpreted widely to include any arrangement creating an enforceable right to such benefits and an arrangement to pay ex-gratia *relevant benefits* (although the latter type of arrangement is not approvable unless the benefit is in the form of a lump sum and satisfies certain conditions). Employee includes an ex-employee. "Employees" and "employee" are replaced by

"scheme members" and "scheme member" in *subsection (3)* and *(4)(b)* of *section 611* and *subsection (b)* defines "scheme member" as including both employees and ex spouses.'

Section C

Non-registered pension schemes

5.122   From 6 April 2006 pension schemes which are not registered pension schemes will be employer-financed retirement benefit schemes ('EFRBS'). Essentially, all existing pre A-Day unapproved pension schemes will come under the tax regime applicable to EFRBS.

Existing unapproved arrangements

5.123   Prior to A-Day, unapproved pension schemes were established by employers to top up benefits for employees whose benefits were limited by legislation. This applied, in particular, to employees subject to the so-called 'earnings cap' (see 5.100 above). There were two types of unapproved schemes – funded unapproved retirement benefit schemes ('FURBS') and unfunded unapproved retirement benefit schemes ('UURBS').

FURBS

5.124   In broad terms, the pre A-Day tax treatment of a FURBS can be summarised as set out below.

(*a*)   Contributions by the employer were allowable against corporation tax as soon as they were made.

(*b*)   The employee was taxed on the employer's contributions as a benefit in kind.

(*c*)   National Insurance contributions ('NICs') were payable on the contributions made.

(*d*)   Investment returns were subject to tax at the basic rate on income (provided the FURBS was established for the sole purpose of providing 'relevant benefits', as defined in *section 612* of *ICTA 1988*, as applicable prior to 6 April 2006), and capital gains were subject to capital gains tax (with tapering relief available).

(*e*) Benefits payable to the employee were subject to income tax when paid as a pension; however, there was no liability to income tax if the benefits were paid as a lump sum (as long as the employer's contributions had been taxed on the employee as a benefit in kind when they were paid in). In practice, all benefits paid from FURBS on an employee's retirement have been paid as a tax-free lump sum in order to avoid the double tax charge. No NICs were payable on the lump sum.

(*f*) Lump sum benefits on the death of an employee were free from liability to income tax and also free from inheritance tax, provided that the benefits were paid under a discretionary trust and the FURBS qualified as a 'sponsored superannuation scheme' (as defined in *section 624* of *ICTA 1988*, as applicable prior to 6 April 1988).

UURBS

5.125   The pre A-Day tax treatment of an UURBS is considerably more straightforward than that of a FURBS and can be summarised as set out below.

(*a*) Payments of benefit made to an employee were deductible for corporation tax when made.

(*b*) The employee was subject to income tax on payment of the benefit (whether paid as a lump sum or a pension).

(*c*) Lump sum benefits on the death of an employee were free from inheritance tax if they were provided from a 'sponsored superannuation scheme' under a discretionary trust; however, income tax was payable on the benefit (unless it was insured – i e 'funded').

EFRBS from A-Day

5.126   As EFRBS are not registered pension schemes, they will not be subject to the new taxation regime set out in *FA 2004*, the key provisions of which are detailed in section A of this chapter.

The introduction of the new regime has a significant impact on pre A-Day unapproved schemes. In view of the flexibility of the new regime to allow for (potentially) unlimited pensions within registered schemes, the only limit being on how much tax relief is given, the Government's view is that non-registered arrangements as separate top-up vehicles are no longer essential, unless the aim is to provide benefits that would not be allowed under a registered scheme. Consequently, under the new taxation regime, although non-registered pension schemes will be allowed to continue, they will not receive any particular tax-favoured status. In particular, it should be noted that the exemptions from inheritance tax previously afforded to 'sponsored superannuation schemes' will no longer apply (see 5.129 below).

A summary of the tax treatment of EFRBS from 6 April 2006 is set out below.

(*a*)   The value of the individual's benefits will not be taken into account for the purpose of testing against the lifetime allowance (see 5.7 above).

(*b*)   Contributions will not be subject to the annual allowance charge (see 5.18 above).

(*c*)   All contributions paid after 5 April 2006 will be treated as if made to an employee benefit trust. This means that there will be no income tax or NICs payable when contributions are made, but also no corporation tax relief for the employer on those contributions. When the benefits are paid, income tax will be charged and relief from corporation tax given.

(*d*)   So long as the employment relationship between employer and employee has ceased, it would appear from draft regulations that there will be no National Insurance charge on the benefits paid from an EFRBS, provided that the benefits are within the limits of benefits that can be paid under a registered scheme. As registered pension schemes may only pay a lump sum retirement benefit of up to a maximum of (broadly) 25 per cent of the value of the scheme benefits (see 5.42 above), this means that, in order to avoid any National Insurance charge, the lump sum must not exceed 25 per cent of the fund.

(*e*)   The taxation of investment income is being aligned with the rates paid by higher rate taxpayers. Investment returns, whether income or capital gains, will be taxed at 40 per cent (dividends at 32.5 per cent). Tapering relief will continue to be available on capital gains tax.

(*f*)   There will be no automatic relief from inheritance tax (see 5.129 below).

Unfunded EFRBS

5.127   It can be seen from the above summary that the tax treatment of EFRBS is similar to the tax regime to which UURBS were subject prior to A-Day. Consequently, there will continue to be a place for unfunded EFRBS under the new regime. Indeed, if an employee already has, or is likely by retirement to have, benefits that exceed the lifetime allowance, an unfunded EFRBS could be a viable option for providing retirement benefits in excess of this amount. The rate of tax on benefits payable under the EFRBS (currently 40 per cent) is less than the penal 55 per cent applied to lump sums in excess of the lifetime allowance payable from a registered scheme.

The attraction to the employee of an unfunded EFRBS will depend upon his view as to security. An unfunded benefit promise is only of value to the extent that the employer remains in existence and is able to pay the benefit. One way of addressing this concern is to provide some form of security for the promise, such as a charge over certain assets. Under the pre A-Day taxation regime, there was some doubt as to whether, if an UURBS promise was secured, the security provided would be considered by HMRC as providing funding for the UURBS, with a resultant tax charge upon the employee (see 5.124 (*b*) above). The legislation that gave rise to this concern (*section 386(1)* of *ITEPA 2003*) has, from 6 April 2006, been repealed, as the provisions are not required under the new taxation regime. This is because employees will now be taxed on receipt of benefits from an EFRBS whether the scheme is funded or unfunded.

With regard to those employees who have existing UURBS arrangements in place at 6 April 2006 whose retirement benefits are not likely to exceed the lifetime allowance (or in relation to benefits up to the lifetime allowance), there is no reason why these benefits cannot now be provided under an employer's registered pension scheme. Any UURBS in place before 6 April 2006 can be consolidated and rolled into a registered scheme. If this is done before 6 July 2006, the increase in the value of the registered scheme benefits resulting from the inclusion of the UURBS benefits will not count towards the annual allowance when the employer 'capitalises' the pension promise. If unfunded benefits are rolled into a registered scheme at any other time (other than in the tax year in which the individual becomes entitled to the benefits), they will count against the individual's annual allowance in the tax year in which benefits are included in the registered scheme.

In connection with any proposal to roll unfunded benefits into a registered pension scheme, it should be borne in mind that, were the registered pension scheme to enter into the Pension Protection Fund (see chapter 17), there is a cap on benefits which is initially set at £25,000 per year (in the tax year 2005/2006). A secured unfunded EFRBS, as referred to above, might therefore be a more attractive option.

Funded EFRBS

5.128   The absence of any tax relief on contributions paid by an employer after 5 April 2006 to an EFRBS makes funded EFRBS an unattractive option (at least for employers). There are, however, transitional protections for pre-6 April 2006 FURBS. Benefits under an EFRBS that were accrued before 6 April 2006 may still be payable as a tax-free lump sum, provided that the employee was taxed on the employer's contributions paid into the arrangement (see 5.124 (*b*) and (*e*) above). If contributions continue to be paid into an EFRBS after 5 April 2006, the emerging lump sum will be apportioned between the pre-6 April 2006 (tax-free) and post-5 April 2006 (taxable) elements. Consequently, it seems likely that most employers will seek to cease paying contributions into EFRBS (which were previously FURBS) after 5 April 2006 and investigate other options for compensating the employee.

Inheritance tax

5.129   Pension schemes established under trust are settled property for inheritance tax ('IHT') purposes. A number of specific exemptions take registered pension schemes outside the usual charges on this type of settlement for IHT purposes (see 5.81 above). Prior to 6 April 2006, most FURBS were also able to obtain these exemptions by virtue of being 'sponsored superannuation schemes' (*section 151(1)* of *IHTA 1984*). In practice, this required the payment of a separately identifiable administration charge by the employer. However, the exemption for sponsored superannuation schemes has, from 6 April 2006, been repealed (by *section 203(4)* of *FA 2004*). This means that EFRBS will be subject to the periodic charge and exit charge applicable to settlements without interest in possession (referred to in 5.81 above). Transitional IHT protection is available for pre-6 April 2006 funds.

Chapter 6

Protection for early leavers

Introduction

General

6.1　One of the main sources of dissatisfaction with occupational pension schemes historically has been the treatment of members who leave such schemes (usually because they have left employment) before normal pension age. (The meaning of 'normal pension age' is discussed in 6.23 below.)

Consequently, legislation has introduced the following protections for early leavers relating to 'preservation' (see 6.2 below), revaluation (see 6.3 to 6.5 below) and transfer values (see 6.6 below).

Preservation requirements

6.2　The preservation requirements set out the benefits which occupational pension schemes are required to provide for early leavers. These requirements are summarised in 6.10 to 6.29 below.

The preservation requirements were first introduced by the *Social Security Act 1973* with effect from 6 April 1975, but have since been amended to give increased protection to leavers. They are now consolidated in *Chapter I* of *Part IV* (i e *sections 69* to *82*) of the *Pension Schemes Act 1993* (*PSA 1993*) and the *Occupational Pension Schemes* (*Preservation of Benefit*) *Regulations 1991* (*SI 1991 No 167*) ('the *Preservation Regulations*').

Revaluation

6.3　An early leaver's scheme entitlement under the preservation requirements (see 6.2 above) will most typically take the form of a deferred pension from the scheme, prospectively payable from his normal pension age.

Legislation requires the calculation of any such pension to be revalued in respect of the period of deferment. Two separate types of revaluation apply, depending on whether or not the benefit concerned is a 'guaranteed minimum pension' earned in relation to pre-6 April 1997 contracted-out employment (see chapter 4).

Revaluation of benefits other than guaranteed minimum pensions

6.4   This is governed by *Chapter II* of *Part IV* (i e *sections 83* to *86*) of *PSA 1993*. (These requirements were first introduced by the *Social Security Act 1985*, but have since been revised; they are discussed in 6.30 to 6.41 below).

Revaluation of guaranteed minimum pensions

6.5   This is governed by *Chapter III* of *Part IV* (i e *sections 87* to *92*) of *PSA 1993*. These requirements (which were originally introduced by the *Health and Social Security Act 1984*) are summarised in chapter 4.

Transfer values

6.6   *Chapter IV* of *Part IV* (i e *sections 93* to *101*) of *PSA 1993* sets out certain statutory entitlements for an early leaver to require that a sum representing his rights under the scheme be used in one of a number of ways (for example, transferred to another scheme or used to buy him an annuity). This right (first introduced by the *Social Security Act 1985*) is covered further in 6.43 below.

Chapter V of *Part IV* (i e *sections 101AA* to *101AI*) of *PSA 1993* was inserted by *section 264* of *PA 2004* with effect from 6 April 2006. These provisions will give those leaving service with at least three months' pensionable service, but without any vested rights, the opportunity to take a cash transfer sum as an alternative to a refund of contributions. This is covered further in 6.59 below.

Scope of early leaver legislation

Schemes affected

6.7   The legislation referred to in 6.1 to 6.6 above applies to occupational pension schemes (as now defined in *PSA 1993*). The High Court, in the case of *Royal Masonic Hospital v Pensions Ombudsman [2001] 01 PBLR (9)* overturned the decision of the Pensions Ombudsman concerning the scope of the preservation requirements. The court held that *section 69* of *PSA 1993* did not cover unfunded private sector schemes as the pension promise was merely a contractual one that would be met in the future from the general assets of the employer rather than from an accrued fund.

Relationship of early leaver legislation to scheme rules

6.8   *Chapter I* of *Part IV* of *PSA 1993* (which relates to preservation) effectively requires that scheme rules contain provisions which comply with the preservation requirements (summarised in 6.10 to 6.29 below). However, *Chapter I* does not actually go so far as to override the scheme rules if they do not comply. [*PSA 1993, s 131*]. Nevertheless, even though *Chapter I* does not override the scheme rules, employers and trustees can still be challenged by members and beneficiaries for operating a scheme whose rules do not fulfil the preservation requirements (see 6.9 below). In particular, it should be noted that *section 132* of *PSA 1993* requires trustees, where their scheme's rules do not meet the preservation requirements, to take such steps as are open to them for rectifying this.

By contrast, *Chapters II, III, IV* and *V* of *Part IV* of *PSA 1993* (which relate to revaluation and transfer values) do override the scheme rules (subject to limited exceptions). [*PSA 1993, s 129*].

Enforcement of preservation legislation

6.9   Until 6 April 1997 the Occupational Pensions Board ('OPB') had certain functions relating to preservation, including the power to determine whether a scheme's rules complied with the preservation requirements and powers to modify scheme rules so as to ensure compliance with those requirements.

However, the OPB was dissolved on 5 April 1997, and the functions of the OPB relating to preservation were not transferred to any other regulatory body. A member who is not satisfied that his scheme complies with preservation can instead seek recourse against the employer and/or the trustees through an application to the Pensions Ombudsman (see chapter 16) or through the courts.

Preservation

Defined terms

6.10   *PSA 1993* uses a number of defined terms in relation to the preservation requirements. These are broadly summarised below.

'2 years' qualifying service'

6.11   This is defined in *section 71(7)* of *PSA 1993*. It means two years (whether a single period of that duration or two or more periods, continuous or discontinuous, totalling two years) in which the member was at all times employed either:

(*a*)   in 'pensionable service' (see 6.12 below) under the scheme; or

(*b*)   in service in employment which was contracted out by reference to the scheme; or

(*c*)   in 'linked qualifying service' (see 6.13 below) under another scheme.

There are special provisions in relation to periods of service previously terminated. [*PSA 1993, s 71(9)* and the *Preservation Regulations (SI 1991 No 167), reg 21*].

'Pensionable service'

6.12   This is defined in *section 70(2)* of *PSA 1993*. In effect, pensionable service means actual service in employment to which the scheme relates which qualifies the member (assuming it continues for long enough) for retirement benefits at normal pension age.

There are detailed regulations regarding breaks in pensionable service. [*Preservation Regulations (SI 1991 No 167), reg 21*]. In particular, the service before and after the break must be added together (in ascertaining whether there are two years' qualifying service – see 6.11 above) where one or more of the following conditions are satisfied:

(*a*)   the break does not exceed one month; or

(*b*)   the break corresponds to the member's absence from work wholly or partly because of pregnancy or confinement and the member returns to pensionable service no later than one month after returning to work in exercise of her statutory rights to return to work; or

(*c*)   the break corresponds to the member's absence from work in furtherance of a 'trade dispute' as defined in the *Social Security Act 1975*.

(Whether or not the break counts towards pension benefits is determined not only by the rules of the scheme, but also by any relevant employment and pensions legislation – particularly where the period is a period of maternity leave (see chapter 9).)

'Linked qualifying service'

6.13   Linked qualifying service is relevant where the scheme has accepted a transfer payment from another occupational pension scheme or a buy-out policy. The qualifying service under the transferring scheme or noted in the buy-out policy, is added to qualifying service in the scheme receiving the transfer payment. The trustees will be given certified details of the qualifying service as part of the conditions for accepting the transfer payment. The detailed definition of linked qualifying service is contained in *section 179* of *PSA 1993*. This includes restrictions on what can and cannot count as linked qualifying service. For example, regard can only be had to 'actual service'.

'Normal pension age'

6.14   Normal pension age is defined in *section 180* of *PSA 1993* and is discussed in detail in 6.23 below. The term is relevant to the questions as to whether a member is an early leaver and when a preserved pension for him becomes payable.

'Long service benefit'

6.15   Long service benefit is defined in *section 70(1)* of *PSA 1993*. It can broadly be seen as those:

(*a*)   retirement benefits for a member at normal pension age; and

(*b*)   benefits for his spouse, civil partner, dependants or others on his attaining normal pension age or, if later, death,

which would have been payable under the scheme had the member remained in pensionable service until normal pension age.

'Short service benefit'

6.16   Short service benefit is the benefit which a scheme may be required to provide in respect of an early leaver unless one of the prescribed 'alternatives to short service benefit' (see 6.24 to 6.27 below) applies instead. The definition is contained in *section 71* of *PSA 1993*.

Qualifying for short service benefit

6.17   Under *section 71(1)* of *PSA 1993*, a scheme must provide short service benefit (consisting of benefit of any description which would otherwise have been payable as long service benefit) where a member's pensionable service is terminated before normal pension age and:

(*a*)   he has at least two years' qualifying service; or

(*b*)   a transfer payment in respect of his rights under a personal pension scheme has been made to the scheme.

The short service benefit is generally payable from the member's normal pension age or age 60 if later (see 6.23 below).

Calculating the short service benefit – an overview

6.18   The method of calculation of short service benefit is set out in *section 74* of *PSA 1993*.

Same basis as long service benefit

6.19   *Section 74(1)* of *PSA 1993* requires that, except where the principle of 'uniform accrual' applies (see 6.20 below), 'a scheme must provide for short service benefit to be computed on the same basis as long service benefit'.

The application of this requirement to defined contributions benefits is relatively simple. If a scheme provides long service benefit on a defined contributions basis, the corresponding short service benefit should also be defined contributions and computed on the same basis. Further details regarding defined contributions benefits are contained in *regulation 14* of the *Preservation Regulations* (*SI 1991 No 167*).

Where long service benefits are calculated by reference to a member's salary at normal pension age, short service benefits must also be calculated in a corresponding manner by reference to the member's salary at the date of termination of pensionable service. Similarly, if the member's salary is averaged over a specified period before normal pension age when calculating his long service benefits, a period of the same duration must be used to average the member's salary for the purpose of calculating short service benefits. [*PSA 1993, s 74(7)*].

The calculation of short service benefit in relation to defined benefits can be illustrated by the following example:

A member's pension, calculated at normal pension age, is ¹⁄₆₀th of final pensionable salary for each year of pensionable service. Final pensionable salary is defined as the average of the member's salary over the three years immediately preceding normal pension age. The member joins the scheme at age 30 and his normal pension age is 65. The calculation of his pension will be as follows:

(a)   if the member stays to normal pension age, and so completes 35 years of pensionable service, his long service benefit will be a pension of $^{35}\!/_{60}$th of final pensionable salary, calculated by averaging his salary over the three years immediately preceding normal pension age; but

(b)   if the member leaves pensionable service, say, at age 40, having completed ten years of pensionable service, his short service benefit will be a pension of $^{10}\!/_{60}$th of final pensionable salary, calculated by averaging his salary over the three years immediately preceding the date of leaving pensionable service. This pension will be payable from the scheme at the normal pension age of 65.

Uniform accrual

6.20   There are a number of circumstances where the legislation requires that short service benefits be computed on the basis of 'uniform accrual' rather than as set out in 6.19 above. [*PSA 1993, s 74(6)*]. In particular, uniform accrual must be applied where the following situations arise, namely:

(a)   the long service benefit formula is not related to the length of pensionable service or the number or amount of contributions paid (*PSA 1993, s 74(4)*); or

(b)   the long service benefit accrues at a higher rate or otherwise more favourably if the member's pensionable service is of some specified minimum length or if he remains in pensionable service up to a specified minimum age (*PSA 1993, s 74(3)*).

The common strand running through those instances where uniform accrual is required is that there is no obvious accrual rate in the scheme rules or the only accrual rate available would give an anomalous result.

The principle of uniform accrual is that benefits accrue evenly over the period of pensionable service (thus creating a notional accrual rate). This is best illustrated by way of an example:

A member joins a scheme at age 30 and is promised a pension of two-thirds of his salary on retirement at age 60. This formula is not related to his length of pensionable service and so, under *sections 74(4)* and *74(6)* of *PSA 1993*, uniform accrual applies. The principle of uniform accrual treats the 'two-thirds' pension, which he will receive at age 60 if he remains in pensionable service, as accruing uniformly throughout the 30 years of his pensionable service (i e from age 30 to age 60). If the member leaves at age 45, he will have completed one half of this 30 year period (i e 15 years), so his short service benefit will be one half of the 'two-thirds' pension which he would have received had he stayed to age 60 (i e one-third of his salary at the date of termination of pensionable service).

Uniform accrual also applies (in a slightly different way) to any part of a member's long service benefit which derives from a benefit improvement granted in relation to previous pensionable service. In these circumstances, the benefit improvement is treated as accruing uniformly over the period from the date when the improvement was granted to the attainment of normal pension age. [*PSA 1993, s 75(5)*].

Death in service benefits not preserved

6.21 It should be noted that the definition of 'long service benefit' contained in *section 70* of *PSA 1993* does not cover death in service benefits. Consequently a scheme is not required by the preservations laws to provide death benefits where an early leaver subsequently dies before normal pension age (although many schemes do provide some level of benefit in these circumstances).

Discretionary benefits

6.22 A further question which arises is how far discretionary benefits must be preserved. *Section 72(1)* of *PSA 1993* provides that a scheme must not contain any rule which could result in an early leaver being treated less favourably for any purpose relating to short service benefit than he would have been treated for the same purpose relating to long service benefit if he had stayed in service. However, this does not apply to a rule which merely confers discretion on the trustees or some other person, so long as the rule does not specifically require the discretion to be exercised in any discriminatory manner against members in respect of the short service benefit. [*PSA 1993, s 72(3)*]. It is therefore arguable that a scheme rule relating to discretionary augmentation which provides that the trustees cannot consider deferred members is discriminatory.

Date of payment of preserved benefits

6.23 Short service benefits are payable from 'normal pension age' or age 60 (whichever is the later). [*PSA 1993, s 71(3)*].

A member's 'normal pension age' is defined in *section 180* of *PSA 1993* as the earliest age at which the member is entitled to receive benefits (other than a guaranteed minimum pension), on his retirement from any employment to which the scheme applies. Where the scheme only provides a guaranteed minimum pension, the normal pension age is the earliest age at which the member is entitled to receive the guaranteed minimum pension on retirement from such employment.

For the purposes of determining a member's normal pension age, any special provision as to early retirement on grounds of ill-health or otherwise must be disregarded. [*PSA 1993, s 180(2)*]. The former OPB's interpretation of this (which is still generally followed) was that a member's normal pension age would be the earliest date on which the member had an unqualified right to retire on an unreduced pension (other than on special grounds such as ill-health or redundancy). For example, if the rules of a scheme specify a normal retirement date of age 65 but allow a member to retire, without the consent of the trustees or his employer and without any actuarial reduction, at any time after age 62, the member's normal pension age will be 62.

Alternatives to short service benefits

6.24   *Section 73(2)* of *PSA 1993* permits the rules of a scheme to provide one or more of a number of alternatives to short service benefits.

Transfer payments

6.25   A member's accrued rights may be transferred to another occupational pension scheme, or to a personal pension scheme, with a view to acquiring rights for the member under the receiving scheme. [*PSA 1993, s 73(2)(a)*]. Furthermore, a scheme may provide for the member's accrued rights to be transferred, if the member consents, to an overseas arrangement. 'Overseas arrangement' means a scheme or arrangement, other than an occupational pension scheme, which:

(*a*)   has effect, or is capable of having effect, so as to provide benefits on termination of employment or on death or retirement to or in respect of earners;

(*b*)   is not an appropriate scheme; and

(*c*)   is administered wholly or primarily outside the UK. [*Preservation Regulations (SI 1991 No167), reg 11A*].

6.26 *Protection for early leavers*

Except in limited circumstances (see 12.42 below), the consent of the member must be obtained if a transfer is to be made as an alternative for providing short service benefits within the scheme. [*PSA 1993, s 73(4)*].

Early retirement

6.26 The rules of a scheme may permit payment of benefits to commence before normal pension age. In such a situation, the benefits payable may be of different amounts, and be payable to different recipients, than applies in relation to short service benefit. [*Preservation Regulations (SI 1991 No 167), reg 8(1)*].

However, where a scheme provides an early retirement pension as an alternative to short service benefits, the following requirements will apply:

(*a*)   the benefits must include a benefit payable to the member (*Preservation Regulations (SI 1991 No 167), reg 8(1)*);

(*b*)   it must be the case that either:

●   the member's earning capacity is destroyed or seriously impaired by physical or mental infirmity; or

●   the member has become incapable of following his normal employment because of physical or mental infirmity; or

●   the member has attained age 50 or is within ten years of normal pension age (*Preservation Regulations (SI 1991 No 167), regs 8(2), 5(2), (3) and (4)*);

(*c*)   the member's consent must be obtained unless:

●   his earning capacity is destroyed or seriously impaired because of physical or mental infirmity; and

●   in the opinion of the scheme's trustees, he is incapable of deciding whether it is in his interests to consent (*Preservation Regulations (SI 1991 No 167), regs 7(2) and 8(3)*); and

(*d*)   the relevant scheme rule must require the trustees to be reasonably satisfied that the total value of the benefits when they become payable is at least equal to the value of the accrued benefits which they replace. [*Preservation Regulations (SI 1991 No 167), regs 8(4) and 11*].

Late retirement

6.27 The rules of a scheme may also permit payment of benefits to commence after normal pension age as an alternative to short service benefits. The benefits payable may be of different amounts, and be payable to different recipients, than applies in relation to short service benefit. [*Preservation Regulations (SI 1991 No 167), reg 8(1)*].

In this situation, the following requirements will apply:

(a)   the benefits must include a benefit payable to the member (*Preservation Regulations (SI 1991 No 167), reg 8(1)*));

(b)   the member's consent to this alternative must be obtained (*Preservation Regulations (SI 1991 No 167), reg 7(2)*)); and

(c)   the relevant scheme rule must require the trustees to be reasonably satisfied that the total value of the benefits when they become payable is at least equal to the value of the accrued benefits which they replace. [*Preservation Regulations (SI 1991 No 167), regs 8(4) and 11*].

Bought-out benefits

6.28   A scheme may provide for a member's benefits to be appropriately secured or 'bought out' by the purchase of an annuity contract or insurance policy from an insurance company. The benefits provided may be different from those required to constitute short service benefit. If this option is to be exercised the trustees must be reasonably satisfied that the payment made to the insurance company is at least equal to the value of the benefits that have accrued to or in respect of the member under the rules. [*Preservation Regulations (SI 1991 No 167), regs 9 and 11*].

Generally the consent of the member is required before benefits can be bought out. [*Preservation Regulations (SI 1991 No 167), reg 7(2)*]. However, consent is not required if the insurance policy or annuity contract to be purchased satisfies certain prescribed conditions (set out in the *Preservation Regulations (SI 1991 No 167), reg 9(4)(a)*) and either:

(a)   the scheme is being wound up; or

(b)   the member has less than '5 years qualifying service' (as defined in *paragraph 7* of *Schedule 16* to the *Social Security Act 1973* immediately before the coming into force of *section 10* of the *Social Security Act 1986* (changes to preservation requirements); or

(c)   the trustees consider that, in the circumstances, it is reasonable for the benefits to be bought out without member consent. [*Preservation Regulations (SI 1991 No 167), regs 9(4)(b) and 9(5)*].

In the case of (b) and (c) above, the following further requirements must be satisfied:

(i)   the member's rights under the scheme must not include protected rights (see chapter 4);

(ii) at least twelve months must have elapsed between the purchase of the insurance policy or annuity contract and the termination of the member's pensionable service;

(iii) the trustees must generally give the member at least 30 days' written notice of their intention to take out the policy or enter into the contract; and

(iv) when the trustees actually take out the policy or enter into the contract there must be no outstanding application by the member for a cash equivalent (see 6.51 below). [*Preservation Regulations (SI 1991 No 167), reg 9(6)*].

Defined contributions benefits

6.29   A scheme may provide defined contributions benefits as an alternative to short service benefits. The relevant scheme rule must require the trustees to be reasonably satisfied that the total value of the benefits when they become payable is at least equal to the value of the accrued benefits which they replace. [*Preservation Regulations (SI 1991 No 167), regs 10* and *11*]. The member's consent is required if this alternative is to be provided. [*Preservation Regulations (SI 1991 No 167), reg 7(2)*]. In practice this alternative is not widely used.

None of the alternatives to short service benefits discussed above may include a return of contributions except in limited circumstances relating to service completed before 6 April 1975. [*PSA 1993, s 73(5)*].

Revaluation

Background

6.30   In spite of the preservation legislation described from 6.10 above, there was for many years a continuing dissatisfaction with the law's failure to protect members' preserved pensions from the impact of inflation in respect of the period from leaving pensionable service to normal pension age.

Chapters II and *III* of *Part IV* of *PSA 1993* now provide for an element of revaluation in respect of this period. Effectively, two separate systems of revaluation apply:

(*a*)   guaranteed minimum pensions accrued by reference to contracted-out employment before 6 April 1997 are subject to revaluation under *Chapter III* of *Part IV* (this is summarised in chapter 4);

(*b*)   revaluation of other benefits is as set out in *Chapter II* of *Part IV* of, and in *Schedule 3* to, *PSA 1993*. It is these provisions which are summarised in 6.31 to 6.41 below.

General application of the revaluation requirements

6.31   Under *section 83(1)(a)* of *PSA 1993*, the revaluation requirements of *Chapter II* apply where benefits are payable to or in respect of a member of an occupational pension scheme and:

(*a*)   his pensionable service ends on or after 1 January 1986;

(*b*)   when his pensionable service ends, he has accrued rights to benefits under the scheme;

(*c*)   there is a period from his date of leaving to his normal pension age of at least a year (see 6.23 above for meaning of 'normal pension age'); and

(*d*)   in the case of benefits payable to any other person in respect of the member, the member dies after normal pension age.

However, revaluation is not required to be applied separately in respect of the 'alternatives to short service benefit' referred to in 6.24 above. [*PSA 1993, s 85*].

For the purposes of the revaluation requirements, where 'normal pension age' is before the age of 60, it is taken to mean the age at which short service benefit is made payable under the scheme rules (see 6.23 above). [*Occupational Pensions Schemes (Revaluation) Regulations 1991 (SI 1991 No 168)*, reg 3].

Determining which method of revaluation applies

6.32   There are four different methods of revaluation:

(*a*)   the 'average salary method';

(*b*)   the 'flat rate method';

(*c*)   the 'money purchase method'; and

(*d*)   the 'final salary method'. [*PSA 1993, s 84* and *Sch 3*].

The first step in revaluing a particular benefit is to decide which of these four methods is to apply.

The average salary method

6.33   The average salary method applies where the benefit is an average salary benefit (i e one whose rate or amount is calculated by reference to a member's average salary over the period of service on which the benefit is based) and the trustees consider it appropriate to use the average salary method. [*PSA 1993, s 84(2)*].

The average salary method itself is set out in *paragraph 3* of *Schedule 3* to *PSA 1993*. Average salary benefits are now relatively rare and so this method does not often apply in practice.

The flat rate method

6.34   The flat rate method applies where the benefit is a flat rate benefit (i e one whose rate or amount is calculated by reference solely to the member's length of service) and the trustees consider it appropriate to use the flat rate method. [*PSA 1993, s 84(2)*].

Again, the flat rate method will rarely apply in practice. The method itself is set out in *paragraph 4* of *Schedule 3* to *PSA 1993*.

The money purchase method

6.35   Where the benefit is a defined contributions benefit, the money purchase method must be used. This method is discussed in 6.37 below. [*PSA 1993, s 84(3)*].

The final salary method

6.36   In all other cases, the final salary method applies. This is described in 6.38 to 6.41 below. [*PSA 1993, s 84(1)*].

The money purchase method

6.37   The money purchase method is set out in *paragraph 5* of *Schedule 3* to *PSA 1993*. Effectively, the money purchase method requires the trustees to apply investment yield and bonuses arising from contributions paid by and on behalf of the member towards the provision of benefits, in the same way which would have applied had the member not left pensionable service.

The final salary method

General

6.38   The final salary method is set out in *paragraphs 1* and *2* of *Schedule 3* to *PSA 1993*. This method introduces the concept widely known as limited price indexation or 'LPI'. The effect of applying LPI to a benefit is to increase it in line with cost of living increases over a given period, subject to a maximum of 5 per cent per annum.

Precisely how LPI applies in this context is dealt with in the following paragraphs. Depending on the precise dates of the member's pensionable service, LPI will not always be applied in full (see 6.41 below).

The 'revaluation percentage'

6.39   *Paragraph 2* of *Schedule 3* to *PSA 1993* requires the Secretary of State, in each calendar year, by order to specify a 'revaluation percentage' for each period which is a 'revaluation period' in relation to that order.

A 'revaluation period' is a period which:

(*a*)   begins with 1 January 1986 or with an anniversary of that date falling before the making of the order; and

(*b*)   ends with the next day after the making of the order which is 31 December.

The 'revaluation percentage' in relation to a given revaluation period is the lesser of:

(i)   the percentage which appears to the Secretary of State to be the percentage increase in the general level of prices in Great Britain during that revaluation period; and

(ii)   five per cent compound per annum.

Calculating the 'appropriate relevant percentage'

6.40   The 'appropriate relevant percentage' is the revaluation percentage (see 6.39 above) specified in the last calendar year before the date on which the member reaches normal pension age for a period of the same length as the number of complete years from the member's leaving pensionable service to his reaching normal pension age. [*PSA 1993, Sch 3, para 2(7)*].

Applying the 'appropriate revaluation percentage'

6.41   The final salary method of revaluation is to add to the amount that would otherwise be payable an amount equal to the whole or part of the appropriate revaluation percentage (see 6.40 above) of the benefit which has accrued on the date when pensionable service ends. *[PSA 1993, Sch 3, para 1]*.

Where pensionable service ends on or after 1 January 1991 or all pensionable service falls on or after 1 January 1985 the whole amount is added. *[PSA 1993, Sch 3, para 1(1)(a)]*. In any other case, a proportionate amount is added. The proportion is calculated by reference to the proportion which the member's post-31 December 1984 pensionable service bears to his total pensionable service. *[PSA 1993, Sch 3, para 1(1)(b)]*.

In either case, guaranteed minimum pensions are excluded from the benefit for the purpose of this calculation. These are revalued separately (see chapter 4).

Transfer values – introduction

6.42   Occupational pension schemes have always been able to offer a transfer payment as an alternative to providing benefits from the scheme. However, the *Social Security Act 1985* introduced legislation giving early leavers a statutory right to have the 'cash equivalent' of their benefits transferred to another pension arrangement. This statutory right overrides any inconsistent provisions in the scheme's governing documentation (other than those relating to the winding up of the scheme), but this does not prevent a scheme from being more generous.

The legislation is now consolidated in *sections 93* to *101* of *PSA 1993* (as amended by *sections 152* to *154* of *PA 1995*) and the *Occupational Pension Schemes (Transfer Values) Regulations 1996 (SI 1996 No 1847)* ('the *Transfer Regulations*'), as amended by the *Personal and Occupational Pension Schemes (Miscellaneous Amendments) Regulations 1997 (SI 1997 No 786)* and the *Occupational Pension Schemes (Transfer Values and Miscellaneous Amendments) Regulations 2003 (SI 2003 No 1727)*.

The right to a cash equivalent

When does a member acquire a right to a cash equivalent?

6.43   Broadly speaking, before 6 April 1997, a member of an occupational pension scheme acquired a statutory right to a cash equivalent if he terminated pensionable service after 1 January 1986 and at least one year before normal pension age (see 6.23 above). The ambit of the legislation was extended by *PA 1995* to include members who terminated pensionable service before 1 January 1986. [*PA 1995, s 152*]. However, the legislation does not apply to a member of a defined benefits scheme who terminated his membership before 1 January 1986, if all his pension benefits have been revalued by at least the rate of inflation. [*Transfer Regulations (SI 1996 No 1847), reg 2(b)*].

A major change introduced by *PA 1995* was the concept of a 'guaranteed cash equivalent'. As from 6 April 1997, the 'cash equivalent' of the benefits to which a member of a defined benefits occupational pension scheme is entitled must be guaranteed for a certain period. As a consequence of this change, the time at which a member acquires a right to a cash equivalent now differs depending on whether the scheme is defined contributions or defined benefits.

A member of a defined contributions occupational pension scheme acquires a right, when his pensionable service terminates, to the cash equivalent of any benefits which have accrued to or in respect of him under the rules of the scheme or any overriding legislation. [*PSA 1993, s 94(1)(a)*].

A member of a defined benefits scheme acquires the right to a 'guaranteed' cash equivalent if he has received a statement of entitlement (see 6.44 below) and has made a relevant application (see 6.51 below) within three months of the 'guarantee date'. [*PSA 1993, s 94(1)(aa)*].

Guaranteed statement of entitlement

6.44   On the application of a member of a defined benefits scheme, the trustees must provide him with a written statement, as at a 'guarantee date', of the amount of the cash equivalent of any benefits which have accrued to or in respect of him under the rules of the scheme or any overriding legislation. This statement is referred to in the legislation as a 'statement of entitlement'. [*PSA 1993, s 93A(1)*].

The guarantee date specified in the statement of entitlement must generally be within three months of the date of the member's application. However, this period can be extended for a reasonable period (of up to six months) if, for reasons beyond their control, the trustees are unable to obtain the information required to calculate the cash equivalent. [*Transfer Regulations (SI 1996 No 1847, reg 6(1))*].

The statement of entitlement must be given to the member within ten days (excluding weekends, Christmas Day, New Year's Day and Good Friday) of the guarantee date. [*Transfer Regulations (SI 1996 No 1847), reg 6(2)*]. For example, if a member terminates his pensionable service on 30 June 1997 and requests details of his cash equivalent on 18 October 1997, the trustees must supply him with a statement of his cash equivalent which has a guarantee date of no later than 17 January 1998. If the guarantee date chosen is, say, 15 January, the statement must be given to the member by 29 January; similarly if the guarantee date chosen were 10 December 1997, the statement would have to be given to the member by 23 December 1997.

A member cannot make more than one request for a statement of entitlement within any twelve-month period unless the rules of the scheme specifically provide for this or the trustees otherwise allow it. [*Transfer Regulations (SI 1996 No 1847), reg 6(3)*]. Any trustee who fails to take all reasonable steps to provide a statement of entitlement to any member who requests it can be fined up to £1,000 in the case of an individual or £10,000 in any other case. [*PSA 1993, s 93A(4)* and the *Transfer Regulations (SI 1996 No 1847), reg 20*]. (See appendix I regarding penalties generally).

Partial cash equivalents

6.45   If a member leaves pensionable service but does not leave service (i e he ceases to be a member of his employer's scheme but remains an employee), he only acquires a right to that part of his cash equivalent which is attributable to his post-6 April 1988 pensionable service; it is only when he ceases to be an employee that he has a statutory right to the remaining part of his cash equivalent (assuming employment terminates at least one year earlier than what would have been the member's normal pension age). [*PSA 1993, s 98* and the *Transfer Regulations (SI 1996 No 1847), regs 3* and *4*].

In practice many schemes do not restrict a member's cash equivalent, preferring to avoid the unnecessary administration costs associated with providing two cash equivalent calculations; instead of relying on the statutory provision, the scheme's governing documentation will specifically allow a member to take a cash equivalent in respect of all of his pensionable service, even if he remains in service.

Losing the right to a cash equivalent

6.46   *Section 98* of *PSA 1993* provides that the right to a cash equivalent is lost if:

(a)   it is not exercised before the 'last option date', i e at least one year before the date on which the member attains normal pension age or, within six months of terminating pensionable service, whichever is the later; or (*b*)   the scheme is wound up. There is some doubt as to whether this means the commencement or the completion of the winding-up process, but the generally held view is that it is the latter.

Calculating the cash equivalent

The basic cash equivalent transfer value calculation

Defined benefits

6.47   The cash equivalent transfer value of any defined benefits must be calculated and verified in a manner approved by the scheme actuary (i e the actuary appointed in accordance with *section 47(1)(b)* of *PA 1995*), or, if the trustees are exempt from the requirement to appoint a scheme actuary, by a Fellow of the Institute or Faculty of Actuaries. [*Transfer Regulations (SI 1996 No 1847), reg 7(1)*]. The methods and assumptions used must either be determined by the trustees or notified to them by the actuary. In either case, the methods and assumptions used must be certified by the actuary as:

(*a*)   being consistent with the statutory requirements relating to the calculation of transfer values (as set out in *section 97* of *PSA 1993* and the *Transfer Regulations (SI 1996 No 1847)*;

(*b*)   being consistent with the guidelines set out in the actuarial Guidance Note 'Retirement Benefit Schemes – Transfer Values' (GN11) issued by the Institute of Actuaries and the Faculty of Actuaries;

(*c*)   being consistent with the methods and assumptions used when granting rights and benefits in respect of a transfer payment accepted by the scheme; and

(*d*)   providing, as a minimum, the amount that would be provided if the methods and assumptions adopted in valuing liabilities for the purpose of the minimum funding requirement (see chapter 11) were used. [*Transfer Regulations (SI 1996 No 1847), reg 7(3)*].

Defined contributions benefits

6.48   A cash equivalent, or any portion of it, which relates to defined contributions benefits must be calculated and verified in a manner approved by the trustees of the scheme and in accordance with methods consistent with the requirements of the legislation. [*Transfer Regulations (SI 1996 No 1847), reg 67(5)*]. Generally the cash equivalent transfer value available in respect of defined contributions benefits will simply be the accumulated value of the contributions made by and in respect of the member plus the investment growth of those contributions.

Requirement to take into account customary discretionary benefits

6.49   Unless the trustees decide otherwise, a cash equivalent transfer value must take account of any additional benefits customarily granted at the discretion of the trustees or the employer. [*Transfer Regulations (SI 1996 No 1847), reg 8*]. The trustees cannot decide to exclude such additional benefits unless, within the three months before making the decision, they have obtained the advice of their actuary. The advice must be in the form of a written report on the funding implications of making such a decision. In particular, the report must include the actuary's advice as to whether or not, in his opinion, there would be any adverse implications for the funding of the scheme if the trustees did not make a direction to exclude discretionary benefits. [*Transfer Regulations (SI 1993 No 1847, reg 8(3)*)].

The requirement to obtain actuarial advice before deciding whether or not to include an allowance for discretionary benefits was introduced on 6 April 1997; before then it was solely a trustee decision which was, in practice, difficult to challenge. The introduction of the requirement for a funding report means that it will be difficult for trustees to exclude customary discretionary benefits unless they can justify doing so on the basis that the funding of the scheme will not permit them to do otherwise.

A common discretionary benefit for which allowance must be made is where early retirement is permitted without actuarial reduction but subject to employer consent. If it would be usual for the employer to consent to any such retirement after, say, age 62, there would be an established custom of granting the additional benefits. The calculation of any cash equivalent should therefore reflect this unless the trustees direct otherwise, taking into consideration the funding of the scheme.

Reduction of cash equivalents

6.50   If a scheme is subject to the minimum funding requirement (see 11.14 to 11.31 below), a cash equivalent may be reduced in certain circumstances. For any transfer value calculated with a guarantee date on or after 6 April 2005 where the 'GN11 insufficiency conditions' are met, then the transfer value for a particular category of liabilities can be reduced in line with the actuary's most recent GN11 report. The GN11 insufficiency conditions are that the latest GN11 report shows that:

(*a*)   the scheme had insufficient assets to pay cash equivalents in full in respect of all members; and

(*b*)   that there were insufficient assets to pay in full the cash equivalent in respect of a category of liabilities relevant to that particular transfer value.

In such a case the trustees may reduce any part of the cash equivalent payable in respect of that category of liability by a percentage not exceeding the relevant percentage deficiency shown in the GN11 report. This is provided that the amount of any cash equivalent after the reduction is not less than the minimum amount required under *regulation 7(3)(b)(iv)* to satisfy the liabilities referred in *section 73(3)* of *PA 1995* (preferential liabilities on winding up) as modified by *regulation 3* of the *Winding-Up Regulations*. [*Transfer Regulations (SI 1996 No 1847), reg 8(4)*].

In the case of a scheme which satisfies the 'MFR insufficiency conditions' then the transfer value for a particular category of liabilities can be further reduced in line with the MFR percentage deficiency. The MFR insufficiency conditions are that:

(*a*)   the latest MFR valuation shows that the scheme had insufficient assets to fund the minimum amount of the cash equivalent in respect of the liabilities referred to in *section 73* of *PA 1995*; and

(*b*)   the assets were insufficient to pay in full any category of liabilities to which that order applies that are liabilities for benefits in respect of which the member's cash equivalent is being calculated.

In such a case the trustees may reduce any part of the minimum cash equivalent payable in respect of that category of liability by a percentage not exceeding the relevant percentage deficiency shown in the MFR valuation. [*Transfer Regulations (SI 1996 No 1847), reg 8(4)*].

Although trustees are generally not obliged to reduce cash equivalents simply because the scheme is in deficit, they could be criticised for not doing so, particularly if a winding up was at the time envisaged (or had even commenced) or where the remainder of members' benefits would be severely jeopardised if cash equivalents were not reduced. Indeed, it is arguable that *regulation 8(12)* of the *Transfer Regulations (SI 1996 No 1847)* does require such a reduction where winding up has started before the guarantee date.

If the benefits to which a cash equivalent relates have been surrendered, commuted or forfeited before the trustees are required to comply with the member's request (see 6.54 below) the cash equivalent can be reduced or extinguished accordingly. Where a scheme is wound up, a cash equivalent can be reduced to the extent necessary to comply with the provisions of *PA 1995* relating to the benefits which must be secured on a winding-up (see chapter 12).

Once a cash equivalent has become a guaranteed cash equivalent it generally cannot be reduced unless either the scheme begins to be wound up or benefits have been surrendered, commuted or forfeited. [*Transfer Regulations (SI 1996 No 1847), reg 8(1)*]. The trustees could not, for example, make a direction that the cash equivalent will not allow for discretionary benefits after they have informed the member of his guaranteed cash equivalent. A guaranteed cash equivalent can be recalculated and either increased or reduced, as appropriate, if it transpires that it was not originally calculated in accordance with the statutory requirements. Where a guaranteed cash equivalent is reduced or increased a new 'guarantee date' will apply and the appropriate time limits will start again.

Exercising the right to a cash equivalent

Making a relevant application

6.51   The right to a cash equivalent can be exercised at any time after termination of pensionable service; it does not have to be exercised coincident with, for example, the date on which the member leaves service. A member exercises his right to a cash equivalent by making a relevant application, i e an application, in writing, to the trustees requiring them to use the cash equivalent by transferring it to a specified arrangement. [*PSA 1993, s 95* and the *Transfer Regulations (SI 1996 No 1847), reg 12*]. The legislation provides that an application is taken to have been made if it is delivered to the trustees personally or sent by post in a registered letter or by recorded delivery. [*PSA 1993, s 95(9)*]. However, in practice this requirement is often waived.

Broadly speaking, in the case of an APSS approved arrangement, a member can ask for his cash equivalent to be paid to any other suitable APSS approved arrangement which is able and willing to accept a transfer. However some restrictions apply, particularly in relation to transfers from schemes contracted out of the State earnings-related pension scheme. [*PSA 1993, s 95* and the *Transfer Regulations (SI 1996 No 1847), reg 12*]. Generally a transfer will be used to:

(*a*)   acquire transfer credits under the rules of an occupational pension scheme which is exempt approved (or awaiting approval) by the APSS under *Chapter I* of *Part XIV* of the *Income and Corporation Taxes Act 1988 (ICTA 1988)*;

(*b*)   acquire transfer credits under the rules of a personal pension scheme approved by the APSS under *Chapter IV* of *Part XIV* of *ICTA 1988*; or (*c*) purchase an annuity from an insurance company chosen by the member.

The application must specifically identify the receiving arrangement. An application which does not do this will simply be treated as an enquiry (or possibly a request for a statement of entitlement) and not a relevant application.

In the case of a defined benefits scheme a member must make a relevant application within three months of the guarantee date. [*PSA 1993, s 94(1)(aa)*]. If the member makes a relevant application outside of this three-month period, the application is treated as a request for a statement of entitlement. [*Transfer Regulations (SI 1996 No 1847), reg 6(4)*]. As not more than one request for a statement of entitlement can be made within any twelve-month period unless the rules of the scheme specifically provide for this (or the trustees otherwise allow it (see 6.44 above)), a member who fails to make a relevant application within the three-month period could find that he cannot require the trustees to take any action for another nine months.

A member may withdraw an application for a cash equivalent at any time before the trustees are committed to complying with the member's request. [*PSA 1993, s 100*]. A member could not, therefore, withdraw his application if the trustees have already made a transfer or entered into a binding agreement with a third party, such as an insurance company. A member who withdraws an application is not prevented from making another application at some future date.

'Splitting' a cash equivalent

6.52 A cash equivalent can be 'split' between a number of arrangements. For example, a member can transfer part of his cash equivalent to an occupational pension scheme and part to a personal pension scheme. [*PSA 1993, s 96(1)*]. This is most commonly done where the transfer is from a contracted-out scheme to a contracted-in scheme which cannot accept assets representing the member's contracted-out rights (but due to changes in the contracting-out system (see chapter 4) this is likely to become less common in the future).

Although a cash equivalent can be split between different arrangements, a member must generally take his whole cash equivalent. [*PSA 1993, s 96*]. There are, however, two qualifications to this: first, where the member's cash equivalent is restricted because he terminated pensionable service without terminating service (see 6.45 above); and, secondly, where his cash equivalent includes contracted-out rights which the receiving arrangement (not being contracted out) is unable or unwilling to accept. [*PSA 1993, s 96(1)(b) and (2)*].

Benefits to be provided by the receiving arrangement

6.53 The benefit which the receiving arrangement provides in respect of a cash equivalent will depend on the rules of that arrangement. A defined benefits scheme may provide a fixed amount of pension, similar to a revalued preserved pension. Alternatively the money may be invested in the same way as a member's additional voluntary contributions, or it may be translated into 'added years'. In the case of a defined contributions scheme a transfer value will usually simply be invested along with other contributions.

Trustees' duties after member exercises his right

Complying with the member's request

6.54   The trustees must do what is necessary to carry out the member's request, in the case of a defined benefits scheme, within six months of the guarantee date or (if earlier) the date on which the member reaches normal pension age. [*PSA 1993, s 99(2)*]. As the six-month period is from the guarantee date the trustees will have a minimum period of three months and a maximum period of six months in which to make the transfer payment (depending on how quickly the member requests the guaranteed cash equivalent).

In any other case, the necessary action must be taken within six months of the date on which the trustees received the application, or (if earlier), the date on which the member reaches normal pension age.

Pension liberation

6.55   Concern by the APSS over the practice of 'pension liberation' led to the amendment of the Practice Notes to impose new requirements in respect of transfers. 'Pension Liberation Schemes' usually involve a scheme member requesting a transfer to a receiving scheme where he has become a 'sham employee' on the books of a sponsoring employer. Once the transfer payment has been received by the receiving scheme, the member is given a lump sum representing that transfer payment minus the commission charged by the operation carrying out the 'liberation'. Commission can often be as high as 30 per cent of the transfer payment and if the APSS discovers the payment the member may also suffer a tax charge of up to 40 per cent of the transfer payment.

Since 1 July 2002 all schemes have had to implement the APSS's requirements in respect of transfers.

Before meeting a transfer the trustees or administrator must satisfy themselves that the receiving scheme is a 'tax advantaged' scheme or arrangement that falls within paragraph 10.23(a)–(d) of the Practice Notes, these are:

(*a*) occupational schemes approved under *ICTA 1988, Chapter I, Part XIV*, including free-standing additional voluntary contribution schemes;

(*b*) approved personal pension schemes,

(*c*) relevant statutory schemes and annuity contracts to which *ICTA 1988, s 431B(2)(d)* or (*e*) applies.

Where a transfer payment is requested, the trustees or administrator (or persons acting on their behalf) must, before making the transfer, ascertain the type of scheme or arrangement that the member has asked the transfer be paid to. Different rules then apply depending on the type of scheme or arrangement to which it is going to be made.

The following table summarises the rules.

Receiving scheme	Requirements
Insured scheme	Payment should only be made to the life office insuring the benefits.
SSAS	Before making the transfer, the transferring scheme must obtain written confirmation from the Pensioneer Trustee of the receiving SSAS that the transfer is to go ahead and the payment is to be made directly into a SSAS bank account of which the Pensioneer Trustee is a mandatory co-signatory. If the transferring scheme still has doubts about the transfer request then it is at liberty to make further enquiries of the Pensioneer Trustee. The prior written consent of the Inland Revenue must still be obtained before making a transfer payment of any kind to an SSAS.
Self-administered scheme (other than a SSAS)	The receiving scheme is required to give the transferring scheme written permission authorising the APSS to give the transferring scheme confirmation that the receiving scheme is/is not a tax approved self-administered scheme. If the transferring scheme has reason to believe the transfer request is suspect then it may write to the APSS (enclosing the authority) asking for confirmation of the receiving scheme's status.

Personal pension schemes	If the receiving personal pension scheme is underwritten by a life office than payment must be made to the life office only. If there is no life office or the receiving scheme is partly non-insured than if the scheme provider falls within ICTA 1988, s 632(1) then the transfer should be made to the life office or administrator as appropriate. If neither of these apply then the receiving scheme must provide the transferring scheme with written permission authorising the APSS to confirm its tax approved status to the transferring scheme. Again, if the transferring scheme has any doubts about making the transfer, it may write to the APSS (enclosing the authority) for confirmation of the tax approved status.

From 17 May 2002 transfers are no longer permitted to go through an independent broker.

HMRC may consider withdrawing approval from a scheme making a transfer to a 'trust busting' arrangement. Before approval is withdrawn, the trustees or administrator will be given an opportunity to demonstrate that they were acting in good faith.

If an approved scheme knowingly makes a suspicious transfer payment it may suffer an obligation to deduct tax under PAYE and additionally failure to comply with the PAYE Regulations may result in penalties and interest charges.

With effect from 6 April 2006 the detailed rules set out above will no longer apply. The Registered Pension Schemes Manual produced by APSS (at *RPSM14107010*) requires that, when considering making a transfer, the 'scheme administrator should make sure that the person to whom they are transferring monies is someone with a position of responsibility in the receiving scheme'. In addition, where the receiving scheme is an insured scheme the scheme administrator will be liable to a penalty of up to £3,000 if the transfer payment is not made directly to the scheme administrator of the receiving scheme or an insurance company issuing policies under the receiving scheme. Only transfers made to other registered schemes or qualifying recognised overseas schemes will be 'recognised transfers', a transfer to any other arrangement will incur a tax penalty.

New provisions dealing with pensions liberation were introduced with effect from 6 April 2005 by *sections 18* to *21* of *PA 2004*. Where money has been transferred out of a pension scheme on the basis that it would be used in an 'authorised way' and it has not or is not likely to be used in that way the Regulator may apply to the court for an order of restitution to recover the money, or assets of an equivalent value, from the recipient (*section 19* of *PA 2004*). An 'authorised way' means either, where it is a statutory transfer such as the exercise of the right to take a cash equivalent, then a way authorised under the relevant statutory provisions. Where the transfer is made pursuant to the scheme rules, then an 'authorised way' is as allowed under the scheme rules. As an alternative to applying to the court for a restitution order, the Regulator has power to take action itself. *Section 20* of *PA 2004* allows the Regulator to make a restraining order over any account which it is satisfied contains money which has been liberated, pending consideration of a repatriation order. *Section 21* of *PA 2004* provides that where a restraining order is in place and the Regulator is satisfied that the restrained account does contain money liberated from a pension scheme it may direct the person holding the account to pay the money to another pension scheme, towards an annuity or to the scheme member affected.

Variations and extensions of time limits

6.56   Under section *99(4)* of *PSA 1993* and *regulation 13* of the *Transfer Regulations* (*SI 1996 No 1847*), the Regulator may grant an extension of the time limits for making the transfer payment in certain circumstances, including where:

(*a*)   the member disputes the amount of the cash equivalent;

(*b*)   the scheme is being wound up or is about to be wound up;

(*c*)   the scheme is ceasing to be a contracted-out scheme;

(*d*)   the interests of the members of the scheme generally would be prejudiced if the trustees acted on a member's request within the statutory time limit;

(*e*)   the trustees have not been provided with the information they reasonably require to carry out properly what the member requires.

An application for an extension must be made during the period within which the trustees should have complied with the member's request.

If disciplinary or court proceedings are brought against a member within twelve months of the termination of his pensionable service and there is a likelihood that his benefits may be forfeited as a result, the period within which the trustees are required to comply with the member's request is extended to three months after conclusion of the disciplinary or court proceedings. [*PSA 1993, s 99(3)*].

Consequences of delay

6.57   If the trustees fail to do what is needed to carry out the member's request within the appropriate time frame, and cannot establish grounds for an extension, they must notify the Regulator of the failure to comply. In making their notification to the Regulator the trustees should give an explanation, since the Regulator then has power to impose a financial penalty (of up to £1,000 in the case of an individual or £10,000 in any other case) if the trustees have failed to take reasonable steps to ensure compliance. [*PSA 1993*, s 99(7)].

A member's cash equivalent must be increased if the trustees delay implementing the member's request for more than six months. If there is a reasonable excuse for the delay, the cash equivalent must be recalculated, and increased as appropriate, as if the date on which the trustees carry out the member's request had been the guarantee date (in the case of a defined benefits scheme) or the date on which the trustees received the member's application for a cash equivalent (in any other case).

If there is no reasonable excuse for the delay, either the cash equivalent must be recalculated as above, or interest must be added to the original cash equivalent at one per cent above base rate (as defined in the *Local Government Pension Scheme Regulations 1995 (SI 1995 No 1019)*) if this would produce a greater amount. [*Transfer Regulations (SI 1996 No 1847), reg 10*].

Discharge of trustees

6.58   Once the trustees have done what is needed to carry out the member's request, they are discharged from any obligation to provide benefits to which the cash equivalent relates. [*PSA 1993, s 99(1)*].

Cash transfer sums

6.59   Employees leaving service on or after 6 April 2005 before normal retirement age with at least three months' pensionable service but no vested rights (usually less that two years' pensionable service) will be entitled to choose a 'cash transfer sum' as an alternative to a refund of their contributions. The provisions are introduced by *section 264* of *PA 2004* which inserts new *sections 101AA* to *101AI* into *PSA 1993*.

The cash transfer sum is defined in *section 101AB* of *PSA 1993* as being the cash equivalent value of the benefits that would have accrued for the member had there not been a rule requiring a minimum period of service before vesting of those rights. This means that early leavers will be able to benefit from the value of their employer's contributions after three months rather than the current period of two years (although the rules of some schemes may already provide for a vesting period of less than two years). The *Draft Occupational Pension Schemes (Early Leavers: Cash Transfer Sums and Contribution Refunds) Regu-*

lations 2006 provide for the cash equivalent to be reduced in certain circumstances including scheme underfunding based on a GN11 report (see 6.50 above).

As is currently the case, schemes will not be required to offer members the option of a deferred pension until they have completed two years' qualifying service. The option to take a cash transfer sum will not be available once a scheme has commenced winding up (*regulation 5* of the *Occupational Pension Schemes (Winding Up etc) Regulations 2005 (SI 2005 No 706)*).

A member may use a cash transfer sum to acquire rights under another occupational pension scheme or a personal pension scheme, for purchasing one or more appropriate annuities or subscribing to such other registered pension schemes.

Section 101AC of *PSA 1993* requires trustees to provide relevant departing members with information regarding the nature and amount of the rights acquired and details of what he must do to exercise those rights. The *Draft Occupational Pension Schemes (Early Leavers: Cash Transfer Sums and Contribution Refunds) Regulations 2006* provide for other detailed information to be given to relevant members including the details and reasons for any reduction, details of any tax liability and the possibility of any reduction if the scheme were to commence winding up before payment is made.

The Regulator has issued a draft Code of Practice setting out proposed time limits for the various stages of the process. This proposes the following:

● Trustees should notify a member of his rights at least within two months of leaving service. Good practice would be to give the member written notice of his rights on his last day of service.

● Members should be given at least three months from the date the statement is given to them in which to make their election.

● Trustees should complete the transfer or refund without unjustifiable delay and usually within three months of receiving the election.

Disclosure requirements

6.60   Active members of any scheme and deferred members of defined contributions schemes are entitled to certain information regarding cash equivalents and transfer values. [*Transfer Regulations (SI 1996 No 1847), reg 11* and *Sch 1*]. In particular, a statement of whether or not a cash equivalent or other transfer value is available, or would be available if the member terminated pensionable service, must be provided. Trustees must also supply the following information as soon as practicable and in any event within three months of the request being made:

(*a*)   an estimate of the amount of the cash equivalent (calculated on the basis that the member's service terminated or will terminate on a particular date);

(*b*)   details of the accrued rights to which the cash equivalent relates;

(*c*)   details of how far discretionary or customary benefits have been taken into account and, if the trustees have exercised their right to direct that such benefits are not taken into account, the fact that the trustees have been obliged to obtain an actuary's report before excluding such benefits and that the member is entitled to ask for a copy of that report; and

(*d*)   if the amount of the cash equivalent has been reduced, a statement of that fact and of the amount by which the cash equivalent has been reduced, an explanation of the reason for the reduction (which shall refer to the paragraph of *regulation 8* of the *Transfer Regulations (SI 1996 No 1847)* relied upon), an estimate of when an unreduced payment would be available and a statement of the member's right to obtain further estimates.

A member is only entitled to this information once in every twelve-month period. Similar information must be given in respect of any non-statutory transfer value that may be available to the member.

When a member is given a statement of entitlement to a cash equivalent transfer value certain information must be given in addition to that referred to above. In particular, the member must be given a statement explaining:

 (i)   that the member can only request a statement of entitlement once in every twelve-month period unless the trustees allow otherwise or the scheme rules permit more frequent requests;

 (ii)   that if the member wishes to exercise his right to take the guaranteed cash equivalent he must submit a written application to that effect so within three months of the guarantee date; and

(iii)   in exceptional circumstances the guaranteed cash equivalent may be reduced and the member will be informed if his cash equivalent is reduced.

Any trustee who fails to take all reasonable steps to comply with these disclosure requirements can be fined up to £1,000 in the case of an individual or £10,000 in any other case. [*PSA 1993, s 93A* and the *Transfer Regulations (SI 1996 No 1847), reg 20*]. See appendix I regarding penalties generally.

Hybrid schemes

6.61   The *Transfer Regulations (SI 1996 No 1847)* make special provisions for 'hybrid schemes', i e schemes which are defined benefits but under which some of the benefits which may be provided are defined contributions benefits or vice versa. In relation to such schemes a member has a right to:

(*a*)   a guaranteed cash equivalent in respect of his defined benefits; and

(*b*)   a cash equivalent which is equal to the defined contributions benefits. [*Transfer Regulations (SI 1996 No 1847), reg 19*].

In exercising his rights, the member must take the whole of his cash equivalent, i e both the guaranteed and non-guaranteed element.

Summary of guaranteed cash equivalent procedure

6.62

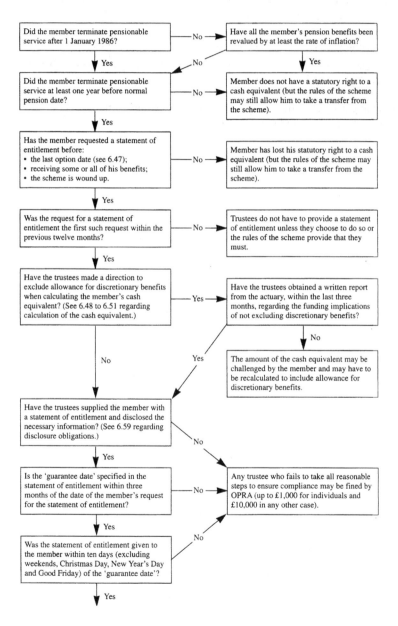

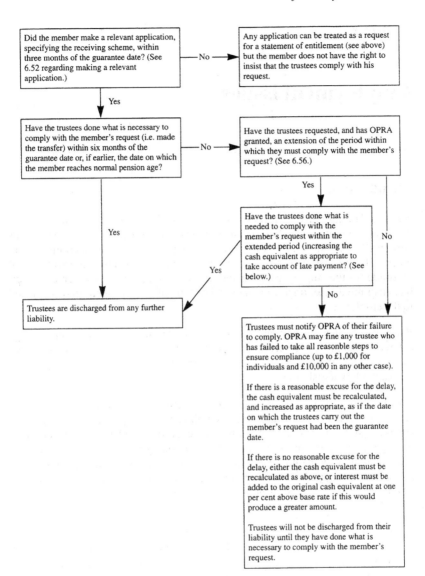

Did the member make a relevant application, specifying the receiving scheme, within three months of the guarantee date? (See 6.52 regarding making a relevant application.)

— No → Any application can be treated as a request for a statement of entitlement (see above) but the member does not have the right to insist that the trustees comply with his request.

Yes

Have the trustees done what is necessary to comply with the member's request (i.e. made the transfer) within six months of the guarantee date or, if earlier, the date on which the member reaches normal pension age?

— No → Have the trustees requested, and has OPRA granted, an extension of the period within which they must comply with the member's request? (See 6.56.)

Yes

Have the trustees done what is needed to comply with the member's request within the extended period (increasing the cash equivalent as appropriate to take account of late payment? (See below.)

No

Yes

Yes

No

Trustees are discharged from any further liability.

No

Trustees must notify OPRA of their failure to comply. OPRA may fine any trustee who has failed to take all reasonble steps to ensure compliance (up to £1,000 for individuals and £10,000 in any other case).

If there is a reasonable excuse for the delay, the cash equivalent must be recalculated, and increased as appropriate, as if the date on which the trustees carry out the member's request had been the guarantee date.

If there is no reasonable excuse for the delay, either the cash equivalent must be recalculated as above, or interest must be added to the original cash equivalent at one per cent above base rate if this would produce a greater amount.

Trustees will not be discharged from their liability until they have done what is necessary to comply with the member's request.

Chapter 7

Employment issues

Introduction

7.1   Traditionally, lawyers attempted to keep pension schemes and employment issues entirely separate, but the distinction between pension rights deriving from a trust and contractual employment rights is becoming more blurred. In the past, pensions were seen as being provided by employers out of gratitude for the employee's long and dutiful service. The employer, as settlor, had absolute discretion as to what level or type of benefits were to be provided to the employee.

Pension schemes are now an integral part of the total remuneration package offered by employers (pension provision is often a key recruitment and retention issue) and the provision of pension benefits is heavily regulated by statute and secondary legislation.

There is currently no legislation requiring an employer to run a pension scheme (except in limited circumstances for ex-public sector employees, although such rights are statutory and not the norm). However, from 8 October 2001, employers of five or more employees are required to designate a stakeholder pension scheme which their employees may elect to join, and to arrange for salary deductions to be made and contributions paid directly to the provider on behalf of employees (*Welfare Reform and Pensions Act 1999, s 1* (as amended by *PA 2004*)).

As a consequence of the *Social Security Act 1986* (now *section 160* of the *Pension Schemes Act 1993*), an employer can no longer make membership of a pension scheme compulsory. There is no minimum or maximum level of benefits that may or should by law be provided, except that a contracted-out scheme must provide certain minimum benefits required by statute (see chapter 4); an exempt approved scheme must not provide benefits which exceed HMRC limits (although this is subject to imminent change in April 2006 under *FA 2004*) (see chapter 5) and final salary schemes must meet the minimum funding requirement or the scheme specific funding requirements (as and when applicable to each scheme) (see chapter 11). None of the tax, preservation, revaluation or contracting-out legislation states that the contract of employment should contain any rights for the employee as against the employer; the employee's rights are ostensibly against the trustees of the pension scheme alone. Moreover, it is understandable that an employer would wish to exercise as much control as possible over a scheme which it operates and funds (particularly following the extension of the *Occupational Pension Schemes (Deficiency on Winding Up etc) Regulations 1996 (SI 1996/3128)* ('the *Deficiency Regulations*') and the introduction of the minimum funding requirement under *PA 1995.*)

An employee does have specific rights against his employer but these are only in the areas of sex, race, religion of belief, sexual orientation and disability discrimination, equal pay, maternity absence and, as of 6 April 2003, paternity and adoption absence and even then these rights are statutory rather than contractual. It is true that *Barber v Guardian Royal Exchange [1990] 2 CMLR 513* (as subsequently clarified by *Coloroll Pension Trustees Ltd v Russell [1995] All ER (EC) 23*) confirmed that pensions are pay, but that is only in the context of the equality provisions of *Article 141 (formerly Article 119)* of the *Treaty of Rome*, as regards access to pension schemes and the benefits to be provided for men and women. In addition, although defined pension contributions and benefits were also recognised as pay by the Central Arbitration Committee, this was only in respect of trade union recognition for collective bargaining purposes (*UNIFI v Union Bank of Nigeria plc [2001] IRLR 712*). Neither *Barber* nor *UNIFI* answer the more fundamental question of whether (and if so, to what extent) pensions are an employment right and neither does *PA 1995*.

What is the employee promised?

Wording of the employment contract

7.2 The wording of an employment contract generally provides little or no guidance as to the pension rights (if any) of the employee. *Section 1* of the *Employment Rights Act 1996 (ERA 1996)* states that within two months of the commencement of employment, the employer must provide a written statement of the essential terms of the employment and must include any terms and conditions (see *ERA 1996, s 1(4)(d)(iii)*) relating to 'pensions and pension schemes'. Generally the information given will be limited, as *ERA 1996* in reality requires information to be given on access to a pension scheme, as opposed to the benefits which will be provided if an employee joins the pension scheme. Indeed it would be risky for an employer to give express commitments in the employment contract as to the benefits to be provided under a final salary scheme as, until the winding up of a pension scheme and the crystallisation of its liabilities, an employer cannot be certain that there will be sufficient funds to meet the pension promise. There is less of a problem with money purchase arrangements.

Although the precise wording would have to be checked in any individual case, usually a contract will state that an employee may join the pension scheme if eligible to do so (for example, upper and lower age limits may be imposed, or a requirement to have completed a year's service) and membership will be subject to the provisions governing the scheme from time to time, which are summarised in the scheme booklet. The contract may also reserve to the employer the right to amend or terminate the pension scheme, or alternatively an employer may rely on the reference to the scheme booklet (which should, if properly drafted, contain such a caveat). In most instances, and as clarified by the High Court in *ITN v Ward [1997] PLR 131*, the trust deed will override the booklet in cases of inconsistency.

When it comes to employing a senior executive, the employer is likely to take more time over the drafting of its particular service contract (which is less likely to follow a standard form) and one of the important clauses will usually deal specifically with the pension benefits to be provided (as opposed merely to access to the scheme).

In most cases the wording of the employment contract is unlikely to be of assistance in analysing pension rights, and it is designed to comply with statutory minimum requirements. The only employment 'right' is likely to be a right to join the scheme, if the employee satisfies the eligibility criteria.

In reality, an employee will obtain clearer information from the trustees of any occupational scheme, pursuant to the trustees' obligations under *PA 1995* disclosure requirements (for further details see chapter 3 and appendix II), than he will from his employer. Basic information about the scheme (*Disclosure Regulations (SI 1996 No 1655), reg 4*)) must be provided as a matter of course to each prospective member or, if this is not practicable, within two months of his becoming a member.

The pension scheme documentation

7.3   The explanatory booklet or announcement will usually be designed to comply with the disclosure requirements of *PSA 1993*, *PA 1995* and the *Disclosure Regulations (SI 1996 No 1655)*. It will usually state that the scheme is established under a trust and is managed by trustees, that the booklet is explanatory only, and that the employees' rights are set out in the trust deed and rules, which is available for inspection or copies of which are available on application to the trustees. In practice it is uncommon for employees to exercise their rights to inspect the deed.

In addition, a statement will usually be incorporated saying that whilst the company has every intention of continuing the scheme it does reserve the right to modify or discontinue it at any time.

The application for membership will usually authorise the company to deduct any contributions payable by the employee from his remuneration and to remit these contributions to the trustees. This authority (which must be in writing and precede the first deduction) is required under *section 13* of *ERA 1996* (a consolidation of the *Wages Act 1986* provisions) and may not be specifically incorporated within the contract of employment. This is an important fact which must be remembered when considering the amalgamation of two or more schemes or the transfer of a group of employees into a new scheme. The authority to deduct contributions may be specific to the former scheme and may have to be renewed for the new scheme before any deductions are made.

The trust deed and rules will generally establish that the employee, if he joins the scheme and becomes a beneficiary of the trust, will become entitled to benefits in defined circumstances. The formal documentation will contain a power of amendment, exercisable by the employer with the consent of the trustees, or vice versa, or (less commonly) by one party solely. Rights already accrued may also be expressly protected (see also 7.10 below).

The employer will usually have power to discontinue contributions, following which the scheme will normally be wound up, although the trustees may have power to continue it as a closed scheme (see chapter 12 for further details regarding winding up of pension schemes). The benefits provided on winding up will depend on the liabilities at that date, the value of the assets and the cost of purchasing annuities. Certain classes of member, starting with existing pensioners, will have priority over other classes of member. Employed members are often at the bottom of the list of priorities and, in cases of significant underfunding, may receive nothing, irrespective of their current age and length of pensionable service. It is at that stage that the employee will be looking to the employer to make good his loss, and either the *Deficiency Regulations* (*SI 1996 No 3128*) or, as the case may be, the *Occupational Pension Schemes* (*Employer Debt*) *Regulations* (*SI 2005 No 678*) will come into play. It should be noted that the *Deficiency Regulations* (*SI 1996 No 3128*) only apply in the case of schemes that have begun to wind up before 6 April 2005 or, unless the scheme is a money purchase scheme, if a debt arose under *section 75* of *PA 1995* before that date. The *Deficiency Regulations* (*SI 1996 No 3128*) are otherwise replaced by the *Occupational Pension Schemes* (*Employer Debt*) *Regulations 2005* (*SI 2005 No 678*). These two sets of Regulations value benefits on different bases, depending on the date of winding up and the status of the employee and therefore, in certain circumstances, employees will not receive their full entitlement. In addition, the employer's debt under these Regulations is an unsecured debt owed to the trustees from the employer, so if the employer is insolvent the employee will potentially receive nothing. However, the employee does have some security on an ongoing basis as a result of the current minimum funding requirements and will have improved security under the new scheme specific funding regime (see chapter 11) and the statutory priorities on wind up (see chapter 12).

PA 2004 has improved member security to an extent, with the introduction of the Pension Protection Fund ('PPF'), which is designed to protect members of private sector defined benefits schemes in the event that their employer becomes insolvent with insufficient funds in the scheme. In summary, it is intended that members of the scheme who have reached normal retirement age will receive in full the pension to which they are entitled under the scheme and that members below retirement age will receive 90 per cent of the pension accrued to them prior to the assessment date, revalued to the date of payment but subject to an overall cap of £25,000 at age 65. The PPF is financed by a levy on defined benefit schemes calculated on the basis of 'scheme factors' and 'risk factors'. In order to offset the cost of the levy, the Limited Price Indexation cap on index-linked pensions was reduced from 5 per cent to 2.5 per cent with effect from 6 April 2005.

For a pension scheme established under trust, the employee's security therefore depends on a number of factors including the continued payment of contributions by the employer, to ensure sufficient funding, and investment performance. It is difficult to ascertain what the employee's 'rights' against an employer are. His pension entitlement is enforceable against the trustees, who will look to the employer for additional funding, if required. If the scheme is in deficit, the employee's enforceable rights against the employer are statutory, and statute does not guarantee that a full pension (i e as promised under the trust documentation) will be paid.

What are the employer's obligations?

General

7.4   The employer must comply with the rights and obligations set out in the trust deed and rules governing the scheme. However, these do not cover every eventuality, and it is often necessary to look to case law for guidance.

Fiduciary duties — Mettoy and Icarus

7.5   *Mettoy Pensions Trustees Ltd v Evans [1990] 1 WLR 1587* acknowledged (although the case did not hinge on this) that an employee's rights under a pension scheme trust are of a commercial and contractual origin; they derive from the contract of employment, with benefits being earned by virtue of service with the employer under those contracts and, where the scheme is contributory, by virtue of those contributions. Employees can therefore only benefit from a pension scheme by virtue of their employment, which in turn is governed by the employment contract. Similar issues were previously raised in

Kerry v British Leyland [1986] CA Transcript 286 and *Mihlenstedt v Barclays Bank International [1989] IRLR 522*, in which the judge stated that the scheme was 'established against the background of such employment and falls to be interpreted against that background'.

The judge in the *Mettoy* case concluded that the power apparently vested in the company to decide what to do with a surplus on winding up was a fiduciary power (ie a power conferred on the employer as 'trustee' of the power, effectively being one which had to be exercised in the best interests of the members and putting the employer in the same position as a trustee as regards the duties owed to members).

A similar decision was made in *Icarus (Hertford) v Driscoll (1990) PLR 1*, where the employer remained as trustee of the scheme following its insolvency (this was prior to the legislation requiring an independent trustee to be appointed in such a situation). It is therefore logical that the judge held the employer to be in a fiduciary position, as the employer was the actual, as opposed to a quasi, trustee. There was held to be a fiduciary power which the employer had to exercise in good faith, 'in the sense that he cannot act for reasons which are irrelevant or perverse'.

Employers should, therefore, bear in mind that the powers which they exercise may be those which a court would consider to be fiduciary in nature and should seek to ensure compliance with the associated duties accordingly.

Duty of good faith — the Imperial case

7.6   It is well established that under the contract of employment there exists a reciprocal duty of good faith on behalf of both employers and employees. As a consequence of the *Imperial* case this principle extends to the exercise of all the employer's powers and obligations under a pension scheme (*Imperial Group Pension Trust v Imperial Tobacco [1991] 2 All ER 597*). In *Imperial* it was held that the company was under an implied contractual obligation of good faith in the exercise of its rights and powers under the pension scheme. The court also established the principle that the trust deed and rules were subject to the implied limitation that any rights or powers of the company should only be exercised in accordance with the obligation not seriously to undermine the relationship of trust and confidence existing between the employer and the employee. This duty of good faith is not the same as a fiduciary duty (see 7.5 above); the judge (Sir Nicholas Browne-Wilkinson V-C) explained that the company can have regard to its own interests (financial and otherwise) but only to the extent that in doing so it does not breach the obligation of good faith to its employees.

The decision in *Imperial* can be seen as the judiciary importing employment law concepts into the pensions arena. Arguably, good faith means little more than the employer having to act in a reasonable manner and it remains to be seen how far this concept will be taken by the courts and by the Pensions Ombudsman. The duty of good faith must also be distinguished from a fiduciary duty which would require an employer to act in the beneficiaries' best interests.

Post Imperial

7.7 The rights and obligations of an employer were considered by the High Court in May 1996 in the case of *Engineering Training Authority v Pensions Ombudsman (1996) PLR 409*, this case being an appeal from a determination by the Pensions Ombudsman of maladministration on the part of the employer. The Ombudsman had jurisdiction at that time to consider the position of an employer's functions in relation to a pension scheme under the *Personal and Occupational Pension Schemes (Pensions Ombudsman) Regulations 1991 (SI 1991 No 588)* (which have subsequently been revoked and replaced by the *Personal and Occupational Pension Schemes (Pensions Ombudsman) Regulations 1996 (SI 1996 No 2475)*). The member was made redundant in May 1993. If he had been made redundant in September 1993, at age 50, he would have been entitled to an early retirement pension. In negotiations the employer agreed to keep the employee on its books until age 50 (agreeing that he could obtain an immediate pension without actuarial reduction) and the employee consented to this (by countersigning a letter to him from the employer). He then complained to the Ombudsman that the employer had not provided him with an enhancement (of six years' pensionable service) which was payable, at the employer's discretion, to employees retiring after age 47 and that he had been 'coerced' into signing away his pension enhancement rights. The court held that the Ombudsman does not have power 'to investigate complaints about the ordinary contractual relations between employer and employee', which are matters for an employment tribunal or a court. The Ombudsman's jurisdiction to investigate is confined to the employer's functions relating to the pension scheme.

Although this case deals essentially with the clarification of the jurisdiction of the Ombudsman, it is indicative of the uncertainty of the overlap between pension and contractual promises. Interestingly, in the appeal the Ombudsman tried to argue that even if the employer was not guilty of maladministration, the complaint should be upheld as the employer had breached the *Imperial* duty of good faith. The court was referred to the decision of the Court of Appeal in *Harris v Shuttleworth (1994) PLR 47* which stated that for an employer to dismiss an employee and thus deprive her of an ill-health pension 'might very well amount to a breach of good faith on the part of the employer, giving the employee a separate remedy'. The judge thought that these submissions were inappropriate in the context of the appeal (having not been considered by the Ombudsman in his determination). However, it is possible in situations such as this that the employee concerned could (time limits permitting) launch a separate action.

The *Imperial* duty continues to be an extremely important legal principle, in both High Court cases and in the Ombudsman's jurisdiction. For example, the judge (Knox J) in *Hillsdown Holdings plc v Pensions Ombudsman (1996) PLR 427* found that the employer had been in breach of the duty of good faith by threatening to suspend contributions and flood an overfunded scheme with new entrants if the trustees did not agree to merger proposals put forward by the employer. Similarly, the Ombudsman determined, in a complaint brought against the National Grid by two pensioners, that the power vested in an employer to distribute surplus had to be exercised in good faith and that, as the power was vested solely in the employer, the obligation approached a fiduciary duty, calling for the power to be exercised in the best interests of the scheme as a whole, without preferring the employer's interests. Inevitably, given the financial significance of the Ombudsman's determination, National Grid appealed the decision. The appeal (*1997 PLR 161*) was heard by the High Court simultaneously with a summons taken out by National Power, upon whom the *National Grid* determination would have impacted. Part of the appeal hinged on the Ombudsman's view of the duty to distribute surplus approaching a fiduciary duty. Walker J concluded that there is an essential distinction between the duty of good faith and a fiduciary duty, being the right of the employer to look at his own interests. He stated that the Ombudsman had 'lost sight of that essential distinction', and felt that if the *Imperial* case had been heard before the *Mettoy* case, the judge in *Mettoy* could have come to a different conclusion. Although the duty of good faith may have aspects in common with a fiduciary duty, Walker J saw no reason to blend them together; he concluded that no evidence had been put before the Ombudsman to suggest that the National Grid was in breach of its duty of good faith, and that the Ombudsman had therefore erred in law. The Ombudsman's directions were consequently set aside by the High Court, but this decision was reversed by the Court of Appeal judgment (*1999 PLR 37*) which in turn was reversed in the House of Lords in favour of the employers. However, the appeal was not concerned with the distinction between the duty of good faith and fiduciary duties, so the judgment of Walker J in that regard is still good law.

Later decisions emphasise the limits of the *Imperial* principle. In *University of Nottingham v Eyett [1999] IRLR 87* an employer was not obliged to warn an employee that he had not chosen the most advantageous course of action, where the employee was aware of his entitlement to a benefit and was taking a decision on ways to maximise it. In *Outram v Academy Plastics [2000] IRLR 499*, the Court of Appeal struck out a claim that an employer owed a duty of care to an employee who had resigned after 20 years' service and later re-joined the employer. Employers, it was held, do not owe a duty of care to advise scheme members faced with choices about pension matters, nor do they owe a wider duty in tort than in contract. If, however, an employer voluntarily undertakes to provide such advice, an implied duty not to give inaccurate, negligent or misleading advice may apply. *Outram* was cited in *Wirral Metropolitan Borough Council v Evans and another [2001] OPLR 73* and that judgment followed. It was held that there was no duty on the administrators to give advice to Mr Evans which would have prevented him from transferring his pension benefits to the scheme on unfavourable terms.

Crossley v Faithful & Gould Holdings Limited [2004] EWCA Civ 293, [2004] ICR 1615 is the most recent case on this matter and Dyson LJ, presiding, usefully analysed previous cases and concluded in paragraph 44 of the judgment that:

> 'The employer is not required to have regard to the employee's financial circumstances when he takes lawful business decisions which may affect the employee's economic welfare. There is no reason to suppose that he will even be aware of the details of those circumstances. Nor is it the function of the employer to act as his employee's financial adviser, that is simply not part of the bargain that is comprised in the contract of employment. There are no obvious policy reasons to impose on an employer the general duty to protect his employee's economic wellbeing. The employee can obtain his own advice, whether from his union or otherwise.'

Nevertheless, if an employer assumes the responsibility for giving financial advice to its employee, it is under a duty to take reasonable care in the giving of that advice. This principle was confirmed in the recent case of *Lennon v Metropolitan Police Commissioner [2004] EWCA Civ 130, [2004] 2 All ER 266,* and cited in the *Crossley* case.

Can an employer contract out of the Imperial duty?

7.8   This issue was considered by the Ombudsman in a determination issued in May 1997 (*Poole v Trustees of the Cytec Industries (UK) Limited Case reference F00088*). The Interim Trust Deed of the Cytec Scheme contained a provision which stated that 'in exercising any discretion, or power, or giving its agreement or consent under the Plan, an Employer may act in its absolute unfettered discretion and in its sole and exclusive interests'.

The Ombudsman determined that this provision could not operate to nullify the implied obligation of good faith, particularly as it appeared in an agreement made between two parties (the employer and the trustees), to the exclusion of the complainant. Additionally the Ombudsman held that the provision cannot be allowed to operate so as to enable the employer to contract out of the Ombudsman's jurisdiction in respect of injustice caused by maladministration. He also commented that the exclusion was unusual and oppressive.

Would the Ombudsman's decision have been different if the offending provision had been printed in the booklet? Probably not, for the reasons set out in 7.19 below, but there is a lesson for employers here: if you wish to rely on a provision, make sure that it is drawn to the employees' attention, in a booklet or other scheme literature distributed to employees.

To whom is the Imperial duty owed?

7.9   In the *National Bus* determination (*1997 PLR 1*) the Pensions Ombudsman stated that the duty of good faith was owed by the employer to the trustees as well as to the employees. The duty is therefore also enforceable by the trustees against the employer. It seems likely that a court would hold that the duty is also owed to ex-employees and by implication, to those claiming through employees (i e spouses and dependants). This is yet to be tested.

In the words of Walker J, 'the scope and limits of the *Imperial Tobacco* duty will no doubt be worked out, on a case by case basis, in coming years'. Employers must therefore take care when exercising their powers.

Termination and reduction of benefits

7.10   In ascertaining the cross-over between pension and employment rights it is useful to focus on a scenario whereby the employer wishes to alter the level of benefits, either by terminating the pension scheme or by providing less beneficial benefits for future (or past) service. From a pure pensions viewpoint the employer would have to consider the terms of the power of amendment (which may be jointly vested in the trustees and the employer and may have certain restrictions on how the power can be exercised), and the limitations imposed by *PA 1995, s 67*. In addition to these aspects, an employer would have to act in accordance with case law; in particular with the *Imperial* duty of good faith.

From an employment law perspective the situation is more complicated.

Termination

7.11   Arguably, termination of a pension scheme (other than cases of insolvencies, where a wind-up would often be automatically triggered), is the real test as to how far an employee has contractual rights against the employer, in addition to the established rights against the trustees under the trust deed and the employee's statutory rights. There is no clear case law on this issue.

As a point of law the question is whether the employer would be in breach of contract by deliberately discontinuing the scheme, or whether it can rely on the express enabling power to terminate contained in the trust deed and (generally) referred to in the booklet. In practice an employer can terminate a pension scheme provided it acts in accordance with the termination procedures contained in the governing documentation. Employers must, however, act very carefully to minimise the risk of any claims by employees and must have a valid reason for wishing to terminate the pension scheme. The most compelling reason will be that the employer simply cannot continue to operate the scheme because of its cost (a reason which has become more commonplace due to the additional costs arising under *PA 1995*).

It would generally be impracticable for an employer to seek the consent of all of the employees who are active scheme members, although this option may sometimes be chosen where the scheme has very few members. Unless the scheme is in deficit, the position of the deferred members and pensioners will be unaffected. A period of consultation may be appropriate, as may negotiations with any trade unions. This will give an employer the opportunity to make the reason for the changes clear, and will also make it more likely that a court would consider that the employer had complied with the *Imperial* duty of good faith. (Consideration should also be given to consultation with employees who are eligible to join the scheme but have so far chosen not to do so.) From April 2006 consultation with employees will be phased in as a statutory requirement in respect of 'listed changes' to occupational and personal pension schemes, of which one is the cessation of future accrual (see 7.12 below).

Alternatively the employer could terminate all existing contracts of employment (by giving the appropriate notice) and issue new contracts, reflecting the less favourable pension provision. There is a risk that, as this is a more aggressive tactic, employees may be able to argue that the unilateral change in their terms of employment constitutes a fundamental breach of contract by the employer which would entitle them to resign and claim constructive dismissal. Additionally, the employer must have a good and substantial reason for wishing to act in this way and the method of implementation must be fair. Also, if the employer has 20 or more employees at an establishment and their employment is terminated within a period of 90 days or less, it would have additional 'collective' information and consultation obligations.

Reduction in benefits in an ongoing scheme

7.12   It has always been generally inadvisable to reduce an employee's past service benefits and in many instances this option will be precluded by the scheme's documentation. In addition, accrued rights and entitlements have been protected (from 6 April 1997) by *section 67* of *PA 1995* (see 12.18 below). The meanings of 'accrued rights' and 'entitlements' are considered in 12.1 below.

If an employer wishes to reduce benefits for future service, for example, by converting a final salary scheme to a money purchase basis, similar considerations to those in 7.9 and 7.10 above will apply. Generally, when a scheme's trust deed or rules are amended, an announcement will be issued to the members. In the context of a diminution of benefits, this course of action is probably not sufficient, and consultation with trade unions or employee representatives (if any) (or under the *Information and Consultation of Employees Regulations 2004 (SI 2004 No 3426)*) may be required and should be considered. It is vital that the impact of the changes is made entirely clear to the employees, to avoid any subsequent rejection of the new terms and conditions and any hostility and suspicion. To try to minimise friction within a workforce, open question and answer sessions or counselling from an external (i e independent) third party is often chosen by employers.

Additionally, pursuant to *sections 259* to *261* of *PA 2004* and the *Occupational and Personal Pension Schemes (Consultation by Employers and Miscellaneous Amendment) Regulations 2006*, a new consultation requirement is being introduced, imposing a duty on employers to consult with existing and prospective members of occupational and personal pension schemes before introducing certain changes to a scheme. Consultation will have to be initiated by employers at least 60 days before the date on which they intend to make a 'listed change'. Listed changes are set out in *regulations 8* and *9* and include increasing the normal pensions age; closure of the scheme to new members; preventing future accrual of benefits; changing some or all of the benefits provided under a defined benefits scheme to money purchase benefits; or changing the contributions required from members or provided by the employer.

The Regulations require employers to initiate the consultation process by providing specified written information to all affected members and representatives of those members describing the change and the effects it will have and providing relevant background information. In the absence of there being existing employee representatives, employers will have to arrange for their appointment or elections. If the employees do not appoint or elect representatives, employers will have to consult with all affected employees individually. Employers must consider the comments made by employee representatives during the consultation, although the final decision will rest with them. There is no definition of 'consultation' although the Regulations state that 'the relevant employer and any person consulted are under a duty to work in a spirit of co-operation, taking into account the interests of both sides'.

The new consultation requirement will be phased in over a two-year period starting from 6 April 2006. It will apply to employers with 150 or more employees from 6 April 2006, employers with 100 or more employees from 6 April 2007 and employers with 50 or more employees from 6 April 2008. Employers with fewer than 50 employees will not be affected by the new requirements.

The issue of reduction of accrued rights was considered by the High Court in *Lloyds Bank Pension Trust Corporation v Lloyds Bank plc (1996) PLR 263*. In that case the power of amendment was vested jointly in the trustee and the employer, but precluded (*inter alia*) alterations which would in the opinion of the actuary decrease 'the pecuniary benefits secured to or in respect of … members under the scheme'. The trustee and company brought the court application to determine whether the trustee could agree to equalise benefits in accordance with a proposal put forward by the employer. The proposal effectively equalised male benefits up to the female level for the period 17 May 1990 to 30 April 2000 (at a cost of £100 million), but equalised female benefits down to the previous male level for the period 1 May 2000 onwards. The scheme also contained express provisions requiring member consent to any alterations. Although this case turns on its own facts and the peculiarity of the amendment power, the legal reasoning is of interest. The judge considered that, except with the requisite level of member consent, no amendment could be made either affecting accrued rights or future benefits and, accordingly, the court would not endorse the amendment.

Similar issues were considered by the Pensions Ombudsman in his determination in respect of the dissolution of the National Bus Company (*National Bus Company* – Determination of the Pensions Ombudsman, 6 September 1996 *(1997) PLR 1)*. The power of amendment was, subject to trustee consent, vested in the company, and contained a proviso that accrued rights could not be affected without obtaining written member consent. As part of a package offered by the company the trustee agreed to alter the basis of indexation on wind up. The Ombudsman considered that the indexation changes affected 'at least some members' benefits' and that accordingly consent had been required. As the trustee, even if acting innocently, had altered benefits in contravention of the power of amendment, the trustee was under an obligation to recover surplus monies paid to the Department of Transport, which inherited the rights and obligations of the company on its dissolution. On 1 June 1999, John Prescott, Deputy Prime Minister, announced that the Government had reached a settlement with the trustees and on 1 August 1999 paid over £355.77 million. What followed was the lengthy and difficult task of several court applications to assist the trustees to ensure the fair and equitable distribution of the returned monies. The final distribution to eligible members is now in progress.

Although it is now beyond doubt, following *Barber* and *Coloroll*, that pensions are deferred pay, whether the employer has obligations (whether fiduciary or contractual or arising from the duty of good faith) not to restrict, reduce or terminate the possibility of earning that future pay has yet to be tested in the courts. Given the wording of (or at least what could be considered to be the intention of) *PA 1995*, a successful challenge seems unlikely. However, in certain circumstances resulting from the particular drafting of scheme documents, such as highlighted in the *Lloyds Bank* case and the *National Bus Company* determination, nothing can be taken for granted. Both of these cases indicate how carefully scheme documents have to be drafted and construed by trustees and employers, as a narrow interpretation is likely to be imposed by a court or the Pensions Ombudsman in the event of a dispute.

How do the trustees fit in?

General

7.13   The trustees of a pension scheme have an overriding duty to act in the best interests of the beneficiaries, which usually means their best financial interests (see chapter 3). If the power of amendment is vested solely in the employer, the trustees cannot control the outcome, save to ensure that the amendment complies with the requirements of *PA 1995, s 67* (except perhaps by way of court application in extreme circumstances, which could either be an injunction to prevent an amendment being made or an application for directions). When the power of amendment is vested in the trustees (or the trustees have to consent to the exercise of a power vested in the employer), the trustees must confine their considerations to the implications for the existing members (including deferred members and pensioners) only. Depending on the particular circumstances, the trustees may also wish to take into account the position of prospective beneficiaries (for example, if there was a waiting period before employees could join the scheme).

Whatever action the trustees take will depend very much on the circumstances; say, trustees are faced with a future reduction in benefits (for example, 60ths accrual to 80ths or final salary to money purchase). They may be persuaded that the amendment is in the interests of all members if the only other alternative is that the scheme will be discontinued because the employer cannot (for sound commercial reasons) afford to continue the current level of promised benefits. In all but the rarest of cases it must be in the beneficiaries' best interests to have an ongoing scheme. This was highlighted in *Re Courage Group Pension Schemes [1987] 1 All ER 528* where the judge stated that 'it is important to avoid fettering the power to amend the provisions of the scheme, thereby preventing the parties from making those changes which may be required by the exigencies of commercial life'.

The trustees may often find themselves in the position of arbitrators between an employer and employee if a dispute over a pension issue arises. Often trust deeds confer upon the trustees the power to reach decisions on any matter of doubt arising under the scheme documentation. Since 6 April 1997, the trustees have had to put in place an internal dispute resolution procedure in accordance with *section 50* of *PA 1995*. (For further details see chapter 3). This requirement for a dispute resolution procedure does not, however, extend to disputes between a member and an employer. The trustees may delegate their obligations to deal with the initial query to another 'person' (this is not defined in *PA 1995* or the regulations made under *section 50* but could be one of the trustees). However, the trustees must take a final decision if the outcome of the initial investigation is not to the satisfaction of the employee. (It is worth noting that *section 273* of *PA 2004* was due to make a number of changes to how schemes will deal with dispute resolution from April 2006, which the DWP has since decided not to bring into effect. The intended requirements did not however change the type of complaints that could be brought under the IDRP process.)

In cases of dismissal or leaving service

7.14 When an employment contract is terminated, the leaving service rules of the scheme will apply and the employee will become a deferred member. The trustees will be obliged, if the ex-employee so requests, to provide details of his options under the trust deed in accordance with the requirements of the *Disclosure Regulations (SI 1996 No 1655)* and the *Preservation Regulations (SI 1991 No 167)*. If the employee takes no action to exercise an option available to him he will simply continue to be treated as a deferred member.

Depending on whom the power to augment is vested in, the trustees may have to liaise with an employer on dismissal or redundancy packages (see 7.15 below).

Entitlements in cases of dismissal or redundancy

Redundancy

7.15 If an employee is entitled to a statutory redundancy payment, such a payment will be based upon his age, length of continuous employment and his gross average weekly pay (subject to a maximum of £280 a week with effect from 1 February 2005). For the purposes of *ERA 1996*, pay means either the remuneration payable under his contract or, alternatively, his pay based on his average hourly rate.

The *ERA 1996* definition of 'a week's pay' does not include any element relating to an employer's contributions to a pension scheme. Therefore, an employee's pension entitlement on redundancy will depend upon the wording of the scheme documentation. Generally, if the employee has been a member for less than two years he will be entitled to a return of his contributions (less tax as calculated under the new provisions of *section 204, Schedules 31* and *36* of *FA 2004*), otherwise he will become a deferred member. It is also worth bearing in mind that many schemes, particularly ex-public sector ones, retain beneficial redundancy/early retirement provisions.

The employer should also consider its rights under *section 158* of *ERA 1996* and the *Redundancy Payments Pensions Regulations 1965 (SI 1965 No 1932)* to reduce or extinguish a redundancy payment in certain circumstances where a pension is payable immediately from the scheme.

Unfair dismissal

7.16   Unfair dismissal is the dismissal of an employee entitled to protection under *ERA 1996* without a potentially fair reason or without following a fair procedure.

If an employee establishes that he has been unfairly dismissed (the burden of proof being on the employee to establish dismissal and on the employer to establish the reason for the dismissal and, effectively, that it was fair) he will usually be awarded compensation comprising a basic award, based on his weekly pay (subject to the statutory cap), age and length of service, and also to a compensatory award. Other alternative remedies include reinstatement or re-engagement, but are less common. The effect of a reinstatement or re-engagement order is that the previous terms and conditions remain in force so, for pension purposes, the employer and employee will simply have to pay arrears of contributions. This, of course, presupposes that the rules of the scheme allow the employee to rejoin.

The maximum basic award for claims where the effective date of termination is on or after 1 February 2006 is currently £8,700 and does not include benefits in kind. Under *sections 123* and *124* of *ERA 1996* the compensatory award is such an amount as the employment tribunal considers just and equitable in all the circumstances, having regard to the loss sustained by the complainant, including loss of any pension benefit, subject to a current maximum of £58,400. The above figures are normally adjusted on 1 February every year. The tribunal has discretion to reduce any award if it believes that the complainant has caused or contributed to his dismissal or has failed to mitigate his loss by securing suitable alternative employment. An additional award is payable where reinstatement or re-engagement orders have not been complied with. This latter award does not include allowance for loss of pension benefits.

In practice, an employee may suffer loss of pension rights if he fails to find new employment or if his new employer does not operate a pension scheme or operates a less beneficial scheme. Compensation for loss of pension rights is often difficult to quantify. Until recently employment tribunals were happy to use as a starting point a 'rough and ready' style of calculation found in guidelines originally prepared in 1990 by the Government Actuary's Department in consultation with three employment tribunal chairmen ('Industrial Tribunals – Compensation for Loss of Pension Rights'). These guidelines, now known as 'the simplified approach', were last updated in 2003. They are used in the majority of employment tribunal cases, requiring a loss to be viewed in three stages, namely:

(*a*)   between the date of the dismissal and the date of the hearing (being the actual loss sustained, for example, the difference between an old and a new employer's benefit provision or, if the complainant is unemployed, between the scheme benefits and State scheme benefits);

(*b*) the loss of future pension rights to the date of retirement (which is essentially speculation on the part of the employment tribunal – it may even conclude that the employee's future earnings and benefits will never match his old package, thus the loss may continue over the remainder of his working life); and

(*c*) the enhancement of accrued pension rights.

The report also provides guidance on how tribunals should reach a just and equitable sum for compensation. It allows the parties to adduce actuarial evidence and breaks down the calculation into three areas:

(i) when attempting to calculate the loss of rights which would have accrued between the date of dismissal and the hearing, reference should be made to the contributions which the employer would have made during that period (although the report admits that this method is not technically correct);

(ii) for the calculation of loss of future pension rights between the date of the hearing and the date of retirement, the employment tribunal should estimate how long it will take for the applicant to enter equivalent employment;

(iii) when calculating the loss of enhancement of the pension rights accrued to the date of dismissal, no enhancement should be granted where the applicant is in any public sector scheme, where he is within five years of retirement or where the employment would have been terminated within one year. Otherwise a multiple (as set out in the report) will be utilised and the employment tribunal may also, at its discretion, apply a withdrawal factor, based on the likelihood of the complainant leaving service, being made redundant or fairly dismissed.

In a few cases, where it is generally considered that the employee will suffer a quantifiable continuing loss and where, for example, the employment was stable and unlikely to have been affected by economic cycles, where the employment lasted a considerable period of time and where the employee reached an age where he was less likely to seek new employment, the guidelines recommend the use of 'the substantial loss approach'. The substantial loss approach involves the use of actuarial tables to assess the capitalised value of the pension rights which the employee would have accrued up to retirement. The actuarial tables use factors that are similar to those in the Ogden Tables for personal injury and fatal accident cases, although some of the assumptions used are different. Calculation under the substantial loss approach automatically includes compensation for loss of enhancement of accrued pension rights at the date of dismissal and for loss of pension rights from the date of dismissal to the date of the hearing, as well as for loss of future pension rights from the date of the hearing.

What calculation method is used is a crucial issue, as the different methods can produce different results and make a substantial difference to the amount of compensation awarded in respect of pension losses. The guidance makes it clear that the ultimate decision as to the method of calculation to be used always rests with the employment tribunal.

Before the publication of the updated version of the guidance, the Employment Appeal Tribunal had ruled that there was no duty on employment tribunals to give precise effect to the guidelines (*Bingham v Hoboun Engineering Ltd [1992] IRLR 298*). Following the increase of the maximum compensatory award under all heads from £10,000 to £50,000 (£56,800 from 1 February 2005) (*ERA 1996, s 124(1)*), loss of earnings may now be less likely to be the major component of any compensatory award and arguably it is becoming more necessary for pension loss calculations to be precise.

Indeed, in *Clancy v Cannock Chase Technical College [2001] IRLR 331*, the Employment Appeal Tribunal noted that the guidelines were drawn up at a time when the compensatory award was set at £10,000. In the EAT's opinion, the significant raising of the cap meant that an accurate compensation for loss of pensions will be relevant (rather than reliance on the guidelines) in many more cases in the future. Evidently, this is not the view taken by the Government Actuary's Department.

Wrongful dismissal

7.17   If an employer dismisses an employee without good cause in breach of an obligation to give notice (either statutory or contractual) and the employee suffers loss as a result it will be liable to pay to that employee damages for wrongful dismissal. The primary remedy is damages, normally equal to loss of earnings and other contractual benefits up to the earliest date upon which the contract could have been lawfully terminated by the employer. The aim of damages is to put the employee in the same position as he would have been had the contract been performed, although the employee is usually under a duty to mitigate his loss.

It is unlikely that an employer could successfully argue that it should not pay damages by reference to the pension scheme on the grounds that it could have been terminated by it at any time in accordance with the trust deed. However such a claim could be effective in respect of a single employee scheme.

In practice, most compensation payments will be negotiated between the employer and employee. For example, if a fixed-term contract was terminated two years before it could lawfully have been terminated, this period will be the starting point for the assessment of loss of pay and other benefits.

With a final salary arrangement, the employee would have been entitled to two years' additional pensionable service, perhaps taking into account an assumed pay rise if provision for this was made in the contract. If pay increases were not provided for in the contract, these will not be taken into account (i e the actual salary at the date of termination will be used), nor will any element of discretionary increases. The following three methods can be used to calculate the loss:

(*a*) The award of an additional two years' notional pensionable service to the employee under the rules of the scheme, dealing with the award under the augmentation provisions. The trustees would require payment of an additional contribution (generally a lump sum) by the employer to cover this (an actuary would be required to advise on the payment of this contribution, and, depending on the employee's age, it may not be simply a case of utilising the general scheme contribution rate as the nearer an employee is to normal retirement date, the more costly this becomes).

(*b*) The most straightforward way of calculating the damages to be paid directly to the employee would be by reference to the employer contribution rate over the two-year period. This would not produce an accurate result (effectively younger employees may be over-compensated) and is more appropriate for money purchase arrangements. If it is used for the basis for calculating damages, it should be subject to grossing up and discounting for early receipt if it is paid directly to the employee.

(*c*) Loss can also be calculated by reference to the difference in capital value of the benefits accrued to the effective date of dismissal and the capital value of the benefits which would have been accrued up to the end of the notice period. This is the most accurate method and actuarial advice will be required.

In a money purchase arrangement, the compensation will be calculated on the basis of the employer contributions which would have been made in the two-year period and an assumed investment return and (potentially) an allowance for salary increases. Similarly, discounting may apply.

Alternatively, an HMRC concession permits the compensation for loss of pension rights to be paid as a contribution to the pension scheme. This may be more tax efficient for the employer (HMRC could seek to disallow a proportion of a payment made directly to an employee on the grounds that it is not made wholly and exclusively for the purposes of the employer's trade). It may also be advantageous to the employee, if, for example, he is approaching retirement.

If the employee is over age 50 it may be worth considering early retirement, to be funded by an additional amount of the damages being paid into the scheme. This can be tax efficient from both an employer and employee viewpoint (although care has to be taken to ensure that the employee does not become liable to tax on the payment into the scheme as a benefit in kind). However it may be less attractive if the augmentation does not compensate for the use of actuarial reduction factors. It would be necessary to involve the pension scheme trustees, as this would be an augmentation of the employee's pension benefits and in all likelihood either trustee or company consent would be required for the early retirement to go ahead (if there is not a consent mechanism and the employee is entitled to pension benefits as of right under the trust deed, *Hopkins v Norcross (1994) PLR 18* confirmed that pension payments cannot be deducted from a wrongful dismissal award, thus leading to an element of double compensation). The advice of an actuary on the scope of the augmentation will also be required.

The employer's aim should ultimately be to negotiate a settlement which should be full and final to preclude the bringing of further claims.

The express pension promise and GPPs

7.18   It is highly unusual for an employer to give an express contractual commitment to provide specified pension benefits in a contract of employment, except perhaps in the case of senior executives. If such a commitment is made, the employee's pension rights, in the event of dismissal or redundancy, will depend entirely on the wording of the pension promise. If, for example, the contract states that the executive shall be entitled to a pension of two-thirds of his salary at the date he leaves the employer, the executive will have a contractual right against the employer if those precise benefits are not paid, and it may be necessary for an employer to provide partially unapproved benefits (see chapter 5) if HMRC or scheme limits prevent the commitment being met out of the approved scheme.

Following 6 April 2006, however, when HMRC limits and the distinction between approved and unapproved benefits cease to apply, employers are likely to have more flexibility in paying such benefits (see chapter 5 in relation to changes to HMRC limits and approved/unapproved benefits).

It is, however, unlikely that a pension promise would be so widely drafted. Generally the promise will be contingent upon the executive remaining with the company until his normal retirement date, the benefits will be payable from his normal retirement date, they will often be subject to HMRC limits and termination conditions will usually be incorporated. The lesson for employers is to take great care in drafting the contract of employment, and not to make any oral commitments.

A more common example of a contractual pension promise in today's climate is a Group Personal Pension, or GPP. This is a straightforward contractual arrangement between employer and employee. The employee joins the GPP, which will be administered by an insurance company. The employer's only commitment is to pay contributions on a fixed basis (for instance, a stated percentage of pensionable salary) for so long as the employee is employed by the employer.

Exclusion in deed and rules

7.19   Many trust deeds contain a clause to the effect that an employer has no liability to compensate employees for loss of pension rights on termination of employment. Case law makes it clear that the *Unfair Contract Terms Act 1977 (UCTA 1977)* applies to contracts of employment (for example, *Brigden v American Express Bank Ltd [2001] IRLR 94*). This means that it is unlikely that such a clause will be effective, as either it is not a term of the contract of employment (being contained in the rules of the pension scheme only and not referred to in the employment contract) or, if it is part of the contract, it will fail the test of reasonableness under *section 3* of *UCTA 1977*.

In addition, *section 203* of *ERA 1996* provides that, subject to a number of exceptions, any agreement precluding an individual from making an unfair dismissal claim is void (the most relevant exception to this – that a fixed-term contract of one year or more can exclude an employee's right to bring an unfair dismissal claim – has been removed by *ERA 1999, s 18* with effect from 25 October 1999). Such a clause is therefore unlikely to afford any real protection to an employer.

Lump sum death in service benefits

7.20   Is an employer liable for the payment of a lump sum benefit if an employee dies following a dismissal which is wrongful or unfair? Providing death in service benefits can be costly and most insurance policies will lapse when an employee leaves service (although for larger schemes which self-insure, the provisions of the trust deed will apply).

In wrongful dismissal cases the employer would be liable if the employee died during the notice period, although it is likely that the duty to mitigate loss would apply. In certain cases the trustees of a scheme may also be liable, as the Pensions Ombudsman ruled in the complaint by *Mrs E Richards* in connection with the Merchant Navy Ratings Pension Fund (May 1999). Consequently, an employee should make his own arrangements (and be compensated for the cost of so doing in his damages award) unless he is uninsurable as a single life (for example, he may be unable to pass a medical). Any action would subsist for the benefit of the estate of the deceased.

The situation is less clear cut in cases of unfair dismissal. In such a situation the tribunal will make an award which it considers to be fair and reasonable, but bearing in mind the limits on compensation a wise employee would arrange his own life cover following the dismissal.

If an employee obtains a reinstatement or re-engagement order his employer should double-check the policy or rules to ensure that life cover continues and that the free cover limit is not breached.

Business reorganisations

Purchase of a company with its own scheme

7.21   If a company purchases the entire issued share capital of another company, the employees' pension rights will not be affected if the latter company operates its own pension scheme, as the scheme will simply remain in place after the sale.

Purchase of a business

7.22   The situation is different if an employer purchases a business or part of a business, in circumstances where the *Transfer of Undertakings (Protection of Employment) Regulations 2006 (SI 2006 No 246) (TUPE)* apply. These *TUPE* regulations came into force on 6 April 2006 replacing the *Transfer of Undertakings (Protection of Employment) Regulations 1981 (SI 1981 No 1794) (TUPE 1981)*. The provisions relating to occupational pensions in *TUPE and TUPE 1981* are substantially the same. In such a scenario, following the 'relevant transfer' the transferring employees become the employees of the purchasing employer. Their employment contracts are not terminated, and the rights and obligations under the contracts pass to the purchasing employer. Until 6 April 2005, most rights under 'supplementary pension schemes' did not transfer as a result of an exclusion contained in *regulation 7* of *TUPE 1981* (now *regula tion 10* of *TUPE*). However, the position changed on 6 April 2005.

The law up to April 2005

7.23   *Regulation 10* of *TUPE* (previously *regulation 7* of *TUPE 1981*) excludes 'supplementary pension schemes' from the 'automatic transfer' effect of the regulations. *TUPE 1981* was intended to implement the *Acquired Rights Directive* (*Council Directive 77/187/EEC*) which states that protection will not be granted to supplementary company pension schemes but nevertheless expressly requires Member States to adopt 'the measures necessary' to protect the scheme members. This has been reinforced by an amending *Acquired Rights Directive* (*Council Directive 2001/23/EC*), adopted on 12 March 2001, which effectively gives Member States the option of protecting pension rights under national legislation.

There have been a number of cases on the scope of *TUPE 1981*. In January 1992 in the case of *Warrener v Walden Engineering Co Ltd (1992) PLR 1*, the Hull Employment Tribunal was asked to consider employees' pension rights when, following a business sale the new employer decided to discontinue all pension arrangements. The Tribunal stated that the benefits provided by the scheme had been 'part of the contract of employment' and that if a pension scheme is terminated an employee has a contractual right to an equivalent scheme, providing benefits no less beneficial, being set up in its place. This case was based on the argument that, as the pension scheme was contracted out of the State earnings-related pension scheme, it was not a supplementary pension scheme for the purposes of *regulation 7* of *TUPE 1981*.

In December 1992 came the case of *Perry v Intec Colleges Ltd (1993) PLR 56* in the Bristol Employment Tribunal. The decision in the case was reached on a different interpretation of *TUPE*; the complainant argued that *TUPE 1981* had failed to translate the aims of the *Acquired Rights Directive* into UK law (i e the subsidiary aim to protect employees). After the transfer no pension provision was to be made for the employees. It was held that the complainant was entitled to pension provision at least as beneficial as that which he had received prior to the transfer. It was suggested that to compensate the employee adequately, the employer should make an equivalent percentage contribution to a personal pension scheme and should also make a lump sum payment to compensate for lost opportunity to enhance accrued pension benefits. In effect, the Tribunal was advocating double recovery.

In June 1993 the Employment Appeal Tribunal overturned the first instance decision in *Warrener* (*Walden Engineering Co Ltd v Warrener [1993] PLR 295*); meaning that an employer does not have to maintain the pension benefits enjoyed by employees prior to a business sale. The Employment Appeal Tribunal stated that a contracted-out scheme is a supplementary scheme (i e supplementary to the basic State scheme) for the purposes of *TUPE 1981*, and accordingly, the employer was protected under the *regulation 7* exclusion. In January 1996 this approach was sanctioned by the High Court in the case of *Adams & Ors v Lancashire County Council & Ors [1996] All ER 473*. The judge stated that *TUPE* required protection to be given to accrued rights only (which are protected as deferred benefits in the transferor employer's scheme by the preservation requirements now set out in *PSA 1993*). On 15 May 1997 the High Court Decision was upheld by the Court of Appeal (*[1997] IRLR 436*).

In *Hagen v ICI Chemicals and Polymers Ltd [2001] 64 PBLR, [2001] All ER (D) 273 (Oct)*, the High Court held that a transferor had made a negligent misrepresentation when persuading its employees to accept a *TUPE* transfer, when it stated that their pension rights after the transfer would be 'broadly comparable' to their pre-transfer rights. The court held that 'broadly comparable' meant no more than 2 per cent difference whereas, in practice, some claimants would have been 5 per cent worse off. Liability for misrepresentations normally passes from transferor to transferee under *TUPE 1981 (regulation 5(2)(a))*. However, since the misrepresentation related to pension entitlement, and was caught by *regulation 7*, liability remained with the transferor only.

One important exception to the exclusion of pension rights from *TUPE* comes under *regulation 10(2) (regulation 7(2) of TUPE 1981)* which attempts to implement *Article 3(3)* of the *Acquired Rights Directive* (now *Article 3(4)* of the *Acquired Rights Directive 2001*). *Article 3(4)* excludes from the automatic transfer provisions 'employees' rights to old-age, invalidity or survivors' benefits under supplementary company or inter-company pension schemes ...'. *Regulations 10(1)* and (2) of *TUPE* stipulate that contractual provisions on occupational pension schemes do not transfer from the transferor to the transferee, except that 'any provisions of an occupational pension scheme which do not relate to benefits for old-age, invalidity or survivors shall be treated as not being part of the Scheme'. For many years, it was unclear whether certain benefits provided under occupational pension schemes (for example, enhanced redundancy terms on early retirement, life assurance etc) fall within *regulation 10(2)*. This question has been dealt with, to some degree, by the ECJ in *Beckmann v Dynamco Whicheloe Macfarlane Ltd, Case C-164/00 [2002] 64 PBLR; [2002] All ER (D) 05 (Jun)*. The ECJ ruled that the exceptions contained in *Article 3(4)* of the *Directive* ought to be interpreted narrowly so as to apply only to old-age, invalidity or survivors benefits under occupational pension schemes falling due at the end of 'normal working life'. Other benefits, such as early retirement benefits and redundancy payments are excluded. (The decision in *Beckman* has recently been approved in *Martin and others v South Bank University C 4/01, [2004] 1 CMLR 472, [2003] All ER (D) 85 (Nov)*. See 16.15 for further elaboration on this topic.)

The Government has also made specific provisions regarding transfer of pension rights in the context of public sector transfers. (See chapter 16 for further elaboration on this topic.)

The law after April 2005

7.24   Following extensive consultation exercises since 1998, the Government has introduced new pensions provisions which give limited protection to employees where the transferring employer has an occupational pension scheme. The protection extends to both scheme members and those eligible to join. Under *sections 257* and *258 of PA 2004* and the *Transfer of Employment (Pension Protection) Regulations 2005 (SI 2005 No 649)*, which came into force on 6 April 2005, transferee employers must offer transferring employees:

(*a*) membership of the transferee employer's occupational defined contribution or defined benefit pension scheme or a stakeholder scheme and make into the scheme matching contributions of up to 6 per cent of an employee's basic pay; or

(*b*) membership of an occupational defined benefit pension scheme which provides benefits the value of which is equal to no less than 6 per cent of an employee's pensionable pay (as set out in the scheme rules) for each year of employment together with the total amount of an employee's contributions. Employees will not be required to make contributions in excess of 6 per cent of their pensionable pay; or

(*c*) membership of an occupational defined benefit pension scheme which satisfies *section 12A* of *PSA 1993* (i e the reference scheme test for contracting out).

There is some uncertainty over how arrangements (*b*) and (*c*) will operate in practice and it is expected that each scheme and transfer scenario will have to be considered on its own facts.

It is interesting to note that the reference scheme test requirement may provide higher benefits than the transferring employer's scheme provided. It is also important to note that because the *Transfer of Employment (Pension Protection) Regulations 2005 (SI 2005 No 649)* have not amended and are not incorporated into *TUPE*, the employer and employee can agree that the above protections will not apply and that different pension arrangements will operate.

Employers should always be cautious in situations where *TUPE* applies; if inferior pension provision is to be offered following a relevant transfer, providing the employees with alternative compensation may be the safest route and will go some way to forestalling industrial unrest. Transferor employers would be well advised to seek indemnity cover; although the judge in *Adams* confirmed that he did not believe that employees could claim against the transferor employer, this point has not yet been tested.

Purchase of a subsidiary participating in its parent's scheme

7.25 Similar considerations to those outlined at 7.22 above would apply on the sale of a company which participates in a holding company pension arrangement although *TUPE* itself would not apply. In practice if a new employer is unable to provide equivalent pension provision, alternative methods of compensation (for example, pay rises) should be considered.

Employer's lien

7.26   Many pension schemes permit a lien to be placed on benefits payable where the employee or ex-employee owes money to the employer or the trustees of a scheme resulting from criminal, negligent or fraudulent acts or omissions. Liens are now governed by *sections 91 to 94 of PA 1995*, and are an exception to the general rule that pension benefits can not be assigned or forfeited. However, a lien rule can only operate with the agreement of the employee unless a court or arbitrator has made an order or award in the employer's favour (*sections 91(5)(d) and 93(3)) of PA 1995*). As an employee can insist on his statutory rights to payment of a guaranteed cash equivalent (see chapter 6), trustees may be forced to pay benefits out before a court or arbitrator has considered the lien issue unless they obtain a time extension for the payment of the cash equivalent.

It should be borne in mind that a lien cannot attach to benefits deriving from transfer credits (unless the transfer is attributable to employment with the same or an associated employer and the transferring scheme contained an appropriate lien rule) (*Occupational Pension Schemes (Assignment, Forfeiture, Bankruptcy etc) Regulations 1997 (SI 1997 No 785), reg 3*), and no part of a guaranteed minimum pension or protected rights may be subject to deduction. The amount that can be recovered is limited to the lesser of the actuarial value of the employee's actual or prospective benefits and the amount of the monetary obligation owed to the employer or trustees of a scheme (*section 91(6) of PA 1995*).

Due to the restrictions referred to above, and in particular the need for consent or a court order or decision of an arbitrator, lien rules are often difficult to operate in practice.

Discrimination

Equality generally

7.27   The issue of sex equality is covered in detail in chapter 9, but it is worth mentioning here the impact of *PA 1995*. *Section 62 of PA 1995* (which came into force on 1 January 1996) implies overriding equality provisions into the rules of occupational pension schemes, to ensure that men and women are treated equally (in terms of both access to benefits and the benefits to be provided). The trustees are empowered, irrespective of the power of amendment contained in the trust documentation, to make whatever amendments are required to ensure compliance with *PA 1995* equal treatment requirements.

The position in respect of transsexuals has been unclear for some time, but in 2004 much awaited ECJ guidance was given. In December 2000, the Court of Appeal referred to the European Court of Justice the question of whether the exclusion of the female-to-male transsexual partner of a female member of the NHS Pension Scheme, which limits the material dependent's benefit to her widower, constitutes sex discrimination in contravention of *Article 141* of the *Rome Treaty* and the *Equal Treatment Directive* (*KB v National Health Service Pensions Agency C-117/01 [2004] ICR 781, ECJ*). The ECJ has ruled that it is unlawful under *Article 141* of the *Rome Treaty* to prevent a female-to-male transsexual from benefiting under the pension scheme of his female partner due to national legislation which prevents transsexuals from marrying.

It is important to note that the ECJ stated that the mere limitation on payment of benefits to married persons is not discriminatory under *Article 141*, as this would apply equally to men and women. The discrimination in the present case arose from the fact that, under the law, transsexuals, in contrast to heterosexuals, are prevented from getting married. However, it is up to the British courts to determine if a person in the applicant's position can rely on *Article 141* to ensure that she can nominate her partner as a beneficiary of her scheme.

In principle, it is a matter for the Court of Appeal to decide how to implement the ECJ's judgment. However, in respect of future rights, as of April 2005, under the *Gender Recognition Act 2004*, transsexuals have a right to lawfully marry under UK law (see 7.35 below).

Part-time workers

7.28   Under the *Part-Time Workers* (*Prevention of Less Favourable Treatment*) *Regulations 2000* (*SI 2000/1551*), which came into force on 1 July 2000, part-time workers (not only employees) ought not to be treated less favourably than comparable full-time workers in their terms and conditions, unless a difference is objectively justified. In particular, this means that from 1 July 2000 part-time workers are entitled to have the same access to occupational pension schemes. The level of benefits offered also needs to be equal but pro-rated under general principles of equality law. For a difference in treatment to be objectively justifiable, the employer is likely to have to show that its policy corresponds to a real business need; is an appropriate method of achieving that objective; and is necessary in order to achieve that objective. Claims under the Regulations may only be made against an employer. The retrospective two-year limit on the remedies which employment tribunals may award (currently *regulation 8*) has been declared incompatible with EU law in *Preston & others v Wolverhampton*

Healthcare NHS Trust [2001] 2 WLR 448 and has been removed with effect from 1 October 2002 by the *Part-time Workers (Prevention of Less Favourable Treatment) Regulations 2002 (SI 2002 No 2035)*. This decision has now been codified by the *Occupational Pension Schemes (Equal Treatment) (Amendment) Regulations 2005 (SI 2005 No 1923)*. Under the Regulations:

- part-time employees have the right to recover backdated scheme benefits going back to 8 April 1976, or the date of commencement of their employment, if later;

- time for making claims is extended to six months from the date of termination of the employment or the end of a stable employment relationship; but

- employers will no longer have to meet the cost of employee contributions in backdated claims.

The Regulations came into force on 1 August 2005. Full details are set out in chapter 9. For claims to succeed, a part-time worker must establish that a comparable full-time worker was treated differently.

In respect of claims preceding 1 July 2000, the question of whether a part-time employee is entitled to be granted pension scheme access depends on whether or not denial of membership constitutes indirect sex discrimination (on the basis that most part-time employees are women). If not, there is no breach of the overriding equal treatment rule and if so, membership may still be denied if the exclusion can be objectively justified by factors unrelated to sex. If indirect discrimination is established, future pension benefits of affected employees will have to be calculated with reference to their periods of service from the latter of 8 April 1976, being the date of *Defrenne v Sabena (No 2) [1976] ECR 445* and the date of commencement of employment (*Preston & others v Wolverhampton Healthcare NHS Trust [2001] 2 WLR 448*).

A number of other important principles continue to emerge in relation to the rights of part-time workers, as a result of the ongoing litigation in *Preston*. Thus in *Preston & Others v Wolverhampton Healthcare NHS Trust (No3), [2004] All ER (D) 175 (Feb)*, the Employment Appeal Tribunal ('EAT') ruled that:

(i) The exclusion of a part-time employee from membership in a pension scheme, where such membership had been compulsory for full-time employees, was unlawful. This is the case even if the part-time employee would not have joined the scheme had she been eligible.

(ii) However, *Article 141* of the *Rome Treaty* would not be breached where pension scheme membership is compulsory for full-time workers but only optional for part-time employees. A requirement that a part-time employee opts into the scheme does not contravene the requirement of equality. In addition, Information Bulletin 9 of the Employment Tribunal makes it clear that where membership by full-time employees was optional and part-time employees were excluded, a part-time employee would not have a claim if she did not join the scheme once the rules changed or soon afterwards.

(iii) There is no continuing breach of *Article 141* by an employer failing to inform a part-time employee of his or her entitlement to join the pension scheme, unless that failure was itself on discriminatory grounds. However, employees may have a breach of contract claim in such circumstances on the basis of the employer's implied obligation to inform employees of advantageous contractual terms (*Scally and others v Southern Health and Social Services Board, [1991] 4 All ER 563*).

(iv) The six-month time limit for bringing a claim under the *Equal Pay Act 1970*, in the context of 'stable employee relationships' begins to run when:

   • either party indicates that further contracts will not be offered or accepted;

   • either party acts in a manner which is inconsistent with the relationship continuing;

   • the employer does not offer a new contract in circumstances where 'the periodicity of the preceding cycle of contracts indicates that it should have been offered';

   • either party stops treating the relationship as stable; or

   • the terms under which work is to be done alter radically;

(v) Since liabilities for occupational pension schemes do not transfer under *TUPE*, liability under the *Equal Pay Act 1970* and *Article 141* of the *Rome Treaty*, for the transferor's failure to provide equal access to a scheme, remains with the transferor.

(vi) Following a *TUPE* transfer, time for bringing a claim against the transferor begins to run from the date the employee's employment with the transferee comes to an end. This point has been subjected to a prolonged appeal process. The House of Lords gave judgment on 8 March 2006 (*[2006] UKHL 13*) ruling that time for bringing a claim begins to run from the date of the transfer.

Inland Revenue Pension Update No 131 confirms the Treasury's position that tax relief will only be available on employees' back contributions up to 15 per cent of remuneration in the tax year in which the contribution is actually paid. Scheme rules may allow for higher contributions in excess of the 15 per cent but they will attract no tax relief. Payments may, with the agreement of the trustees, be made in instalments to spread the tax relief. If the member has left the relevant employment but is being allowed to make retrospective contributions, no tax relief at all is given.

Employers' contributions to fund back service will be allowable for tax purposes in the normal way under *section 592(4)* of *ICTA 1988*.

Lump sum compensation payments outside the pension scheme will not be taxable as income under *Schedule E* but may attract capital gains tax – the usual annual exemptions will apply.

Where a member has already retired and taken benefits an additional lump sum may not be paid but if a transfer payment has been made an additional supplementary transfer can be paid (see PSO Update No 40).

With regard to the limits on employer and employee contributions mentioned above, it should be noted that, under *FA 2004*, from 6 April 2006 the current limits on contributions will disappear.

Fixed-term (temporary) workers

7.29   EU *Council Directive 1999/70/EC* on *Fixed Term Work* prohibits employers from treating fixed-term workers less favourably than comparable permanent workers, unless a difference is objectively justified. The UK Government has implemented the Directive under the *Fixed-Term Employees* (*Prevention of Less Favourable Treatment*) *Regulations 2002* (*SI 2002 No 2034*). The *Regulations* came into force on 1 October 2002. Essentially the *Regulations* require employers not to discriminate against fixed-term employees (not 'workers' as per the Directive) as compared with permanent employees, in the terms of their contract, unless the difference can be objectively justified. It needs to be appreciated that under the *Regulations* employers are not obliged to offer an identical package of terms as long as, on the whole, the contract is no less favourable.

The Government was of the opinion that the Directive does not apply to pay and occupational pension schemes. The *Regulations* do cover pay and occupational pension schemes, however, and thus access to pension arrangements and level of benefits offered. In the pensions context, therefore, employers are required to offer fixed-term employees the same rights of entry to the pension scheme and the same benefits under it as they do for permanent employees. One difficulty is the two-year vesting period. Many employees on contracts fixed for less than two years might well not want to contribute to the scheme if the only benefit will be a return of contributions. The administrative costs to the employer also might be disproportionate to the benefit (although balanced against this might be the death in service benefit). However, not to offer participation would be a high risk strategy. There may also be *Imperial* type issues which arise – would an employer inviting a fixed-term employee to join a scheme, knowing that at the end of it all they would get back is their net contributions, be breaching its obligation of trust and confidence? Any employer opening its scheme to employees on contracts for less than two years should consider some form of disclaimer and issue a recommendation that the employee seeks independent advice before joining.

If an employer cannot offer entry to the main pension scheme for employees on fixed-term contracts, it might consider offering to make equivalent contributions to a personal arrangement to allow for better portability. However, there may be a difficulty in showing that this benefit is 'at least as favourable' as that offered to permanent employees. A further alternative would be for fixed-term employees, whom the employer does not want to admit to the pension scheme, to be paid a salary bonus equivalent to the value of the scheme membership, although this could give rise to industrial relations problems where permanent employees then ask for the bonus instead of scheme membership.

It should be noted that there is no direct claim under the *Regulations* by employees against trustees. However, this is an issue which trustees of schemes excluding fixed-term employees may wish to raise with the sponsoring employers.

Disability discrimination

7.30   In brief, the *Disability Discrimination Act 1995* (*DDA 1995*) makes it unlawful (with effect from 2 December 1996) for employers to discriminate without objective justification against disabled persons:

(*a*)   in the arrangements made for deciding who should be offered employment; or

(*b*)   in the employment terms; or

(*c*)   by refusing to offer or deliberately not offering employment.

'Employment terms' include access to and benefits provided by a pension scheme. An employer discriminates against a disabled person if it treats that person less favourably than it treats (or would treat) others to whom that reason does not (or would not) apply (unless it can show that the treatment is objectively justified). The protection is diluted by the justification defence: unequal treatment may be justified if it is 'material to the circumstances of the case and substantial'. In respect of pension arrangements a justification may be that the cost of providing the disabled person with benefits (for instance, life assurance benefits) would be substantially greater than the cost for employees who do not have the disabling condition.

It is important to note that, in addition, as of 1 October 2004, *DDA 1995* prohibits direct disability discrimination, namely less favourable treatment on grounds that a person is disabled. This form of unlawful treatment cannot be justified, unlike discrimination for a reason related to disability.

DDA 1995 implies an overriding 'non discrimination rule' into pension schemes in respect of 'disabled people' (see *section 17* of *DDA 1995*). This is similar to the *PA 1995* equal treatment rule (see 7.27 above), and trustees or managers of pension schemes must not commit any acts or omissions which would amount to unlawful discrimination. This may cause trustees difficulties if there are costs involved in complying with *DDA 1995*, and it is not clear whether the trustees may also take advantage of the justification defence.

A person who believes that he has been discriminated against may bring a claim to an employment tribunal or, alternatively, against the trustees under the scheme's internal dispute resolution procedure (see chapter 3).

Provisions implementing the *Equal Treatment 'Framework' Directive (Council Directive 2000/78/EC)* in so far as it relates to disability discrimination have been made under the *Disability Discrimination Act 1995 (Amendment) Regulations 2003 (SI 2003 No 1673)* and the *Disability Discrimination Act 1995 (Pensions) Regulations 2003 (SI 2003 No 2770)* ('the *Pensions Regulations*'), which came into force on 1 October 2004. One of the major amendments introduced by the regulations is the abolition of the small employer (i e one with 15 or fewer employees) exemption, following which the *DDA 1995* applies to all employers, regardless of the number of employees they have.

Under the *Pensions Regulations*, *DDA 1995* is amended so trustees and managers of occupational pension schemes are prohibited from discriminating against or harassing disabled members or prospective members of the scheme in carrying out their functions under the scheme. Thus, a non-discrimination rule will be implied into every occupational pension scheme, and all the scheme's provisions will be read subject to that rule. However, the non-discrimination rule does not apply to rights accrued and benefits which are payable in respect of periods preceding the date the *Pensions Regulations* come into force (1 October 2004). Still, communications with members and prospective members about such rights and benefits are subject to the non-discrimination rule.

In addition, trustees and managers of occupational pension schemes have a duty to make reasonable adjustments in relation to provisions, criteria or practices (including scheme rules) which place a disabled member/prospective member at a substantial disadvantage compared with non-disabled members/

prospective members. There is also a requirement, in such circumstances, to make any necessary reasonable adjustments to physical features of premises occupied by the trustees/scheme managers.

Breach of the *Pensions Regulations* can result in a complaint to the employment tribunal against the trustee/scheme managers (with the employer being joined as a party). A tribunal may make a declaration (except where the claim is brought by pensioner members) that the complainant has a right to be admitted to the scheme. The tribunal may not award damages, other than for injury to feelings or if there is a failure, without reasonable justification, to follow a recommendation made by the employment tribunal.

DDA 1995 will be amended again with effect from 5 December 2005, by the *Disability Discrimination Act 2005* (*DDA 2005*). Amongst other things, *DDA 2005* extends the definition of disability to include, from the point of diagnosis, persons who have cancer, HIV infection or multiple sclerosis. In addition, the requirement that a mental impairment ought to be a clinically well-recognised illness will be removed, thus further extending the scope of persons who will be covered by the legislation.

Maternity, paternity, adoption and parental absence

7.31   This issue is covered in detail at chapter 9. The provisions of the *Social Security Act 1989* have been in force since 23 June 1994. Briefly these provisions require that pension benefits for a woman who is on paid maternity leave must accrue in the same way as for a woman who is working normally. Death in service benefits must similarly remain in place. An employee who is absent on maternity leave is required to contribute, but on the basis of the actual statutory or contractual maternity remuneration received. Similar provisions for employees on paid paternity or adoption leave came into force on 6 April 2005 under the *PA 2004* (amending the *Social Security Act 1989, Sch 5*) to bring periods of paid paternity and adoption leave in line with paid maternity leave. Although statutory parental leave is unpaid leave and, thus, falls outside *Article 141* of the EU *Equal Pay* and *Equal Treatment Directives*, *regulation 18A* of the *Maternity and Parental Leave etc Regulations 1999* (*SI 1999 No 3312*) (as amended) does appear to provide full rights to pension accrual for those returning from parental leave on a similar basis to those returning from ordinary maternity leave.

Same sex partners

7.32   The *Employment Equality (Sexual Orientation) Regulations 2003* (*SI 2003 No 1661*) ('the *Sexual Orientation Regulations*') implement the provisions of the *Equal Treatment 'Framework' Directive* (*Council Directive*

2000/78/EC). The *Regulations*, which came into force on 1 December 2003, outlaw discrimination on the grounds of sexual orientation. This includes a prohibition on less favourable terms and conditions of employment based on an employee's sexual orientation. In the context of pensions, the *Regulations* (as amended by the *Employment Equality (Sexual Orientation) (Amendment) Regulations 2003 (SI 2003 No 2827))* make it unlawful for trustees and managers of occupational pension schemes to discriminate against, or subject harassment to, any members or prospective members in carrying out their functions under the scheme (except in relation to rights accrued or benefits payable in respect of period of service preceding 1 December 2003). Every occupational scheme will thus be treated as including a non-discriminatory rule on the grounds of sexual orientation and trustees and scheme managers have the power to alter the scheme to ensure that it is non-discriminatory (regardless of the terms of the scheme).

Breach of the non-discrimination rule can result in a claim to the employment tribunal against trustees and scheme managers (and the employer may be joined as a party). If the claim is successful, a tribunal may make a declaration (except where the claim is brought by a pensioner member), for example, that the complainant has a right to be admitted to the scheme. The tribunal may not award damages, however, other than for injury to feelings or in respect of a failure, without reasonable justification, to follow a recommendation made by the tribunal.

Of particular importance is *regulation 25* of the *Sexual Orientation Regulations* which allows discrimination on grounds of marital status (for example, limiting payments under a pension scheme to the spouse of a member). This provision has been the subject of judicial review proceedings on the ground that it contradicts EC law. The High Court rejected this argument and held that the provision was lawful. The decision has not been appealed against. It is also arguable that the *regulation* contravenes *Articles 8* and *14* of the *European Convention on Human Rights (ECHR)* and, on the basis of the decision in *KB v National Health Service Pensions Agency [2004] All ER (D) 03 (Jan)* breaches *Article 141* of the *Rome Treaty*. Note that once the *Civil Partnership Act 2004* came into force on 12 December 2005, the scope of *regulation 25* was extended to include civil partners.

The *Civil Partnership Act 2004* is designed to give same sex couples the same rights as are currently available to married couples. The Act contains a number of pensions provisions which came into force on 5 December 2005. In respect of employment after 6 April 1998, the Act requires employers to make contributions to provide surviving civil partners with the same contracted-out benefits as are offered to surviving spouses in relation to contracted-out occupational schemes and personal pension schemes.

In addition, the Act implies into every occupational pension scheme an overriding non-discrimination rule which prohibits less favourable treatment of civil partners compared with spouses. This means that discrimination in the provision of pension benefits or lump sum is prohibited. This prohibition relates to service from 5 December 2005 only. However, the Act does not prohibit schemes from differentiating between members who are married or are civil partners and members who are not. Finally, the pension sharing provisions have been amended to apply to the dissolution of civil partnerships in the same way as they apply to divorce.

Religion or belief discrimination

7.33 The *Employment Equality (Religion or Belief) Regulations 2003 (SI 2003 No 1660)* ('the *Religion or Belief Regulations*') implement the provisions of the *Equal Treatment 'Framework' Directive (Council Directive 2000/78/EC)* on discrimination on grounds of religion or belief. The *Regulations*, which outlaw discrimination on these grounds, came into force on 2 December 2003. Like the *Sexual Orientation Regulations*, the *Religion or Belief Regulations* outlaw less favourable treatment, victimisation and harassment, in the employment context, on grounds of religion or belief.

In the context of pensions, the *Religion or Belief Regulations* introduce obligations on trustees and fund managers, identical to those which are contained in the *Sexual Orientation Regulations* (see 7.32 above). However, there is no equivalent provision to *regulation 25* of the *Sexual Orientation Regulations*.

Age discrimination

7.34 The *Equal Treatment 'Framework' Directive (Council Directive 2000/78/EC)* also outlaws discrimination on grounds of age. The UK is due to implement this aspect of the Directive by October 2006. A Government consultation paper ('Age Matters') was published in July 2003. The *Employment Equality (Age) Regulations 2006 (SI 2006 No 1031)* were made in March 2006 and are due to come into force on 1 October 2006. Under the regulations discrimination, harassment and victimisation on grounds of age are prohibited. In addition, retirement ages below the age of 65 are to be outlawed, except where they can be objectively justified.

The Regulations contain specific provisions dealing with occupational pension schemes. In brief, trustees and managers must not discriminate against or harass members on grounds of age in the carrying out of their functions in relation to the scheme. The Regulations imply a non-discrimination rule into every occupational pension scheme and give power to trustees and managers to modify a scheme to comply with this rule (subject in certain circumstances to employer consent). Many age-related pension scheme rules are excluded from the scope of the Regulations by *Schedule 2*, with the result that many schemes are expected to continue to operate largely as they currently do. For example, even after the Regulations come into force employers will be able to apply a minimum/maximum age criteria as conditions for admission into a scheme and to fix a minimum/maximum age for entitlement to benefits. Provisions which may not be allowed to continue without objective justification include requiring accrual to cease at a certain age and non-uniform accrual in defined benefit schemes.

The Regulations are not retrospective and apply only to benefits accrued through service on or after 1 October 2006.

In October 2003 the EAT overturned an employment tribunal's decision that the statutory upper age which applies to complaints of unfair dismissal and for statutory redundancy pay was unlawful as being indirectly discriminatory on grounds of sex (*Rutherford v Secretary of State for Trade and Industry [2003] IRLR 858, [2003] All ER (D) 67 (Oct)*). This decision has now been approved by the House of Lords (*[2006] UKHL 19*). In any event, the current statutory age limit is to be abolished under the *Employment Equality (Age) Regulations 2006*.

Transsexual employees

7.35   In July 2002, the European Court of Human Rights found the UK to be in breach of *Article 8* of the *ECHR* in failing to deal with the legal implications which arise as a result of gender reassignment (*Goodwin v UK [2002] IRLR 664*). In *Goodwin*, a male-to-female transsexual brought various complaints, including that she had been refused a State pension at 60 as she was treated as a man for National Insurance purposes contrary to *Article 8*. In the opinion of the European Court the uncertain legal position of transsexuals in the UK was no longer sustainable. In *KB v National Health Service Pensions Agency [2000] All ER (D) 2279 (Jan)* the ECJ agreed with the UK Government that restricting access to certain benefits to married couples did not constitute discrimination on grounds of sex. However, the ECJ found *Article 141* of the *Rome Treaty* was nonetheless violated, since UK law, in breach of the *ECHR*, prohibited trans-sexuals from marrying. This UK legislature has now rectified this position with *The Gender Recognition Act 2004* which came into force on 4 April 2005 to enable transsexuals to marry a person of the opposite sex.

Additional changes

Time off for performance of duties and for training

7.36   Under *section 58* of *ERA 1996* (originally *section 42* of *PA 1995*), an employer must permit any employee who is a trustee of a scheme to take time off during working hours to allow him to perform all of his duties as a trustee or to undergo relevant training. The amount of time off, and any conditions imposed by the employer, must be reasonable having regard to the employer's business and the effect of the employee's absence. Any employee is entitled to be paid for any time taken off pursuant to this provision (*section 59 of ERA 1996*). A common criticism of *PA 1995* is that trustee training is not mandatory. This criticism is due to be rectified, however, by the trustee knowledge and understanding requirements under *sections 247 to 249 of PA 2004*, due to come into force on 6 April 2006. Trustees will be required to have 'knowledge and understanding' of the law relating to pensions and trusts and the principles relating to funding and investment. This issue is covered in detail in chapter 3.

An employee can bring a complaint to an employment tribunal if he believes that his employer has failed to give him time off and failed to pay him (*section 60 of ERA 1996*). He has three months from the date when the failure occurred in which to present his complaint, but the tribunal will have the power to extend this period if it is satisfied that it was not reasonably practicable for the complaint to be presented within the period.

If an employee's complaint is upheld, the tribunal can award such compensation at it considers just and equitable.

Right not to suffer detriment or to be unfairly dismissed

7.37   *Section 46* of *ERA 1996* (previously *section 46 of PA 1995*) states that an employer is not permitted to victimise an employee simply on the ground that he performed or proposed to perform his functions as a trustee of a scheme which relates to his employment.

Further, if an employee is dismissed and the reason (or the principal reason) for the dismissal is that the employee performed any functions as a trustee, the dismissal is to be regarded as automatically unfair and the employee may be entitled to compensation (*ERA 1996, s 102*).

Any provision in the contracts of employment which purports to exclude or limit the right not to suffer detriment or to be unfairly dismissed is void (*ERA 1996, s 203(1)*).

Conclusion

7.38   It is difficult to classify pension provisions or an entitlement to pension benefits as an employment 'right', as in most instances employers do not have to provide pension arrangements. There are certain exceptions to this (for example, ex-members of public sector arrangements have statutory 'protected person' status, meaning that on privatisation they must be offered membership of the mirror-image, industry-wide schemes) but these rights are of a statutory nature and therefore uncommon. However, as a result of *PA 2004*, employees are now given a degree of protection following a business transfer. In addition, *PA 2004* improved rights in relation to paternity and adoption leave and introduced rights for civil partners.

On becoming a member of a pension scheme, an employee does obtain rights and entitlements, but primarily against the trustees of the scheme. The only contractual 'right' of the employee is to join the pension scheme if eligible to do so. Otherwise, it is easier to classify the rights of a member as being either statutory (for example, not to be discriminated against on various grounds) or common law rights, for example, the *Imperial* duty of good faith. Some of the cases referred to in this chapter clearly indicate the difficulties of differentiating between pension and employment issues. However, the basis of pension provision is likely, in time, to move further towards a contractual as opposed to 'trusts' basis.

Chapter 8

Pensions and divorce

Introduction

8.1   Over the years there have been fundamental changes in the treatment of pension benefits in the context of divorce proceedings. These have arisen out of two different concepts for the treatment of pensions: earmarking and pension sharing, which have been introduced by *PA 1995* and the *Welfare Reform and Pensions Act 1999* (*WRPA 1999*) respectively. This legislation has not only increased the awareness of divorcing couples of the comparatively high value that pension benefits may have in the context of the matrimonial assets as a whole, but has introduced sufficient flexibility to enable a fair settlement to be reached, whatever the divorcing parties' general and financial circumstances.

It was not until the introduction of *PA 1995* that the family law courts were finally granted jurisdiction over pension schemes in the context of divorce settlements (*Brooks v Brooks [1995] All ER 257, HL* is the notable exception, but it is likely that this judgment is, in any case, confined to its own facts and has now been superseded by the legislation mentioned briefly above). That is not to say that the pension rights of parties to divorce proceedings were not taken into consideration prior to *PA 1995*, merely that the courts did not have the jurisdiction to make orders against pension schemes' trustees or scheme members, in respect of their pension benefits, when deciding how the parties' assets were to be split. This lack of options in law for the treatment of pension rights on divorce had long been a cause for dissatisfaction and was the subject of various reports which, in essence, recommended that the courts should have the power to split the pension rights on divorce, thereby creating a separate entitlement for the ex-spouse.

So why, with this obvious desire for change, did it take so long for the legislation to appear on the statute books? The reason lies in the nature of pension schemes themselves. The majority of pension schemes were designed to be eligible for tax approval (see chapter 5). The requirements for obtaining exempt approved status prevent benefits being paid to any person who is not a member or a 'dependant' (as defined in the Glossary to the Revenue's Practice Notes, IR12 (2001)) of a member, and specifically prevent pensions from being assignable (subject to certain statutory exceptions) (IR12 (2001) PN 7.31). This had proved the main obstacle for the courts in the past because the governing trust deed of an exempt approved scheme would always contain a specific provision that benefits cannot be assigned. There was no mechanism to assign benefits to an ex-spouse so that they would become payable to the ex-spouse as of right, nor indeed to provide for the ex-spouse on the death of the scheme member unless, first, the ex-spouse fell within the definition of 'dependant' and, secondly, the trustees exercised their discretion to pay the benefits to him or her in that capacity.

These problems have now been overcome. However, it may still be appropriate for parties in some circumstances to leave the pension benefits intact and it is, therefore, useful to look at the issues which were relevant prior to the introduction of *PA 1995*.

Position prior to PA 1995

8.2   Prior to the introduction of *PA 1995* the treatment of property on divorce in England, Wales and Northern Ireland was governed by *sections 21* to *25* inclusive of the *Matrimonial Causes Act 1973* (*MCA 1973*) (as amended by the *Matrimonial and Family Proceedings Act 1994*).

Section 25A(1) of *MCA 1973* required the court to consider whether the financial obligations of each party towards the other can be terminated as soon after the grant of the decree as the court considers just and reasonable. This is known as a 'clean break'. It put the onus on the court to consider lump sum payments and property adjustment orders, rather than periodical payments orders (commonly known as maintenance payments), wherever possible and, if a maintenance payment order is made, to limit its duration if appropriate. A clean break will usually be appropriate where the couple is young, both are working and have no children or where the couple's assets are sizeable enough that they can be split in such a way that the ex-spouse will have sufficient resources on which to live.

Prior to amendment by *PA 1995, section 25(2)* of *MCA 1973* stated that the court should, when considering financial provision orders, have particular regard, amongst other matters, to the following:

'(*a*)   the income, earning capacity, property and other financial resources which each of the parties to the marriage has or is likely to have in the foreseeable future, including in the case of earning capacity any increase in that capacity which it would in the opinion of the court be reasonable to expect a party of the marriage to take steps to acquire;

...

    (*h*)   in the case of proceedings for divorce or nullity of marriage, the value to each of the parties to the marriage of any benefits (for example, a pension) which by reason of the dissolution or annulment of the marriage, that party will lose the chance of acquiring.'

However, a problem of interpretation arose with the use of the words 'in the foreseeable future' in the then *section 25(2)(a)* of *MCA 1973*. The approach adopted by the courts resulted in consideration being given only to those assets which a party could expect to acquire within the next ten years. Consequently, where a party to the divorce was more than ten years away from retirement, the value of his pension entitlements would not be taken into account. In any event, the court had no power over either the trustees or the assets of a pension scheme and so could not make an order re-allocating assets or obliging the trustees to make a payment to an ex-spouse. Therefore, even where pension rights fell within the definition of matrimonial property their value could only be taken into account in relation to the distribution of non-pension assets.

Under *section 25(2)(h)* of *MCA 1973* the court was required to have regard to the value of any pension that a party to a divorce loses the chance of acquiring. It was not clear, however, to which benefits these provisions referred, i e to the member's pension, any cash lump sum payable on retirement, a spouse's pension payable on the death of the member and/or lump sum on a member's death in service.

The courts' inability to divide pension assets was problematical, particularly where there were insufficient non-pension assets to provide for the ex-spouse's needs. A common result was that in the divorce settlement the ex-spouse would be allocated the matrimonial home whilst the scheme member retained the pension rights. This often created both long and short-term problems; the party with the matrimonial home had realisable assets but no income on retirement, whereas the scheme member retained pension rights, to which he could not gain access to set up a new home, but was guaranteed a certain level of future income. An even worse scenario was where the pension rights were the only or the largest asset and, consequently, the court was unable to make any order which would adequately compensate the ex-spouse. Therefore, in many cases, this was not satisfactory for either party. It was against this background that *section 166* of *PA 1995* was introduced.

Earmarking – impact of PA 1995

General jurisdiction

8.3   The concept of earmarking was introduced by *section 166* of *PA 1995*. In general terms earmarking introduced a means by which pension benefits could be used to pay either maintenance or a capital sum from the pension scheme direct to the ex-spouse on the member's behalf, but which would only become payable when entitlement arose under the pension scheme in respect of the member.

The powers of the courts regarding financial provision on divorce are still contained in *MCA 1973* but s*ection 25* was amended to introduce a concept of earmarking. *Section 166* of *PA 1995* inserted new s*ections 25B* to *25D* with effect from 1 August 1996 which applied to petitions presented on or after 1 July 1996. *WRPA 1999* has subsequently made certain refinements to these sections which are reflected below. In essence the earmarking provisions provide that the courts:

(*a*)   must have regard to pension benefits which either party has or is likely to have or stands to lose the chance of acquiring because of the divorce and must ignore the words 'in the foreseeable future' contained in s*ection 25(2)(a)* of *MCA 1973* for this purpose (*section 25B(1)* of *MCA 1973*);

(*b*)   have jurisdiction to make orders against the person responsible for the pension arrangement for payment of financial provision from a member's pension benefits to the other party when payment of those benefits falls due to the member (s*ection 25B(4)* of *MCA 1973*) The term 'person responsible' was introduced by s*ection 46(2)* of *WRPA 1999* and means, in the case of occupational pension schemes or personal pension schemes, the trustees and managers of the scheme. In the case of a retirement annuity contract it means the provider of the annuity and, in the case of an insurance policy, the insurer. The term 'pension arrangement' was introduced by s*ection 46(1)* of *WRPA 1999* and means an occupational pension scheme, personal pension scheme, retirement annuity contract, an annuity or insurance policy which is to give effect to the rights of an occupational pension scheme or a personal pension scheme or an annuity purchased for the purpose of discharging liability for a pension credit (as discussed in more detail under 8.12 below);

(*c*)   have power to direct a member as to the extent to which he may commute payments, thereby reducing the pension benefits payable to him, and have power to order payment of any lump sum following commutation to be made to the ex-spouse (s*ection 25B(7)* of *MCA 1973*);

(*d*)   can direct trustees to exercise their discretionary powers in the event of the death of a member or pensioner in favour of the ex-spouse in whole or in part, and can also require a member to nominate his ex-spouse for all or part of a lump sum payable on his death (s*ection 25C* of *MCA 1973*).

Essentially, the type of order that the court is empowered to make was not changed by *PA 1995*, merely the source of the payment. The order is in the form of either a deferred periodical payments (or maintenance) order or a lump sum order. The member's pension benefits remain in the scheme and are still attributable to the member but a proportion is payable directly to the ex-spouse. No separate entitlement is created in the scheme for the ex-spouse so payments only become due to the ex-spouse when they become due to the member and will stop automatically on the death of the member. As with all periodical payment orders, either party can apply to the court to have the amount varied (*section 31* of *MCA 1973*) and payments will cease on the re-marriage or death of the ex-spouse.

The amount due to the ex-spouse must be expressed as a percentage of the total amount of pension due to the member (*section 25B(5)* of *MCA 1973*). Such total amount can include the value of the member's GMP by virtue of the exclusion of the provisions relating to inalienability of GMPs (*section 91* of *PA 1995*) under *sections 166(4)* and *(5)* of *PA 1995*. Any lump sum payment made by the persons responsible for the pension arrangement shall discharge them of any liability to the member to the extent of the amount of the payment (*sections 25B(6)(a)* and *25C(3)* of *MCA 1973*) and, in the case of pension payments, any payments made by the person responsible for the pension arrangement shall be treated as a payment made by the member towards the discharge of his liability under the court order (*section 25B(6)(b)* of *MCA 1973*).

The duty of the court to consider a clean break was not affected by the changes introduced by *PA 1995*. In practice, therefore 'earmarking' orders against pension payments are likely only to be made where a clean break is not possible and a periodical payments order is appropriate. Such an order, however, gives the ex-spouse additional comfort and security because, instead of obtaining a deferred maintenance order payable by the member in retirement, the ex-spouse will now receive payments directly from the pension scheme. This removes direct dependency on the member for financial support and avoids the potential problems caused by non-compliance with an order by the member.

The amendments to *MCA 1973* by *PA 1995* (and *WRPA 1999*) specified the schemes against which the court can make orders. These are referred to as 'pension arrangements' and include not only occupational pension schemes of all nature as well as personal pension schemes, retirement annuity contracts, annuities and *section 32* buy-out policies (*section 25D(3)* of *MCA 1973*).

It is considered unlikely that any inheritance tax ('IHT') liability will attach where the court has made an order for a lump sum payment on death. The HMRC statement of practice E3 relating to the provisions of the *Inheritance Tax Act 1984* states that pension scheme benefits will not be liable to IHT if the executors or administrators do not have a legally enforceable claim to the benefits. Therefore, whilst lump sum benefits which are subject to an earmarking order are no longer payable at the sole discretion of the trustees of the pension scheme, the lump sum payment nevertheless passes outside the will or intestacy of the deceased member.

Valuation of benefits for earmarking purposes

8.4   The question of the valuation of pension rights for earmarking is dealt with in the *Divorce etc (Pensions) Regulations 2000 (SI 2000 No 1123)* (although it should be noted that the precursor Regulations (*SI 1996 No 1676*) still apply in respect of divorce and nullity proceedings commenced before 1 December 2000). *Regulation 3* of the *2000 Regulations* provides that, for the purposes of earmarking, benefits under a pension arrangement shall be calculated in the manner set out in *regulation 3* of the *Pensions on Divorce etc (Provision of Information) Regulations 2000 (SI 2000 No 1048)*.

Regulation 3 of the *Pensions on Divorce etc (Provision of Information) Regulations 2000 (SI 2000 No 1048)* specifies that the basis of valuation depends on the category of member in question:

(*a*)   For active and deferred members of occupational pension schemes, members of personal pension schemes and a person with rights contained in a retirement annuity contact, the statutory cash equivalent transfer value basis ('CETV') must be applied. Generally, the effective date for calculating the CETV is the date on which the request for the valuation was received by the person responsible for the pension arrangement. However, it should be noted that under *regulation 3* of the *Divorce etc (Pensions) Regulations 2000 (SI 2000 No 1123)* the court can specify another date, if it considers it appropriate, such date not to be earlier than one year before the date of the petition and not later than the date on which the court is exercising its powers.

(*b*)   In any other circumstances *regulation 3 (SI 2000 No 1048)* specifies that the value of benefits shall be calculated and verified by a qualified actuary (*regulation 3(7)* of *SI 2000 No 1048*) by adopting methods and making assumptions certified as being consistent with 'Retirement Benefit Schemes – Transfer Values' (GN11) as published by the Institute of Actuaries and the Faculty of Actuaries and current at the date on which the request for the valuation is received (*regulation 8 of SI 2000 No 1048*). *Regulation 9 (SI 2000 No 1048)* provides for certain specific provisions to apply to money purchase benefits.

Transfers of, and notices in relation to, earmarked benefits

8.5   Given that the courts' powers enable orders to be made for deferred maintenance payments, payable at some date in the future, it was necessary to make provisions permitting the transfer of the orders on the transfer of the member's accrued benefits to a new scheme (*section 25D(1)(a)* of *MCA 1973*). The *Divorce etc (Pensions) Regulations 2000 (SI 2000 No 1123)* provide for the person responsible for the transferring arrangement to give notice to the person responsible for the receiving arrangement in circumstances where an earmarking order is in force against a member who wishes to transfer his pension benefits. The effect of this notice is that the earmarking order will attach to the transfer credits granted in the receiving scheme and will be enforceable against the trustees of the receiving scheme.

Regulation 4 (SI 2000 No 1123) sets out the content of the notices which must be given to the receiving arrangement and the ex-spouse and the period within which they must be given. Notice must be given within the period provided by *section 99* of *PSA 1993* for the person responsible for the transferring arrangement to effect a transfer (usually six months) and before the expiry of 21 days after the person responsible for the transferring arrangement has made all required payments to the person responsible for the receiving arrangement (*regulation 4(5)* of *SI 2000 No 1123*).

The notice to the ex-spouse must contain the following particulars:

(*a*)   the fact that the pension rights of the member have been transferred;

(*b*)   the effective date of the transfer;

(*c*)   the name and address of the person responsible for the new arrangement; and

(*d*)   the fact that the order made under *section 23* of *MCA 1973* is to have effect as if it had been made in respect of the person responsible for the new arrangement.

The notice to the person responsible for the new arrangement shall consist of:

(i)   every order made under *MCA 1973* imposing a requirement on the person responsible for the transferring arrangement in relation to the rights transferred;

(ii)   any subsequent orders varying the original order;

(iii)   all information or particulars supplied by the ex-spouse under *rule 2.70* of the *Family Proceedings Rules 1991 (SI 1991 No 1247) (as amended)* (for example, address and bank details);

(iv)   any notice given by the ex-spouse to the transferring trustees relating to a change of personal details or re-marriage; and

(v)   where the rights of a member under the transferring scheme derive from a transfer from a previous scheme, any notices to the person responsible for the previous arrangement on the former transfer.

Under *regulation 5 (SI 2000 No 1123)* notice is also required to be given by the person responsible for the arrangement to the ex-spouse, within 14 days of the occurrence of an event, when:

(*a*)   there has been a significant reduction in the benefits payable under the scheme in respect of the member (save where transfer of all benefits has been made or where market conditions have affected the value of the scheme's assets) (*regulation 5(1)* of *SI 2000 No 1123*); and/or

(*b*)   a partial transfer of the member's accrued benefits has been made (*regulation 5(3)* of *SI 2000 No 1123*).

This notice shall state the nature of the event which has occurred and the extent of the reduction in benefits and, in the case of a partial transfer, the name and address of the person responsible for the receiving arrangement.

It should be noted that in the event of a partial transfer the order will remain with the original scheme and this may therefore give the member scope for the avoidance of the order. Nevertheless, because notice is given to the ex-spouse by the scheme, this gives the ex-spouse an opportunity to apply to the court for a variation of the original order.

An ex-spouse is required to give notice (*regulation 6* of *SI 2000 No 1123*) within 14 days to the person responsible for the arrangement subject to a court order where the particulars supplied by her cease to be accurate; where the ex-spouse has remarried or where, for any other reason, the order has ceased to have effect. The person responsible for the arrangement will be discharged of any liability to the ex-spouse to the extent of a payment where, by reason of the inaccuracy of the particulars supplied by the ex-spouse or the ex-spouse's failure to give notice of a change in details, it is not reasonably practicable for the person responsible for the arrangement to make a payment as required by the order and a payment is therefore made to the member instead (*regulation 6(4)* of *SI 2000 No 1123*).

Ambit of court orders

8.6   The courts were empowered to make deferred maintenance orders from 1 August 1996 where applied for in petitions presented after 1 July 1996, although any orders made could not take effect before 6 April 1997. In addition to making a deferred maintenance order from the pension arrangement the court can also require a member to commute his pension when he retires, with part or all of the lump sum being paid to the ex-spouse (*section 25B(7)* of *MCA 1973*, see 8.3 above). Similarly in respect of benefits payable on the member's death, the court has the power to order the allocation of any lump sum and, even where payment of the lump sum is discretionary, the persons responsible for the pension arrangement can be ordered to pay all or part of it to the ex-spouse. In cases where the member himself has the power to nominate a beneficiary, the member can be required to nominate the ex-spouse.

As mentioned above the order must express the amount due to the ex-spouse as a percentage of the total amount due to the member. The order may also state the rate at which the payment is to increase annually and this may vary from the rates stated in the scheme rules. In relation to orders prior to 1 December 2000 which were made for a fixed amount, it would also be necessary to consider whether or not allowance would need to be made for re-valuation up to retirement and, further, to consider what the position would be were a member to retire and whether or not this earlier payment should be reflected in the ex-spouse's pension.

Charging for earmarking orders

8.7   Charges by pension arrangements in relation to earmarking orders are permitted pursuant to *section 24* of *WRPA 1999* by reference to *regulation 10* of the *Pensions on Divorce etc (Charging) Regulations 2000 (SI 2000 No 1049)*. It is stated that the charges which a person responsible for a pension arrangement may recover in relation to an earmarking order are those charges which represent the reasonable administrative expenses which have been incurred or are likely to be incurred by reason of the order.

Regulation 3 (SI 2000 No 1049) deals with charges recoverable in respect of the provision of basic valuation information and provides that the persons responsible for the pension arrangement may also recover the reasonable costs of providing such information to the extent that they would not have been required to provide such information in the ordinary course of disclosure in accordance with the *Occupational Pension Schemes (Disclosure of Information) Regulations 1996 (SI 1996 No 1655)* ('the *Disclosure Regulations*').

Disclosure

8.8   The current provisions governing disclosure in relation to earmarking orders can be found under the *Pensions on Divorce etc (Provision of Information) Regulations 2000 (SI 2000 No 1048)*. *Regulation 2* deals with the provision of the basic information which the person responsible for a pension arrangement can generally be required to disclose on request. These provisions apply equally to pension sharing and are set out in detail at 8.24 below.

Regulation 10 (SI 2000 No 1048) deals with the provision of information after receipt of an earmarking order. The person responsible for the pension arrangement must, within 21 days of receipt of the earmarking order, issue to both parties to the marriage a notice that includes the following, as appropriate:

(*a*)   for an order in respect of pension rights not in payment, a list of the circumstances in respect of any changes of which the member or the ex-spouse must notify the person responsible for the pension arrangement;

(*b*)   where the pension is in payment:

   (i)   the value of the member's pension rights;

  (ii)   the amount of those pension rights after the order has been implemented;

 (iii)   the first date when a payment under the order is to be made; and

 (iv)   the circumstances in respect of any changes of which the member or the ex-spouse must notify the person responsible for the pension arrangement;

(*c*)   the amount of charges which remain unpaid by each party pursuant to *regulation 3* of the *Pensions on Divorce etc (Charging) Regulations 2000 (SI 2000 No 1049)* (see 8.7 above) and in respect of complying with the order;

(*d*)   information as to how and when these charges will be recovered.

Pension sharing

Introduction

8.9   The concept of pension sharing was first introduced, but not implemented, by the *Family Law Act 1996*. A lengthy consultation process then followed which culminated in the provisions contained in *WRPA 1999*.

In brief, the term pension sharing is used to signify a clean break approach towards dealing with pension rights. The aim is that the capital value of the pension will be divided between the parties with the effect that the rights of the member will be reduced by way of a 'pension debit' and the ex-spouse will be granted a 'pension credit' of the same amount. The primary advantage of pension sharing to an ex-spouse is that her rights are independent of those of the member and, in contrast with earmarking, will, therefore, continue beyond the death of the member and after the ex-spouse's remarriage.

The relevant sections of *WRPA 1999* came into force on 1 December 2000 and were in the form of insertions and amendments to *MCA 1973*, the provisions of *Part III* of *WRPA 1999*, and a number of statutory instruments.

Pension sharing is only available in proceedings commencing on or after 1 December 2000, the effective date for the new legislation (*Welfare Reform and Pensions Act 1999 (Commencement No 5) Order 2000 (SI 2000 No 1116)*). The provisions only apply to proceedings for divorce or nullity of marriage, and do not extend to judicial separation (*section 24B(1)* of *MCA 1973*). Subsequent case law has made it clear that the question of whether a decree nisi could be rescinded, to allow new divorce proceedings to be issued after 1 December 2000 thus enabling a pension sharing order to be made, is one for judicial discretion. In *S v S [2002] All ER (D) 58 (Mar)* the court allowed rescission where both parties consented. However, in *Rye v Rye [2002] EWHC 956 (Fam)* the husband (who had the pension) successfully objected to rescission. The court held that *WRPA 1999* provides a clear cut-off date and in the absence of consent by both parties it would be an impermissible exercise by the court of its discretion to circumvent the statutory provision by rescinding the decree nisi.

The amendments made to *MCA 1973* mean that the courts now have the option to consider the possibility of granting a sharing order, if deemed appropriate, when considering ancillary relief (*section 24B(1)* of *MCA 1973*). Whilst it is open to the courts to make more than one sharing order in relation to a given set of divorce proceedings, the courts cannot make a pension sharing order in relation to a pension arrangement which is already the subject of a pension sharing order in relation to that marriage (*sections 24B(3)* and *(4)* of *MCA 1973*). Moreover, the court cannot make a pension sharing order in respect of pension benefits which are already subject to an earmarking order.

Section 21A of *MCA 1973* states that a sharing order involves the court ordering that the 'shareable rights' of the member be shared for the benefit of the ex-spouse, with the order specifying the value of those rights to be transferred as a percentage of the total rights attributable to the member.

Section 27(2) of *WRPA 1999* sets out the definition of 'shareable rights' as any rights under a 'pension arrangement' other than non-shareable rights of a description specified in regulation*s*. As detailed at 8.3 above the *WRPA 1999* definition of 'pension arrangement' (*section 46(1)*) is broadly termed. Due to the adoption of the *PSA 1993 (section 1)* definition of 'occupational pension scheme', benefits under unfunded and unapproved schemes are included as shareable rights, as are benefits under the state earning related pension scheme. Indeed, the only exceptions to date appear to be excepted public sector schemes (*section 27(1)(3)* of *WRPA 1999*) by reference to the *Pension Sharing (Excepted Schemes) Order 2001 (SI 2001 No 358)* (being the schemes relating to the Prime Minister, Lord Chancellor and Speaker of the House of Commons) and the basic State pension.

Pension debits and credits

8.10   The person responsible for a pension arrangement is not required to implement the pension debit and pension credit until the pension sharing order has taken effect (*section 29(1)(a)* of *WRPA 1999*). Pension sharing can also be provided under a 'qualifying agreement' between the parties to the marriage which takes effect on the dissolution of the marriage under the *Family Law Act 1996* (*section 28(1)(b)*). (A 'qualifying agreement' has yet to be defined in regulations but, when it is, the sharing legislation will apply equally to it as to court orders.)

A sharing order cannot take effect unless the decree pursuant to which it has been made has been made absolute (*section 24B(2)* of *MCA 1973*). In addition *section 24C* (by reference to *regulation 9* of the *Divorce etc* (*Pensions*) *Regulations 2000* (*SI 2000 No 1123*)) provides that the order cannot come into effect earlier than seven days after the end of the period for filing notice of appeal against the order.

Once the sharing order has become effective the member's shareable rights under the arrangement become subject to a 'debit' of the specified amount and the ex-spouse becomes entitled to a 'credit' of a corresponding amount, held as a right against the person responsible for the arrangement (*section 29(1)* of *WRPA 1999*).

Pension debits

8.11   The pension debit operates by reducing the member's current and future benefits under the pension arrangement by a specified percentage (*section 31(1)* of *WRPA 1999*) on the transfer day (i e the date on which the order takes effect). The benefits to be reduced must be 'qualifying benefits' (*section 31(3)*). A benefit is a qualifying benefit if the member's cash equivalent includes an amount in respect of it.

When a benefit is reduced by a pension debit each part of the benefit is reduced equally. Thus, for example, the GMP benefits of a member are reduced by the same percentage as the excess over GMP. *Section 31(2)* of *WRPA 1999* clarifies how the percentage deduction rule applies for members who are in pensionable service on the transfer day. The debit is applied to the deferred pension to which the member would have been entitled had he left pensionable service on that day. The benefits of active members to be reduced by the pension debit therefore exclude any elements which would not be included in his deferred pension, such as a death in service lump sum.

Pension credits

8.12   The ex-spouse becomes entitled to the corresponding amount as a pension credit, made up of the same elements and in the same proportions as the benefits of the scheme member. An arrangement which is the subject of a pension sharing order may discharge its liability for the pension credit by conferring appropriate rights under that arrangement (an 'internal transfer') or by transferring the pension credit to another qualifying pension scheme or arrangement (an 'external transfer') (see 8.14 below).

Implementation period

8.13   The person responsible for the arrangement has a specified period within which to give effect to the provisions of the pension sharing order – this is known as the implementation period and is a period of four months beginning with the later of the day on which the pension sharing order takes effect, and receipt by the person responsible for the arrangement of certain matrimonial documents (for example, the order itself and the order or decree of the divorce or annulment), and the information set out in the *Pensions on Divorce etc (Provision of Information) Regulations 2000 (SI 2000 No 1048)* (this includes the names, addresses, dates of birth and National Insurance numbers of the divorcing couple) (*section 34(1)* of *WRPA 1999*). A further pre-condition of implementing the sharing order may be the payment of any charges due from the divorcing couple (see 8.25 below).

In the event that the order has not been implemented by the trustees of an occupational pension scheme within the implementation period they shall be required to notify the Pensions Regulator ('the Regulator') within 21 days beginning with the day immediately following the end of the implementation period (*regulation 2* of the *Pension Sharing (Implementation and Discharge of Liability) Regulations 2000 (SI 2000 No 1053)*)) and s*ection 10* of *PA 1995* shall apply. The Regulator may, therefore, impose civil penalties if the trustees failed to take all such steps as were reasonable to discharge liability for the pension credit before the end of the implementation period. On application by the trustees, the Regulator may extend the implementation period under certain circumstances (*section 33(4)* of *WRPA 1999*). These circumstances are set out in *regulation 3* of the *Pension Sharing (Implementation and Discharge of Liability) Regulations 2000 (SI 2000 No 1053)* and include the scheme being in wind up; ceasing to be contracted out or where an extension is in the financial interests of the members of the scheme generally. The implementation period may also be suspended or postponed where one of the parties has made an application for leave to appeal out of time (*regulation 4* of *SI 2000 No 1053*).

Discharging liability for the pension credit

General position

8.14   The main body of the pension sharing legislation is aimed at the means by which the liability of the person responsible for the pension arrangement which is subject to a pension sharing order can be discharged in respect of the pension credit created. The relevant provisions can be found in *section 35 of WRPA 1999* by reference to *Schedule 5*, together with the *Pension Sharing (Implementation and Discharge of Liability) Regulations 2000 (SI 2000 No 1053)*.

Schedule 5 deals with funded (*paragraph 1*), unfunded (*paragraphs 2* and *3*) and 'other' (*paragraph 4*) pension arrangements. This chapter will concentrate on the description of 'funded' schemes in *Schedule 5, paragraph 1*, i e pension credits derived from a funded occupational pension scheme or a personal pension scheme.

Schedule 5 (paragraph 1(2)) states that the trustees or managers of these types of arrangements may discharge their liability in respect of the pension credit by conferring rights under the relevant scheme on the ex-spouse, with his or her consent or otherwise in accordance with regulations. This is known as the 'internal transfer' option. Alternatively, under *Schedule 5, paragraph 1(3)* the liability may be discharged by paying the amount of the pension credit to the person responsible for a 'qualifying arrangement' (defined widely in *Schedule 5, paragraph 6*) with the ex-spouse's consent or otherwise in accordance with regulations. This is known as the 'external transfer' option.

The *Pension Sharing (Implementation and Discharge of Liability) Regulations 2000 (SI 2000 No 1053)* set out the detail of these procedures under *regulation 7*. In summary, for internal transfers (*regulation 7(1)*) the consent of the ex-spouse must be obtained unless the ex-spouse has failed to provide this consent and has also failed to specify a suitable recipient scheme under the external transfer route.

An external transfer (*regulation 7(2)*) must be made with the ex-spouse's consent unless the ex-spouse fails to provide this consent and he or she has also failed to consent to an internal transfer or the trustees did not offer the internal transfer route as an option in the first instance.

Schedule 5 (paragraph 1(4)) specifies that any consent to be given by the ex-spouse to an internal transfer option will be invalid unless it is given after receipt of a written notice of an offer to discharge liability by way of an external transfer and the consent is not withdrawn within seven days of receipt of such notice.

Death of ex-spouse prior to discharge of liability

8.15   *Regulation 6 (SI 2000 No 1053)* specifies how a pension credit liability can be discharged when the ex-spouse dies after the liability has arisen but before it has been discharged. Essentially, any benefits the scheme provides must, subject to the rules of the scheme, be in the form of a lump sum payment; payment of a pension; payment of both a lump sum and a pension and/or the purchase of an annuity contract or insurance policy with a 'qualifying arrangement' (defined in *regulation 11 (SI 2000 No 1053)*).

Small self-administered schemes

8.16   It should be noted that *regulation 2* of the *Retirement Benefits Schemes (Restriction on Discretion to Approve)* (*Small Self-administered Schemes*) (*Amendment*) *Regulations 2000* (*SI 2000 No 1086*) confirms that, whilst an ex-spouse participant who is offered an internal transfer will count as a scheme member for general purposes, an additional member of this type in the scheme will, nevertheless, not count towards the total number of members for determining whether the scheme can qualify as a small self-administered scheme ('SSAS') (i e less than twelve members).

Pros and cons of internal v external transfer options

8.17   When pension sharing was first introduced there was much debate about which option trustees should adopt as their policy for securing pension credits. Arguments against internal transfers are the added costs and the administrative burdens of an extra membership category; extended ongoing disclosure requirements and the need for extensive rule amendments to incorporate a new benefit structure and category of member. Moreover, the external option sits more easily with the 'clean break' motivation that gave rise to the pension sharing legislation in the first place.

The majority of funded occupational pension schemes have expressed a preference for the external transfer option, which avoids the problems outlined above. Concerns were, however, raised about the ability of trustees who were not authorised under *FSA 1986* (now *FSMA 2000*) to select a default external transfer destination without contravening *section 191* of *FSA 1986* (now *article 37* of the *Financial Services and Markets Act 2000* (*Regulated Activities*) *Order 2001* (*SI 2001 No 1544*). However, the position has subsequently been clarified somewhat by the Financial Services Authority which, in a letter to the NAPF dated 2 February 2001, stated that, where trustees pay the pension credit to a designated default option provider, this will not amount to the purchasing of an investment which will be held for the purposes of the scheme and so falls outside the ambit of the definition of a specified activity for the purposes of the financial services legislation.

The question of the availability of a suitable 'qualifying arrangement' to receive external transfers (without the need for the ex-spouse's signature on a proposal form) remains, at the time of writing, a problem. In relation to the default option, generally the Department for Work and Pensions ('DWP') has clarified a few points that had arisen regarding the type of vehicle available for the default option:

(a) The default option should not be available until the former spouse has been given adequate opportunity to make his or her choice or to make a further choice where payment cannot be made in accordance with his or her wishes. Where the default option, nevertheless, comes into play the only options available are either an internal transfer or the purchase of an annuity or insurance policy.

(b) This gives rise to the question as to the type of annuity and insurance policy available for this purpose. A deferred annuity can be purchased but it is not clear what other 'insurance policy' can be used. It is not possible to transfer the credit to a personal pension scheme or stakeholder schemes without the consent of the former spouse.

(c) *Section 32* buy-out contracts would also seem not to be an option. This is because only pension *benefits* can be transferred to a *section 32* buy-out contract (GN Practice Note 6A.21) so it would only be in the event that an ex-spouse were to acquire a 'pension credit benefit' in the scheme that this could then be transferred out – and even in that case the consent of the ex-spouse would be required. In most cases there will be no pension credit benefit, only a pension credit liability to be discharged by the trustees. This appears to leave the purchase of an annuity as the only available external default option.

In practice this issue seems to have posed less of a problem than anticipated. An ex-spouse who agrees to a pension sharing order as part of the divorce settlement will have been notified of the trustees' policy and, where only an external transfer option is offered, is likely already to have made suitable arrangements before agreeing to such an order.

Pension credit benefits

General benefits and transfers

8.18 Where the trustees of a scheme choose to offer ex-spouses an internal transfer option, and the ex-spouse does not elect to transfer the pension credit to another arrangement, the ex-spouse will become an ex-spouse participant and will become entitled to pension credit benefits in the scheme.

Section 37 of *WRPA 1999* inserts new *sections 101A to 101Q* in *PSA 1993*, setting out the requirements relating to pension credit benefits under occupational pension schemes. The protection given to ex-spouses with pension credit benefits broadly reflects the existing provisions for early leavers from occupational pension schemes, including similar transfer rights to those of a deferred member. This legislation is supplemented by the *Pension Sharing (Pension Credit Benefit) Regulations 2000 (SI 2000 No 1054)*.

Pension credit benefits are payable at 'normal benefit age', which means the earliest date at which a person who has a pension credit right is entitled to receive a pension by virtue of those rights (disregarding provisions as to early payment on grounds of ill-health). Normal benefit age must be between 60 and 65 and benefits cannot be taken in lump sum form before that age except in prescribed circumstances (*section 101C* of *PSA 1993* and *Part II* of *SI 2000 No 1054*). Essentially this is where the ex-spouse is suffering from serious ill-health prior to normal pension age (i e a life expectancy of less than one year) or where the benefits can be trivially commuted.

Members with pension credit benefits are entitled under *section 101F* of *PSA 1993* to request that their cash equivalent be transferred to another occupational pension scheme or personal pension scheme which satisfies the necessary criteria, or be used to purchase an annuity, subject to certain requirements and restrictions set out in *Part III of SI 2000 No 1054*. *Section 101H* of *PSA 1993* provides, in relation to salary related schemes, that a statement of entitlement must be provided by the trustees or managers, on the application of an eligible member, following which the eligible member has three months within which to request a transfer (*section 101G(1)*). The exceptions to this general rule are that an eligible member may not take a transfer if there is less than a year remaining before the member reaches normal benefit age or where any part of the benefit attributable to the member's pension credit rights has or must become payable. Where the trustees receive a transfer notice (i e a request for transfer) from an eligible member *section 101J* of *PSA 1993* requires the trustees to comply with the notice within six months of the valuation date or the date on which the member reaches normal benefit age, if earlier. *Regulation 26 (SI 2000 No 1054)* states that extensions may be applied for from the Regulator in similar circumstances to those referred to at 8.13 above in relation to the extension of the implementation period. Otherwise, failure to comply with the transfer notice must be reported to the Regulator within 21 days beginning with the day immediately following the end of the period for compliance (*regulation 25* of *SI 2000 No 1054*). The Regulator may then impose civil penalties under *section 10* of *PA 1995* if the trustees failed to take all such steps as were reasonable to ensure that the notice was complied with.

Indexation

8.19 *Regulations 32 to 35* of the *Pension Sharing (Pension Credit Benefit) Regulations 2000 (SI 2000 No 1054)* provide that occupational pension schemes must apply indexation to the pension credit benefit derived from safeguarded rights (see 8.27 below) and/or post-April 1997 rights excluding AVCs. The indexation to be applied is 5 per cent per annum or the increase in the Retail Prices Index, whichever is lower in respect of pensions in payment prior to 6 April 2005 or where entitlement to the pension credit arose before that date and 2.5 per cent per annum where entitlement to the pension credit arose on or after 6 April 2005.

MNT legislation

8.20   Ex-spouse members with pension credit benefits under the scheme do not count as 'qualifying members' for the purpose of the statutory consultation procedures relating to MNTs or MNDs under *PA 1995 (WRPA 1999, Sch 12, paras 45* to *49)*. These procedures no longer apply from 6 April 2006.

Section 67 of PA 1995

8.21   *Paragraph 53* of *Schedule 12* to *WRPA 1999* amended *section 67* of *PA 1995* to include pension credit benefits on the list of rights protected by that section. Any amendment of the scheme's rules, however, to give effect to the trustees' pension sharing policy and enable the application of a pension debit is excepted from *section 67* by virtue of *subsection 67(5)* and to accommodate pension credits and pension credit rights by virtue of *section 68(2)(da)*.

The *PA 2004* revised s*ection 67* provisions carry forward this exemption at new *subsection 67(3)* by excluding from the 'subsisting rights provisions' modifications for a purpose connected with pension debits under *section 29(1)* of *WRPA 1999*.

Treatment on winding up

8.22   In the case of a scheme to which s*ection 73* of *PA 1995* applies (see chapter 12), from 6 April 2005 the position of pension credits in the statutory order of priorities on winding up is referred to under *section 73(8)(b)* where it is stated that benefits derived from pension credits are not to be treated as derived from voluntary contributions for the purposes of that section.

In the case of all other schemes, pension credits are to be accorded the same treatment on winding up as the rights of a pensioner member if they have come into payment and the rights of a deferred member if they have not come into payment (*section 38(2)* of *WRPA 1999*). This section overrides the provisions of the scheme to the extent that they conflict with it.

371

Valuation

8.23   In creating pension debits and credits under s*ection 29* of *WRPA 1999* the pension sharing order is applied to the statutory cash equivalent of the member's benefits (*section 30* of *WRPA 1999*). The specified percentage for reduction of a member's benefits is therefore the percentage of his or her cash equivalent of the relevant benefits on the valuation day (*section 29(2)* of *WRPA 1999*). 'Valuation day' is defined in s*ection 29(7)* of *WRPA 1999* as such day within the implementation period for the credit as the person responsible for the arrangement may specify by notice in writing to the member and ex-spouse.

For active members of occupational pension schemes the statutory cash equivalent is calculated in respect of the benefits to which the member would have been entitled to had his pensionable service been terminated on the day immediately prior to the transfer day, i e the day on which the pension sharing order takes effect (s*ection 29(4)*). *Section 30* of *WRPA 1999* provides for the calculation of the cash equivalent of these benefits to be carried out in accordance with the provisions set out in the *Pension Sharing (Valuation) Regulations 2000 (SI 2000 No 1052)*.

Regulation 4 (SI 2000 No 1052) provides that cash equivalents are to be calculated by a qualified actuary (*regulation 4(1)*) in accordance with GN11. In the case of an active member his cash equivalent is required to be calculated on the assumption that the member had made a request for an estimate of cash equivalent as if his pensionable service were to terminate on the transfer day. The methods and assumptions used to calculate the cash equivalent of the benefits must not only comply with GN11 but also be consistent with the methods and assumptions used by the scheme for someone who is acquiring transfer credits under the scheme.

Regulation 5 (SI 2000 No 1052) provides for the possibility of increasing or, indeed, reducing cash equivalents in certain circumstances to provide, for example, for the inclusion of discretionary benefits or, conversely, the reduction of the cash equivalent where a scheme to which the scheme funding requirements in *Part 3* of *PA 2004* apply meets the GN11 insufficiency conditions (*regulation 5(3)*). It is important to note, however, that a reduction cannot be applied in circumstances where the pension credit liability is to discharged by way of internal transfer or by way of external transfer without the ex-spouse's consent.

Disclosure of information

8.24   *Section 23(1)(a)* of *WRPA 1999* provides for regulations to impose requirements on the person responsible for a pension arrangement to supply information to certain parties in connection with the power to provide financial relief under *MCA 1973*. The *Pensions on Divorce etc (Provision of Information) Regulations 2000 (SI 2000 No 1048)* set out the details of these requirements.

At the beginning of the divorce process the person responsible for the arrangement must, on the request of a scheme member, spouse or the court, ensure that the following information is provided in connection with the divorce in accordance with *regulation 2*:

(*a*)   a valuation of the pension rights or benefits accrued under the pension arrangement, if requested by the member or the court;

(*b*)   a statement that, if a member or the court requests, a valuation of the member's accrued benefits will be provided to the member or the court;

(*c*)   a statement summarising the way in which any such valuation of the benefits disclosed is calculated;

(*d*)   a statement of benefits included the valuation;

(*e*)   a statement as to whether the person responsible for the arrangement intends to offer membership of the scheme to a person entitled to a pension credit (i e internal transfer) and, if so, the type of benefits available to the pension credit member under that arrangement;

(*f*)   a statement as to whether the person responsible for the arrangement intends to discharge liability for a pension credit other than by offering membership to a person entitled to a pension credit (i e external option only);

(*g*)   the schedule of charges to be levied by the person responsible for the arrangement; and

(*h*)   any other additional information relevant to the sharing order requested by the court.

Therefore the valuation of a member's accrued benefits can only be provided by the arrangement to a member or the court. Once requested it must be provided within three months beginning with the date of receipt of the request; or within six weeks of the date of receipt of the request if the member has notified the trustees that it is required in connection with financial relief in divorce proceedings; or within a shorter period if so ordered by the court.

All the other items of information set out above must be supplied within one month of receipt of the request (as long as the request makes it clear that this is a request in connection with divorce). These provisions are contained in *regulation 2* of the *Pensions on Divorce etc (Provision of Information) Regulations 2000 (SI 2000 No 1048)*.

Regulation 4 sets out the information to be provided within 21 days of a notification that a pension sharing order or provision may be made, as follows:

(*a*) the full name and address of the pension scheme;

(*b*) whether the scheme is in winding up and, if so, the effective date of winding up and the contact details of the trustees or administrators;

(*c*) whether cash equivalents are subject to deductions;

(*d*) whether the trustees are aware of any other relevant court orders;

(*e*) any elements of the member's pension rights which are not shareable;

(*f*) details of how charges are to be paid;

(*g*) whether the member is a trustee of the scheme;

(*h*) whether the scheme may request details of the member's health from the member, if the order were to proceed; and

(*i*) whether the scheme requires any further information before implementation of the order.

Regulation 5 sets out the information required by the person responsible for the pension arrangement before the implementation period begins, as follows:

(i)   In relation to the member – all names and former names; date of birth; address; National Insurance number; name of scheme to which the order relates and membership/policy number.

(ii) In relation to the ex-spouse – all names and former names; date of birth; address; National Insurance number; if the ex-spouse is also a member of the scheme from which the pension credit is derived, the membership/policy number.

(iii) Where the ex-spouse is transferring to another arrangement – the full name and address of that arrangement; the membership or policy number; details of the person able to discharge liability for the pension credit; in the case of rights transferring from an occupational pension scheme which is in winding up with a deficit, whether the ex-spouse has indicated she wishes to transfer the pension credit rights; and any further information the receiving arrangement may require.

Regulation 6 sets out the information to be provided after the death of the ex-spouse prior to liability having been discharged.

Regulation 7 sets out the information to be provided after receipt of the pension sharing order or provision and *regulation 8* the information to be provided after the implementation of a pension sharing order.

Charging

8.25   *Section 41* of *WRPA 1999* and the *Pensions on Divorce etc (Charging) Regulations 2000 (SI 2000 No 1049)* provide for persons responsible for pension arrangements to recover charges in respect of pension sharing costs.

Costs are not recoverable unless the divorcing parties have been informed in writing by the person responsible for the pension arrangement of the intention to recover costs and a written schedule of the charges has been provided. Charges cannot, however, be recovered for the provision of basic information about pensions and divorce and for the provision of information in response to a notification that a pension sharing order may be made (*regulations 2* and *4* of the *Pensions on Divorce etc (Provision of Information) Regulations 2000 (SI 2000 No 1048)*) unless that information has already been provided on the previous twelve-month period; the member has reached normal retirement age or is within twelve months of normal retirement age. Charges also cannot be recovered for the provision of a cash equivalent which is provided in accordance with *section 93A* or *94* of *PA 1995* or in accordance with the *Disclosure Regulations*.

Where charges are recoverable they can only be for the reasonable administrative expenses the arrangement will incur in connection with the implementation of the pension sharing order or the provision of information in connection with the divorce proceedings and must be directly related to the individual case (*regulation 5* of *SI 2000 No 1049*). The legislation does not define, however, what is meant by 'reasonable'. The National Association of Pension Funds has issued guidance on this point to its membership (see 8.26 below).

Section 24D of *MCA 1973* has been introduced to give the courts power to include a provision in the order relating to the apportionment of charges between the parties. To the extent that the court is silent on the issue *section 41(3)(b)* of *WRPA 1999* provides that the charges shall be attributable to the scheme member.

Regulation 7 (SI 2000 No 1049) permits the postponement of the start of the implementation period for a sharing order until specified charges are paid, provided that appropriate notice has been given to the parties in accordance with that regulation.

Regulation 9 provides for certain methods of recovery of the charges by the person responsible for the pension arrangement. Where the charges are not paid in cash, recovery can be by way of deduction from the pension credit; deduction from the member's accrued rights; deduction from pension where the pension is in payment; and deduction from payments of pension credit benefits (subject to certain conditions having been satisfied).

Reference should be made to the *Pensions on Divorce etc (Charging) Regulations 2000 (SI 2000 No 1049)* for full details of the conditions and restrictions relating to the charging for information and pension sharing activities.

In relation to earmarking orders, charges for the provision of information are dealt with as described above. In relation to the costs associated with the implementation of an earmarking order *regulation 10* of *SI 2000 No 1049* provides that the person responsible for the pension arrangement recovers reasonable administrative expenses which have been or are likely to be incurred by reason of the order.

NAPF recommended scale of charges

Pension sharing costs for active and deferred members
8.26

Step	Lower limit	Upper limit	Notes
Produce CETV quotation	£0	£0	1. This is a standard entitlement under regulations. 2. CETV refers to 'cash equivalent transfer value' – the value of pension rights from the scheme.
Additional CETV quotations	£150	£200	Any more than one quotation a year can be charged for.
Provision of other information	£0	Up to £250	Information which does not have to be provided free may be charged for. Cost will depend upon the nature and complexity of the inquiry.
Processing a pensions sharing order ('PSO') – internal transfer, in DB or hybrid scheme	£1,950	£2,350	Includes allowance for future scheme admin costs approximately £1,000.
Processing a PSO – internal transfer, DC scheme	£1,800	£2,200	It is recommended that if trustees will pay for annuity purchase advice on retirement an extra £500 can be charged.
Processing a PSO – external transfer, DB or hybrid scheme	**£1,100**	**£1,550**	

Step	Lower limit	Upper limit	Notes
Processing a PSO – external transfer, DC scheme	*£1,050*	*£1,450*	

Pension sharing costs for pensions in payment

Step	Lower limit	Upper limit	Notes
Produce CETV quotation	£500	£800	There is no entitlement to this information under regulations.
Additional CETV quotations	£500	£800	There is no entitlement to this information under regulations.
Provision of other information	£0	Up to £250	Information which does not have to be provided free may be charged for. Cost will depend upon the nature and complexity of the inquiry.
Processing a PSO – internal transfer, in DB or hybrid scheme	£2,000	£2,550	Includes recalculation of CETV and recovery of pension arrears if the full amount is paid for a time after the pension sharing order.
Processing a PSO – external transfer	£1,300	£1,900	

Safeguarded rights

8.27   *Section 36 of WRPA 1999* inserts new *sections 68A to 68D into PSA 1993* with the effect that 'safeguarded rights' are created where rights to future benefits under the scheme are attributable to a pension credit which is or includes contracted-out (or safeguarded) rights. The safeguarded rights shall form the same percentage of the pension credit as the contracted-out (or safeguarded) rights form of the member's cash equivalent. Despite the different terminology, safeguarded rights are treated in broadly the same way as contracted-out rights. The detailed provisions can be found in the *Pension Sharing (Safeguarded Rights) Regulations 2000 (SI 2000 No 1055)*, including restrictions on the transfer or discharge of the safeguarded rights.

Family Proceedings Rules

8.28   The procedures to be followed to obtain either an earmarking or sharing order are set out in *rule 2.70* of the *Family Proceedings Rules 1991 (SI 1991 No 1247) (as amended)*.

The rule applies to applications for ancillary relief and sets out the obligations of the parties with regard to the provision of information relating to benefits which a party has or is likely to have under a pension scheme. For both earmarking and pension sharing the order must be specifically applied for on Form A or Form B. The court will then fix an appointment and, within seven days after receiving notification of the date of that appointment, the member must request that the person responsible for the pension arrangement(s) under which the member has or is likely to have benefits provides basic information set out in *regulation 2(2)* and *2(3)(b)* to *(f)* of the *Pensions on Divorce etc (Provision of Information) Regulations 2000 (SI 2000 No 1048)* (see 8.24 above).

Within seven days of receiving this information the member shall send a copy of it to the other party together with the name and address of the person responsible for the pension arrangement(s). *Rule 2.70(4)* states that, where the member is already in possession of, or has requested, a relevant valuation of his benefits under the pension arrangement in question, then this request for disclosure need not be made (for these purposes a relevant valuation is one which has been furnished to the member within the preceding twelve months).

If notice is given of intention to proceed with an application for a pension sharing order, the applicant must send a copy of Form A to the person responsible for the pension arrangement (*rule 2.70(6)*). In the case of an application for an earmarking order the applicant must send the person responsible for the pension arrangement a copy of Form A; an address for the service of any notices on the applicant by the person responsible for the pension arrangement; an address to which payments can be remitted; and, if that address is a bank, sufficient details to enable payment to be made into the applicant's account (*rule 2.70(7)*).

Within 21 days after service of a notice of application for an earmarking order under *rule 2.70(7)*, the person responsible for the pension arrangement has the right under *rule 2.70(8)* to require a copy of the statement in Form E supporting the application to be provided and they may provide to the applicant, respondent and the court a statement in answer. *Rule 2.70(8)* and *(9)* provides the relevant time limits. If the earmarking order is being applied for by way of consent order the relevant information, together with a copy of the draft order, must be provided to the persons responsible for the pension arrangement and the order shall not be made until 21 days have elapsed without objections being made or the court has considered any objections (*rule 2.70(11)* and *(12)*).

Under *rule 2.70(13)* any order for ancillary relief, whether by consent or not, which includes either a provision for pension sharing or for earmarking must:

(*a*)   in the body of the order state that there is to be provision by way of pension sharing or earmarking in accordance with the annex to the order; and

(*b*)   be accompanied by an annex setting out specified information in relation to each of the pension arrangements under consideration.

On being asked to review the contents of either a pension sharing or earmarking order it is *rule 2.70* of the *Family Proceedings Rules 1991 (SI 1991 No 1247)* (as amended) to which reference should be made.

Scheme documentation

8.29   PSO Update 62 and HMRC's model rules cover pension sharing on divorce. Any new scheme which was seeking HMRC approval after 10 May 2000 needed to provide for pension sharing on divorce, although in most cases the model rules will need significant tailoring in order to fit in with any particular provisions of the scheme (HMRC has confirmed that this was the intention when issuing the model rules). For any schemes fully approved before 10 May 2000, PSO Update 62 states that pension sharing legislation is overriding but there is an expectation that schemes will take the opportunity to incorporate the pension sharing provisions as soon as reasonably practicable and, in any case, when submitting a deed of amendment on another topic to HMRC, the scheme's examiner will wish to ensure that provisions for pension sharing have been included.

Overlap between earmarking and pension sharing

8.30   *Section 24B(5)* of *MCA 1973* states that a pension sharing order may not be made in relation to the rights of a person under a pension arrangement if there is in force an earmarking order in relation to any of the member's benefits under the relevant schemes.

Section 25B(7B) of *MCA 1973* states, similarly, that the power to make an earmarking order may not be exercised in relation to a pension arrangement which is the subject of a pension sharing order in relation to the marriage in question or has been the subject of a pension sharing between the parties to the marriage. In addition, *section 25C(4)* also extends this prohibition on to lump sum orders where the pension arrangement is subject to a pension sharing order in relation to the marriage or has been the subject of pension sharing between the parties to the marriage.

Civil partnerships

8.31 The *Civil Partnership Act 2004* (*CPA 2004*) came into force on 5 December 2005 and provides the opportunity for same-sex couples to obtain legal recognition of their relationship by registering as civil partners. The general principles behind *CPA 2004* are that registered civil partners will have access to rights and responsibilities similar to those of married couples including employment and pension benefits, the duty to provide maintenance for a civil partner, the duty to provide maintenance for children of the partnership and recognition under intestacy rules. See 9.31 below for more information.

A civil partnership is formed by signing a civil partnership document in the presence of witnesses and a civil partnership registrar, following which the civil partnership will end only on death, dissolution or annulment. *Schedule 5* to *CPA 2004* makes provision for financial relief in connection with civil partnerships that corresponds to the financial relief available in connection with divorces after marriage under *MCA 1973*. *Part 4* of *Schedule 5* to *CPA 2004* sets out full details in relation to pension sharing orders available on the dissolution or nullity of a civil partnership and these provisions mirror in essence those set out in the preceding paragraphs of this chapter in relation to divorce. *Part 6* of *Schedule 5* to *CPA 2004* sets out the provisions in relation to earmarking orders.

Consequential amendments have been made, therefore, to all relevant statutes and regulations referred to in the preceding paragraphs of this chapter to extend the provisions to apply on the dissolution of a civil partnership including, in particular, amendments to *MCA 1973* and *WRPA 1999*.

Chapter 9

Sex equality

Introduction

9.1 In the UK, differential pension provision for men and women was, prior to the 1990s, the norm rather than the exception. Two main factors contributed to this situation: the differing life expectancies of men and women, and the work patterns of men and women in paid employment. A further contributing factor in the UK has been the discriminatory retirement ages in the State scheme, although this is now in the process of being equalised.

The effect of European Community ('EC') law in prescribing requirements for equal treatment in pension schemes could no longer be ignored in the UK when the Court of Justice of the European Communities ('ECJ') confirmed in the *Barber* case (*Barber v GRE Assurance Group [1990] ECR I-1889*) that pensions were 'pay' for the purposes of the equal pay requirements of *Article 141* of the *Treaty of Rome* (formerly *Article 119* but renumbered by the *Treaty of Amsterdam* with effect from 1 May 1999).

Article 141 of the *Treaty of Rome* provides that:

'1. Each Member State shall ensure that the principle of equal pay for male and female workers for equal work or work of equal value is applied.

2. For the purpose of this Article, "pay" means the ordinary basic or minimum wage or salary and any other consideration, whether in cash or in kind, which the worker receives directly or indirectly, in respect of his employment, from his employer.

Equal pay without discrimination based on sex means:

(*a*)   that pay for the same work at piece rates shall be calculated on the basis of the same unit of measurement;

(*b*)   that pay for work at time rates shall be the same for the same job.'

The action in *Barber* was against the employer, not the pension scheme, as it was founded on the equal pay concept. In brief, Mr Barber was made redundant at the age of 52, and received various cash benefits, but was only entitled to a deferred pension payable from his normal retirement date. A woman in the same position as Mr Barber would have been entitled to an immediate retirement pension in addition to redundancy pay. The total value of the benefits payable to a woman in these circumstances exceeded the amount paid to Mr Barber. Mr Barber claimed successfully in the European Court that pensions should be treated as pay under *Article 141* and that, in consequence, he should be entitled to the same benefits as a woman of the same age. However, the European Court's decision was not retrospective and persons were not permitted (unless legal proceedings had already begun) to claim entitlement to a pension effective from a date prior to the date of judgment, i e 17 May 1990.

The *Maastricht Protocol (No 2)* ('the *Maastricht Protocol*') annexed to the *Treaty of European Union* (7 February 1992) was ratified by the Member States in October 1993 and amended *Article 141* constraining its application (in relation to pensions) to benefits accrued after 17 May 1990.

Although decisions of the ECJ are not legislative in nature, they are binding upon those to whom they are addressed (see *Article 249 (formerly Article 189)*). Where EC law has direct effect, it will generally override UK law. The principle that *Article 141* had direct effect was established on 8 April 1976 by the *Defrenne (No 2)* case which stated that 'direct effect' means that the protections given under *Article 141* apply directly to UK law without the need for any further national or European legislation. This was confirmed in the *Coloroll* case, which also made it clear that *Article 141* can be relied upon by both employees and their dependants against trustees who are bound to observe the principles of equal treatment.

The *Pensions Act 1995 (PA 1995)* incorporates the general requirements for equal treatment in pension schemes (see *sections 62 to 66*). These cover not only the terms on which scheme members are treated but also the terms on which employees are admitted to membership. Thus *section 62(3)* of *PA 1995* provides that in relation to such a 'term' that is '... less favourable to the woman than it is to the man, the term shall be treated as so modified as not to be less favourable'. These provisions came into force on 1 January 1996, but their operation is to some extent retrospective, as explained below. These requirements are overriding so schemes must comply with them, irrespective of the actual provisions in their governing documentation. *Section 65* of *PA 1995* also empowers trustees of schemes with inadequate amendment powers in their governing documentation to make whatever rule amendments are necessary to ensure compliance with the equal treatment requirements without employer consent.

PA 2004 also contains equal treatment provisions. *Section 171, which comes into force on 6 April 2006, provides for the equal treatment of men and women in relation to the 'payment function' of the Board of the Pension Protection Fund.

The Explanatory Notes to *PA 2004* state that *section 171* provides the mechanism to ensure that there is no discrimination between men and women arising from the use of the scheme rules when calculating entitlement to pension compensation.

A 'payment function' is a function of the Board of the Pension Protection Fund relating to 'pension compensation', 'duty to pay scheme benefits unpaid at assessment date' and the 'discharge of liabilities in respect of money purchase benefits' (see chapters 12 and 17).

It can be seen that there has been no clear policy or decision of principle underlying the development of UK law in this area. Indeed, it had been thought that the implementation of sex equality in pension schemes was simply not practicable. The cost issue alone was a significant deterrent to equalisation. Pension matters were expressly excluded from the equal pay and sex discrimination legislation passed in the 1970s and 1980s. Thus, the law has grown in fits and starts, very much in reaction to developments in Europe. It is an area of law in which most of the major issues have now been resolved, although a few anomalies remain. Commenting on the DWP's report on women and pensions in November 2005, the then Minister for Women and Secretary of State for Culture, Media and Sport, Tessa Jowell said:

'The role of women in society and in the workplace has changed dramatically since the war and this change is now reflected in most of our institutions, inside and outside of work. However, many women are left disadvantaged by a pension system that is based on a view of society that is nearly 60 years old and which is largely predicated on women relying on their husbands for their retirement income, so it is right that Government alongside others considers how best we address this.'

The DWP's report states that the issue of women's pensions is central to the National Pensions Debate and that the report will raise further questions for consideration alongside the work of the Pensions Commission.

A summary of relevant legislation and case law (UK and European) is set out at the end of the chapter.

Access/eligibility

General

9.2   The principle of equal access to pension scheme membership was established by the *Social Security Act 1973*, with detailed provision contained in regulations (the *Occupational Pension Schemes (Equal Access to Membership) Regulations 1976 (SI 1976 No 142)*). These Regulations were subsequently superseded by the *Occupational Pension Schemes (Equal Treatment) Regulations 1995 (SI 1995 No 3183)* (the *'Equal Treatment Regulations'*). The relevant provisions of the *Social Security Act 1973* were re-enacted in *PSA 1993* (see *section 118*, now repealed), and are now covered in *sections 62* to *66* of *PA 1995*, and associated regulations.

The ECJ, in the 1994 judgments of *Vroege v NCIV Instituut C-57/93 [1994] ECR I-4541* and *Fisscher v Voorhuis Hengelo BV C-128/93 [1994] ECR I-4583*, unequivocally stated that the right to join an occupational pension scheme falls within the scope of *Article 141* of the *Treaty of Rome*, and is therefore covered by the prohibition on sex discrimination laid down by that *Article*. Therefore, this means that the direct effect of *Article 141* could be relied upon to claim (retrospectively) equal treatment from 8 April 1976 (the date of the *Defrenne* case when it was established that *Article 141* had direct effect). In these two judgments the ECJ confirmed the earlier decision in *Bilka-Kaufhaus GmbH v Weber von Hartz C-170/84 [1986] ECR 1607* that discriminatory entry conditions which could not be objectively justified on grounds that related to the needs of the business, and not to the gender of the employee, were in breach of *Article 141*.

Part-time employees

Exclusion from membership – general

9.3   The exclusion of part-timers from scheme membership may infringe *Article 141* if it can be shown that there has been indirect sex discrimination.

There are two types of sex discrimination: direct and indirect. Direct sex discrimination occurs where, for example, women are denied entry to pension schemes but men are not. Indirect sex discrimination occurs where, for example, the pension scheme eligibility requirements are such that they are to the detriment of a significantly greater proportion of women than men because considerably fewer women can comply with them. By applying such restrictions (without objective justification not dependent on sex), women are being indirectly discriminated against on grounds of sex because considerably more women than men are being detrimentally affected.

It has generally been the case that considerably more women than men work part-time and, thus, may suffer indirect discrimination. Unfortunately, the ECJ did not expand on what it meant by 'a much greater number', nor did it specify a minimum number of hours that a part-timer must work in order to qualify for membership. Some light was shed on the latter point by the ECJ decision in *Nolte v Landesversicherungsanstalt Hannover C-317/93 [1996] All ER (EC) 212*, where it was decided that it was permissible to avoid granting pension benefits to employees who work less than 15 hours per week, where the reason is to achieve a social policy unrelated to any discrimination on grounds of sex. Here, the ECJ agreed that the fostering of 'minor' employment, for which there was a social demand, was practicable only if it was excluded from the relevant compulsory insurance provisions.

In the case of *Regina v Secretary of State for Employment ex parte Seymour-Smith and Another Case C-167/97 [1999] ICR 447*, the Advocate General considered among other questions the test for determining whether a measure adopted by a Member State had 'such a disparate effect as between men and women as to amount to indirect discrimination'. The Advocate General opined that the best approach to this issue was to compare statistical evidence of the proportion of men able to satisfy the condition at issue and those unable to do so and to compare those proportions. If the statistics indicated that a 'considerably smaller percentage' of women than men were able to satisfy the condition, there was indirect sex discrimination unless the measure was justified by objective factors. He also said that a lesser but persistent and relatively constant disparity over a long period between men and women who satisfied the particular condition at issue could also amount to indirect sex discrimination.

Exclusion from membership with justification

9.4   Even if the workforce statistics suggest that there might be discrimination, a scheme will not have to admit part-timers if the employer can demonstrate that the exclusion can be explained by objectively justified factors unrelated to any discrimination on grounds of sex. In the *Bilka-Kaufhaus* case, the first case to consider the issue of part-timers becoming members of an occupational pension scheme, it was accepted that a rule that incidentally adversely affects more women than men may nevertheless be lawful. It is for national courts to decide whether a particular rule is or is not justifiable, but guidelines laid down by the ECJ suggest that the onus is on the employer to show that:

(*a*)   the grounds put forward do not relate to the employee's sex;

(*b*)   the grounds put forward relate to a real need of the employer; and

(*c*)   the measures taken are appropriate and necessary to achieve the desired end.

An employer who can show, for example, that there is a genuine need to encourage full-time working patterns because they increase productivity or that part-timers will gain very little or nothing by joining a scheme that is contracted out instead of remaining with the State Second Pension, may be able to exclude part-timers without infringement of *Article 141*.

Part-timers' claims

9.5   The *Equal Treatment Regulations* came into force on 1 January 1996 to supplement the requirements for equal treatment relating to occupational pension schemes provided for in *sections 62 to 66 of PA 1995*. The regulations extended the scope of the *Equal Pay Act 1970* to cover pensions and consequently (in accordance with the then provisions of the *Equal Pay Act*) any claim had to be brought within six months of the end of the employment to which the claim related. In addition, claims were limited to two years' backdated membership.

The *Equal Treatment Regulations* also imposed the full cost of funding the excluded employee's benefits after 31 May 1995 on the employer.

The ECJ reviewed the validity of these time limits in *Preston v Wolverhampton Healthcare NHS Trust [2000] All ER (EC) 714*. This was followed by a referral to the House of Lords (*Preston (No 2) [2001] IRLR 237, HL*). The House of Lords confirmed that any national legislation was unlawful if it prevented any service from being taken into account that was earlier than two years before the date of the claim. Therefore, pension benefits payable after the date of claim now have to be calculated by reference to all periods of service for which the employee should have been a scheme member (or, if later, from 8 April 1976). The House of Lords also held that the rules of procedure under the *Equal Pay Act 1970* which required that a claim for membership of an occupational pension scheme must be brought within six months of the end of the employment to which the claim relates, were not less favourable than those applying to a breach of contract claim. Therefore the six-month limitation did not breach the community law principle of 'equivalence'. The significance for employees of this decision is that claims must, at the latest, be filed within six months of leaving employment. Employers also have to be aware that claims may arise not only from current part-time workers, but also from those who have ceased employment within the last six months or those who left employment more than six months previously but filed their claims within the six-month period. The House of Lords made it clear that a series of short-term contracts can amount to a stable employment relationship and therefore employment does not terminate at the end of each individual contract. Further, time starts to run for bringing a claim only when that relationship is broken.

A Directions hearing was subsequently held in November 2001 in which further issues relating to the *Preston* decision were raised and test cases were selected for a full hearing. These hearings took place in June and July 2002 and certain aspects of the employment tribunal's decision were appealed to the Employment Appeal Tribunal ('EAT'). The EAT (*Preston v Wolverhampton Healthcare NHS Trust (No 3) [2004] IRLR 96*) made the following determinations:

(*a*) There is a breach of the *Equal Pay Act 1970* where membership of a scheme is compulsory for full-time workers but part-time workers are excluded.

(*b*) There is no breach of *Article 141* of the *Treaty of Rome* where membership of the scheme is compulsory for full-time workers but part-time workers are given the option of joining or not joining the scheme.

(*c*) There is no continuing breach of *Article 141* by an employer failing to inform a part-time employee of his entitlement to join the pension scheme, unless that failure was itself on discriminatory grounds. However, employees may have a breach of contract claim in such circumstances on the basis of the employer's implied obligation to inform employees of advantageous contractual terms.

(*d*) The six-month time limit for bringing a claim under the *Equal Pay Act 1970* begins to run when:

   (i) either party indicates that further contracts will not be offered or accepted;

   (ii) either party acts in a manner which is inconsistent with the relationship continuing;

   (iii) the employer does not offer a new contract in circumstances where the periodicity of the preceding cycle of contracts indicates that it should have been offered;

   (iv) either party stops treating the relationship as stable;

   (v) the terms under which work is to be done alter radically;

   (vi) since liability for occupational pension schemes does not transfer under the *Transfer of Undertakings (Protection of Employment) Regulations 1981 (SI 1981 No 1794)* ('*TUPE*'), liability under the *Equal Pay Act 1970* and *Article 141* for the transferor's failure to provide equal access to a scheme remains with the transferor; and

   (vii) following a *TUPE* transfer, time for bringing a claim against the transferor begins to run from the date the employee's employment with the transferee comes to an end. Although the EAT commented that an employee may be advised to take action shortly after a relevant transfer to lessen the risk of the transferor going out of business and 'disappearing'.

The last finding relating to *TUPE* was appealed. The House of Lords (upholding the Court of Appeal) found that the time for bringing a claim begins to run from the date of the transfer (*Powerhouse v Burroughs [2006] UKHL 13*).

A settlement model has been agreed between HM Treasury and six public sector trade unions for the calculation of backdated employee contributions. This model may be used by employers and trustees to assist them in calculating the appropriate contribution required in order for part-time service to be reinstated. There is no requirement for the model to be followed. It can be accessed at www.employmenttribunals.gov.uk/england/ptsettlement.html.

The Occupational Pension Schemes (*Equal Treatment*) (*Amendment*) *Regulations 2005* (*SI 2005 No 1923*) implement the rulings in the *Preston* case. The *Regulations* amend provisions of the *Equal Pay Act 1970*, *PA 1995* and the *Equal Treatment Regulations*. In accordance with the decision in the *Preston* case, the *Regulations* remove the two-year limit on backdating successful claims. In addition, the *Regulations* make the six-month time limit for bringing claims comply with EC law in that claims must be brought within six months of leaving employment or the end of a stable employment relationship. Finally the *Regulations* remove an obligation on the employer to meet the cost of employee contributions where backdated access is granted.

In *Deutsche Telekom v Schroder [2000] ECR I-743* the ECJ confirmed that the *Defrenne* time limit does not prevent more favourable national legislation which may allow even further backdating of periods of service, i e prior to 8 April 1976, thereby going further than European legislation itself.

The right of access to a pension scheme for contract workers arose in the case of *Allonby v Accrington and Rossendale College [2001] IRLR 364 (CA)*. In 1996 the college terminated Mrs Allonby's part-time contract and employed her services through an employment agency instead. Mrs Allonby complained, inter alia, that she was no longer eligible for membership of the Teachers' Superannuation Scheme and that this amounted to discrimination. The Court of Appeal held that by virtue of *section 1(2)(a)* of the *Equal Pay Act 1970*, Mrs Allonby was in a contract of employment for occupational pension purposes. The appeal was allowed on the grounds that the employment tribunal had not adopted the correct approach to the question of whether the impact of the condition for continuous employment was proportionate and justifiable, and the case was remitted back to the employment tribunal for a further hearing on whether the employer had discriminated against the employee as a contract worker. The Court of Appeal also referred certain questions to the ECJ and on 13 January 2004, the ECJ gave its judgment in *Allonby v Accrington and Rossendale College (Case C-256/01 [2004] IRLR 224)*. The ECJ considered and gave judgment on the questions referred to it by the Court of Appeal as outlined below:

(a) The first question concerned whether Mrs Allonby could bring an equal pay claim identifying a male full-time employee as her comparator (Mr J). The ECJ held that Mr J could not be a comparator for Mrs Allonby. Mr J was paid by the college and Mrs Allonby by an employment agency.

There was no basis on which the differences in pay between Mrs Allonby and Mr J could be attributable to a single source. There was therefore no single body responsible for the inequality.

(*b*) The ECJ considered whether Mrs Allonby was entitled to the right to equal pay conferred by *Article 141*. The ECJ held that the right extends to all 'workers' but does not cover an independent provider of services who is not in a relationship of subordination with the person who receives those services.

(*c*) Where an equal pay claim relates to a private occupational pension scheme a 'worker' must identify, in the same undertaking, workers of the opposite sex who perform or have performed comparable work.

(*d*) Where the pension scheme is statutory, an equal pay claim could be pursued where the statistics support it, even in the absence of an actual comparator. This is on the basis that the legislation is the sole source of the unequal treatment, i e there is no requirement for the comparator.

(*e*) In order to succeed, Mrs Allonby would have to show that, among teachers who are 'workers' and fulfil all of the scheme's membership conditions except that of being employed under a contract of employment, there is a much higher percentage of women than men. It would be open for the college objectively to justify the difference in treatment.

In light of the ECJ's judgments, the Court of Appeal held, on 25 November 2004, that it would be appropriate to remit the case to the employment tribunal for determination of outstanding matters. It was held that the following issues required determination; (a) whether Mrs Allonby was a worker as ruled by the ECJ; (b) if so, whether the pension scheme had an adverse impact on her on the grounds that she was a woman; and (c) whether any such impact was justified.

The decision in *Allonby* was referred to recently in the case *British Airways Plc v Jessica Starmer [2005] IRLR 862*. It was held by the EAT that the employment tribunal was correct in finding that the decision of British Airways not to allow Mrs Starmer to work 50 per cent of her hours was a provision, criterion or practice which had a disparate impact and was not justified.

However, the *Allonby* decision was distinguished in *Shaikh v Department for Constitutional Affairs [2005] All ER (D) 154*. The claimant was a part-time tribunal chairman. He claimed equal access to the pension provision available to full-time chairmen. However, the respondents denied the claim and stated that there were no comparable female chairmen engaged in like work or work of equal value. Relying on the decision in *Allonby* the claimant asserted that there was no requirement for a comparator in this case as statute was the source of the unequal treatment. However, distinguishing *Allonby*, the EAT stated that there had to be a female comparator.

In the case of *Dacas v Brook Street Bureau (UK) Ltd [2004] EWCA Civ 217*, Mrs D worked for a local authority through an agency. She claimed unfair dismissal against both the agency (Brook Street) and the local authority. Brook Street appealed the EAT's decision that it was her employer. The Court of Appeal held that Brook Street was not Mrs Dacas' employer. It went on to say that there might be an implied contract of employment between Mrs Dacas and the local authority. If the local authority had been a party to the appeal then that question would have been remitted to the employment tribunal for decision. The importance of this decision for pensions is that the Court of Appeal is indicating that agency workers could be employees of the organisation they provide their services to. This is a move away from the previously generally held view that the individual's only contractual relationship was with the agency. If such workers can establish implied contracts of employment then they may well also, as employees, have rights to membership of pension schemes.

In *Astbury v Gist [2005] ALL ER (D) 165 (Apr)* the *Dacas* case was applied when the EAT found that the employment tribunal had been wrong in not carrying out a detailed factual assessment before reaching a conclusion as to whether or not there was an implied contract of employment between the worker and the end user.

It may be possible for employees who are excluded from schemes and who are outside the statutory time limits to complain to the Pensions Ombudsman, meaning that longer time limits may therefore apply. The Ombudsman has indicated that such exclusion could constitute maladministration and, consequently, he may investigate equal access complaints and indeed took this view in his determination of *Mrs D Copnall (Case No F00828, 28 September 2000)*. He determined that failure to admit part-timers retrospectively to a pension scheme was maladministration. However, this finding was overturned on appeal to the High Court in *Glossop v Copnall [2001] PLR 263* on 5 July 2001 when Sir Andrew Morritt held that a trustee's failure to comply with the requirements of legislation is not of itself maladministration (in fact, Mrs Copnall had not complained of the matter which the Ombudsman held to be maladministration). The High Court held that trustees acted properly in waiting for the relevant decisions by the European Court before granting backdated benefits.

The benefit of making a complaint to the Pensions Ombudsman is that the more generous limitation period of three years applies. The Ombudsman can also extend the three-year limitation period in exceptional cases where the complainant was unaware of the event giving rise to the complaint or if it was not reasonably practicable for the complaint to be made or referred within the three-year time limit. However, the Ombudsman is precluded from investigating complaints if proceedings have already been brought before the courts, and this includes employment tribunal claims (*PSA 1993, s 146(6)*).

With regard to the backdating of employee contributions where retrospective membership of a scheme has been granted, HMRC indicated (see HMRC Update No 26, March 1997) that in the case of schemes approved before 27 July 1989, if prescribed circumstances are satisfied, any employee granted back-dated membership of a pension scheme who is required to pay a contribution to purchase past service benefits, may pay contributions in excess of 15 per cent of remuneration. The same treatment applies to schemes approved on or after 27 July 1989 under HMRC's discretionary powers. Tax relief for the contributions will be limited to 15 per cent of the individual's earnings for the tax year in which the payment is made. The Occupational Pensions Board (before it was dissolved) confirmed that National Insurance contributions may be refunded to both employers and employees where retrospective contracted-out membership has been granted. Pension Update No 131 dated 23 April 2002 noted the position on the tax treatment of pension contributions of part-time employees who are given rights following the decision in *Preston*. This Update confirms the Treasury's position that tax relief will only be available on employees' back contributions up to 15 per cent of remuneration in the tax year in which the contributions were actually paid. The Update also provides that, where a member has already retired and taken benefits, an additional lump sum may not be paid, but if a transfer payment has been made an additional supplementary transfer can be paid. The HMRC subsequently announced that Update 131 would be amended to permit pensioners to take a second lump sum and this announcement was given effect to in Pensions Update No 135, 'Lump Sums', dated 20 December 2002.

In the context of the limits on employee contributions mentioned above, it is worth noting that following *FA 2004* from April 2006 the current limits on contributions will disappear (see chapter 5).

Membership conditions

9.6   Some schemes/employers may impose membership conditions that indirectly discriminate against part-timers. An example of this type of practice was challenged in the complaint of Mrs E M Shillcock which was determined by the Pensions Ombudsman (*No F00317, [1997] PLR 207*). In that complaint, the scheme rules required the lower earnings limit for national insurance contributions ('LEL') to be deducted when determining pensionable salary. Employees who earned less than the LEL were not eligible to join the scheme.

The Pensions Ombudsman ruled that this practice amounted to indirect discrimination against part-time employees earning less than the LEL. He said that only part of the LEL should have been deducted, representing the proportion that the employee's part-time hours bore to full-time hours. The decision was appealed to the High Court and the decision was overturned. It was held that the

Pensions Ombudsman did not have jurisdiction to entertain a complaint regarding death in service benefits. In addition, the LEL offset was not discriminatory and had it been so, the intention to provide integration with the State scheme would have been sufficient objective justification (*Uppingham School v Shillcock [2002] EWHC 641 (Ch), [2002] 2 CMLR 39*).

The Part-time Workers Regulations

9.7 *The Part-time Workers (Prevention of Less Favourable Treatment) Regulations 2000 (SI 2000 No 1551)* came into effect on 1 July 2000 and implemented *Directive 97/81/EC* as extended to the UK by *Directive 98/23/EC*. The *Regulations* require employers to treat part-time workers no less favourably than they treat full-time workers in respect of the same type of employment contract. In addition, employers may not treat less favourably an employee who, having worked full time, returns to work on a part-time basis after absence, compared with the way the employee was treated when he or she worked full time. This is subject to the defence of objective justification. It will not be necessary for a part-timer to prove indirect sexual discrimination in order to claim entitlement to the same benefits as full-time workers. So, for example, part-time workers cannot be excluded from a pension scheme which full-time workers are entitled to join unless this exclusion can be objectively justified. Employers will have to ensure that there are no restrictive conditions relating to access to, and benefits under, the pension scheme for part-time workers.

However, treating part-timers less favourably than full-timers can be justified on objective grounds provided that it can be shown that the less favourable treatment is (*a*) to achieve a legitimate objective (for example, genuine business objective); (*b*) necessary to achieve that objective; and (*c*) an appropriate way to achieve that objective.

To reflect the ruling in *Preston* (see 9.5 above), the *Part-time Workers (Prevention of Less Favourable Treatment) Regulations 2000 (Amendment) Regulations 2002 (SI 2002 No 2035)* came into force 1 October 2002. The *2000 Part-time Regulations (regulation 8(8))* had limited the backdating of a claim to two years from the date upon which the complaint was presented. *Regulation 2* of the *Amendment Regulations* removes this restriction. In addition, the distinction between fixed-term and permanent contract employees has been removed with the result that part-time workers on a fixed-term contract can now compare themselves with full-time workers on a permanent or fixed-term contract.

The first case under *the Part-time Workers Regulations 2000* to reach the Court of Appeal was *Matthews v Kent & Medway Towns Fire Authority [2004] EWCA Civ 844*. Mr Matthews worked as a part-time fire-fighter and complained that he was discriminated against compared with full-time fire-fighters, in particular by not being granted access to the pension scheme. The employment tribunal had dismissed the fire-fighters' claims on the basis that the part-time fire-fighters were employed on a different type of contract to full-time fire-fighters and the part-time fire-fighters were not engaged in the same or broadly similar work as full-time fire-fighters. The EAT dismissed the fire-fighters' appeal and their appeal against the EAT decision was dismissed by the Court of Appeal. The Court of Appeal found that the part-time fire-fighters were employed under the same type of contract as their full-time colleagues but that the Tribunal was correct in finding that the full-time fire-fighters carried out additional job functions not carried out by the part-time workers.

In the DWP's report on women and pensions it was noted that women who work part time are still at the greatest risk of having an employer who does not offer a pension scheme. Around 40 per cent of women employed part time say their employer does not have a pension scheme compared with 25 per cent of women employed full time.

The Fixed-term Employees Regulations

9.8   *The Fixed-term Employees* (*Prevention of Less Favourable Treatment*) *Regulations 2002* (*SI 2002 No 2034*) came into force on 1 October 2002. The *Regulations* require employers to treat fixed-term employees no less favourably than permanent employees of the same employer who are doing similar work, unless there is an objective justification for the difference in treatment. The *Regulations* also provide that if a fixed-term employee is employed on a number of successive contracts for four years or more then their contract has the effect of a permanent contract unless the employer can objectively justify continuing employment on a fixed-term basis. The *Regulations* cover all employees under a fixed-term contract with the exclusion of apprentices, agency workers, the armed forces and those employed under a Government training scheme. It is worth noting that under *regulation 8*, continuous employment can commence (under a new or renewed contract) from 10 July 2002 for the purpose of calculating the four-year period of a fixed-term contract (this is because the *Regulations* had to be implemented in the UK by 10 July 2002).

The *Regulations* cover, in addition to other contractual terms, pay and occupational pension schemes and thus access to pension arrangements and levels of benefits offered. However, the *Regulations* do not require term-per-term equality, providing the overall package offered is broadly comparable. Therefore, whilst in principle employers are required to offer fixed-term employees the same rights of entry to the pension scheme and the same benefits under it as they do for permanent employees; it may, however, be possible, in certain circumstances, to offer access on different terms, providing that the overall package of rights is comparable (see chapter 7).

Benefits

General

9.9   Although the matter of equal access to pension schemes has presented many difficulties, many more questions have been raised over the issue of equality in benefits and contributions. This arises, in the main, by the fact that benefit design and computation have been dictated by actuarial science which takes into account, among other matters, the differing mortality rates of the sexes. The *Barber* decision (17 May 1990) meant that immediate action had to be taken, and various measures were adopted to implement equalisation. Many, but not all, of the issues raised by the *Barber* decision were clarified in subsequent ECJ decisions (notably, the 1994 *Coloroll* decision (*Coloroll Pension Trustees Ltd v Russell C-200/91 [1994] ECR I-4389*)). It had been feared by employers that the equalisation of benefits would have to be fully retrospective, although the ECJ in the *Coloroll* case confirmed that retrospection is only required in relation to benefits payable for periods of service from 17 May 1990. This is known as the 'accruals' basis. The reason for this limitation on equalisation of benefits for men and women is because it was held that Member States could argue that they had been led to believe that such discrimination was acceptable because of parallel EU legislation. In the case of *Quirk v Burton Hospital [2002] 24 PBLR* the Court of Appeal upheld the judgment of the EAT which held that the limitation is correct and equal treatment under *Article 141* in relation to scheme benefits does not apply to service prior to 17 May 1990.

The ECJ required employers and trustees to consider three time periods in respect of measures to equalise benefits under their schemes:

(*a*)   the period up to 17 May 1990, when benefits need not be equalised;

(*b*)   the period from 17 May 1990 to the date when scheme benefits are equalised, when benefits must be 'levelled up' (i e increased to the level enjoyed by the advantaged sex); and

(*c*)   the period after the date when scheme benefits are equalised. Although *Article 141* itself permits benefits to be 'levelled up' or 'levelled down' in respect of this period, the UK decision in the *Lloyds Bank* case should be noted at this point (*Lloyds Bank Pension Trust Corporation Ltd v Lloyds Bank plc [1996] OPLR 181*). In this case, the High Court decided that future accrual rates could not be reduced to meet equalisation objectives. This may be a decision turning on the particular facts of the case (summarised in the table of cases at the end of this chapter), and certainly flows against the tide of the other main cases, notably *Smith v Avdel Systems Ltd C-408/92 [1994] ECR I-4435*.

Derived rights

9.10   The requirement for equality in pay and pensions applies also to spouses, survivors, dependants and others who are entitled to claim benefits through an employee's membership of a scheme. In *Ten Oever v Stichting Bedrijfspensioenfonds voor het Glazenwassers-en Schoonmaakbedrijf [1993] ECR I-4879* the ECJ confirmed that a survivor's pension falls within the scope of *Article 141*. Thus, any scheme benefit provided for the wife of a male member must also be provided for the husband of a female member. The ECJ in the *Coloroll* case confirmed that, as for members' benefits, this requirement for equal treatment only applies in relation to service from 17 May 1990, except for those claims brought before this date.

Transfers

9.11   Schemes which accept transfer payments in respect of benefits accrued since 17 May 1990 will bear the burden of equalisation as a consequence of any inadequacy in the transfer payments received. The ECJ considered (in *Coloroll*) that the rights accruing to an employee from *Article 141* cannot be affected by the fact that he changes his job and has to join a new scheme, with his accrued pension rights being transferred to the new scheme. However, in the event of an inadequate transfer payment being made, the ECJ envisaged the receiving scheme making a claim (under national law) against the transferring scheme for the additional sums required to equalise the benefits to be paid. In practice trustees of the receiving scheme will also obtain an indemnity from the transferring scheme to cover such additional sums as may be required.

It may be that transferring employees have a claim against both the trustees of the transferring scheme and of the receiving scheme. The *Acquired Rights Directive (77/187/EEC)* was designed to safeguard employees' rights and ensure continuing employment following a transfer of a business undertaking. However, provisions contained in a contract of employment or collective agreement relating to an occupational pension scheme are specifically excluded. There have been a number of challenges to this pensions exclusion over the years. The case of *Beckmann v Dynamco Whicheloe Macfarlane Ltd, Case C-164/00 [2002] 64 PBLR; [2002] All ER (D) 05 (Jun)* held that benefits payable on redundancy do transfer under the *Acquired Rights Directive*. The effect of this judgment appears to be that redundancy benefits payable under an occupational pension scheme and other benefits payable before normal retirement date may transfer. The decision in *Beckmann* was approved in the case of *Martin v South Bank University [2004] IRLR 74* where it was decided that only benefits paid from the time when an employee reaches the end of his normal working life can be classified as 'old age' benefits within the meaning of

Article 3(3) and are thus excluded from automatic transfer under *TUPE*. With effect from April 2005, *PA 2004* introduced a basic level of pensions protection for employees on a *TUPE* transfer. This protection is contained in the *Transfer of Employment (Pension Protection) Regulations 2005 (SI 2005 No 649)* (see chapter 7).

The position of money purchase schemes which receive unequalised transfer payments is uncertain. Clearly, there would be serious practical difficulties in complying with the obligation to equalise, possibly entailing the re-allocation of funds in individual members' accounts. Arguably, the *Coloroll* decision does not encompass money purchase schemes (see 9.15 below) but pending clarification of the issue, the trustees of such schemes should act with great caution. For example, trustees should consider very carefully whether this would be an appropriate circumstance in which they should exercise any discretion (in the provisions of the scheme) to refuse transfers.

Bridging pensions

9.12   Bridging pensions aim to achieve a form of equality between men and women in the pensions received where men have retired before State pension age, by taking into account the earlier date from which women are eligible to receive the State pension. Thus, bridging pensions could be paid to both men and women who take early retirement at, say, age 55, and stop at age 60 for women, but to continue to age 65 for men. In *Birds Eye Walls v Friedl M Roberts [1993] PLR 323*, the pension for a female ex-employee was reduced when she reached age 60, whereas a man would have received a full pension to age 65. The ECJ was asked whether bridging pensions where in breach of *Article 141*. The ECJ held that bridging pensions were not discriminatory because they were designed to remove an existing inequality arising as a consequence of the different ages that State pension commences for men and women. This decision can be criticised, however, in that it allows employers to reduce a pension on the assumption that a woman is in receipt of a full State pension, whether or not that is in fact the case. It is to be noted that *section 64(2)* of *PA 1995* and the *Equal Treatment Regulations* exclude bridging pensions paid in these circumstances from the ambit of the equal treatment rule contained in *section 62* of *PA 1995*. In addition, *FA 2004* allows scheme pensions to be reduced when a member begins to receive a State retirement pension (*Schedule 28, para 2*).

The decision in *Birds Eye* is difficult to consider against the decision in *Bestuur van het Algemeen Burgerlijk Pensioenfonds v Beune [1995] All ER (EC) 97* where the ECJ held that it was unlawful for a scheme to make deductions in respect of the State pension where it had the effect of producing a lower pension for men but not women from the scheme. In the Netherlands, the Dutch State scheme gives married men a higher pension than married women.

Actuarial factors

9.13   The use of actuarial factors in funded final salary occupational pension schemes which vary according to sex was held by the ECJ in *Coloroll* not to fall within the scope of *Article 141*. This was so even though the amount of a transfer value for a man would be lower than for a woman in consequence of the actuarial factors used in the assessment of the capital sum transferred that are based on life expectancy which differs between men and women.

The issue of unequal transfer values had previously been considered in *Neath v Hugh Steeper Ltd [1993] ECR I-6935*, in which the ECJ decided that lump sum payments and transfer values were not 'pay' within *Article 141*. It considered that it is only the employer's commitment to the payment of a periodic pension at a particular level which constitutes pay within the meaning of *Article 141*. It decided that the funding arrangement by which the pension was to be secured falls outside the scope of *Article 141*. (Although this was confirmed in the *Coloroll* decision, the ECJ has made the position clear only in relation to final salary schemes.)

It was confirmed in *Neath* that as employees' contributions were deducted from salaries, employees' contribution rates must be the same for both men and women as they constitute an element of pay within *Article 141*. Thus, although contributions made by employees must be equal as between men and women, as these contributions are an element of their pay, employers' contributions are pitched to ensure the adequacy of the funds necessary to secure the future payment of periodic pensions and may be unequal due to the use of sex-based actuarial factors. Inequalities in the amounts of capital benefits or substitute benefits (for example, where a dependant's pension is payable in return for surrender of part of the member's annual pension or where a reduced pension is paid on early retirement) whose value can be determined only on the basis of the arrangements chosen for funding the scheme, were likewise considered to be outside the scope of *Article 141*.

PA 1995 (*section 64*) and the *Equal Treatment Regulations* (*regulation 15*) expressly permit the use of actuarial factors which differ for men and women. It is stated that the equal treatment rule does not operate in relation to actuarial factors which differ for men and women in respect of the differences in the average life expectancy of men and women and which are determined with a view to providing equal periodical pension benefits for men and women. The difference in treatment is permitted only in relation to certain prescribed benefits as set out in *regulation 15*.

Additional voluntary contributions

9.14   Equality principles apply to all pension benefits under a scheme and it is irrelevant whether they are attributable to employers' or employees' contributions. However, where the scheme does no more than provide the necessary arrangements for the management of contributions and payments of the resulting benefits (in relation to money purchase additional voluntary contributions) those resulting benefits are not covered by *Article 141*. Consequently additional benefits deriving from contributions paid by employees on a voluntary basis are not covered by *Article 141*, as these additional contributions are to secure benefits over and above those which they are entitled to expect by reason of their employment and cannot, therefore, be regarded as pay within the meaning of *Article 141*.

Money purchase benefits

9.15   In money purchase schemes, the pension commitment of the employer is an obligation to pay a defined level of contribution. The ECJ has not directly decided how the principle of equal treatment is to be applied to money purchase schemes. What has been established is that the commitment or 'promise' to the employee, which must be equal between men and women, is to be distinguished from the funding considerations, which are not covered by *Article 141*.

Whilst it is clear that employee contributions must be equal as between men and women, the position in relation to employer contributions is less certain. It is generally accepted that, as the employer in a money purchase scheme does not promise any particular level of benefit, the commitment is the contribution, and as such these must be equal. In schemes which use sex-based actuarial factors, it is not possible to have both equal contributions and equal benefits. If the *Neath* case applies to money purchase schemes, women are most likely to be the disadvantaged sex. This is because the capital sum built up will not secure the same amount of pension for a woman as for a man. Her periodic pension will be lower as it will take account of the expectation that she will live longer. *Article 6* of the *Equal Treatment Directive* specifically allows a differential where the ultimate aim is to achieve equality.

The DSS directed that where trustees have been responsible for providing or securing a pension, this must be equal. Where a member exercises an open market option provided under the provisions of the scheme, the DSS considered the benefit to be the capital sum, which again must be equal. This appears to be a distinction without a difference, but until unisex actuarial factors are an accepted norm in the insurance domain, it would be safer for schemes to make the open market option available to members and let them make the arrangements for securing their benefits with the insurer of their choice. The member is not subject to the same constraints on trustees in securing a pension. On taking his capital sum from the scheme, the trustees are released from any further liability to the member, and it is for the member to buy the best pension he can in the annuity marketplace.

Retirement ages

State pension age and contractual retirement age

9.16 State pension age is being equalised over a ten-year period commencing in the year 2010. The new pension age of 65 for women will apply to those born on or after 6 March 1955. However, the Turner Report (the Second Report of the Pensions Commission published on 30 November 2005 entitled 'A New Pension Settlement for the Twenty-First Century') suggests raising State pension age for men and women to 68 years by 2050. It has been suggested that any such attempt may be undermined by an agreement reached in October 2005 between the Government and public sector trade unions that (in relation to their occupational scheme) public sector workers would not be required to work until 65. At the time of writing a Government White Paper is awaited. The public sector has had to offer equal pension ages since the coming into effect of *Directive 76/207/EEC* in 1976, as the ECJ in *Marshall v Southampton & SW Hampshire Area Health Authority [1986] ECR 723* held that the *Directive* had direct effect on the employer in that case as the employer was an 'emanation of the State'. It was held that the exception to the prohibition on sex discrimination in the *Directive* applied only to the determination of pensionable age for the purposes of granting old-age and retirement pensions. However, a policy involving the dismissal of a woman because she had reached State pension age (which is different for men and women) constituted discrimination contrary to the *Directive*.

Ascertaining the contractual retirement age is not as straightforward as it seems. If the contract of employment is silent on the retirement age the established custom and practice will be looked at to determine when employees have retired in the past in relation to that particular position. However, the contractual retirement age must not be different for men and women doing the same job.

The *Equal Treatment 'Framework' Directive (2000/78/EC)* outlaws discrimination on the grounds of age, although the UK is not due to implement this aspect of the *Directive* before 2006. The *Employment Equality (Age) Regulations 2006 (SI 2006 No 1031)* are designed to implement the age discrimination requirements. The *Regulations* are to come into force on 1 October 2006 and include, in their current form, some exemptions for certain types of potentially age discriminatory differences in treatment in UK occupational pension schemes. For more detail see chapter 7.

In the ECJ case *Kutz-Bauer v Freie und Hansestadt Hamburg [2003] All ER (D) 327 (Mar)*, provisions allowing workers over 55 to work part-time applied only until the date on which the worker became entitled to a statutory old age pension. For most women this was 60 and for most men it was 65. It was held that this was capable of breaching the *Equal Treatment Directive* and it was for the national court to determine whether there was in fact indirect discrimination which could not be objectively justified.

In October 2003, in the case of *Secretary of State for Trade and Industry v Rutherford, Bentley and Harvest TownCircle Limited EAT [2003] 78 PBLR*, the EAT overturned a tribunal's decision that the statutory upper age limit which applies to complaints of unfair dismissal and for statutory redundancy pay was unlawful for being indirectly discriminatory on grounds of sex. Mr Rutherford was over 65 when he was dismissed. He was not given redundancy pay nor was he able to claim for unfair dismissal. At the Court of Appeal, it was held that the complainant had not established indirect discrimination against men and there was no need for the court to consider the issue of objective justification (*Rutherford v Secretary of State for Trade and Industry [2004] 72 PBLR*). This was upheld by the House of Lords in May 2006. The Government has announced its intention to abolish these statutory age limits under the *Employment Equality (Age) Regulations*.

The contractual retirement age of British Airways' employees has recently come under the scrutiny of the EAT in *Cross v British Airways [2005] 26 PBLR*. The case arose when several employees were dismissed on full pension at the age of 55 in accordance with BA's retirement policy. Claimants wanted to be allowed to continue working until age 60. Some of the employees framed their claims on the basis that they had a retirement age of 60 following a historic *TUPE* transfer. Other employees alleged sex discrimination due to certain historic practices of BA. Interestingly, in light of the current moves towards later retirement, BA presented considerable evidence that it would be more expensive to allow the employees to continue to work than to retire them.

It is possible (and permissible) for employers to have differing retirement ages for different positions, as long as the demarcation of positions is not sex discriminatory (whether direct or indirect). This principle was upheld in *Bullock v The Alice Ottley School [1992] IRLR 564* in which the Court of Appeal decided that a school's grounds and maintenance staff (who had a retirement age of 65) could have a different retirement age from its domestic staff (who had a retirement age of 60). However, where different groups of employees are treated in this way, the court will look very closely at the reasons given to justify the difference.

Retirement age under the pension scheme

9.17 Although the *Barber* case established beyond doubt that pensions were 'pay' and, in consequence, that pensions had to be equal for men and women, the questions as to how and from which date equalisation was to be implemented were not answered until later. These issues were addressed by the

ECJ in the *Coloroll* and *Smith v Avdel* cases. In the *Smith v Avdel* case, the employer proposed to implement the *Barber* decision by raising the retirement age of women to that of the men, and including the period prior to the date of the *Barber* decision. The ECJ held that until equalisation measures had been taken, the only proper method of compliance with *Article 141* was to confer upon the disadvantaged sex those advantages enjoyed by the favoured sex, in respect of service after 17 May 1990.

Thus, from 17 May 1990 until the date of the equalisation of retirement ages, the pension rights of the men had to be enhanced to correlate with the lower retirement age of the women, i e 60. For the period prior to the date of the *Barber* decision, the ECJ determined that there was no requirement to equalise benefits.

With regard to the period following the date of equalisation, the ECJ stated that *Article 141* did not preclude equalisation measures which had the effect of reducing the benefits of the (previously) advantaged sex. *Sections 62* to *66* of *PA 1995* (which aim to bring into statute the effect of *Barber* and the subsequent cases) do not preclude this either. However, neither *Article 141* nor *PA 1995* overrides trustees' duties to act in their members' best interests (or an employer's duty of good faith) and so these duties must still be borne in mind.

The equal treatment requirement was not, therefore, a victory for women. Where retirement ages have been equalised upwards, women will have to work for longer or face the risk of a reduction in their pensions if they still wish to retire at age 60. Further, as the decisions in *Coloroll* and *Neath* confirm, sex-based actuarial factors may be applied which could further reduce the amount of pension received. This would affect transfer values, which on transfer to a money purchase scheme would lead to unequal benefits. However, where a prospective pensionable service factor is used, for example, on ill-health early retirement, this can increase the resultant pension.

Conclusions and practical issues

General

9.18   Although most of the equality issues raised by the *Barber* case have now been settled, a few anomalies remain. There is also an increasing realisation that equalisation does not necessarily lead to equity. The main difficulty which has confronted many employers and trustees is how to implement the equal treatment requirement in their schemes.

Employers and trustees

9.19   It was unclear from the *Barber* decision whether *Article 141* imposed an obligation both on the trustees and the employer in respect of equal treatment. Whilst the primary obligation to implement equalisation falls upon the employer, the position of trustees was clarified by the ECJ in the *Coloroll* case. The ECJ confirmed that trustees in the exercise of their powers and in the performance of their obligations are also bound to observe the principles of equal treatment. Although the ECJ decisions are overriding, *PA 1995* clearly envisages schemes being able to be amended so as to comply with the equal treatment provisions. *Section 65* of *PA 1995* empowers trustees or managers of occupational pension schemes to make amendments by resolution where either they do not have the necessary amendment powers to implement the equal treatment requirements, or they do have powers available but the procedure for implementation is 'liable to be unduly complex or protracted' or 'involves the obtaining of consents which cannot be obtained, or can only be obtained with undue delay or difficulties'.

Review of scheme documentation

9.20   In as much as the equal treatment cases are overriding, clarity and consistency in the day to day application of the equal treatment principles is only likely to be achieved when scheme documentation is brought into line with the current law. Areas requiring careful consideration include:

(*a*)   conformity of the (equalised) normal retirement age under the scheme and the contract of employment;

(*b*)   equality in early retirement terms, survivors' benefits, and transfer arrangements; and

(*c*)   allowing trustees the discretion to grant enhanced benefits in individual cases.

Scheme amendments

9.21   As stated above (see 9.9 and 9.17 above), employers and trustees must consider three time periods in respect of measures to equalise benefits under their schemes:

(*a*)   the period up to 17 May 1990, when benefits need not be equalised;

(*b*)   the period from 17 May 1990 to the date equalisation takes place, when benefits must be 'levelled up'; and

(*c*)   the period after the date equalisation takes place, when benefits can be levelled up or down.

Careful scrutiny of the power of amendment will be necessary to ensure that any changes made are a valid exercise of that power. Amendment powers often contain an express restriction that accrued rights cannot be reduced without members' consent. Even in the absence of specific wording to that effect, such a restriction is consistent with a trustee's fiduciary duty to act in the best interests of the members and it is generally accepted to be consistent with the employer's duty of good faith towards its employees. Further, *PA 1995, section 67* imposes restrictions on scheme amendments which reduce the accrued rights and entitlements of members. However, with effect from April 2006, *section 67* is amended by *PA 2004*. Under the new provisions, although schemes will not be able to reduce the value of a member's accrued rights, they will be able to make changes to the nature of the rights. It is intended that employers and trustees will be able to replace one accrued right with another provided that the overall actuarial value of the affected person's accrued rights is not reduced (see chapter 12).

Where there is no amendment power, or inadequate provision, the power conferred by *PA 1995, section 65* must be used to implement the equal treatment requirements. The exercise of the statutory power may place the employer in a vulnerable position, as it is a power to be used by the trustees alone, and not, as is usually found in scheme provisions, either an employer's power or a joint power of the employer and the trustees.

The power of amendment is a fiduciary power and, as mentioned above, its exercise is, therefore, subject to a duty of good faith to the beneficiaries of the scheme. Thus, in seeking to amend the scheme to comply with the equal treatment requirements, the best interests of the whole membership must be considered. Following the decision in *Van den Akker v Stichting Shell PF [1994] ECR I-4527*, it is not possible to 'red circle' groups of members, i e to apply preferential benefits to a group of members who were exclusively women or men, unless the group delineation was objectively justified and, thus, not sex discriminatory.

Employment law considerations

9.22   In considering how to implement the equal treatment requirements, careful review must be made of the employees' contracts of employment and the precise wording of the 'pension promise' (if any) contained in them. Changes made by an employer to contracts (for example, amending the normal retirement date from 65 to 60), could give rise to a claim of breach of contract by the employee, although loss would have to be shown to substantiate a claim for damages. Where possible, and particularly where terms of employment are clearly worsened, the consent of the employees should be sought.

New employees

9.23   Employers are not constrained to deal with new employees in the same way as existing employees. Thus, new employees may be employed on terms differing from those of current employees, including a different (but equal between men and women) retirement age. This may give rise to problems relating to indirect age discrimination (see chapter 7).

Ill-health early retirement

9.24   Where the provisions of a scheme calculate ill-health pensions as inclusive of prospective service to normal pension age, a lowered normal pension age will operate to reduce the amount of pension payable. It is to be noted that in respect of the 'levelling up' period described at 9.9(*b*) above, benefits calculated by reference to a member's prospective service to normal retirement age must be calculated by reference to the higher normal retirement date.

Single-sex schemes

9.25   The *Coloroll* case confirmed that *Article 141* does not apply to schemes which have at all times had members of only one sex nor could *section 62* of *PA 1995* give rise to a claim in such a case. However, it is not permitted to establish a scheme open to only one sex.

Transfers

9.26   The ECJ in *Coloroll* stated that benefits on transfer must be equalised by the receiving scheme if the transfer value does not take into account any inequality for service from 17 May 1990 to the date of transfer. This applies to group transfers and individual transfers alike, and the ECJ has confirmed that, if necessary, a claim can be made by a receiving scheme against the transferring scheme under national law in respect of any additional liability. In the case of individual transfers, it is unlikely that a discharge form signed by a member in favour of a transferring scheme will constitute an effective defence, unless it can be shown that the member fully understood that he was waiving any claim he might have following the *Barber* decision. Unequalised transfer values should not be accepted by a scheme.

Actuarial issues

9.27   The use of unisex actuarial factors is permitted. Unisex tables appear to be logical, and the aim of achieving equal contributions and equal benefits would seem to be desirable. However, as long as insurance companies remain outside the constraints of *Article 141* in their assessments of risk, this disparity with company pension schemes would distort the market.

Unisex annuity rates are already required in securing the protected rights element of contracted-out money purchase schemes and personal pension schemes (see chapter 4). Similarly, HMRC has introduced unisex commutation rates to ascertain the maximum benefits available from exempt approved schemes (see chapter 5 as concerns HMRC limits). In respect of pre-*Finance Act 1989* Continued Rights members, schemes are permitted to switch to or, indeed, keep, unisex rates provided these do not exceed either 12:1 or the existing permitted rates for male members. For other members, the maximum 12:1 commutation factor applies to both male and female members (see 5.6 above).

HMRC requirements

9.28   HMRC Update (No 27) on Equal Treatment dated 2 May 1997 had immediate and, if desired, retrospective effect. Where a member has different normal retirement ages for different periods of service, as envisaged by the ECJ, HMRC will only take into account the current normal retirement age and apply this age to all services.

This is likely to be of particular concern to members subject to the pre-1989 tax regime who are treated as taking early retirement (for example, where a woman retires at age 60 in a scheme which has now equalised retirement ages at age 65, but which preserves a previous right to retire at age 60 with unreduced benefits). This is due to the fact that HMRC would normally calculate maximum benefits by reference to the higher retirement age which, in applying the usual N/NS formula (i e the ratio of completed to potential service) would reduce the maximum approvable benefits under the scheme. However, in circumstances like these, the HMRC Update contains an easement which would allow potential service to be calculated and paid on the basis that the unequalised normal retirement date still applied to that member. Men would have to be treated in the same way, at least in respect of service after 17 May 1990, so as to comply with the equal treatment requirements.

Update No 27 also allows, where despite the application of the easements unequal benefits are still yielded in respect of equal service, the benefits of the disadvantaged sex to be calculated on the same basis as the advantaged sex even if normal HMRC limits related to the old or new normal retirement age would be exceeded for that member.

From a procedural viewpoint, HMRC has confirmed that advance clearance of changes to effect an equalised normal retirement age is not required, provided that the new normal retirement age is not less than 60. Once the change has been made, HMRC will need to be notified.

Update No 27 was clarified by Update No 68 dated 29 August 2000, which provides that the easements apply to members with continued rights in schemes where the normal retirement ages for males and females have been equalised. This includes all members with continued rights and members who joined after equalisation and those still to join an equalised scheme.

With effect from 6 April 2006, current limits on the maximum approvable benefits will no longer apply in accordance with the provisions of *FA 2004* (see chapter 5).

Contracted-out schemes/guaranteed minimum pensions (GMPs)

9.29 The issue of equalisation of GMPs (see chapter 4) is fraught with difficulty, and the relevant provisions of *PA 1995, s 126* deal only with the future equalisation of the contracting-out arrangements. Neither the ECJ nor the Government has addressed all the difficulties that arise as a result of the fundamental design of GMPs correlating to the State scheme with its discriminatory pension ages. Specifically, the difficulties arise out of the methods of calculation and revaluation applied to the GMP element of a pension before and after State pension age is attained. The *Equal Treatment Regulations* permit pension increases to be paid at different rates on GMPs and pensions in excess of GMPs, in so far as the difference does not exceed the SERPS increase for the same period. The *Equal Treatment Regulations* do not, however, legalise the differences in benefits caused by the contracting-out legislation.

The determination by the Pensions Ombudsman in *Williamson* dated 7 January 2000 (*No: H00177*) restated the requirement to equalise GMPs. The Pensions Ombudsman directed that the trustee and the company equalise GMPs in compliance with the equal treatment rule under *section 62* of *PA 1995*. However, he did not make any directions as to how this should be done and noted that:

> 'Parliament apparently concluded that salary-related schemes should have the flexibility and freedom to make their own arrangements as to how equalisation should be achieved.' (paragraph 37)

Furthermore he expressed the view that the method of equalisation chosen should not be one that could lead to some members of the scheme being adversely affected.

The *Williamson* determination was subsequently overturned in the High Court in *Marsh Mercer Pension Scheme v Pensions Ombudsman [2001] 16 PBLR (28)* on the basis that the Ombudsman cannot make a direction relating to the equalisation of GMPs and compliance with the equal treatment rules in *section 62* of *PA 1995* as the question was too wide-ranging and the nature and effect of the Ombudsman's direction was so uncertain that he was in error making it. The Ombudsman's jurisdiction did not extend to his making a decision on the question of equalisation of GMPs as this matter had an impact on other members of the scheme without allowing them the opportunity to put their case. Rimer J added that GMPs in isolation did not have to be equalised on the basis that they are not a distinct part of a pension scheme. However, the position as to whether total benefits should be equalised was undecided. Therefore, the issues as to the application of *Article 141* and the method of equalisation of GMPs remain undetermined and trustees currently attempting to wind up contracted-out final salary schemes are left with little guidance as to how to proceed.

In its Update 3, 'Winding Up', dated August 2003, Opra recognised that trustees have concerns regarding GMP equalisation. The Update states that, although Opra does not endorse any particular approach taken to resolving the question of GMP equalisation, it expects trustees to consider the funding position of their scheme and the costs to the fund of equalising benefits, and comments that 'the cost and time involved in devising and implementing a methodology for equalisation may well outweigh the value in terms of benefits to members'.

The Regulator stated in response to a telephone inquiry that generally trustees should consult with their advisers in order to arrive at a solution that is suitable for their scheme in relation to GMP equalisation. The Regulator stated that it does not endorse any particular method and would encourage trustees not to delay in making decisions about equalisation. When coming to a decision the trustees should ensure that they are acting in the best interests of members.

The rulings of the European Court in *Bestuur van het Algemeen Burgerlijk Pensioenfonds v Beune [1995] All ER (EC) 97* and *Birds Eye Walls v Friedl M Roberts [1993] PLR 323* (see 9.12 above) appear contradictory in deciding whether a scheme may provide unequal benefits to men and women to remove an existing inequality as a result of the different ages that State pension commences for men and women. These two cases were considered by the High Court in *Uppingham School v Shillcock [2002] EWHC 641 (Ch), [2002] 2 CMLR 39* in its ruling that an LEL offset to integrate with the State scheme was not indirect sex discrimination and, had it been so, that it would have been objectively justified. This case would appear to support the argument that unequal GMPs are objectively justifiable if the intention is to integrate with the State scheme.

In the recent case of *Leadenhall Independent Trustees Limited v Welham [2004] All ER (D) 423 (Mar)*, the scheme was winding up with a surplus and the trustee sought directions as to whether it had the power to allocate funds in such a way as to neutralise the gender discrimination of GMPs. The court said that the trustee could augment deferred benefits as there was express power in the governing documentation to do so. In the case of existing pensioners (for which there was no express power of augmentation) the court was not willing to say whether or not the trustee could augment benefits, nor was it prepared to state whether overriding EC equal treatment law could be applied. The court suggested that if the trustee did decide to go ahead and augment benefits for pensioners, it should consider taking out trustee insurance.

Alan Pickering's review of pension schemes, the Pickering Report ('A Simpler Way to Better Pensions') published July 2002 recommended a new, simpler reference scheme test ('RST') for contracted-out salary-related schemes and that schemes should be able to convert all benefits including GMPs to RST benefits, thereby removing equalisation issues. *PA 2004* contains modifications to the payment of contracted-out benefits but the general simplification of these benefits previously put forward by the Government has not been included.

Same-sex partners

9.30   The legal position of same-sex partners was examined in the case of *Grant v South-West Trains Limited [1998] All ER (EC) 193*. This was an employment case involving the granting of travel concessions. South West Trains refused to give travel concessions to Ms Grant's same-sex partner when she was promoted to a post at South-West Trains previously occupied by an employee whose opposite sex partner had obtained such concessions. The ECJ found that the refusal of the employer to grant the travel concessions in this case did not constitute discrimination prohibited by *Article 141* of the *EC Treaty* or *Council Directive 75/117/EEC* of 10 February 1975 as the condition imposed by South-West Trains applied in the same way to female and male workers. The ECJ said that Community law as it stands at present does not cover discrimination based on sexual orientation. If the ECJ had decided in favour of Ms Grant, this would have had implications for pension benefits provided for unmarried couples which would have to be the same for all such couples irrespective of gender.

The European *Equal Treatment 'Framework' Directive (2000/78/EC)*, establishing a general framework for equal treatment in employment and occupation, requires Member States to enact legislation to prohibit discrimination on the grounds of religion or belief, disability, age and sexual orientation. The time limit for compliance was December 2003 for discrimination on the grounds of religion or belief or sexual orientation, and 2006 for discrimination on the grounds of age and disability. In the context of sexual orientation discrimination, the *Directive* provides that pension schemes which recognise unmarried heterosexual partners will be required to recognise same-sex partners. However, a loophole in the *Directive* allows pension schemes which recognise married couples only to continue to do so.

The *Employment Equality (Sexual Orientation) Regulations 2003 (SI 2003 No 1661)* (as amended) are designed to implement the *Directive* in respect of sexual orientation discrimination and outlaw discrimination in employment and vocational training on grounds of sexual orientation. The *Regulations* came into force on 1 December 2003 and protect heterosexuals, homosexuals and bisexuals.

The *Regulations* prohibit direct discrimination (i e treating people less favourably than others on grounds of sexual orientation) and indirect discrimination (i e applying a provision, criterion or practice which disadvantages people of a particular sexual orientation and which is not justified in objective terms) (*regulation 3*). The *Regulations* also prohibit unwanted conduct that violates people's dignity or creates an intimidating, hostile, degrading, humiliating or offensive environment (harassment) (*regulation 5*) and the treatment of people less favourably because of action they have taken under or in connection with the new legislation (victimisation) (*regulation 4*).

As with other anti-discrimination legislation, the *Regulations* cover the terms of a person's employment. As is established law, this extends to the field of occupational pensions. The primary target of the *Regulations* as they apply to pension schemes would seem to be to prevent discrimination in respect of dependant's pensions (i e where the scheme rules provide that a pension may be paid to an unmarried opposite sex partner but not to a partner of the same sex). If a scheme provides benefits to opposite sex unmarried partners but not same-sex partners, then this would constitute direct discrimination.

The *Employment Equality (Sexual Orientation) (Amendment) Regulations 2003 (SI 2003 No 2827)* amended the *Regulations* to extend their provisions to the trustees and managers of occupational pension schemes. The amended *Regulations* make provision for every occupational pension scheme to be treated as including a 'non-discrimination' rule prohibiting discrimination contrary to the *Regulations*.

Originally the *Regulations* provided that, if the scheme provides benefits to married partners but not unmarried opposite sex partners, then there would be no actual discrimination as *regulation 25* states that it will not be unlawful discrimination if access to benefits is prevented or restricted by reference to marital status. This 'loophole' arises out of the Government's interpretation of the *Directive's* provision that it is without prejudice to national laws on marital status and benefits dependant thereon.

Six unions sought a judicial review of the *Regulations* backed by the Trades Union Congress. The most significant aspect of the legal challenge was centred on *regulation 25*. The unions stated that because it allows UK pension schemes to continue to discriminate in favour of married people, *regulation 25* is allowing indirect discrimination against homosexuals as they are not able to marry their partners. A further aspect of the challenge related to *regulation 7(3)* which allows for sexual orientation discrimination where someone works for an organised religion. The unions argued that the law may allow employers to stop gay, lesbian or bisexual people from working at church groups and other religious organisations. It was reported on 26 April 2004 that the trade unions lost both aspects of their challenge. The High Court upheld the legality of the *Regulations* and refused to condemn them as 'incompatible' with European law.

In any event, from 5 December 2005 *regulation 25* has been amended by the *Civil Partnership Act 2004* (*Amendments to Subordinate Legislation*) *Order 2005* (*SI 2005 No 2114*). The new *regulation 25(a)* preserves the existing exemption for benefits which are dependent on marital status where the right to the benefit accrued or the benefit is payable in respect of periods of service prior to the coming into force of the *Civil Partnership Act 2004*. *Regulation 25(b)* permits benefits to be conferred on married people and civil partners to the exclusion of all others.

In addition a new paragraph has been inserted into *regulation 3* to ensure that the status of a civil partner is comparable to that of a spouse. The effect of the amendment is that if a spouse receives different treatment to a civil partner, the employer or training provider etc cannot successfully argue that there is no discrimination because married persons are not comparable to civil partners.

Civil partnerships

9.31 The *Civil Partnership Act 2004* received Royal Assent on 18 November 2004. The *Act* provides for same-sex couples to obtain legal recognition of their relationship by registering as civil partners. Registered civil partners will have access to rights and responsibilities including, for example:

- employment and pensions benefits;
- the duty to provide maintenance for a civil partner;
- the duty to provide maintenance for children of the partnership; and
- recognition under intestacy rules.

There are certain eligibility requirements that must be satisfied before couples can register as civil partners. The couple must be of the same sex, both parties must be over 16 years, neither party can be legally married or already a civil partner and the partner cannot be 'within prohibited degrees of relationship' (i e blood ties).

There are also various formalities involved in registering a civil partnership. The register has to be signed by the couple in the presence of the civil partnership registrar and two witnesses (see *Part 2, Chapter 1*).

In a similar way to divorce, a civil partnership can only be dissolved or nullified by a court order (see *Part 2, Chapter 2*).

The *Act* impacts on pensions in a number of areas including:

- state pensions;

- survivor benefits;

- pension sharing; and

- *section 67* issues.

Section 255 of the *Act* contains an enabling power to allow a Minister of the Crown to amend by statutory instrument, primary and secondary legislation relating to pensions in order to achieve the main purpose of the *Act*.

There are numerous statutory instruments that have been implemented in relation to the Act. In particular, the *Civil Partnership (Pensions and Benefit Payments) (Consequential, etc, Provisions) Order 2005* provides for a number of amendments to *PSA 1993*, *PA 1995* and *PA 2004*. In addition, the *Civil Partnership Act 2004 (Amendments to Subordinate legislation) Order 2005 (SI 2005 No 2114)* makes changes to the *Employment Equality (Sexual Orientation) Regulations 2003 (SI 2003 No 1661)* and the *Paternity and Adoption Leave Regulations 2002 (SI 2002 No 2788)*.

State pensions

9.32 The *Civil Partnership Act 2004* makes a number of amendments to the *Social Security Contributions and Benefits Act 1992* and the Explanatory Notes to the *Act* summarise the position as follows:

- Currently, a married woman (but not a married man) can use her husband's National Insurance contribution record to qualify for a lower rate (60 per cent) basic State pension when they have both reached State pension age. Amendments ensure that civil partners (like married men) will be able to qualify for these pensions when their civil partners or wives who were born on or after 6 April 1950 reach State pension age.

- Civil partners who reach pension age on or after 6 April 2010 will be able to qualify for a State pension by virtue of the contributions of their deceased civil partner, consisting of a basic pension plus additional pension (a percentage of SERPS depending on when the spouse reached pensionable age and 50 per cent of any State Second Pension).

- Civil partners whose partner dies before reaching pension age to be able to receive a State pension at any time if in the past they were entitled to a bereavement allowance or widowed parent's allowance when over age 45 and have not married or formed a civil partnership following the death. This is payable only as additional pension and, if aged 45 to 54 when bereaved, it is reduced on a sliding scale.

- Civil partners to be able to receive a State pension based on their deceased civil partner's contribution record if both civil partners are over State pension age when the first one dies. This provision will apply to civil partners who reach pensionable age between the implementation date and 5 April 2010.

Survivor benefits

9.33 In contracted-out schemes a civil partner must be entitled to an equivalent widower's pension on the death of a member if the spouse will be entitled to a GMP (post 5 April 1988), protected rights or statutory reference scheme benefits on the death of a member. The changes to the contracting-out legislation are made by the *Civil Partnership (Contracted-Out Occupational and Appropriate Person Pension Schemes) (Surviving Civil Partners) Order 2005 (SI 2005 No 2050)*. Non-contracted-out benefits for civil partners must be provided in respect of pensionable service from 5 December 2005. Contracted-out schemes may need to amend their rules to comply with the new requirements. However, the provisions in relation to non-contracted out benefits are overriding. Employers and trustees may also want to consider whether they wish to grant civil partners benefits in excess of the statutory minimum, i e benefits for all service back to April 1988 or benefits for all pensionable service.

Pension sharing

9.34 *Part 4* of *Schedule 5* to the *Civil Partnership Act 2004* provides the court with a power to make a pension sharing order on making a dissolution or nullity order in respect of the civil partnership and at any time afterwards.

It is provided under *Part 4* that a pension sharing order is an order which provides that one civil partner's 'shareable rights' under a 'specified pension arrangement' are to be subject to pension sharing for the benefit of the other civil partner. A 'specified pension arrangement' includes occupational and personal pension schemes. There is also power for the court to make earmarking orders (*Part 6* of *Schedule 5*).

Section 67

9.35 Before trustees and employers amend their schemes to give effect to the *Civil Partnership Act 2004*, regard must be had to the provisions of *section 67*.

As mentioned above, the requirement to treat civil partners in the same way as spouses from 5 December 2005 is overriding. However, the requirement to backdate contracted-out benefits is not overriding. Therefore, schemes will need to amend their rules (although some schemes may not need to where the rules contain a provision stating that they will comply with the contracting-out legislation as amended from time to time).

Therefore, consideration will have to be given to *section 67* in this respect and also in cases where the employer and trustees wish to provide beyond the statutory minimum and grant benefits for civil partners for all pensionable service or all pensionable service back to 1988.

Generally, trustees and employers should consult with their actuary and have regard to the provisions of their scheme. It had appeared that *section 67* is likely to be most problematic in circumstances where the scheme rules provide that where there is no spouse then children's pensions are payable or are increased. This is because incorporating benefits for civil partners may have the effect of reducing the benefit payable to the child or may mean that no children's pensions are payable at all. However, the *Occupational Pension Schemes (Modification) Regulations 2006 (SI 2006 No 759)* exclude certain such amendments from the ambit of *section 67*.

Gender Recognition Act 2004

9.36 Case law and, more recently, the *Gender Recognition Act 2004* have developed the law relating to transsexuals. In the case of *Goodwin v United Kingdom [2002] IRLR 664,* the European Court of Human Rights held that UK law was in breach of the *European Convention on Human Rights* in not allowing Ms Goodwin to marry or enjoy the benefits and burdens of her new gender. In particular, it was held that Ms Goodwin was entitled to the pension rights available to members of her new gender.

In its judgment of 10 April 2003 in *Bellinger v Bellinger [2003] UKHL 21, [2003] 2 All ER 593* the House of Lords considered the position of Mrs Bellinger, a transsexual woman who had undergone a marriage ceremony to a man in 1981. The Court of Appeal had declined to grant a declaration that the marriage was valid. The House of Lords held that the marriage was not a valid marriage but declared that the non-recognition of gender reassignment for the purposes of allowing transsexuals to marry was incompatible with the right to respect for private and family life and the right to marry guaranteed by *Articles 8* and *12* of the *European Convention on Human Rights.*

Also, in the case *KB v National Health Service Pensions Agency [2004] All ER (D) 03 (Jan),* the ECJ confirmed that national legislation which prevents marriage (and therefore the enjoyment of certain pension benefits) to individuals who have undergone a sex change is in breach of EU law.

The *Gender Recognition Act 2004* received Royal Assent on 1 July 2004 and the *Act's* provisions came into force on 4 April 2005.

Under the *Act*, a person over 18 may make an application to a Gender Recognition Panel for a gender recognition certificate on the basis of living in the other gender, or having changed gender under the law of a country outside of the UK. Where a gender recognition certificate is granted, then the applicant's gender becomes for all purposes the acquired gender. The *Act* will allow transsexuals on acquiring a gender recognition certificate to marry in their acquired gender and be given birth certificates that recognise the acquired gender.

Temporary workers

9.37   On 20 March 2002, the European Commission adopted a proposal for a Directive of the European Parliament and the European Council on working conditions for temporary workers.

The aim of the Directive was to provide a protective framework for temporary workers engaged via employment agencies which does not impede the development and creation of small businesses. It was stated that: 'The basic working and employment conditions applicable to temporary workers should be at least those which would apply to such workers if they were recruited by the user undertaking to occupy the same job.'

However, on 27 September 2005 the European Commission delivered results from its 'better regulation initiative'. The initiative on better regulation consists of three elements:

- withdrawal or modification of pending proposals;
- simplification of existing EU law; and
- better quality of new Commission proposals.

After screening 183 proposals for EU laws pending at the European Parliament and Council, the Commission announced its decision to 'scrap' more than a third. The press release states that in relation to the proposal on temporary workers the Commission will 'reconsider the proposal in the light of future discussions on other proposals'.

In response to the announcement from Brussels the TUC issued a press release stating that:

> 'Today's announcement is a major setback for temps across Europe. For four years the agency workers' directive has been blocked by various governments including our own and now it is destined to sit on a Brussels shelf for many more years to come. Agency workers deserve a better deal ...'

Maternity provisions

General

9.38   Some form of favourable treatment is afforded to women in the area of maternity provision. The requirements for the equal treatment of women on maternity leave, contained in the *Third Equal Treatment Directive 86/378/EEC*, led to the passing of the *Social Security Act 1989*, the relevant provisions of which came into effect on 23 June 1994. These provisions provide for benefits under occupational pension schemes to accrue for women on paid 'ordinary' maternity leave in the same way as for women working normally, and by reference, therefore, to their full remuneration. Members pay contributions based upon their actual pay received.

Generally, all pregnant employees who satisfy certain conditions (mainly in relation to notifications) are entitled to a period of 'ordinary' maternity leave. During this period, most employees will be entitled to statutory maternity pay from their employer (depending on their earnings and period of continuous employment) or to maternity allowance, paid by the State. The right to 'ordinary' maternity leave applies regardless of the number of hours a woman works or her length of service (except that they must give notice, and thus be employed, by the 15th week before the expected week of childbirth) (see *section 71* of *ERA 1996*.)

The *Employment Act 2002* has introduced measures designed to enhance and simplify the rules on maternity leave and pay. The *Act*'s regime applies to employees whose expected week of childbirth began on or after 6 April 2003. Thus, from 6 April 2003, 'ordinary' maternity leave was increased from 18 weeks to 26 weeks and the period in respect of which statutory maternity pay is payable was also extended to 26 weeks (see 9.35 below).

In the case of *Boyle & others v Equal Opportunities Commission (C411/96) [1998] All ER (EC) 879*, it was stated that a condition limiting accrual of pensionable service to periods of paid 'ordinary' maternity leave was contrary to *Article 12* of the *Pregnant Workers Directive (EU Directive 92/85/EEC)*. The court said that the *Directive* required that the period of 'ordinary' maternity leave was to be pensionable regardless of whether the woman concerned is in receipt of pay. This means that the pensionable service of any woman who is a pension scheme member but who is not entitled to either contractual or statutory maternity pay (perhaps because she has recently become an employee) must continue during this minimum period (see *section 71(4)* of *ERA 1996*).

As a result of changes introduced by the *Employment Act 2002*, from 6 April 2003 the qualifying period for 'additional maternity leave' was reduced from one year to six months and the period of leave was increased to 26 weeks.

With the exception of 'ordinary' maternity leave (discussed above) the continuation of pension rights whilst an employee is absent on maternity leave is dependent upon whether or not the employee is entitled to be paid during that period, be it statutory maternity pay or pay under the contract of employment. This is because the *Social Security Act 1989* requires that membership of an employer's pension scheme should continue during any period of paid maternity leave.

There is no statutory right to pay during additional maternity leave. Therefore, only if the employee has a specific right in her contract of employment to pay during this period will pension treatment be the same as for ordinary maternity leave, i e the employee will be entitled to pension benefits as if she were working normally.

Under the *Employment Relations Act 1999* which implements the European *Directive* on parental leave, qualifying employees with one year's continuous service have a right to take up to 13 weeks' unpaid leave in respect of a child for whom they have parental responsibility, provided the child was born or adopted on or after 15 December 1994. This right must be exercised before the child's 5th birthday (18th if the child is disabled).

The employee has no statutory right to be paid for this period of leave. If parental leave is unpaid, it is assumed that the employee is not entitled to accrue pension benefits. An employee may, however, have a contractual right to parental leave and remuneration. If so, pension benefits continue to accrue on the basis of actual pay received.

The *Employment Act 2002* and regulations made under it give certain qualifying employees (of either sex) the right to two weeks' paid paternity leave in respect of a child born, or whose expected week of birth begins, on or after 6 April 2003, and in respect of a child matched for adoption, where the adopter was notified of the match or the placement took effect on or after 6 April 2003. Continuity of employment will be preserved during this period of leave.

The *2002 Act* also provides a new right of adoption leave (some of which is paid) for certain qualifying employees.

Section 265 of *PA 2004* adds two new paragraphs to *Schedule 5* to the *Social Security Act 1989*. These new paragraphs relate to periods of paid paternity leave and paid adoption leave. The new provisions provide that in respect of any period of paid paternity leave or paid adoption leave, a member shall only be required to pay pension contributions on the amount of contractual remuneration or statutory pay actually paid to or for him in respect of that period. Employer pension contributions during periods of paid paternity or adoption leave should be made as if the member were working normally.

Maternity pay

9.39   Statutory maternity pay ('SMP') is only payable where an employee has completed six months' continuous service with the same employer by the 15th week before the expected week of childbirth. This requirement continues to apply under the *Employment Act 2002*. Employees with an expected date of childbirth falling on or after 6 April 2003 will receive SMP for a maximum of 26 weeks. The payment of contractual remuneration, i e payment under the employee's contract of employment, affects pension rights only in respect of maternity leave in excess of 26 weeks or if the contractual pay is higher than SMP.

Contractual remuneration

9.40   Although the protection of pension rights during maternity absence can depend upon the payment of 'contractual remuneration', it is not clear what this includes. Employment legislation defines remuneration as comprising cash payments, whereas tax legislation includes benefits in kind within the definition. The safer approach is to treat remuneration as including all benefits in kind, for example, a company car. What has been confirmed, in the case of *Gillespie v Northern Health & Social Services Board [1996] AER (EC) 284*, is that bonuses or pay increases granted during paid maternity absence, but which are backdated to the relevant pre-absence period, are to be reflected in the remuneration of those on paid maternity leave. SMP will also have to be recalculated if a backdated pay increase affects the average earnings which underlie the calculation of SMP.

Essentially, the *Gillespie* case underlines the requirement in the *Social Security Act 1989* that pension rights accruing during a period of paid maternity absence reflect any increase to 'normal pay'.

In the last 12 months, the UK and European courts have had to revisit the so-called 'contractual remuneration during leave' question. These cases have taken the issues much further than in *Gillespie*. A number of these decisions have been reflected in recent amendments to the *Equal Pay Act 1970*.

In relation to pay rises, the ECJ in *Alabaster v (1) Woolwich plc; (2) Secretary of State for Social Security Case C-147/02 [2005] All ER (EC) 490* ruled that any pay rise, awarded from the time a woman falls pregnant and up to the end of her maternity leave, must be reflected in her higher SMP rate, contractual maternity pay, and the rate of pay on which she returns to work. This is the case even if the pay rise takes effect after the end of the period during which the higher rate SMP is payable. It is important to note that, as things currently stand, the law only applies to SMP payments made after 5 April 2006. However, this may change once the ECJ considers this point in early 2006, and there is a possibility that employers may be required to make retrospective payments.

The recent decision in *Hoyland v Asda Stores Ltd [2005] IRLR 438* dealt with bonus entitlements during maternity leave. The EAT ruled that a woman must not be deprived of contractual bonus payments which are awarded to reflect work performance done at the time: (a) before the woman went on leave; (b) during which the woman was on a statutory compulsory leave period; and (c) after the woman returned to work following maternity leave. It is important to note that the EAT limited its decision to contractual bonus provisions but failed to distinguish between discretionary and non-discretionary policies. The decision is subject to an appeal to the Court of Appeal and is due to be heard on 16 March 2006.

Finally, the ECJ has recently decided that employers are not required to give full pay to women absent from work for a maternity-related illness, provided that they are treated in the same way as male employees on sick leave and that the level of pay they receive is not 'too low' so as to undermine the objective of protecting pregnant women. In the case in question (*North Western Health Board v McKenna [2006] All ER (EC) 455*) the employee's sick pay amounted to half of her contractual pay. It, therefore, seems safe to assume that sick pay that is equal to half of an employee's contractual pay will not be regarded as being too low. However, it is far from clear whether lower pay, including the current level of statutory sick pay, would be 'too low'.

Final salary schemes

9.41   The *Social Security Act 1989* provides for periods of paid 'ordinary' maternity absence to count as pensionable service as if the woman was working normally, and for the accrual of benefits to continue on the basis of the pre-absence level of remuneration. As the employee's contributions are based upon actual pay and full final salary benefits accrue during the periods of paid absence, the employer will incur an additional cost to fund those benefits to compensate for any reduction in the amount of contribution paid by the employee.

Money purchase schemes

9.42   The position here is less certain, but money purchase schemes are not excluded from the scope of the legislation. Although the employee can only be required to contribute on the basis of actual pay received, the employer has to contribute at the full rate appropriate to the employee's pre-absence remuneration. It is also arguable that, as with the final salary schemes, the employer has to make good any shortfall in contributions (i e the difference between the contributions actually paid by the employee and those that would have been paid by her if she had been working normally) but this point is far from certain.

Death benefits

9.43   Benefits on death are treated in the same way as pension benefits, in that they must be continued during periods of paid maternity absence. On the death of an employee during such absence, death benefits will be calculated by reference to full pre-absence remuneration as if the employee had been working normally.

All of the requirements for equal treatment are clearly subject to the special provisions relating to paid maternity and family leave.

Tables of relevant legislation and case law

9.44   The following tables list relevant UK and European legislation and its main effect. The table of cases lists the main issues decided.

UK legislation	
Legislation	*Main effect*
Equal Pay Act 1970	Did not encompass pension schemes; *section 6(1A)* provides 'An equality clause ... shall not operate in terms related to death or retirement ...'. (Amended by the *Occupational Pension Schemes (Equal Treatment) Regulations 1995 (SI 1995 No 3183)*, see below.)
Social Security Act 1973	Required schemes to provide equal access to membership for both men and women (re-enacted in *PSA 1993* and now covered by *PA 1995*).

Employment Protection *(Consolidation) Act 1978*	Preserved contractual terms and conditions of employment during the maternity leave period (but did not confer right to remuneration). (Re-enacted in the *Employment Rights Act 1996*).
Sex Discrimination Act 1986	Removed the exemption from the *Sex Discrimination Act 1975* relating to occupational pension schemes, and required equal retirement ages for men and women in contracts of employment.
Social Security Act 1989	This was designed to implement the requirements of *Directive 86/378/EEC* on equal treatment (see below).
Pension Schemes Act 1993	Consolidated previous pensions legislation (*Social Security Act 1973, Social Security (Pensions) Act 1975, Social Security Act 1990*).
Pensions Act 1995	Imposes equal treatment requirements on scheme provisions in relation to pensionable service after 17 May 1990, and covers both access to schemes and benefits under schemes. It also empowers trustees to make changes unilaterally for the purpose of implementing equal treatment.
Occupational Pension Schemes *(Equal Treatment)* *Regulations 1995 (SI 1995 No 3183)*	The *Regulations* supplement the requirements for equal treatment relating to occupational pension schemes provided for in *sections 62 to 66 of PA 1995.*
Employment Rights Act 1996	Consolidated previous employment legislation.
Part-time Workers (Prevention of Less Favourable Treatment) Regulations 2000 (SI 2000 No 1551) (implementing *Directive 97/81/EC*)	The *Regulations* give part-time workers the right not to be treated less favourably than full-time workers working for the same employer under the same type of employment contract. Workers who change from full-time to part-time are also protected as they are to be treated no less favourably than they were before going part-time. The *Regulations* apply where the less favourable treatment is applied to a part-time worker which cannot be justified on objective grounds.
Part-time Workers (Prevention of Less Favourable Treatment) Regulations 2000 (Amendment) Regulations 2002 (SI 2002 No 2035)	The *Regulations* remove the provision which had limited the backdating of a claim to two years from the date on which the complaint was presented. Additionally, provisions for comparators have been amended, removing the distinction between fixed-term and permanent contracts.

Fixed-term Employees (Prevention of Less Favourable Treatment) Regulations 2002 (SI 2002 No 2034) (implementing *Directive 2000/78/EC*)	The *Regulations* give fixed-term employees the right not to be treated less favourably than permanent employees of the same employer who are doing similar work unless there is an objective justification for the difference.
Employment Act 2002	The *Act* provides a number of family-friendly provisions including measures designed to simplify maternity leave and pay, a right to paid adoption leave, a right to paid paternity leave, improvements to the employment tribunal process, introduction of an equal pay questionnaire and provisions to implement the *Fixed-term Workers Directive*.
The Employment Equality (Sexual Orientation) Regulations 2003 (SI 2003 No 1661) (implementing *Directive 2000/78/EC*)	The *Regulations* are designed to implement the *Directive* in respect of sexual orientation discrimination and outlaw discrimination in employment and vocational training on grounds of sexual orientation. The *Regulations* came into force on 1 December 2003 and protect heterosexuals, homosexuals and bisexuals.
The Employment Equality (Sexual Orientation) (Amendment) Regulations 2003 (SI 2003 No 2827)	These *Regulations* extend the provisions of the *Sexual Orientation Regulations* to the trustees and managers of an occupational pension scheme. The *Amendment Regulations* make provision for every occupational pension scheme to be treated as including a 'non-discrimination' rule prohibiting discrimination contrary to the *Regulations.*
Pensions Act 2004	The *Act* received Royal Assent on 18 November 2005. The provisions of the *Act* are coming into force in stages. April 2005 saw the introduction of the PPF and the Regulator. The new scheme funding requirements are effective from 30 December 2005 and in April 2006 provisions relating to MNTs and the trustee knowledge and understanding requirements will come into force.
Gender Recognition Act 2004	Under the *Act*, a person over 18 may make an application to a Gender Recognition Panel for a gender recognition certificate on the basis of living in the other gender, or having changed gender under the law of a country outside of the UK. Where a gender recognition certificate is granted, then the applicant's gender becomes for all purposes the acquired gender.

Civil Partnership Act 2004	The *Act* provides for same-sex couples to obtain legal recognition of their relationship by registering as civil partners.
The Occupational Pension Schemes (Equal Treatment) (Amendment) Regulations 2005 (SI 2005 No 1923)	These *Regulations* amend the provisions of the *Equal Pay Act 1970, PA 1995* and the *Equal Treatment Regulations* to reflect the *Preston* decision.
The Transfer of Employment (Pension Protection) Regulations 2005 (SI 2005 No 649)	These *Regulations* provide a basic level of pensions protection for employees on a *TUPE* transfer who were prior to the transfer members of or entitled to be members of an occupational pension scheme.

European legislation	
Legislation	*Main effect*
Treaty of Rome 1957 – Article 141 (formerly 119)	Each Member State shall ensure and subsequently maintain the application of the principle that men and women should receive equal pay for equal work.
Directive 75/117/EEC on equal pay	Requires Member States to introduce equal pay laws.
Directive 77/187/EEC on acquired rights	Ensures continuing employment following a transfer of the business undertaking (but excludes pension rights).
Directive 76/207/EEC on equal treatment	Requires Member States to prohibit sex discrimination in employment, but made no specific reference to pensions or social security (made under *Article 235*).
Directive 79/7/EEC on statutory benefits	Requires Member States to implement equal treatment in statutory social security schemes but excludes retirement ages, survivors' benefits, derived rights and maternity provisions.
Directive 86/378/EEC on equal treatment	Requires Member States to implement equal treatment in pension schemes and includes access, calculation of contributions and of benefits, retirement ages and maternity provisions. [NB following the various ECJ decisions on equal treatment, a revised directive has been issued – see below.]
Directive amending *Directive 86/378/EEC* (above)	Transposes the ECJ decisions on equal treatment onto the *1986 Directive*. Thus, those parts of the *1986 Directive* which provide for derogations from the principle of equal treatment are invalid as far as paid employees are concerned. However, the provisions of the *1986 Directive* relating to self-employed workers remain valid.

Directive 98/50/EC on acquired rights	Reinforces *Directive 77/187/EEC* and effectively gives Member States the option of protecting pension rights under national legislation.
Directive 2000/78/EC on equal treatment.	This *Directive*, establishing a general framework for equal treatment, requires Member States to enact legislation prohibiting discrimination on grounds of religion or belief, disability, age or sexual orientation.
Directive 2001/23/EC on acquired rights	Codified and replaced previous acquired rights *Directives*.
Directive 2002/73/EC on equal treatment	Amends *Directive 76/207/EEC* in respect of sex discrimination and introduces two new definitions of harassment.

Cases		
Decision	*Date*	*Main issues decided*
Defrenne v The Belgian State Case No 80/70 [1971] ECR 445	1971	Distinguished between statutory pension provision and private occupational pension schemes, in that the former did not come within the scope of *Article 141*. Payments from the latter were not, in principle, to be excluded from the concept of 'pay' for the purposes of *Article 141*.
Defrenne v Sabena (No 2) Case No 43/75 [1976] ECR 455	1976	Determination that *Article 141* had direct effect, and consequently could be enforced by individuals in Member States without the need for further legislation to implement it.
Bilka-Kaufhaus GmbH v Weber von Hartz Case No 170/84 [1986] ECR 1607	1986	Exclusion of part-timers from scheme membership is unlawful where the reason for exclusion is discriminatory on grounds of sex. Here, the exclusion affected ten times as many women as men and could not be explained by any reason other than one based on sex discrimination, i e it was not 'objectively justified'.
Marshall v Southampton & SW Hampshire Area Health Authority Case No 152/84 [1986] ECR 723	1986	State employers were required to have equal contractual retirement ages (as the *1976 Directive* had direct effect on 'emanations of the State'), but discriminatory normal pension ages were not outlawed.

423

Barber v GRE Assurance Group *Case No C-262/88* *[1990] ECR I-1889*	17 May 1990	Decided that a pension paid from a UK occupational pension scheme was 'pay' for the purposes of *Article 141* which requires equal pay for equal work. Also decided that the same retirements benefits 'package' available to a woman who is made compulsorily redundant, should also be available to a man in like circumstances, and that each element (as opposed to the totality) of a pay package must be equal.
Bullock v The Alice Ottley School *[1992] IRLR 564*	1992	Employers are permitted to have a variety of normal retirement ages for different types of workers, provided that the reason for the differences is not based upon direct or indirect sex discrimination.
Ten Oever v Stichting *Case No C-109/91* *[1993] ECR I-4879*	6 Oct 1993	Temporal limitations of the *Barber* judgment clarified in that the direct application of *Article 141* can only substantiate a claim in respect of benefits (in this case, a widower's pension) relating to periods of employment on or after 17 May 1990, unless the claim is brought before that date.
Birds Eye Walls v Friedl M Roberts *Case No C-132/92* *[1993] PLR 323*	9 Nov 1993	'Bridging' pensions do not infringe *Article 141*, as they are designed to remedy inequality (in this case, in taking into account the differing ages at which State pensions became payable).
Neath v Hugh Steeper Ltd *Case No C-152/91* *[1993] ECR I-6935*	22 Dec 1993	Under a final salary scheme, it is the employer's commitment (i e the amount of pension promised) that must be equal, even though the use of sex-based actuarial factors may require unequal contributions from the employer to meet the funding requirements of the scheme.

Coloroll Pension Trustees Ltd v Russell Case No C-200/91 [1994] ECR I-4389	28 Sep 1994	Determined that: • both employees and their dependants may rely on the direct effect of *Article 141* against a scheme's trustees (who are required to observe the principles of equal treatment); • equal treatment may be implemented by the 'levelling down' of benefits (i e reduction of the advantages enjoyed by one group of members to the level received by a less advantaged group) from the date of scheme equalisation; • retrospection is only in relation to benefits (including survivors' benefits) for periods of service after 17 May 1990; • the receiving scheme must make good any inadequacy in respect of an unequalised transfer payment made to it; and • AVC's and single sex schemes do not fall within the scope of *Article 141*.
Smith v Avdel Systems Ltd Case No C-08/92 [1994] ECR I-435	28 Sep 1994	Retirement ages for women could not be raised to that of men for the period from 17 May 1990 to the date of equalisation, although this measure would not infringe *Article 141* in respect of service completed after the date of the change.
Van den Akker v Stichting Shell PF Case No C-28/93 [1994] ECR I-4527	28 Sep 1994	*Article 141* does not allow a uniform retirement age to be set whilst maintaining an advantage for women members. Equality can only be achieved by the 'levelling up' of benefits, i e for men to enjoy the same advantages of women members, for service after *Barber* to the date of equalisation.
Algemeen Burgerlijk PF v Beaune Case No C-7/93 [1994] ECR I-4471	28 Sep 1994	Civil service pension schemes do come within the scope of *Article 141*.
Vroege v NCIV Instituut Case No C-57/93 [1994] ECR I-4541	28 Sep 1994	The right to join an occupational pension scheme is covered by *Article 141*, but falls outside the temporal limitations of the *Barber* judgment. This right continues to be governed by the *Bilka-Kaufhaus* judgment.

Fisscher v Voorhuis Hengelo BV Case No C-128/93 [1994] ECR I-4583	28 Sep 1994	As for *Vroege*, but also decided that administrators must comply with *Article 141*. Further, it confirmed that employees can claim retrospective membership although they cannot avoid paying backdated contributions.
Nolte v Landesversicherungsanstalt Hannover Case No C-317/93 [1996] All ER (EC) 212	14 Dec 1995	Exclusion of part-timers from membership is permissible, even where to do so affects more women than men, where the reason is to achieve a social policy unrelated to any discrimination.
Lloyds Bank (EC) Pension Trust Corporation Ltd v Lloyds Bank plc [1996] OPLR 181	24 Apr 1996	The rules of the scheme provided that 'pecuniary benefits secured' for members could not be reduced without their consent. The court refused to permit the trustees to amend the rules to reduce future benefits.
Gillespie v Northern Health & Social Services Board Case No 342/93 [1996] AER (EC) 284	13 Feb 1996	Where maternity pay is calculated by reference to the pre-absence salary, it must include pay rises (if backdated to the relevant pre-absence period) during the period of maternity absence.
Regina v Secretary of State for Employment ex parte Seymour-Smith and Another Case C-167/97 [1999] ICR 447	9 Feb 1999	The Advocate General considered, among other questions, the test for determining whether a measure adopted by a Member State had 'such a disparate effect as between men and women as to amount to indirect discrimination'. The Advocate General opined that the best approach to this issue was to compare statistical evidence of the proportion of men able to satisfy the condition at issue and those unable to do so and to compare those proportions. If the statistics indicated that a 'considerably smaller percentage' of women than men were able to satisfy the condition, there was indirect sex discrimination unless the measure was justified by objective factors.

Grant v South-West Trains Limited [1998] All ER (EC) 193	17 Feb 1998	This was an employment case involving the granting of travel concessions. South-West Trains refused to give travel concessions to Ms Grant's same-sex partner when she was promoted to a post at South-West Trains previously occupied by an employee whose opposite sex partner had obtained such concessions. The ECJ said that Community law as it stood did not cover discrimination based on sexual orientation.
Preston v Wolverhampton Healthcare NHS Trust Case No C78/98 [2000] All ER (EC) 714 and [2001] IRLR 237 HL	16 May 2000 and 8 Feb 2001	Claims by part-timers in respect of unlawful exclusion from scheme membership have to be made within six months of leaving service as required under national UK law. However, the maximum of two years' backdated benefits that can be awarded under the UK legislation is not valid and backdated benefits can be claimed going as far back as of April 1976. However, Member States are permitted to require that individuals making a claim pay any past contributions which they would have had to pay had they belonged to the scheme throughout the relevant period.
Deutsche Telekom v Schroder [2000] ECR I-743	10 Feb 2000	The *Defrenne* time limit of 8 April 1976 (backdated benefits can be claimed as far back as this date) does not prevent national legislation being even more generous and backdating claims even further.
Marsh Mercer Pension Scheme v Pensions Ombudsman [2001] 16 PBLR 28	23 Feb 2001	The Pensions Ombudsman could not make a direction relating to the equalisation of GMP's and compliance with equal treatment rules in *section 62* of *PA 1995* as the matter was too wide-ranging for determination in such a manner. The Ombudsman was wrong to determine that the dispute was one affecting the scheme and all the members generally and also his direction requiring the rewriting of the scheme affected all the members. It was not within the jurisdiction of the Ombudsman to purport to decide equalisation of GMPs on behalf of all the other members of the scheme.

Allonby v Accrington & *Rossendale College* *[2001] IRLR 364*	23 Mar 2001	Claim brought by a part-time lecturer who was no longer eligible for membership of the scheme by virtue of change in employment status – the lecturer's services were changed by the employer from being employed on a one year renewable contract with the employer to being employed through an employment agency while doing the same work. It was held by the Court of Appeal that the part-time lecturer was in a contract of employment for occupational pension purposes. As there could be a possible conflict with *Article 141 Allonby* was referred to the ECJ.
Glossop v Copnall *[2001] PLR 263*	5 Jul 2001	The Pensions Ombudsman's determination that the trustees' failure to comply with *Article 141* amounts to maladministration was incorrect. A mere error of law could not amount to maladministration.
Quirk v Burton Hospital *[2002] 24 PBLR*	*12 Feb* *2002*	Mr Quirk, a male nurse, had been excluded by scheme rules from rights available to female nurses. Mr Quirk complained that the decision in *Barber* should be retrospective. It was held that the reason for the limitation on equalisation of benefits to 17 May 1990 was because Member States could reasonably have believed that such discrimination was lawful on the basis of parallel EU legislation. Therefore the limitation in *Barber* is correct and equal treatment under *Article 141* in relation to scheme benefits does not apply to service prior to May 1990.
Uppingham School v *Shillcock* *[2002] EWHC 641 (Ch),* *[2002] 2 CMLR 39*	19 Apr 2002	The case overturned the decision of the Pensions Ombudsman and held that an LEL offset to integrate benefits with the State scheme was not indirect discrimination and, had it been so, it would have been objectively justified.

Beckmann v Dynamco Whicheloe Macfarlane Ltd Case C-164/00, [2002] 64 PBLR, [2002] All ER (D) 05 (Jun)	4 Jun 2002	This case held that benefits payable on redundancy under the *NHS Compensation for Early Retirement Regulations* transfer under *TUPE* and the *Acquired Rights Directive* despite the fact that they are calculated by reference to the same rules used to calculate normal pension benefits. Early retirement benefits and benefits intended to enhance the conditions of such retirement, paid before the end of a 'normal working life' in the event of dismissal for redundancy are not 'old age, invalidity or survivors' benefits' within the meaning of *Article 3(3)* of the *ARD* and thus are not subject to exclusion from transfer.
Goodwin v UK [2002] IRLR 664	11 Jul 2002	The European Court held that the UK was in breach of *Article 8* (right to respect for private and family life) and *Article 12* (right to marry and to found a family) of the *European Convention on Human Rights*. The UK had failed legally to recognise that Ms Goodwin who underwent 'gender re-assignment' surgery was female. Ms Goodwin was therefore required pay NICs until age 65. Had her sex change been legally recognised, NICs would have ceased at age 60.
Bellinger v Bellinger [2003] UKHL 21, [2003] 2 All ER 593	10 Apr 2003	The House of Lords held that the marriage was not a valid marriage but declared that the non-recognition of gender reassignment for the purposes of allowing transsexuals to marry was incompatible with the right to respect for private and family life and the right to marry guaranteed by *Articles 8* and *12* of the *European Convention on Human Rights*.
Kutz-Bauer v Freie und Hansestadt Hamburg [2003] ECRI-2741	20 Mar 2003	Provisions allowing workers over 55 to work part-time applied only until the date on which the worker became entitled to a statutory old age pension. For most women this was 60 and for most men it was 65. It was held that this was capable of breaching the *Equal Treatment Directive* and it was for the national court to determine whether there was in fact indirect discrimination which could not be objectively justified.

Allonby v Accrington and Rossendale College [2004] IRLR 224	13 Jan 2004	The ECJ's judgment on matters referred to it by the Court of Appeal following the 2001 *Allonby* case.
Martin v South Bank University [2003] [2004] IRLR 74	6 Nov 2003	It was decided by the ECJ that only benefits paid from the time when an employee reaches the end of his normal working life can be classified as 'old age' benefits within the meaning of *Article 3(3)* and are thus excluded from automatic transfer under *TUPE*.
Secretary of State for Trade and Industry v Rutherford, Bentley and Harvest TownCircle Limited EAT [2003] 78 PBLR	2 Oct 2003	The EAT overturned a tribunal's decision that the statutory upper age limit that applies to complaints of unfair dismissal and for statutory redundancy pay was unlawful as being indirectly discriminatory on grounds of sex.
Preston v Wolverhampton Healthcare NHS Trust (No. 3) [2004] IRLR 96	19 December 2003	Decision of the Employment Appeal Tribunal on a number of part-timer issues raised by the 2002 *Preston* case.
KB v National Health Service Pensions Agency [2004] All ER (D) 03 (Jan)	7 Jan 2004	The ECJ confirmed that national legislation which prevents marriage (and therefore the enjoyment of certain pension benefits) for individuals who have undergone a sex change is in breach of EU law.
Leadenhall Independent Trustees Ltd v Welham [2004] All ER (D) 423 (Mar)	19 Mar 2004	The trustee of a scheme in surplus sought directions as to whether it had the power to augment benefits to neutralise the gender discrimination of GMPs.
Dacas v Brook Street Bureau (UK) Ltd [2004] EWCA Civ 217	19 Mar 2004	Court of Appeal decision indicating that agency workers could be employees of the organisation they provide services to.
Matthews v Kent & Medway Towns Fire Authority [2004] EWCA Civ 844	2 Jul 2004	Case brought before the Court of Appeal under the *Part-time Workers* (*Prevention of Less Favourable Treatment*) *Regulations 2000 (SI 2000 No 1551)*. The EAT had held that a part-time fire fighter had not suffered less favourable treatment than full-time fire fighters despite being excluded access from the pension scheme. The fire-fighters' appeal to the Court of Appeal was dismissed.

Preston v Wolverhampton Healthcare NHS Trust (No 3) [2004] EWCA Civ 1281	At the time of writing the decision of the House of Lords is awaited.	Decision of the Court of Appeal which allowed the appeal in relation to the point at which the time limit for a part-timer's claim begins to run following a *TUPE* transfer.
Cross v British Airways [2005] 26 PBLR	23 Mar 2005	This case looked at the expense involved in allowing employees to work later.
Astbury v Gist Ltd [2005] ALL ER (D) 165 (Apr)	14 Apr 2005	Application of the *Dacas* case in relation to agency workers.
British Airways Plc v Jessica Starmer [2005] EAT	6 July 2005	Application of the *Allonby* case.
Shaikh v Department for Constitutional Affairs [2005] ALL ER (D) 154 (Sep)	31 Aug 2005	Case distinguishing the *Allonby* decision in relation to the requirement for a 'comparator'.
Alabaster v (1)Woolwich plc; (2) Secretary of State for Social Security C-147/02 [2005] ALL ER (EC) 490	2005	Case looking at contractual remuneration during periods of absence from work. Any pay rise awarded from the time a woman falls pregnant and up to the end of her maternity leave must be reflected in her statutory maternity pay and contractual maternity pay.
Hoyland v Asda Stores Ltd [2005] IRLR 438	2005	Case looking at bonus entitlement during maternity leave.
North Western Health Board v McKenna [2005] ALL ER (D) 47	2005	ECJ decision that employers are not required to give full pay to a woman absent from work on a maternity-related illness provided that she is treated in the same way as male employees on sick leave.

Chapter 10

Investment

Introduction

10.1   One of the fundamental duties of any trustee is to invest the monies under his control so as to produce income for his trust. In doing so a trustee must act within the boundaries imposed on him by the trust instrument, by statutory restrictions and by case law. The duties and obligations are onerous and consequently many trustees prefer to delegate their powers to professional fund managers.

This chapter deals with the powers of trustees regarding the investment of the funds for which they are responsible and the duties imposed on them when exercising those powers. It considers how, and to whom, trustees may delegate their powers and briefly discusses the implications of the *Financial Services and Markets Act 2000* (*FSMA 2000*). Finally it examines the protection afforded to trustees in respect of investment decisions. This chapter is particularly relevant to trustees of self-administered schemes, whether large or small, who will be more directly involved with investment activities than trustees of insured schemes.

Following the publication, on 6 March 2001 of the report by Paul Myners, 'Institutional Investment in the United Kingdom: A Review', the Government issued a voluntary Code of Best Practice on 2 October 2001, containing ten or so key principles which relate to the setting of investment objectives, and the method by which pension trustees should take investment decisions.

Although the Code of Practice is voluntary, the Myners review recommended that there should be a subsequent review, to be commenced in March 2003, to establish how effective the voluntary Code had been in bringing about change. The Government said that, if change has not occurred in the methods by which trustees reached investment decisions by March 2003 on a voluntary basis, the Government would legislate. *PA 2004* introduces new knowledge and understanding requirements, which are dealt with at 10.51 below together with the Myners' Code of Practice.

The meaning of investment

10.2   The classic statement of the legal meaning of the words 'invest' and 'investment' was given in the case *Re Wragg* in which Mr Justice Lawrence said that:

> 'Without attempting to give an exhaustive definition of the words "invest" and "investment" I think that the words "to invest" when used in an investment clause may safely be said to include as one of its meanings "to apply money in the purchase of some property from which interest or profit is expected and which property is purchased in order to be held for the sake of the income which it will yield".'
> (*Re Wragg [1919] 2 Ch 58* at page 64)

On a strict interpretation, an asset purchased for some reason other than deriving an income would therefore not be an investment; for example, land that is purchased for the financial gain it will produce when it is sold will not be an investment unless it is let for a rent or produces some other income.

In recent years there have been indications of greater flexibility in the definition of investment. In *Marson v Morton* Sir Nicolas Browne Wilkinson V-C recognised that in the modern financial arena 'new approaches to investment have emerged putting the emphasis in investment on the making of capital profit at the expense of income yield'. [*Marson v Morton [1986] 1 WLR 1343* at page 1350]. He gives the purchase of short-dated stocks (which give a capital yield but no income) and works of art as examples of common ways of investing and concludes that the mere fact that land is not income-producing should not be decisive on the question of whether it was bought as an investment.

The Pension Law Review Committee used the term investment to mean 'any application of assets, whether or not investments in the technical sense, and thus [including], for example, stock lending and borrowing' (Report of the Pension Law Review Committee, page 342). Unfortunately this approach was not adopted in *PA 1995*, which does not define 'investment'. Consequently there remains doubt as to the modern meaning of the term. The cautious approach must be to adopt the strict interpretation set out in *Re Wragg* in the absence of a more definitive modern definition.

Trading or investing?

10.3   Broadly speaking, exempt approved schemes are not liable for income tax or capital gains tax on the investments they make. [See 5.25 to 5.27 above for details of the taxation of pension schemes]. However, in certain circumstances, HMRC may argue that trustees are not investing but are in fact trading. If a pension scheme is found to be trading, rather than investing, the transaction will fall outside the scope of the statutory tax exemptions and the trustees will be liable for the appropriate income tax. It is, therefore, important to determine whether the proceeds of the sale of an asset constitute the realisation of an investment, or are the profits of a trade.

Badges of trade

10.4   The 1954 Royal Commission (Cmd 9474, paragraph 116) identified 'six badges of trade' as being relevant in deciding whether a transaction is, or is not, to be treated as a trading transaction. These 'badges' are discussed below.

The subject matter of the realisation

10.5   Generally property which does not yield an income is more likely to have been acquired for the purpose of trading rather than as an investment. A one-off transaction of the purchase of a type of property which yields no income followed by a profit on a sale has been held to be trading. (*IRC v Fraser (1942) 24 TC 498.*) However, dealing with an asset which does not produce an income, does not of itself necessarily imply trading; an asset can quite legitimately be purchased solely for the capital profit it will yield. (*Marson v Morton [1986] 1 WLR 1343.*) Some forms of property, such as manufactured articles, are usually purchased for trading and can only very exceptionally be an investment.

The length of the period of ownership

10.6   There is an inference of trading where property is realised within a short time of acquisition. However, if trustees can show a good reason for their actions the presumption that the trustees are trading may be rebutted. There is no doubt, however, that a quick sale helps to support the finding of trading, especially where other indications of trading are present. (*Turner v Last (1965) 42 TC 517; Eames v Stepnell Properties Ltd (1966) 43 TC 678.*)

The frequency or number of similar transactions by the same person

10.7   If there are repeated instances over a period of the same type of activity being carried out by trustees then the number of transactions may in itself give rise to a presumption of trading. In some cases it may be conclusive proof. (*Pickford v Quirke (1927) 13 TC 251.*) However, much will depend on the reasons for the sale.

Supplementary work on or in connection with the property realised

10.8   If land is purchased and then developed for sale there is often a suggestion that the trustees are to sell the property soon and thus enter into a transaction in the nature of trade. However, this is not necessarily the case; trustees may well refurbish a property simply in order to retain its marketability in the long term, which most prudent investors would, and probably should, do.

The circumstances that were responsible for the realisation

10.9   There are many situations that may arise which call for an asset to be sold very shortly after its purchase, for example, changes in market conditions or the payment of a large cash benefit. In such a situation it would be sensible for the trustees or their investment advisers to record in writing the reason for the sale so that any suggestion of 'trading' can be rebutted.

It should be remembered that one of the prime duties of a trustee is to exercise his duty of investment with diligence and prudence. Even if there may be a potential tax charge on grounds of trading, trustees should realise an asset, where appropriate, if not to do so would be a breach of trust. The duty of a trustee to invest prudently can be a very powerful weapon against allegations of trading.

Motive

10.10   The intention or motive of the trustees can be an important factor. There are cases in which the purpose of a transaction is clearly discernible, but where this is not so it may be sensible for the trustees or their investment advisers to note the reason for the purchase or the sale of an asset. In the absence of direct evidence of the trustees' intentions, motive can be inferred from the surrounding circumstances.

Application of the badges of trade

10.11   The 'badges of trade' are of general application to all types of transactions, where tax mitigation may be in question; they were not drawn up to apply solely to trustees or to pension schemes, and so may not always be relevant to dealings by pension scheme trustees. The onus of proving trading is, in reality, on HMRC, as far as occupational pension schemes are concerned (*Salt v Chamberlain (1979) 53 TC 143*) and there are presumptions to assist trustees who are accused of trading.

Presumption against trading

10.12   It is common practice for frequent changes to be made in a scheme's portfolio of Stock Exchange securities. Normally no inference of trading would be drawn from such changes. However, if there is evidence of a large turnover of a scheme's holdings, which appears to have been carried out pursuant to a deliberate and organised plan of buying and selling with a view to profit-making, it may be possible to infer that trading has taken place. (*Cooper v C & J Clarke Ltd (1982) 54 TC 670.*)

In the case of *Clark v British Telecom Pension Scheme [1999] 06 PBLR 21*, Lightman J overturned the earlier decision of the Commissioners of the Inland Revenue that profits received from the sub-underwriting of share issues by the trustees were not profits from trade rather than gains from investments and hence were not subject to tax. Lightman J found instead that the trustees had been involved in operations of a 'commercial character' for a period of years and the activity had all the hallmarks of trade being 'frequent (or habitual) and organised as well as extensive, business-like and for profit' (paragraph 31). However, the trustees of British Telecom Pension Scheme appealed and the Court of Appeal (*[2000] 21 PBLR 13*) held that the sub-underwriting activities of the trustees were an integral and indissoluble part of their investment activities. Income from the sub-underwriting was not therefore trading income and was exempt from tax by virtue of *ICTA 1988, s 592*. Lightman J's decision was therefore reversed. Appeal to the House of Lords was refused.

Powers given under the trust instrument

10.13   The majority of trust deeds governing pension schemes contain wide powers permitting investments in many areas. Trustees may also be given power to trade, but when such a power is missing there is a very strong argument against any allegation of trading; it is unlikely that a trustee will knowingly commit a breach of trust in order to trade.

Power of investment

10.14   A trustee's power of investment will derive from two sources; statute and the trust instrument.

Statutory power to invest

10.15   Prior to 6 April 1997, statutory powers of investment were conferred on trustees by the *Trustee Investments Act 1961* (*TIA 1961*), and to a small extent, the *Trustee Act 1925*. Even before *PA 1995* it was rare for a pension scheme to rely solely on the powers conferred by these Acts as they are very restrictive in the types of investments they permit. So far as pension scheme trustees are concerned, the provisions of *TIA 1961* have largely been replaced or superseded by the provisions of *PA 1995* and so are no longer generally relevant.

Section 34(1) of *PA 1995* confers a wide power of investment on trustees by providing that they have the same power to 'make an investment of any kind as if they were absolutely entitled to the assets of the scheme; subject only to any restriction imposed by the scheme'. This provision, which takes effect as if it was contained in the scheme's governing documentation, was intended to aid trustees who were prevented from making some types of investment by an overly restrictive power of investment. However, the wording of the provision causes problems which were not intended. If the term 'investment' is narrowly construed then certain traditional assets including, for example, group life policies, are not investments under *PA 1995,* so *section 34* alone would not permit trustees to purchase them. Consequently, trustees still need a carefully drafted investment power, allowing them specifically to undertake transactions, or to purchase assets, which fall outside the meaning of investment used in *Re Wragg [1919] 2 Ch 58*.

The trust instrument

10.16   It is common for trustees to be given power to invest, or otherwise apply the monies under their control in any manner which they could do if they were absolutely and beneficially entitled to the assets of the scheme and in any manner which they could do as trustees of a pension scheme. The second limb is necessary to allow trustees to invest in those investments, such as exempt unit trusts which are only available to trustees of funds which are not liable for income or capital gains tax. The ability to 'apply' the fund allows trustees to purchase assets which are not, perhaps, technically investments.

Trustees will generally be given specific power to purchase certain assets such as traded options, financial futures, life assurance contracts and assets which are to be held for capital growth rather than for the income they produce. Trustees may also be given power to underwrite new issues on the Stock Market and possibly the power to engage in stock lending. Trustees are sometimes given specific power to trade, but this is less common (see 10.13 above).

Trustees may also be given the power to commingle the assets of their scheme with the assets of one or more other schemes in a common investment fund, which will usually be set up under an independent trust. In order to continue to benefit from the tax advantages available to 'exempt approved schemes', all schemes participating in such a fund must themselves be exempt approved schemes.

It is also advisable to have express power in the trust deed to lease, charge and otherwise deal in and conduct the management of real property, and to have a general power to give indemnities and guarantees.

Notwithstanding the supposedly wide power of investment given in *PA 1995*, the investment provisions contained in most trust deeds will probably continue to spell out the powers of the trustees, since, if they do not, there is the possibility of the trustees exceeding their powers by inadvertently purchasing an asset which is not an investment and which cannot, therefore, be purchased under the power given by *section 34* of *PA 1995*.

Duties of trustees when exercising their investment power

10.17   When exercising their investment power, trustees must consider the duties imposed on them under the trust instrument, by statute and by case law. The main duties are set out in 10.18 to 10.22 below.

The duty to act in the best interests of the beneficiaries

10.18   One of the fundamental duties of a trustee is to exercise his powers in the best interests of the beneficiaries of the scheme and to act fairly between different classes of beneficiaries. In the context of an investment power, a beneficiary's best interests will generally mean his best financial interests. Consequently an investment power must generally be exercised so as to produce the best return possible, having regard to the level of risk involved. (*Cowan v Scargill [1984] 2 All ER 750.*)

The prudent man test

10.19   The basic duty of a trustee, when exercising his investment power, is to choose investments which are within the terms of his trust and, in selecting those investments, to 'take such care as an ordinary prudent man would take if he were minded to make [an investment] for the benefit of other people for whom he felt morally bound to provide'. (*Re Whiteley (1886) 33 Ch D 347.*)

The House of Lords decision in *Learoyd v Whiteley* sets out the principles which trustees must consider when exercising their investment power as follows:

'As a general rule the law requires of a trustee no higher degree of diligence in the execution of his office than a man of ordinary prudence would exercise in the management of his own private affairs. Yet he is not allowed the same discretion in investing the money of the trusts as if he were a person *sui juris* dealing with his own estate. Business men of ordinary prudence may, and frequently do, select investments which are more or less of a speculative character; but it is the duty of a trustee to confine himself to the class of investments which are permitted by the trust, and likewise to avoid all investments of that class which are attended with hazard.'
(*Learoyd v Whiteley (1887) 12 AC 727*, Lord Watson at page 733)

Sir Robert Megarry has reiterated and clarified the standard required of a trustee in exercising his powers of investment, making it clear that, in addition to the above, the duty 'includes the duty to seek advice on matters which the trustee does not understand, such as the making of investments, and on receiving that advice to act with the same degree of prudence'. (*Cowan v Scargill [1984] 2 All ER 750* at page 762).

Sections 247 and *248* of *PA 2004* contain provisions, which are due to come into effect in April 2006, concerning the 'requirement for knowledge and understanding' of trustees and introduce more specific and onerous requirements for trustees of occupational pension schemes. This is dealt with further at 10.51 below.

However wide the provisions of an express investment power may be, the trustees are not absolved from their duty to consider whether a proposed investment is such that it is prudent and right for them, as trustees, to make it. The mere fact that a certain type of investment is authorised by the trust instrument or by statute does not mean that it is necessarily proper to invest in it. Even though under *PA 1995* trustees have power to invest at their absolute discretion and as if they were absolute owners, they should remember that they must act as trustees in exercising that power. Moreover, *PA 2004* amends *section 36* of *PA 1995* to ensure compliance with *Article 18(1)* of the European *Pensions Directive (2003/41/EC)*. This directive requires investments to be carried out in accordance with the 'prudent person principle' as defined in the Directive. The detailed requirements are contained in the *Occupational Pension Schemes (Investment) Regulations 2005 (SI 2005 No 3378)* ('the *2005 Investment Regulations*'). The *2005 Investment Regulations* replace the *1996 Investment Regulations* with effect from 30 December 2005, together with the changes to *sections 35* and *36* of *PA 1995* and the insertion of new *section 36A*.

When exercising their investment power, *section 36* of *PA 1995* requires trustees (and any fund manager to whom a discretion has been delegated) to consider the need for diversification (see 10.20 below) and the suitability of the investments proposed. As a result of the *PA 2004* amendments, the requirements are now contained in the *2005 Investment Regulations*. These *Regulations* require that the trustees of a trust scheme (and any fund manager to whom any discretion has been delegated) must exercise their powers of investment, in accordance with the provisions of *regulation 4*:

- The assets must be invested in the best interests of members and beneficiaries and, in the case of a potential conflict of interest, in the sole interest of members and beneficiaries.

- The powers of investment, or the discretion, must be exercised in a manner calculated to ensure the security, quality, liquidity and profitability of the portfolio as a whole.

- Assets held to cover the scheme's technical provisions must also be invested in a manner appropriate to the nature and duration of the expected future retirement benefits payable under the scheme.

- The assets of the scheme must consist predominately of investments admitted to trading on regulated markets; investments in assets which are not admitted to trading on a regulated market must in any event be kept to a prudent level.

- The assets of the scheme must be properly diversified in such a way as to avoid excessive reliance on any particular asset, issuer or group of undertakings and so as to avoid accumulations of risk in the portfolio as a whole. Investments in assets issued by the same issuer or by issuers belonging to the same group must not expose the scheme to excessive risk concentration.

- Investment in derivative instruments may be made only in so far as they:

  (*a*)   contribute to a reduction of risks; or

  (*b*)   facilitate efficient portfolio management (including the reduction of cost or the generation of additional capital or income with an acceptable level of risk),

  and any such investment must be made and managed so as to avoid excessive risk exposure to a single counter party and to other derivative operations.

Note that *regulation 4* does not apply to a scheme that has fewer than 100 members but regard must still be had to the need for diversification of investments, in so far as appropriate to the circumstances of the scheme. *Regulation 9* of the *2005 Investment Regulations* also partially disapplies *regulation 4* in respect of schemes being wound up.

Section 36 of *PA 1995* also requires trustees to obtain and consider 'proper advice' before making any investment in order to ascertain whether the investment is suitable, having regard to the need for diversification (see 10.20 below) and whether it is in accordance with the statement of investment principles (see 10.23 below). *Section 36* (as amended by *PA 2004*) will require 'proper advice' to be taken on the question of whether the investment is satisfactory taking into account the requirements of the *2005 Investment Regulations*, some of which are referred to above, so far as relating to the suitability of the investments.

Broadly speaking, proper advice is advice from a person authorised under *FSMA 2000* in relation to investments covered by that Act. In any other case proper advice must be obtained from a person whom the trustees reasonably believe to be qualified by his ability in, and practical experience of, financial matters and to have the appropriate knowledge and experience of the management of the investments of pension schemes. Trustees must ensure that they obtain confirmation of the 'proper advice' given in writing in order to comply with the requirements of *PA 1995*.

Failure to comply with the requirements set out in *section 36* of *PA 1995* could result in a trustee being fined and/or removed or, in extreme cases, disqualified from acting as a trustee (see appendix I). Changes to *section 36* of *PA 1995*, to be introduced by *PA 2004,* provide for civil penalties to be levied but not the removal of a trustee.

The duty to diversify

10.20 Before exercising any investment power, trustees (and any fund manager to whom the trustees' discretion has been delegated) must 'have regard to the need for diversification of investments, in so far as appropriate to the circumstances of the scheme'. This duty to diversify is contained in *section 36(2)* of *PA 1995*.

These requirements are contained in the *2005 Investment Regulations*, and the existing *section 36(2) of PA 1995* has been repealed.

In addition to the above requirements, *PA 2004* inserted a new *section 36A* into *PA 1995* concerning restrictions on borrowing by trustees, or the fund manager to whom any discretion has been delegated under *section 34* of *PA 1995*. The *2005 Investment Regulations* provide that they cannot borrow money or act as a guarantor in respect of the obligations of another person where the borrowing is liable to be repaid, or liability under a guarantee is liable to be satisfied, out of the assets of the scheme. This is stated not to preclude borrowing made only for the purposes of providing liquidity for the scheme and on a temporary basis.

The requirement imposed on the trustees to diversify is also important from the actuary's standpoint, particularly in mature schemes. Although the actuary does not advise between one investment and another he may, and frequently does, become involved in deciding investment policy and asset allocation of the scheme. The actuary will ascertain the liabilities of a scheme and will advise on the short, medium and long-term liabilities. He should then be able to advise on the various types of investment and, for example, how they should be split to allow the trustees sufficient cash funds to provide lump sum and pension benefits for the beneficiaries as they fall due.

The trustees, or more likely the fund managers, will look at the strategy for the short, medium and long-term cash needs which the actuary has mapped out and should select investments that suit the aim. Not only must they look at diversification from that standpoint but they must also look at diversification on a second level. Clearly if a certain percentage of the fund has to be put in short-term investments, they would not put all of the fund designated for such purpose into one investment; they would spread the risk amongst a group of investments.

Moral and ethical considerations

10.21   There has been much discussion on the ability of trustees legitimately to consider moral and ethical considerations in preference to financial return on any particular investment.

Decided case law indicates that trustees cannot invest other than on the usual criteria (financial returns, security and diversification) but there is no reason why they cannot consider other factors, including social and moral criteria. If, for example, trustees wish to make an ethically acceptable investment which will produce a financial return that is at least as good as that produced by any other suitable (although perhaps not so ethically sound) investment, there is no reason why they cannot do so. Essentially they must act with the standard of care and prudence required by the law. What the trustees cannot generally do is subordinate the interests of the beneficiaries to ethical or social demands (see *Cowan v Scargill [1984] 2 All ER 750*; *Bishop of Oxford v Church Commissioners (1991) PLR 185*; *Martin v The City of Edinburgh District Council (1989) PLR 9*). In some circumstances trustees 'may even have to act dishonourably (though not illegally) if the interests of their beneficiaries require it'. (*Cowan v Scargill [1984] 2 All 750* at page 761.)

However, although trustees cannot allow their own political, social and moral views to override financial considerations when making investments, they can in some circumstances be influenced by the views of the beneficiaries of the scheme. If all the beneficiaries are known to hold strong moral views on a matter '… it might not be for the "benefit" of such beneficiaries to know that they are obtaining rather larger financial returns under the trust by reason of investments in those activities than they would have received if the trustees had invested the trust funds in other investments'. (*Cowan v Scargill [1984] 2 All ER 750* at page

761.) The circumstances where this principle could apply in relation to a pension scheme must be very limited due to the inevitable divergence of opinions of a large number of beneficiaries.

The debate over whether trustees can, or even should, invest in so-called ethical or socially-responsible investments has moved on. The *Occupational Pension Schemes (Investment, and Assignment, Forfeiture, Bankruptcy etc) Amendment Regulations 1999 (SI 1999 No 1849)* amended the *Occupational Pension Schemes (Investment) Regulations 1996 (SI 1996 No 3127)* and came into force on 9 August 1999, except for the provisions relating to ethical/social/ environmental investment policies and voting which came into force on 3 July 2000. These require the trustees to state in their Statement of Investment Principles (a) the extent (if at all) social, environmental or ethical considerations are taken into account in the selection, retention and realisation of investments; and (b) their policy (if any) in relation to the exercise of the rights (including voting rights) attaching to investments. At *regulation* 2 of the *2005 Investment Regulations* similar requirements for inclusion of reference to social, environmental or ethical considerations are provided.

Duty to review investments

10.22   A trustee's responsibility does not stop once he has made an investment; trustees have a duty to review the investments of the scheme from time to time. Although this is a continuing duty it will be particularly relevant in a scheme which is close to winding up as it may be advisable to match the investments of the fund with the liabilities of the scheme. Even where a scheme is wholly insured trustees should still review the position from time to time as it may be sensible for the trustees to consider changing the insurance company or to become self-administered.

Under *section 36* of *PA 1995* trustees must consider at what intervals they should obtain 'proper advice' in respect of investments they retain and must then obtain and consider such advice accordingly (see 10.19 above regarding the meaning of 'proper advice'). In determining the appropriate intervals the trustees must consider the circumstances of the case and, in particular, the nature of the investment. It might, for example, be appropriate to review the scheme's gilt portfolio less frequently than its equity portfolio as equities are a more volatile investment than gilts.

Statutory obligations

Statement of investment principles

10.23   Under *section 35* of *PA 1995* trustees must ensure that there is prepared, maintained and from time to time revised, a written statement of the principles governing their decisions about investments. Trustees (or the fund manager acting on their behalf) must then exercise their investment power with a view to giving effect to the principles contained in the statement, so far as reasonably practicable. [*PA 1995, s 36(5)*].

The original *section 35* wording was repealed and a new *section 35* has been substituted with effect from 30 December 2005 (*section 244* of *PA 2004*) but this is likely to be by the end of 2005. The new *section 35* should be read together with the provisions of *regulation 2* of the *2005 Investment Regulations*. Under these new provisions the trustees of the scheme must secure:

- that a statement of investment principles is prepared and maintained for the scheme; and
- that it is reviewed at least every three years and without delay after any significant change in investment policy.

The statement must cover, among other matters, the trustees' policy for securing compliance with *section 36* of *PA 1995* (see 10.19 and 10.20 above), the provisions of *PA 1995* relating to the minimum funding requirement (see 11.13 to 11.31 below) and their policy about:

(*a*)   the kinds of investments to be held;

(*b*)   the balance between different kinds of investments;

(*c*)   risk;

(*d*)   the expected return on investments; and

(*e*)   the realisation of investments.

The *2005 Investment Regulations* contain similar provisions to the existing *section 36* of the *PA 1995* as to the matters to be covered in the statement except that (*c*) risk (above) is expanded so that reference must be made to 'risks, including the ways in which risks are to be measured and managed'. In addition, reference to the minimum funding requirement is deleted.

The agreed investment strategy set out in the statement of investment principles must accord with the general law discussed in 10.17 to 10.22 above and be devised to reflect the liability position of the scheme in question. Schemes approved under *section 615(6)* of the *Income and Corporation Taxes Act 1988*, small self-administered schemes, wholly insured schemes, unapproved schemes and schemes whose solvency is guaranteed by a Minister of the Crown are exempt from having a statement of investment principles. [*Investment Regulations, reg 10*].

Regulation 6 of the *2005 Investment Regulations* contains disapplications of *section 35*. The requirements for a statement are disapplied for a scheme which has fewer than 100 members, or a scheme which is established by or under an enactment (including a local Act) and is guaranteed by a public authority. *Section 35* and the relevant regulations are also modified in respect of wholly insured schemes as defined by *regulation 8* of the *2005 Investment Regulations*.

Before a statement of investment principles is prepared or revised, trustees must:

(i)   obtain and consider the written advice of a person whom they reasonably believe to be qualified by his ability in, and practical experience of, financial matters and to have the appropriate knowledge and experience of management of the investments of pension schemes; and

(ii) consult the scheme's sponsoring employer.

The requirement to consult previously contained in *section 35* of *PA 1995* has now moved to *regulation 2* of the *2005 Investment Regulations*.

Where a scheme has more than one sponsoring employer, all the participating employers may nominate a person to represent them, in which case the trustees need only consult that person. Where the employers do not nominate a representative, each employer must be consulted individually unless all the employers notify the trustees to the contrary.

The Act does not define what is meant by 'consult'. Consultation does not mean consent; in fact *PA 1995* specifically prohibits the exercise of any investment power being subject to the consent of the employer. To comply with their duty to consult trustees should allow the employer sufficient time to make representations and should ensure that they consider suggestions put forward by the employer with an open mind. If the trustees are obliged to consult all the employers they may specify a reasonable period (which cannot be less than 28 days) within which the employers must make representations regarding the statement of investment principles; any representations made after the specified date can be ignored by the trustees.

The extent of the requirement to consult was considered in the recent case of *Pitmans Trustees v the Telecommunications Group plc [2004] PBLR 32, [2004] All ER (D) 143*. The Vice-Chancellor ('V-C') confirmed the above views, namely that to comply with the consultation requirements in *section 35(5)(b)* of *PA 1995* trustees must go further than simply giving notice to the employer of the proposed changes to the statement of investment principles. Although no timeframe is prescribed in *section 35(5)(b)* it was held that it is necessary to give adequate time for the employer to obtain and consider advice of its own on the proposals and to comment on the proposals. The V-C held that prior consultation is a pre-condition to the existence and exercise of the trustees' powers in *section 35* of *PA 1995* and, therefore, if prior consultation has not taken place then this pre-condition has not been satisfied, the power has not yet arisen and a purported exercise of it will be of no effect. The adoption of any revised statement of investment principles will be invalid as a result.

Trustees must confirm in their annual report whether they have produced a statement of investment principles in accordance with *section 35* of *PA 1995* and must also include a statement providing details of any investments which were not made in accordance with the statement of investment principles giving the reasons why and explaining what action has been or will be taken to resolve the position. A copy of the statement of investment principles must be provided to any member or beneficiary who requests it. [*Occupational Pension Schemes (Disclosure of Information) Regulations 1996 (SI 1996 No 1655), reg 6*]. Similar provisions are contained in the draft *Occupational Pension Schemes (Disclosure of Information) Regulations 2006* which are due to come into force on 6 April 2006.

A failure to take all reasonable steps to prepare or maintain a statement of investment principles or to take advice from an appropriately qualified person could result in a trustee being fined and/or removed. [*section 35(6)* of *PA 1995*]. See appendix I. Changes to *section 35* of *PA 1995* to be introduced by *PA 2004* provide for civil penalties to be levied but not the removal of a trustee.

Restrictions on employer-related investment

10.24   Trustees are under a statutory duty to ensure that not more than 5 per cent of the current market value of the resources of the scheme is invested in employer-related investments. Furthermore, none of the resources of a scheme may be invested in an employer-related loan or in any employer-related investment if it would involve the trustees entering into a transaction at an undervalue (see *section 40* of *PA 1995* and *regulation 5* of the *Investment Regulations (SI 1996 No 3127)*). The provisions of *regulation* 12 of the *2005 Investment Regulations* restate these restrictions.

In summary, employer-related investments are defined under *section 40* of *PA 1995* as:

(a)   shares or other securities issued by the employer or by any person who is connected with, or an associate of, the employer (for definition of connected employers see the table at 13.3 below and for associated employers see the diagram at 13.10 below);

(b)   land which is occupied by, or used by, or subject to a lease in favour of, the employer or by any person who is connected with, or an associate of, the employer;

(c)   property (other than land) which is used for the purposes of any business carried on by the employer or by any person who is connected with, or an associate of, the employer;

(*d*)   loans to the employer or any person who is connected with, or an associate of, the employer;

(*e*)   other prescribed investments.

In addition, *regulation 4* of the *Investment Regulations (SI 1996 No 3127)* sets out additional employer-related investments including:

• the obligations of any employer, or any person who is connected with, or an associate of, the employer, to the extent that they have been guaranteed or secured by the trustees;

• loans to any person where repayment depends on the employer's actions (unless the trustees did not intend to financially assist the employer);

• the appropriate proportion of any collective investment scheme which would have counted as an employer-related investment had it been made by the scheme directly.

The *2005 Investment Regulations* contain the list of investments prescribed as employer-related investments at *regulation 11*.

If any sums due and payable by a person (including, but not limited to, an employer) to the trustees of a scheme remain unpaid they are to be regarded, for the purposes of *section 40* of *PA 1995*, as a loan made to that person by the trustees and may consequently be treated as an employer-related investment.

The provisions under *PA 1995* relating to employer-related investments do not apply to unapproved schemes. Nor do they apply to small self-administered schemes if the rules of the scheme provide that before any investment is made in an employer-related investment, each member must agree in writing to the making of that investment. (See chapter 13 for details of restrictions on investment for small self-administered schemes.) The *2005 Investment Regulations* contain an exemption for small schemes and there are also further investments to which these restrictions do not apply in *regulation 13* (see below).

Certain insurance policies and additional voluntary contributions may be invested in an employer-related investment with the written agreement of the member who paid the contributions. [*Investment Regulations (SI 1996 No 3127), reg 6*]. The *2005 Investment Regulations* contain relaxations to the restrictions on employer-related investment at *regulation 13*. These include the two relaxations mentioned concerning certain types of insurance policies and additional voluntary contributions.

Regulation 7 of the *Investment Regulations (SI 1996 No 3127)* sets out transitional provisions for existing loans and employer-related investments. Generally, so long as any conditions relating to the loan or investment remained unchanged, the transitional period lasted until 5 April 2002. The *2005 Investment Regulations* contain transitional provisions at *regulation* 14.

Under *PA 1995* if the resources of a scheme are invested in employer-related investments in excess of the maximum allowed, sanctions, in the form of a fine and/or removal, could apply to any trustee who fails to take all reasonable steps to ensure compliance with the Act. Further, a trustee who agrees to make an employer-related investment is guilty of an offence and may be liable, in extreme cases, to imprisonment (see appendix I). The position concerning sanctions has not changed by virtue of *PA 2004* but breach of this section will not render the trustees subject to the Regulator's prohibition (ie removal) powers.

The Financial Services and Markets Act 2000

10.25 The *Financial Services and Markets Act 2000* (*FSMA 2000*) came into effect on 1 December 2001. Its purpose is to provide for the regulation of the whole of the UK financial services and banking industry by a single regulator, the Financial Services Authority ('FSA'). The FSA has assumed responsibility for banking supervision from the Bank of England and HM Treasury, and for the admission of securities to the official List from the London Stock Exchange. With effect from 1 December 2001 the FSA took over the regulatory duties of IMRO, SFA and PIA and those of the Building Societies Commission and the Friendly Societies Commission.

Transitional arrangements were in force until 30 June 2002 to enable the business rules operated by the previous regulatory bodies to be harmonised with the new conduct of business rules made by the FSA. The purpose of the transitional provisions was to assist firms to achieve a smooth transfer from one regulatory regime to another.

Professional firms (solicitors, accountants and actuaries) who do not undertake FSA regulated activities such as providing investment advice will be exempt from direct regulation by the FSA.

Such firms will also be exempt if they only carry out certain restricted activities arising out of, or incidental to the provision of professional services.

It should be noted that in February 2004 the Government published a consultation paper entitled 'Financial Services and Markets Act two year review: Changes to secondary legislation – Proposals for Change'. The deadline for submissions was 28 May 2004. One outcome of the review was the removal of the word 'routine' from 'routine and day to day' in relation to the managing of investments by trustees – see 10.30 below. Another outcome is the *Financial*

Services and Markets Act 2000 (Financial Promotion) Order 2005 (SI 2005 No 1529) which allows employers to promote group personal pension plans and stakeholders (*article 72*).

Objectives of the FSA

10.26 The FSA has four principal objectives under *FSMA 2000*:

(*a*)   maintaining market confidence;

(*b*)   promoting public understanding of the financial system;

(*c*)   the protection of consumers; and

(*d*)   reducing financial crime, i e by the regulation of investment activities and persons authorised to carry on such activities.

Investment managers

10.27 From 1 December 2001, investment managers providing financial services to pension scheme trustees have re-classified their trustee clients as 'Intermediate Customers' under the new regime, instead of 'non-private clients' under the *FSA 1986* regime. Such clients no longer have access to the complaints handling ombudsman and are required to take up their complaints with an independent senior executive within the investment house.

Prohibited activities

10.28 It is a criminal offence under *FSMA 2000, s 24* to carry out a 'regulated activity', without authorisation or exemption from authorisation.

What constitutes a regulated activity?

10.29 *FSMA 2000* and specifically the *Financial Services and Markets Act 2000 (Regulated Activities) Order 2001 (SI 2001 No 1544)* ('the *Regulated Activities Order*') specify a wide range of regulated activities which include the following activities, namely:

(*a*)   dealing in investments;

(*b*)   arranging deals in investments;

(*c*)   managing investments;

(*d*)   giving investment advice;

(*e*)   establishing, operating or winding up a collective investment scheme or a stakeholder pension scheme; and

(*f*)   safeguarding and administering investments.

Specified investments, for the purposes of *FSMA 2000*, include shares and stocks, debentures, Government and public securities, certificates representing securities, units in collective investment schemes, rights under a stakeholder pension scheme, options, futures, contracts for differences and rights under contracts of insurance (*Part III* of the *Regulated Activities Order*). Land and cash are not investments for the purposes of *FSMA 2000*.

The position of the trustees

10.30   Ordinarily, where trustees deal, arrange deals or give advice in relation to investments, they are likely to benefit from the exclusions contained in the *Regulated Activities Order*. However, *article 4* of the *Financial Services and Markets Act 2000 (Carrying on Regulated Activities by Way of Business) Order 2001 (SI 2001 No 1177)* ('the *Business Order*') provides that trustees will be treated as carrying out the activity of managing investments by way of business, where assets are held for the purposes of an occupational pension scheme. An exception to this is where all 'day-to-day' decisions in the carrying on of that activity (except for certain exclusions in *article 4(6)* of the *Business Order*) relating to securities or contractually based investments are taken by an authorised or exempted person or an overseas person who does not require authorisation. The reference to 'routine' in the context of the exclusion for 'day-to-day' decisions was revoked from 6 April 2005 by the *Financial Services and Markets Act 2000 (Carrying on Regulated Activities by Way of Business) Amendment Order 2005 (SI 2005 No 922)*. Most commonly trustees seek to benefit from this provision by delegating investment management activities to duly authorised fund managers

Where a trustee undertakes investment management activities himself, he will need to be authorised under *FSMA 2000* and regulated by the FSA. The rules of the FSA are intended to ensure that those managing pension scheme assets are adequately trained and supervised and meet competence thresholds; that adequate records are kept; that proper investment contracts are entered into; and that adequate procedures exist to safekeep assets.

In supervising a fund manager (see 10.34 below), trustees must ensure that they do not inadvertently end up taking day-to-day investment decisions which would require them to be authorised under *FSMA 2000*. The Securities and Investments Board issued a guidance note 'Pensions Advice and Management under the Financial Services Act 1986' in March 1988, confirming that if the trustees limit their investment to the strategic level, for example, by deciding on an overall investment plan but not specific investments, they will not be regarded as taking any day-to-day decisions and, therefore, would be exempt. It is anticipated that a similar position will prevail under *FSMA 2000* and the FSA is currently updating its guidance on investment activities relating to pension schemes. The publication of this guidance has been delayed but is expected in the near future. The involvement of most trustees extends to deciding on an investment policy, which will generally be reflected in the statement of investment principles required under *section 35* of *PA 1995* (see 10.23 above), and monitoring the performance of the fund manager against the market generally. This will not constitute day-to-day decision-making but if, for example, the trustees direct the fund manager to purchase specific investments, they may have to be authorised.

Certain exemptions apply in relation to small self-administered pension schemes where all of the scheme members are trustees (see also 13.14 below).

Trustees should also beware of breaching the provisions of *section 98* of *FSMA 2000* which prohibits the issuing of investment advertisements unless their contents are approved by an authorised person.

Care should also be taken when investing in common investment funds. These are usually established where an employer operates more than one pension scheme and it is decided to place all of the schemes' investments in one vehicle. Usually such arrangements are established to enable the participant schemes to benefit from the additional purchasing power, reduction in costs and wider market exposure that a larger investment arrangement may offer.

The selection and supervision of investment advisers

10.31   Quite apart from the *FSMA 2000* implications discussed in 10.25 to 10.30 above, many trustees will lack either the time or skill to manage directly their scheme's portfolio, and so will delegate their investment power to a professional fund manager. Although it is a fundamental rule of trust law that a trustee cannot delegate his powers and discretions, there are statutory exceptions to the rule and it can be overridden by the trust documents.

Position before PA 1995

10.32   *Section 23* of the *Trustee Act 1925* (now repealed) allowed trustees to employ and pay an agent to transact any business required in the execution of a trust. However, this provision did not allow a trustee to delegate the exercise of a discretion. The trustees still had to decide on the investments to be sold and purchased; the agent simply implemented the decisions made.

Section 23 of the *Trustee Act 1925* has now been replaced by *section 11* of the *Trustee Act 2000*, which allows trustees to authorise any person to exercise any or all of their 'delegable functions' as their agent. Trustees may delegate any function other than:

(*a*) a function relating to the distribution of the assets of the trust;

(*b*) a power to decide whether payments from the trust funds should be made out of income or capital;

(*c*) a power to appoint trustees; or

(*d*) a power conferred by any other enactment or the trust instrument which permits the trustees to delegate their functions or to appoint a person to act as a nominee or custodian.

Section 25 of the *Trustee Act 1925* allows trustees to delegate the exercise of their discretions for a period of up to one year under a power of attorney but does not explicitly allow for the remuneration of the person to whom the discretion has been delegated.

Due to the constraints of the statutory power to delegate, trustees are generally given power to delegate investment decisions and to appoint and remunerate advisers and agents, including investment advisers and fund managers, in their scheme's documentation.

Position after PA 1995

10.33   The statutory power allowing trustees to appoint agents and delegate the exercise of their investment power has been significantly extended from 6 April 1997 by *PA 1995*.

Section 34 of *PA 1995* effectively permits delegation of investment decisions by the trustees where the delegation is:

(*a*) to a fund manager who is authorised under *FSMA 2000*;

(*b*) to a fund manager who is not authorised under *section 19* of *FSMA 2000* so long as any decisions made by that fund manager would not constitute activities of a specified kind under *FSMA 2000*;

(*c*) to a sub-committee of two or more trustees;

(*d*) in accordance with *section 25* of the *Trustee Act 1925* (see 10.32 above).

Trustees cannot otherwise delegate any investment decision. [*PA 1995, s 34(2)(b)*]. As the provisions of *PA 1995* are overriding in this regard, even if the trust instrument permits delegation in other circumstances, it appears that the trustees cannot delegate outside of the four situations referred to above. In the case of (*c*) and (*d*) above, the trustees' ability to delegate may be further restricted by the requirements of *FSMA 2000* (see 10.25 to 10.30 above).

Section 34(2) of *PA 1995* permits trustees to delegate any discretion to make any decision about investments to a fund manager who is authorised under *FSMA 2000*. Provided that the trustees take all reasonable steps to satisfy themselves that the fund manager has the appropriate knowledge and experience for managing the investments of the scheme and is carrying out his work competently and complying with *section 36* of *PA 1995*, they will not be responsible for the acts or defaults of the fund manager. (See 10.19 above regarding the requirements of *section 36,* and see 10.34 below regarding supervision of a fund manager.)

Section 34(5) provides that, subject to any restrictions imposed by the scheme, trustees may delegate investment decisions to a sub-committee of two or more of the trustees. However, in practice, the requirements of *FSMA 2000* may restrict the circumstances in which such a delegation would be appropriate. The trustees, or a person on their behalf, may also delegate decisions which do not constitute carrying on a regulated activity (within the meaning of *FSMA 2000*) to a fund manager who is not authorised under *FSMA 2000*. Trustees will remain liable for any acts or defaults of the sub-committee or the fund manager to whom the discretion has been delegated. However, if the trustees, or the person who delegated the discretion on their behalf, take all reasonable steps to ensure that such a fund manager is an appropriate person to appoint, the trust documents can exclude or restrict the liability of the trustees for the acts and defaults of the fund manager. (See 10.50 below for discussion on restricting liability of trustees.)

Although *section 34* of *PA 1995* gives trustees a power to delegate investment decisions, it does not give trustees explicit authority to remunerate any fund manager to whom such decisions have been delegated. The cautious approach is to ensure that the trust instrument contains power to remunerate fund managers although, arguably, there is an implicit power to do so. Although the statutory power to delegate investment discretions has certainly been widened by *PA 1995*, most trust deeds will probably continue to include some form of express powers of delegation. The relationship between the trustees and the fund manager they appoint is, and will continue to be, governed to a large extent by the terms of the agreement entered into between them.

Section 47 of *PA 1995* requires an individual or a firm to be appointed by or on behalf of the trustees as fund manager if the assets of the scheme consist of or include investments (within the meaning of *FSMA 2000*) (see 10.29 above). The appointment of the fund manager must be made in writing and must specify the date on which the appointment is due to take effect, to whom the fund manager is to report and from whom the fund manager is to take instructions. [*Occupational Pension Schemes (Scheme Administration) Regulations 1996 (SI 1996 No 1715), reg 5*].

Neither the Act nor the regulations made under *section 47, PA 1995* impose any requirements or restrictions regarding the qualifications or experience required of a person to be appointed as a fund manager. He does not, for example, have to be authorised under *FSMA 2000*. In reality trustees are likely to appoint the person to whom they have delegated their investment decisions but this is not a requirement of the Act. Indeed, on a literal reading of *PA 1995*, a fund manager appointed under *PA 1995, section 47* need play no role in the scheme whatsoever.

Supervision of a fund manager

10.34　　Trustees have a general duty to supervise and monitor the performance of a fund manager. In particular, trustees should ensure that the fund manager is carrying out his work competently and complying with the requirements of *PA 1995* if they wish to benefit from the statutory exoneration provision contained in *section 34(4)* which is applicable where an FSA authorised manager is appointed (see 10.33 above and 10.50 below). Supervising does not imply that the trustees should continually check up on their fund manager but it does impose an obligation to review his appointment from time to time. If the fund manager is regularly performing below the market performance or is outside the benchmark set by the trustees, the trustees should ask why this is and, if appropriate, consider whether they wish to continue their arrangement with that fund manager.

The liability of investment advisers

Duties arising from the agreement

10.35　　As a matter of general contract law, a fund manager is obliged to act in accordance with the terms of his contract and must not exceed his authority or he will be liable for a breach of contract even if he acted in his client's best interests. (*Fray v Voules [1859] 1 E&E 839.*) A fund manager may be required to follow the trustees' instructions, but he cannot be obliged to commit an illegal act. It is not enough for the fund manager simply to follow the trustees' instructions and to observe to the letter the terms of his written agreement; he is in addition contractually bound to act with due care and skill. As a fund manager is remunerated for his services he must perform his duty exercising the care, skill and diligence which it is usual, necessary and proper for professional fund managers to employ.

FSA 1986 and now *FSMA 2000* have, to an extent, dictated the terms of the contractual relationship between fund manager and trustees. Under the FSA Rules a fund manager cannot generally manage the investments of trustees on a discretionary basis unless there is in place an investment management agreement regulating the rights and liabilities of the trustees and the investment manager. 'Standard' terms and conditions for discretionary fund management are now published by the Investment Management Association ('IMA'). We are informed by the IMA that the most recent edition of the standard terms was published in January 2006. Many fund managers do, however, prefer to use their own 'standard' terms and conditions. The fact that such contracts are described as 'standard', however, should not dissuade trustees from questioning their terms or seeking additional protections.

The agreement will also contain a schedule setting out specific investment guidelines agreed upon by the fund manager and the trustees. Some of the 'standard' terms deal specifically with the fiduciary duties imposed upon fund managers and, where appropriate, these are considered in 10.42 to 10.47 below. The following provisions in the standard terms are examples of provisions which could cause concern for trustees, particularly in light of *PA 1995*.

Investment discretion

10.36   The fund manager and the trustees must agree on any restrictions or objectives to be imposed on the fund manager. Trustees should consider supplying the fund manager with a copy of the investment power they are delegating to ensure that the fund manager does not inadvertently make an investment which is outside the scope of the power. Trustees may also wish to clarify the details of their statement of investment principles with the fund manager and to append it to the written agreement to seek to ensure that he exercises the investment power with a view to giving effect to the principles contained in the statement of investment principles. (See 10.23 above and *section 36(5)* of *PA 1995*.)

Liability

10.37   Typically fund managers will attempt to limit their contractual liability. In particular they will look to exclude liability for indirect or consequential loss (even where they have had prior notice of special circumstances concerning the possibility of such loss arising). It is not uncommon for managers to attempt also to avoid responsibility for the acts and omissions of delegates and agents. Trustees should be concerned to obtain protection in respect of these 'third parties' given that they will have little involvement in their selection and may have no direct contractual relationship with them.

Uninvested cash

10.38 The IMA's standard terms allow a fund manager to hold uninvested cash in a bank account. Trustees should ensure that in doing so, the fund manager is obliged to comply with the requirements of *PA 1995* relating to the retention of money in a bank account. [*PA 1995, s 49* and the *Occupational Pension Schemes (Scheme Administration) Regulations 1996 (SI 1996 No 1715), reg 11*]. Consideration should also be given to the application of the 'FSA's Conduct of Business Rules' concerning the treatment of client money.

Voting

10.39 The IMA's standard terms refer to the way in which a fund manager may exercise any voting rights attaching to investments. Trustees should consider whether they should impose any specific conditions on the fund manager in light of their possible duties to exercise voting rights (see 10.49 below).

Valuation and reports

10.40 Trustees will need to consider when they require reports to be made regarding the valuation of investments. In agreeing on a suitable time frame they should bear in mind their duty to supervise the fund manager and in particular whether the timing is appropriate to ensure that they are satisfied that the fund manager is carrying out his work competently and complying with *section 36* of *PA 1995* (see 10.19 above). It may also be appropriate to require the fund manager to disclose other documents and information in his possession on the reasonable request of the trustees and to allow auditors or other advisers to inspect these documents. Trustees should also take care over clauses which provide that, following a specified period after the trustees have received a valuation or report, they may no longer bring an action against the manager for any breach which occurred during the period to which the valuation or report relates.

Custodianship

10.41 If the fund manager is to make use of the services of a custodian (who may or may not be a party to the investment management agreement), the trustees should ensure that they have formally appointed that custodian (i e in accordance with *section 47* of *PA 1995* and *regulations 4* and *5* of the *Occupational Pension Schemes (Scheme Administration) Regulations 1996 (SI 1996 No 1715))* as otherwise they will not be able to rely on his skill or judgment without the risk of incurring sanctions in the form of a fine and/or removal (see appendix I).

The debate as to whether trustees must also appoint sub-custodians was closed as a result of the publication of the *Occupational Pension Schemes (Scheme Administration) Amendment Regulations 1998 (SI 1998 No 1494)* which relieve trustees of this obligation and enable them to rely on the skill and judgment of sub-custodians appointed by the custodian provided that written disclosure of the extent to which (if any) the custodian accepts liability for its sub-custodians' actions is made in the custody agreement. Any changes to the liability position must be immediately notified to the trustees by the custodian. The trustees should also check that the custodian they appoint has the appropriate *FSMA 2000* authorisation.

Where the custodian is not a party to the investment management agreement, it is likely that there will be a separate 'global custody agreement'. Whether custody is dealt with in the investment agreement or otherwise, it will be necessary to deal with a number of key areas in addition to core custody, including: settlement of transactions (contractual or actual); cash management; liability for sub-custodians; and foreign exchange transactions.

Investment management and custody agreements should always be carefully reviewed by trustees and their advisers before being entered into, as some of their terms (for instance, the extent to which the agreement seeks to exempt the fund manager or custodian from liability) can expose the scheme to considerable liabilities.

Fiduciary duties

10.42 Because the fund manager is handling trust monies, it may be argued that his duties are not only contractual, but also fiduciary, i e they may have to be exercised in the best interests of the members. In effect, this means that the following duties may be implied.

Duty not to delegate

10.43 The general duty not to delegate applies not only to trustees but also to their agents. An agency relationship is based on the confidence one person has in another, and so an agent is in principle prohibited from delegating his authority to another person or even appointing a sub-agent. (See *Allam & Co Ltd v Europa Poster Services Ltd [1968] 1 All ER 826.*) Delegation is, however, permitted in certain circumstances. For example, where the employment of a sub-agent is usual in managing a client's investments and is not unreasonable or inconsistent with the express terms of any written agreement; or where the act delegated is purely administrative and one which does not require or involve confidence or discretion.

Usually the investment management agreement will expressly permit a fund manager to delegate or appoint sub-agents, often without the consent of the trustees. Fund managers will often include a provision to the effect that they are not liable for the actions of their sub-agents unless they are 'connected companies'. As trustees may have no direct contractual relationship with the sub-agent it is advisable for them to ensure that, if the fund manager is to be allowed to delegate or appoint agents, he remains liable to the trustees for their acts or defaults.

The fund manager must not put himself in a position where his duties to the trustees conflict with his own interests

10.44 This is no more than the application of the equitable maxim that a person in a position of trust must not put himself in a situation in which his interest and his duty would be in conflict. An extreme example is where a fund manager seeks to buy an asset from the trustees. He would be attempting to achieve the impossible: trying to achieve the highest price for the trustees and at the same time endeavouring to pay the lowest possible price himself.

The IMA's standard terms specifically address potential conflicts of interest. They allow the fund manager to effect transactions where conflicts arise but provide that the fund manager must ensure that such transactions are effected on terms which are not materially less favourable to the trustees than if the potential conflict had not existed. Despite this there may be situations where the fiduciary duty should, and does, override the contractual provision.

A fund manager appointed under *section 47(2)* of *PA 1995* must, on being appointed, confirm that he will declare any conflict of interest affecting his relationship with the trustees immediately he becomes aware of it or, if he is regulated under *FSMA 2000*, in accordance with the rules of the FSA. However, many managers will interpret the rules to allow them to give generic style disclosures in the investment management agreement, thus avoiding the impracticality of making prior disclosure on a case-by-case basis.

Duty not to accept bribes

10.45 This duty is self explanatory. If a fund manager accepts a payment which could constitute a bribe and conducts himself in the way proposed by the person offering the bribe, it will be presumed that he has been influenced by the bribe and has breached his duty to the trustees. This presumption is not rebuttable and the trustees' loss is considered to be at least the amount of the bribe.

The person offering the bribe, as well as the fund manager who receives it, will be criminally liable. The fund manager will have to repay or forego any commission, profit or remuneration to which he would otherwise have been entitled from the trustees. (*Andrews v Ramsey & Co [1903] 2 KB 635.*) The trustees will be able to dismiss the fund manager without notice (*Bulfield v Fournier [1895] 11 TLR 282*) and claim for the amount of the bribe plus interest from the date upon which the bribe was received.

The fund manager has a duty not to take advantage of his position or the trustees' property in order to acquire a benefit for himself

10.46   An investment manager is liable to account to the trustees for any profits he makes using confidential information acquired in the course of his appointment. (*Peter Pan Manufacturing Corporation v Corsets Silhouette Ltd [1963] 3 All ER 402.*) The provisions relating to insider dealing contained in the *Criminal Justice Act 1993* may also be relevant. Broadly speaking, dealings in securities of a company by an individual who holds unpublished price-sensitive information in respect of that company by virtue of his connection with the company are prohibited. There are similar provisions with regard to advising others to deal in the shares or debentures of the company, and in respect of the communication of unpublished price-sensitive information to others where that person might reasonably be expected to make use of it for the purpose of dealing.

Ultra vires

10.47   If trustees make an investment which under their investment power is barred or outside its scope they are acting *ultra vires*. *Hazell v Hammersmith and Fulham London Borough Council [1990] 2 WLR 17* raised the concept of *ultra vires* in connection with a local authority's funds as certain of the activities were beyond those permissible by the relevant Local Government Act. An act which is *ultra vires* is generally void and may not be ratified. Fund managers should be made aware of the powers of the trustees on whose behalf they are acting as otherwise they may enter into *ultra vires* arrangements. Equally, trustees are advised to ensure that they restrict fund managers from inadvertently acting outside the trustees' powers by ensuring that the investment management agreement contains appropriate investment restrictions.

Liability for breach of trust by agents

10.48   It is possible for an agent of trustees to be held liable in respect of a breach of trust committed by the trustees for whom he is acting, and which he, as agent, has facilitated. To be liable, the fund manager would have knowingly to commit a wrongful act in relation to the scheme's assets; in effect, he would have to know that the trustees did not have authority to give the instructions he followed or take the action he took. A fund manager may also be liable where he turns a blind eye to what is an obvious breach of trust where an honest and reasonable man would have considered it such.

Unless fund managers are either aware that a breach of trust is being committed by the trustees concerned, or the situation is such that it is, or should be, obvious to any competent fund manager that this is the case, they are entitled to assume that the instructions given are bona fide and within the powers of the trustees. If a fund manager follows an investment policy which he knows to be outside the powers of the trustees he renders himself liable to an action for breach of trust.

The most crucial factor on which liability of a fund manager depends is the precise terms of the investment powers given to the trustees and whether the fund manager is aware of them. Consequently trustees should ensure that the fund manager is fully apprised of any restrictions on their powers of investment and appropriate restrictions should be built into the investment management agreement.

Voting rights as a consequence of share ownership – is it a trust asset?

10.49   In the UK approximately a third of all shares in publicly quoted companies are held by pension funds. Trustees have traditionally exercised their voting rights only in exceptional cases but the sheer size of their voting power begs the question: are trustees and any fund managers to whom they have delegated their discretions in some way responsible for the actions of the companies in which they invest?

The Cadbury Committee recommended that institutional investors should make positive use of their voting rights and should also disclose their policies on the use of voting rights. The National Association of Pension Funds has recommended that trustees should decide on their voting policy and that voting policy should be made public. Trustees should then exercise their votes prudently and in the interests of scheme beneficiaries.

There is no doubt that in the US this idea has progressed further than in the UK. Pension funds in the US have been obliged to exercise their voting rights since 1988 in respect of US companies. This duty was extended in 1994 to include overseas companies and the effect of this duty is being felt in the UK. (See 10.51 below.)

The legislators in the UK have, to date, resisted attempts to impose a similar obligation on trustees. The previous Government successfully resisted an attempt by the then opposition to include such a duty in *PA 1995*. Although it was felt that imposing a mandatory duty to exercise voting rights was contrary to the general aim of deregulation and would be too difficult to enforce, it was accepted that trustees, or fund managers on their behalf, should be encouraged to exercise their voting rights.

Even in the absence of a statutory duty to exercise voting rights, there is a strong case for arguing that some form of duty exists. Trustees have a clear duty to act in the best interests of their members and this includes protecting the value of, and the income derived from, an investment. There may be circumstances where this can only be achieved by voting for or against certain proposals and in such situations trustees may be open to attack if they simply make no voting decision whatsoever. It should be remembered that positively abstaining from voting can be a legitimate voting decision. The duty is perhaps not necessarily to vote but to consider whether, and if so how, to vote.

Arguably, fund managers to whom discretionary investment responsibilities have been delegated have fiduciary responsibilities similar to the responsibilities of trustees. Accordingly, if trustees have a duty to consider exercising voting rights, it follows that fund managers must also concern themselves with the running of companies in whom they invest trustees' monies.

In 2002, the Government gave its response (its 'consultation document') to the Myners Review in which it stated at Principle 6 on Activism:

> 'The mandate and trust deed should incorporate the principle of the US Department of Labor Interpretative Bulletin on activism. Trustees should also ensure that managers have an explicit strategy, elucidating the circumstances in which they will intervene in a company; the approach they will use in doing so; and how they measure the effectiveness of this strategy.'

In October 2002, the Institutional Shareholders Committee (which consisted of the Investment Management Association, the Association of British Insurers, the National Association of Pension Funds and the Association of Investment Trust Companies) unveiled the publication of a new Statement of Principles entitled, 'The Responsibilities of Institutional Shareholders and Agents – Statement of Principles'. It develops the principles set out in its 1991 statement 'The Responsibilities of Institutional Shareholders in the UK' and expands on the Combined Code of Corporate Governance of June 1998. It sets out best practice for institutional shareholders and/or agents in relation to their responsibilities in respect of investee companies. The Statement comments in relation to intervention, that if boards do not respond constructively when institutional shareholders and/or agents intervene, then institutional shareholders and/or agents will consider on a case-by-case basis whether to escalate their action. The Government said that it welcomed the publication of the Statement of Principles and that it would review its impact after two years to see 'whether this non-legislative approach has been successful in delivering change'. At this stage, we are not aware of any proposed legislation on this subject.

Trustee liability and protection

10.50   The ultimate responsibility for investment decisions lies firmly with the trustees. The duties placed on trustees regarding investment are onerous, and becoming more so, not only in terms of the legal principles governing the propriety of their actions, but also in terms of the types of investment vehicles now available. It would be a foolish trustee who did not take specialist advice regarding the exercise of his investment power. However, taking advice will not, on its own, necessarily protect the trustee; he must still act honestly with reasonable care and prudence. The increased responsibilities of trustees in *PA 2004* should also be noted (see further at 10.51 below). The fiduciary duties and liability of fund managers are discussed at 10.42 and 10.48 above but the following particular points arise in relation to investment decisions.

Trustees will be liable for the acts or defaults of the fund manager if they fail to take reasonable care in choosing the fund manager or in fixing or enforcing the terms of his engagement. (*Steel v Wellcome Custodian Trustees Ltd [1988] 1 WLR 167*.)

Section 23 of the *Trustee Act 2000* gives trustees some protection by providing that a trustee is not liable for any act or default of an agent, nominee or custodian, or a permitted substitute, when entering into or reviewing the arrangements under which that person acts, unless the trustee has failed to comply with the applicable duty of care.

Case law considers 'wilful default' to include both positive acts and a 'want of ordinary prudence'. (*Speight v Gaunt (1883) 22 Ch D 727; Re Chapman [1896] 2 Ch 763*.) There have been cases to the effect that 'wilful default' should be interpreted in the company law context so that it includes a deliberate or reckless breach of duty but not a negligent breach of duty. (*Re Vickery [1931] 1 Ch 572*.) However, the safer and the generally more acceptable view of trustees' responsibilities is the former definition.

It is common sense that trustees should take care when selecting their advisers and agents, as would any man with common prudence, and further exercise reasonable and responsible supervision.

Many trust deeds attempt to mitigate trustees' responsibilities by widely drafted exoneration clauses. However, *section 33* of *PA 1995* limits the extent to which liability in respect of investment decisions may be excluded by providing that liability for breach of an obligation to take care or exercise skill in the perform-ance of any investment functions exercisable by the trustees (or by a person to whom that function has been delegated under *section 34* of *PA 1995*) cannot be excluded or restricted by any instrument or agreement. *Section 33* of *PA 1995* does not prevent trustees being exonerated under the provisions of the trust deed from liability for the actions of a fund manager to whom the trustees have delegated an investment discretion under *section 34(5)* of *PA 1995* (see 10.33 above).

However, *PA 1995* also offers some exoneration for trustees who delegate their investment discretion to a fund manager authorised under *FSMA 2000* in accordance with *section 34(2)* of *PA 1995*. The trustees will not be liable under *PA 1995* for the acts or defaults of such a fund manager provided they have taken all reasonable steps to satisfy themselves that he has the appropriate knowledge and experience and is acting competently and complying with the requirements of *section 36* of *PA 1995* (see 10.19 and 10.20 above). [*PA 1995, s 34(4)*].

Myners' Report: voluntary Code of Practice

10.51   A brief summary is set out below of the proposed principles which the Myners' Report suggests should be adopted on a voluntary basis by the trustees of defined benefit schemes when taking investment decisions. There is a separate set of principles applicable to defined contribution schemes. The Government allowed schemes two years to comply with Myners (or explain why they could not) and it stated that it intended to conduct an 'audit' of Myners compliance in 2003. The Department for Work and Pensions published a report on compliance with Myners in Autumn 2003 which set out the extent to which 14 schemes have voluntarily complied with Myners. Voluntary compliance is most visible in relation to quantifiable targets, such as asset allocation and performance measurement, and there has been less progress towards effective decision-making, shareholder activism and socially responsible investment. Larger schemes seem more compliant than smaller ones.

• *Effective decision-making*

>   *Trustees should have sufficient expertise and appropriate training to be able to evaluate critically any investment advice they may receive. They should also ensure that they have sufficient in-house staff to support them in their investment responsibilities. It is good practice to have an investment sub-committee to provide focus. Trustees should adopt a forward-looking business plan and arrange to conduct a*

self-assessment of their skills and their investment processes to ensure that they carry out their role effectively. Myners' view is that trustees should be paid.

- *Clear objectives*

   Trustees should set investment objectives which take into consideration the trustees' view of what is necessary to meet the fund's liabilities taking account of the fund's overall income, and the trustees' attitude to risk (and, specifically, their willingness to accept under-performance by their fund manager due to market conditions). Investment objectives set by trustees must relate to the fund's specific liabilities, not in relation to peer group performance.

- *Focus on asset allocation*

   Trustees should pay significant attention to strategic asset allocation, and recognise its importance in helping the trustees to achieve the fund's investment objectives. Trustees should take advantage of the full range of investment opportunities available to them to meet their objectives, including investment in private equity.

- *Expert advice*

   Contracts for actuarial and investment advice should be open to separate competition.

- *Explicit mandates*

   Trustees should agree explicit written mandates with their fund managers, covering topics such as objectives, benchmarks, risk, the manager's investment approach and the timescales for measurement and evaluation of the manager's performance. Myners does not believe that a fund manager's mandate should be terminated before its term expires for under performance alone, at least where such underperformance results from adverse market conditions. No financial instruments should be excluded from the fund manager's mandate without clear justification. Trustees must seek to understand how transaction related investment costs including commissions are incurred and should put in place controls to monitor investment costs. Trustees should not permit soft commissions to be paid in respect of their investment transactions.

• *Activism*

　The US Department of Labor Interpretative Bulletin on activism (ie the investor's policy on proxy voting, or guidelines) should be incorporated into the fund manager's mandate and the scheme's trust deed. Trustees and their fund managers should agree explicitly the circumstances in which the manager will be required to intervene in a company which the trustees hold as an investment.

• *Appropriate benchmarks*

　Trustees and their fund managers should agree appropriate benchmarks, avoiding sub-optimal investment strategies. Trustees should consider, in relation to each asset class, whether active or passive management is more appropriate and allow managers to pursue active strategies (if chosen) to achieve higher investment returns.

• *Performance measurement*

　Trustees must arrange to measure their fund's performance regularly and carry out a regular formal assessment of their own investment procedures and decisions together with a review of the procedures and investment decisions delegated to their advisers and fund managers.

• *Transparency*

　Trustees should produce a more detailed Statement of Investment Principles than the existing SIP, showing:

　• who takes investment decisions and why the investment structure used by the scheme has been selected;

　• the fund's investment objectives;

　• the fund's asset allocation strategy, and how this has been reached;

　• details of the mandates agreed with each of the fund's *advisers* and managers;

　• the fee structures agreed with managers and with *advisers* and managers and, why these fee structures have been selected.

• *Regular reporting*

　The fund's Statement of Investment Principles should be published, together with the results obtained from monitoring the performance of advisers and fund managers. A summary of key information taken from

> *the Statement of Investment Principles and the performance results of the scheme's managers should be sent to scheme members, together with an explanation of why the fund has decided to depart from any of the key principles set out above.*

Given the increasingly complex investment decisions which trustees are required to make, it seems entirely sensible that trustees should seek to increase their knowledge and understanding of how investment markets work, and in particular, how charges operate in relation to investment decisions made by the trustees.

However, it seems equally valid that, where investment managers, with a full discretionary mandate involve pension scheme trustees in complex financial transactions, or instruments, they should clearly communicate the value of entering into such transactions in relation to their trustees' particular circumstances.

The Government threatened to legislate to incorporate Paul Myners' principles into trustees' investment decision-making. This has resulted in the provisions contained at *sections 247* to *249* of *PA 2004* which set out the level of knowledge that the Government now expects of trustees. The new legislative provisions are expected to come into force in April 2006. Trustees and where there is a trustee company, each individual who exercises any function which the company has as trustee of the scheme, must be 'conversant with':

- the trust deed and rules of the scheme;
- any statement of investment principles;
- any statement of funding principles; and
- any other document recording policy for the time being adopted by the trustees relating to the administration of the scheme generally.

They must also have 'knowledge and understanding of':

- pensions and trust law; and
- principles relating to funding of occupational pension schemes and the investment of the assets of schemes.

The degree of knowledge and understanding required is that appropriate for the purposes of enabling the individual properly to exercise the function in question. A draft Code of Practice has been issued by the Regulator to provide guidance on how trustees are expected to comply with these new requirements. This Code is due to come into effect in April 2006.

Chapter 11

Funding, deficits and surpluses

Introduction

11.1   Most private sector occupational pension schemes in the UK are funded; assets are set aside, in advance, to provide a fund to meet the benefits ultimately payable (although it is not uncommon for death in service benefits to be insured). Public sector schemes are often unfunded or partially funded as they are, instead, backed by a Government guarantee. It has become increasingly common for higher-paid employees to be provided with benefits from an unapproved top-up scheme (which may be unfunded) (see chapter 5). However, changes to simplify the tax treatment of pension schemes (see chapter 5) may well affect their popularity. In general, unfunded occupational schemes are the exception rather than the rule even though, before *PA 1995* came into force, there was little in the way of legislation relating to funding.

The first part of this chapter deals with the legal requirements imposed on trustees and employers regarding funding and, in particular, it considers the new scheme specific funding provisions contained in *PA 2004*. The second part of this chapter considers the implications of excessive funding and discusses the ways in which a 'surplus' can be reduced.

Pre-PA 1995 requirements relating to funding

11.2   Until *PA 1995* there was no legislation which specifically required an employer to fund a pensions promise in advance. An employer could, quite legitimately, promise a pension to an employee and then make no financial provision for the benefit until it became payable. However, there were several controls which had implications in respect of funding which are discussed in 11.3 to 11.5 below.

HMRC requirements

11.3   HMRC will not grant an occupational pension scheme exempt approved status unless that scheme has some element of employer funding.

Although HMRC has no hard and fast rules, it looks for at least 10 per cent of the total contributions to be provided by the employers, unless of course there is an employer contribution holiday in place. This requirement will cease to apply from 6 April 2006 and it does not appear that there will be any specific HMRC requirements for employers to contribute to registered occupational pension schemes.

At the other end of the scale, HMRC aims to restrict funding by limiting the tax reliefs available in respect of overfunded schemes (see 11.46 below). This is to be removed with effect from 6 April 2006 and replaced by a tax charge of 35 per cent on any payment to an employer.

Contracting-out requirements

11.4 Before the changes introduced by *PA 1995*, contracted-out defined benefits schemes were required to obtain an actuarial certificate at least once every three years which confirmed that, in the actuary's opinion, the assets would be sufficient to ensure that members' guaranteed minimum pensions would be paid in full if the scheme were to be wound up during the following three-and-a-half years. This requirement was intended to ensure that contracted-out schemes were sufficiently funded to provide at least guaranteed minimum pensions and any benefits which, on the winding up of the scheme, would have to be secured in priority to guaranteed minimum pensions. (For the latest position see 11.36 below.)

Disclosure requirements

11.5 Under the *Occupational Pension Schemes* (*Disclosure of Information*) *Regulations 1986* (*SI 1986 No 1046*), trustees of Inland Revenue approved schemes were required to produce an annual report which had to include an actuarial statement. The statement had to set out information on long-term funding, including:

(*a*)   whether members' accrued benefits were covered by the assets held;

(*b*)   the long-term contributions required to provide the benefits; and

(*c*)   the key assumptions adopted by the actuary.

Where the assets were not sufficient to cover the accrued benefits, the statement had to indicate what percentage of the benefits was covered and when the assets were expected to be sufficient to cover all of the accrued benefits.

The disclosure requirements were superseded by the requirements of *PA 1995* (see 11.10 below) and schemes completing valuations under the scheme specific funding provisions will become subject to new disclosure requirements prescribed under *PA 2004* (see 11.28 below).

Funding practice

11.6   Generally employees prefer not to rely on their employer having the financial resources available to meet the pension commitment by the time benefits become payable. With an unfunded scheme, an individual could find that, when he comes to retire, the employer he worked for 20 years previously and who had promised him a pension, has gone out of business. A funded scheme alleviates this concern and ensures members will (or should) receive the pension due to them at retirement.

From the employer's perspective, making provision for future benefits as they accrue (as opposed to when they fall due) means that the employer can control its cash flow more easily and plan ahead; it is not faced with having to provide a costly benefit when its financial position may be such that it can ill afford it. Also, in the case of exempt approved schemes (or registered schemes from 6 April 2006), the tax advantages available in respect of contributions to the scheme and income and capital gains on assets held by the scheme (see chapter 5) mean that the overall cost of providing benefits is reduced. This will be even more important from 6 April 2006 when unfunded schemes lose the tax advantages they previously enjoyed.

Most occupational pension schemes are funded in a way that aims to ensure that, by the time each member reaches retirement, there are sufficient funds to provide the benefits that have been promised. A scheme's governing documentation will normally contain rules specifying how the contributions payable by both the employer and the employees are to be determined. In most defined benefits schemes employees' contributions are fixed, with the employer meeting the balance required to pay the benefits promised (a 'balance of cost' scheme). The question of who determines the contribution rates (the trustees, the employer or, in some cases, the actuary) generally depends upon the scheme rules. Typically, no matter who has the responsibility under the trust deed to decide the contribution rate, the advice of an actuary will be sought and generally followed. The scheme specific funding provisions contained in *PA 2004* require most funding decisions to be made by the trustees with the consent of the employer, overriding the provisions of scheme rules. These requirements are subject to modification depending on the exact provisions of the scheme rules and this is dealt with in more detail in 11.28 below.

The minimum funding requirement – Pensions Act 1995

The need for a solvency standard

11.7 The Goode Committee considered the issue of funding in some detail and concluded that a statutory funding requirement was desirable. After discussing the arguments put forward both for and against a minimum solvency standard, the Committee concluded:

> 'In assessing these various arguments we have taken as our basic premise the need to ensure that scheme members are not faced with a reduction in their accrued benefits. We take the view that the purpose of a funded pension scheme is that, no matter what happens to the sponsoring employer, the scheme members' accrued rights will be inviolate. We have therefore concluded that the introduction of a statutory minimum solvency requirement is necessary to provide security for the accrued pension rights of scheme members.' (Report of the Goode Committee, paragraph 4.4.16)

During the passage of *PA 1995* through Parliament, the 'minimum solvency requirement' became the 'minimum funding requirement' but the change in name was not the only alteration. Many of the proposals put forward by the Committee were adopted in principle, but the test itself became less stringent. The minimum funding requirement does, however, play a pivotal role in the working of many of the provisions of *PA 1995*.

The minimum funding requirement

11.8 *PA 1995* introduced a requirement that 'the value of the assets of the scheme is not less than the amount of the liabilities of the scheme'. This requirement is referred to as the minimum funding requirement ('MFR').

Details of the MFR are contained in *sections 56* to *61* of *PA 1995*, the *Occupational Pension Schemes (Minimum Funding Requirement and Actuarial Valuations) Regulations 1996 (SI 1996 No 1536)* (the '*MFR Regulations*') and a professional Guidance Note, 'Retirement Benefit Schemes – Minimum Funding Requirement', GN27, issued by the Institute and Faculty of Actuaries and revised most recently in January 2003.

Compliance with the MFR, however, does not always guarantee that the assets of the scheme will be enough to meet its liabilities. This is because there will be timing differences between applying the MFR test and taking action in response

470

to the results of the test. Also, the test does not seek to guarantee that schemes will always have sufficient funds to provide for benefits by purchasing annuities from an insurance company.

The MFR does not apply to all occupational pension schemes, the main exemptions being:

(*a*)   defined contribution schemes (which for the purposes of *PA 1995* includes a defined contributions scheme which also provides salary related death benefits (*Personal and Occupational Pension Schemes (Miscellaneous Amendments) Regulations 1997 (SI 1997 No 786),* reg 2));

(*b*)   certain public service pension schemes and government guaranteed schemes;

(*c*)   unapproved schemes;

(*d*)   schemes established in the UK under trust in respect of non-UK businesses which provide benefits in respect of individuals employed outside the UK;

(*e*)   schemes with less than two members; and

(*f*)   schemes which provide only death benefits.

[*section 56(2) of PA 1995 and MFR Regulations, reg 28*].

The MFR was a cyclical process consisting of three components: valuations, contribution schedules and annual certification.

The MFR has, in relation to valuations with an effective date on or after 22 September 2005, been replaced by the statutory funding objective (see 11.20 to 11.40 below). Schemes are not required to obtain an actuarial valuation under the new provisions until the next due date for an MFR valuation (usually three years from the effective date of the previous valuation) so schemes may continue to operate under MFR valuations until September 2008, subject to the transitional provisions described in 11.39 below.

The requirements relating to the MFR as set out below will continue to apply to schemes operating under MFR until they have in place their first schedule of contributions under the statutory funding objective (the savings to the *MFR Regulations* are set out in *Schedule 4* to the *Occupational Pension Schemes (Scheme Funding) Regulations 2005 (SI 2005 No. 3377)* ('the *Scheme Funding Regulations*')).

Record keeping

11.9   As part of the MFR procedure, under *regulation 19* of the *MFR Regulations*, trustees are required to keep records of:

471

(*a*)   all contributions made to the scheme, showing separately:

   (i)   the aggregate of the contributions paid by or on behalf of active members and the dates on which they were paid;

   (ii)   the voluntary contributions paid by each member; and

   (iii)   the aggregate of the contributions paid by or on behalf of each employer and the dates on which they were paid;

(*b*)   all contributions and payments made to secure any increase required to meet a serious shortfall;

(*c*)   any action taken by trustees to recover:

   (i)   any contributions which are not paid on the date on which they are due;

   (ii)   any debt which has arisen as a result of any failure to deal with a serious shortfall within the required time frame; and

   (iii)   any debt that has arisen as a consequence of an employer's insolvency.

Disclosure

11.10   A copy of the latest statement and the latest actuarial valuation must be disclosed to any member, potential member, the spouse of any member or potential member, any beneficiary or any recognised trade union who requests it. [*Occupational Pension Schemes (Disclosure of Information) Regulations 1996 (SI 1996 No 1655), reg 7*].

Extension of schedule period

11.11   Opra had a discretion to extend the schedule period if it is satisfied that the circumstances justify it. Exact details of the requirements which have to be met are set out in *regulations 25* to *27* of the *MFR Regulations*. Any extensions approved by Opra before 6 April 2005 remain valid and applications for extensions after that date may be made to the Regulator.

Supervision by the Regulator

11.12   If the contributions due in accordance with a schedule of contributions are not paid, trustees must give notice of that fact to the Regulator within 30 days of the due date (unless payment has been made within ten days beginning with the due date, and the default is only the first or second such default in the period of twelve months ending on and including the due date) (*MFR Regula-*

tions, reg 23). This requirement has effectively been modified by the Regulator's Briefing (see below). Notice must then be given to members within 90 days of the due date (unless payment has been made within 60 days of the due date). Any contributions which remain unpaid become a debt due from the employer to the trustees for which the trustees may choose to sue the employer if the funding of the scheme is at risk. [*PA 1995, s 59(2)*].

The Regulator issued Briefing No 1 in May 2005 which provides guidance about the circumstances in which trustees should report late payments of contributions. The Briefing provides that, unless there is a more serious or wider problem requiring an earlier report:

- trustees do not normally need to report any contributions paid late but received within 90 days of the due date; and

- trustees should report all contributions outstanding at the end of the 90-day period.

Examples in the Briefing of situations where an earlier report should be made include cases where the employer is using the contributions to alleviate cash flow difficulties, where the employer does not have suitable systems or procedures in place or where the trustees believe the problem may pose an immediate or potentially significant risk to members' benefits.

Failure to pay contributions in accordance with the schedule of contributions may also be a breach of law requiring a report to the Regulator under *section 70 of PA 2004* (see 2.14 above).

Annual certification

11.13   Where the most recent MFR valuation shows funding at less than 100 per cent the trustees must obtain an 'annual certificate' not earlier than 21 days before, and not later than 21 days after, each anniversary of the signing of the schedule of contributions (*MFR Regulations, reg 18*). In the certificate the scheme actuary must state whether or not, in his opinion, the contributions payable are adequate for the purpose of securing that the MFR will continue to be met throughout the schedule period, or will be met by the end of the period. He must also indicate any relevant changes that have occurred since the last MFR valuation was prepared.

Trustees must forward a copy of the certificate to the employer within seven days. The exact form of the actuary's statement and actuary's certificate is set out in *Schedule 3* to the *MFR Regulations*.

If the actuary certifies that, in his opinion, the contributions payable are not adequate to ensure that the MFR is, or will be, met throughout the schedule period, and the value of the scheme's assets is less than 90 per cent of its liabilities, the trustees must either obtain an MFR valuation or revise the schedule of contributions within six months of the date on which the certificate was signed. In practice it is likely that the scheme actuary will notify the trustees of any potential problems before issuing a negative certificate. This will give the trustees an opportunity to take remedial action, if appropriate, before the certificate is issued.

Serious under-provision

11.14   Where an MFR valuation shows that the value of a scheme's assets is less than 90 per cent of the amount of its liabilities, the employer must increase the value of the assets within a set period to a level which (taken with any contributions paid) reaches the 90 per cent level. This can be done either by the employer making an appropriate payment to the trustees or (if the trustees so decide within twelve weeks of the signing of the valuation) by one of the following 'prescribed' methods:

(*a*)   a guarantee, in writing, from a bank or building society that it will meet the shortfall should the employer become insolvent or the scheme wind up;

(*b*)   the payment of the required sum into a deposit account held in the names of the trustees and designated as an account that complies with the regulations made under *PA 1995*;

(*c*)   a charge over any assets which are otherwise free from any encumbrance, provided that the charge is registrable under a statutory provision. [*PA 1995, s 68*; *MFR Regulations, reg 22*].

Schedule 4 to the *MFR Regulations* specifies conditions relating to each of the above methods for securing the required increase.

If the required increase is to be secured by the making of an appropriate payment, the payment must be made within twelve months of the signing of the MFR valuation. In all other cases the employer has three months within which to secure the increase. The Regulator has the power to extend these periods if circumstances justify such action.

If the employer fails to secure the required increase, the shortfall becomes a debt on the employer and the trustees are obliged to notify the Regulator and members of the scheme within 14 days. [*PA 1995, s 60(4), (5)*].

If the MFR is not met and between MFR valuations the funding of the scheme deteriorates the trustees must prepare a report stating the reasons for the failure to meet the MFR and for the deterioration in the funding of the scheme. Such a report must be made available to any member or prospective member and their spouses, any beneficiary or prospective beneficiary and any independent trade unions recognised for the purposes of collective bargaining in relation to the scheme. [*MFR Regulations, reg 21*].

Modifications of MFR in respect of certain schemes

Multi-employer schemes

11.15 Where a scheme has several employers and each employer effectively operates a distinct section of the scheme, for the purposes of the MFR, each section is treated as a separate scheme. [*MFR Regulations, Sch 5, paras 1* and 2].

Frozen or paid-up schemes

11.16 Where there are no active members, references to the employer are taken as references to the person who was the employer on the date on which there was last an active member. [*MFR Regulations, Sch 5, para 3*].

Shared cost scheme

11.17 Shared cost schemes are defined as schemes where, if there is a shortfall, the rates of both employer and employee contributions are increased by the same proportion. In such a scheme, in the case of serious under-provision, both the employer and the employees are required to meet any shortfall. [*MFR Regulations, reg 24*].

Consequences of non-compliance

11.18 If trustees fail to take all reasonable steps to secure compliance with the various requirements of the MFR legislation summarised above, they face being fined (maximum of £5,000 for an individual or £50,000 for a company) and/or removed as a trustee. The sanction on the employer is that if contributions are not paid within a certain time frame they become a debt due to the trustees for which the trustees could sue the employer. The burdens placed on trustees are fairly onerous, but they have few statutory powers if the employer does not co-operate. They are responsible only to the extent that they have not taken 'all reasonable steps'.

Trustees and employers alike should remember that, in its current form, the MFR is intended to provide only a minimum level of funding. If, instead, the legislation had based the MFR on the cost of securing benefits by the purchase of annuities, the test would have been considerably stricter in terms of funding, but would provide members with greater security.

Replacement of the MFR

Initial reforms

11.19   Pending the introduction of the new statutory funding objective, the Government made a number of amendments to regulations as the first stage of the reform of the MFR by the *Occupational Pension Schemes (Minimum Funding Requirement and Miscellaneous Amendments) Regulations 2002 (SI 2002 No 380)* which came into force on 19 March 2002. The amendments included:

(*a*)   an extension of the periods within which any deficit in funding must be made good – to three years for schemes where there is serious under-provision (see 11.14 above) for them to reach the 90 per cent MFR funding level and to ten years for schemes to reach the 100 per cent MFR funding level (this applies only to new schedules of contributions certified after 19 March 2002);

(*b*)   the removal of the requirement for annual re-certification of schemes that are 100 per cent funded (see 11.13 above);

(*c*)   the extension of the 'transitional period', as defined in the *MFR Regulations, reg 1* to 31 December 2004 (subsequently further extended to 5 April 2006);

(*d*)   a change in the MFR equity market value adjustment from 3.25 per cent to 3 per cent; and

(*e*)   the introduction of stricter conditions in cases where the pension scheme of a solvent employer is voluntarily wound up, so that the debt on the employer includes the actual costs of winding-up, the purchase of immediate annuities for pensioners and the provision of cash equivalent transfer values for non-pensioner members.

Pensions Act 2004 – statutory funding objective

The statutory funding objective

11.20   The statutory funding objective ('SFO') is the latest legal funding standard that replaces the MFR. In contrast to the 'one size fits all' approach adopted by the MFR, it is intended that the SFO will enable individual schemes to adopt a funding strategy that is more appropriate to their specific circumstances. The provisions governing the SFO are set out in *sections 221* to *233* of *PA 2004* and the *Occupational Pension Schemes (Scheme Funding) Regulations 2005 (SI 2005 No 3377)* ('the *Scheme Funding Regulations*'). They came into force on 30 December 2005 but apply to actuarial valuations with an effective date on or after 22 September 2005. These provisions are supported by a Code of Practice issued by the Regulator which was laid before Parliament in December 2005. In October 2005 the Regulator issued a draft statement for consultation dealing with the manner in which it intended operating its powers in relation to scheme funding (see 11.30 below).

The SFO will apply to all defined benefit schemes unless exempted by regulations. The effect of the *Regulations* is broadly that those schemes that are currently exempt from the MFR will also be exempt from the new requirement. The exemptions, listed in *regulation 17* of the *Scheme Funding Regulations*, are:

- statutory schemes guaranteed by a public authority;

- pay-as-you-go schemes;

- House of Commons pension scheme;

- certain schemes for overseas employees;

- an unapproved or unregistered scheme with fewer than 100 members;

- a *section 615(6)* scheme which has fewer than 100 members;

- a scheme which has fewer than two members;

- a scheme which has fewer than 12 members, where all the members are trustees of the scheme and either:

   – the provisions of the scheme provide that all decisions which fall to be made by the trustees are made by the unanimous agreement of the trustees who are members of the scheme; or

   – the scheme has a trustee who is an independent trustee in relation to the scheme for the purposes of *section 23* of *PA 1995* and is on the Regulator's register;

- a scheme which has fewer than 12 members, where a company is a trustee of the scheme and all the members of the scheme are directors of the company and either:

   – the provisions of the scheme provide that any decision made by the company in its capacity as trustee is made only by the unanimous agreement of the directors who are members of the scheme; or

   – one of the directors is a trustee who is independent in relation to the scheme for the purposes of *section 23* of *PA 1995* and is on the Regulator's register;

- a scheme under which the only benefits provided for (other than defined contributions benefits) are death benefits, if the death benefits are secured by insurance policies or annuity contracts;

- a scheme which is the subject of a scheme failure notice under *section 122* or *130* of *PA 2004* (PPF);

- a scheme which is being wound up (see 11.32 below), or

- the Chatsworth Settlement Estate Pension Scheme.

The new overriding statutory funding requirement is set out in *section 222* of *PA 2004*. It requires that a scheme must have 'sufficient and appropriate assets to cover its technical provisions'. The term 'technical provisions' means the 'amount required, on an actuarial calculation, to make provision for the scheme's liabilities'.

PA 2004 includes little detail about how the SFO will work in practice. The *Scheme Funding Regulations* set down some requirements as to how to value assets and liabilities. The technical provisions are to be calculated in accordance with prescribed methods and assumptions. The *Scheme Funding Regulations* require that this must be an 'accrued benefits funding method' but it will be for the trustees to decide exactly which methods and assumptions are used for their scheme. In reaching this decision, the trustees will have to take into account certain matters. This will include taking advice from the actuary and in most cases obtaining the employer's agreement (see 11.28 below).

The statement of funding principles

11.21 Trustees will be required to prepare, and from time to time review and if necessary revise, a statement of funding principles. This is a written statement setting out the trustees' policy for securing that the SFO is met.

Certain details to be included in the statement are set out in *section 223* of *PA 2004*. In particular, it must record any decisions by the trustees about the actuarial methods and assumptions to be used for calculating the scheme's technical provisions and the period within which any failure to meet the SFO is to be made good. *Regulation 6* of the *Scheme Funding Regulations* lists further matters to be covered in the statement and sets out the timescales within which the statement has to be prepared, reviewed and if necessary revised (see 11.27 below).

Actuarial valuations and reports

11.22 Currently trustees are usually only required to obtain an MFR actuarial valuation every three years. *Section 224* of *PA 2004* requires trustees either: (a) to obtain an actuarial valuation annually, or (b) if they obtain 'actuarial reports' each year, they can obtain an actuarial valuation every three years.

An actuarial report is a written report from the scheme actuary 'on developments affecting the scheme's technical provisions since the last actuarial valuation was prepared'.

The trustees must ensure that the SFO actuarial valuation or actuarial report is obtained by them within a prescribed period after the effective date. The *Scheme Funding Regulations* specify 15 months (but see 11.27 below). The trustees are then obliged to ensure that a copy is made available to the employer within seven days of the trustees receiving it.

Certification of technical provisions

11.23   *Section 225* of *PA 2004* requires that when an actuarial valuation is carried out, the calculation of the technical provisions must be certified by the scheme actuary. The actuary must certify that, in his opinion, the calculation of the technical provisions complies with the *Scheme Funding Regulations*. The certificate must also include the actuary's estimate of the solvency of the scheme (*regulation 7(4)* of the *Scheme Funding Regulations*). This will usually be on a buy-out basis but, where this is not possible, the actuary may substitute an alternative appropriate basis. The certificate should be included as part of the actuarial valuation document (see 11.22 above).

If the actuary cannot certify that the relevant legal requirements have been satisfied, he must report the matter in writing to the Regulator within a reasonable period following receipt of the valuation by the trustees. The Code of Practice proposes ten working days as a reasonable period.

Recovery plan

11.24   As with MFR, there is statutory provision for making good any shortfall. Where an actuarial valuation shows that the SFO is not met on the effective date, *section 226* of *PA 2004* requires that the trustees prepare a recovery plan or, if there is already a recovery plan in place, review and revise the existing plan as necessary. The recovery plan must set out the steps to be taken to meet the SFO and the period over which this is to be achieved. The recovery plan must be 'appropriate having regard to the nature and circumstances of the scheme' (*section 226(3)* of *PA 2004*). The recovery plan must include provisions for it to be reviewed and revised (for example, following a further actuarial valuation).

Regulation 8 of the *Scheme Funding Regulations* requires the trustees to take account of the following:

- the asset and liability structure of the scheme;
- its risk profile;
- its liquidity requirements; and
- the age profile of the members.

The Code of Practice provides that when devising a recovery plan trustees should aim to eliminate the shortfall as quickly as the employer can reasonably afford. The trustees should ensure that the recovery plan is appropriate for the scheme. The Code of Practice lists matters the trustees should take into account including:

- the employer's business plan and the likely effect any recovery plan would have on future viability;
- the scheme's membership profile and any proposed changes;
- the ability of the trustees to pursue an employer should the scheme wind up;
- the employer's expenditure commitments; and
- the likely outcome for members of the employer's insolvency.

The recovery plan must include the date by which the shortfall is expected to be eliminated (*section 226(2)* of *PA 2004*). The Code of Practice suggests that it should also include the date by which the amount of additional contributions to be made is half the amount of all the contributions due under the recovery plan (i e when half the shortfall will be eliminated). A copy of the recovery plan has to be sent to the Regulator except in certain circumstances as set out in the regulations. Failure by trustees to take all reasonable steps to comply with this requirement can lead to civil penalties.

Schedule of contributions

11.25 It will continue to be necessary for trustees to prepare, and from time to time review, a schedule of contributions (*section 227* of *PA 2004*). The schedule of contributions will have to show:

- the rates of contributions payable by the employer and active members of the scheme; and
- the due dates on or before which the contributions have to be paid.

The actuary is required to certify that the schedule of contributions is consistent with the statement of funding principles and either:

- the scheme meets the SFO and can be expected to do so for the period covered by the schedule; or

- the scheme can be expected to meet the SFO by the end of that period.

If the actuary is unable to give this certificate, a report has to be made to the Regulator. Where the SFO was not met on the effective date of the most recent actuarial valuation, the trustees will need to submit the schedule to the Regulator. The schedule must be signed by the trustees. Where employer consent is required (see 11.28 below) the schedule must also be signed by the employer.

Where the actuary considers that because of the possibility of significant changes in the value of scheme assets or technical provisions since the effective date of the latest valuation he is unable to certify the schedule as described above, he may sign a modified certificate. The form of the modified certificate is set out in *Schedule 1* to the *Scheme Funding Regulations*.

The schedule of contributions must be sent to the Regulator within a 'reasonable period' of its completion. The Code of Practice suggests that this would be within ten days of the actuary certifying the schedule.

Failure to make payments

11.26   Requirements, similar to those which apply under MFR, provide for the trustees to report late payment of contributions that are due under a schedule of contributions. *Section 228* of *PA 2004* requires a report of late payment to be made to the Regulator and the members where the trustees have reasonable cause to believe that the failure to pay on time is 'likely to be of material significance in the exercise by the Regulator of any of its functions'. The Code of Practice sets out situations which are likely to be of material significance. These include where the employer appears to have been involved in fraudulent evasion, where there is an immediate risk to members' benefits and where contributions remain unpaid for 90 days. Situations unlikely to be of material significance include failures stemming from administrative lapses which have been remedied and cases where a claim has been made to the Redundancy Payments Service. Reports to the Regulator should usually be made within ten working days, or earlier where an immediate report is required. Reports to members should be made within one month.

As under the MFR, any contributions that remain unpaid become a debt due from the employer to the trustees (*section 228(3)* of *PA 2004*).

Timing

11.27   The *Scheme Funding Regulations* set out an overall 'longstop' period of 15 months from the effective date of the actuarial valuation in which the trustees must obtain the actuarial valuation, produce a statement of funding principles, set a schedule of contributions and (if necessary) produce a recovery plan. Schemes with an effective date for valuation between 22 September 2005 and 29 December 2005 have an overall period of 18 months. This is so that those schemes should not be prejudiced by the delay in implementing the legislation.

The Code of Practice suggests that trustees draw up an action plan factoring in time for contingencies and to make allowance for taking actuarial advice, reaching agreement with the employer (from April 2006 the employer may be required to consult employees (see chapter 7) and considering any recovery plan.

Role of the employer

11.28   The intention behind the new scheme funding requirements is for there to be a partnership approach with the trustees working with the employer to develop an appropriate funding strategy for their scheme. A number of the requirements set out in the legislation are primarily the responsibility of the trustees. However, under *section 229* of *PA 2004*, trustees are required to obtain the consent of the employer in relation to the following key issues:

- any decision about the methods and assumptions underlying the technical provisions;
- the content of the statement of funding principles;
- any recovery plan; and
- the schedule of contributions.

A universal requirement for employer consent in relation to the schedule of contributions would cut across any existing trustee powers in the scheme rules to set contributions without reference to the employer. This point was debated at length as the provisions of *PA 2004* were going through Parliament. Baroness Hollis of Heigham, the Government spokesman in the House of Lords confirmed:

> '… where trustees already have the power, it will not be diluted. Where employers have full power there will in future be a collaborative process between the employer and the trustee.'

In order to seek to achieve this, the *Scheme Funding Regulations* modify the provisions of *PA 2004*, depending on the provisions in the scheme rules on setting the contribution rate (*Schedule 2, paragraph 9* of the *Scheme Funding Regulations*):

- where the trustees have unrestrained power under the scheme rules to determine contribution rates (and no one else is permitted to reduce the rate or suspend contributions) then the consent requirements set out above are replaced by a requirement for the trustees to *consult* with the employer only;

- where the trustees have power, subject to conditions, to set the contribution rate (and no one else is permitted to reduce the rate or suspend contributions) then, providing the conditions are satisfied, the consent requirements set out above are replaced by a requirement for the trustees to *consult* with the employer only.

The Regulations also impose the following additional conditions:

- Where the scheme rules provide for the contribution rate to be determined by or 'in accordance with the advice of' someone other than the trustees, and without the agreement of the employer, then the trustees must obtain the employer's consent and the trustees must take account of the recommendations of that other person on the methods and assumptions for calculating the technical provisions and on the preparation of any recovery plan (but not the schedule of contributions itself or the statement of funding principles) (*regulations 5(3)* and *8(2)(e)* of the *Scheme Funding Regulations*). Issues may arise as to what is meant in the *Regulations* by 'in accordance with the advice of'. Will it apply only in cases where the trustees are bound by the scheme rules to follow the advice, or will it also catch schemes where the trustees are obliged only to take into account that advice but retain a discretion to make the determination themselves? In the latter case, the trustees may then be obliged only to consult with the employer (under *section 229*, as modified by *Schedule 2, paragraph 9* of the *Scheme Funding Regulations*) and follow the recommendations of the other person. The impact of the modifications is not clear; further guidance from the Regulator on this point is awaited and ultimately it may in some cases be an issue on which the courts must decide.

- Where the scheme actuary has the power under the scheme rules to determine the contribution rate without the agreement of the employer then the trustees must determine the rate with the consent of the employer (in accordance with *section 229* of *PA 2004*) with an additional requirement that the actuary may only certify the schedule of contributions if the contributions are no less than they would have been had the actuary determined the rate (*Schedule 2, paragraph 9(5)* of the *Scheme Funding Regulations*).

In many schemes the application of the above provisions may not be straightforward and detailed advice may be required at the outset in order to establish which procedures the trustees are required to adopt.

Where it is necessary to obtain the consent of the employer, what happens where the employer does not agree? There are two consequences of failing to agree which are set out in *section 229* of *PA 2004*:

- the trustees may modify future service accrual by resolution, with the employer's consent; and

- the trustees must report the failure to agree to the Regulator who has wide powers to intervene.

Where modification for future accrual is being considered and the trustees have power under the scheme rules to fix contributions, then they need only consult the employer with regard to the proposed changes (*Schedule 2, paragraph 9* of the *Scheme Funding Regulations*). Any modification must not affect subsisting rights. Modifications must be in writing and must be notified to the active members within one month of the modification taking effect. Where trustees have unilateral power of amendment under the scheme's trust deed and rules then this is may not be diluted by *section 229* and in those circumstances the trustees could exercise the power of amendment without the consent of or consulting the employer.

With effect from April 2006 employers may have to consult with employees on certain 'listed changes' to pension schemes (see chapter 7). The draft Regulations on employer consultation include modifications made under *section 229* as a 'listed change' and, if the Regulations are enacted in their present form, consultation will be required for relevant employers (the draft Regulations require employers with over 150 employees to consult from 6 April 2006). Trustees should ensure that they allow sufficient time for any statutory consultation (a minimum of 60 days) within the overall 15-month period for putting the funding arrangements in place. In any event, trustees and employers would need carefully to consider the employee relations consequences (and possible legal consequences in relation to contracts of employment) of such a change before going ahead.

Role of the actuary

11.29   *Section 230* of *PA 2004* sets out certain circumstances where trustees must obtain the advice of an actuary. The trustees must obtain advice before:

- making any decision about the methods and assumptions to be used in calculating the scheme's technical provisions;

- preparing or revising the statement of funding principles;

- preparing or revising a recovery plan;

- preparing or revising the schedule of contributions; and

- modifying the scheme as regards future accrual of benefits in the event of failure to agree with the employer.

The Regulations require the actuary to have regard to professional guidance. The Institute and Faculty of Actuaries has issued GN49 dealing with this.

As mentioned in 11.28 above, where the actuary has the power under the scheme rules to fix the contribution rate then the Regulations provide for the trustees to fix the rate with the consent of the employer with an additional requirement that the actuary must certify that the contributions are no less than they would have been had the actuary fixed the rate. In addition, where the scheme rules require that the contribution rate be determined by, or on the advice of, someone other than the trustees or employer then that person's recommendations (and in many cases that person will be the actuary) must be taken into account when calculating the technical provisions and preparing a recovery plan.

Powers of the Regulator

11.30   The Regulator has a range of new powers designed to ensure that the new scheme funding requirements are complied with by trustees and employers. These powers are set out in *section 231* of *PA 2004* and include the ability to modify future service benefits and to impose a schedule of contributions, a statement of funding principles or a recovery plan where the trustees have failed fully to comply with the statutory requirements.

The Regulator's Code of Practice provides guidance on the steps that it expects the trustees to take in order to reach agreement with the employer before reporting to the Regulator.

In October 2005 the Regulator issued a draft statement on how it intends exercising its powers in relation to scheme funding. It sets out the principles underpinning its regulatory approach and deals with how it might identify schemes which pose the greatest risk.

The suggested principles under which it will operate are:

- **protecting members** – schemes should aim to be funded so that they can pay all benefits promised to members as they fall due;

- **scheme specific** – each scheme needs to take account of its specific circumstances, including the strength of the employer;

- **risk-based** – regulatory function should be focused on those schemes that pose the greatest risk (see below);

- **proportionate** – trustees are required to correct any shortfall as quickly as the employer can reasonably afford;
- **preventative** – where possible, to act before risks materialise;
- **practicable** – to operate within the constraints of the information and resources available and to minimise additional burdens on schemes;
- **referee not player** – it is the responsibility of trustees and employers, with the help of their advisers, to ensure that schemes are fully funded.

In order to identify schemes at risk the proposal is that the Regulator will look for two triggers, one based on a scheme's funding target and the other based on the recovery plan. The draft statement proposes that the funding trigger will be schemes where the funding target is between 70 per cent and 80 per cent of full buy out. The triggers the Regulator will look for in relation to recovery plans are:

- the recovery period is ten years or longer;
- the recovery period is less than ten years but the employer could reasonably eliminate the shortfall in a shorter period; or
- the recovery plan is significantly back end loaded.

Where the Regulator does decide to investigate further it may:

- ask the trustees to demonstrate they have taken all appropriate factors into account;
- scrutinise the assumptions in the light of actuarial advice;
- consider the specific circumstances of the scheme and the employer;
- consider whether the trustees or employer have taken any other steps to mitigate funding risk.

The Regulator has confirmed that it will be publishing specimen scheme funding documents (including a statement of funding principles and a schedule of contributions). These are available on the Regulator's website, www.thepensionsregulator.gov.uk.

Multi employer schemes

11.31 The *Scheme Funding Regulations* modify *PA 2004* so that where there is a sectionalised scheme the SFO provisions apply to each section as if it were a separate scheme. A sectionalised scheme is one where contributions and assets are allocated to a particular section and cannot be used for the purposes of any other section.

For non-sectionalised multi-employer schemes provision is made for a single employer (nominated by the other employers or under the scheme rules) to agree matters with the trustees. If no nomination is made then the agreement of all employers must be sought (subject to 1.9 above). An employer may waive its right to agree to the modification of future accrual. [*Schedule 2, paragraphs 1 and 2 of the Scheme Funding Regulations*].

Schemes in winding up

11.32   Schemes which commence winding up before 30 December 2005 will not be subject to the new scheme funding regime. Schemes which commence winding up on or after 30 December 2005 are subject to a limited requirement to obtain from the scheme actuary an annual estimate of the solvency position. [*regulation 18 of the Scheme Funding Regulations*].

Schemes with fewer than 100 members

11.33   Schemes with fewer than 100 members on the effective date of the most recent actuarial valuation made under SFO need not obtain annual actuarial reports nor issue annual funding statements between their triennial valuations. If the membership reaches 100 at any time during a year then an annual report will be required. Members for this purpose include active, deferred, pensioner and pension credit members. [*Schedule 2, paragraph 11 of the Scheme Funding Regulations*].

Cross-border schemes – European Union

11.34   Stricter funding requirements apply to these schemes. The European *Directive 2003/41/EC on the Activities and Supervision of Institutions for Occupational Retirement Provisions* ('IORP') requires that a scheme operating cross border within the EU must be 'fully funded at all times'. The *Scheme Funding Regulations* require that such schemes must meet the SFO requirements at all times and have annual actuarial valuations, each valuation must be signed by the actuary and received by the trustees within one year of its effective date. Schemes already operating cross-border as at 30 December 2005 have until 22 September 2008 to become fully funded. The Regulator may revoke cross-border authorisation for cross-border schemes falling below SFO where it is of the view that the SFO will not be met within two years of the effective date of the relevant actuarial valuation. [*Schedule 2, paragraph 6 of the Scheme Funding Regulations*].

Transfer values – removal of MFR underpin

11.35 Under the MFR regime cash equivalent transfer values could not be reduced below the MFR level. The *Scheme Funding Regulations* have removed this underpin with effect from 30 December 2005, not only for schemes which have adopted the SFO, but also for schemes still operating under MFR. [*Schedule 3, paragraph 5* of the *Scheme Funding Regulations*].

Contracting out

11.36 Where a scheme is contracted out on the 'reference scheme' basis, either the resources of the scheme must be sufficient to enable the scheme to meet the statutory funding objective provided for in *section 222(1)* of *PA 2004*, or the actuary must have certified that in his opinion the rates shown in the schedule of contributions are such that the statutory funding objective can be expected to be met by the end of the period specified in the recovery plan. [*Occupational Pension Schemes (Contracting-Out) Regulations 1996 (SI 1996 No 1172), reg 18*]. Schemes still operating under MFR must either satisfy the MFR test, or must be on track to satisfy the test by reference to the schedule of contributions.

Reporting to the Regulator

11.37 The following must be reported to the Regulator:

- The actuary must report if he is unable to certify that the calculation of technical provisions is made in accordance with the Regulations. The Code of Practice suggests that this should be done within ten working days of the deadline for certifying the technical provisions.

- The actuary must report if he is unable to certify the schedule of contributions. The Code of Practice suggests that this should be done within ten working days of the deadline for certifying the schedule.

- A copy of any recovery plan must be sent (see 11.24 above).

- Failure to pay in accordance with the schedule of contributions (see 11.26 above).

- Failure to agree any matter with the employer (see 11.28 above).

Failure to report could give rise to civil penalties.

Disclosure to members – annual funding statement

11.38 The *Scheme Funding Regulations* include amendments to the *1996 Disclosure Regulations* which provide for an annual funding statement to be sent as a matter of course to all members and beneficiaries of schemes subject to the SFO. The *1996 Disclosure Regulations* are due to be replaced, with effect from 6 April 2006, by new *Disclosure Regulations* but it is likely that these new provisions will be included in similar form in those new Regulations. The annual funding statement must contain:

- a summary, based on the most recent valuation, of the extent to which the assets were sufficient to cover the technical provisions;

- an explanation of any change in the funding position since the date of the last funding statement (or in the case of the first funding statement, since the last actuarial valuation);

- an estimate by the actuary of the solvency position (buy out) as contained in the most recent valuation;

- a summary of any recovery plan;

- information as to whether the scheme has been modified at the direction of the Regulator, or subject to directions of and or bound by a schedule of contributions imposed by the Regulator together with an explanation of the circumstances in which this occurred;

- whether any payment of surplus has been made to the employer; and

- a statement that further information about the scheme is available, and the address from where it can be obtained.

The trustees must make available to members and beneficiaries on request (either to inspect or provide copies):

- the statement of funding principles;

- actuarial valuations and reports;

- any recovery plan; and

- the certified schedule of contributions.

Transitional provisions

11.39   The broad policy of the DWP is said to be to minimise additional administrative costs by allowing trustees to bring in SFO in line with their existing valuation cycles. The transitional provisions and savings are set out in *Schedule 4* to the *Scheme Funding Regulations*. Schemes that wish to transfer to SFO earlier may bring forward their valuation dates if appropriate.

Schemes will be required to obtain their first SFO valuation with reference to an effective date no later than the third anniversary of their last MFR valuation preceding 22 September 2005. The latest effective date for an SFO valuation should therefore be 22 September 2008. Schemes then have 15 months in which to put in place all the elements of the SFO. So the latest that SFO will be up and running should be 22 December 2009.

Where there is no previous MFR valuation, schemes will be required to obtain an SFO valuation with an effective date no later than 30 December 2006.

Schemes with effective dates for valuation between 22 September 2005 and 29 December 2005 have 18 months in which to put in place all the elements of the SFO.

Where an MFR valuation is required with an effective date before 22 September 2005 the trustees are still required to obtain that valuation and put in place a schedule of contributions in accordance with the MFR requirements, even if the deadline for trustees receiving the valuation falls after 30 December 2005.

The MFR requirements relating to schedules of contributions, record keeping and late contributions will continue to apply until the trustees have put in place a new schedule of contributions following their first SFO valuation.

Where the trustees are required to obtain a new actuarial valuation because the actuary has certified the schedule of contributions to be inadequate (*section 57(2) of PA 1995*), or as a result of an employer leaving a multi-employer scheme, and the trustees decide that the new valuation should have an effective date on or after 22 September 2005, then the new valuation must be obtained on an SFO basis and not MFR.

Extensions to contribution periods approved by Opra prior to 6 April 2005 will still apply. Applications for extensions to contribution schedules relating to an actuarial valuation with an effective date prior to 23 September 2005 may be made to the Regulator.

Other actuarial valuations

11.40 *PA 2004* has introduced two new statutory actuarial valuations. The first, referred to as a '*section 143* valuation', applies only to those schemes being considered for entry to the Pensions Protection Fund ('PPF') and its purpose is to ascertain whether the scheme has sufficient assets to cover its liabilities for benefits at the PPF level as well as the expenses of winding up.

The second is referred to as a '*section 179* valuation' and will be required for all schemes eligible for the PPF for the purpose of calculating each scheme's risk-based levy. Schemes may submit a *section 179* valuation to the PPF by 31 March 2006 if they wish it to be taken into account for the purposes of the 2006/2007 levy. Schemes not submitting a *section 179* valuation by that date will be assessed on the basis of a modified version of the most recent MFR valuation. It is intended by the PPF that all schemes will be required to submit a full *section 179* valuation by 31 March 2008. Trustees should consider discussing with their actuary the relative merits of submitting an MFR valuation or *section 179* valuation in relation to 2006/2007 and 2007/2008.

Schemes in deficit

11.41 The position of deficits in schemes in winding-up, or where an employer ceases to participate, is dealt with in chapter 12.

There are also a number of consequences for an ongoing scheme which is in deficit. The exact impact will depend upon the basis upon which the deficit has been assessed. For example:

- schemes in deficit on an SFO basis will be subject to a recovery plan (see 11.24 above) and those with a funding target of less than 70 or 80 per cent of full buy out may come under the scrutiny of the Regulator (see 11.30 above);

- schemes funded at less than 125 per cent on a PPF (*section 179*) basis (see 11.40 above) will be subject to the PPF risk based levy, and the greater the deficit, the higher the levy will be subject to a cap (proposed at 0.5 per cent of liabilities);

- schemes showing a deficit on an MFR or *section 179* basis will be required to report more notifiable events than those which do not (see 2.14 above);

- schemes showing a deficit on an FRS17 basis may be subject to clearance applications under the moral hazard provisions (see 11.30 above).

What is a surplus?

11.42 Although the expression 'surplus' is widely used, it is not a legally defined term and often has misleading connotations. By way of a general definition, a surplus is said to exist when the actuarially estimated value of a scheme's assets at a certain date exceeds the actuarially estimated value of its liabilities at that date.

When a scheme is winding up, a surplus is easy to identify as the cost of securing the liabilities of the scheme in a given manner will ultimately be known, as will the value of the assets of the scheme. On a winding-up, a surplus will exist if there are any funds remaining after all the benefits have been secured.

The position is different with an ongoing scheme as the actuary will have to make certain assumptions as to future events. Depending on the method adopted and the assumptions used for the valuation, a scheme could be either in deficit or in surplus at any given time. A 'surplus' in an ongoing scheme is therefore simply the actuary's prediction, based on a given method and on a certain set of assumptions that the scheme will have more than sufficient assets to cover its liabilities over a certain period.

An employer may tend to see a surplus in an ongoing scheme as representing past overfunding. Trustees may see it as representing a reserve fund, providing security in the event of the cost of the benefits being more than the actuary anticipated or the investments of the scheme failing to perform to the level hoped for. Members, on the other hand, will sometimes regard a surplus in an ongoing scheme as 'spare' money that could be used for immediate benefit increases. However, arguably there can be no certainty of a surplus unless and until the scheme is wound up and all benefits secured. Any surplus in an ongoing scheme is notional as any number of events could happen which would totally eradicate it.

Why surpluses are an issue

11.43   During the 1980s a huge growth in the value of investments, coupled with a reduction in the workforce, led to many schemes having substantial surpluses. Where these forces combined to produce a large surplus in a scheme, even the suspension of contributions by employers and employees was sometimes insufficient to eliminate it over a foreseeable period. Many employers began to look for ways to extract what appeared to be unrequired assets in their pension schemes.

At the same time, the Government became concerned that the tax advantages conferred on occupational pension schemes meant that it was losing valuable tax revenue from the assets in these overfunded schemes. The *Finance Act 1986* removed some of the tax advantages available to schemes with excessive surpluses by imposing tax on the income and gains arising from scheme assets in excess of a certain prescribed limit. Some employers saw the introduction of the legislation as a mandate to remove a surplus from a scheme. Others were encouraged to take contribution holidays or improve scheme benefits to eradicate surplus.

The combination of the factors outlined above caused some members and trustees of pension schemes to become increasingly concerned that employers were unjustly appropriating part of their schemes' funds, resulting in the reduction of scheme security and the loss of any possibility of increased benefits. Consequently the treatment of a surplus in an ongoing scheme gave rise to controversy and continues to do so.

In recent years surplus has become much less of an issue as many defined benefit schemes have moved into deficit.

Who owns a surplus?

Ongoing schemes

11.44   Although a surplus in an ongoing scheme may be considered notional, the debate over the ways in which such a surplus can be used is very real. In most defined benefits schemes the employer's contribution will be the balance of the cost of providing the benefits promised. One of the easiest ways of dealing with a surplus is, therefore, simply to adjust the employer's contribution rate. However, trustees and beneficiaries may argue that if there is a surplus in a scheme it will not necessarily have arisen because the employer has paid excessive contributions; it could be due to high investment growth on the assets purchased by both the employer's and members' contributions or to members leaving a scheme at a faster rate than that assumed by the actuary for the purposes of his valuation. In such a situation the issue of who owns the surplus is inevitably raised.

There have been a number of cases in which the courts have been asked to consider the use of a surplus and, in particular, the members' right to share in the surplus. These cases have generally recognised that, in a defined benefits scheme where an employer would be required to meet any deficit it would be inequitable for the employer not to benefit at all from any surplus. There has, however, been a gradual shift away from the proposition that any surplus belongs solely to the employer while the scheme is ongoing.

In *Re Courage Group's Pension Schemes [1987] 1 All ER 528* the view of Millet J (as he then was) was that although members did not have an absolute legal right to participate in the surplus in their scheme, they were entitled to have the surplus dealt with by consultation and negotiation between them and the employer. He rejected the argument that members were entitled, as of right, to a contributions holiday, directing that any surplus arising from past overfunding in a balance of cost scheme did not arise from the employer and members pro rata, but arose primarily from the employer. The judge did, however, draw a distinction between the employer using a surplus to fund a contributions holiday and it requiring a payment out of the scheme. In the latter situation the trustees could, and should, press for generous treatment of members and the employer could be expected to be influenced by the desire to maintain good industrial relations with its workforce.

When considering how to deal with a surplus, it should be remembered that an employer can have regard to its own interests (financial and otherwise) but only to the extent that in doing so it does not breach the obligation of good faith to its employees (*Imperial Group Pension Trust Ltd v Imperial Tobacco Ltd [1991] 2 All ER 597*). (See chapter 7 for discussion of the employer's obligations in this regard.)

The issue of who owns a surplus continues to be subject to debate. The starting point should of course be the terms of the trust deed and rules of the particular scheme. The position would currently seem to be that members may have a legitimate expectation of benefit improvements, particularly where the trustees have a discretion as to the use of a surplus and there is a possibility of a payment to the employer, but this is not to say that they have an absolute right to any surplus. When considering the use of a surplus the employer is, however, obliged to keep an open mind and consider arguments put forward on behalf of the members. (See *Stannard v Fisons Pension Trust Ltd [1992] 1 PLR 27* and *LRT Pension Fund Trustee Co Ltd v Hatt [1993] PLR 227*.) Much will depend on the respective powers of the trustees and the employer under the scheme's governing documentation and the relative bargaining position of the parties.

The Goode Committee Report pointed out 'if employers were to be debarred from taking contribution holidays, they might well feel impelled to freeze the scheme or wind it up altogether and, in relation to new schemes, to fund at a level designed to avoid a surplus arising'. This point was accepted by the judge in *The National Grid Company plc v Laws [1997] PLR 157*, who said:

'... any general exclusion of employers from surplus would tend to make employers very reluctant to contribute to their pension schemes more than the bare minimum that they could get away with. That would be unfortunate, and it would be even more unfortunate if employers were driven to abandon defined benefits, balance of cost schemes and were instead to turn to defined contributions schemes which may in the long term prove less advantageous to the beneficiaries.'

Since 1997 the *National Grid* case progressed to the Court of Appeal and, in 2001, to the House of Lords. The Court of Appeal best summarised the current law on the matter with the words:

'The solution lies within the terms of the scheme itself, and not within a world populated by competing philosophies as to the true nature and ownership of actuarial surplus.'

This view was supported by the Court of Appeal in the *Stevens v Bell (British Airways) [2002] PLR 247* case. The judgement again explored the use of surplus although the emphasis was again placed on the specific construction of the relevant trust documentation.

Interestingly, despite Myners' suggestion that the Law Commission should review the issues involved in the ownership of surpluses, the Government, in the Green Paper 'Simplicity, Security and Choice: Working and Saving for Retirement', concluded that for the time being there will be no steps made towards legislation. This may, in part, be due to the fact that in the current economic climate surpluses have become less of a concern.

Schemes which are winding up

11.45 A scheme's trust deed and rules will generally include a rule setting out how the fund is to be distributed on a winding-up. This rule should include a provision relating to how any assets remaining after all the liabilities have been secured are to be used. Usually there will be a power to increase benefits up to HMRC limits and/or make a payment to the employer. It is important to check whether this power is given to the employer, or to the trustees, or to both jointly. In some instances the provision will simply provide that all assets remaining should be paid to the employer.

If the rules do not contain provisions regarding the use of a surplus, perhaps because the scheme is being wound up whilst still governed by interim documentation, the general principles of trust law will have to be considered. Essentially, where funds are transferred to a trust and it subsequently transpires that those funds are not needed for the purposes of the trust, the trustees hold those funds for the benefit of the person who provided them on a 'resulting trust'. A resulting trust does not arise where the person who provided the money never intended to receive any of it back, so if the rules of the scheme specifically provide that no payment can be made to an employer (on a winding-up or otherwise) a resulting trust cannot arise.

How a surplus should be dealt with in the absence of a valid rule was considered by Scott J in *Davis v Richards Wallington Industries Ltd [1991] 2 All ER 563*. A resulting trust in favour of the members of the scheme was excluded largely on the grounds that, as the scheme provided salary related benefits, two members who paid in the same monetary amount in contributions could be entitled to benefits of a different value. A resulting trust was therefore unworkable as between the different groups of beneficiaries. A resulting trust in respect of transfer payments was also excluded; it was clear that the transferring schemes were divesting themselves once and for all of the transferred funds and had not intended to receive any of it back. Consequently any resulting trust had to be in favour of the employer.

Consideration was also given by Scott J as to how much of the surplus derived from employer contributions, how much from the contributions of members and how much from transfer values. In his opinion, it was wrong to consider that the surplus was attributable to all three sources proportionately. The employer's obligation was to pay whatever was necessary to fund the benefits over and above that provided from other sources. It was, therefore, logical to treat the benefits as being funded first by the contributions made by members and by the transfer payments and only secondly by the employer's contributions. Consequently any surplus was to be treated as being provided first and foremost by the employer's contributions.

HMRC requirements relating to the reduction of surpluses

11.46   Considerable tax advantages are available in respect of exempt approved occupational pension schemes. An employer is entitled to deduct contributions made to such schemes before calculating its profits for tax purposes, and the income and gains of such a scheme are generally not taxable. When large surpluses arose during the 1980s, the Government, concerned at the loss of potential tax revenue, introduced measures to ensure that the tax advantages available to pension schemes with large surpluses were restricted. These measures were consolidated in *sections 601* to *603* of, and *Schedule 22* to, the *Income and Corporation Taxes Act 1988* and the *Pension Scheme Surpluses (Valuation) Regulations 1987 (SI 1987 No 412)* ('the *Surplus Regulations*'). These provisions set down detailed requirements for the valuation of surpluses and the procedures for reducing them.

This legislation is due to be repealed with effect from 6 April 2006 (see 5.1 above) and will be replaced with a straightforward tax charge of 35 per cent on payments to employers (*sections 177* and *207* of *FA 2004*) combined with the requirements of *section 37* of *PA 1995* (see 11.47 below).

Pensions Act 2004 – position from 6 April 2006

Ongoing schemes

11.47   *Section 37* of *PA 1995* introduced with effect from 6 April 1997 certain requirements which had to be satisfied before a repayment of surplus could be made to an employer. These included an increase in all pensions by 5 per cent LPI and requirements to give advance notice to members. Further details were set out in the *Occupational Pension Schemes (Payments to Employers) Regulations 1996 (SI 1996 No 2156)*.

Section 250 of *PA 2004* substitutes a new *section 37* of *PA 1995*. This provision is due to come into force on 6 April 2006. The new *section 37* provides that where power is conferred on the employer, or any other person, to make payments to the employer then that power may be exercised only by the trustees. The power to repay surplus may only be exercised if:

- the trustees have obtained a written valuation prepared and signed by an actuary (usually the scheme actuary);

- there is a certificate in force which meets prescribed requirements (see below) and specifies the maximum amount which may be paid to the employer;

- the payment does not exceed the maximum amount specified in the certificate;

- the trustees are satisfied that it is in the interests of the members that the power is exercised in the manner proposed;

- there is no freezing order in force under *section 23* of *PA 2004*; and

- notices have been given to members in accordance with prescribed requirements.

The draft *Occupational Pension Scheme (Payments to Employer) Regulations 2006* (the 'draft *Payments to Employers Regulations*') were issued for consultation in January 2006. The draft *Payments to Employers Regulations* provide that valuation methods similar to those under the *Scheme Funding Regulations* should be adopted. Alternatively trustees may rely on an SFO valuation (see 11.22 above) for 15 months from the effective date of the valuation. The maximum amount of any refund payment to the employer will be the amount by which the value of the assets exceeds the estimated costs of full buy out (*regulation 6* of the draft *Payments to Employers Regulations*).

Where the trustees intend making a payment to the employer then the draft prescribed requirements for the notice (*regulation 10* of the draft *Payments to Employers Regulations*) are:

- a statement that the trustees have decided to make a payment;

- the payment amount;

- the date the payment is to be made (at least three months from the date of the notice);

- a statement that the trustees are satisfied that it is in the best interests of the members, and the reason for that view;

- a copy of the relevant valuation certificate; and

- a statement that the scheme is not subject to a freezing order.

Where a payment is made notice must be given to the Regulator within one week (*regulation 11* of the draft *Payments to Employers Regulations*).

Where the scheme is an insured money purchase scheme a payment may be made to the employer where all the liabilities in respect of the relevant member, beneficiary or estate have been satisfied and there are assets remaining in relation to that member (*regulation 7* of the draft *Payments to Employers Regulations*).

Transitional powers in *section 251* of *PA 2004* provide trustees with a power to amend existing scheme rules to allow payments in accordance with the new *section 37*. Any such amendments must be made within five years of the provisions coming into force and are subject to notice being given to the employer and members.

Schemes in winding up

11.48   If an exempt approved scheme commences winding up on or after 6 April 1997, any power which is conferred on the employer or the trustees to distribute assets to the employer on a winding up, cannot be exercised unless the requirements set out in *sections 76* and *77* of *PA 1995* and *regulations 7 to 10* of the *Occupational Pension Schemes (Payments to Employers) Regulations 1996 (SI 1996 No 2156)* are satisfied. These can be summarised as follows:

(*a*)   the liabilities of the scheme must have been fully discharged;

(*b*)   where there is any power under the scheme to distribute surplus assets to any person other than the employer, that power must have been exercised or a decision must have been made not to exercise it;

(*c*)   the annual rate of pensions payable under the scheme (excluding any guaranteed minimum pension or any defined contributions benefits) must have been increased by the appropriate percentage (removed from 6 April 2006); and

(*d*)   notice must have been given, in accordance with the prescribed requirements, to members of the scheme of the proposal to exercise the power.

The notice requirements in respect of a scheme which is winding up are similar to those for ongoing schemes.

The position is slightly different where a scheme contains a prohibition on the distribution of assets to the employers on a winding up (see *section 77* of *PA 1995*). If such a scheme has assets remaining undistributed after all the liabilities have been fully discharged, and after any power to distribute assets has been either exercised or a decision has been made not to exercise it, the trustees must use the remaining assets for the purposes of providing additional benefits or increasing the value of the benefits up to HMRC limits. Only then may the trustees distribute any remaining assets to the employer. There are no notice requirements.

From 6 April 2006, *section of 76 PA 1995* will continue to apply as set out above, with the requirement to increase benefits by an appropriate percentage removed, but the draft *Payment to Employers Regulations* will replace the *Occupational Pension Schemes (Payment to Employers) Regulations 1996 (SI 1996 No 2156)*.

Where the trustees or employer propose to exercise the power to make a payment they must take all reasonable steps to ensure that each member is sent two notices. The first notice must:

- inform the member as to the trustees' estimate of the value of assets remaining and the persons or classes of person to whom it is proposed that they should be distributed and whether the requirements of *section 76(3)* of *PA 1995* are satisfied;

- invite the member to make written representations before a specified date (not earlier than two months from the date the notice is given); and

- advise the member that a second notice will be issued if they intend to proceed with the proposal and that no assets will be distributed until at least three months after the date on which the second notice is furnished to him.

The second notice must:

- contain the information referred to in the first point above, including any modifications to the proposal; and

- advise the member that he may make written representations to the Regulator before a specified date (not earlier than three months from the date on which the second notice is furnished to him) if he considers *section 76(3)* of *PA 1995* is not satisfied.

Where the Regulator receives written representations, or obtains from any other source information sufficient to raise a doubt as to whether the requirements of *section 76(3) PA* of *1995* are satisfied, the Regulator may notify the trustees or employer (as appropriate) that the power should not be exercised until the Regulator has confirmed in writing that he is satisfied. Where the three-month time limit has expired and the trustees or employer have heard nothing from the Regulator, they should ask the Regulator for written confirmation that it has not received any representations or information (draft *regulation 17*).

Schemes with more than one employer

11.49   Where a scheme has more than one employer and is divided into two or more sections and the provisions of the scheme are such that:

(*a*)   different sections of the scheme apply to different employers or groups of employers;

(*b*)   contributions payable to the scheme by an employer or by its employees are allocated to that section; and (*c*)   a specified part or a proportion of the assets of the scheme is attributable to each section and cannot be used for the purposes of any other section,

the requirements of the Act relating to payments to the employer for both ongoing schemes and schemes which are winding up apply as if each section of the scheme were a separate scheme. [draft *regulation 8* of the *Payments to Employers Regulations*].

Trust law requirements relating to the reduction of surpluses

Powers under the trust instrument

11.50   Although HMRC permits some flexibility in respect of how a surplus is reduced, the ways in which a reduction may be achieved can be restricted by the terms of a scheme's trust deed and rules. Usually a scheme's governing documentation will be wide enough to let the employer and the trustees decide on benefit improvements or a contributions holiday. However, the trust deeds of many schemes established before 1970 include a restriction on the power of amendment to the effect that no amendment can be made which would permit scheme funds to be paid to the employer. It is debatable whether such a restriction can be validly removed so as to allow a payment to be made to the employer, much will depend on the circumstances of the case and the exact wording of the power of amendment. Before agreeing to a payment to the employer, trustees should carefully check all previous trust deeds to ensure that the power of amendment has not been inappropriately amended in the past.

Even if the amendment is possible, trustees must consider whether, in agreeing to the amendment, they are acting in the best interests of the beneficiaries. Trustees may be faced with the offer of benefit improvements for the beneficiaries in return for making the amendment and subsequently making a payment to the employer. In such a situation, trustees must balance the security of members' interests in the fund against the benefit improvements on offer when deciding whether to agree to the amendment. The decision is not easy and trustees must consider carefully the propriety of making the amendment when the benefit improvements on offer are relatively small.

Exercise of trustees' powers

11.51   Before agreeing to a payment of surplus to the employer (or, where the trust deed requires their agreement, to an employer's contributions holiday) trustees should obtain independent legal advice and should also consider whether they are subject to any conflicts of interest. For example, a trustee who is also a director of the employer may have difficulty maintaining his impartiality and fulfilling his duties as a trustee. In some circumstances it may be necessary to appoint independent trustees.

In exercising their powers, trustees must act in the best interests of the beneficiaries and must act impartially between the different groups of beneficiaries. If, for example, an agreement was reached between the employer and the employees' representatives, it would indicate that active members find the proposal satisfactory, but the trustees would still have to consider the interests of deferred members and pensioners. Trustees have a duty to negotiate the best bargain they can in the circumstances, taking into consideration the relative balance of power between themselves and the principal employer (see *Re Courage Group's Pension Scheme [1987] 1 All ER 528*). The employer also has obligations to the membership; it must ensure that it is not acting in breach of its implied obligation of good faith (see *Imperial Group Pension Trust Ltd v Imperial Tobacco Ltd [1991] 2 All ER 597*). In practice it is difficult to see how the trustees can justify making any payment to the employer unless they have also secured some clear advantage (usually benefit improvements) for the beneficiaries.

Chapter 12

Reconstruction and winding up

Introduction

General

12.1　In this chapter the word 'reconstruction' is used to denote some significant change in the nature or structure of an employer's pension arrangements. Such a reconstruction will typically involve:

(*a*)　a scheme amendment;

(*b*)　a bulk transfer of assets and liabilities between different schemes operated by the same employer (or by employers within the same group); and/or

(*c*)　the winding up of a scheme.

Amendments

12.2　Examples of scheme amendments which are significant enough to be regarded for the purposes of this chapter as reconstructions include:

(*a*)　converting a defined benefits scheme into a defined contributions scheme;

(*b*)　closing a scheme to future entrants;

(*c*)　amending a scheme so that no further benefits accrue under it; or

(*d*)　amending a scheme as part of a wider exercise, so as to enable the parties to make bulk transfer payments to other schemes (see 12.3 below) and/or wind up the scheme (see 12.4 below).

Scheme amendments are dealt with further in 12.8 to 12.21 below.

Bulk transfers

12.3   Bulk transfers of assets and liabilities between schemes operating within the same group of employers have become increasingly common in recent years. Typical cases include:

(*a*)   bulk transfers from a defined benefit scheme to a defined contribution arrangement; or

(*b*)   bulk transfers between defined benefit schemes operating within the same group of employers, so as to replace two or more defined benefit schemes with a single, larger defined benefits scheme. Some of the advantages of having a single, larger scheme are that:

   (i)   it avoids the inefficiency for employers of operating some over-funded schemes and some underfunded schemes;

  (ii)   administrative costs for a single scheme should be lower owing to economies of scale;

 (iii)   a single, larger fund may justify the trustees in pursuing some investment opportunities which might be considered too risky in relation to a smaller fund; and

 (iv)   less time and resources overall need be spent on compliance with statutory requirements as there will be only one scheme (rather than several) in relation to which these requirements need to be met.

Bulk transfers are considered further in 12.30 to 12.47 and 12.64 to 12.69 below.

Winding up

12.4   A winding up occurs when a scheme is terminated and its assets are used to secure the scheme's benefits through other means (typically, by pur-chasing annuities or making transfer payments to other schemes).

The circumstances in which schemes go into winding up are varied, but some examples are:

(*a*)   where the purpose of the winding up is to make a bulk transfer to another scheme, often for one of the purposes referred to in 12.3 above;

(*b*)   where the employers can no longer afford to run the scheme. The employ-ment law implications of this are considered in chapter 7; or

(*c*)   where a scheme (perhaps with few, if any, remaining active members) has become too small to justify the cost of continuing to operate it as a separate scheme.

Winding up is dealt with in more detail at 12.48 to 12.68 below.

Before dealing further with these areas, it is worth looking at some of the key considerations which will determine how far it is possible to achieve a scheme reconstruction.

Key considerations

Powers

12.5   The trustees and the employers need to be certain that they have the necessary powers to carry out any proposed reconstruction. If, for example, the trustees were to accept a bulk transfer from another scheme in circumstances where they had no power under their trust deed to do so, they could subsequently be challenged by the members and held liable for resulting losses even though the trustees had at the time taken all available steps to ensure that the arrangement was in the members' best interests.

The question of whether the parties have the necessary powers will be determined primarily by the scheme's trust deed and rules. If therefore it is intended, for instance, to amend a scheme, it should be checked that the governing documentation does not impose restrictions on the power of amendment which the proposed alteration would infringe.

The *Pensions Act 2004* (*PA 2004*) has a further bearing on whether the parties have the necessary powers. The effect of the Act in some areas is to restrict the exercise of certain powers which a scheme's rules (when read in isolation) appear to confer, and in other areas the effect is to give wider powers to the trustees. For instance:

(*a*)   *section 67* of the *Pensions Act 1995* (*PA 1995*) introduces certain restrictions on the exercise of the power of amendment, which is modified by *section 262* of *PA 2004* with effect from 6 April 2006 (dealt with further in 12.18 below); and

(*b*)   where an approved defined benefit scheme begins to be wound up after 5 April 1997, any power in the trust deed to apply the assets in respect of pensions or other benefits becomes exercisable by the trustees (even if the trust deed confers that power on another party, such as the employer) (*section 73A(9)* of *PA 1995*).

It is not sufficient, however, for the employers and the trustees simply to have the necessary powers to carry out the reconstruction; they must ensure that in exercising those powers they act in a manner consistent with their duties as employers (see 12.6 below) and trustees (see 12.7 below) respectively.

Employers' duties

12.6 Many scheme reconstructions are initiated by employers, often prompted by funding concerns. An employer should ensure that its proposals do not contravene its contractual commitments towards its employees in relation to pensions. These commitments will be set out primarily in employees' written terms and conditions of employment (although references to pensions in such documents are usually brief). There will, in addition, be written announcements or booklets issued to the employees explaining the scheme, which the courts are increasingly inclined to regard as contractually binding. (The legal nature of these written particulars is considered further in 7.2 above.)

Employers are also under an implied contractual duty of good faith (*Imperial Group Pension Trust Ltd v Imperial Tobacco Ltd [1991] 1 WLR 589*). The nature of this duty is that both employers and employees are obliged to act in a manner which is consistent with a relationship of mutual trust and confidence between them. Failure to do so can amount to a breach of contract.

This implied duty of good faith (unlike the more onerous duties placed on trustees) does not require the employer to act solely in the best interests of those to whom the duty is owed; an employer is entitled also to take its own commercial interests into account. It is not possible to give a definitive statement as to what would and would not amount to a breach of that duty. However, the following instances, which can be expected to amount to a breach of the duty of good faith, may be useful as guidelines:

(*a*) a refusal by the employer even to consider (as opposed to considering and then rejecting) alternative proposals put forward by the trustees;

(*b*) putting forward proposals which discriminate between employees (or groups of employees) without justification;

(*c*) threatening to suspend contributions unless the trustees agree to the proposals (*Hillsdown Holdings plc v Pensions Ombudsman (1996) PLR 427*); or

(*d*) threatening never to grant further pension increases unless the parties agree to the proposals (*Imperial Group Pension Trust Ltd v Imperial Tobacco Ltd [1991] 2 All ER 597*).

chapter 7 considers the duty of good faith in further detail (from 7.6 above).

Trustees' duties

12.7 Trustees' powers are of a fiduciary nature, which means that they must exercise them in the best interests of the persons for whose benefit those powers were conferred. In most cases, this will be the scheme's present and past members (and any of their family or dependants who may have an interest in the scheme as a consequence of their membership).

Trustees may also owe a duty towards the employer when exercising certain of their powers. For instance, if the scheme rules give the trustees a discretion to pay surplus assets to the employer on winding up, they must at least take the employer's interest into account. However, their duties towards scheme members are undoubtedly more onerous than an employer's duty of good faith towards its employees (described in 12.6 above).

This mismatch between the trustees' duties and those of the employer can give rise to a potential conflict of interests between the two sides and trustees should, therefore, seek separate advice wherever such a conflict exists. In the absence of separate advice, trustees may find themselves vulnerable to criticism if their decisions are subsequently called into question by scheme members; even if the trustees have acted entirely in their beneficiaries' best interests, it may be harder to convince the Pensions Ombudsman (or a court) of this if independent advice has not been obtained.

The terms of the trust deed (as qualified by *PA 1995* and *PA 2004* – see 12.5 above) will be relevant, in that any conflict is likely to be less of an issue if the trustees simply have no power to do anything other than implement the employer's proposals; however, such instances are rare (and will become even more so in the future as *PA 2004* shifts the balance of power further from the employer to trustees).

Conflicts can arise not only as between employers and trustees, but also as between the trustees of separate schemes. This may happen where a bulk transfer of assets and liabilities from one scheme to another is under consideration, as the trustees of the two schemes will owe their duties to different groups of beneficiaries. Where there is a conflict, separate advice should again be sought.

Amendments

General

12.8 Scheme reconstructions very often involve amending a scheme, either because the reconstruction itself takes the form of a fundamental change to the scheme's rules, or because an amendment is required to enable the employers or the trustees to make (or receive) a bulk transfer and/or wind up the scheme.

The main ways in which an occupational pension scheme may be amended are:

(*a*)   in accordance with a power of amendment contained in the scheme's trust documents;

(*b*)   by a court order;

(*c*)   by means of a modification order granted by the Pensions Regulator ('the Regulator'); or

(*d*)   by a trustees' resolution passed under a specific provision in *PA 1995* or *PA 2004.*

The first of these methods is by far the most common, but it is worth summarising the others before considering the scheme's own power of amendment in more detail.

Court order

12.9   A court order to vary the terms of a trust may be available in the following limited circumstances:

(*a*)   On application by the trustees (or, less likely, a beneficiary) under *section 57* of the *Trustee Act 1925*. The basis for any such application must be that the trustees do not have the necessary investment or administrative powers which they need to deal in some particular way with the trust property. The court will need to be convinced that the proposed transaction is expedient.

(*b*)   On application to the court under the *Variation of Trusts Act 1958*. This Act (which is not normally used in relation to pension schemes) enables the court to approve amendments on behalf of beneficiaries.

(*c*)   Under the court's inherent jurisdiction to vary trusts. The court will generally only exercise this jurisdiction in circumstances where some matter concerning the scheme has in any event come before the court.

Modification orders

12.10   The Regulator has powers under *sections 69* to *71A* of *PA 1995* to grant orders for the modification of occupational schemes (other than public service schemes) in certain circumstances.

There are two purposes for which the Regulator may grant an order in this context (*section 69* of *PA 1995*), as illustrated in the following table.

	Who may apply for order	Orders which may be granted
Where the purpose, in the case of a registered scheme which is being wound up, is to enable assets remaining after the liabilities have been fully discharged to be distributed to the employer (and all other relevant requirements for that distribution have been met).	The trustees.	● Order authorising the trustees to modify the scheme; or ● order modifying the scheme.
Where the purpose is to enable the scheme, for the period from 6 April 1997 to 5 April 1999, to be so treated that an employment to which it applies may be contracted out (see chapter 4).	The trustees, the employer or any person other than the trustees who has power to alter the rules of the scheme.	● Order authorising such persons (not restricted to parties to the application) as the Regulator thinks appropriate to modify the scheme; or ● order modifying the scheme.

The Regulator may only make such an order if it is satisfied that the desired result cannot be achieved without one, or that it can only be achieved in accordance with a procedure which is liable to be unduly complex or protracted (or involves the obtaining of consents which cannot be obtained without undue delay or difficulty) (*section 70* of *PA 1995*).

There is provision for such a modification to be retrospective. The modification order may be made or complied with even if the scheme rules or other legal requirements would otherwise prevent it (*section 71* of *PA 1995*).

Where an application is made to the Regulator under the *Winding up Notices and Reports Regulations* (*SI 2002 No 459*) such application will be subject to the following conditions:

(*a*)   it must set out the modification required and specify what effect (if any) it may have on benefits;

(*b*)   it must specify the reasons for the modification;

(*c*)   it must identify any previous application for a modification order made to a court or to the Regulator;

(*d*)   it must confirm that the employer is subject to an insolvency procedure;

(*e*)   it must specify whether the modification order will reduce the value of the assets; and (*f*)   it must contain a statement that notices have been given to members of the scheme and any other relevant persons together with the relevant date(s) where such notice is given.

A member of the scheme in respect of which a notice has been given has the right to make representation to the Regulator within one month of any notice to request a modification order. Before the Regulator considers any application for a modification order it will require:

(i)   a copy of the documents which govern the scheme;

(ii)   a copy of any actuarial advice on the effect or otherwise of the modification order on the scheme's assets;

(iii)   a copy of any legal advice in relation to the application for a modification order;

(iv)   a copy of any court determination in relation to the application for a modification order or any similar order; and

(v)   a copy of any determination by trustees or managers to wind up the scheme.

Trustees' statutory power to amend

12.11   Subject to limited exceptions (primarily public service schemes), trustees have power under *section 68* of *PA 1995* to amend a scheme by resolution with a view to achieving any of the following purposes:

(*a*)   (subject to the consent of the employer) to extend the class of persons who may receive benefits in respect of the death of a member;

(*b*)   to enable the scheme to conform with arrangements required by *PA 1995* prior to 6 April 2006 and by *PA 2004* with effect from 6 April 2006 in respect of the appointment of member-nominated trustees or member-nominated directors (see chapter 3);

(*c*)   to enable the scheme to comply with requirements imposed by the Pension Protection Fund in relation to any payment to be made by that body; or

(*d*)   to enable the scheme to conform with certain other specified provisions of *PA 1995 and PA 2004*.

The *Occupational Pension Schemes* (*Modification of Schemes*) *Regulations 2006* (*SI 2006 No 759*) prescribe additional circumstances in which trustees have the power to modify schemes under *section 68* of *PA 1995*. These are to take into account the provision of *FA 2004* and to adopt provisions relating to survivors' benefits for civil partners. There are further sections of *PA 1995* and *PA 2004* and their accompanying regulations which enable the trustees to modify the scheme by resolution for specific purposes. For example, *section 65* of *PA 1995* enables trustees to alter the scheme in line with the requirements for equal treatment as between men and women (see chapter 9).

Scheme's own power of amendment – general

Need for power

12.12   An occupational pension scheme may well continue in operation for several decades. During that time, it will almost certainly need to be adapted to cater for circumstances which could not reasonably have been predicted at the outset. For this reason, it is essential that the documents governing the scheme contain a power of amendment.

If no amendment power is included in the interim deed, it may still be possible to adopt a suitable power in the scheme's definitive deed, to take effect retrospectively to the date of the interim deed. (*Re Imperial Foods Ltd Pension Scheme [1986] 2 All ER 802.*)

The consequences of omitting the power from the definitive deed will be more serious and render it unlikely that a power of amendment can validly be inserted into the documents at a future date. It may still be possible subsequently to adopt a power of amendment, if it can clearly be shown that it had always been intended to include the power but that it was omitted by mistake; however, this would involve a court application.

Exercise of power

12.13   The exercise of any power of amendment must be carried out by the persons, and in accordance with any requirements (for instance, that there be a deed), specified in the provision conferring that power. The vast majority of amendment powers require some involvement by both the principal employer and the trustees before the scheme may be amended.

To the extent that an employer is involved in the exercise of the power, it must act in accordance with its implied duty of good faith towards its employees (see 12.6 above). In the rare cases where an employer has power to amend without requiring the agreement of the trustees, the courts can be expected to scrutinise the exercise of that power particularly strictly.

The trustees' duties are more onerous, as mentioned earlier in 12.7 above. Some examples of the sorts of amendments which trustees may and may not properly agree to are considered in 12.23 to 12.29 below. At this point, however, it is enough to say that trustees must not, as a matter of trust law, agree to amendments which reduce benefits earned before the amendment power is exercised (whether or not immediately payable).

Whoever exercises the power of amendment must do so for the purpose for which it was conferred, namely (unless the trust deed indicates otherwise) to promote the purposes of the scheme. Any statement in the trust deed as to the scheme's main purpose may therefore be relevant to the validity of a subsequent amendment. However, this purpose need not remain fixed indefinitely, and it was recognised in the *Courage* case that a scheme's underlying purpose may change gradually as a scheme evolves over a period of time. (*Re Courage Group's Pension Schemes [1987] 1 WLR 495.*)

The *Courage* case itself provides an example of scheme amendments which were successfully challenged in court as not promoting the schemes' purposes. There were three schemes involved, whose principal employer had recently been acquired by a new owner. The aim of the amendments was to enable the new owner (who had no genuine relationship with the members and was already negotiating to sell the existing principal employer) to be substituted as the schemes' new principal employer, and so gain some benefit from the schemes' surplus funds. This conflicted with the purpose for which the schemes had been established, which was the provision of retirement benefits. The judge specifically commented upon the fact that the new owner was not recognisably the successor to the business or workforce of the company for which it was intended to be substituted.

The case of *Harwood-Smart v Caws [2000] PLR 101* arose following the compulsory liquidation of the employer. The trustees asked the court to determine whether they had to use any surplus to increase benefits to Revenue maxima prior to making any repayment to the employers. It was found in favour of the beneficiaries rather than the employers. The original trust provisions on winding up had required any surplus to be used to enhance benefits to Revenue maxima prior to making any payment to the employers. The power of amendment contained a specific prohibition on paying any part of the fund back to the employers. However, the power of amendment had itself been subsequently amended and been used to amend the winding-up provisions to permit refunds to be paid to the employers without increasing members' benefits in excess of their entitlement. The court found that this power of amendment was invalid.

In the other recent case of *Bestrustees v Stuart [2001] PLR 283*, the BAI pension scheme amended its normal retirement age to 65 for all members following the case of *Barber v GRE [1990] ECR I-1889* in the European Court of Justice in 1990. This case arose around the ambiguity of how and when the decision was made to amend the rules to effect equalisation. As the employer was also trustee, the issue of consent by the other party did not arise. The amendment to the rules was found to be of limited effect. The scheme was in deficit and in the process of being wound up while its assets were used to apply for a decision in circumstances where it was suggested that the professional trustees should have exercised their discretion.

Effect of winding up

12.14   It is unlikely that a power of amendment can be exercised once winding up has started, unless the terms of that power and the other provisions of the scheme rules indicate a contrary intention. (*Thrells v Lomas (1992) PLR 233.*) However, a power of amendment can probably be exercised (unless the scheme rules indicate otherwise), after an employer has given notice to wind up a scheme, but before that notice has expired (*Municipal Mutual v Harrop [1998] PLR 149*).

Many trust deeds include wording to the effect that the trusts of the scheme will cease once winding up begins, and this can be taken to include any amendment power. Others include a provision to the effect that amendments may be made during the winding-up stage, in which case the power will continue to be exercisable.

If a scheme's winding-up rule has not been triggered, but the scheme has become closed to new entrants or benefits have ceased to accrue, the power of amendment remains exercisable unless the scheme rules suggest that it does not.

Retrospective amendments

12.15   A power of amendment may be worded so as to permit scheme amendments to take effect from a date earlier than the date on which they are made. Retrospective amendments may validly be made under such a power, although the requirements of *section 67* of *PA 1995* (as amended by *section 262* of *PA 2004*) will usually apply (see 12.18 below).

If the power of amendment does not expressly allow retrospective alterations, the position is less certain. In reality, a court's decision on the validity of a purportedly retrospective amendment in these circumstances may depend on the nature of the change. A retrospective amendment made simply to ensure compliance with some statutory requirement would probably be upheld; a more controversial alteration might not.

Not surprisingly therefore, the judge in *Municipal Mutual v Harrop [1998] PLR 149* disallowed a retrospective amendment which would have taken away vested rights. He also decided that the amendment could not be upheld on the grounds that its purpose was to correct an error in the scheme rules.

Restrictions

12.16   An amendment will not be valid if it infringes restrictions written into the amendment power under which it is made. Some of the more common restrictions found in amendment powers are as follows:

(*a*)   That no amendment may be made which would alter the main purpose of the scheme. This reflects the general law on scheme amendments (see 12.13 above).

(*b*)   That no amendment may be made which would result in surplus assets being returned to the employers. Such restrictions were built into some older trust deeds in order to comply with requirements of tax approval which no longer apply. *PA 1995* has introduced provisions to overcome restrictions of this nature in certain circumstances (see 12.10 above).

(*c*)   That no amendment may reduce pensions in payment or accrued benefits. This adds nothing to existing trust law principles; the position is now reinforced by *PA 1995* (see 12.18 below).

(*d*)   That amendments (or amendments of a certain nature) may be made only with the members' consent. Sometimes the members concerned are simply not contactable; *PA 1995* helps to relieve this problem.

Of course, an amendment will not be valid if it infringes overriding legislation.

Amending a power of amendment

12.17   The presence of unwanted restrictions in an amendment power raises the question of whether those restrictions can be removed by amending the power of amendment.

If the trust deed states that the amendment power can itself be amended, then this should be possible. However, if the restriction being removed is one which can only serve to protect members' interests, the change may be hard for the trustees to justify.

If there is no express power to amend the power of amendment, it will generally not be possible (without a court order or modification order) to remove restrictions which have been there since the scheme was established; widening the amendment power in this way would be like introducing an amendment power where none had previously existed.

However, removing a restriction which did not exist at the scheme's inception but was introduced at a later date may present less of a problem. The nature of the restriction being removed, how it arose, and how long it has been in place, are likely to be relevant.

It is not usual for the parties to wish to introduce restrictions where none previously existed. Were the trustees to do so, they would be in breach of the general trust law duty not to fetter their own discretion (although it is possible for that duty to be excluded by an express provision in the trust deed).

Statutory protection of entitlements and accrued rights

General

12.18 Since 6 April 1997, under *section 67 of PA 1995*, any power conferred by an occupational pension scheme (other than a public service pension scheme) to modify the scheme could not be exercised 'in a manner which would or might affect any entitlement, or accrued right, of any member of the scheme acquired before the power is exercised' unless the statutory requirements were satisfied. These provisions were replaced from 6 April 2006 by *section 262* of *PA 2004*, which replaces *section 67 of PA 1995*.

Under the original provisions of *section 67* of *PA 1995*, consideration had to be given to whether an amendment would or might affect accrued rights or entitlements. Under the *new section 67*, the question is whether the power to modify is being used to make what is called a regulated modification. A regulated modification is either:

(*a*)   a protected modification; or

(*b*)   a detrimental modification,

or is both.

A protected modification is a modification which would or might result in the reduction of any pension in payment; and/or a modification which involves converting defined benefit rights into defined contribution rights.

A detrimental modification is a modification that would or might adversely affect the subsisting rights of any member of the scheme or any survivor of a member of the scheme. A detrimental modification is the type of modification under the original *section 67* provisions that can only be made if member consent is obtained.

Any exercise of a power to make a regulated modification is voidable unless certain conditions are satisfied. These conditions are as follows:

(*a*) In the case of each affected member for protected modifications (converting defined benefit rights into defined contribution rights or reducing pensions in payment) the consent requirement must be satisfied and for detrimental modifications (those which would or might adversely affect subsisting rights) either the consent requirement or the actuarial equivalence requirement must be satisfied.

(*b*) In respect of all regulated modifications the trustee approval requirements and the reporting requirement must be satisfied.

(*c*) In summary there are three pre-conditions to make a regulated modification which are consent or actuarial equivalence requirements, trustee approval requirement and reporting requirement.

Under the new provisions the consent requirement is made up of two components which are the informed consent requirement and the timing requirement.

The consent requirement

12.19   The consent requirement is satisfied if the trustees give information to members explaining the proposed modification, the trustees notify members that they may make representations to the trustees about the modification, members are notified that the consent requirements apply and the member then gives his consent to the proposed modification in writing.

Once the member has given his consent, the timing requirement is satisfied if the modification takes effect within a reasonable period after the giving of consent.

The actuarial equivalence requirement

12.20   The actuarial equivalence requirement applies in relation to a detrimental modification that is not a protected modification (i e a modification which would involve or might adversely affect subsisting rights but not a modification which involves converting defined benefit rights into defined contribution rights or reducing pensions in payment) and where the trustees determine that this test is to apply.

The actuarial equivalence test has three aspects which are the information requirement, the actuarial value requirement and the actuarial equivalence statement requirement.

(*a*)   *The information requirement*

This involves the trustees giving information in relation to the proposed modification in writing to members and allowing members to make representation to the trustees.

(*b*)   *The actuarial value requirement*

This requirement is satisfied if the trustees have taken steps to secure that 'actuarial value' will be maintained. Actuarial value is maintained if the actuarial value, immediately after the time at which the modification takes effect, of the member's subsisting rights is equal to or greater than the actuarial value of his subsisting rights immediately before that time.

(*c*)   *The actuarial equivalence statement*

This is a statement by the scheme actuary certifying that actuarial value has been maintained.

Civil penalties

12.21   The new *section 67* provides that, where a modification is held to be voidable, then civil penalties under *section 10* of *PA 1995* may be applied to any trustee who has failed to take all reasonable steps to secure that the modification was not voidable.

Affected schemes

12.22   The new *section 67* applies to any power conferred on any person by an occupational pension scheme to modify the scheme. The new provisions do not apply to a public service pension scheme or a 'prescribed scheme' or a scheme of a 'prescribed description'.

Examples

12.23   The following examples consider some of the scheme amendments which an employer might wish to make, and whether the trustees could properly agree to them.

It is assumed for this purpose that the scheme's amendment power is wide enough to allow the amendments proposed but that agreement between the employer and the trustees is required.

The employer's decision to make these amendments and whether such decision accords with its contractual obligations will be governed by the principles outlined in 7.6 to 7.10 above.

Reduction of past service benefits

12.24 Trustees should think carefully before agreeing to an amendment which reduces any benefit earned before the amendment power is exercised (whether payable immediately or from some time in the future). If the trustees were to agree to such amendment, it would arguably be a breach of trust (quite apart from the requirements of *section 67* of *PA 1995*).

Sometimes an employer will propose a method of recalculating all past service benefits which appears to represent a general benefit improvement but, on closer examination, disadvantages a small number of members. The trustees should not agree to the proposals unless they are revised to remove that detriment; it is no defence to a breach of trust action brought by a disadvantaged minority that the arrangements benefit the majority.

Reduction of future service benefits

12.25 Trustees should not agree to a reduction in future benefit accrual without compelling reasons. For example, if the likely outcome of the trustees refusing to agree to the reduction is that the employer will arrange for the scheme to be wound up, the trustees may take the view that they are acting in the best interests of their members by agreeing to the change. Trustees do also owe a duty to the employer (see chapter 3), and are not required to push the company into paying more than it can genuinely afford. This is also a matter which may need to be considered when negotiating scheme funding (see chapter 11)

Amending the scheme so that no further benefits will accrue in the future

12.26 This is simply a more drastic version of 12.25 above, and so the same principles apply.

Closing the scheme to future entrants

12.27 The proposal here will be that an amendment is made to the scheme's eligibility rule so that no further members may join the scheme in the future. This will not necessarily cause the trustees significant problems as the main effect of the amendment will be to exclude individuals who have never belonged to the scheme and to whom the trustees will, therefore, not normally owe a duty. It may raise age discrimination issues for the employer.

However, some schemes impose a 'waiting period' for membership, so that an employee has to complete, say, six months' service before he is allowed to join the scheme. Individuals currently serving this 'waiting period' can be regarded as being contingently entitled to benefits from the scheme, and the trustees would usually, therefore, be well advised (unless the scheme is seriously underfunded) to insist that the closure to new entrants does not affect these particular individuals.

Introduction of different benefits for future joiners

12.28   The concern here is very often that the new benefits package is (or is capable of being) less generous than the one for current members. The issues which this raises for trustees are similar to those in 12.27 above, in that the individuals to be affected by the amendment will not yet be scheme members. The same considerations as regards anyone serving a 'waiting period' will apply.

Conversion to defined contribution

12.29   An employer may continue to operate its defined benefits scheme on the existing basis for current members, but decide that future joiners should be admitted to membership on a defined contribution basis only. This is an example of the sort of amendment described in 12.28 above.

The trustees will face harder decisions if they are asked to agree to an amendment which will convert the current defined benefit scheme members to a defined contribution basis for future accrual (and possibly also for past service benefits).

The trustees, acting on actuarial advice, should not hesitate where appropriate to seek from the employer improvements in the defined contribution benefits being offered. This might take the form of:

(*a*)   a more generous method of conversion (if it is proposed to convert past service benefits);

(*b*)   an increase in the employer's future contributions; or

(*c*)   possibly even some form of 'defined benefit underpin' for the members involved, so that their eventual benefits will not dip below a given level.

The employer may be prepared to compromise on at least some of these points in order to see the conversion go ahead. The improvements will also make the exercise easier for the employer to justify to its employees.

The trustees should seek actuarial advice as to how the employer's proposals will compare with the existing defined benefit basis. Applying the principles set out in 12.24 and 12.25 above, the position will normally be as follows:

(i)   The trustees should have no difficulties in agreeing to the proposals in relation to any member whom those proposals will clearly benefit.

(ii) The trustees should not agree to the proposals in relation to any member for whom the risks or other disadvantages of those proposals outweigh any advantage.

(iii) If neither of the above applies in relation to a member, the trustees should generally be reluctant to permit the conversion to take place without his consent. In seeking his consent, the position should be explained fully to him in terms which he can understand and which clearly draw his attention to any risks involved. He should also be advised to seek independent financial advice. If he decides to consent, he should be asked to sign a consent form which states that the decision reached is his own and that the trustees will not be held responsible for it.

In some circumstances, the trustees may justifiably go further than this towards accommodating the employer's proposals (for instance, if the future service benefits offered are genuinely the best which the employer can afford). However, in no circumstances should the trustees allow a reduction in the value of a member's accrued benefits. The conversion of past service defined benefits to a defined contribution basis will be a protected modification and require consent under *section 67* of *PA 1995* (see 12.18 above).

Bulk transfers – general

Background

12.30   Some of the reasons for making bulk transfers of assets and liabilities between schemes operating within the same group of employers were outlined in 12.3 above. The matters that arise in relation to bulk transfers vary to some extent according to whether or not the transferring scheme has begun to be wound up before the time of the transfer (see 12.45 to 12.47 and 12.64 to 12.69 below). Here, however, some general issues are considered.

Members' consents to transfer

12.31   An advantage of obtaining members' consents to the transfer is that, if matters have been properly and clearly explained to the members, they are less likely to feel aggrieved about the transfer arrangements later on.

However, the fact that members' consents are being sought in no way relieves the trustees of the responsibility to ensure that the arrangements are in the members' best interests. The consent form which members are asked to sign may contain a statement discharging the transferring trustees from any further liability, but it may not be possible for trustees to rely on this discharge if it is later shown that they did not take proper steps to protect their members.

In seeking consents, care should be taken not to give unauthorised investment advice contrary to the *Financial Services and Markets Act 2000* (explained further in 10.25 above) and members should be encouraged to seek independent financial advice before taking a decision.

In reality, however, obtaining the consent of the entire membership will often be impractical, particularly in relation to deferred pensioners, some of whom are likely to have moved house and not advised their former employer or the trustees of their new address. Transfers to other occupational pension schemes (but not to personal pension schemes) are therefore permissible without the need for members' consents, but only if:

(*a*)   either:

   (i)   the scheme rules expressly permit transfers to be made without consent; or

   (ii)   the transferring scheme is an approved defined benefit scheme, the transfer follows the commencement, after 5 April 1997, of the winding up of that scheme and the requirements dealt with in 12.57 to 12.59 below are met; and

(*b*)   either:

   (i)   both schemes apply to employment with the same employer (which is generally taken to mean that the two schemes must have at least one participating employer in common); or

   (ii)   it is a bulk (as opposed to an individual) transfer, either resulting from a financial transaction between the employers or where the employers are 'connected' for the purposes of the legislation (*regulation 12(2)* of the *Occupational Pension Schemes (Preservation of Benefit) Regulations 1991 (SI 1991 No 167)* ('the *Preservation Regulations*'));

(*c*)   an actuarial certificate (often called a 'GN16', this being the number of the Guidance Note issued by the Institute and Faculty of Actuaries regulating the preparation of such certificates) is given to the effect that:

   (i)   the transfer credits in the receiving scheme for each member are broadly no less favourable than the rights being transferred; and

   (ii)   there is good cause to believe that the award of discretionary benefits (or discretionary benefit increases) in the receiving scheme will be broadly no less favourable than any established custom of awarding discretionary benefits (or discretionary benefit increases) in the transferring scheme (*regulation 12(3)* of the *Preservation Regulations (SI 1991 No 167)*). For this purpose, the actuary may make an allowance for any amount by which the transfer credits under the receiving scheme are more favourable than the rights to be transferred; and

(*d*)   in relation to contracted-out arrangements (see chapter 4) the transfer is not of such a kind that members' consents are required as set out in 4.33 above. These requirements used to be particularly onerous in relation to protected rights but the *Protected Rights (Transfer Payment) (Amendment) Regulations 2005 (SI 2005 No 2906)* permit, from 28 November 2005, the bulk transfer of protected rights to a contracted-out defined contributions scheme or the defined contribution section of a mixed benefit scheme, without members' consent; provided that the amount is at least equal to the value of the cash equivalent and transferring members must either be given at least three months' notice and have the opportunity to object, or be given at least one month's notice; subject to an actuary's statement that a member's rights will be broadly no less favourable (see chapter 4). At the time of writing, it is arguable (but by no means certain) that these requirements do not apply so long as the transferring scheme is an approved defined benefits scheme, the transfer follows the commencement, after 5 April 1997, of the winding up of that scheme and the requirements dealt with in 12.57 to 12.59 below are met.

Where a transfer is to be made without consent, information about the proposed transfer and details of the value of the rights to be transferred (including rights in respect of death in service benefits and survivors' benefits) must be given to each member affected not less than one month before the proposed transfer is due to take place (*regulation 12(4B)* of the *Preservation Regulations (SI 1991 No 167)*).

The ability to transfer without consent in these circumstances applies only to past service benefits. Future service benefits cannot accrue without consent in the receiving scheme; this would amount to compulsory scheme membership contrary to *section 160* of the *Pension Schemes Act 1993 (PSA 1993)*.

Even where all the above conditions are met, the trustees may not exercise a discretion to make a transfer unless they are satisfied that it is in their members' best interests.

Issues for trustees to consider

12.32   The matters to be borne in mind by the trustees in deciding whether they are doing the best for their members will vary according to the circumstances, but the following issues are amongst those which will most commonly arise. It is assumed here that the trustees have some discretion as to whether the transfer takes place.

Benefits

12.33   The employers may offer benefit improvements in order to encourage the trustees to agree to the transfer. If improvements are not offered, the trustees should seek them (particularly if, without any, there is no advantage for their members in the transfer going ahead). This is potentially an issue for both the transferring and receiving trustees.

The transferring trustees should examine closely the benefits which are offered in respect of the transfer and guard against the possibility of agreeing to proposals which result in any person's benefits being reduced. Trustees' duties in relation to changes in benefits were considered in 12.23 to 12.29 above in the context of scheme amendments. The same principles apply in relation to transfers, so that trustees will be in breach of trust if they agree to a transfer which reduces any person's past service benefits, and only exceptionally may they agree to a transfer which reduces future benefits (for instance, in the circumstances outlined in 12.25 above).

Funding disparity

12.34   Another issue is the comparative funding levels of the transferring and receiving schemes. If, for example, the trustees of an ongoing scheme are considering whether to make a bulk transfer, they should seek advice as to the solvency of both the transferring and receiving schemes respectively. If the transferring scheme is significantly better funded than the receiving scheme, the transferring trustees should question whether they can justify making a transfer which would, in effect, put their members into a worse funded scheme than the one to which they presently belong.

How much of an issue this is will depend not only on the extent of the funding disparity but also on other factors. For instance, both schemes might be well funded, but the receiving scheme only slightly less so than the transferring scheme. In these circumstances the transferring trustees could properly take the view that the modest funding disparity was outweighed by any more significant advantages of the transfer, such as:

(*a*)   better benefits to be provided by the receiving scheme;

(*b*)   provisions in the receiving scheme's rules creating greater scope than under the transferring scheme for surplus assets to be used for benefit improvements; or (*c*) a likelihood of the receiving scheme's future investment performance significantly outstripping that of the transferring scheme (perhaps because the receiving scheme is much larger – see 12.36 below).

If the funding disparity remains an issue, the transferring trustees should impose conditions upon the employers (and, where appropriate, the receiving trustees) before agreeing to make the transfer. These conditions might typically include one or both of the following:

(i) That a benefit improvement be granted in respect of the members to be transferred.

(ii) That any surplus to be transferred from the transferring scheme be subject to some measure of 'ringfencing' in the receiving scheme. The aim of ringfencing is to ensure that assets transferred from the transferring scheme are subject to safeguards for the benefit of the transferring members in the receiving scheme. This is done by amending the rules of the receiving scheme, so as (in this context) to give the transferring members prior rights over other members as regards the transferred assets in relation to such matters as:

- any use of surplus assets to grant benefit improvements;

- the calculation of future transfer values paid from the receiving scheme; and/or

- the distribution of assets on a winding up of the receiving scheme. However, such an amendment may be partly or wholly ineffective if the receiving scheme subsequently goes into winding up with insufficient assets to meet all its liabilities. This is because of the winding-up requirements in *PA 1995* and *PA 2004* which, at least to some extent (as explained further in 12.61(*c*) below), override the scheme's rules.

The employer may well insist that any 'ringfencing' provisions only remain effective for a specified period of time. In agreeing to a suitable period, the trustees should consider actuarial advice as to how long the surplus might otherwise have lasted in the transferring scheme.

The transferring trustees are likely to have less negotiating power, however, if their scheme has gone into winding up.

If, conversely, the receiving scheme is better funded than the transferring scheme, then similar considerations in reverse will have to be borne in mind by the receiving scheme's trustees before they exercise any discretion under the terms of their trust deed to accept the transfer.

Comparison of balance of powers

12.35 The trustees of an ongoing scheme ought also, before agreeing to make a transfer, to consider the 'balance of powers' (as between the employers, on the one hand, and the trustees, on the other) under the provisions of their own scheme and compare it with the corresponding balance in the receiving scheme. If the receiving scheme's balance of powers is overall less favourable towards the trustees (and therefore the beneficiaries) than under the transferring scheme, then the transferring trustees should again question whether they can properly make the transfer.

An unfavourable shift in the balance of powers may be compensated for by other factors; for instance, if the receiving scheme is significantly better funded than the transferring scheme, provides better benefits, or (as mentioned in 12.36 below) has better prospects for future growth. If this is not the case, however, then the trustees should consider obtaining from the employer some benefit or safeguard for their members before agreeing to the transfer. This might take the form of:

(*a*)   an immediate benefit improvement in respect of the transferring members; or

(*b*)   amendments to the receiving scheme to make its balance of powers more favourable to the trustees, at least in so far as that scheme will ultimately relate to the transferring members. Where surplus assets are being transferred, any such amendment will be another form of 'ringfencing' as referred to in 12.34(ii) above. The difference here, however, is that the purpose of the ringfencing will be to protect the transferring members' interests against those of the employers (rather than against those of the other members).

The issue will not be as acute for the transferring trustees if their scheme is already in winding up.

Long-term future of schemes

12.36   It is increasingly difficult to predict the long-term stability and growth of any pension scheme, but it is nevertheless an issue which trustees should bear in mind. The overall financial circumstances of a scheme's sponsoring employers may give a clue as to the scheme's future. Another factor is the scheme's size.

Many transfers of the sort discussed in this chapter are from smaller schemes to larger schemes. Larger funds tend to bear proportionately lower administrative costs (owing to economies of scale) and may be able to pursue a successful investment strategy which might not realistically be available to a smaller scheme. However, trustees should be wary of relying too heavily on this to justify a transfer which would not otherwise be in their members' best interests.

It is comparatively rare for trustees to be asked to agree to a transfer to a smaller scheme within the same group of employers. The trustees should make certain that there is a clear advantage for their members (most probably in the form of benefit improvements) should this happen.

Of course, if the transferring scheme is already being wound up, that scheme will not have any long-term future for the trustees to consider.

Other ways of securing benefits on a winding up

12.37 If the transferring scheme is in the course of being wound up, some of the issues mentioned above may be less relevant, as members will not have the alternative simply of remaining in the transferring scheme. Instead, the transferring trustees should satisfy themselves that any bulk transfer will be on terms which serve their members at least as well as the other courses of action available (such as transfers to personal pension schemes or purchasing annuities).

Contracted-out schemes

12.38 Further requirements apply in relation to contracted-out schemes. These requirements are dealt with in 4.42 above.

Transfer agreement

12.39 It is advisable for the parties involved to enter into a formal transfer agreement where the terms of the arrangement which has been entered into can be clearly set out. The parties will usually be the trustees of the two schemes and each scheme's principal employer. The terms of any such agreement will vary enormously depending on the circumstances, but 12.40 to 12.44 below describe the provisions which will most often be included.

Some of these are in reality scheme amendments. The parties could, as an alternative, deal with these areas in separate deeds of amendment relating to the two schemes, but it is often more convenient to deal with all matters relating to the transfer in a single document. Care should be taken to ensure that, if the transfer agreement is to amend either of the schemes, it complies with all the relevant requirements of that scheme's power of amendment (for instance, by being in the form of a deed).

The agreement will typically cover the following areas.

Amendments to the transferring scheme

12.40   Amendments to the transferring scheme may be necessary to:

(*a*)   permit the parties to make the transfer; and/or

(*b*)   grant any benefit improvements which the transferring trustees require as a condition of their making the transfer.

Transfer amount

12.41   This may be stated as a specific sum (subject to a market value adjustment and/or increase for late payment) or the agreement may simply set out the method by which the amount is to be calculated (perhaps by reference to an actuary's letter appended to the agreement). If the agreement provides for the transferring scheme's entire assets to be transferred, then the precise calculation of the amount becomes less of an issue.

Past service benefits

12.42   The benefits to be provided in the receiving scheme in relation to the transfer payment should be clearly stated.

Amendments to the receiving scheme

12.43   Amendments may be required in relation to the receiving scheme, for instance, to:

(*a*)   permit the parties to accept the transfer;

(*b*)   incorporate any special future service benefits in relation to the transferring members which have been agreed;

(*c*)   grant any benefit improvements for the receiving scheme's existing members which the receiving trustees require as a condition of their accepting the transfer; and/or

(*d*)   incorporate any 'ringfencing' provisions (as referred to in 12.34(ii) and 12.35(*b*) above) which have been agreed between the parties as a condition of the transfer being made.

Indemnity

12.44   The transferring trustees may seek an indemnity from the receiving trustees in relation to any claims which might be brought against them in relation to the transferring members. The receiving trustees should of course consider how this might affect their own members' interests. Any such indemnity will normally exclude matters where there has been an element of bad faith or dishonesty by the transferring trustees and be limited, for instance, to that part of the receiving scheme's assets which is attributable to the transfer payment.

To the extent that these assets may be insufficient fully to indemnify the transferring trustees, one or more of the employers may agree to indemnify the transferring trustees for the difference; however, care should be taken not to infringe the provisions of *sections 309A* to *309C* of the *Companies Act 1985* (inserted with effect from 6 April 2005 by the *Companies (Audit, Investigations and Community Enterprise) Act 2004* to replace *section 310* of the *Companies Act 1985*) (referred to further in chapter 3 – see 3.61 above) regarding companies indemnifying their own officers. In future indemnities must be a 'qualifying third party indemnity' to be valid.

Bulk transfers – specific issues where winding up has not commenced

Background

12.45   The questions of whether there is power to make a bulk transfer, and how any transfer payment is to be calculated, will attract different answers depending on whether or not the transferring scheme has gone into winding up at the time of the transfer. The date on which a scheme commences to be wound up for this purpose is governed by *section 124(3A)–(3E)* of *PA 1995* (or for schemes commencing winding up before 6 April 2005 by *regulation 2* of the *Occupational Pension Schemes (Winding Up) Regulations 1996 (SI 1996 No 3126)* ('the *Winding-up Regulations*')).

Where winding up has not commenced (or is not even expected to happen), the position is as set out in 12.46 and 12.47 below. (The corresponding position where winding up has commenced is dealt with in 12.64 to 12.68 below.)

Power to make bulk transfers

12.46   Whether there is power to make a bulk transfer out of a scheme which is not in winding up depends upon the terms of that scheme's trust deed and rules. If there is power to make the transfer, much will depend on whether the trust deed and rules place that power primarily with the employers or with the trustees. For instance:

(*a*)   the principal employer might have power to direct the trustees to make a transfer, with the trustees having no right of refusal;

(*b*)   the principal employer might have power to request the trustees to make a transfer, with the trustees having a discretion as to whether or not they act on that request;

(*c*)   the trustees might have power to initiate a transfer, subject only to the employer's consent. This gives the trustees a greater degree of control than in (*b*) above since, in putting their proposals to the employer, the trustees are effectively requiring the employer to consider those proposals in a manner consistent with its implied duty of good faith (see 12.6 above);

(*d*)   the trustees might have power to make a transfer, subject only to consultation with the employer. So long as a genuine consultation procedure is carried out, this does not require the trustees actually to obtain the employer's consent; or

(*e*)   the trustees might have power to make a bulk transfer without any form of reference to the employer being required.

Amount to be transferred

12.47   Similarly, the calculation of the transfer amount is governed by the trust deed and rules, subject to members' statutory entitlements to a minimum of the cash equivalents of their accrued benefits (see 6.44 above) (although underfunding in the transferring scheme may justify a reduction of cash equivalents – see 6.51 above for further details on the reduction of cash equivalents).

Trust deeds vary considerably as to how the transfer amount is to be calculated. Some examples are as follows:

(*a*)   The matter might be left entirely to the discretion either of the principal employer or of the trustees, often subject to the requirement that they first consider the advice of the actuary (which advice the trust deed may or may not require them to accept, but in practice may be hard to reject without good reason).

(*b*)   More commonly, the deed will leave the decision as to the amount to one of the two parties – either the principal employer or the trustees – subject to the consent of the other.

(*c*)   The trust deed might (particularly if it is an older one) have the effect of requiring that the transfer payment represent a share of the overall fund in respect of the members being transferred. In an underfunded scheme, this would mean the transferring members bearing a proportion of the brunt of any overall deficit in the transferring scheme. In an overfunded scheme, by contrast, the transfer payment would have to include a share of any surplus.

(*d*)   The trust deed might (especially if it is a relatively modern one), seek to give the employers maximum control in relation to active members by specifying that the transfer payment be the lesser of:

    (i)   their statutory cash equivalents; and

    (ii)   the amount which would be available to be applied in respect of them were the scheme to be wound up,

    (which is, effectively, the minimum which the law will allow) subject to the principal employer's sole discretion to direct a greater amount.

Schemes are seldom overfunded when valued on the basis used by HMRC for determining if the scheme has a statutory surplus, but there may be difficulties in transferring a share of the surplus in the rare cases where this is so.

The position with regard to these issues will be rather different where the transfers take place after winding up has commenced. Before looking at this further (see 12.64 below), however, it is necessary to consider the winding-up procedure as a whole.

Triggering a winding up

Triggering events

12.48   The events which will trigger a winding up of a scheme will depend upon the scheme's governing trust deed and rules. These might typically provide for a winding up of the scheme to be triggered upon the earliest of:

(*a*)   the expiry of a notice to the trustees by the principal employer, requiring that the scheme be wound up;

(*b*)   the trustees resolving to wind the scheme up and notifying the principal employer accordingly;

(*c*)   the principal employer being in arrears in its contributions to the scheme and failing to rectify the position within a specified period of the trustees formally requesting it to do so;

(*d*)   the principal employer going into liquidation; and

(*e*)   the expiry of a specified period from the date on which the scheme was established.

Many trust deeds and rules will, in some of these circumstances, give the trustees a discretion to continue operating the scheme (with a new principal employer, where appropriate) rather than wind it up immediately; this is dealt with further in 12.50 below.

Application to the Regulator

12.49   In the unlikely event of the employer or the trustees wishing to wind up a scheme and there being no power in the trust deed enabling them to do so, the Regulator may, under *section 11* of *PA 1995*, authorise or direct a winding up if:

(*a*)   the scheme (or any part of it) ought to be replaced by a different scheme;

(*b*)   the scheme is no longer required; or

(*c*)   it is necessary in order to protect the interests of the generality of the scheme members.

It should only rarely be necessary to resort to an application to the Regulator, and the Regulator is unlikely to make such an order without a compelling case being made to it. Alternatively, it may in exceptional circumstances be necessary to apply to the court for directions to wind up a scheme.

Disclosure requirements

12.50   The intention of the Regulator's disclosure requirements is to shorten the time between the instigation of termination of a pension scheme and its completion. An outline of the Regulator's requirements is as follows:

(*a*)   the trustees must notify the Regulator where a scheme has been in the process of winding up for more than three years;

(*b*)   the trustees must notify the Regulator in writing every twelve months about current progress;

(*c*)   the trustees must provide a member of the scheme with a copy of any report sent to the Regulator within two months of a request being made;

(*d*)   the Regulator has the power to speed up the winding-up process of a scheme, where it deems it appropriate;

(*e*)   the scheme's sponsor or administrator must notify the Regulator in the absence of an independent trustee where an independent trustee is required;

(*f*)   an independent trustee must be appointed by the official receiver or insolvency practitioner where relevant within three months of the date such appointment was required;

(*g*)   the trustees must notify the Regulator within one month in the absence of an independent trustee where an independent trustee is required;

(*h*)   the administrator must notify the Regulator within one month where the scheme has no trustees;

(*i*)   the trustees and the employer (if appropriate) must keep a written record of any decisions to wind up a scheme;

(*j*)   the trustees can seek a modification order from the Regulator to wind up a scheme.

Where the trustees have not complied with the requirements to wind up a scheme, they will have to provide justified reasons to the Regulator for not doing so. This may include copies of statements from the scheme's actuary or auditor. Delays in winding up which are allegedly caused by awaiting information from HMRC on contracting-out issues are expected to be reduced. Trustees may be fined by the Regulator in the event of unjustified delays in winding up a scheme.

Deferral of winding up by trustees

Power under scheme rules

12.51   Some scheme rules give the trustees power, even after the winding-up rule has been triggered, to defer winding the scheme up. Examples of circumstances where the trustees might wish to defer winding up are:

(*a*)   where annuity rates are low at the time when the winding-up rule is triggered and the trustees wish to wait for them to rise, so placing the fund in a better position to secure the benefits with an insurance company;

(*b*)   where the trustees are awaiting a clarification of the law without which winding up may prove risky (the initial uncertainty over the European Court's *Barber* decision – see chapter 9 – being an example); or

(*c*)   where the scheme's winding-up rule has been triggered by the principal employer going into receivership and the trustees expect the business to be sold to a new owner who is committed to the continued funding and operation of the scheme.

A scheme rule enabling the trustees to defer winding up in these circumstances may or may not permit the trustees to take steps during the deferral period (for example, requiring further employers' contributions) which would create further liabilities for the employers.

Statutory power

12.52   Where winding up has not commenced before 6 April 1997, there is in some circumstances a statutory power to defer winding up for those trustees who do not have such a power under their scheme rules.

This statutory power is conferred by *section 38(1)* of *PA 1995* and is available only where (in particular):

(*a*)   there is no power to defer winding up in the scheme's trust deed and rules (*section 38(1)*);

(*b*)   it is not a defined contribution scheme (*section 38(3)(a)*);

(*c*)   the scheme:

- has at least two members;

- is approved (or formerly approved) or a relevant statutory scheme; and

- is not a tax approved (or formerly tax approved) small self-administered scheme (see chapter 13) [*Winding-up Regulations (SI 1996 No 3126), reg 10(1)*]; and

(*d*)   a 'relevant insolvency event' has occurred in relation to any of the scheme's employers and that event is, under the scheme rules, an event triggering a winding up of the scheme. A 'relevant insolvency event' is defined in *section 75* of *PA 1995*, but in broad terms it means the commencement of an employer's bankruptcy or an employer going into liquidation. If the scheme has no active members, anyone who was an employer in relation to the scheme when the scheme last had active members will count as an employer for this purpose. [*Winding-up Regulations (SI 1996 No 3126), reg 10(1)(a) and (2)*].

Where trustees exercise this new power, they may not allow new members to join the scheme during the deferral period. However, *section 38(2)* of *PA 1995* does allow them to decide:

(i)   that contributions will not continue to be payable; or

(ii)   that benefits will not continue to accrue,

during deferment, but not to stop increases to accrued rights.

Winding-up priorities

12.53   Whilst winding up is being deferred, some active members are likely to become deferred pensioners, others to become pensioners, and so on. These changes of status are important because, should the scheme be wound up with insufficient assets to secure all the benefits, some membership categories (such as pensioners) may have preferential rights over others. This is less important since new statutory winding up priorities were introduced from 6 April 2005. [See 12.61 below].

Trustees who defer winding up now have a limited degree of scope under *regulation 5* of the *Winding-up Regulations (SI 1996 No 3126)* for deciding the date at which membership status (for instance, whether a person is an active member or a pensioner) is to be determined for this purpose.

Disclosure requirements

12.54   Any decision to defer winding up (whether reached under the scheme rules or under *section 38* of *PA 1995*) or to fix a date for determining winding-up priorities (whether reached under the power referred to in 12. 53 above or under any other power) must be recorded and members must be informed of the decision within one month. [*Winding-up Regulations (SI 1996 No 3126), reg 11*].

If the trustees do not defer winding up, or when any period of deferral comes to an end, the winding-up process will start.

The winding-up process

Overview

Methods of securing the liabilities

12.55   The securing of the scheme liabilities where a scheme is being wound up varies accordingly to when the winding up began. There are three time periods to consider as set out below.

Winding up begins before 6 April 1997

12.56   Where winding up started before 6 April 1997, the winding-up process for securing the benefits was governed primarily by the scheme rules. The winding up of pension schemes can take many years so there may still be a handful of schemes where a pre-1997 winding-up has not yet completed. There will be a difference between one scheme and another but the following matters will usually be covered in scheme rules.

(*a*) *Expenses*

Most scheme rules will provide for an amount to be set aside out of the assets to cover scheme expenses. The costs will depend upon a number of factors including the complexity of the scheme, the size of the scheme and any problems encountered in the winding-up.

(*b*) *Purchase of annuities*

From the remaining assets, the rules will normally provide for the trustees to secure the benefits by purchasing annuities from an insurance company. Where there are insufficient assets, an order of priorities in accordance with which the trustees must apply the assets will normally be established and this is set out in the rules.

(*c*) *Transfers*

As an alternative to purchasing annuities, most schemes will allow the trustees to transfer benefits to other retirement benefits schemes or personal pension schemes or other approved arrangements.

Winding up begins after 5 April 1997 and before 6 April 2005

(*a*) *Statutory power to secure benefits*

Where the winding up of a scheme commences after 5 April 1997, *section 74* of *PA 1995* gives trustees of an approved defined benefits scheme, the power to secure members' benefits.

(*b*) *Options available*

Section 74 of *PA 1995* and the *Winding-up Regulations (SI 1996 No 3126)* provide that trustees of defined benefits schemes which commenced winding up after 5 April 1997 are treated as having discharged any liability in respect of scheme benefits so long as they have arranged for the discharge of that liability in one or more of the following ways:

- by making transfer payments to other occupational pension schemes (*section 74(3)(a) of PA 1995*);

- by making transfer payments to personal pension schemes (*section 74(3)(b) of PA 1995*);

- by purchasing annuities from insurance companies (*section 74(3)(c)* of *PA 1995*);

- by transferring the benefits of an annuity contract or insurance policy to the member concerned (or his dependant) (*regulation 8(4)* of the *Winding-up Regulations (SI 1996 No 3126)*);

- in certain limited circumstances, relating to insolvent contracted-out schemes, paying sums to the Department of Work and Pensions (*regulation 8(5)* of the *Winding-up Regulations (SI 1996 No 3126)*),

provided that any transfer value quotation issued to a member must be accompanied by a statement informing him that the value of his guaranteed cash equivalent may be affected by the winding up of the scheme, that a decision to take a guaranteed cash equivalent should be given careful consideration and that the member should consider taking independent financial advice prior to any transfer payment from the scheme being made.

(*c*)   *Notice to members*

When securing a member's benefits in accordance with *section 74* of *PA 1995* trustees must also give to the member to whom the liabilities relate (or if the member is deceased to his beneficiaries), a notice in writing of the proposed discharge (a 'discharge notice') (*regulation 6(2)(a)* of the *Winding-up Regulations (SI 1996 No 3126)*.

(*d*)   *Statutory discharge*

In order to be discharged when securing members' benefits, the *Winding-up Regulations (SI 1996 No 3126)* provide that the trustees must comply with the requirements relating to: (i) the contents of the discharge notice (*regulation 7* of the *Winding-up Regulations* as mentioned above; and (ii) other prescribed requirements, such as whether the individual's consent is required (*regulations 6* and *8* of the *Winding-up Regulations*).

12.57   *Regulation 9* of the *Winding-up Regulations (SI 1996 No 3126)* confirms that these requirements are in addition to (and do not replace) certain requirements of *section 32A* of *PSA 1993* in relation to the discharge of protected rights on winding up and any scheme rules reflecting those requirements.

Winding up begins on or after 6 April 2005

12.58   If the scheme began to wind up on or after 6 April 2005, it is necessary to consider the extent to which the changes introduced by *PA 2004* impact on the methods of securing members' benefits. In particular, the extent to which: (i) the Pension Protection Fund; and (ii) the Financial Assistance Scheme are relevant.

Impact of the Pension Protection Fund ('PPF')

(*a*) *The PPF was established on 6 April 2005*

12.59 The legal framework is set out in *sections 107* to *220* of *PA 2004*, *Schedules 5* to *9* to *PA 2004* and associated regulations.

In summary, schemes eligible for protection by the PPF have to pay the PPF levies. In return, members of those schemes may be entitled to compensation from the PPF if the employer becomes insolvent. Where the employer cannot become insolvent in a normal sense (for example, public bodies or unincorporated charities), the trustees or the Regulator must inform the PPF when they become aware that the employer is unlikely to continue as a going concern. The PPF represents an additional method of securing members' benefits if the sponsoring employer is insolvent. For this to be possible certain qualifying conditions have to be satisfied.

(*b*) *Conditions for entry*

There are a number of conditions for entry in *Part 2* of *PA 2004* and related regulations – in particular the *Pension Protection Fund (Entry Rules) Regulations 2005 (SI 2005 No 590)*.

(i) *Eligible schemes*

PA 2004 provides that certain pension schemes will not be considered an eligible scheme for the purposes of gaining entry to the PPF. In order to be considered to be eligible, the pension scheme:

- must not be a defined contributions scheme (*section 126(1)(a)* of *PA 2004*);

- must not be a prescribed scheme (*section 126(1)(b)* of *PA 2004* and *regulation 2* of the *Pension Protection Fund (Entry Rules) Regulations 2005 (SI 2005 No 590)*);

- must not have started winding up before 6 April 2005 (*section 126(2)* of *PA 2004*). The date on which a scheme starts to wind up is usually determined by reference to the scheme rules; and

- except in certain circumstances, must not have entered into a legally enforceable compromise agreement, in connection with a debt payable by the employer under *section 75* of *PA 1995* (Deficiencies in the assets).

The circumstances when a *section 75* debt can be compromised without preventing a pension scheme from being an eligible scheme are set out in *regulation 2(2)* to *2(7)* of the *Pension Protection Fund (Entry Rules) Regulations 2005 (SI 2005 No 590)*. In summary this is where one of the following applies:

- the PPF has validated an actuarial statement that the compromise is above the PPF level of benefits; or

- the compromise was part of an arrangement under *section 425* of the *Companies Act 1985* (power of company to compromise with creditors or members); or

- the PPF Board acting as creditor of the pension scheme has entered into a legally enforceable agreement with the employer on behalf of the trustees; or

- a prescribed arrangement is in place pursuant to regulations made under *section 75A* of *PA 1995* (debt due from the employer in the case of multi-employer schemes).

(ii) *Qualifying insolvency events*

For a scheme to be considered for entry to the PPF, a qualifying insolvency event must occur in relation to the sponsoring employer. The insolvency event must have occurred on or after 6 April 2005. (This is discussed in more detail in chapter 17.)

Multi-employer schemes

12.60   Where a solvent employer ceases to participate in a multi-employer scheme on or after 2 September 2005, either it will become liable for a debt on a buy-out basis, or it will have to enter into a withdrawal arrangement with one or more guarantors.

Where a withdrawal agreement is put in place the departing employer will remain liable for a debt on the minimum funding requirement basis (less the value of any liabilities relating to its former employees which have been transferred out) plus the expenses associated with its withdrawal. The guarantors may either be responsible for the balance of the buy-out debt as at the date the employer withdrew or the amount that would be payable had the employer withdrawn at a future 'guarantee time' – the guarantee time being the date the scheme commences winding up, the date no solvent employers remain or a date when the Regulator directs the guarantors to pay. A withdrawal agreement will remain in force until the scheme has completed winding up, the Regulator issues a notice stating that it is no longer required or it is replaced by another withdrawal agreement.

The terms of the withdrawal agreement must be approved by the Regulator. It can only be approved where the Regulator is of the opinion that the agreement satisfies the conditions laid down in legislation and that the guarantors have sufficient resources such that the debt is likely to be met. When an approved withdrawal agreement is in force the guarantors must notify the Regulator of certain events including any decision which would result in the debt not being paid in full or any change in control of the guarantor.

Order in which benefits are secured

12.61   The order in which the trustees must secure members' benefits when a scheme is being wound up varies according to when the winding up began. There are four time periods to consider:

- before 6 April 1997;
- 6 April 1997 to 9 May 2004;
- 10 May 2004 to 5 April 2005; and
- on or after 6 April 2005.

A statutory priority order was introduced for the first time by *PA 1995*. The policy intention behind having a statutory priority order is that when a scheme is wound up in deficit, the assets are divided amongst scheme members as fairly as possible.

The provisions of *section 73* of *PA 1995* (preferential liabilities on winding up) and the *Winding-up Regulations (SI 1996 No 3126)* imposed a statutory overriding priority order from 6 April 1997 where a scheme was winding up and it was subject to the statutory minimum funding requirement.

A new transitional priority order was introduced for schemes that commenced winding up after 9 May 2004 (the *Occupational Pension Schemes (Winding Up) (Amendment) Regulations (SI 2004 No 1140)*).

PA 2004 introduced changes to *section 73* of *PA 1995*. A different winding-up priority order therefore applies for schemes where winding up starts after 6 April 2005.

(a)   Time at which winding up starts

The relevant legislation determines the time at which the wind up starts. The relevant legislation is *regulation 2* of the *Winding-up Regulations (SI 1996 No 3126)* and *section 124(3A)* to *(3E)* of *PA 1995*.

(i) *Scheme rules*

If the scheme is winding up under the scheme rules, then it is necessary to consider whether the rules specify a time for the winding up to start. If they do not, the *Winding-up Regulations (SI 1996 No 3126)* provide that the time at which winding up starts is the later of:

(*a*)   the time when the trustees (or whoever has the power) decide that the scheme wind up starts; and

(*b*)   the earliest date when there are no members in pensionable service.

If the rules do specify a time and the trustees have decided not to defer the winding up of the scheme, the winding up starts on the later of:

(*a*)   the date as specified in the scheme rules; and

(*b*)   the earliest date when there are no members in pensionable service.

(ii) *Order of the Regulator*

If the winding up has been triggered by the Regulator, then the time at which winding up starts depends on whether or not a time is specified in the relevant order. If a time is specified, then this is the time for winding up to start. If the order is silent, the winding up will start on the effective date of the order.

(iii) *PPF assessment period*

If an assessment period has been triggered in relation to the scheme, then the PPF rules set out in *PA 2004* will apply in relation to the time at which winding up starts. This is discussed at 12.55 above.

(*b*)   *Before 6 April 1997*

(i) *No statutory framework*

Prior to *PA 1995*, there was no statutory framework to govern how the assets of a pension scheme were to be allocated where there was a deficit. Contracted-out defined benefit schemes were required to adopt an order of priorities which afforded higher priorities to guaranteed minimum pensions over the non-guaranteed minimum pensions element of deferred pensioners' benefits. Most pension schemes had a winding-up rule that included a list of priorities in accordance with which the assets of the scheme were to be distributed on a winding up.

(ii) *Typical priority order*

Typically the order of priorities in a contracted-out scheme might be as follows:

(*a*)   pensions and other benefits in payment together with benefits payable to those over normal pension age and still in service;

(*b*)   guaranteed minimum pensions not yet in payment, equivalent pension benefits under the *National Insurance Act 1965* and State scheme premiums;

(*c*)   deferred pensions and other benefits for early leavers;

(*d*)   deferred pensions and other benefits for scheme members when the winding up began as if they had left service;

(*e*)   augmentation of benefits within Inland Revenue limits;

(*f*)   payment of any remaining surplus to the employers.

Additional voluntary contributions normally have absolute priority on winding up provided certain conditions are met. The purpose of these conditions is to ensure that the additional voluntary contributions fund can be regarded as a totally separate fund, the distribution of which will not affect the ability of the scheme to meet its liability for the basic benefits which the scheme provides.

(*c*)   *Winding up started at any time from 6 April 1997 to 9 May 2004*

The priority order for a scheme that started winding up at any time from 6 April 1997 to 9 May 2004 is set out in *section 73* of *PA 1995*, as modified by the *Winding-up Regulations (SI 1996 No 3126)*.

When considering the provisions of *section 73* of *PA 1995* and the associated provisions of the *Winding-up Regulations (SI 1996 No 3126)*, it is necessary to ignore the changes made to that section by *section 270* of *PA 2004*. This is because the *Pensions Act 2004 (Commencement No 2, Transitional Provisions and Consequential Amendments) Order (SI 2005 No 275)* confirms that *section 270* of *PA 2004* does not come into force for all purposes. The new wording is not effective to the extent that it affects *sections 73* and *74* of *PA 1995* as they apply immediately before 6 April 2005 to a scheme in winding up at that time. The question of whether or not a scheme was in winding up at that time is determined under *regulation 2* of the *Winding-up Regulations (SI 1996 No 3126)* or *section 124* of *PA 1995* (as appropriate).

Section 73(2) of *PA 1995*, as it applies to schemes in wind up before 6 April 2005, requires that the assets of the scheme must be applied first towards satisfying the amounts of the liabilities mentioned in *section 73(3)* of *PA 1995*. If the assets are insufficient to satisfy the amounts in full then the earlier paragraphs of *section 73(3)* of *PA 1995* take priority over the later paragraphs.

Any assets remaining after allocating these amounts in this way must then be used to satisfy any remaining liabilities, in the order of priorities set out in the scheme's own rules (*section 73(4) of PA 1995*).

The priority order in *section 73(3)* of *PA 1995* is as follows:

First priority – additional voluntary contributions benefits

Either in defined contributions form or added years. If added years, the benefits must be identified by the trustees as being accrued by reference to additional voluntary contributions.

Second priority – pre-1997 insurance policies

These are the liabilities secured where:

- the trustees are entitled to benefits under an insurance contract entered into:
    - *before* 6 April 1997; and
    - in order to secure all or part of the scheme's liability for any benefit payable in respect of one particular person whose entitlement to payment of a benefit has arisen (and for any benefit which will be payable in respect of him on his death); and
- either:
    - the contract may not be surrendered; or
    - the surrender value does not exceed the liability secured (excluding liability for pension increases).

This exemption for insurance policies only applies to policies taken out *before* 6 April 1997 and where they have been taken out after this date, they may need to be surrendered in order to comply with *section 73* of *PA 1995*.

Third priority – liability for benefits to which entitlement to payment has arisen and benefits which will be payable in respect of the person so entitled upon his death (excluding pension increases)

This will cover pensions in payment from the scheme and should also cover postponed pensioners (where a member has postponed taking benefits after normal retirement age) and any lump sum death benefits that arose prior to the commencement of the winding up.

Fourth priority – contracted-out benefits and refunds of contributions

Fifth priority – liabilities for increases to pensions referred to in the second and third priorities above

Where the increases to the pension arose prior to the date on which the winding up started, then they form part of the benefit liability as at that date and enjoy higher priority than post-wind up increases.

Sixth priority – liabilities for increases to pensions referred to in the fourth priority above

Seventh priority – other liabilities for accrued benefits (including pension increases)

This category is mainly for the deferred pensioners (including those with pension credits). Where the scheme is contracted out, it will cover non-guaranteed minimum pension benefits (as the contracted-out benefits currently have higher priority). For schemes that are not contracted out, a much larger proportion of the benefits will fall into this priority.

It also covers future pensions or other future benefits attributable (directly or indirectly) to pension credits (including increases to pensions).

(d)   Winding up started at any time from 10 May 2004 to 5 April 2005

A new transitional priority order was introduced for schemes that commenced winding up after 9 May 2004.

The main changes from the priority order that applied before 10 May 2004 is that: (i) increases on pensions in payment now fall below deferred benefits; and (ii) no priority is given to contracted-out benefits.

The transitional priority order is as follows:

First priority – additional voluntary contributions benefits

Either in defined contributions form or added years. If added years, the benefits must be identified by the trustees as being accrued by reference to additional voluntary contributions.

Second priority – pre-1997 insurance policies

These are the liabilities secured where:

- the trustees are entitled to benefits under an insurance contract entered into:

    - before 6 April 1997; and

    - in order to secure all or part of the scheme's liability for any benefit payable in respect of one particular person whose entitlement to payment of a benefit has arisen (and for any benefit which will be payable in respect of him on his death); and

- either:

- the contract may not be surrendered; or
- the surrender value does not exceed the liability secured (excluding liability for pension increases).

This exemption for insurance policies only applies to policies taken out *before* 6 April 1997 and where they have been taken out after this date, they may need to be surrendered in order to comply with *section 73* of *PA 1995*.

Third priority – liability for benefits to which entitlement to payment has arisen and benefits which will be payable in respect of the person so entitled upon his death (excluding pension increases)

This will cover pensions in payment from the scheme and should also cover postponed pensioners (where a member has postponed taking benefits after normal retirement age) and any lump sum death benefits that arose prior to the commencement of the winding up.

Fourth priority – liabilities for pensions or other benefits which have accrued to or in respect of any members of the scheme (excluding increases to pensions) and refunds of contributions

- Future pensions, or other future benefits, attributable (directly or indirectly) to pension credits (but excluding increases to pensions); and
- refunds of contributions for members with less than two years' service.

Fifth priority – liabilities for increases to pensions referred to in the second and third priorities above

Where the increases to the pension arose prior to the date on which winding up started, then they form part of the benefit liability as at that date and enjoy higher priority than post-wind up increases.

Sixth priority – liabilities for increases to pensions referred to in the fourth priority above

(e)   Winding up started on or after 6 April 2005

Section 270 of *PA 2004* replaces *section 73* of *PA 1995*. The new provisions only apply for schemes that start to wind up on or after 6 April 2005. The *Occupational Pension Schemes (Winding up etc) Regulations 2005 (SI 2005 No 706)* ('the *Winding-up Regulations 2005*') have been issued pursuant to the revised *section 73* of *PA 1995*, also with effect from 6 April 2006.

The intention behind the new requirements is to ensure that the winding-up provisions work in harmony with the provisions of *PA 2004* and associated regulations that establish the PPF and its procedures. The changes are intended to ensure that individual scheme members will be no worse off where their scheme winds up than they would be if the PPF were instead to assume responsibility for the scheme and pay compensation to members.

Sections 73, 73A and *73B* of *PA 1995* do not apply in relation to any liability for an amount by way of pensions or other benefits which a person became entitled to payment of, under the scheme rules, before the start of the winding up (*section 73B(6)* of *PA 1995*).

The new statutory priority order now set out in *section 73(4)* of *PA 1995* is as follows:

First priority – pre-1997 insurance contracts

This is a contract of insurance entered into before 6 April 1997 to secure certain scheme liabilities which may not be surrendered, or the amount payable on surrender does not exceed the liability secured by the contract (*section 73(5)* of *PA 1995*).

Second priority – liability for benefits to the amount of the corresponding PPF liability

This is the cost of securing the benefits that would be payable to a member under the pension compensation provisions if the PPF assumed responsibility for the scheme in accordance with *PA 2004* (*section 73(5)* of *PA 1995*). This means the pension compensation provisions set out in *PA 2004* are modified in certain respects (*section 73(4)(b)* of *PA 1995*).

Third priority – additional voluntary contributions benefits

Under the post-2005 priority order additional voluntary contributions benefits have been demoted from their top priority position to a lower priority. This is linked to the compensation mechanism within the PPF. The PPF compensation formula swallows up payments from additional voluntary contributions. As a result of this additional voluntary contributions (except those that have been turned into added years) fall behind the benefits for which PPF compensation is paid.

Fourth priority – any other liability in respect of pensions or other benefits

Once the PPF liabilities have been given priority, all other remaining benefits of members of the scheme are secured. In practice, this means that contracted-out benefits have no priority which fits with the position under the PPF. The fourth priority order will simply apply to all remaining benefits which are to be secured by the scheme.

Moving down the priority order

12.62 Once it has been established which priority order applies when securing members' benefits, the trustees have to work down the priority order securing benefits until they run out of funds. It is important to establish which category of membership applies to each individual member of the scheme – this is done by reference to the 'crystallisation date'. It is then necessary to decide how much to apply to each category. *PA 2004* has given the trustees new powers to make adjustments to the benefits of certain members that have to be secured which in turn has an impact on the amount to be applied for those members.

(*a*)   *Crystallisation date*

It is important to note that the status of the beneficiary (i e pensioner, deferred member) as at the date the scheme starts to wind up dictates the level of priority. This date is referred to as the 'crystallisation date'. *Regulation 4* of the *Winding-up Regulations (SI 1996 No 3126)* confirms the meaning of the crystallisation date. This is the date when the scheme starts to wind up; or if the trustees have determined to postpone winding up, such earlier date, prior to the actual winding up which is fixed by the rules of the scheme.

(*b*)   *How much to apply to each category*

Regulation 4 of the *Winding-up Regulations (SI 1996 No 3126)* sets out how the liabilities are calculated under *section 73* of *PA 1995*. A number of amendments have been made to *regulation 4* of the *Winding-up Regulations* as the amount to be applied to each category has increased over time.

(i)   *The sum needed to secure pensions in payment plus minimum funding requirement value* of *other benefits*

This amount applies where the members' rights crystallised before 19 March 2002. It also applies where all of the participating employers in the scheme immediately before the start of the winding up were insolvent.

The liabilities for benefits other than pensions in payment should be calculated in the manner specified in *regulations 7(2)*, *(3)* and *(7)* to *(10)* and *8(2)* of the *Occupational Pension Schemes (Minimum Funding Requirement and Actuarial Valuations) Regulations 1996 (SI 1996 No 1536)*. The liabilities do not include the expenses involved in meeting them and therefore the actuary should include no allowance for the buy-out costs.

(ii)   *Buy-out costs for pensions in payment and future increases plus minimum funding requirement value of other benefits*

This is the amount to apply to each category where:

- the rights crystallised on or after 19 March 2002, but before 11 June 2003; and

- the participating employers were not insolvent immediately before the start of winding up.

The amount to apply for pensioners is calculated as the cost of buying annuities in the market. The calculation of the minimum final requirement liabilities is as set out above but expenses are included. This reflects the position set out in the *Winding-up Regulations* (*SI 1996 No 3126*).

(iii) *Buy-out costs for all benefits*

This is the amount to apply to each category under *regulation 4* of the *Winding-up Regulations* (*SI 1996 No 3126*) where:

- the winding up started on or after 11 June 2003;

- the date chosen for calculating the statutory winding-up debt falls on or after 15 March 2004; and

- the participating employers were not insolvent immediately before the start of the winding up.

This change was introduced in March 2004 but was made retrospective to June 2003 because this is the time at which the change to buy-out costs was first announced by the Government.

Further changes were made in February 2005, so that if the winding up commences on or after 15 February 2005, the amount to apply is the buy-out costs for all benefits whether or not the employer participating in the scheme is solvent or insolvent. The buy-out costs for this purpose include full winding-up expenses.

(iv) *Actuarial Guidance Note GN19*

The scheme actuary calculates the value of the liabilities for the purposes of *section 73* of *PA 1995*. Actuarial Guidance Note GN19 gives the actuary guidance with regard to calculation of the scheme liabilities and any *section 75* debt arising. The actuary must certify that the calculation made of the liabilities is made in accordance with GN19.

(c) *New powers for trustees to make adjustments*

Sections 73A and *73B* of *PA 1995* confirm that during the winding-up period, no benefits may accrue to members under the scheme rules and no new members can be admitted to the scheme. The benefits to be secured are those that apply on the crystallisation date. However, the *Winding-up Regulations* (*SI 1996*

No 3126) permit the trustees to make adjustments to certain scheme liabilities in limited circumstances. These powers are intended to prevent the amount of the scheme's liabilities being increased after the date on which the winding up starts. This is consistent with the PPF rules in *PA 2004*.

(i) *Early leavers*

Members of the scheme who have completed more than three months' pensionable service but less than two years' pensionable service at the time that the scheme starts to wind up, are deemed to have chosen the contribution refund option on the day that winding up commenced (*section 73(9)* of *PA 1995* and *regulation 5* of the *Winding-up Regulations 2005* (*SI 2005 No 706*)). The trustees must therefore provide benefits for them on this basis.

(ii) *Discretionary awards*

If someone has exercised a power under the scheme rules to pay a discretionary award to a member in the winding-up period, the trustees can reduce the member's benefits if the effect of the discretionary award is to increase the scheme's liabilities. The adjustment will ensure that the total benefits for that member do not exceed the amount of their benefits immediately before the day that winding up commenced (*section 73A(7)* and (*8*) of *PA 1995* and *regulation 6* of the *Winding-up Regulations 2005* (*SI 2005 No 706*)). If the date of winding up is backdated because an assessment period has been triggered and a withdrawal notice given, the adjustment takes effect from the date that the award takes effect, rather than the date on which winding up is treated as having started.

Where a discretionary award takes effect during the winding-up period, the trustees must provide the affected member with a notice in writing within one month explaining that the trustees may make an adjustment to the award at a future date.

(iii) *Survivors' benefits*

If a member dies during the winding-up period and a survivor's pension comes into payment, the trustees can reduce the survivor's benefits if the effect of the payment is to increase the scheme's liabilities. The adjustment will ensure that the total benefits payable in respect of the member do not exceed the amount of the member's benefits immediately before the day that winding up commenced (*section 73A(7)* and (*8*) of *PA 1995* and *regulation 7* of the *Winding-up Regulations 2005* (*SI 2005 No 706*)). If the date of winding up is backdated because an assessment period has been triggered and a withdrawal notice given, the adjustment takes effect from the date that the entitlement to benefits arises, rather than the date on which winding up is treated as having started.

Where the entitlement to a survivor's benefit arises during the winding-up period, the trustees must provide the affected member a notice in writing within one month explaining that the trustees may make an adjustment to the benefits at a future date.

(iv) *Death benefits*

Where a member dies before winding up commenced but the trustees do not confirm a beneficiary's entitlement to death benefits until after the start of the winding up, then those benefits will be treated as having arisen before the commencement of winding up (*section 73B(8)* of *PA 1995* and *regulation 8* of the *Winding-up Regulations 2005 (SI 2005 No 706)*). This means that they will be excluded from the scheme liabilities for the purposes of the winding-up provisions in *section 73* of *PA 1995*.

(v) *Benefits discharged during an assessment period*

The PPF rules in *Part 2* of *PA 2004* allow certain liabilities to be validly secured during an assessment period. Where this happens those liabilities will be excluded from the scheme liabilities for the purposes of the winding-up provisions in *section 73* of *PA 1995* (*section 73B(6)* of *PA 1995* and *regulation 10* of the *Winding-up Regulations 2005 (SI 2005 No 706)*).

Defined contributions schemes

12.63 *Sections 73, 73A, 73B* and *74* of *PA 1995* do not apply and defined contributions schemes are not eligible for PPF protection. In normal circumstances at retirement the trustees will have purchased for existing pensioners an annuity with their money purchase 'pot' and this will be transferred into the name of the member on winding up. Deferred members' 'pots' will then be applied to purchase an annuity or will be transferred to another approved arrangement. The issue of 'priorities' is therefore not strictly relevant.

A facility enabling the trustees to deduct winding-up costs from members' defined contributions accounts prior to applying them for transfer/buy-out needs to be included. Schemes where there is a defined benefits and defined contributions section should make it clear that defined contributions assets cannot be used to subsidise a deficiency in the defined benefits section. By the same token defined contributions members may not necessarily expect to share in a defined benefits surplus.

Bulk transfers – specific issues where winding up has commenced

Preliminary

12.64 It is now appropriate to return to the subject of bulk transfers and address the questions of whether there is power to make a bulk transfer, and how any transfer payment is to be calculated, from a scheme that has begun to be wound up. (The corresponding position where the transferring scheme has not gone into winding up is dealt with in 12.45 to 12.47 above).

Power to make bulk transfers on winding up

Winding up started before 6 April 1997

12.65 In these circumstances, the existence of a power to make bulk transfers on winding up, and the question of who may exercise that power, is governed by the scheme's trust deed and rules.

Care should be taken to check whether any bulk transfer out power under those documents may be exercised during the winding-up stage. A transfer out power which is intended for use whilst the scheme is ongoing may well cease to be exercisable after winding up has commenced, depending on the exact wording of the scheme documents.

Winding up started after 5 April 1997

12.66 *Section 74* of *PA 1995* gives the trustees of approved defined benefit schemes which commence winding up after 5 April 1997 power to make bulk transfers even if there is no power to do so in the scheme rules (so long as the requirements in 12.61 above are met). Whether trustees have power to make a transfer from a scheme to which *section 74* of *PA 1995* does not apply will continue to depend upon the trust deed and rules.

Many schemes' rules give the principal employer a power to direct the trustees to make a bulk transfer. Any such power in an approved defined benefit scheme where winding up has started after 5 April 1997 needs to be considered in the context of *section 73(5)* of *PA 1995*. If it amounts to a power 'to apply the assets of the scheme in respect of pensions or other benefits', as the power will no longer be exercisable by the principal employer and will be exercisable by the trustees instead.

Amount to be transferred on a winding up

Winding up started before 6 April 1997

12.67   The amount to be transferred in these circumstances will depend upon the trust deed and rules. However, a minimum of the statutory cash equivalents of members' accrued benefits (see 6.40 above) must be transferred (although cash equivalents may be reduced to take account of underfunding – see 6.47 above for further details on the reduction of cash equivalents).

In the unlikely event of the transferring scheme being regarded by HMRC as overfunded, there may be difficulties in transferring the surplus to another scheme.

Winding up started after 5 April 1997

12.68   The position as set out in 12.67 above is subject to two further points in relation to approved defined benefits schemes where winding up instead commences after 5 April 1997:

(*a*)   if the scheme is underfunded, the amount of the transfer payment in respect of any given person must be consistent with the sums required to be allocated towards the scheme's various liabilities under the new statutory order of priorities (*section 73* of *PA 1995*, summarised in 12.61 above); and

(*b*)   under *PA 1995*, any power given by the scheme's rules to a person other than the trustees (the principal employer, for instance) 'to apply' scheme assets during winding up 'in respect of pensions or other benefits' will become exercisable by the trustees and not by that person. *PA 1995* prevents an employer from directing the trustees to transfer less than the amounts required under the new statutory order of priorities (see 12.61 above) but does not affect an employer's power under the scheme rules to decide whether the transfer amount should include any surplus.

Bulk transfers – overview

12.69   The following table provides an overview of the requirements governing bulk transfers as described in this chapter.

	1. Where the transferring scheme has not gone into winding up	**2. Where the transferring scheme has gone into a winding up which commenced before 6 April 1997**	**3. Where the transferring scheme has gone into a winding up which commenced after 5 April 1997**
A. Issues for trustees	Before exercising any discretion enabling the transfer to go ahead, issues which the trustees should consider may include: ● the effect of the transfer on members' benefits (issue for transferring trustees and receiving trustees – see 12.33); ● any disparity between the funding position of the transferring scheme and that of the receiving scheme (issue for transferring trustees and receiving trustees – see 12.34); ● the 'balance of powers' in the receiving scheme as compared with that in the transferring scheme (issue for transferring trustees – see 12.35); ● the long-term futures of the transferring and receiving schemes (issue for transferring trustees – see 12.36); and ● if the transferring scheme is already being wound up, the comparative merits of other ways of securing benefits (issue for the transferring trustees – see 12.37).		

B. Members' consents	Members' consents are required unless: ● scheme rules permit non-consent transfers; ● either: (*a*) both schemes relate to employment with the same employer; or (*b*) it is a bulk transfer either resulting from a financial transaction between the employers or where the employers are 'connected'; ● actuarial certificate GN16 is given; ● members are notified at least one month before transferring; and ● contracting-out requirements do not require members' consents.	Members' consents are required unless: ● either: (*a*) both schemes relate to employment with the same employer; or (*b*) it is a bulk transfer either resulting from a financial transaction between the employers or where the employers are 'connected'; ● actuarial certificate GN16 is given; ● members are notified at least one month before transferring; and ● either: (*a*) scheme rules permit non-consent transfers; or (*b*) the transferring scheme is an approved defined benefits scheme and the requirements mentioned in 12.61 are met; and ● any contracting-out requirements for members' consents are met.
C. HMRC approval	HMRC permission should be sought prior to 6 April 2006 in advance of transfer. If the transferring scheme is overfunded on HMRC basis, HMRC may refuse to agree to the transfer of that surplus to another scheme.	
D. Contracting out	Further requirements may apply if either the transferring scheme or the receiving scheme is contracted out, depending on the circumstances (see 4.33).	As for columns 1 and 2, except that, if the transferring scheme is an approved defined benefits scheme, it may be sufficient to meet the requirements by notifying the Regulator.

E. Do trustees have power to make a bulk transfer?	Depends on scheme rules.	Depends on scheme rules.	If transferring scheme is an approved defined benefits scheme, yes. Otherwise, depends on scheme rules.
F. Can the employ-er(s) *require* the trustees to make a bulk transfer?	Depends on scheme rules.	Depends on scheme rules.	Depends on scheme rules *except* that, if any such power of the employer (in an approved defined benefits scheme) amounts to a power 'to apply the assets of the scheme in respect of pensions or other benefits', that power becomes exercisable by the trustees and not by the employer(s).
G. How is the transfer payment calculated?	As set out in the scheme rules, but subject to: ● H below where the transferring scheme is in deficit; and ● C above where the transferring scheme has a surplus.	As set out in the scheme rules, but subject to: ● H below where the transferring scheme is in deficit; and ● C above where the transferring scheme has an HMRC surplus.	As set out in scheme rules, but subject to: ● H below where the transferring scheme is in deficit; ● C above where the transferring scheme has a surplus; and ● the fact that, if an approved defined benefits scheme's rules give to any person other than the trustees (e g the employers) power 'to apply the assets of the scheme in respect of pensions or other benefits', that power ceases to be exercisable by that person and becomes exercisable instead by the trustees.

H. Deficit: may the scheme rules provide for the transfer payment to be reduced to take account of underfunding in the transferring scheme?	Yes, so long as members are not denied their statutory cash equivalents. Some reduction of cash equivalents is, however, permissible in cases of underfunding (see 6.51).	Yes, so long as members are not denied their statutory cash equivalents. Some reduction of cash equivalents is, however, permissible in cases of underfunding (see 6.51).	Yes, subject: ● (in relation to an approved defined benefits scheme) to complying with the statutory order of priorities (as explained in 12.61); and ● (in relation to other schemes) as set out in column 2.
I. Surplus: may the scheme rules provide for the transfer payment to include a share of any surplus in the transferring scheme?	Yes, but see C above where there is a surplus.	Yes, but see C above where there is a surplus.	Yes, but subject to: ● C above where there is a surplus; and ● the fact that, if an approved defined benefits scheme's rules give to any person other than the trustees (e g the employers) power 'to apply the assets of the scheme in respect of pensions or other benefits', that power ceases to be exercisable by that person and becomes exercisable instead by the trustees (see 12.60).

Sanctions against trustees under PA 1995

12.70   Trustees who disregard the provisions of *PA 1995* as summarised in this chapter may be subject to prohibition orders and civil penalties. Further details appear in the table set out in appendix I.

Chapter 13

Small self-administered schemes

Introduction

13.1   Small self-administered schemes ('SSASs') were first developed in the early 1970s as a result of the decision to permit private company directors to join occupational pension schemes (*Finance Act 1973*). SSASs were promoted as a means of providing directors with their own pension fund whilst, at the same time, allowing some of the money in the fund to continue to work for the business by way of loans and leasebacks.

As with other pensions arrangements, the rules for SSASs will change radically from April 2006. The new legislation will no longer use the term 'SSAS', but it is retained for this chapter, for convenience.

HMRC estimated in April 2004 that there were almost 38,000 SSASs then in existence, with almost 90,000 members.

SSASs are occupational defined contributions schemes. Very few are operated on a defined benefits basis. SSASs operate under a legal and regulatory structure which differs in a number of respects from larger schemes, for example:

(*a*)   one trustee must (until April 2006) be a pensioneer trustee (see 13.4 below);

(*b*)   the investment rules for some small schemes are different (see 13.14 to 13.27 below);

(*c*)   some *PA 2004* provisions do not apply, particularly if (as is usual) all members are appointed trustees (see 13.31 below); and

(*d*)   the requirements for reporting to APSS have been stricter.

This chapter aims to focus on those issues which arise most in practice.

There have been six main sources of information for those involved with advising on SSASs:

(i) statutes, particularly *Part XIV* of the *Income and Corporation Taxes Act 1988* and *PA 1995*;

(ii) a number of statutory instruments, referred to below;

(iii) Part 20 of 'Occupational Pension Schemes Practice Notes', booklet IR12 (2001) ('PN') published by HMRC;

(iv) HMRC's internal manual 'SSAS Guidance Notes' published under the Open Government rules;

(v) regular APSS practice statements, formerly called Joint Office Memoranda and Pension Schemes Office ('PSO') Updates, and now called Pensions Updates; and

(vi) regular Newsletters published for members by the former Association of Pensioneer Trustees (the 'APT').

Development of the regulatory framework

History

13.2 Typically, the directors (and shareholders) of the sponsoring company and the members and trustees of the SSAS will all be the same people. This close identity of interests provided some scope for abuse, prompting the APSS's concern that SSASs may in some cases be operated other than for the sole purpose of the provision of benefits on retirement. This concern led to the APSS's first attempt to regulate SSASs as a specific group, codified in its Memorandum No 58 (issued in February 1979). This Memorandum represented a general guide to the exercise of APSS discretion in approving SSASs.

The *Retirement Benefits Schemes (Restriction on Discretion to Approve) (Small Self-Administered Schemes) Regulations 1991 (SI 1991 No 1614)* ('the *SSAS Regulations*') then set out a regulatory framework within which SSASs must be administered on a day-to-day basis. These *SSAS Regulations* were amended in 1998 by two further sets of regulations, and main aim of the changes was to tighten up on the role of the APSS's 'watchdog', the pensioneer trustee. The *Regulations* have been further amended by the *Retirement Benefits Scheme (Restriction on Discretion to Approve (Small Self Administered Schemes) Regulations (Amendment) Regulations 2000 (SI 2000 No 1086)*.

The *Retirement Benefits Schemes (Information Powers) Regulations 1995 (SI 1995 No 3103)* (amended by the *Retirement Benefits Schemes (Information Powers) (Amendment) Regulations 2002 (SI 2002 No 3006)*) introduced a requirement for reports to be made to the APSS of certain investment transactions by SSASs.

PSO Update 69, published on 29 August 2000, enhanced the role of the pensioneer trustee in relation to SSASs (see 13.15 below).

Changes affecting pension schemes generally have also affected SSASs – as, for instance, the introduction of self-assessment tax returns, changes in data protection legislation, and changes resulting from the *Financial Services and Markets Act 2000* (*FSMA 2000*).

The April 2006 changes (stemming from the *Finance Act 2004*) remove the requirement for a pensioneer trustee. Special treatment is, however, retained for schemes which are broadly those previously defined as SSASs – those with fewer than twelve members, where all members are trustees and trustees' decisions are unanimous.

Over the years, practitioners saw the need to come together to negotiate jointly with the APSS, the Department for Work and Pensions and other official bodies. As a result, the APT was formed in the early 1980s. It was the practice of the APSS to consult with the APT on many proposals for changes relating to SSASs, with a view to ensuring that the changes will be clear and workable in practice. In 2005 the APT merged with the SIPP Providers Group, to form the Association of Member-Directed Pension Schemes ('AMPS').

Formal definition of an SSAS

13.3 A SSAS was defined (under *regulation 2* of the *SSAS Regulations* (*SI 1991 No 1614*)) as a scheme:

(*a*) with some or all of its income and other assets invested otherwise than in insurance policies;

(*b*) where the number of active members is below twelve (although there are a few instances where the APSS may treat a scheme as an SSAS where there are more than twelve members); and

(*c*) where at least one scheme member (i e a current active member) is 'connected' to:

- another member; or

- a trustee of the scheme; or

- a person who is an employer in relation to the scheme.

Before 6 April 2006 an investment company could not set up an SSAS, but this will now change.

In place of the 'SSAS' definition, the Government appears to be using more widely the definition 'self-directed pension schemes' to refer to those arrangements (such as an SSAS or a Self-invested Personal Pension Scheme ('SIPP')) where investment decisions are made by the member.

Pensioneer trustee

13.4   Up until 2006 there is a requirement for an SSAS to have a pensioneer trustee (*regulation 9* of the *SSAS Regulations (SI 1991 No 1614)*). Approval criteria for pensioneer trustees were restated in PSO Update 69. A pensioneer trustee is an individual or body recognised by the APSS as:

(*a*)   being widely concerned with SSASs;

(*b*)   having evidenced that knowledge in relation to at least 20 SSASs; and

(*c*)   having given confirmation to the APSS in the form set out in PSO Update 69. The pensioneer trustee must agree not to consent to any action that he considers infringes any approval requirement in relation to an SSAS, and not to consent to the termination of the SSAS otherwise than in accordance with the approved terms of the winding-up rule. A company which is a pensioneer trustee must demonstrate that a person with the required experience and knowledge (see (*a*) and (*b*) above) is in a position of authority with the company, so that the company is able to comply with its obligations to the APSS (IR12 (2001) PN 20.6).

In practice the pensioneer trustee (or another company in the same group) sometimes carries out administrative, consultancy, actuarial, investment management and legal work in relation to the SSAS. Sometimes these roles are split between two or more advisers. Different arrangements are adopted by different practitioners.

Since 1998 the pensioneer trustee has been prohibited from terminating his appointment to a given scheme, unless he dies, is removed by a court order, the APSS withdraws his pensioneer trustee status, an order by the Regulator (previously Opra), is made, or (most significantly) someone else is willing and able to be appointed as pensioneer trustee in his place. This rule (currently in *regulation 9* of the *SSAS Regulations (SI 1991 No 1614)*) is expected to be changed with effect from 6 April 2006.

In certain circumstances a pensioneer trustee must be appointed to act in respect of a personal pension scheme – see Pensions Update 118, 25 February 2002.

After April 2006, pensioneer trustees will need to decide whether they should continue in office as trustees, or whether they should resign. If they do nothing, then they will remain trustees. If before 6 April 2006 they were the administrator of an existing scheme under *section 611AA* or *section 638(1)* of the *Income and Corporation Taxes Act 1988*, then they will become the 'Scheme Administrator' for the purposes of *section 270* of *FA 2004*.

So the pensioneer trustee will need to decide if he wants the liabilities that go with being the scheme administrator. There is a heavy burden in terms of responsibility for filing reports and returns, liability for taxes and penalties, and other duties.

If the pensioneer trustee accepts these responsibilities, it is suggested that:

● there will be costs in terms of staff training and systems;

● he must have contractual arrangements in place with his clients;

● he must have sufficient control over the scheme to know what payments are being made in and out of the scheme;

● he should probably also be a co-owner of the assets, and a mandatory co-signatory on the scheme bank account, as originally stipulated by Update 69 for pensioneer trustees;

● he must be aware that as a trustee he may incur liabilities to third parties such as banks; and

● he should ensure that the scheme documents are changed to reflect the new position.

He may also want to review the indemnity and exoneration provisions in the scheme documents.

If, on the other hand, the pensioneer trustee wants to resign, he will need (among other things) to:

● check the scheme rules to see the powers of resignation and removal;

● perhaps amend the scheme rules to remove the previous restriction on the pensioneer trustee resigning;

● resign (or be removed) in a way that ensures a discharge for him;

● cease to be a signatory on the scheme bank account;

● cease to be a co-owner of the assets, and reassign to the remaining trustees the legal title to any policies held by the trustees;

● cease to be a party to any scheme borrowing;

● remove any restriction at the Land Registry which prevents a dealing (without his approval) with any property owned by the scheme;

● notify any investment managers with whom an investment management agreement has been signed;

- notify the Information Commissioner's Office; and
- notify HMRC (in accordance with his undertaking to HMRC).

Practice

13.5   Up until 6 April 2006, the provisions of the *SSAS Regulations* (*SI 1991 No 1614*) must be incorporated in all SSAS documentation. After that date, and as a result of what HMRC describes as 'a complete overhaul of the way pensions are taxed', HMRC do not need to see the documents establishing a scheme, when a scheme applies for registration (*RPSM02101020*). Registration does not amount to endorsement by HMRC. There is no particular legal form for a registered pension scheme (*RPSMO2102040*). So there is not the same insistence on certain provisions being in the scheme documents. The emphasis changes to the way in which schemes are operated. Payments into and out of the scheme will have certain tax consequences, whatever the rules may say. However, payment should not of course be made unless the scheme rules permit them to be made.

Because individuals will have more flexibility in deciding how to save for their old age, it will not necessarily be tax factors that govern whether they wish to contribute to an SSAS or to some other pension arrangement. Other factors will come into play for individuals in weighing up different kinds of pension arrangement, including:

- whether they want control over investment decisions;
- whether they want responsibility for running the scheme themselves, with outside help;
- whether they would prefer specialists to run the scheme, with implications for lack of control and lack of individual flexibility;
- the different investment possibilities that are available with different pension arrangements; and
- the comparative cost of different arrangements.

Some have suggested that the element of individual control which an SSAS brings for trustees, coupled with the ability to lend money back to a sponsoring employer which is not available for an SIPP, will ensure the continued success of the SSAS format.

Funding SSASs and payment of benefits

13.6   Before 6 April 2006, SSASs were subject to the usual funding principles which applied to all approved schemes. For instance, employers must be under an obligation to contribute, and contributions must be actuarially justifiable. New maximum funding rules for SSASs came into effect on 1 June 1996. Limited revisions were introduced by Pension Update 137 of 11 March 2003.

After 6 April 2006, there is no limit on the amount of contributions that can be made to a registered pension scheme by a member, an employer or another person (*RPSM05100030*). But there is a limit on the amount of tax relief that may be received.

Historically members have not often contributed to SSASs, but if they do in the future the new annual allowance rules will apply.

For employer contributions, there is no set limit and normal rules as to deductibility of a payment as a business expense apply. The payment must be wholly and exclusively for the purposes of the employer's business (*RPSM05102010*). There is a special rule for contributions by an employer for members who are directors and shareholders. The contribution must be 'in line with the contribution that would have been made to fund the pension provision for an unconnected employee in a similar situation' (*RPSM05102170*).

There are particular rules too for contributions in specie (*RPSM05101020*).

The former requirement for contributions to be justifiable by actuarial valuation reports has fallen away, and there was a relaxation of the requirement to submit AVRs to HMRC in the year leading up to 6 April 2006 – see Pensions Update 155 (16 September 2005).

Spreading

13.7   Given that many SSASs are established by relatively small companies, whose ability to make consistent contributions will often be limited, the APSS's previous insistence that tax relief on special contributions (that is, contributions in excess of the amount set out in the most recent actuarial valuation report) should be spread into future tax years seemed harsh.

As from 1 June 1996 this requirement fell away, ensuring increased flexibility for companies with variable yearly cash flow. Basically, any special contribution below £500,000, once actuarially justified, is permissible. The APSS still reserves the right to spread contributions in excess of £500,000 (*RPSM05102070*).

Deferred annuities

13.8   HMRC originally required that pensions coming into payment under SSASs should be secured as soon as possible by the purchase of an annuity from a life office, with a maximum long-stop period of five years from retirement. Investment restrictions apply during this five-year period.

However, scheme rules may provide for the purchase of the annuity for members and widows and dependants alike to be deferred for longer (up to age 75), and for the pension to be paid in the meantime from the scheme's resources (Memorandum 119; PSO Update 14 (26 March 1996); IR12 (2001) PN 20.38 et seq). The trustees might choose to use this facility if, for example, annuity rates at the time of a member's retirement are unfavourable, or if they prefer for the time being not to pay a capital sum to an insurance company.

Note that annuities generally may be purchased in the name of the member or beneficiary, rather than the names of the trustees.

Pensions must be bought out by age 75. If a member has reached age 75 before 6 April 2006, the APSS's view is that an annuity should be purchased (without the option of an alternatively secured pension) because otherwise any post-6 April 2006 payments will be unauthorised.

Actuary's certificate

13.9   For annuity deferral, the actuary must at the time when the payment of the pension begins and the annuity purchase is to be deferred, certify the amount of pension under the scheme rules which the scheme is capable of providing.

The certificate must compare the pension provided from the scheme with an annuity that could be secured on the open market on the same terms at the time the funds are available. Any difference in excess of 10 per cent between the two amounts must be explained by the actuary.

Loans, share purchases and borrowing

13.10   Where a pension is being paid directly from the scheme, the actuary must ensure that the portion of the fund nominally underpinning the deferred annuity is excluded when calculating the maximum sum available for loans to the employer or associated employers (see 13.21 below regarding loans made by SSASs), or with which to purchase shares in the employer or 'associated' employer.

As with the calculations for loans and share purchases the retired member's fund must be excluded during the deferral period from the scheme assets in calculating the maximum available borrowing limit. There has been a five-year transitional period enabling the trustees to reduce existing borrowings to the acceptable level in the event that a member retires.

If all scheme members (or their survivors) are in receipt of a pension, no new loans to, or share purchases in, the employer or an associated employer are permitted nor any share purchase in any other unquoted company. There is then a five-year transitional period during which all existing loans must be repaid and/or relevant shares sold.

Investment in property and drawdown

13.11   The trustees are still able to invest in property during the deferral period provided sufficient readily realisable assets are available to purchase the annuity from age 70 onwards. This avoids a forced sale situation when the member who has deferred the purchase of an annuity is between 70 and 75 years old and an annuity needs to be purchased.

On 30 June 1999, HMRC introduced a more flexible facility allowing scheme rules of approved SSASs that provide only defined contributions benefits to defer the purchase of an annuity and in the meantime pay pensions by income drawdown (PSO Update 54 (30 June 1999)).

Detailed rules are to be made available covering the position that will apply after 6 April 2006.

Borrowing by SSASs

Before April 2006

13.12   Until 6 April 2006, there is a restriction on the amount of money which trustees may, at any time, borrow on behalf of the scheme. (*SSAS Regulations (SI 1991 No 1614), reg 4*). The total amount borrowed must not, in aggregate, exceed the total of:

(*a*)   three times the 'ordinary annual contributions' paid by the employer;

(*b*)   three times the annual amount of basic or contractual contributions paid by the scheme members in the year of assessment ending immediately before the date on which the borrowing takes place; and

(*c*)   45 per cent of the market value of the investments then held for the purposes of the scheme, (excluding funds notionally underpinning benefits in payment and any outstanding sum borrowed to purchase those investments) (IR 12 (2001) PN 20.62 et seq).

The pensioneer trustee must be a party to borrowings (IR 12 (2001) PN 20.28) although lenders will often agree to exclude the personal liability of the pensioneer trustee to repay the sums borrowed, and interest (see 13.15(*d*) below).

All borrowings must be used to benefit the scheme, and must be reported to the APSS within 90 days on Form PS7015. (Small short-term borrowings, however, need not be reported – IR12 (2001) PN 20.66.)

Where borrowings from a company are proposed, and the trustees are directors of that company, consideration should be given to the *Companies Act 1985* restrictions on loans to directors.

After 6 April 2006

13.13 Borrowing by trustees to acquire an asset is authorised if the trustees are satisfied that the borrowing will benefit the scheme, and that it complies with HMRC's rules. Borrowing includes a situation where a debt is to be paid from the scheme. Borrowings from connected parties will result in a tax charge unless the transaction is at arm's length.

The limit for authorised borrowings is 50 per cent of the net value of the fund, after any existing borrowings. The formula to be applied, which deals with the valuation of pensions in payment, is at *RPSM07104030*. If the value of the fund later drops, there is no need to retest the value against the 50 per cent limit. Borrowings over the limit will be unauthorised, so will attract a scheme sanction charge. Details are at *RPSM07104050*.

Borrowings made before 6 April 2006 will not be 'retested' at that date, although they must be taken into account on any further borrowings (*RPSM07104070*).

Investments by SSASs – general

Financial services regulation

13.14 Trustees should bear in mind the application of the *Financial Services and Markets Act 2000* (*FSMA 2000*).

For self-administered schemes in general it is common for trustees to delegate the exercise of their investment powers to a person authorised under *FSMA 2000*. (In the case of an SSAS, this may be the pensioneer trustee, or an associate of the pensioneer trustee, if in either case he is authorised.) This is so that the trustees do not 'carry on a regulated activity ... by way of business' in contravention of *FSMA 2000, ss 19* and *22*.

Trustees of SSASs may, however, want to rely on a specific exemption from *FSMA 2000*. The *Financial Services and Markets Act 2000 (Carrying on Regulated Activities by Way of Business) Order 2001 (SI 2001 No 1177), art 4* (amended by *SI 2005 No 922*) follows on from the similar exemption that used to apply under *section 191* of the *Financial Services Act 1986*. The exemption provides that a person is not treated as 'managing investments' for the purposes of *FSMA 2000* if he is a member-trustee of an SSAS, or he is a trustee who takes no part in day to day investment management decisions. For the exemption to apply, all members (including for instance deferred and pensioner members) must be trustees, and day-to-day investment decisions must be taken by all (or a majority) of the members, if of course they are not taken by a person who is authorised under *FSMA 2000*.

The FSA has published a detailed guidance note covering the application of *FSMA 2000* to pension scheme trustees generally.

Further regulation came into effect in January 2005, as a result of the *Insurance Mediation Directive 2002/92/EC* and the *Financial Services and Markets Act 2000 (Regulated Activities) (Amendment) (No 2) Order 2003 (SI 2003 No 1476)*. Among other things, these changes affected a pensioneer trustee who, for payment, arranged for SSAS trustees (including himself) to enter into an insurance policy, to be held as an investment of the SSAS.

Co-ownership and co-signatory requirements

13.15 HMRC brought in new rules in August 2000, in PSO Update 69. They were incorporated in IR12 (2001), largely in PN 20.17 to 20.33. The objective of the rules was to encourage greater compliance with HMRC's requirements. The general principles were that where it is legally possible the pensioneer trustee should be a registered co-owner (along with the other trustees) of all the assets; and that the pensioneer trustee's signature should be required to move any funds out of SSAS bank, building society and other types of investment accounts.

As to co-ownership, there were detailed rules. Some assets acquired before 1 October 2000 are not affected. The precise requirements depend on the nature of the asset. For shares, the pensioneer trustee's name must appear on the company's share register. For investment management arrangements entered into by the trustees, shares may be registered instead in the name of the investment manager's nominee company, but only if the shares cannot be transferred out of the investment manager's control without the pensioneer trustee's written approval. (IR 12 (2001) PN 20.23 and 20.24).

For loans made by the SSAS, the pensioneer trustee must be a party to the loan agreement, and similarly with insurance policies the pensioneer trustee's name should appear on the policy.

Particular rules apply for land. The situation is complex for four reasons:

(*a*)   England and Wales, Scotland and Northern Ireland each have different land laws.

(*b*)   With registered land, in England and Wales, an alternative to the pensioneer trustee becoming a registered owner is for a 'restriction' to be registered, to the effect that the land cannot be disposed of without the written consent of the pensioneer trustee.

(*c*)   Ownership of land may bring with it certain liabilities, such as duties in respect of any asbestos, and liability for clearing up costs in the event of contaminated land. The pensioneer trustee will want to avoid taking on such liabilities.

(*d*)   Often land is purchased by an SSAS with the aid of a bank loan (see 13.12 above). The pensioneer trustee must be a party to the borrowing, but will want to avoid becoming personally liable to repay it. The APSS has confirmed, in the answers to the 'frequently asked questions' on PSO Update 69, that: 'the Update does not require the pensioneer trustee to enter into any covenants in favour of the lender to, say, repay the sum borrowed, or to pay interest on that sum. The Update does not require the pensioneer trustee to put itself in a position where it could be sued by the lender.'

As to the co-signatory requirements, the pensioneer trustee must be a mandatory signatory (not merely an optional signatory) on bank current and deposit accounts which hold scheme assets. There is of course a requirement in *PA 1995* for there to be a scheme bank account. Contributions, transfers-in and proceeds of sale of scheme assets must be paid into an account on which the pensioneer trustee is a co-signatory (IR (2001) PN 20.30). All movements of money out of SSAS bank accounts must be authorised by the pensioneer trustee, except:

(i)   regular payments previously authorised by the pensioneer trustee and covered by direct debit or standing order arrangements – examples are given in IR12 (2001) PN 20.31;

(ii)   payments out of loan or overdraft accounts (IR12 (2001) PN 20.31); and

(iii)   transfers between SSAS current and deposit accounts, where the transfer arrangements have been agreed in general by the pensioneer trustee (IR12 (2001) PN 20.29).

From 6 April 2006, since there will be no need for a pensioneer trustee, these co-ownership and co-signatory arrangements (and the protection for the Exchequer which they bring) will no longer be required by tax law. Where

SSASs wish to remove the pensioneer trustee as a co-owner and as co-signatory, new instructions are likely to have to be given in respect of each asset. Holdings of land and of investments will need to be re-registered, re-negotiations with lenders may be required, and new signing instructions will have to be given to banks. Whilst welcoming simplification in general, the AMPS has commented that the new rules will be 'reversing all the good work achieved by PSO Update 69'.

Prohibited investments

Personal chattels

13.16   Originally the tax simplification proposals were intended to allow great flexibility in terms of investments. The prohibition on a scheme acquiring personal chattels which had been in place since 1991 was to be removed. But on 5 December 2005 the Chancellor's Pre-Budget Report stated that as from 6 April 2006 the tax advantages from putting certain assets such as wine, cars, art and antiques in a pension scheme would be removed. The phrase used was 'most forms of tangible moveable property'. Both direct and indirect investment is covered, and the effect of making such an investment will be that the scheme will be subject to an unauthorised member payments charge (*section 208* of *FA 2004*). The total tax charge could be 70 per cent of the value of the assets, with a possible further charge of 40 per cent of the value of the scheme if the scheme is de-registered.

Residential property

13.17   There is also currently a ban on all investments 'directly or indirectly' in residential property.

There are limited exceptions where employees need to occupy residential premises as a condition of employment (for instance, as a caretaker), or as a direct result of occupation of business premises. There are regulations preventing any such permitted occupant being a member or being connected with a member or the employer company (IR 12 (2001) PN 20.72).

Further exemptions cover holdings in authorised property unit trusts, and investments in ground rents and similar interests, where there is no member occupation (IR12 (2001) PN 20.73).

The 2005 Pre-Budget Review also affected investment in residential property. Investments of this kind were originally to be allowed as from 6 April 2006, but this was changed on 5 December 2005. Direct and indirect investment in residential property by self-directed pension schemes is now to result in a tax charge. Indirect investment would include a case where a pension scheme held 100 per cent of the shares in a company which itself owned residential property. Legislation is to be published setting out the detail. It is expected that the limited exceptions to the existing rules (set out above) will continue to apply, and that investment in 'genuinely diverse commercial vehicles that hold residential property or other prohibited assets' will be allowed. An example of those vehicles given by the Treasury is an investment in the proposed new form of real estate investment trust. Another might be holdings in authorised property unit trusts, which are permitted currently.

Substantial shareholdings

13.18 Investments were formerly prohibited in shares in unlisted companies which carry with them in excess of 30 per cent of the voting power or dividend rights of the company *(SSAS Regulations (SI 1991 No 1614), reg 5)*.

This no longer applies. In order to avoid an unauthorised payments charge and a scheme sanction charge, the market value of shares acquired in a sponsoring employer should not exceed 5 per cent of the value of the assets of the scheme. Shares in more than one sponsoring employer may be acquired, but the overall limit is 20 per cent *(RPSM07105020)*.

Transactions between approved and non-approved schemes

13.19 Many transactions between tax-approved schemes and non-approved schemes were formerly prohibited. This prohibition caught shared investments, preventing (for instance) an SSAS and a funded unapproved retirement benefit scheme ('FURBS') buying a property jointly, particularly where a member of the SSAS (or a person connected with him) has an interest in the FURBS. It also caught sale purchase and lease transactions between an SSAS and a FURBS. For details it is necessary to refer to PS Update 102 and IR12 (2001) PN 20.77 to 20.79.

Transactions with members or connected persons

13.20 Purchase, lease or sale transactions directly, or indirectly, with a scheme member or someone 'connected' with that member are also banned before 6 April 2006 *(SSAS Regulations (SI 1991 No 1614), reg 8)*.

The ban on transactions with scheme members (or persons 'connected' with them) applies so that the trustees cannot purchase property which has, at any time in the last three years, been owned by a member or 'connected' person.

Similarly the trustees should not sell property which will in the next three years be sold on to a member or 'connected' person (IR 12 (2001) PN 20.67 and 20.69).

Loans to members or 'connected' persons are prohibited (*SSAS Regulations (SI 1991 No 1614), reg 6*). This prevents the amount available for pensions being artificially reduced, and any attempt to circumvent this ban by means of a back-to-back arrangement would result in scheme approval being withdrawn.

'Members' has a wide meaning here, and can include deferred and pensioner members, ex-spouse members and even former members if they are still in the service of a participating employer.

The APSS reviews transactions in order to satisfy itself that they do not involve a member or 'connected' person. Note, however, that by the *SSAS Regulations (SI 1991 No 1614), reg 11*, the restrictions on assets held by an SSAS in 1991 are looser in some respects than the restrictions affecting subsequently acquired assets.

The rules change as from 6 April 2006. *RPSM07012110* makes clear that: 'there is no objection in principle to a registered pension scheme entering into transactions with a member or a person/company connected with a member. However, various tax charges are imposed where any investment transactions entered into by the scheme are not on arm's length terms.'

Loans by SSASs

Permitted loans

13.21   Loans by SSASs are generally permitted, subject to the ban on loans to members and persons connected with them and subject to the overall requirement of prudence. Loans should be made on a commercial basis. In particular, loans are permitted to employers and other 'associated' employers for the purpose of the borrower's business, subject to the restrictions below and the self-investment restrictions. Interest on loans can now be paid gross (*Finance Act 2002, s 94*).

For loans, there are 'grandfathering' provisions such that if a loan made by a pension scheme was valid according to the rules in place before 6 April 2006, then the loan will not be subject to the new rules applying after 6 April 2006, so long as there are no changes in the repayment terms after that date. A 'rollover' for no more than five years will, provided other conditions are satisfied, not be treated as a change to the repayment terms for this purpose.

13.22 *Small self-administered schemes*

The meaning of loan is extended to include guarantees given by the scheme, but excludes loan stock and debentures and instruments offered to the public.

Loans made after 6 April 2006 will fall into one of three categories, and each category is treated differently.

(*i*) *Loans to members and parties connected with members*

Loans to members, and parties connected with members or with sponsoring employers, should be avoided as they are unauthorised payments and will result in a scheme sanction charge. 'Connected' for this purpose is defined in *section 839* of the *Income and Corporation Taxes Act 1988 (ICTA 1988)*.

(*ii*) *Loans to sponsoring employers*

These are authorised employer payments so long as the terms of *section 179* of *ICTA 1988* are complied with. Five tests must all be satisfied. These relate to:

- the taking of **security** – the loan must be secured by a first charge;

- **interest** rate – the minimum rate is 1 per cent above clearing bank base rates (dealt with in the *Pension Schemes (Prescribed Interest Rates for Authorised Employer Loans) Regulations 2005 (SI 2005 No 3449))*;

- the **term** of the loan – it must be no longer than five years;

- the maximum **amount** of the loan – no more than 50 per cent of the value of the net assets of the scheme; and

- the **repayment** terms – the loan must be repaid to the scheme by equal capital and interest instalments over the period of the loan.

Any loan that does not satisfy each of these tests will result in an unauthorised payment charge.

(*iii*) *Loans to separate and independent third parties*

These are permissible. They should be made on an arm's length basis and at a commercial rate.

Rollovers

13.22 Rollovers of loans are permitted for a period of up to five years. RPSM should be checked for the rules relating to rollovers of loans made before 6 April 2006, as the rules for these loans are slightly different.

Investment in shares

13.23 Investments by pension schemes in shares, listed or unlisted, issued by companies in the UK or overseas, are permitted. But there is a restriction on the number of shares in a sponsoring employer that can be acquired by a pension scheme.

The limit is on the percentage of the value of the net assets of the pension scheme that can be invested in the shares of any one sponsoring company. The limit is 5 per cent. If the scheme wishes to buy shares in more than one sponsoring company it can do so, provided the 5 per cent limit for each sponsoring company is not exceeded, and provided the total invested in shares in sponsoring companies does not exceed 20 per cent. There are provisions dealing with the method of valuation.

There is no separate limit on the percentage of the share capital in any one company that can be acquired. So a pension scheme could buy 50 per cent of the shares in a company, so long as the value was still less than 5 per cent of the net assets of the scheme.

Any investments in excess of the 5 per cent and 20 per cent limits will be subject to an unauthorised payments charge, and a scheme sanction charge.

Shares in a sponsoring employer held before 6 April 2006 may continue to be held.

Self-investment

13.24 Until 6 April 2006, both loans to and the purchase of shares in an employer or 'associated' employer, are subject to APSS limits on self-investment (*SSAS Regulations (SI 1991 No 1614), reg 7*). The requirements are that:

(*a*) for the first two years of a scheme's life self-investment does not exceed 25 per cent of the market value of the scheme assets derived specifically from contributions from the employer and employee since the date of establishment; and

(*b*) from two years onwards self-investment must not exceed 50 per cent of the market value of all the scheme assets. (The key difference, therefore, apart from the percentage increase, is that for the first two years transfers-in cannot be taken into account.)

It should also be noted that the APSS applies these self-investment limits to loans to and shares in other persons and companies connected with the scheme via a member, trustee or employer.

An exemption from the 5 per cent limit on employer-related investments for SSASs was originally in the *Occupational Pension Schemes (Investment) Regulations 1996 (SI 1996 No 3127)*. This exemption is in general continued by the *Occupational Pension Schemes (Investment) Regulations 2005 (SI 2005 No 3378)*. The exemption applies to 'small schemes', which are defined broadly as schemes:

- with less than twelve members;
- who are all trustees; and
- either the rules provide for all decisions to be made unanimously by the member-trustees, or there is an independent trustee appointed under *section 23* of *PA 1995*. (This exception is not the same as providing for a pensioneer trustee).

There are corresponding provisions covering cases where a small scheme has a corporate trustee, of which all members are directors.

A check should be made to ensure that scheme rules permit the investment.

From 6 April 2006, there is a fixed limit of 5 per cent on the value of the scheme assets which can be invested in shares in a single employer – see 13.18 above.

Investment in real property

Prohibitions

13.25 Before 6 April 2006, there was a general prohibition on investment in residential property (see 13.17 above). It is now possible, but subject to heavy tax charges – see **13.17** above. The former ban on transactions with members and 'connected' persons is lifted, but there are tax charges where transactions are not at arm's length (see **13.20** above).

Permitted investments

13.26 Commercial property has been a popular investment for trustees of pension schemes. The APSS has for a long time emphasised that while property may be a good long-term investment the trustees should bear in mind the need to have liquid funds to pay pensions. It points out that if a property is purchased which forms an important part of the employer's business premises, it may be difficult to realise.

Trustees also need to be aware that the holding of property brings with it liabilities under statute and liabilities to third parties – such as liabilities under the *Control of Asbestos at Work Regulations 2002 (SI 2002 No 2675)*.

Trustees should also be wary of investing in limited liability partnerships – see *RPSM 04103010*.

Value-shifting

13.27 Trustees of SSASs will need to be particularly aware of the new value-shifting provisions (*FA 2004, s 174*). HMRC considers that value can be shifted out of a pension scheme to a member or a connected person without making an actual payment, and that this can be done either by increasing the value of an asset, or decreasing the liability of a member or employer. A transaction other than on arm's length terms which falls into this category can be treated as an unauthorised payment, with severe tax consequences.

Examples could include changing the rights attaching to shares, or changing rights and restrictions relating to property held by the scheme.

It may be that trustees will need to be more careful to obtain independent valuations before entering into transactions that could fall foul of the value-shifting rules.

Tax avoidance and the bona fides of the scheme

General

13.28 The practice of the APSS before 6 April 2006 was in general only to interfere with the trustees' exercise of their power of investment where:

(*a*)   tax avoidance is suspected; or

(*b*)   scheme investments seem irreconcilable with the bona fide sole purpose of the scheme being to provide retirement benefits (IR12 (2001) PN 20.51).

The APSS has expressed concern about investment by SSASs in certain overseas arrangements which appear to be promoted with tax avoidance in mind, and which (in return for a large fee) promise that members can receive assets from the SSAS tax free. Serious doubts have been expressed about whether these schemes work.

Withdrawal of approval and de-registration

13.29   Until 6 April 2006, the APSS's power to withdraw the approval of a scheme (*section 591B(1)* of *ICTA 1988*) will be operated on a purely discretionary basis.

Approval may be withdrawn for serious rule breaches. In addition, in certain instances the APSS has set specific time limits for regulatory changes in scheme documentation. Failure to comply with these deadlines could have serious effects. *Section 61* of the *Finance Act 1995* introduced a 40 per cent tax charge on the market value of a scheme's assets if the scheme loses approval for any reason. This penalty could include non-deliberate failings of the trustees, for example, to keep the trust documentation up to date in line with APSS regulations.

The so called 'trust busting' provisions, introduced by the *Finance Act 1995,* should also be borne in mind. A 40 per cent tax charge will result if SSASs are used as a method of tax avoidance. The general consequences of approval being withdrawn before 6 April 2006 include:

(*a*)   lump sum benefits paid will generally not be tax free;

(*b*)   employees become liable to tax on any subsequent contributions by the employers;

(*c*)   from the date of withdrawal all applicable exemptions or reliefs cease;

(*d*)   the capital gains tax exemption is withdrawn on any capital gains realised on or after withdrawal of approval (IR 12 (2001) PN 19.3.)

After 6 April 2006, withdrawal of approval is replaced by de-registration. A scheme can be de-registered if HMRC consider that there is a failure to pay tax or provide information, or in certain other cases. Reference should be made to *section 174* of *FA 2004*. The 40 per cent tax charge on the assets of the scheme which applied on the loss of approval before 6 April 2006 will also apply on de-registration after 6 April 2006. Other tax charges may also apply.

Trading

13.30   *Section 592(2)* of *ICTA 1988* exempts income from investments and deposits held for the purposes of the scheme from income tax. Any income which is considered by the APSS to be derived from trading does not, however, benefit from this exemption.

The issue of trustees' trading is something which concerns not only the APSS but HMRC generally. Trustees may trade, but if they do then there may be a tax liability.

If in any doubt trustees should seek professional advice at the earliest point.

PA 1995

13.31 Generally speaking *PA 1995* is limited in its application to SSASs as SSASs are specifically exempted from many of the provisions. Practice since the advent of *PA 1995* has illustrated that the bulk of its protective requirements are largely unsuitable for SSASs where there is such community of interest between members, trustees and employers.

The Green Paper, 'Partnership in Pensions', published by the Government in December 1998, looked in detail at the relevance of *PA 1995* to SSASs. It acknowledged that application of the legislation to SSASs was complex, inconsistent, confusing and generally inappropriate and recommended a widening of the exemptions.

Those areas of *PA 1995* specifically exempting SSASs or treating them differently from other schemes are as set out in the table below.

Application of PA 1995 to SSASs and small schemes

13.32 Until 6 April 2006 a number of exemptions for SSASs apply. After this date the definition of SSAS is not needed, so the scope of some of the exemptions will change. Under the *Occupational Pension Schemes (Scheme Administration) Regulations 1996 (SI 1996 No 1715)* ('the *Scheme Administration Regulations*') (as amended), the exemption applies to schemes with fewer than twelve members where all members are trustees and either decisions are made unanimously by the member-trustees or there is a statutory independent trustee. There is an equivalent exemption for small schemes which have a sole corporate trustee of which all members are directors, and all decisions are either made by all the member-directors unanimously, or where there is a statutory independent director.

Subject	Position for SSASs	Authority
Advisers	An auditor must be appointed in accordance with the requirements of *PA 1995* and the *Scheme Administration Regulations* (*SI 1996 No 1715*) (as amended) unless the small scheme exemption above applies or the scheme only has one member. An actuary is not needed for a defined contributions scheme.	*PA 1995, ss 47* and *48* and *Scheme Administration Regulations 1996 (SI 1996 No 1715)*.

Compensation scheme/PPF	Exempt where only one member or all members are trustees and their decisions can (by the rules) only be made by unanimous agreement. This exemption continues for the Pension Protection Fund.	*PA 1995, s 81(1)* and *Compensation Regulations* (*SI 1997 No 665*).
Disclosure	Exemption where one member only, and trustees have no disclosure obligations to members where all members are trustees.	*Disclosure Regulations* (*SI 1996 No 1655*).
Disputes	Exempt where either only one scheme member or all members are trustees.	*Dispute Regulations* (*SI 1996 No 1270*).
Equal treatment	No exemption unless one member only.	*PA 1995, ss 62 to 66* and *Equal Treatment Regulations* (*SIs 1995 No 1215* and *1995 No 3183*).
Independent trustee appointment	Exempt from appointing independent trustee if a defined contributions scheme. In defined benefits schemes, appointment required where not all members are trustees.	*Independent Trustee Regulations* (*SI 1997 No 252*).
Investment	Exempt from self-investment restrictions under *PA 1995*, but different restrictions apply. Statement of investment principles not needed where the small schemes exemption above applies.	*PA 1995, ss 34* and *35* and *Investment Regulations* (*SI 1996 No 3127*). *OPS Investment Regulations 2005* (*SI 2005 No 3378*).
Member-nominated trustees	Exempt.	*MNT Regulations* (*SI 1996 No 1216*).
Payment schedules, and scheme funding requirements	Broadly the small scheme exemption above applies.	*Scheme Administration Regulations 1996* (*SI 1996 No 1715*) and *OPS* (*Scheme Funding*) *Regulations 2005* (*SI 2005 No 3377*).
The Regulator	Trustees may be liable to suspension, disqualification, fines and imprisonment.	Various. *PA 1995, ss 6, 9* and *10*.
Pensions Ombudsman	No exemption from Pensions Ombudsman's jurisdiction.	*PA 1995 ss 156 to 160* and *SI 1991 No 588*.

Registration	Exempt if only one member.	*Register of Occupational and Personal Pension Schemes Regulations 2005 (SI 2005 No 597).*
Transfers	No exemption.	*PA 1995, ss 152 to 154* and *SI 1996 No 1847.*
Winding up	*Section 73* does not apply to small schemes mentioned above.	*Occupational Pension Schemes (Winding-up, etc) Regulations 2005 (SI 2005 No 706).*

Future

13.33   It is clear that a small defined contributions scheme under the new post-April 2006 rules will be very different to an SSAS pre-April 2006. Administration requirements will increase, and in particular those who deal with small schemes will need to watch carefully the potential for tax charges, and for liabilities on administrators.

For those who have the option to choose between membership of an SSAS and membership of an SIPP, a number of factors will need to be taken into account in selecting the right format (see **13.5** above). However, SSAS providers are confident that some clients will continue to find the SSAS format attractive.

Chapter 14

Personal pension and stakeholder schemes

Introduction

14.1   This chapter describes personal pension schemes, self-invested personal pension schemes and stakeholder schemes. Unless stated otherwise, the descriptions given in this chapter with regard to personal pension schemes (with the exception of self-invested personal pension schemes) also apply to stakeholder schemes.

14.2   This chapter deals with HMRC approved personal pension and stakeholder schemes and many of the conditions and restrictions referred to are as a consequence of tax legislation, most notably *ICTA 1988*. The changes introduced by *FA 2004*, which came into force on 6 April 2006, represented a significant change to legislative framework that supports personal pension schemes and many of the conditions and restrictions found in this chapter therefore, also changed from 6 April 2006. From that date personal pension schemes will be governed by the unified and simplified tax regime contained in *FA 2004*.

Much of this chapter represents a historical picture, which will nonetheless remain relevant by virtue of the fact that an appreciation of past regimes remains vital in understanding and operating pension schemes, be they occupational or personal pension schemes. Instead, going forward, much of the statutory framework relating to personal pension schemes will be found in *FA 2004* and, therefore, chapter 5 of this book.

14.3   The forerunner of the personal pension scheme was the 'retirement annuity contract' ('RAC'). RACs were first introduced in the 1950s. They subsequently became governed by *section 226* of the *Income and Corporation Taxes Act 1970* and consequently are often referred to as *section 226* policies. The most significant distinctions between RACs and personal pension schemes are:

(*a*)   RACs were only available to the self-employed and those in non-pensionable employment (i e broadly speaking, employment where the employer did not provide a pension scheme); an individual could not leave an occupational pension scheme and take out an RAC if he remained employed by the sponsoring employer of that occupational scheme;

(*b*)   an individual's employer is not permitted to contribute to an RAC but can contribute to a personal pension scheme (*ICTA 1988, s 620*); and

(*c*)   insured personal pension schemes allow individuals to contract out of the Second Tier State Scheme ('S2P') (formerly the State Earnings Related Pension Scheme ('SERPS')) via an 'Appropriate Personal Pension Scheme' ('APPS') – there was no such facility under an RAC. [*PSA 1993, s 43(1)*].

Although RACs are still in existence and contributions can still be made to them, it has not been possible to establish a new RAC since 1 July 1988.

Personal pension schemes first became available on 1 July 1988, although the concept of personal pensions was originally brought in by the *Social Security Act 1986*. The main reason for the introduction of personal pensions was to allow individuals who did not have access to a company sponsored group scheme (or who wanted to leave such a scheme whilst still employed by the sponsoring employer i e to 'opt out') the opportunity of building up their own pension entitlement. The power of an employee to leave their occupational scheme whilst remaining an employee was one of the major factors in the pensions mis-selling scandal and has resulted in many providers of personal pension schemes having to pay substantial compensation in order to re-instate those individuals' mis-sold personal pensions back into their previous occupational schemes. Personal pension schemes were also designed to give individuals the opportunity (at their own volition) to contract out of SERPS on an individual basis.

The introduction of the concept of the Self-Invested Personal Pension Scheme ('SIPP') in the 1989 Budget led to individuals having even more choice in retirement provision by giving the member the opportunity to become involved in decisions about the investment of contributions. SIPPs have tended to attract higher earners because of the higher costs of administration and membership and the general complexity of such arrangements. SIPPs are not suitable vehicles for contracting out and, therefore, if a SIPP member wishes to contract out of S2P this should be achieved by taking out a separate APPS for this purpose. Originally, the requirements for a SIPP (in addition to those personal pension requirements already set out in HMRC's Practice Notes) were outlined in Memorandum No 101 published in October 1989. However, this Memorandum was superseded by the Personal Pension Schemes Practice Notes IR76 (2000) and in particular by the *Personal Pension Schemes (Restriction on Discretion to Approve) (Permitted Investments) Regulations 2001 (SI 2001 No 117)* which came into force on 6 April 2001. For more details regarding these Regulations see 14.59 below.

14.3 *Personal pension and stakeholder schemes*

Personal pension schemes, like occupational pension schemes, had to be approved by HMRC if they were to benefit from the full range of tax advantages. The *Finance (No 2) Act 1987* introduced legislation governing the approval and tax treatment of personal pension schemes. This legislation is now consolidated in *sections 630 to 655 of ICTA 1988* which, as mentioned above, will be repealed from 6 April 2005. Although, for many years, it was anticipated that the then Inland Revenue would publish a separate set of Practice Notes that would deal specifically with the requirements relating to SIPPs this has not happened. However, the Practice Notes IR76 (2000) describe in much greater detail than previously APSS's specific requirements in relation to SIPPs. Previously, the Personal Pension Schemes Practice Notes were drafted very much from the perspective of insured personal pension schemes. That anomaly has been largely addressed.

Stakeholder schemes were introduced by the Government in an attempt to considerably increase pension coverage for the UK working population. One of the main driving forces was that stakeholder schemes were to be low cost personal pension schemes. They were originally introduced by the *Welfare Reform and Pensions Act 1999* and the first stakeholder schemes were available from April 2001. It is a requirement that a stakeholder scheme, in order to be recognised as such, has to be registered with the Regulator and approved by HMRC. Stakeholder schemes were also approvable under *Chapter IV* of *Part XIV* of *ICTA 1988* in the same way as personal pension schemes and will therefore come under the auspices of *FA 2004* from 6 April 2006. Stakeholder schemes were registrable from 1 October 2000 but they could only commence from 6 April 2001.

In order that the Government's objective for stakeholder schemes is met, the *Welfare Reform and Pensions Act 1999* stated that, in many cases, an employer must offer access to a stakeholder pension scheme. This is known as the 'Employer Access Requirement'. Unless exempt, an employer has to select a stakeholder pension scheme that the employees could join if they so wish. Membership of the scheme is not compulsory. In addition an employer does not have to contribute on behalf of the employee. The exemptions, whereby, if one of them is satisfied, there is no obligation upon the employer to arrange access to a stakeholder scheme are to be found in *regulation 22* of the *Stakeholder Pension Schemes Regulations 2000 (SI 2000 No 1403)* (as amended). These exemptions include:

(*a*)   The employer already offers an occupational pension scheme that all staff are eligible to join within one year of commencing work for the employer.

(*b*)   The employer employs less than five people. In determining this all employees must be counted which may include company directors (but does not include any self-employed persons). If the employer has five or more employees but fewer than five meet the conditions to have access then these employees must be given access to a stakeholder scheme.

(*c*)   If the employer already offers to make contributions to a personal pension scheme in respect of that employee, providing that the scheme:

   (i)   is receiving a contribution from the employer of at least 3 per cent of the employee's basic pay (note that an employer does not have to count overtime, commission or bonuses when calculating this figure);

   (ii)   does not penalise members for ceasing contributions or transferring their entitlements;

   (iii)   is offered to every employee who would in law have access to a stakeholder scheme (ignoring anyone under age 18).

The Regulator

14.4   One major change introduced by *PA 2004* of particular relevance to personal pensions has been that the Regulator, the successor body to Opra, now includes personal pensions as well as occupational pensions within its remit. In turn, this means that the Regulator will be able to use the raft of new powers that are available to it under *PA 2004* in relation to personal pension schemes. These powers are discussed in chapter 2.

HMRC approval of the scheme

Personal pension scheme providers

14.5   A personal pension scheme will currently only be approved by HMRC if it is established by a permitted 'Provider' (*ICTA 1988, s 632*). The list shown below applies from 6 April 2001. It also applies to stakeholder schemes established under contract.

'(1) ...

(a)   a person who has permission under Part 4 of the Financial Services and Markets Act 2000 to effect or carry out contracts of long-term insurance or to manage unit trust schemes authorised under section 243 of that Act;

(aa)   an EEA firm of the kind mentioned in paragraph 5(d) of Schedule 3 to the Financial Services and Markets Act 2000 which—

   (i)   has permission under paragraph 15 of that Schedule (as a result of qualifying for authorisation under paragraph 12 of that Schedule) to effect or carry out contracts of long-term insurance; and

        (ii)   fulfils any one of the requirements under subsections (5), (6) or (7) of section 659B;

(ab)   a firm which has permission under paragraph 4 of Schedule 4 to the Financial Services and Markets Act 2000 (as a result of qualifying for authorisation under paragraph 2 of that Schedule) to manage unit trust schemes authorised under section 243 of that Act;

(ac)   a person who qualifies for authorisation under Schedule 5 to the Financial Services and Markets Act 2000;

(b)   a building society within the meaning of the Building Societies Act 1986;

...

(c)   a person falling within section 840A(1)(b);

(cc)   a body corporate which is a subsidiary or holding company of a person falling within section 840A(1)(b), or is a subsidiary of the holding company of such a person;

...

(e)   an institution which—

        (i)   is an EEA firm of the kind mentioned in paragraph 5(a), (b) or (c) of Schedule 3 to the Financial Services and Markets Act 2000;

        (ii)   qualifies for authorisation under paragraph 12(1) or (2) of that Schedule, and

        (iii)   has permission under Financial Services and Markets Act 2000 to manage portfolios of investments.

(1A) The Board may approve a personal pension scheme established by any person other than a person mentioned in subsection (1)(a) to (e) if the scheme is established under a trust or trusts.

(2) In subsection (1)(a) above "contracts of long-term insurance" means contracts which fall within Part II of Schedule 1 to the Financial Services and Markets Act 2000 (Regulated Activities) Order 2001.

(2A) In subsection (1)(cc) above "holding company" and "subsidiary" are to be construed in accordance with section 736 of the Companies Act 1985 or Article 4 of the Companies (Northern Ireland) Order 1986.

...

(3) Subsection (1) above shall not apply in relation to a scheme approved by APSS by virtue of section 620(5) if it was established before 1 July 1998.'

[ICTA 1988, s 632]

'Authorised Corporate Directors' of OEICs can also become a 'Provider' by virtue of paragraph 2.2 of IR76 (2000) subject to certain conditions.

After 6 April 2006, both trust and non trust based personal pension schemes will have to be established by one of the entities listed in *FA 2004*. These can be found in 5.1 above.

The Administrator

14.6   In addition, HMRC also require there to be a person resident in the United Kingdom who is responsible for the management and administration of the scheme. [*ICTA 1988, s 638(1)*]. This person, known as the administrator, can be any corporate body or individual appointed for the purpose, including the Provider, an employee of the Provider or the trustees of a scheme established by trust.

Once again, after 6 April 2006, the appointment of an administrator will be governed by *FA 2004*. See 5.3 above.

Applying for approval

Personal pension schemes

14.7   The provider of a personal pension scheme must apply to HMRC on the appropriate form (PSPP101) to have the scheme approved. Approval, prior to 6 April 2006, is granted under *Chapter IV* of *Part XIV* of *ICTA 1988*.

In order to obtain HMRC approval, it is necessary (under *section 633* of *ICTA 1988*) to satisfy HMRC that the sole purpose of the scheme is the provision of benefits on retirement or death (see 14.14 below) and to comply with HMRC's requirements relating to how these benefits are provided. The HMRC has published Model Rules (coded IMR 2003) for personal pension schemes and, if these are incorporated in full without amendment, the scheme will usually be granted approval very quickly.

There are four versions of IMR 2003. These are:

(*a*)   IMR 2003 (this covers all types of schemes);

(*b*)   IMR 2003 PP (abridged version – cannot be used for contracted-out personal schemes or stakeholder schemes);

(*c*)   IMR 2003 CO (to be used by contracted-out personal pension schemes (but not stakeholder)); and

(*d*)   IMR 2003 SHP (to be used by contracted-out personal pension schemes that are also stakeholder schemes).

If a SIPP is being established the documentation will need to include the relevant additional provisions for conditions applicable to SIPPs in addition to the Model Rules. A version of IMR 2003 should have been adopted and in place by 6 April 2004 if, for no other reason, to demonstrate compliance with the *Personal Pension Sharing* (*Restriction on Discretion to Approve*) (*Permitted Investments*) *Regulations 2001* (*SI 2001 No 117*).

Schemes still operating on the 1995 Model Rules must have adopted a version of IMR 2003 by 6 April 2004.

Various documents have to be prepared when establishing a tax approved personal pension scheme. HMRC has relaxed the amount of documents it requires to review when making application for tax approval but, of course, HMRC expects that the rest of the documentation used in connection with the personal pension scheme fully satisfies the requirements of IR76 (2000). Details of how to apply for the tax approval of a scheme are contained in Part 13 of IR 76 (2000). As mentioned, Form PSPP101 is currently required and this lists the accompanying documentation required when submitting the form.

If anyone knowingly makes a false statement on making an application for approval of a personal pension scheme or for the purpose of obtaining relief from or repayment of tax, a penalty not exceeding £3,000 may be imposed. [*ICTA 1988, s 653*].

Stakeholder schemes

14.8   Unlike personal pension schemes, a stakeholder scheme can be considered to be either an occupational scheme (where, as a consequence, the majority of *PA 1995* would then apply) or a personal pension scheme. This is because a stakeholder scheme can either be established on a contract basis or a trust basis. If a trust basis is selected then most of the *PA 1995* applies. Where a stakeholder scheme has been established purely for a specific employer or group of employers then occupational pension scheme rules will apply. In the majority of cases stakeholder schemes will be established under contract and, because the majority of individuals and employers are likely to be joining a scheme already set up by a financial institution (for example, an insurance company) the scheme will be governed by a deed (as is sometimes also the case for personal pension schemes where the provider is an insurer and the investments under the scheme consist purely of insurance products) or a board resolution. Careful consideration would need to be given when establishing a stakeholder scheme under trust because much of the regulatory framework that some employers will be trying to avoid by not establishing a pure occupational pension scheme will, in fact, apply equally to a trust based stakeholder scheme. For example, a trust based stakeholder scheme needs to appoint a scheme auditor and the requirement to ensure that there is suitable diversification of investments as described in *PA 1995*. Industry-wide stakeholder schemes must be established under trust.

When making an application for a stakeholder scheme the applicant needs to obtain the standard application pack for 'Establishing a Stakeholder Pension Scheme' from HMRC (this is also available on its website). All stakeholder pension schemes must be capable of accepting a transfer of pension rights for any member. Such a transfer could include 'contracted-out rights' and therefore the application must include an election to contract out of S2P. As stated previously registration for stakeholder schemes commenced from 1 October 2000 but the effective date of approval could not have been earlier than 6 April 2001. HMRC had discretion to issue approval notices before 6 April 2001 but this did not mean that the stakeholder scheme could be operated before 6 April 2001. There is also a standard stakeholder registration application that the applicant needs to complete and send to the Regulator. The governing rules for stakeholder schemes are, as with personal pension schemes, IMR 2003.

Once the registration forms to both HMRC and the Regulator have been submitted, if HMRC decides that the scheme is approvable they will then consult with the Regulator and then either confirm to the applicant that the scheme qualifies as a stakeholder scheme or, alternatively, that it does not and refuse the application. In the event of the application being refused it is not a question of simply amending the application already made – a fresh application for registration would have to be submitted in these circumstances. HMRC will also inform the appropriate tax offices for both the provider and the administrator that approval has been granted. [paragraph 13.17 of IR76 (2000)].

After 6 April 2006, all pension schemes seeking 'registration' will follow the same process. This is to be found in *section 153* of *FA 2004* and *RPSM02101010*, which details the information that must be submitted by the scheme administrator. This is also highlighted in 5.3 above.

Membership of a personal pension scheme and stakeholder scheme

Conditions for membership

14.9   An individual may become a member of a personal pension scheme or stakeholder scheme only if he has not attained age 75. With effect from 6 April 2001 it was no longer essential that an individual always had 'net relevant earnings' in order to make contributions to a personal pension scheme (IR76 (2000) PN 3.7). This means that any individual who is under age 75 and is either:

(*a*)   resident and ordinarily resident in the UK at sometime in the relevant tax year; or

(*b*)   a Crown servant; or

(*c*)   the spouse of a Crown servant,

may, subject to requirements relating to a person who is also accruing benefits under a tax-approved occupational pension scheme, join a personal pension scheme. If the individual does not have any 'relevant earnings' or does not fall under the concession described above, he may become a member of a personal pension scheme so that it can receive a transfer payment, but in this situation, no contributions can be made to the scheme by or in respect of the individual until he has 'relevant earnings'.

Concurrency

14.10   With effect from 6 April 2001, there are provisions (IR76 (2000) PN 3.16) in force relating to what is known as 'concurrency', i e where a person accrues benefits under an occupational pension scheme and, at the same time, is permitted to pay contributions to a personal pension scheme. The individuals that are permitted to do this must fall under at least one of the following categories.

The individual:

(*a*)   is being provided with death in service benefits only under the occupational pension scheme (IR76 (2000) PN 3.20); or

(*b*)   is joining the personal pension scheme solely for the purpose of contracting out of S2P (IR76 (2000) PN 3.21); or (*c*)   can satisfy all of the following requirements in relation to the year in question:

    (i)   at some time in the year, the individual is either resident and ordinarily resident in the UK, or is overseas, a Crown servant or the spouse of a Crown servant;

    (ii)   is not, and has not been a 'controlling director' of a company at any time in the year or in any of the five tax years preceding it (note: tax years prior to 2000/2001 do not count); and

    (iii)   in at least one of the five tax years preceding the year in question, the individual has had an 'aggregate grossed up remuneration' not exceeding the 'remuneration limit' for that earlier year (again, tax years prior to 2000/2001 do not count). (The 'remuneration limit' is described in *section 632B(4)* of *ICTA 1988* and can be amended by Treasury Order.)

An individual who satisfies the above conditions is then permitted to contribute to a personal pension scheme up to the earnings threshold. Another important concession here is that where concurrent membership takes place in accordance with these provisions then the individual's personal pension scheme benefits can be ignored when assessing his maximum benefits (in accordance with HMRC limits) under the occupational scheme. A member of a personal pension scheme must immediately notify the scheme administrator if they join an occupational pension scheme. If this notification is not given at the time of joining it must be given the next time they make a contribution to the personal pension scheme.

In relation to a new stakeholder scheme the following employees are not entitled to access to a stakeholder scheme in accordance with *regulation 23* of the *Stakeholder Pension Schemes Regulations 2000* (as amended) even where the employer has a basic obligation to provide a stakeholder scheme for certain of its employees, i e where that employee:

(*a*)   is already a member of the employer's occupational pension scheme or would be qualified to be a member if he had been employed by that employer for a period of more than twelve months; or

(*b*)   has worked for the employer for less than three months in a row; or

(*c*)   has not been able to join the occupational scheme of the employer solely because the scheme does not permit employees under the age of 18 or where the employee is already within five years of that scheme's normal pension age;

(*d*)   has earnings that have fallen below the National Insurance lower earnings limit for a period of one or more weeks within the last three months;

(*e*)   would have been eligible to join the occupational pension scheme but has opted not to or ceased to be a member of that occupational pension scheme; or

(*f*)   is not eligible to join a stakeholder scheme because an APSS condition means he is not eligible.

An employee of the type listed above will not be a 'relevant employee' for the purposes of *section 3* of *WRPA 1999*.

The employer is obliged to discuss with eligible employees and any representative organisations the employer's plans for the stakeholder pension scheme. There is flexibility here in how this is achieved, for example, by way of a meeting or by giving details in writing and then asking for feedback. Once the consultation process is completed it is the employer who makes the final decision. The employees may, despite the employer setting up a stakeholder scheme, decide to join a different stakeholder scheme. Of course, if an employee already contributes to another pension scheme that can continue or they may choose to transfer to the employer's new stakeholder scheme.

'Relevant earnings'

14.11   Relevant earnings are defined in *section 644* of *ICTA 1988* as any earned income which is chargeable to income tax for the year of assessment in question and which falls within one of the following categories:

(*a*)   general earnings from an office or employment held by the individual (unless *section 645* of *ICTA 1988* applies);

(*b*)   income from any property which is attached to, or forms part of, the emoluments of an office or employment held by him or her (unless *section 645* of *ICTA 1988* applies);

(*c*)   income chargeable under *Part 2* of the *Income Tax (Trading and Other Income) Act 2005* immediately derived from the carrying on or exercise of a trade, profession or vocation (either as an individual or as a partner acting personally or in a partnership);

(*d*)   income from patent rights which is treated as earned income by virtue of *section 833(5B)* of *ICTA 1988*.

However, certain elements of remuneration are specifically excluded from the definition of 'relevant earnings', including:

(i)   anything arising from the acquisition or the disposal of shares or an interest in shares or from a right to acquire shares and which is chargeable to tax under *ITEPA 2003*; and

(ii) payments and benefits on the termination of employment and anything else that is chargeable to tax by virtue of *Chapter 3* of *Part 6* of *ITEPA 2003*.

Other items that do not count as relevant earnings include pension benefits in payment and benefits paid by the state. A useful list of those items that constitute relevant earnings and those that do not constitute relevant earnings are to be found in Appendix 2 and 3 of IR76 (2000).

Miscellaneous membership requirements

14.12 With the exception of the concurrency rules described above (effective from 6 April 2001) it has always been possible for an individual to be a member of more than one personal pension scheme in respect of the same source of income. However, the additional establishment and administration costs which may be incurred usually do not make this an attractive or viable option. The maximum percentage limit of contributions (see 14.32 below) must be adhered to irrespective of the number of schemes.

If an individual has more than one source of income he may be a member of a personal pension scheme in respect of one source and a member of an occupational pension scheme in respect of another source. Similarly, the individual could enter into several personal pension arrangements, having a separate one for each source of income. In this situation a separate maximum percentage limit of contributions will then apply to each separate occupational/personal pension arrangement.

Membership after 6 April 2006

14.13 From 6 April 2006, as with many of the changes introduced by *FA 2004*, the issue of 'membership' will be largely removed. Instead, *FA 2004* seeks to ascertain which individuals ('relevant UK individuals') will be able to claim tax relief in relation to their registered pension scheme. This is dealt with in chapter 5. The concept of 'relevant earnings' will remain as 'Relevant UK Earnings' after 6 April 2006 in order to determine the tax relief available to an individual.

Benefits payable from a personal pension scheme

General

14.14 The benefits that are listed below stem from the provisions of *ICTA 1988* and will be repealed from 6 April 2006. The benefits that can be provided by a registered pension scheme after 6 April 2006 are now covered in chapter 5.

A personal pension scheme is a defined contributions scheme (sometimes also known as a 'money purchase scheme'). The benefits it can provide are determined by the level of contributions paid to it and the amount of investment growth achieved on those contributions. The only control on funding is the level at which contributions may be paid (see 14.31 below). No actuarial calculations and recommendation as to the funding of a personal pension scheme are required. The value of the assets of the scheme at the time of payment of benefits determines the level of benefits to be paid.

The only benefits which a personal pension scheme could provide were, until May 1995, annuities payable to the member on his retirement, annuities payable to his spouse and/or dependants on his death or a lump sum payable on the retirement of the member or on his death. HMRC impose conditions on the type of annuity which may be provided and on the amount of cash lump sum which can be taken (see 14.16 to 14.19 below). Since May 1995 it has been possible for a member to defer purchasing an annuity and instead make income withdrawals (known as 'income drawdown' or 'income withdrawal') from the scheme (see 14.21 below).

Pension date

14.15 The scheme rules of a personal pension scheme will usually allow the member to choose the date on which he retires but the date must generally not be before age 50 nor after age 75 (*ICTA 1988, s 634*). The date on which a member chooses to receive his benefits is referred to as his 'pension date'. HMRC will allow a pension date earlier than age 50 if they are satisfied that the member's occupation is one in which people usually retire before age 50. For example, if HMRC is satisfied that a member is a professional athlete, the rules of the scheme may allow the member to choose a pension date of age 35. The following is a list of occupations where APSS permit a pension date to be set that is lower than age 50. Certain other conditions do also apply (see Appendix 10 of IR76 (2000)).

Profession or occupation	Retirement age
Athletes	35
Badminton players	35
Boxers	35
Cricketers	40
Cyclists	35
Dancers	35
Divers (saturation, deep sea and free swimming)	40

Footballers	35
Golfers	40
Ice hockey players	35
Jockeys – flat racing	45
Jockeys – national hunt	35
Members of the reserve forces	45
Models	35
Motor cycle riders (motocross or road racing)	40
Motor racing drivers	40
Rugby league/union players	35
Skiers (downhill)	30
Snooker/billiards players	40
Speedway riders	40
Squash players	35
Table tennis or tennis (including real tennis players)	35
Trapeze artists	40
Wrestlers	35

From 6 April 2006 it will not be permissible to have a normal minimum pension age of less than 50 (age 55 from 2010) except in cases of ill health (*section 165 of FA 2004*). As such, it will no longer be possible from 6 April 2006 to have the differential normal pension ages applied to certain occupations detailed above. However, where an individual had an existing actual or prospective right to take their benefits earlier than age 50, they may still be able to do so subject to fulfilling certain conditions. These are discussed in *paragraphs 22* and *23* of *Schedule 36* to *FA 2004* and *RPSM03106010*.

Annuity payable to a member

14.16 Before his pension date a member will need to take advice about annuity rates and decide how much of the fund he wishes to take as tax free cash (see 14.17 below). The remaining fund will be used to purchase an annuity (*ICTA 1988, s 634*; see also IR76 (2000) PN 9.2 to PN 9.8). The annuity purchased for the member must satisfy the following conditions:

(*a*) it must be payable by an authorised insurance company situated within the EU which may be chosen by the member (the member is not obliged to choose the provider of the scheme (assuming, of course, the provider is an insurance company) as the insurance company which provides the annuity, although the rules of a scheme may require this);

(*b*) from September 2002 members of a personal pension scheme or stakeholder scheme must be told of the existence of an open market option as well as the general advantages and disadvantages of exercising the option, how the option is exercised and the advisability of seeking professional advice; this is not pertinent to a self invested personal pension scheme;

(*c*) it must commence on the member's pension date, although it may commence earlier if the member retires due to ill-health, and must be payable for life;

(*d*) it may be guaranteed for a specified term not exceeding ten years (although it is more usual for a five-year period to be selected), so that it continues to be paid at the full rate in the event of the member's death during that term or the equivalent of that amount is paid as a lump sum upon the death of the member;

(*e*) it must not be capable of assignment or surrender; the only exception to this is that an annuity which has a guarantee period may be assigned on the death of a member by his will;

(*f*) it may increase in line with the Retail Prices Index or at a fixed percentage per annum or remain at the same level, i e 'static' throughout the period of payment; and

(*g*) it may be payable in advance or in arrears and may be of any frequency of payment.

Tax free cash lump sum payable to the member

14.17 Except where the arrangement consists solely of protected rights or monies transferred from a designated scheme, a member may elect to receive part of his benefit in the form of a tax free cash lump sum (IR76 (2000) PN 9.41 to PN 9.56). If a member wishes to receive a lump sum he must make an election to that effect on or before his pension date. A cash lump sum is payable subject to the following conditions:

(*a*) It must be paid at the same time as the balance of the fund is used to provide the annuity.

(*b*) It must not exceed 25 per cent of the total value of the fund, and in this regard there is a distinction depending on when the scheme was established; in respect of schemes established before 27 July 1989:

- if the arrangement includes separate provision for a spouse's or dependant's annuity, the fund accumulated to provide these benefits must be excluded from the total value of the fund; and

- if the scheme is an APPS the protected rights provided by the scheme may be included in the value of the fund for the purpose of calculating the amount of the lump sum available, but only that part of the fund which does not constitute protected rights may be used to provide the lump sum (consequently a member who has an APPS which is used solely for the purpose of contracting out will not be able to take a cash lump sum from it);

- a smaller maximum amount than 25 per cent may be imposed if a transfer payment has been made to the personal pension scheme from an occupational pension scheme and a controlling director or high earner has been subject to the certification requirements of the *Personal Pension Schemes (Transfer Payments) Regulations 1988 (SI 1988 No 1014)*, now covered under the *Personal Pension Schemes (Transfer Payments) Regulations 2001 (SI 2001 No 119)*. These Regulations limit the amount of tax free cash available under the personal pension scheme to the amount of cash that would have been available to the individual under the occupational pension scheme.

(*c*) In respect of schemes established after 27 July 1989, if the scheme is an APPS, the protected rights provided by the scheme cannot be used for the purposes of calculating the amount of the lump sum. (See *ICTA 1988, s 635* and IR76 (2000)).

(*d*) Pensions Update Number 135 (20 December 2002) allows, in limited circumstances, more than one lump sum to be paid under the same personal pension scheme; this can occur where:

   (i)   there has been pensions mis-selling; or

   (ii) where it is necessary to comply with a court order.

The APSS allow, as a result of a second lump sum being paid, a realignment or adjustment of the annuity or income drawdown already in payment.

Annuity payable after the death of the member

14.18   If a member dies before electing to take his benefits from the scheme, annuities may be provided by the scheme for the member's spouse and/or dependants (*ICTA 1988, s 636* and IR76 (2000) Part 10). Alternatively, when a member reaches his pension date he may choose to make provision for the payment of an annuity to his spouse and/or dependants. In either case an annuity payable after the death of the member is subject to the following conditions:

(*a*) it must be payable by an authorised insurance company situated within the EU which may be chosen by the member or the person in respect of whom the annuity is being purchased ('the annuitant');

(*b*) the annuitant must be the member's spouse or a person who was a 'dependant' of the member at the date of the member's death (a 'dependant' need not be a relative but he or she must be regarded as being financially dependent on the member; a child of the member who is under age 18 or undergoing full-time education or vocational training will always be considered to be a dependant);

(*c*) if the member dies before his pension date, the aggregate annual amount of all annuities payable to the spouse and any dependants must not exceed the highest amount of annuity that would have been payable to the member (ignoring the ability to take a lump sum) if his pension date had been the date of his death;

(*d*) where the member dies after his pension date, the aggregate annual amount of all annuities payable to the spouse and any dependants must not exceed the annual amount of the annuity that was being paid to the member at the date of his death;

(*e*) it may be guaranteed for a specified term not exceeding ten years so that it continues to be paid at the full rate in the event of the annuitant's death during that term;

(*f*) it must not be capable of assignment or surrender; the only exceptions to this is that an annuity which has a guarantee period may be assigned on the death of an annuitant by his will and also in the case of a pension sharing order or provision;

(*g*) it may increase in line with the Retail Prices Index or at a fixed percentage per annum or remain at the same level, i e 'static' throughout the period of payment;

(*h*) it may be payable in advance or in arrears and may be of any frequency of payment;

(*i*) it must generally be payable for life but, in the case of an annuity payable to a spouse, payment may cease on the re-marriage of the annuitant (this is becoming increasingly less common); if the annuity is payable to a child, payment should cease when the child reaches 18 or ceases to be in full-time education or vocational training.

A spouse who, whilst under age 60, becomes entitled to an annuity on the death of a member may elect to defer purchasing the annuity until, at the latest, she or he reaches age 60. This facility is particularly useful where the spouse is relatively young when the member dies and the annuity that could be purchased at that time would produce little income. Where the purchase of the annuity is deferred under this provision income withdrawal is not permitted (see 14.22 below).

Lump sum payable on the death of the member

14.19　When entering into a personal pension scheme, an individual should decide what element (if any) of his contributions he wishes to use to purchase term assurance (i e life cover). [*ICTA 1988, s 637* and IR76 (2000) PN 4.8]. The amount allowable is described in 14.35 below. Any sum assured under a contract purchased from an authorised insurance company can be paid as a lump sum in the event of his death before age 75.

In any event, on the death of a member, any part of the fund not used to purchase an annuity may be paid as a lump sum. The amount of the lump sum must represent no more than a return of the contributions paid by the member (and, where relevant, the member's employer) together with interest at a reasonable rate. However, if the contributions are invested in units under a unit trust scheme the lump sum may represent the sale price of units.

A lump sum can be paid to the member's personal representative, to a beneficiary nominated by the member or at the discretion of the scheme administrator.

Clustering

14.20　Annuity rates move in line with changes in yield on medium term gilts. People retiring in early 1999 faced an annuity income of approximately 40 per cent less than those retiring four or five years earlier with the same size of fund and, currently, the position continues to worsen. To minimise these problems it is possible to write a personal pension as a cluster of policies, colloquially known as 'clustering' or 'segmentation'. The vast majority of both insured personal pension schemes and SIPPs offer this feature. Usually, but not always, the number of segments offered is 1,000. This works by allowing segments of the pension policy or slices of the fund in the insured personal pension scheme or SIPP to be encashed each year to provide a combination (if selected) of a tax free cash lump sum and income withdrawals whilst leaving the remainder to roll-up gross, free in most usual circumstances from inheritance tax should the member die. Using clustering in this way increases the tax efficiency of the whole arrangement and the potential return of capital on death of the member.

Income withdrawal

Background

14.21　Until May 1995, once a member of a personal pension scheme decided to draw his benefits, an annuity had to be purchased at that time from a life office. If annuity rates were low at that time, his resulting pension would be lower (in some cases much lower) than he could have hoped for. This inflexible approach had obvious disadvantages, especially compared with small self-administered schemes (see chapter 13) where the purchase of the annuity could be deferred until age 75. As annuity rates are progressively worsening this difference becomes increasingly more important and, without the introduction of income drawdown, would have meant 'switching' to a personal pension scheme from a small self-administered scheme would have, in all likelihood, become considerably less popular.

The life offices introduced what is known as 'staggered vesting' and managed annuities to get round the problems only to be thwarted by the then Inland Revenue. Subsequent lobbying induced the Chancellor to make proposals in his 1994 Budget that would allow members of personal pension schemes to defer the purchase of an annuity when they retired to age 75 and withdraw amounts during the period of deferral. These proposals were eventually enacted in *section 58* of, and *Schedule 11* to, the *Finance Act 1995* and came into effect on 1 May 1995.

Since May 1995 those personal pension schemes (including SIPPs) which have adopted suitable rules to offer the facility to defer annuity purchase until, at the latest, age 75 and in the interim permit income withdrawal. Those personal pension schemes which have not adopted rules allowing income withdrawal may only pay the benefits outlined in 14.14 above and so must purchase an annuity on the retirement of the member. Part 9 of IR76 (2000) and *section 634A* of *ICTA 1988* contain considerable information in relation to all aspects of operating income drawdown. The paragraphs below describe the main points of these conditions.

Income withdrawal by the member

14.22 Income withdrawal is defined as payment of income from a personal pension scheme otherwise than by way of an annuity. [*ICTA 1988, s 630*]. A member's pension date is still the date the member's annuity first becomes payable between age 50 and 75. The link between the cash lump sum benefit and the commencement of the annuity is totally severed permitting the lump sum to be taken, but the purchase of the annuity to be deferred. The lump sum is, however, only payable on the date on which the election to defer the purchase of the annuity takes effect; it may not be taken later.

If a member elects to defer purchasing an annuity he must withdraw income from the funds during the period of deferral although not, if he so chooses, in the year the annuity is purchased or in which the member dies. All amounts withdrawn are taxable and the administrator is obliged to deduct payment through the PAYE system.

The amounts withdrawn are subject to maximum and minimum limits. [*ICTA 1988, s 634A*]. The maximum is broadly equivalent to the payments which would be made from a level single life annuity and is calculated by reference to tables provided by the Government Actuary's Department ('GAD') for each age and sex. The minimum level of income withdrawal is 35 per cent of the maximum permitted. The calculations take account of the amount of the member's fund available for annuity purchase at pension date with a deduction in the first year for any lump sum benefit paid or to be paid. (*Section 634A(4)* of *ICTA 1988* sets out further conditions.)

Within the maximum and minimum limits, members may choose the level of income withdrawal and vary the amounts from year to year. The scheme administrator is responsible for ensuring withdrawals remain within the limits each year. The initial maximum and minimum withdrawal limits originally applied for the first three years and then were subject to further reviews every three years. The scheme administrator needs to make a fresh calculation (employing the GAD tables) at each specified review date. The calculation is based on the remaining value of the member's fund at that date. The timing of this review is effectively set by what is known as the 'relevant reference date'. There are new provisions in force from 1 October 2000 (known by HMRC as the 'new rule'), which allow greater relaxation on how the relevant reference date is timed. What is known as a '60 day window' was also brought in from that date. Any personal pension scheme approved on or after 1 October 2000 is allowed to choose whether to operate the old or the new income drawdown rules. Alternatively a combination of these rules can be used.

The Practice Notes IR76 (2000) set out in considerable detail the further requirements relating to income drawdown and, in particular, where income withdrawals are taking place from two or more arrangements at the same time (IR76 (2000) PN 9.21 to PN 9.33).

In addition, for the first time, with effect from 14 February 2001, the *Personal Pension Schemes (Transfer Payments) Regulations 2001 (SI 2001 No 119)* permitted transfers to be made to and from personal pension schemes where income drawdown has already been triggered under the paying scheme.

Income withdrawal after 6 April 2006

14.23   It will still be possible to effect income withdrawal after 'A-Day' as an 'unsecured pension' (see Pension Rule 5 in *section 165* of *FA 2004*). This is discussed in chapter 5.

Death benefits

Death of a member on or after pension date

Death where an annuity has already been purchased

14.24   Where an annuity has already been bought by a member and the member then dies, an annuity can be paid to a 'survivor'. HMRC's definition of 'survivor' is:

> '… a widow, widower or dependant of a member who has died.'

'Dependant' is defined as:

> '… a person who is financially dependent on the member or dependent on the member because of disability or who was so dependent at the time of the member's death or retirement. An ex-spouse of the member who was in receipt of payments from the member up to his or her death in respect of, for example, a financial provision order under the *Matrimonial Causes Act 1973* may be regarded as financially dependent on the member. An adult relative who is not, or was not, supported by the member is not that member's dependant.'

IR76 (2000) (within the definition of 'dependant') then continues to describe HMRC conditions with regard to children and states that, in most circumstances, a pension paid to an adult dependant who '… qualifies on grounds of financial dependency or disability …' may continue indefinitely.

It is a matter for the scheme administrators to determine whether a person satisfies the definition of 'dependant'.

In these situations HMRC does not permit a survivor to request income drawdown. This is not surprising as the annuity has already been purchased by the member.

Death where income drawdown had started

14.25   Where the member has died after receiving income drawdown under an arrangement (there may, of course, be other arrangements under the scheme where no such drawdown has commenced) there are four basic options available. These options are available to the 'survivor'. The options are to:

(*a*)   Leave purchasing any annuity until a later date (the maximum age for this purchase is age 75) (IR76 (2000) PN 10.8).

(*b*)   Buy an annuity immediately on the open market (IR76 (2000) PN 10.12 to PN 10.19).

(*c*)   Take income withdrawals in the interim period and then purchase an annuity at a later date (but no later than age 75 under current rules) (IR76 (2000) PN 10.20 to PN 10.21).

(*d*)   Take an immediate lump sum from the arrangement. It should be noted that this will be subject to a tax charge of 35 per cent and the lump sum must be paid within two years of the member's death. The only exception to this would be where the lump sum has arisen as a result of a survivor's death where that survivor had been making income withdrawals. It is the responsibility of the scheme administrator to deduct the 35 per cent tax charge. The administrator would then provide for this within the annual tax return. No reclamation of this tax can be made by any of the survivor's beneficiaries (IR76 (2000) PN 10.32 to PN 10.35).

The same maximum and minimum limits apply to income withdrawal by a spouse or dependant, but the calculations take account of the amount of the fund available at the death of the member. Again the withdrawal limits apply for the first three years from the death of the member and fresh calculations must be made as at the first day of each subsequent three-year period.

Even if a spouse's entitlement ceases on remarriage or a dependant's entitlement ceases at age 18 or on cessation of full-time education, he or she may still opt for income withdrawal during the intervening period.

If a spouse or dependant who has chosen to receive income withdrawals dies within two years of the member's death, provided no annuity has been purchased, the remaining balance in the survivor's fund can be paid as a lump sum if the scheme rules permit it. If the spouse or dependant dies more than two years after the member died and an annuity has not been purchased, the balance in the survivor's fund is forfeit and must be used to meet administration expenses of the scheme.

Any lump sum payable to a spouse or dependant following the death of the member is liable to a tax charge of 35 per cent which is payable by the administrator. [*ICTA 1988, s 648B*].

Death of a member before pension date

14.26   In these circumstances, as with death following pension date, there are varying permutations of potential benefit payable. The main factors which cause these variations will be:

●   Were there any protected rights under the arrangement?

- Was there provision for a survivor's annuity?

- Was there a survivor?

- Had the arrangement received a transfer from what APSS term a 'designated scheme'? The definition of 'designated scheme' encompasses a retirement benefits scheme approved under *Chapter I* of *Part XIV* of *ICTA 1988*, a relevant statutory scheme under *section 611A* of *ICTA 1988* or a '*section 32*' buy-out policy that holds benefits deriving from an occupational pension scheme.

- Have contributions been paid for term assurance which provides a lump sum on death?

Parts 10.3, 10.4, 10.5, 10.6 and 10.7 of IR76 (2000) describe in full the various benefits that can be paid in the circumstances described above and these are summarised below.

Was there provision for a survivor's annuity?

14.27   If the answer to this is 'yes' and the member dies leaving a survivor (and where no transfer-in from a designated scheme has been received) a survivor's annuity can be bought using the whole value of the arrangement at the date of death. This is true even if there are protected rights under the arrangement as well. In addition, any term assurance benefits would be paid as a lump sum under a discretionary trust (in most circumstances) on top of the annuity.

Death with survivor but no specific provision for survivor's annuity

14.28   Where no transfer has been received and there is no specific provision for survivor's annuity (for whatever reason) the benefits can be paid in complete lump sum form (subject to conditions described in IR76 (2000) PN 10.5 and PN 10.6). However, this can only be done where:

(*a*)   if there are protected rights there is no 'qualifying survivor' for the purposes of the contracting-out requirement, or there is a 'qualifying spouse' but the maximum pension payable to that spouse amounts to less than £260 per annum;

(*b*)   there are no protected rights;

In the same circumstances as above but where there happens to be an annuity payable to a qualifying survivor with the protected rights, the entire fund can be used to buy a survivor's annuity or can be used for the purposes of income drawdown. 'Entire fund' means the whole of the fund that the member could have used had he survived.

In addition any lump sum life cover can also be paid subject to the terms of the scheme's governing rules.

Has a transfer been received from a designated scheme?

14.29   In these circumstances the basic choices available are that the scheme administrator must, with that part of the member's fund representing a transfer in from a designated scheme, use it either entirely to buy an annuity or annuities for a survivor or survivors (or survivor's income withdrawal) or pay up to one quarter of the transfer amount as a lump sum and use the remainder to buy a survivor's annuity or to be used for the purposes of the survivor receiving income drawdown (an example is given at IR76 (2000) PN 12.23). In addition there are further detailed requirements set out in the *Personal Pension Schemes (Transfer Payments) Regulations 2001 (SI 2001 No 119)*.

Death benefits after 6 April 2006

14.30   Minor changes are made to some of the important definitions used in these situations after 'A-Day'. For a full discussion of the new death benefit rules in force after 'A-Day' see chapter 5.

Contributions

General

14.31   In the pre 'A-Day' regime, detailed below, both a member and his employer may make contributions to a personal pension scheme, but unlike occupational pension schemes, the employer contributing is purely an option not an obligation (this also applies to stakeholder schemes) (IR76 (2000) PN 4.1).

Unless the 'concurrency' rules apply (see 14.10 above), if the personal pension scheme is an APPS and the member is also a member of an occupational pension scheme which is not contracted out of the S2P the only contributions that can be made are the 'minimum contributions' paid by the NI Contributions Office (see 14.48 below).

When a member's benefit becomes payable either by the purchasing of an annuity or commencing income withdrawal, no further contributions may be paid to the personal pension scheme. [*ICTA 1988, s 638*]. The only exception to this is where the member is under State pension age in which case 'minimum contributions' may continue to be paid to accrue further 'protected rights' until the member reaches State pension age (see 14.49 below). [*Personal Pension Schemes (Deferred Annuity Purchase) (Acceptance of Contributions) Regulations 1996 (SI 1996 No 805)*].

Maximum contributions

14.32   The position described here applies from 6 April 2001 to 5 April 2006.

Contributions up to the 'earnings threshold'

14.33   Any member can contribute up to the earnings threshold irrespective of their age (providing they are under age 75), whether they have earnings or whether they are currently in an occupational pension scheme (although the conditions as described earlier still have to be met).

Contributions higher than the 'earnings threshold'

14.34   Where more than the earnings threshold is to be paid to a personal pension scheme, the aggregate amount of contributions paid into an approved personal pension scheme by a member and his employer (if applicable) must then not exceed the appropriate percentage of 'net relevant earnings' for the year of assessment as determined in accordance with the table set out below. [*ICTA 1988, s 640*].

Age on 6 April	Percentage of net relevant earnings
35 or less	17.5
36 to 45	20
46 to 50	25
51 to 55	30
56 to 60	35
61 or more	40

'Net relevant earnings' is defined in *section 646(1)* of *ICTA 1988*. Essentially, it is the amount of an individual's relevant earnings (see 14.11 above) for the tax year in question less certain deductions including any necessary expenses incurred by the individual as part of his job (for example, travelling expenses, subscriptions to professional bodies).

A partner's 'net relevant earnings' are calculated after necessary business expenses and allowances have been deducted from his share of partnership income.

From 6 April 1989, the 'net relevant earnings' of a member are restricted to the 'permitted maximum' or, as it is colloquially known, the 'earnings cap', imposed by *section 590C* of *ICTA 1988*. This is set at £105,600 for the tax year 2005/2006, and is generally increased in line with the Retail Price Index each year. Any earnings above the earnings cap must be disregarded for the purposes of calculating net relevant earnings. [*ICTA 1988, s 640A*].

From 6 April 2001 there has been a new principle introduced for the purposes of an individual determining their 'net relevant earnings'. This involves the member selecting the 'basis year' for the purposes of calculating their net relevant earnings (*section 646B* of *ICTA 1988*). The 'basis year' can be the current tax year or any of the previous five tax years. An important point to note here is that the 'basis year' can occur in a year where the member did not have a personal pension scheme but that individual must be able to show that he did have net relevant earnings in that selected year.

This basis can then be used for calculating what can be paid by way of contributions to the personal pension scheme. Once the basis year has been selected that, naturally, is the year that has to be used for determining the net relevant earnings applicable. Their age must be the age on 6 April of the current tax year that the contribution is being paid. Clearly this new mechanism gives a potential advantage to those who have earned more in one of the five previous tax years and, therefore, they are able to pay more by allowable contribution to the personal pension scheme than would have ordinarily be the case. Importantly, this figure can then be used for the purposes of contributions in the following five tax years – not just the first tax year that contributions were paid. A member is permitted to change the basis year where, for example, their net relevant earnings are higher than they were by using the original basis year.

In stakeholder schemes where the employee has asked the employer to make payments by way of the employer's payroll the employer must explain within two weeks and in writing how the payroll deductions will be administered. This would include such things as how often the employer can accept changes (this must be available at least once every six months), how the employee can ask for these contributions to be stopped and how notifying changes in the rate of contribution should be communicated to the employer. If the employer cannot accept a request for a change then the employee must be told in writing. An explanation for the refusal should be given and the employee should be reminded that the employee can cancel the deduction from payroll at any time.

The employee has a variety of choice in relation to how he pays, i e the basis by which contributions are deducted from their pay. This can be on the basis of a fixed monetary sum that has been agreed between the parties involved or on a percentage of pay. Where the contribution is to be on the basis of a percentage of pay it obviously needs to be determined in advance on what basis 'pay' is to be calculated. This is very similar, of course, to an occupational pension scheme that would contain a clear definition of, for example, 'pensionable salary' so that the employee clearly understands what elements of pay are being counted for contribution purposes and what elements are being ignored.

Application of contributions

Purchase of life assurance

14.35   Before 6 April 2003 contributions of up to 5 per cent of a member's 'net relevant earnings' for the tax year in question may be used to purchase a term assurance contract to pay a lump sum benefit in the event of the member's death before age 75 (this will often, but not always, be written under discretionary trust so as to mitigate any inheritance tax liability by ensuring that the lump sum does not form part of the member's estate (see also 14.19 above)). From 6 April 2001 the position has been altered so that now the amount of life cover that can be bought can not exceed 10 per cent of what HMRC term 'relevant pension contributions', i e the amount of pension contributions made by the member during the scheme year in question. Further details are given in IR76 (2000) PN 4.14.

Insurance against incapacity – after 6 April 2001

14.36   From 6 April 2001 no individual will be allowed to use any element of contributions to insure against their incapacity where this may lead to a loss of earnings and, therefore, the member would be unable to make contributions. However, if an arrangement to do this was already in place before 6 April 2001 this can continue. This insurance is usually known as 'waiver of contribution'. From 6 April 2001 although it is not possible to provide such insurance within the context of the personal pension scheme itself this can still be arranged but has to be completely separate from the personal pension scheme. Where a pension contract has an option to take out waiver in existence pre-6 April 2001 this option can be exercised after 6 April 2001 but APSS will not allow the scheme to exercise the option – only the member will be permitted to do so [IR76 (2000) PN 4.21].

Insurance against incapacity – pre-6 April 2001

14.37   Scheme rules may allow a member to elect that not more than 25 per cent of his contributions shall be applied as a premium under a contract of insurance which provides that:

(*a*)   his contributions and those of an employer will be waived for any period during which, by reason of incapacity, he is unable to work and for the value of benefits to be maintained as though those contributions have been paid;

(*b*)   an annuity payable to a member whose vesting date has been brought forward because of incapacity will not be reduced on that account.

This means that the scheme may include a lifetime or permanent disability insurance which may be paid in the event of permanent and total incapacity. Any contributions used in this way will not qualify for tax relief (see 14.40 below). [IR76 (2000) PN 4.15 to 4.20].

Contributions paid in error whilst a member of an occupational pension scheme

14.38   Some individuals may have contributed unwittingly to a personal pension scheme at the same time as being members of an occupational pension scheme (unless the concurrency rules apply) being unaware that they were ineligible to make retirement provision via a personal pension scheme in respect of the same source of earnings. Strictly speaking, any contributions paid to personal pension schemes in these circumstances should be refunded. If an occupational scheme provides only modest lump sum benefits (less than £400 for each year of service), an extra-statutory concession (small lump sum retirement benefits schemes: Extra Statutory Concession A95) allowed the contributions to remain with the personal pension scheme without affecting the tax reliefs if the following conditions are satisfied:

(*a*)   the member waives entitlement to the lump sum retirement benefit; or

(*b*)   no lump sum retirement benefits accrue; and

(*c*)   the arrangement under the personal pension scheme is not cancelled.

The concession applies only where the occupational schemes rules provide for no such lump sum to accrue in respect of any period during which the member has paid contributions to the personal pension scheme.

From 6 April 2001 if the total contributions paid are greater than the higher of the earnings threshold and the permitted maximum percentage contribution (see the table in 14.34 above) then all contributions which are not eligible for relief have to be repaid.

Contributions from 6 April 2006

14.39   After 6 April 2006, a member will be entitled to make unlimited contributions to any registered pension scheme. However, tax relief will only be given on a relievable pension contribution made by a relevant UK individual. Even then, the tax relief will only be available where the total of employer and member contributions, or the value of benefits that accrues in any year, do not exceed the annual allowance. These are discussed in more detail in chapter 5.

Tax treatment

Tax relief for member's contributions

14.40   The position stated here applies from 6 April 2001 to 5 April 2006.

A member can obtain tax relief, at his highest marginal rate, on the contributions he makes to a personal pension scheme (*ICTA 1988, s 639*). It does not matter whether the member is an ordinary or higher rate taxpayer, all permitted contributions to a personal pension scheme are treated as being paid net of basic rate tax (*ICTA 1988, s 639(3)*). The administrator of the personal pension scheme must accept the amount paid after this deduction in full discharge of a member's liability and can then recover the amount deducted by making a claim to APSS.

If the member is a higher rate taxpayer he must claim the remaining amount of relief due to him from his local Inspector.

Employers are permitted to contribute to personal pension schemes (subject to the appropriate limits) and they can claim their tax relief by showing such contributions in their accounts which, as it will be shown in calculating taxable profits will usually be permitted as a deduction under Schedule D. The procedures here are not automatic in the same way as they would be for employee contributions and the employer would need to liaise with its tax office in assessing what relief would be made available.

Carrying forward tax reliefs – pre-6 April 2001

14.41   Prior to 6 April 2001, if, in any tax year, the amount of contributions made to all personal pension schemes was less than the allowable maximum, then the balance could be carried forward as 'unused relief' (*ICTA 1988, s 642*). This would then be set off against contributions paid by the individual to personal pension schemes in any of the following six tax years which would otherwise exceed the maximum applicable. Relief would be given for an earlier year before being given for a later year.

Carrying forward tax reliefs – after 6 April 2001

14.42   The carrying forward of tax relief is not available after 6 April 2001 although in some situations this may still be possible in limited circumstances. This is discussed in more detail in IR76 (2000) PN 6.41.

Carrying back contributions

14.43   This section discusses the position as applicable from 6 April 2001 to 5 April 2006.

It was also permissible for a member to 'carry back' contributions by electing to have a contribution or part of a contribution treated as having been paid in the tax year immediately preceding that in which it was actually paid (or, if there are no 'net relevant earnings' in that year, in the previous year). (*ICTA 1988 s 641* and IR76 (2000) PN 6.30). Contributions paid by an employer may not be carried back. If contributions are carried back, it is not possible to exceed the maximum allowable percentage of contributions in the year to which they are carried back. Carry back was abolished by *section 17* of the *Finance Act 2000* after 6 April 2001. Instead *section 641A* was inserted by that same Act to deal with contributions made in the tax year 2001/2002 and thereafter.

Applications to carry back or carry forward contributions must be submitted to APSS on the specified form PP43. Scheme administrators should keep a supply of the forms as members have a right to request them. The wording of PP43 should not be varied unless prior consent from FICO has been obtained (see IR76 (2000) PN 6.38). An election to carry back the contribution must be made not later than three months after the end of the tax year in which the contribution was paid.

Where an individual is electing for a contribution to be treated as if it had been paid in the previous tax year, this can only be done where the contribution had been paid between 6 April and 31 January and the person confirmed that he wished to carry back at the time that contribution was paid.

One major advantage of the option to carry back is that tax relief may be obtained more quickly than if the relief is claimed against the tax year in which the contribution is actually paid. However, care must be taken to ensure that carrying back does not, in fact, lead to relief at a lower rate.

Tax relief for employer's contributions

14.44   Contributions paid by an employer on behalf of a member are not assessable on the employee as a benefit in kind (or liable for National Insurance). [IR76 (2000) PN 4.35].

Taxation of the fund

14.45   Personal pension schemes which are approved by HMRC are exempt from tax on the income from investments or deposits held for the scheme (*ICTA*

1988, s 643(2)) and capital gains tax on gains arising from disposals of investments. A scheme established by an insurance company for the issue of insurance policies or annuity contracts does not obtain relief in this way, but claims an exemption from income tax, corporation tax and capital gains tax, as this is referable to the 'pension business' of the insurance company. [*ICTA 1988, s 438(1)*]. Unlike the vast majority of these concessions, the latter provision is not repealed at 'A-Day' and replaced by *FA 2004*.

Taxation of benefits

14.46   An annuity paid under a personal pension scheme is chargeable to income tax. [*ICTA 1988, s 648A*]. The tax is collected through the PAYE system via the administrator.

No general exemption from income tax is given by the UK tax legislation to recipients of pension who are resident abroad. However, it may be possible to obtain an exemption if there is a double taxation agreement in force in relation to the overseas country involved.

A lump sum paid under a personal pension scheme to a member is not liable to income tax, provided it is within HMRC's limit of 25 per cent of the fund at the date the lump sum is being paid (and assuming no lesser amount has had to be paid as a result of certification (see 14.17 above)). The lump sum must be paid at the same time as the balance of the fund is used to provide an annuity (see also 14.17 above).

Contracting out of the State earnings related pension scheme

Appropriate personal pension schemes (APPS)

14.47   The rules of an APPS may provide for the payment of contributions in addition to 'minimum contributions' (see 14.48 below). An APPS may be used as a vehicle for transfers-in and, if the member has 'relevant earnings' (see 14.11 above) it can also receive ordinary contributions to build up benefits in excess of those provided by protected rights. An individual who is a member of an occupational pension scheme which is not contracted out of the State earnings-related pension may contract out via an APPS. Such an APPS can then only accept 'minimum contributions' (see 14.48 below).

A properly constituted APPS must have a current 'Appropriate Scheme Certificate' in force. Such a certificate can only be issued once a scheme complies with the statutory requirements. [*PSA 1993, s 9(5)*].

An APPS may take the form of any one of the following:

(*a*)   an arrangement for the issue of insurance policies or annuity contracts; or

(*b*)   an authorised unit trust scheme (set up solely for the purpose of providing personal pension schemes); or

(*c*)   a building society deposit; or

(*d*)   a bank account.

Providers of an APPS may be insurance companies, friendly societies, suitably authorised banks or building societies.

There are detailed requirements relating to the continuing supervision of APPSs by NISPI. These include the need to submit an annual return, the need to notify NISPI in writing of any changes in scheme details and the requirement to give members certain information.

Stakeholder schemes must be contracted out. Part 22 of IR76 (2000) deals with how stakeholder schemes contract out of S2P, either as an Appropriate Personal Pension stakeholder pension scheme ('APPSHP') or as a Contracted-out Money Purchase stakeholder pension scheme ('COMPSHP'). Personal pension schemes which are not and are not applying to be stakeholder pension schemes should use HMRC documents 'CA16: Appropriate Personal Pension Scheme Manual: Procedural Guidance' and 'CA16A: Appropriate Personal Pension Scheme Manual: Technical Guidance for Scheme Managers'.

Minimum contributions

14.48   Minimum contributions equate to the contracted-out rebate and the age-related rebate paid by the Department of Work and Pensions ('DWP'). The contracted-out rebate is the difference between the full rate of National Insurance contribution and the reduced, contracted-out rate, payable on 'band earnings', i e earnings between the lower earnings limit and the upper earnings limit. Since 6 April 1997 only an age-related rebate has been payable. No 'flat-rate' rebate is available.

Protected rights benefits

14.49   Unless the rules of the scheme provide otherwise, the whole of the fund will be treated as 'protected rights'. This is inadvisable as it would mean that all the stringent provisions relating to protected rights would then have to apply to all the rights in the scheme. Consequently the rules of the scheme will usually contain a specific definition of what constitutes protected rights. (For a general discussion on protected rights, see chapter 4.)

When a scheme's rules define protected rights, they must include all or any of the following:

(*a*)   minimum contributions;

(*b*)   protected rights transferred from another personal pension scheme or occupational pension scheme;

(*c*)   guaranteed minimum pensions transferred from an occupational pension scheme;

(*d*)   any 'incentive payments' made by the DWP;

(*e*)   payments representing basic rate relief from income tax on the member's share of minimum contributions. [*PSA 1993, s 10*].

Protected rights benefits become payable as a pension through the purchase of an annuity at State pension age. This benefit may not be drawn before State pension age and may only be taken in the form of pension. It may not be commuted to a cash lump sum. Payment of the protected rights pension annuity must be monthly unless the member agrees to a longer interval. The scheme rules must provide for the protected rights pension to be revalued in respect of the amount of protected rights attributable to contributions made before 6 April 1997, in line with the Retail Prices Index or 3 per cent (whichever is less), and in respect of contributions remitted on or after 6 April 1997, in line with the Retail Prices Index or 5 per cent (whichever is less).

Protected rights cannot be assigned, suspended or forfeited.

Death of member and protected rights pension

14.50   In the event of the death of the member, either before or after taking protected rights pension benefits, a spouse's pension will be payable.

If the member dies after the pension has commenced, the spouse's pension will equate to 50 per cent of the pension the member was receiving at his or her death. If the member dies before the pension has commenced, the spouse's pension will equate to 50 per cent of the pension that would have been payable to the member at death.

The spouse's pension must generally be payable until he or she dies or re-marries while under State pension age (but see also chapter 4).

Transfer of protected rights

14.51   Protected rights may be transferred to another pension arrangement which is permitted to accept such a transfer, including:

(*a*)   another APPS or APPSHP;

(*b*)   a contracted-out or previously contracted-out occupational pension scheme including a COMPS (or COMPS part of a COMBS), COMPSHP or COSRS (or COSRS part of a COMBS); or

(*c*)   an overseas occupational pension scheme.

The member must at all times consent to the transfer and the transfer payment must be at least equal to the cash equivalent value of the member's protected rights. [Part 5 of CA16: Appropriate Personal Pension Scheme Manual: Procedural Guidance].

In the case of a transfer of protected rights to a contracted-out defined contributions scheme, the transfer payment must be applied by the receiving scheme and be used to provide protected rights under the scheme for that member. In the case of a transfer of protected rights to a contracted-out defined benefits scheme, the receiving scheme must provide for the member and the member's spouse to be entitled to guaranteed minimum pensions in respect of pre-April 1997 service and benefits calculated on the same basis as for other scheme members for post-April 1997 service.

A transfer from a contracted-out defined benefits scheme is made to an APPS, and pre-April 1997 accrued guaranteed minimum pension rights and any post-April 1997 contracted-out rights must be treated as protected rights in the receiving APPS.

Personal pension protected rights premium

14.52   If an APPS ceases to be contracted-out or if the member wishes to cease being in contracted-out employment, the member may regain the entitlement from SERPS by the payment of a Personal Pension protected rights Premium ('PPRP') to the DWP. The PPRP will be calculated according to the accumulated protected rights fund or, if necessary, by an objective actuarial calculation. The ability to pay a PPRP is not available post-6 April 1997 so the scheme must either retain the protected rights in deferred form, or buy them out by purchasing a suitable annuity.

Transfer values

The right to a cash equivalent

14.53   A personal pension scheme will not be approved unless it includes provisions for transfer payments to be made, accepted and applied in accordance with the statutory provisions. (See *sections 93* to *101* of *PSA 1993* and the *Personal Pension Schemes (Transfer Payments) Regulations 2001 (SI 2001 No 119)* and IR76 (2000) Part 12). Transfers to a personal pension scheme from a (tax approved) occupational pension scheme in respect of a controlling director or an individual whose remuneration exceeds the earnings cap may be restricted to prevent transfers being used to maximise the tax free lump sum from a personal pension scheme.

The right to a cash equivalent (i e the value of all the benefits accrued under the scheme to or in respect of the member) is exercised by the member requiring the administrator to acquire transfer credits for him under an occupational pension scheme or rights under another personal pension scheme.

A transfer payment between schemes must be made from scheme administrator to scheme administrator either directly or through an independent broker. In no circumstances must any transfer payment be made via a member or his employer.

A transfer need not be in cash: it may be made by a transfer of assets such as stocks and shares or property. This is commonly known as a 'transfer in specie'. It is also (usually) possible to assign a policy from one personal pension scheme to another.

Transfers made to a personal pension scheme

14.54   A personal pension scheme may, on the written request of the relevant member, accept transfer payments from any of the following:

(*a*)   another approved personal pension scheme; or

(*b*)   a retirement benefits scheme approved or being considered for approval under *Chapter I* of *Part XIV* of *ICTA 1988*; or

(*c*)   a scheme established by statute (for example, a local authority scheme) (see *section 611A* of *ICTA 1988*); or

(*d*)   an RAC; or

(*e*)   a deferred annuity contract securing benefits which have accrued to the individual by virtue of membership of a retirement benefits scheme or scheme established by statute; or

(*f*)   a *section 608* fund. [IR76 (2000) PN 12.10].

A personal pension scheme is not permitted to accept monies from any other source unless the prior consent of the APSS has been obtained. In addition, if the personal pension scheme is accepting 'minimum contributions' only, then it can only receive a transfer consisting of protected rights from another source.

There are further requirements where a 'regulated individual' has requested the transfer from a 'designated scheme'. The meaning of designated scheme is discussed in 14.26 above, but a 'regulated individual' is a person who:

(i)   is or was in any period ten years prior to the transfer a controlling director; or

(ii) was a person earning above the 'earnings cap' in any one year falling in whole or in part during a six-year period prior to the date the transfer took place *and* was aged 45 or over at the date of transfer.

In these circumstances it is a requirement that the administrator of the transferring scheme has signed a certificate in accordance with *regulation 8(3)* of the *Personal Pension Schemes (Transfer Payments) Regulations 2001 (SI 2001 No 119)*. It should be noted that this regulation does not apply to any *section 32* contracts established before 6 April 2001. In this case there is an HMRC concession in place described in IR76 (2000) PN 12.14.

In addition, 'regulated individual' will have controls in relation to the maximum tax free cash available at pension date and this means that no more than the certified amount of tax free cash available from the 'designated scheme' can be paid by the personal pension scheme at pension date. This will often, but not always, have the effect of reducing the usual 25 per cent tax free cash (i e 25 per cent of the accumulated fund value of the personal pension scheme) to a lesser amount. If the certified amount is greater than 25 per cent of the non-protected rights fund then the 25 per cent limit prevails.

Nil certificates

14.55   Some transfers may be subject to what is known as a 'nil certificate'. This simply means that the transfer either derived from a source which was non-commutable (for example, a free-standing additional voluntary contributions scheme ('FSAVC') or an additional voluntary contributions ('AVC') scheme where AVC's were commenced on or after 8 April 1987). This is designed so that a transfer from such a source (a full list is given in IR76 (2000) PN 12.17) cannot become commutable simply because a transfer to a personal pension scheme has taken place. If the nil certificate is only certifying a proportion of the transfer monies coming across then only that portion is subject to the nil certificate and the excess can be commutable in accordance with the usual 25 per cent personal pension scheme limit for tax free cash transfers made from a personal pension scheme.

Transfer made from a personal pension scheme

14.56   On the written request of the member, the administrator of a personal pension scheme must, if the statutory procedures are complied with, make the requested payment (IR76 (2000) PN 12.3). The transfer can be to any of the following:

(*a*) another personal pension scheme;

(*b*) a retirement benefit scheme approved under *Chapter I* of *Part XIV* of *ICTA 1988* (including a FSAVC or a separately approved AVC scheme) but not a scheme awaiting approval;

(*c*) a relevant statutory scheme (*section 611A* of *ICTA 1988*);

(*d*) an overseas scheme, if:

　　(i) all the conditions in Appendix 22 of IR76 (2000) are satisfied; and

　　(ii) where necessary the prior consent of HMRC has been obtained.

A transfer payment made from an approved personal pension scheme must represent the whole fund accumulated under that arrangement except:

　(i) it need not include any assets which represent protected rights; and

　(ii) any amount which has been, or will be, used to pay a 'personal pension protected rights premium'.

If a cash equivalent is being paid to a contracted-in occupational scheme, or to a personal pension scheme that is not an APPS, the assets representing the member's protected rights cannot be transferred. In such a situation the protected rights element will generally remain in the scheme as a deferred benefit.

Further detailed control, when making transfer payments from a personal pension scheme to prevent 'improper transfers' (i e to sources involved in trust busting) came in with effect from 1 July 2002 under Pensions Update 132 published by HMRC.

Disclosure of information

14.57 The trustees (or the provider) are responsible for disclosing certain information to the member. In particular they must provide certain basic information about the scheme to every new member within 13 weeks of joining. [*Personal Pension Schemes* (*Disclosure of Information*) *Regulations 1987* (*SI 1987 No 1110*) (as amended)].

Information relating, in particular, to the amount of contributions credited to the member, the value of the member's protected rights, and the value of the member's accrued rights other than those protected rights must be given to the member annually. In addition, further information must be given to each member before his retirement.

In relation to each scheme year commencing on or after 1 October 1987, the trustees must make available to every member a copy of an annual statement containing specified information.

Investment

Personal pension and stakeholder schemes in general

14.58   In order to ensure that the sole purpose of a scheme is the provision of benefits on retirement or death (*ICTA 1988, s 633*) (see 14.14 above) restrictions are placed on the investment activities of an approved scheme. The purpose of these restrictions is to ensure the member does not receive benefits from the scheme other than in the prescribed form. The main restrictions are that:

(*a*)   scheme funds must not be used to provide loans to a member or any persons 'connected' with the member;

(*b*)   there must be no investment transaction with a member or persons 'connected' with the member;

(*c*)   schemes must not hold residential property or land directly as an investment. Commercial property which is leased to a business or partnership 'connected' with a member can form part of the assets of the scheme provided that an independent professional valuation is carried out and the terms of the lease are to be termed on a commercial basis. (IR76 (2000) PN 11).

With stakeholder schemes the investment choice is likely to be more restricted than that available under general insured personal pension schemes and, much more restricted than the choice available to SIPPs. This is because of the much stricter control placed on costs with the main control being that the annual management charge levied on a stakeholder scheme cannot exceed 1 per cent of the member fund per year. This will inevitably lead to a limited range on offer. However, that said, stakeholder schemes will be operating in a very competitive market and, as such, providers have been looking to provide innovative ways of attracting stakeholder contributions whilst, at the same time, being imaginative with what is on offer regarding investments under stakeholder schemes. Lifestyle funds, tracker and various types of flexible funds are being made available. It should be noted, however, that members cannot be required to select an investment choice so a stakeholder scheme will need a fallback investment policy to cover those members. Of course, all investment transactions must comply (from 6 April 2001) with the *Personal Pension Schemes (Restriction on Discretion to Approve) (Permitted Investments) Regulations 2001 (SI 2001 No 117)*. All stakeholder schemes are obliged to have a statement of investment principles. Therefore, proper advice must be taken by the trustees or managers to ensure diversification and the appropriateness of the investments selected. Further requirements related to with profits funds (that can be offered under stakeholder schemes) which include the ring fencing of those with profit funds so those funds are only available to stakeholder schemes.

Since 6 April 2005, there has also been a requirement that, for members who joined after that date, their pension is made subject to 'lifestyling' (*regulation 10A* of the *Stakeholder Pension Schemes Regulations 2000 (SI 2000 No 1403)* (as amended)). This will essentially mean that a less 'risky' or volatile investment strategy is adopted at least five years before a member's retirement date.

SIPPs

Member directed investments

14.59   For self-invested personal pension schemes ('SIPPS') (this does not apply to stakeholder schemes) the range of permitted investments has been adapted to provide an opportunity for members to become directly involved in decisions about the investment of contributions. The original requirements relating to the types of investments which members could make were set out in Memorandum No 101. These have subsequently been extended and clarified by the *Personal Pension Schemes (Restriction on Discretion to Approve) (Permitted Investments) Regulations 2001 (SI 2001 No 117)*). The *Schedule* to those Regulations lists the acceptable investments and is worthy of inclusion in its entirety:

'1   Stocks and shares listed or dealt in on a recognised stock exchange.

2   Futures and options, relating to stocks and shares, traded on a recognised futures exchange.

3   Depositary interests.

4   Units in an authorised unit trust scheme.

5   Units in a unit trust scheme which:

   (a)   is an unauthorised unit trust whose gains are not chargeable gains by virtue of section 100(2) of the Taxation of Chargeable Gains Act 1992, and

   (b)   does not hold any freehold or leasehold interest in residential property other than that specified in paragraph 13 or 14 of this Schedule.

6   Eligible shares within the meaning of section 638(11) received by the self-invested personal pension scheme as contributions to the scheme.

7   Shares in an open-ended investment company.

8   Interests (however described) in a collective investment scheme

that is either a recognised scheme or a designated scheme within the meaning of section 86 or 87 of the Financial Services Act 1986

9   Contracts or policies of insurance linked to insurance company managed funds, unit-linked funds or investment funds of an insurance company resident in the United Kingdom or authorised in accordance with Article 4 of Directive 2002/83/EC of the European Parliament and of the Council of 5th November 2002 concerning life assurance.

10   Traded endowment policies transacted with a person regulated by the Financial Services Authority.

11   Deposits in any currency held in deposit accounts with any deposit-taker.

12   A freehold or leasehold interest in commercial property where the interest is acquired from any person other than a member of the scheme or a person connected with him, or the interest is acquired from a member of the scheme or a person connected with him in circumstances in which regulation 9(3) applies.

13   A freehold or leasehold interest in any residential property which is:

   (a)   property which is, or is to be, occupied by an employee, whether or not a member of the self-invested personal pension scheme or connected with a member of the scheme, who is not connected with his employer and is required as a condition of his employment to occupy the property, and

   (b)   property which is, or is to be, occupied by a person who is neither a member of the self-invested personal pension scheme nor connected with a member of the scheme in connection with the occupation by that person of business premises held as an investment by the scheme.

14   Ground rents, rent charges, ground annuals, feu duties or other annual payments reserved in respect of, or charged on or issuing out of, property, except where the property concerned is occupied by a member of the scheme or a person connected with him.'

A number of these will also have specific definitions applicable to them that can be found within those Regulations.

HMRC, within IR76 (2000) (in Appendix 25), also provides a list of prohibited investments and these are as follows:

   (i) Premium Bonds.

(ii) Loans to any party.

(iii) Milk quotas.

(iv) Fishing quotas.

(v) Residential property.

(vi) Gold bullion.

(vii) Shares traded on OFEX.

(viii) Unlisted shares (except in a site maintenance property, for the necessary extent needed to purchase a commercial property).

(xi) Personal chattels (for example, paintings, antiques, fine wine and jewellery).

(xii) Borrowing other than that specified in IR76 (2000) Part 11, paragraph 11.25, 11.28 or 11.29.

SIPP investment requirements

14.60 IR76 (2000) contains (in Part 11) specific details relating to HMRC requirements for SIPP investments. The main principle behind a SIPP is that the member must retain control as to how contributions are to be invested. The members can choose the type of investments (subject, of course, to HMRC requirements (see 14.59 above)), when those investments are disposed of etc. Although there is currently debate within the industry as to the regulatory position of SIPPs, there are usually two basic choices available to a SIPP member:

(*a*)   he makes all day-to-day investment decisions unilaterally; or

(*b*)   investment decisions are made on behalf of the member by an appointed, appropriately regulated, investment manager.

It is a requirement of IR76 (2000) PN 11.4 that the member normally has no legal ownership over the investments (although separate trusts with the member acting as co-trustee are permitted by IR76 (2000) PN 11.5). Where IR76 (2000) PN 11.4 applies the Practice Notes envisage that the investments are held by the scheme administrator although, in practice, legal title to those investments would be held by the trustee of the SIPP on behalf of the member. An important point to note is that, unlike APSS concession for personal pension schemes where the assets comprise of purely insured assets (ie the APSS allows such schemes to be governed by deed), such a concession is not available to a SIPP. A SIPP is required to have assets governed under an irrevocable trust and it follows that, to achieve this, a trustee is required!

IR76 (2000) PN 11.7 makes it clear that HMRC requires trustees of a SIPP to act in a fiduciary manner on behalf of the scheme members, i e to act in their best interest (case law indicates this would mean best financial interest). The trustee should not be attempting to act in the interest of other parties – to do so is likely to threaten the removal of APSS approval to the SIPP.

Investment after 'A-Day'

14.61   The intention, after 6 April 2006, was that the new tax regime would impose few restrictions on investment. *Section 186(1)* of *FA 2004* states simply that 'no liability to income tax arises in respect of: (a) income derived from investments or deposits held for the purposes of a registered pension scheme …'. However, other more generalised restrictions will remain such as limits on the amount of borrowing. Investments are discussed in more detail in chapters 5 and 10.

For SIPPs this would have represented a significant change from the restrictions imposed by the *Personal Pension Schemes (Restriction on Discretion to Approve) (Permitted Investments) Regulations 2001 (SI 2001 No 117)* and discussed at 14.59 above. As a result many professional trustees offering SIPPs were exploring and actively marketing investment in residential properties and exotic investments such as wine and antiques through SIPPs. However, the Government, in the Pre-Budget Report on 5 December 2005, indicated that investments in residential property and exotic investments would not attract tax relief. APSS have produced a technical bulletin indicating that this is to '… prevent people benefiting from tax relief in relation to contributions made into self directed pension schemes for the purpose of funding purchases of holiday or second homes and other prohibited assets for their or their family's personal use'. It is intended that this will only limit direct investment and not indirect investment through, for example, unit trusts. Legislation is awaited to provide details of how this will apply.

Stamp duty

14.62   In relation to property, stamp duty was a document-based tax charged voluntarily up to 30 November 2003.

If a property situated in the UK was purchased by the trustees of a tax approved occupational or personal pension scheme or retirement annuity contract ('RAC') stamp duty was payable on the purchase/sale price or open market value of the property, whichever was higher, at the relevant percentage rate subject to any de minimis exception. If the property was subject to a mortgage, stamp duty was still payable on the equity value and the amount of the debt assumed by the purchaser (Statement of Practice 6/90, 27 April 1990).

Stamp duty may also have been payable on the taking of a lease by the trustees as lessee of any tax approved pension scheme on both the premium and rent payable with the rate varying according to the length of the lease (*section 55* of the *Finance Act 1963* and *section 55* of the *Stamp Act 1891*).

It can be seen from the second and third paragraphs above that the trustees of a SIPP were liable to pay stamp duty in the relevant circumstances.

In specie transfers

14.63   If a property in the UK is owned by the trustees of a tax approved pension scheme and is transferred in specie for no consideration other than the liability of the receiving trustees of another tax approved pension scheme to pay the retirement benefits represented by the value of the property concerned, the value of the property being transferred is exempt from stamp duty (*Category F* in the *Schedule* to the *Stamp Duty (Exempt Instruments) Regulations 1987 (SI 1987 No 516)* ('the *Stamp Duty Exemption Regulations*'). However, the document evidencing the transfer is only subject to the fixed rate of stamp duty of £5.00.

If the property being transferred in specie is subject to a mortgage or legal charge, the mortgage/legal charge value is not exempt from stamp duty as the consideration passing on the transfer comprised 'other consideration', so far as HMRC is concerned, and attracts stamp duty at the relevant percentage rate. Any remaining equity value in the property is exempt from stamp duty in accordance with *Category F* in the *Schedule* to the *Stamp Duty Exemption Regulations*.

If the trustees of a SIPP received a transfer in specie of a property in the UK as part of or the whole of the retirement benefits of the member from:

(*a*)   any tax approved occupational pension scheme; or

(*b*)   another SIPP; or

(*c*)   from a retirement annuity contract;

or they transferred in specie a property in the UK as part or the whole of the retirement benefits of the member to:

(*d*)   any tax approved occupational pension scheme; or

(*e*)   another SIPP;

the value of the property forming part of the transfer is exempt from stamp duty (*Category F* in accordance with the *Schedule* to the *Stamp Duty Exemption Regulations.*

The legal title of a property, which comprised an asset of an occupational or personal pension scheme (including a SIPP) or a RAC, could also have changed in any of the following circumstances:

(i)   a change of name or death of individual trustee;

(ii)   a change of name of a sole corporate trustee;

(iii)   a commercial acquisition by a corporate trustee of a portfolio of SSAS and/or SIPPS from another corporate pension trustee;

(iv)   the divorce of a SSAS/SIPP/RAC member where a separate SSAS or SIPP is established to receive the pension credits.

In (i), (ii) or (iii) above, as the trust vehicle is likely to remain the same, no transfer of property takes place, therefore stamp duty does not apply except for the £5.00 fixed duty charge where appropriate and the mortgage element of any property involved. At (iv) the exemption at *Category F* in the *Schedule* to the *Stamp Duty Exemption Regulations* applies subject to the £5.00 fixed duty charge where appropriate and subject to the mortgage element of any property involved.

Stamp duty land tax (SDLT)

14.64   Stamp duty land tax ('SDLT'), which came into effect on 1 December 2003, is transaction based and no longer a voluntary tax like stamp duty.

Stamp duty, in respect of UK property acquisitions, was abolished with effect from 1 December 2003 and replaced by SDLT (*section 42* of the *Finance Act 2003*). Purchases of property by the trustees of occupational and personal pension schemes and retirement annuity contracts are liable to SDLT at the appropriate percentage rate subject to any de minimis exemptions. If the property is subject to a mortgage, SDLT is payable on the equity value and the amount of the debt assumed by the purchaser (*FA 2003, Sch 4, para 8*).

Stamp duty on the taking of a lease was also abolished with effect from 1 December 2003 and replaced by SDLT (*section 56* of and *Schedule 5* to *FA 2003*). The basis of valuation of the lease to arrive at the SDLT payable is different from stamp duty and the amount of SDLT payable is likely to be greater than the former stamp duty.

The trustees of a SIPP are liable to pay SDLT in the circumstances outlined in the second and third paragraphs above.

In specie transfers

14.65   Where a property in the UK owned by the trustees of a tax approved pension scheme forming part or the whole of an in specie transfer of a member's retirement benefits is transferred between tax approved occupational and personal pension schemes and RACs from 1 December 2003, the value of the property is not liable to SDLT. This is because the assumption by the trustees of the receiving pension scheme to provide retirement benefits does not constitute chargeable consideration for the property transaction in HMRC's view.

If the property being transferred in specie is subject to a mortgage or legal charge, the mortgage/legal charge is not liable to SDLT. This is because HMRC, as a concession, will not treat the assumption of the outstanding debt as chargeable consideration. Any remaining equity value in the property is not liable to SDLT as referred to in the first part of this section.

If the trustees of a SIPPS receive a transfer in specie of a property in the UK as part or the whole of the retirement benefits of the member from:

(*a*)   any taxed approved occupational pension scheme; or

(*b*)   another SIPP; or

(*c*)   from a retirement annuity contract;

or they transfer in specie a property in the UK as part or the whole of the retirement benefits of the member to:

(*d*)   any tax approved occupational pension scheme; or

(*e*)   another SIPP;

the value of the property forming part of the transfer is not liable to SDLT in accordance with the first paragraph of this section.

The legal title of a property, which is an asset of an occupational or personal pension scheme (including a SIPPS) or a RAC, may also change in any of the following circumstances:

(i)   change of name or death of individual trustee;

(ii)   change of name of a sole corporate trustee;

(iii) acquisition commercially by a corporate trustee of a portfolio of SSAS and/or SIPP from another corporate pension trustee; or

(iv)   divorce of a SSAS/SIPP/RAC member where a separate SSAS or SIPP is established to receive the pension credits.

In all of these circumstances, including any such case where a mortgage or legal charge is secured on the property concerned, a charge to SDLT will not arise.

Property transactions covered by (i) to (iv) above do not have to be notified to HMRC, but must be self-certified if registration of the change of title is needed.

HMRC's interpretation of the SDLT legislation as it applies to pension schemes was not made public until after 1 December 2003. It is contained in its own internal SDLT Manual which is available publicly via Open Government. It can be relied upon as a statement of HMRC's policy on SDLT and pension schemes in relation to transfers in specie and related mortgages/legal charges effective from 1 December 2003. It should be noted, however, that transfers between non-trust based arrangements has yet to be resolved.

The taking of a lease by the trustees of any tax approved pension scheme from 1 December 2003 is liable to SDLT.

Withdrawal of HMRC approval

14.66 HMRC has the power to withdraw the approval from a personal pension scheme if the circumstances warrant it. [*ICTA 1988, s 650* and Part 13 of IR76 (2000)]. Approval will be withdrawn from the date when the facts were such as not to warrant the continuance of approval. In such circumstances a notice of withdrawal of approval will be sent to the administrator. The notice must state the grounds on which, and the date from which, approval is withdrawn.

Approval is only likely to be withdrawn where there is a serious breach of legislation or HMRC guidelines, such as where securing the provision of appropriate benefits was not the sole purpose of the member. Unacceptable amendments may also lead to loss of approval, as could payment of excessive lump sum benefits, transactions with connected persons or the acquisition of prohibited investments. Withdrawal of approval would effectively reverse the tax reliefs afforded to personal pension schemes.

HMRC also has the power to refuse to approve a personal pension scheme. The grounds for a refusal are likely to be those which would also involve withdrawal of approval. If approval is either withdrawn or refused the decision may be appealed against. The appeal must be in writing, stating the grounds for the appeal and must be made within 30 days of the original decision. [*ICTA 1988, s 651(1)*]. Other adverse decisions of HMRC relating to personal pension schemes should be pursued by representations to the officer concerned or to a more senior officer. Unresolved problems or complaints may be taken to an HMRC adjudicator.

After 6 April 2006 it will be possible for HMRC to 'deregister' a registered pension scheme. This may occur, for example, where a scheme has made unauthorised payments of more than 25 per cent of the market value of the scheme's assets. This would attract significant tax charges. This is discussed in more detail in chapter 5.

Chapter 15

Commercial transactions

Introduction

General

15.1   This chapter considers the pensions implications of buying or selling a company or business. The value of the pension liabilities concerned can be very substantial and in some cases may exceed the value of the company or business itself, particularly where there is a defined benefit scheme involved. It is therefore essential that the main pensions issues arising from such a transaction are considered and addressed at an early stage in the negotiations. This was never more so than since the enactment of *PA 2004* where the concept of 'moral hazard' in relation to pension schemes was introduced. There are now provisions in *PA 2004* and subordinate legislation that specifically deal with this issue, including a new clearance procedure with the Regulator, whereby parties to a transaction can seek the Regulator's confirmation that it will not issue a contribution notice or financial support direction as a result of the restructuring/ sale/purchase in contemplation. These new provisions are explored in more detail throughout the chapter.

Type of scheme

15.2   Inevitably, much will depend upon the type of scheme involved. However, pensions will tend to feature most prominently in the negotiations where the employees affected by the sale belong to a defined benefit scheme. Most of these schemes are exempt approved under *Chapter I of Part XIV* of *ICTA 1988* (to be known as registered schemes from April 2006 pursuant to the *Finance Act 2004*) and will also frequently be contracted out (see chapter 4).

This chapter is therefore primarily concerned with those transactions where the employees concerned belong to an approved, contracted-out defined benefit occupational pension scheme. The implications for other types of scheme are considered at the end of the chapter.

Type of sale

15.3   The course of the pensions negotiations will depend largely upon:

(*a*)   whether the sale is of shares or of assets (see 15.14 below); and

(*b*)   whether or not the sale will require a transfer of assets and liabilities between schemes. The circumstances which will typically give rise to such a transfer are described further in 15.20 below.

Funding

15.4   A preliminary point to establish, which will set the tone of subsequent negotiations, is the funding position of the scheme providing benefits for the employees of the company or business which is being sold.

Where employees' benefits are to be transferred from the vendor's scheme to a scheme of the purchaser following completion (see 15.20 below), the funding level is likely to affect the sum which is transferred from the vendor's scheme and consequently the level of past service benefits to be granted in the purchaser's scheme following the transfer (unless the purchaser can negotiate a shortfall clause – see 15.44 below).

Where instead the purchaser is to take over the entire scheme (see 15.21 below), the funding level may impact on the profitability of the company or business being purchased. For example, a well-funded scheme may reduce future liability for the company to contribute (so boosting profits) but, conversely, an underfunded scheme may require an immediate injection of cash to raise its funding level.

These situations are likely to affect the negotiation of the contract wording and, of course, the purchase price itself. In some instances, the funding level of the pension scheme may be of such concern to the purchaser that it is not prepared to acquire the target company unless the pension deficit has been addressed. Although the compromise of pension scheme deficits has to date been relatively under-utilised as a means of dealing with funding shortfalls when selling the entire issued share capital of a company, this may become more commonplace in the future as means of ensuring that the transaction proceeds, especially where the target or its holding company are in financial difficulty. These issues are dealt with in more detail below and further information on the new Statutory Funding Objective, which was brought into effect from 30 December 2005 under *PA 2004*, can be found chapter 11.

Warranties and indemnities

15.5   It is common in a sale and purchase agreement for both warranties and indemnities to be agreed to deal with specific issues of concern to the parties, often points which have arisen during the course of negotiations and the due diligence exercise.

A *warranty* is a statement of fact made by one party to the contract (usually the vendor). An example of this may be that the benefits provided by the scheme have been fully equalised as between men and women as required by law (see chapter 9). This statement may then be disclosed against in the disclosure letter (see 15.12 below) to negate the effect of the statement to some extent, for example, by the disclosure that guaranteed minimum pensions have not yet been equalised. In such a circumstance the purchaser may seek to obtain an *indemnity* to the effect that the vendor will indemnify the purchaser for the costs of equalising benefits, should this cost be incurred by the purchaser after completion.

The main difference between a warranty and an indemnity is the level of protection given to the party for whose benefit it is given and the method by which each is enforced. To enforce a warranty, the party seeking to benefit must take steps to enforce the contract. Unless a breach of warranty is agreed by both the parties, this is likely to involve proceedings, incurring costs and delays.

By contrast, an indemnity requires the party who granted the indemnity to reimburse the other party for specified losses which have been incurred. There is no requirement for the indemnified party to mitigate his loss or to take steps to prove any wrongdoing by the indemnifying party. Consequently an indemnity offers not only more protection than a warranty to the purchaser but also considerably less inconvenience in obtaining a remedy.

Due diligence

15.6   Due diligence is the name given to the fact-finding exercise which takes place before and during negotiation of the contract. The purchaser will be concerned to find out as much information as possible about the company or business it is seeking to acquire, to ascertain not only what potential liabilities there are but also to ensure that these are quantifiable and that protection, in the form of warranties and indemnities, is sought from the vendor where appropriate.

In the context of pensions, the purchaser will wish to see, for example, a copy of the trust deed and rules, the scheme's booklet and full details of employees (including salary levels). Where a company with its own scheme is being purchased, as opposed to a transfer payment being received, more extensive information will be sought, as the purchaser will effectively be inheriting the whole scheme. The results of the due diligence exercise may result in re-negotiation of the purchase price or the seeking of further warranties and indemnities. Due diligence is considered in further detail below.

The sale documents

The sale agreement

Parties

15.7   The distinction between share sales and assets sales is considered in 15.14 below, but in either case the main parties to the agreement will be the vendor (seller) and the purchaser (buyer) respectively. There may also be other parties including, for example, guarantors.

The important point to bear in mind, therefore, is that the trustees of the respective pension schemes are unlikely to be parties to the agreement and, consequently, there will be no contractual relationship between them. In any event, trustees may not under normal circumstances fetter a future exercise of their discretion and so making them a party to the agreement would be of little comfort to either the vendor or the purchaser when the calculation of the transfer payment and the granting of past service benefits take place a few months after completion of the agreement. [*Stannard v Fisons Pension Trust Ltd [1992] 1 PLR 27*].

This is relevant when the pensions schedule is negotiated. It may be impossible for a party to agree to procure that a certain event occurs, because the scheme rules place that event in the hands of the trustees. An example of this would be where the rules of the purchaser's scheme provide that past service benefits are granted entirely at the trustees' discretion. Where this is the case, the principal company or an adhering employer cannot guarantee that a certain level of past service benefits will be granted. The most the purchaser is likely to agree to in such circumstances is that it will use its best endeavours to procure that the specified event will take place.

The extent to which the parties can hold out for a greater commitment will therefore generally depend on who has the relevant power under the trust deed and rules and (if it is the trustees) the extent to which the principal employer or an adhering employer (subject to any overriding legislation) has control over the trustees' actions. An exception to this, however, is the transfer payment. In the context of transfer payments, the purchaser should seek to place the vendor in such a position that, should the trustees pay less than the contractually defined transfer payment, the vendor will be bound to make up any shortfall – see 15.44 below.

Warranties

15.8   The pensions warranties will usually appear in the part of the agreement which sets out all the warranties (not just those relating to pensions) being given by the vendor. Sometimes, however, where there is a schedule to the agreement dealing with other pensions issues (typically a transfer payment – see 15.9 below) the pensions warranties may appear in that schedule instead. Where this happens, the vendor should take care to ensure that any clauses in the agreement that limit the scope of the warranties also extend to the warranties in that schedule. The purchaser, on the other hand, may wish to seek to disapply any general limitations from the pension warranties schedule.

It is common for parties to enter into a 'disclosure letter' of the same date as the main agreement (see 15.12 below). To the extent that a warranty is disclosed against, this will negate the effect of the warranty. An example of this has already been given in 15.5 above.

The warranties that a purchaser requires will vary considerably according to the nature of and the circumstances surrounding the transaction and are dealt with later on in this chapter in the contexts in which they arise.

Pensions schedule

15.9 Where the transaction involves a transfer of assets and liabilities from a scheme operating within the vendor's group to one to be set up (or already established) by the purchaser, its holding company or one of its subsidiaries, there will normally be detailed provisions specifying how this is to happen. In the vast majority of cases, these will be set out in a schedule to the agreement, dealing specifically with pensions.

Other provisions

15.10 Other provisions may be included either in the pensions schedule (where there is one) or in the main body of the agreement.

These might include indemnities (see 15.5 above), for instance, in relation to equalisation issues (see chapter 9) or as a consequence of obligations that may be inherited as a result of case law such as the *Beckmann* and *Martin* cases (see below). Another example might be a provision which seeks to adjust the purchase price for any past overfunding or underfunding that may emerge where the purchaser is to inherit the scheme in its entirety (see 15.27 to 15.28 below).

Consistency with scheme rules

15.11 Any action to be taken in connection with the transfer of benefits from one scheme to another will need to be carried out in accordance with the respective scheme's rules. It is therefore important that both parties are aware of the provisions in the schemes' rules governing each particular issue. One example of this is where the transaction involves a transfer payment and the scheme rules require a different method of calculation from that specified in the sale agreement. Other examples are given in the course of this chapter.

The disclosure letter

15.12   As mentioned briefly above, the disclosure letter documents the agreement between the parties on the information which has been provided during the due diligence exercise and acts to limit or negate the effect of the warranties given in the sale and purchase agreement. The disclosure letter is a letter from the vendor to the purchaser which is likely to set out first certain general statements of agreed information (such as records at Companies House) and will then go on to set out specific disclosures against specific warranties.

Purchasers should seek to ensure that the wording of disclosures is specific and to the point. From the perspective of the vendor, by contrast, it will often be desirable to make general disclosures, or make reference to a bundle of documents (thereby making an effective disclosure without drawing attention to specific areas about which the purchaser should be concerned or, at least, aware). From the purchaser's point of view, it is important to receive as much specific information as possible to ensure that it is informed of all potential and actual liabilities and can take these into account when negotiating the sale and purchase agreement.

Actuary's letter

15.13   It will be seen later in this chapter that, particularly where the transaction involves a transfer payment from the vendor's scheme, it may be necessary to agree a calculation method and assumptions for valuing the scheme's liabilities. Although there is no reason in principle why these assumptions cannot be set out in the agreement itself, they will usually be covered separately in a letter from the vendor's actuary to the purchaser's actuary and countersigned by the purchaser's actuary by way of agreement. The letter should be clearly identified in the pensions schedule, attached as an appendix and referred to where relevant.

Shares or assets

The distinction

15.14   For the purposes of this chapter, a share sale takes place when the vendor is selling all of the issued share capital of a company. In such a situation the identity of the company remains the same; it is the underlying ownership of the company which has changed. The purchaser inherits through its ownership of the company all the company's pre-existing contracts including (of particular relevance to pensions) contracts of employment and deeds which the company has entered into in relation to a pension scheme.

An asset sale takes place when all or part of a business is being sold to the purchaser. In such a transaction the purchaser will take on only specific contracts, premises and employees of the company selling the business and will only assume those liabilities specified in the agreement.

Practical implications

Employment aspects

15.15   Following a sale of shares there is no change in the employment relationship between the company and its employees. The employment contracts will stay intact and the employees therefore will enjoy the ongoing benefit of any contractual provisions, including any that relate to pensions.

This contrasts with the position of employees on an asset (or business) sale where their employment contracts are transferred to a new employer. Whilst the *Transfer of Undertakings (Protection of Employment) Regulations 1981 (SI 1981 No 1794)* ('*TUPE*') contains provisions to transfer contractual employment rights to the purchaser, *regulation 7* makes an exception in relation to 'so much of a contract of employment … as relates to an occupational pension scheme'. However, any provisions of an occupational pension scheme which do not relate to benefits for old age, invalidity or survivors are excluded from the *regulation 7* exception described above, and will therefore pass to a purchaser. The first case in which the status of such benefits was raised in the courts was the case of *Frankling v BPS Public Sector Ltd [1999] IRLR 212, [1999] ICR 347, EAT*. The Employment Appeal Tribunal refused the employee's claim that the previous entitlements to early retirement pensions and compensation on redundancy were not part of the scheme and therefore transferred under *TUPE*. The Employment Appeal Tribunal considered that the rights still related to old age, they were just triggered by redundancy. The employee's leave to appeal was granted but the action was settled before it reached appeal.

This was followed by the case of *Beckmann v Dynamco Whicheloe Macfarlane Ltd, Case C-164/00 [2002] 64 PBLR; [2002] All ER (D) 05 (Jun)*. Katia Beckmann was a former NHS employee whose employment transferred to Dynamco Whicheloe Macfarlane under *TUPE*. She was subsequently dismissed on redundancy grounds and claimed entitlement to an early retirement pension and other lump sum benefits, on the basis that these had transferred under *Article 3* of the 1977 *Acquired Rights Directive (77/187/EEC)* (now repealed). *Article 3(3)* excludes the provision of 'employees' rights to old-age, invalidity or survivors' benefits under supplementary company or inter-company pension schemes outside the statutory social security schemes in member states'. A reference was made to the European Court of Justice ('ECJ'), and the ECJ decided that 'it is only benefits paid from the time when an employee reaches the end of his normal working life as laid down by the general structure of the pension scheme … that can be classified as old age benefits, even if they are calculated by reference to the rules for calculating normal pension benefits'. As a result, the right to an early retirement pension on redundancy was held to transfer. The judgment was short and has given rise to concerns amongst pensions professionals.

Beckmann is considered further at 15.50 below.

A new case was subsequently referred to the ECJ in which additional questions were posed. In *Martin v South Bank University [2004] 1 CMLR 472, [2003] All ER (D) 85*, Martin and others transferred into a private pension arrangement following the transfer of their employment from the NHS to South Bank University. The claimants subsequently opted to take early retirement and claim an early retirement redundancy pension.

Nine questions were referred to the ECJ on the assumption that rights contingent upon both dismissal and premature retirement pass under *TUPE*. These included:

(*a*)   Is an employee's right to the payment of early retirement benefits and lump sum compensation:

- on redundancy;

- in the interests of the efficiency of the service;

- on organisational change;

- a right to 'old age, invalidity or survivors' benefit'?

(*b*)   May an employee agree to waive benefits if the purchaser's scheme does not entitle the employee to the same benefits if:

- the employee joins the purchaser's scheme; or

- joins the purchaser's scheme and transfers his past service pension rights to the purchaser's scheme?

(*c*)   Where a purchaser and employee agree that the employee will take premature retirement on less generous terms than under the vendor's scheme, what criteria should a national court use to establish if the transfer is the reason for that agreement (a reconsideration of *Foremn-*

gen v Daddy's Dance Hall [1988] ECR 739 – employment terms can be varied, provided that the transfer is not the reason for the variation)?

When the Advocate General's opinion was handed down it was dubbed 'Beckmann revisited'. Early retirement benefits and benefits intended to enhance the conditions of such retirement, paid in the event of dismissal to employees who have reached a certain age, did not relate to 'old-age, invalidity or survivors' benefits'. The right did therefore transfer.

On the *Daddy's Dance Hall* issue, rights cannot be waived, but could be varied within the parameters of that case – whether the transfer is the reason for the variation can only be answered on all the facts of the case. However, changes in the law or in the purchaser's economic position may suggest that the reason is something other than the transfer.

The Advocate General did not give a view on the impact of a transfer of past service rights.

The ECJ gave its decision on 6 November 2003. It upheld the Advocate General's opinion, but gives no guidance on the issue of in what circumstances the transfer may not be considered to be the reason for the change.

However, as regards waiving rights, the ECJ considered that as the protection was imposed as a matter of public policy, an employee could not waive his rights.

So what will transfer under *TUPE*? It is likely that redundancy benefits payable under an occupational pension scheme will transfer, and it is certainly arguable that other benefits payable before normal retirement date may transfer. The matter will undoubtedly give rise to further litigation, as the issues are clarified in the courts. In the meantime, there are a number of interesting issues raised by the case law.

(*a*) Must benefits be replicated in a purchaser's scheme to in all respects? *Mitie Management Services Limited v French [2002] IRLR 513, [2002] All ER (D) 150 (Sep)* provides some authority for not having to replicate unjust, absurd or impossible features. Replacement benefits, for example salary increases, may need to be offered instead.

(*b*) When is the transfer going to be considered to be the reason for the change? Can it be argued that an employee agreeing to join the purchaser's scheme post transfer constitutes a variation of terms by mutual consent as opposed to a waiver?

(*c*) Does it make a difference whether past rights are transferred? What happens if an employee is told that if his past service benefits are not transferred, any benefits will be limited to future service?

(*d*)   Can *Beckmann/Martin* be distinguished? The *Beckmann* pension was only payable to normal retirement age – the rights under a private sector scheme may be payable for life.

PA 2004 pension protection on the transfer of employment

15.16   Criticisms of the exclusion of occupational pensions from the ambit of *TUPE* (except in relation to *Beckmann* and *Martin*-type benefits) have lead to the introduction of limited protection for employees pursuant to *PA 2004*, introduced with effect from 6 April 2005. Where an employer acquires employees on or after that date as a result of a business purchase governed by *TUPE*, the new employer will be required to provide a minimum level of pension protection where the employee was an active member of or eligible to become a member of the vendor's occupational pension scheme prior to the transfer.

From 6 April 2005, *sections 257* and *258* of *PA 2004* and the *Transfer of Employment (Pensions Protection) Regulations 2005 (SI 2005 No 649)* have therefore brought in limited protections for the pension position of employees who are involved in a business transfer governed by the *TUPE* regulations. To qualify for the protection, certain conditions must be met:

- there must be a transfer of an undertaking or part of an undertaking to which the *TUPE* regulations apply;

- by virtue of that transfer the employees cease to be employed by the transferor and become employed by the transferee;

- at the time immediately before the employee becomes employed by the transferee, there is an occupational pension scheme in relation to which the transferor is the employer;

- the employees being transferred were either active members of the scheme, were eligible to become a member of the scheme or were in a waiting period before becoming eligible; and

- if the transferor's scheme provided money purchase benefits, (i) for active members the transferor was required to make contributions to the scheme or elected to contribute even though there was no requirement for it to do so and (ii) for those who were not active members but were eligible to join or would have been eligible after completing a waiting period, the transferor would have been required to contribute if they had been active members.

If the above conditions are met, the new employer will now be required, as a condition of the employee's contract of employment, to offer the transferred employees membership of:

(*a*)   the transferee employer's occupational defined contribution or defined benefit pension scheme or stakeholder scheme and make into the scheme matching contributions of up to 6 per cent of an employee's basic pay; or

(*b*)   an occupational defined benefit pension scheme which provides benefits the value of which is equal to no less than 6 per cent of an employee's pensionable pay (as set out in the scheme rules) for each year of employment together with the total amount of an employee's contributions. Employees will not be required to make contributions in excess of 6 per cent of their pensionable pay; or

(*c*)   an occupational defined benefit pension scheme which satisfies *section 12A* of the *Pension Schemes Act* 1993 (i e the reference scheme test for contracting out).

Unlike the position generally under *TUPE*, these protections can be disapplied in relation to a contract or contracts of employment if the employee(s) and the new employer agree alternative terms. [*PA 2004, s 258(6)*].

It is worth noting that the definition of occupational pension scheme in *PSA 1993* has been amended by *PA 2004* to the effect that schemes providing only death in service benefits are excluded from the definition. Consequently such schemes will not be covered by the occupational pension scheme exemption and will transfer under *TUPE*.

Employer's debt

15.17   We shall see later in this chapter (see 15.63 onwards below) that, where the vendor's scheme is underfunded, the sale may give rise to a statutory debt payable to the trustees by the purchaser or by the company that it is buying. It will be seen, however, that the extent of this problem will normally be less on an asset purchase than on a purchase of shares (see 15.74 below), unless of course the purchaser as part of a share purchase insists on acquiring the company free of all pension liabilities, in which case further considerations apply, including notifiable events requirements and the possibility of clearance being sought from the Regulator.

Deed of substitution

15.18   Circumstances may arise where an asset sale results in the employment contracts of all of the scheme's active members being transferred to the purchaser. In such a situation it may be appropriate for the entire scheme to become the purchaser's responsibility. This will typically require the execution of a deed substituting the purchaser as the scheme's new principal employer. In most cases, the execution of such a deed will be entirely consistent with *Re Courage Group's Pension Schemes [1987] 1 WLR 495* (outlined in 12.13 above).

A share sale is generally less likely to give rise to a deed of substitution. However, one example of where this might be appropriate would be where the vendor is the scheme's principal employer but the subsidiary being sold employs all or the majority of the scheme's active members.

Whether the sale will give rise to a transfer payment

General

15.19   The scope, nature and extent of the contractual provisions required in the sale and purchase agreement will generally depend on whether or not a transfer payment is anticipated. In most cases, the question of whether there is to be a transfer will be dictated largely by the structure of the pension arrangements and of the sale (see 15.20 and 15.21 below) but the parties may nevertheless be able to agree some alternative approach (see 15.22 below).

Circumstances involving a transfer

15.20   The following circumstances will normally give rise to a transfer payment:

(*a*)   where the company being sold is one of a number of companies which participate in the vendor's scheme; or

(*b*)   on an asset sale, where some but not all of the scheme's active members are to have their employment transferred to the purchaser.

Transactions such as these are discussed further in 15.31 to 15.62 below. Where the scheme is funded below the statutory minimum funding requirement, the sale (particularly if it is a share sale) may give rise to an employer's debt, and this aspect is considered further in 15.63 to 15.67 below.

Circumstances not involving a transfer

15.21   The following circumstances will not usually give rise to a transfer payment:

(*a*)   the sale of a company with its own scheme; or

(*b*)   an asset sale, where all of the scheme's active members are to have their employment transferred to the purchaser and the purchaser is to be substituted as the scheme's new principal employer (see 15.18 above).

In these cases, the purchaser will effectively be taking over the whole of the scheme, as it will be buying (or, alternatively, becoming) its principal employer. This is considered further in 15.23 below.

Other approaches

15.22   The general principles outlined in 15.20 and 15.21 above may sometimes be overridden if the parties agree to structure matters differently.

One example of this would be where the vast majority of the active members were to be affected by the transaction, but not all of them. In these circumstances, rather than provide for a transfer payment to be made in respect of most the scheme's active members, the parties might decide instead to arrange for the purchaser to be substituted as the scheme's principal employer (and then for a transfer payment to be made back to another scheme within the vendor's group in respect of the minority of active members whose employment was to remain with the vendor).

The parties will need to satisfy themselves that the course of action proposed will be one which can be achieved under the terms of the scheme rules (particularly as the co-operation of the trustees, who will not be parties to the agreement, may be required). Even if the scheme rules themselves do not appear to present a problem, the agreement may still fail if it is inconsistent with the purposes of the scheme; *Re Courage Group's Pension Schemes [1987] 1 WLR 495* (see 12.13 above) is perhaps the best known example of this happening.

In some cases, the purchaser may refuse to accept any responsibility for past service benefits at all, so that the employees concerned simply become deferred pensioners in the vendor's scheme. The industrial relations consequences of such a step do of course need to be borne in mind and the employment law position carefully considered in all the circumstances (see chapter 7); in this respect, there may be a difference depending on whether it is a share or asset sale, in view of the employment law distinction mentioned in 15.15 above.

Transactions where the purchaser takes over the whole scheme

Protection of purchaser

General

15.23   Where the purchaser is, in effect, to take over the whole of the vendor's scheme (see 15.21 above), its main concern will be to obtain as much protection as possible from any liabilities associated with it which arose prior to completion. This is especially the case because the scheme will relate not only to those current employees being acquired by the purchaser, but also to past employees with benefits (whether deferred or in payment) under the scheme. It is not surprising, however, that purchasers are becoming increasingly reluctant to acquire companies with defined benefit liabilities. This is a result of many factors, including unpredictability of costs, continually improving mortality rates and low inflation.

Where, however, a scheme is to come within the purchaser's group after completion, protection will take the form of thorough due diligence, warranties and, in relation to areas of particular concern, indemnities. There may also be negotiation on payments into the scheme by the vendor to address funding concerns.

Due diligence

15.24   The purchaser should seek to ensure that its advisers have the opportunity to examine as much as possible of the scheme's documentation at an early stage.

At the very least, this should cover the scheme's governing trust documents, the latest actuarial valuation report (and any subsequent actuarial advice), booklets and announcements issued to members (as well as references to pensions in contracts of employment and service agreements), recent annual reports and accounts and sufficient membership data to enable the purchaser's advisers to take a view on the costs of the scheme's ongoing liabilities.

The purchaser should also seek to obtain copies of the HMRC approval letter and any contracting-out certificates. Other relevant matters are trustees' minutes, copies of investment management agreements (and other advisers' appointment letters), insurance policies, transfer agreements with the trustees of other schemes, the statement of investment principles, the schedule of contributions, documentation relating to member-nominated trustee arrangements and details of the scheme's internal dispute resolution procedure.

Additionally and pursuant to *PA 2004*, the purchaser should also be raising inquiries regarding whether any breaches of the law have been reported to the Regulator by the trustees of the scheme or the vendor (not to mention the scheme's advisers or other persons involved in the administration) under *section 70* of *PA 2004* or if any reportable matters have arisen in relation to the scheme in accordance with *section 69* of *PA 2004* and the corresponding Codes of Practice for both. Purchasers will also want to know if the vendor has been the subject of a contribution notice or if a financial support direction is in place (*sections 38* and *43* of *PA 2004*) in relation to the scheme, as such funding obligations could be inherited going forwards. Both contribution notices and financial support directions are discussed in further detail at **15.65** to **15.70** below.

The aim should be to build up a full picture of the scheme including funding levels, liabilities, the balance of powers between the employers and the trustees and compliance with *PA 1995* and *PA 2004*. This knowledge will all be important as part of the negotiation process.

Warranties

15.25 The more comprehensive the warranties that the purchaser is able to obtain from the vendor, the safer he will generally be. For maximum protection, the agreement may stipulate that the warranties apply not only as at the date of the agreement but also (if later) the date of completion. Even if the vendor gives warranties but then discloses against them, the purchaser will at least be in a better position to know where any problems lie.

Some examples of the warranties that a purchaser should seek are:

(*a*)   that there are no schemes or similar commitments (whether legally binding or not) relating to the employees, except those that have been disclosed;

(*b*)   that the documents provided to the purchaser are true and complete;

(*c*)   that the scheme is an exempt approved scheme and there is no reason why that approval might be withdrawn;

(*d*)   that the scheme is contracted out (where appropriate) (see chapter 4) and the necessary contracting-out certificates have been issued;

(*e*)   that the scheme complies with all legal requirements for the equalisation of benefits as between men and women;

(*f*)   that the scheme, its trustees and the employers have complied with all applicable statutory requirements;

(*g*)   that the information contained in the latest actuarial valuation report is complete and accurate in all respects and that nothing has happened since its effective date which would have an adverse affect on its conclusions;

(*h*)   that none of the employers being acquired is, or may become, liable in respect of any underfunding under *section 59, 60* or *75* of *PA 1995* (as amended);

(*i*)   the rate of employers' contributions;

(*j*)   that all contributions due have been paid in accordance with the trust deed and rules and as required by the scheme's schedule of contributions;

(*k*)   that no changes have been made (or proposed or announced) to the scheme's eligibility requirements, contribution rates or benefits;

(*l*)   that all risk benefits are validly insured with an insurance company of good repute on normal terms for persons in good health;

(*m*)   that there are no court proceedings and no complaints (whether under the scheme's internal dispute resolution procedure, or to The Pensions Advisory Service ('TPAS') or to the Pensions Ombudsman) in progress, pending, threatened or anticipated;

(*n*)   that no contribution notices or financial support directions have been issued by the Regulator in relation to the scheme;

(*o*)   that no employee has ever become employed by the vendor as a result of a transfer pursuant to *TUPE*; and

(*p*)   that no professional adviser has had cause to whistleblow in accordance with *section 48* of *PA 1995* or report breaches of the law in accordance with the requirements of *PA 2004*.

The purchaser may seek more extensive warranties than these and the vendor, conversely, will often aim to limit their scope. For instance, the vendor may wish to restrict the warranties to matters of which it is aware, which in turn may lead to negotiations as to what extent of knowledge the contract should deem the vendor to have. The vendor will be particularly cautious with regard to any funding warranty, as a breach of this can prove extremely expensive.

Indemnities

15.26   Either party may seek indemnity protection from the other in respect of matters where there is some particular risk involved.

Purchasers therefore frequently require indemnities against the costs of benefits not having been equalised as between men and women in respect of past service (see chapter 9). Another area which may give rise to an indemnity is the possibility of an employer's debt becoming payable under *section 75* of *PA 1995* (see 15.63 to 15.73 below) and, more recently, claims relating to *Beckmann/Martin* type benefits where the transaction is subject to the provisions of *TUPE*.

Funding

General

15.27   The importance to a purchaser of having a funding warranty has already been mentioned in 15.25 above.

A separate (but related) issue arises where the scheme is understood to be overfunded or underfunded on an ongoing basis and it is agreed that there should be some payment between the parties following the sale (usually as an adjustment to the purchase price) to compensate. Where this happens, the respective parties' actuaries will normally negotiate a method and assumptions for determining the amount of overfunding or underfunding; the calculation itself is then carried out after completion.

(It is common for these issues instead to be dealt with at an earlier stage, as part of the purchase price negotiations. The most likely reason for dealing with the matter by means of a post-completion adjustment would be that there was insufficient information as to the scheme's funding position at the time of sale.)

Underfunded scheme

15.28   Where the scheme is underfunded on an ongoing basis, the purpose of the compensating payment will, in effect, be to relieve the purchaser of the costs of bringing the funding up to that level.

The sum which the scheme will require, therefore, will be the amount by which the scheme's assets fall short of the value calculated in accordance with the agreed actuarial method and assumptions. The vendor, however, will be reluctant to pay more than is necessary to achieve this, and so (instead of paying the sum directly into the scheme) may propose to pay it to the purchaser net of the standard rate of corporation tax, on the basis that corporation tax relief will become available to the purchaser's group when it is remitted to the trustees. (The vendor may be particularly concerned that the payment should be used to restore the scheme's funding position rather than to benefit the purchaser, and so expressly require that the purchaser pay the sum into the scheme as soon as it is received.)

The purchaser will not necessarily be satisfied with this approach. For instance, the purchaser's group may prove not to be making profits when the time comes, in which case it will derive no benefit from the theoretical availability of corporation tax relief. Alternatively, even if the purchaser is making profits, the sum involved may be treated by HMRC as a special contribution (see chapter 5), in which case the tax relief would have to be spread over a period of years.

A compromise position would be for the payment to be made to the purchaser gross of corporation tax, on condition that the purchaser take steps to avail itself of corporation tax relief on paying the sum into the scheme and account to the vendor for the value of that relief.

Overfunded scheme

15.29   Where the scheme has a surplus on an ongoing basis, the purpose of a compensating payment (which would instead be from the purchaser) is very different, as are the considerations affecting its calculation.

The payment would be a form of recognition that, before the sale, there was an overfunded scheme within the vendor's group from which the vendor might have gained some benefit in the future. Following the sale, the vendor no longer has that opportunity, which has passed to the purchaser instead.

It would probably be inappropriate for the purchaser to pay to the vendor the whole of this surplus. This would presume that it was open to the scheme's employers to acquire the full present value of the scheme's surplus, which is not the case for a number of reasons:

(*a*)   Only in exceptional cases may an employer receive a refund of surplus assets from its scheme, and even then the scheme rules may require that substantial benefit increases be granted first. Previous legislation also required this. From 6 April 2006 pursuant to *section 37* of *PA 1995*, as amended by *sections 250 and 251* of *PA 2004*, before any refund of surplus can be made certain conditions will need to be satisfied. For example, the scheme will need to show that it is funded at buy-out level on an actuarial basis; the trustees will need to confirm that they are satisfied such a payment would be in the best interests of the members; and the Regulator must not have issued a freezing order against the scheme which is in force. Any such refund would, in any event, be subject to a 35 per cent tax charge. [*section 207* of *FA 2004*]. These issues are considered in more detail in chapter 11.

(*b*)   It is more likely that the employer could benefit from the surplus by means of a reduction in its contributions or even a contributions holiday. However, it is by no means certain that the whole of the surplus could be used in this way. For example, if the scheme rules give the trustees a say in the matter, then it is likely that at least some of this surplus would instead have to be used for benefit improvements.

(*c*)   Even if the employer is able to take a contributions holiday in respect of the entire surplus, the benefit of that holiday will only gradually be realised over a period of time. An immediate payment to the vendor in lieu of that contributions holiday, therefore, ought not to be equal to the entire surplus, but should be discounted to take into account the fact that (unlike a contributions holiday) the benefit to the vendor is immediate.

It can be seen from this that agreeing a suitable method for ascertaining the amount of the compensatory payment is likely to prove complex. Often the matter will instead be dealt with between the parties before the sale as part of the purchase price negotiations.

Change of trustees

15.30   Usually, the scheme's trustees will be directors, employees or a subsidiary company of the vendor. If the trustees are to remain with the vendor's group following completion, it will generally be appropriate for them to be replaced as trustees by individuals or by a company within the purchaser's group. The contract may expressly provide for this to be done, and may even require that a deed of removal and appointment of trustees be one of the completion documents.

Considerations may also arise in relation to the issue of member-nominated trustees. This is addressed further in 15.68 below.

Transactions involving a transfer payment

General

15.31   Where the transaction involves a transfer payment (see 15.20 above), the sale agreement may provide for the company being sold (or, in the case of an asset sale, the purchaser) to participate in the vendor's scheme on a transitional basis for a temporary period after completion. This is not always the case, however, and the following paragraphs, from 15.32 to 15.51 below, assume that there is to be no such transitional period.

The further issues which will become relevant if there is to be a transitional period are considered later in this chapter (see 15.52 onwards).

Methods of calculating transfer payments

Past service reserve

15.32   There are several ways of calculating a bulk transfer payment. Of these, a 'past service reserve' calculation is the one which seeks to produce a sum which is sufficient to provide past service benefits which are equal overall to the benefits that the transferring members could otherwise have expected to receive in respect of their completed membership of the vendor's scheme had there been no sale.

A past service reserve transfer payment is calculated by reference to the length of past pensionable service of the members concerned, but with present pensionable salaries being increased by an actuarially assumed rate of future salary growth. The calculation will also require other assumptions to be made, for instance, in relation to the future mortality rates, inflation, rates of withdrawal by members from pensionable service and investment growth.

The figure produced by this calculation will ultimately depend upon the assumptions used. These assumptions should normally therefore be agreed between the respective parties' actuaries before the contract is signed. Two very slightly differing sets of assumptions can produce vastly different results and consequently these negotiations are often hard fought. In reality, the relationships between the assumptions (for instance, the extent by which investment returns are assumed to exceed future salary growth) may have a greater impact on the final calculation than the assumptions themselves.

The purchaser's actuary will normally wish to see a copy of the scheme's most recent actuarial valuation report, so that he can form a view as to whether the assumptions on offer are consistent with the way in which the scheme as a whole is funded. The vendor may refuse to make the valuation report available, but the purchaser may still be able to obtain it through links with members or with trades unions to whom the trustees can be required by law to provide a copy in accordance with the *Occupational Pension Schemes (Disclosure of Information) Regulations 1996 (SI 1996 No 1655)* (to be replaced from October 2006 by the *Occupational Pension Schemes (Disclosure of Information) Regulations 2005*) (see summary at appendix II).

The valuation report may reveal that the assumptions on offer will produce a smaller transfer payment than would the long-term funding assumptions recommended by the actuary for the purpose of calculating employer's contributions. The purchaser may then argue that the scheme's long-term funding assumptions should be used instead. The vendor's likely response would be that a policy decision had been taken to fund the scheme using more cautious assumptions than were strictly necessary or that different assumptions were appropriate to the group of employees being transferred.

Sensitivity about the scheme's funding assumptions is not the only reason why a vendor may prefer not to make a copy of the valuation report available. Other reasons might be that:

(*a*)   the valuation shows that the scheme is in surplus, and this may encourage the purchaser to press for a greater transfer payment; or

(*b*)   the valuation shows that the scheme is weakly funded, which in turn may lead the purchaser to ask for an indemnity in respect of any employer's debt that may arise. This aspect is explained further in 15.63 to 15.67 below.

Past service reserve plus share of surplus

15.33   The purchaser may seek a transfer payment that is calculated on a past service reserve basis but which also includes a proportionate share of any surplus funding in the vendor's scheme over and above that.

Although the scheme rules will be relevant, it has been widely accepted since Walton J's decision in *Re Imperial Foods Ltd Pension Scheme [1986] 2 All ER 802* that there is no reason in principle why a purchaser (or the receiving trustees) should expect the transfer payment to include a share of any surplus. The rationale for this view is that, in an ongoing scheme whose rules will require the employers to increase their contributions to make good any under-funding that arises in the future, a surplus in the scheme as at a given time simply reflects the fact that the employers are temporarily ahead with their contributions. The so-called surplus does not represent 'spare' money that should necessarily be available to a receiving scheme.

Transfer payments including a share of a surplus are therefore now compara-tively rare. However, they can still occur where, for instance, a very substantial proportion of the vendor's scheme's liabilities is to be transferred in circum-stances where the vendor's scheme's rules will make it difficult for the trustees to justify not transferring a share of the surplus, or require a 'share of fund' transfer value to be paid.

Where this does happen, the vendor can be expected to require an increase in the purchase price. The manner in which this should be calculated is complex, but it will be governed by the same considerations as have been mentioned above in the context of 15.29 above.

Cash equivalents

15.34   We saw in chapter 6 that a member's 'cash equivalent' is the statutory amount which he may be entitled by law to require the trustees to transfer to another scheme. For a group of members, their aggregate cash equivalents will broadly speaking be comparable to the amount which is needed to satisfy the statutory minimum funding requirement in respect of their past service benefits.

In most cases, cash equivalents will produce a lower figure than would a past service reserve. This is primarily because the cash equivalent calculation does not provide for future salary growth. (It should be noted, however, that consul-tation took place on changes to the calculation basis of transfer values under Actuarial Guidance Note GN11 and that the original exposure draft EXD54 would, if adopted, be likely significantly to increase transfer values for some members. At the time of writing new professional guidance is expected within the next few months.)

Where a vendor proposes that the transfer payment be restricted to cash equivalents, this may be because the vendor's scheme is too precariously funded to be able to pay more. If this is so, the purchaser may request a shortfall payment from the vendor representing the difference between the cash equiva-lents and the higher amount which a past service reserve calculation would have produced (see 15.45 below) or alternatively seek a reduction in the purchase price. If the vendor is not prepared to accede to either of these requests, then there is likely to be an adverse impact on the past service benefits which the purchaser's scheme will be able to offer, unless the purchaser is prepared to make up the shortfall itself. The employment law and industrial relations of this will have to be considered (see chapter 7), as well as the possibility instead that past service benefits simply be left in the vendor's scheme (rather than transferred).

Sometimes a vendor will offer only cash equivalent transfer payments, even though its scheme can afford to pay more. The scheme rules are likely to be especially relevant in such cases; it may well be that they require the trustees to pay more than the vendor is offering.

Reduced cash equivalents

15.35   In some circumstances, the law may permit the trustees of the vendor's scheme to reduce members' cash equivalent transfer payments, on the basis of the scheme's funding position. The problems which this can raise for the purchaser are essentially the same as those mentioned in 15.34 above, only even more acute. The purchaser should also be particularly concerned about the risk of an employer's debt arising as explained further in 15.63 below.

Other possibilities

15.36   There are, of course, other ways of calculating a transfer payment. For instance, it could be calculated as an agreed percentage of (for example) the amount needed to meet the statutory minimum funding requirement ('MFR') (to be replaced by the statutory funding objective ('SFO') as more fully explained in chapter 11) in respect of the transferring members' past service benefits. So, a scheme which, being funded at 104 per cent of the MFR, could afford to pay more than the statutory cash equivalents but was unable to pay a reasonable past service reserve, might pay transfer payments equal to 104 per cent of the MFR in respect of the members concerned.

Timescales, mechanics and calculation adjustments

Timescales and mechanics

15.37   In the absence of a transitional period (see 15.52 onwards below), the mechanics of the transfer provisions will tend to revolve around two key dates.

The first of these is the date of completion of the sale which, for pension purposes, will be the date on which the relevant employees' pensionable service in the vendor's scheme will terminate.

The second of these is the date on which the transfer payment becomes payable.

The length of time that is to pass between the completion date and the payment date will be determined by the sale agreement. In most cases the agreement will provide for certain steps to be taken between the two dates. In a typical agreement, these might include:

(*a*)   Following the completion date, members are to be invited to join the purchaser's scheme for future service and advised that if they do elect to join they will have a right to transfer their past service benefits to the purchaser's scheme.

(*b*)   The members are to be given a period in which to decide whether to elect for such a transfer. This will normally involve their signing and returning a consent form, and the sale and purchase agreement will often provide for that form to include a discharge from the member to the vendor's scheme's trustees (and possibly the vendor) in respect of any further liability for past service benefits. The information given to members should recommend that they obtain independent financial advice, so as to avoid problems arising under the *Financial Services Act 1986* (see chapter 10).

(*c*)   Once that period has expired, the parties know which members have elected to transfer. The parties then instruct their actuaries to liaise with a view to calculating the transfer payment in accordance with the method of calculation previously agreed between them. There will usually be a set timescale for this.

(*d*)   Once the calculation of the transfer payment has been agreed, there is a short further period allowed for, at the end of which the payment becomes due. If it has been agreed that the transfer be paid in cash, the transferring trustees may need to realise assets during this period. Alternatively, the parties and their actuaries may agree certain in specie transfers of assets.

Timing adjustment

15.38   A past service reserve transfer payment will in these circumstances be calculated as at the date of completion, as that will be the date on which pensionable service terminated and the benefits therefore crystallised.

However, as explained in 15.37 above, the transfer payment will not actually become payable until some time after that. Some provision therefore needs to be included in the agreement specifying how the transfer payment is to be adjusted in respect of the period from completion until the date on which it becomes payable.

An interest calculation can be used, but this may not take proper account of the effects of investment conditions during the period in question. If, for instance, share values were to soar ahead of the agreed interest rate during this period, then the vendor's fund would benefit disproportionately from this, whereas the purchaser's fund would not benefit from it at all. Conversely, were investments instead to fall in value, the effect of an agreed interest rate would be to exacerbate the impact of this upon the vendor's fund, whilst the purchaser's fund would remain insulated from the adverse conditions.

The actuaries may therefore agree a market related 'timing adjustment' in respect of this period. In effect, this means that the past service reserve figure is to be adjusted by a formula representing movements over the period in a notional portfolio consisting of (for instance) 85 per cent equities and 15 per cent gilts. The actuaries will discuss and agree the formula to be used before the sale agreement is signed. The respective schemes' investment strategies can be expected to have some bearing on these discussions.

Interest

15.39 If the transfer payment is not paid until after it has fallen due, a further adjustment will be necessary in respect of the period of late payment.

This may be dealt with simply by continuing to apply the timing adjustment for that further period, but the purchaser may consider that the sale agreement should require a more punitive adjustment as payment by that stage will be overdue. One approach would be to continue to apply the timing adjustment, but to make the sum resulting from it subject to an agreed rate of interest in respect of the period of delay.

Voluntary contributions

15.40 The agreement should also provide for the transfer of assets arising from the payment of money purchase voluntary contributions by those members who elect to transfer their past service benefits. Because of the money purchase nature of these, this will be a simpler provision than those parts of the agreement dealing with the transfer of defined benefit liabilities.

Disputes clause

15.41 There may be circumstances in which, following the sale, the actuaries are unable to agree the calculation of the transfer payment as required by the sale agreement. Alternatively, the sale agreement may require that the past service benefits to be granted by the purchaser's scheme should be equal in overall value to the amount of the transfer payment; this is another area where the actuaries may fail to agree.

Most pensions schedules therefore include a clause providing for disagreements of this nature to be referred to an independent actuary. The clause will normally provide for the independent actuary to act as expert (rather than as arbitrator) as this is generally suitable for disputes of this nature and is less formal than arbitration. The agreement should also make provisions as to who is to bear the expert's costs; for example, whether these are to be borne between the parties equally or, alternatively, as the expert may direct.

Revenue issues

Consent to bulk transfer

15.42   The consent of HMRC should be sought before making a bulk transfer payment to or from an approved scheme, and the pensions schedule should accordingly make it clear that any obligations in relation to the transfer are subject to this approval being obtained.

The application to HMRC should be made on form PS 295. In practice, HMRC is unlikely to object except in the very rare cases where a scheme has such a large surplus that HMRC requires it to be reduced.

This requirement ceased on 6 April 2006.

Continued rights

15.43   We saw in chapter 5 (see 5.6 onwards) that Revenue limits may (subject of the member's precise circumstances) be more generous for a member who joined a scheme before 17 March 1987 or 1 June 1989 than if he had joined on or after those dates. Members who joined before these dates are said to have 'continued rights'.

HMRC should therefore be asked to confirm that these members of the vendor's scheme may carry on being treated as having 'continued rights' after they join the purchaser's scheme. The *Occupational Pension Schemes (Transitional Provisions) Regulations 1988 (SI 1988 No 1436)* and the *Retirement Benefits Schemes (Continuation of Rights of Members of Approved Schemes) Regulations 1990 (SI 1990 No 2101)* respectively provide for such treatment. It is not strictly necessary to seek HMRC's approval in all cases but it is generally safest to do so, and should certainly be sought where members already had continued rights in the vendor's scheme arising from a previous transfer in.

This no longer applies from 6 April 2006 but the purchaser should try to establish whether any members will be transferring with transitional protection of existing rights under *FA 2004* (see chapter 5).

Contracting out

15.44   Separate requirements apply to the transfer of contracted-out benefits. The relevant law is summarised in chapter 4, starting at 4.75.

Shortfall and excess clauses

Shortfall clause

15.45   As has been mentioned already, the trustees will not be a party to the sale agreement and so will not be bound by its terms. Consequently, except in those cases where the vendor's scheme's rules enable the vendor to direct the amount of the transfer payment, there can be no guarantee that the trustees of that scheme will in fact transfer the amount provided for in the sale agreement. The purchaser will have particular cause for concern if the funding position of the vendor's scheme suggests that its assets may prove insufficient to justify the transfer payment which the parties have negotiated.

The purpose of a shortfall clause, therefore, is to protect the purchaser (and the purchaser's scheme) from the possibility of the trustees transferring less than the amount which the vendor and the purchaser have agreed. The clause will require a payment by the vendor itself (or by a company in its group) to achieve this. The principles surrounding the shortfall payment (including the tax considerations) will be those that have already been considered in the context of 15.28 above.

Excess clause

15.46   An excess clause is essentially the converse of a shortfall clause. Whereas a shortfall clause requires a payment from the vendor, should the trustees of the vendor's scheme pay less than the agreed transfer payment, an excess clause requires a payment from the purchaser should they pay more.

A vendor might insist that, in order to be even-handed, any shortfall clause in the agreement should be accompanied by a mirror-image excess clause. The purchaser, however, may take the view that the vendor's trustees will only exceed the negotiated transfer payment if they are satisfied that their scheme can afford it. Consequently, many excess clauses are expressed so as only to apply to the extent that the trustees have transferred the excess by mistake.

The purchaser's scheme

Type of scheme

15.47   The course of action which ought to create the least disruption to the continuing accrual of members' pension benefits will be a properly funded transfer payment to a defined benefit scheme of the purchaser, containing similar provisions to those of the vendor's scheme.

Often, however, the purchaser will not have an existing defined benefit scheme and the number of employees to be transferred may simply not be enough to make the establishment of a defined benefit scheme specifically for them financially viable. In these circumstances, the purchaser might instead offer membership of a money purchase scheme or agree to pay contributions to personal pension schemes in relation to the employees concerned.

The vendor will normally require a commitment in the sale agreement that the receiving scheme should be approved (or at least capable or receiving approval), so that the vendor's scheme may properly make the transfer to it. The contracted-out status of the purchaser's scheme should also be addressed, in view of the requirements referred to in 15.44 above.

One related point concerns announcements which the vendor may have made about the purchaser's scheme. When contemplating making announcements to members about an impending sale, vendors will need to bear in mind the case of *Hagen v ICI Chemicals and Polymers Ltd [2001] 64 PBLR, [2001] All ER (D) 273 (Oct)*. This has already been referred to at 7.22 above. In the light of this case, the vendor may want to leave as much detail as possible to be explained by the purchaser, whilst still complying with its duty to provide certain disclosures under *TUPE*. The vendors should ensure that communications are as far as possible recorded in writing and that they take legal advice.

Past service benefits

15.48   If the sale agreement provides for a past service reserve transfer payment to a defined benefit scheme, the vendor is likely to require some commitment as to what past service benefits the purchaser's scheme will provide. The vendor may prefer that these be determined in the same manner as applies for the calculation of benefits under the vendor's scheme, but this could prove impractical for the purchaser if its own scheme has a different benefit structure.

Instead, the purchaser may (if it is satisfied that the transfer payment will be sufficient) be prepared to agree that the past service benefits will be broadly equivalent (or, if the purchaser agrees to go further than that, at least equal in value) overall to those earned in the vendor's scheme; the vendor, in turn, may consider that this should be tightened so as to apply separately in respect of each member. The agreement may have to make it clear how benefits are to be valued for this purpose.

A more stringent line that a vendor could take would, in effect, be to insist that the whole of the transfer payment is used to provide past service benefits in respect of the employees concerned. This would prevent the purchaser from using any part of the sum to fund a reduction in employers' contributions or to provide benefits for other scheme members. Much will depend upon the trust deeds and funding positions of the respective schemes, but a purchaser may well be reluctant to accept such a suggestion on the ground that it places a more onerous obligation upon it than would previously have applied under the vendor's scheme.

Indeed, the purchaser may be reluctant to give any commitments as to the level of past service benefits at all if it has doubts about the adequacy of the transfer payment being offered.

Where the transfer is to be made to a money purchase scheme, the question of past service benefits is less controversial. These will normally be whatever the value of each member's portion of the overall transfer payment provides.

Future service benefits

15.49 Purchasers are generally reluctant to commit themselves in the sale agreement to a specific level of benefits in respect of future service. This is partly because to do so would in most cases be a more onerous obligation than the vendor itself had ever assumed, but more particularly because it would fetter the future running of their business.

A purchaser which has decided initially to provide defined benefits might, therefore, be prepared to commit itself to a particular benefits structure as at the date when the employees join the scheme, but reserve the right to amend or discontinue the scheme at any time after that. In the comparatively rare cases where the purchaser agrees to maintain a particular benefit structure (perhaps because it is receiving a generous transfer payment), this will only normally apply for a limited period.

Transfer agreement

15.50 The nature of the purchaser's scheme and the benefits under it will generally tend to be of greater concern to the transferring trustees than they are to the vendor itself. These trustees may even have adopted a practice of requiring receiving trustees to enter into a transfer agreement with them, dealing specifically with these issues, before they will agree to make a particular transfer payment. The ability of trustees to take such a stance will depend on the balance of powers in the transferring scheme.

However, where this is the case, the vendor may require that a form of transfer agreement is attached to the sale agreement and that the vendor's obligations in relation to any transfer are dependent upon the purchaser's scheme's trustees entering into such an agreement with the vendor's scheme's trustees.

Transfer agreements, and examples of the matters that they will frequently cover, are considered in chapter 12, at 12.35 onwards.

Due diligence, warranties and indemnities

15.51 Where the purchaser will not be inheriting the whole of the vendor's scheme, it may not require the same level of warranty protection as described in 15.25 above. This is particularly so in the absence of a transitional period (see 15.31 above), as the purchaser (or, in the case of a share purchase, the company it is buying) will not be participating in the vendor's scheme following completion.

The purchaser should still, however, request a complete copy of the scheme's trust deed and rules and obtain a warranty as to its accuracy. There are two main reasons for needing to see this. The first is to enable the purchaser to satisfy itself that its provisions will not be such as to prevent the agreed pensions schedule from being implemented. If, therefore, the rules show that the power to make bulk transfer payments rests solely with the trustees, then (particularly if the scheme appears to be poorly funded) the purchaser will be forewarned of the importance of obtaining a shortfall clause (see 15.45 above).

The other reason is to enable the purchaser to ascertain the contributions and benefits structure in the vendor's scheme; with this in mind, the purchaser should also seek to obtain copies of members' booklets and should also require a warranty that no changes to the information shown have been proposed or announced. This (together with appropriate membership data) should enable the purchaser's actuary to assess the likely costs to the purchaser of providing the same benefits for future service and suggest what alternative approaches might be available. This information should also reveal any particular expectations the members may have that could prove expensive for the purchaser, such as generous early retirement provisions on redundancy.

The purchaser ought also to request a copy of the latest actuarial valuation report and obtain warranties to the effect that nothing has happened since its effective date which might adversely affect its findings. An understanding of the scheme's funding position will help the purchaser to take a view as to how large a transfer payment it can realistically negotiate. Where there is some indication of underfunding, this will again alert the purchaser to the possible need for a shortfall clause (see 15.45 above) and an indemnity in respect of any employer's debt that may arise (see 15.63 to 15.73 below).

Warranties should also be sought as to the vendor's scheme's tax position (as an approved scheme is not permitted by HMRC to accept a transfer payment from a scheme that is not approved) and also its contracted-out status (because of the requirements referred to briefly in 15.47 above and set out in chapter 4).

Another area of concern is the equalisation of benefits as between men and women as required by law (see chapter 9). The purchaser should seek a warranty that these requirements have been met, as a member who is entitled to bring a claim based on a scheme's failure to equalise can also sue the trustees of another scheme to whom the benefits in question have been transferred. If successful, such a claim can prove expensive. It is therefore common for purchasers also to seek an indemnity against this eventuality.

The current state of concern arising from the case of *Beckmann v Dynamco Whicheloe Macfarlane Ltd, Case C-164/00 [2002] 64 PBLR; [2002] All ER (D) 05 (Jun)* (see 15.15 above) may lead to purchasers and vendors negotiating who will bear the commercial risk that a particular scheme benefit will pass following this case. Purchasers may seek indemnities or an adjustment to the purchase price in this connection. They should consider relevant provisions of the vendor's scheme very carefully and ask their actuary to cost these pension rights.

Transitional periods

General

15.52   Transactions involving a transfer payment fall into two main categories, depending upon whether the employees concerned:

(*a*)   cease to be active members of the vendor's scheme from the completion date; or (*b*)   continue to be active members of the vendor's scheme for a transitional period following the completion date.

The purchaser may wish to have the benefit of a transitional period if it has no suitable scheme in place to receive the transfer payment (or provide future service benefits) and requires a period of time in which to establish one.

In the context of a company sale, this will simply be a case of the company continuing to participate in the scheme for a temporary period after it has been sold out of the vendor's group. In an asset sale, by contrast, it will mean the purchaser (or employer of the transferring employees) being admitted to the vendor's scheme as a participating employer, but only for the agreed transitional period commencing on the completion date.

Previously in this chapter we have considered only those cases where there is no transitional period. Where there is to be a transitional period, further considerations will apply.

HMRC

15.53   Currently, any period of participation in these circumstances by an employer which is not (or has ceased to be) associated with the scheme's principal employer will require the agreement of HMRC. The sale and purchase agreement should be drawn up in a manner which recognises this. In the past HMRC has usually agreed to a period of participation not exceeding 12 months.

The requirement that an employer has to be associated with the principal employer to participate in a scheme falls away with effect from 6 April 2006 when it will be possible to admit non-associated employers to participate in a scheme and/or allow previously associated employers receiving a transfer of employees following a business transfer to participate for longer than the existing permitted period (12 months) on completion of the transaction. This may give rise to 'balance of power' issues (for example, is admission subject to trustee consent under the trust deed and rules governing the scheme?) and consideration will be required as to whether the participation of a non-associated employer would be consistent with the main purpose of the scheme (i e where the scheme in question has been established for the benefit of the employees and directors of the principal and associated employers).

Role of trustees

15.54   Before agreeing to a period of temporary participation, the vendor should check its scheme rules to see if the trustees have a discretion as to whether or not to permit this. If so, then the vendor will not be in a position to *procure* a transitional period in the sale agreement, and should ensure that the level of commitment required of it under the sale agreement is consistent with those rules.

In most instances, the trustees should be amenable to the agreement of a transitional period of participation, but circumstances may arise where they are not (for instance, if the trustees anticipate that the temporary employer intends to grant artificially high pension increases, to the detriment of the scheme's funding position).

The sale agreement will normally seek to regulate the terms upon which the company or purchaser is to be permitted to participate, as we shall see below. This is another area, therefore, where the rules of the vendors' scheme and the scheme's actuarial assumptions will need to be checked. This can be particularly relevant in the context of contributions, which is considered next.

Employers' contributions

15.55 The parties may either leave the question of contributions during the transitional period to be determined in accordance with the scheme rules, or they can agree a specific rate.

If, for example, the vendor's scheme is overfunded and the participating employers are enjoying a contributions holiday, the vendor is likely to prefer to specify a fixed contribution rate, probably equal to the long-term contribution rate which the actuary would be recommending if the scheme was evenly funded on an ongoing basis. This, of course, is because the purchaser will have made no contribution towards the surplus that has arisen and so the vendor will not wish to see the purchaser derive any benefit from it.

Conversely, the employers may all be paying very high contributions following an unfavourable actuarial valuation report. In these circumstances, the purchaser can be expected to request a lower, specified rate.

Even where a specified rate of contribution is agreed, it may in fact be the vendor's scheme's trustees (rather than the vendor) who have the power to decide contribution rates under the scheme rules. If, therefore, the parties have agreed a fixed rate which tends to favour the purchaser, then the purchaser may also seek an indemnity from the vendor against the possibility of the trustees requiring a higher rate.

Expenses

15.56 Expenses arising during the transitional period may take the form of:

(*a*)   administrative expenses; or

(*b*)   the cost of insuring risk benefits.

They may form part of the contribution rate required to be paid by the purchaser during the transitional period, or be specified in the agreement as a further sum to be paid in addition to those contributions.

Limit on salary increases

15.57   One of the actuarial assumptions by reference to which the vendor's scheme is funded will relate to future salary increases. A transitional period presents some risk to the vendor of the temporarily participating company granting salary increases during that period which significantly exceed this assumption.

Such an increase will inflate the vendor's liabilities for deferred pensions in respect of those members affected by the transaction who elect not to transfer to the purchaser's scheme. It may also increase the amount of the transfer payment, depending on the circumstances (see 15.60 below). This, of course, will be detrimental to the funding of the vendor's scheme.

The vendor may therefore insert a provision requiring the purchaser to procure that pay increases do not rise by more than a certain percentage during the transitional period (often a percentage consistent with the scheme's assumptions). Whether this presents a problem for the purchaser will depend on whether it anticipates granting such increases. If not, then the purchaser may choose to accept the restriction, but with the qualification that the increases may be granted with the consent of the vendor (that consent not to be unreasonably withheld or delayed).

Other obligations of the purchaser during the transitional period

15.58   The sale agreement may also require the purchaser to procure that, during the transitional period, it (or, where appropriate, the participating employer owned by it):

(*a*)   will comply with all the provisions of the vendor's scheme which apply to it as a participating employer;

(*b*)   will not exercise any discretion which it may have in relation to the vendor's scheme without the vendor's consent (usually not to be unreasonably withheld or delayed);

(*c*)   will not by any act or omission prejudice the scheme's exempt approved or contracted-out status;

(*d*)   will not take any steps which might increase the transfer payment; and

(*e*)   will nominate the vendor to act on its behalf in relation to the member-nominated trustee arrangements and its right to be consulted about the scheme's statement of investment principles.

Obligations of the vendor during the transitional period

15.59   Obligations of the vendor under the sale agreement in respect of the transitional period might be as follows:

(*a*)   to keep the scheme in full force and effect;

(*b*)   not to increase benefits in relation to the members concerned; and

(*c*)   not to take any steps which might reduce the transfer payment.

Date as at which past service liabilities are calculated

15.60   The date as at which the transfer payment should be calculated may be either:

(*a*)   the completion date; or

(*b*)   the end of the transitional period.

One of these alternatives may be more consistent with the scheme's trust deed and rules than the other. A number of issues will arise depending upon which of the two dates is to apply:

 (i)   If the completion date is used, an addition should be made to the calculation of the transfer payment representing the contributions paid by the participating employer in respect of the transferring members, and by the transferring members themselves, during the transitional period (less any part of the employer contributions which relates to the expenses mentioned in 15.56 above).

 (ii)   If the end of the transitional period is used, then the issue of salary increases during the transitional period (see 15.57 above) becomes particularly relevant, as increases in excess of the assumptions will inflate the calculation of the transfer payment.

(iii)   If the end of the transitional period is used, then the timing adjustment (which, in the absence of a transitional period, would operate from the completion date – see 15.38 above) should instead operate from the end of the transitional period.

Admission of new members during the transitional period

15.61   If during the transitional period the purchaser does not have any other scheme in place, it may wish to have new members employed by it (who were not members before completion) admitted to the vendor's scheme during that period. The vendor's views on this are likely to depend on the administrative implications.

It may be that the vendor will draw a distinction between:

(*a*)   applicants who were employed by the company (or within the business) before completion but were at that time serving a 'waiting period' before they could become eligible to join; and

(*b*)   applicants who are recruited as employees by the new owners after completion,

and agree only to admit the first of these two groups.

Due diligence, warranties and indemnities

15.62   The purchaser should obtain the same information, and seek the same protections, as mentioned in 15.51 above.

In addition, however, the fact that there will be a temporary period of participation in the vendor's scheme will necessitate a careful review of the participating employers' obligations under the scheme's trust deed. The issues in relation to employers' contributions have already been mentioned (see 15.55 above) including the possible need for an indemnity from the vendor. A review of the scheme's latest actuarial valuation report may (depending on how recent it is) give some indication as to whether this is likely to be an issue.

The purchaser should also check to see whether the trust deed (or any other document) contains an indemnity by the participating employers in favour of the trustees. If so, more extensive warranties may be necessary to satisfy the purchaser that there is no matter in respect of which it might become liable under that indemnity.

Employer's debt

General

15.63   We saw in chapter 12 (see 12.68 onwards) that there are certain circumstances where *section 75* of *PA 1995* may render an employer liable for a debt to the trustees of an underfunded scheme.

Some of those circumstances are especially relevant in the context of this chapter. The *Occupational Pension Schemes (Employer Debt) Regulations 2005 (SI 2005 No 678)* (the *'Employer Debt Regulations'*), as amended by the *Occupational Pension Schemes (Employer Debt etc) (Amendment) Regulations 2005 (SI 2005 No 2224)* came into force in April 2005 and replaced (for schemes winding up on or after 6 April 2005) the *Occupational Pension Schemes (Deficiency on Winding Up etc) Regulations 1996 (SI 1996 No 3128)* (the *'Deficiency Regulations'*). The *Employer Debt Regulations* set out the level of debt due from an employer on insolvency, scheme wind up or withdrawal from a multi-employer scheme.

As set out in 15.52 above, purchasers may, in some circumstances, want to participate in a vendor's pension scheme if they do not have appropriate arrangements for the transferring employees to join on completion. Similarly, when a company is being sold which is a participating employer in a multi-employer defined benefit pension scheme, that company will, at the time of completion, withdraw from those arrangements. Parties to such transactions need to be aware that the withdrawal of a company from a defined benefit arrangement may give rise to a *section 75* debt if:

(*a*)   the scheme is one to which *section 75* relates (which in practice covers most approved defined benefit pension schemes – see 12.69 above);

(*b*)   the employer ceases to be an employer employing persons in a description of employment to which the scheme relates whilst at least one other employer continues to do so (a 'cessation event'); and

(*c*)   the scheme is at that time underfunded by reference to the statutory minimum funding requirement (currently still the 'MFR' but due to move to the statutory funding objective ('SFO')) (see chapter 11 for details regarding the new SFO).

A statutory debt will be triggered under *section 75* of *PA 1995* (*regulation 6* of the *Employer Debt Regulations*) and the company being acquired will have to make an immediate payment to fund part of the statutory debt on a full buy-out basis (with effect from 2 September 2005 pursuant to the *Occupational Pension Schemes (Employer Debt etc) (Amendment) Regulations 2005 (SI 2005 No 2224)* (the *'Employer Debt Amendment Regulations'*)) together with any 'cessation expenses' (see *regulation 7* of the *Employer Debt Regulations*). Alternatively, the withdrawing employer can pay the MFR debt if a withdrawal arrangement is agreed between the purchaser and the trustees and approved by the Regulator. Withdrawal arrangements are discussed in further detail at 15.71 to 15.74 below.

Amount of the debt

15.64   A *section 75* debt can arise when an employer participating in a group defined benefit scheme ceases to participate in a multi-employer scheme or on a business sale when the company *'ceases to be an employer employing persons in the description of employment to which the scheme relates'* (*regulation 6(4)* of the *Employer Debt Regulations*) at a time when there are remaining employers in the scheme. As a general rule, the amount of debt triggered will depend upon the proportion of the scheme's liabilities that relate to that employer divided by the liabilities of the scheme that relate to all employers multiplied by the amount of the debt.

Regulation 6(1)(e) of the *Employer Debt Regulations* provides, broadly, that *section 75(4)* of *PA 1995* applies on the basis that the employer is only liable for its share of the debt. *Regulation 6(2)* of the *Employer Debt Regulations* defines the share of the debt as being:

'(a)   such proportion of the total difference as, in the opinion of the actuary after consultation with the trustees or managers, the amount of the scheme's liabilities attributable to employment with that employer bears to the total amount of the scheme's liabilities attributable to employment with the employers; or

(b)   if the scheme provides for the total amount of the debt to be otherwise apportioned amongst the employers, the amount due from that employer under that provision.'

Included in the withdrawing employer's share of the debt are any 'cessation expenses attributable to the employer' and the employer's share of the debt, in accordance with *regulation 6(1)(e)* of the *Employer Debt Regulations*.

For the purposes of *regulation 6(2)* of the *Employer Debt Regulations*, the total amount of the scheme's liabilities which are attributable to employment with the employers and the amount of the liabilities attributable to employment with one employer are such amounts as determined, calculated and verified by the actuary in accordance with the guidance provision in Faculty & Institute of Actuaries Guidance Note 'Retirement Benefit Schemes – Winding up and Scheme Asset Deficiency' (otherwise known as 'GN19').

The *Employer Debt Amendment Regulations* came into force on 2 September 2005 and changed the debt payable by an employer following a cessation event where that employer participated in a multi-employer defined benefit pension scheme. The position now is that on the withdrawal of an employer from a multi-employer defined benefit scheme on or from 2 September 2005, the calculation of the debt will be on a full buy-out basis, unless there is an alternative arrangement in place (in accordance with *paragraph 1(1)(a)* of *Schedule 1A* to the *Employer Debt Regulations*) which the trustees have agreed and the Regulator has approved. This will have the effect of reducing debt to the MFR (later the SFO) basis (see 15.71 to 15.73 below for further details).

On a business and asset sale, no debt on the new employer is likely to arise as long as the purchaser is not admitted to participate in the vendor's scheme for a transitional period. However, if the purchaser does participate in the vendor's scheme, then as some of the liabilities will be attributable to employment with that employer, it could be liable for some of any statutory debt that may arise when it ceases to participate.

Money purchase arrangements are generally excluded from the provisions of *section 75* but *regulations 10* to *13* of the *Employer Debt Regulations* will apply to such arrangements when the general levy has not been paid or where the assets have reduced as a result of crime. In both cases the employer becomes liable to the extent that it cannot be paid out of unallocated assets.

Clearly the possibility of a *section 75* debt arising will have a significant impact on the viability of a proposed transaction and the value of a withdrawing company. The *Employer Debt Regulations* are in themselves a complex piece of legislation and should be considered in detail in the event that the purchaser is acquiring a company which participates in a multi-employer scheme.

See also chapter 12 above regarding when multi-employer schemes are treated as being divided into separate schemes for debt purposes.

Moral hazard

15.65   With effect from April 2005 the Regulator has had new powers to prevent employers 'dumping' their defined benefit liabilities upon the Pensions Protection Fund and to increase member security. These so-called 'moral hazard' provisions and resultant Regulator's powers are of particular relevance to corporate transactions. Two of the Regulator's new powers include the ability to issue contribution notices, requiring specified persons to make contributions to pension arrangements, and to issue financial support directions, requiring certain persons to put in place financial support arrangements for a pension scheme. These new powers together with the new 'clearance procedure' for corporate transactions are set out in further detail below.

Contribution notices

15.66   The Regulator may, in accordance with *section 38* of *PA 2004*, issue a contribution notice to an employer or person *connected* with or an *associate* of the employer (see 15.67 below) where it is of the opinion that the person was a party to an act or deliberate failure to act where the main purpose or one of the main purposes of the act or failure to act was:

(a)   to prevent the recovery of the whole or any part of the *section 75* debt; or

(b)   otherwise than in good faith, to prevent such a debt becoming due, to compromise or otherwise settle such a debt, or to reduce the amount of the debt that would otherwise become due.

These provisions do not apply to money purchase schemes or other prescribed schemes.

The contribution notice will require the person to pay a specified sum into the scheme. This contribution could be of an amount up to the total shortfall of any *section 75* debt (or even where there is no debt yet due, the total assessed shortfall as if a *section 75* debt were due from a solvent employer, i e in practice this would mean the full buy-out cost).

The Regulator can only impose a contribution notice if it is reasonable to do so. When deciding what is reasonable, it must have regard to 'such matters as the Regulator considers relevant including where relevant, the following matters':

●   the degree of involvement of the person in the act or failure to act;

●   the relationship which the person has or has had with the employer (including where the employer is a company, whether the person has had control of the employer within the meaning of *section 435(10)* of the *Insolvency Act 1986*);

●   any connection or involvement which the person has or has had with the scheme;

●   if the act or failure to act was a notifiable event for the purposes of *section 69* of *PA 2004*, any failure to notify;

●   all the purposes of the act or failure to act (including whether a purpose of the act or failure was to prevent loss of employment);

●   the financial circumstances of the person; and

●   such other matters as may be prescribed.

The legislation is retrospective and the Regulator can issue a contribution notice in relation to an act or failure to act which occurred on or after 27 April 2004 and before any assumption of responsibility for the scheme by the Pension Protection Fund Board. Purchasers should therefore be seeking confirmation from the vendor that no contribution notices have been issued by the Regulator and remain unpaid in relation to a pension scheme if acquiring the entire issued share capital of the target company. See 15.25 above for further details on suggested warranties.

'Connected' and 'associated'

15.67   The Regulator can only issue a contribution notice to a person if that person was at any time in the relevant period:

(*a*)   an employer in relation to the scheme; or

(*b*)   a person connected with, or an associate of, the employer.

These are complex definitions. In summary, a person is '*connected*' with a company if:

(i)   he is a director or shadow director of the company or an associate of such a director or shadow director;

(ii)   he is an associate of the company.

'*Associate*' is defined widely and includes corporate bodies and private individuals such as husbands, wives and relatives. The definition is complex and includes as associates partners, trustees, employers and employees and companies if the person has control or if he and his associates have control of the company. For example, a person can be associated with a company if he and one or more of his associates jointly hold one third of the company's voting rights in that company or in another company which has control of it. A company can also be an associate of another company where a person controls one company and his associate (or he and his associate jointly) controls the other. The definition is drawn widely and could therefore potentially catch a number of individuals or companies within a group structure – even unrelated companies could be treated as associated with each other and potentially brought into the scope of the Regulator's powers.

Financial support directions

15.68   *Sections 43* to *50* of *PA 2004* provide the Regulator with new powers to issue a financial support direction to the employer and persons connected and associated with the employer. The purpose of a financial support direction is to ensure that groups of companies stand behind their pension liabilities and do not leave them with the weakest member of the group and, in turn, with the Pension Protection Fund.

The Regulator may issue a financial support direction if it is of the opinion that an employer to the scheme is a 'service company' or is 'insufficiently resourced'.

A company will be a *service company* if, at the relevant time, it is an employer in the group and its turnover is 'solely or principally derived from amounts charged for the provision of the services of the employees of [this company] to other members of the group'.

A company is *insufficiently resourced* if, at the relevant time:

- the employer has insufficient net assets to enable it to meet the amount which is a prescribed percentage (50 per cent) of the estimated *section 75* debt in relation to the scheme; and

- there is at that time a person who qualifies under the legislation and whose resources are not less in value than the amount which is the difference between:

  - the value of the resources of the employer; and

  - the amount which is the prescribed percentage (50 per cent) of the estimated *section 75* debt.

The P*ension Regulator* (*Financial Support Directions etc*) *Regulations 2005* (*SI 2005 No 2188*) ('the *FSD Regulations*') came into force on 1st September 2005.

A financial support direction ('FSD') in relation to the scheme is a direction which requires the person or persons to whom it is issued to secure:

(*a*)   that financial support for the scheme is in place within the period specified in that direction;

(*b*)   that thereafter financial support or other financial support remains in place while the scheme is in existence; and

(*c*)   that the Regulator is notified in writing of prescribed events in respect of the financial support as soon as reasonably practicable after the event occurs.

PA 2004 provides that financial support arrangements can mean making all the members of a group jointly and severally liable for the whole or part of an employer's pension liabilities or making a holding company liable for the whole or part of a subsidiary employer's pension liabilities.

To make an FSD the Regulator has to be satisfied it is reasonable to do so. Among the factors the Regulator has to take into account to decide whether it is reasonable to make an FSD is 'the value of any benefits received directly or indirectly by that person from the employer'.

Where there is a disposal of an employer the Regulator may need to be informed of this as the disposal is a notifiable event. If the Regulator thinks an FSD is appropriate both vendor and purchaser would be included as 'associates' and the relevant event would usually be fixed as the disposal date. In accordance with *regulation 5* of the *FSD Regulations*, a company remains 'associated' for twelve months after the disposal. Accordingly, companies planning a disposal may wish to apply to the Regulator for clearance.

Purchasers therefore need to be aware that the company they are acquiring could potentially be the subject of an FSD for up to twelve months after the transaction has completed. Careful and early due diligence will be required of the corporate structure and any pension schemes relating to the company in question to put this matter beyond doubt and where necessary, relevant warranties and indemnities should be sought from the vendor.

Clearance

15.69   As a consequence of the new powers of the Regulator brought into effect by *PA 2004*, a statutory clearance procedure has been introduced to give greater certainty to parties considering transactions involving companies with defined benefit schemes. Assurance can be gained by the persons involved by requesting and obtaining a clearance statement from the Regulator to the effect that the actions in contemplation will not later cause the Regulator to exercise its powers to issue a contribution notice or FSD. According to the Guidance issued by the Regulator,

'Clearance was introduced with the underlying aims being:

- the protection of jobs, particularly where clearance is needed to prevent the employer becoming insolvent; and
- the continuation of appropriate deal activity involving employers with defined benefit schemes.'

Clearance applications are voluntary but they do provide certainty to those who may be liable to the imposition of a contribution notice or financial support direction. There is no time limit stipulated within which the Regulator must issue the statement except that it must be issued 'as soon as reasonably practicable'. Once issued the clearance statement will bind the Regulator unless there is a material change in circumstances or if the circumstances described in the application are not correct.

The Guidance advises that clearance will be considered only in relation to schemes in deficit on an FRS17 basis, the implication being that schemes in excess of this level will not generally be subject to contribution notices or FSDs. Parties wishing to apply for clearance should complete the Regulator's standard application form (available on the Regulator's website: www.thepensionsregulator.gov.uk) and provide the information requested, which includes:

- details of the event giving rise to the request for clearance and its effect on the scheme;
- details of discussions between employer and trustees;

- details of the employer's corporate structure and financial information; and

- information on scheme funding and membership.

The standard form issued by the Regulator for use for a clearance application invites the applicant to request that the Regulator issues one or more of the following statements:

In the Pensions Regulator's opinion:

- The applicant would not be, for the purposes of *subsection (3)(a)* of *section 38* of *Pensions Act 2004*, a party to an act or a deliberate failure to act falling within *subsection (5)(a)* of the section;

- It would not be reasonable to impose any liability on the applicant under a contribution notice issued under *section 38*; and/or

- it would it would not be reasonable to impose the requirements of a financial support direction, in relation to the scheme, on the applicant.

The Guidance issued provides examples of the circumstances in which clearance statements will be given for various types of corporate activity. Broadly the approach that the Regulator is going to take is to focus on 'specified events' which are events affecting an entity which are financially detrimental to the ability of a defined benefit scheme to meet its pension liabilities. For clearance purposes the Regulator is going to adopt a risk-based approach, operating the clearance procedure generally only where the scheme is not 100 per cent funded on an FRS17 basis. The Guidance does say, however, that FRS17 should only be used where there is no doubt the employer can continue as a going concern. If there is doubt a buy-out funding basis should be used. However, in most circumstances, if a scheme is fully funded on an FRS17 basis there should be no exposure to a contribution notice or a FSD.

Classification of events

15.70   The Guidance divides various types of corporate activity into three types:

(a)   **Type A** are events that do affect the pension creditor. These are specified events which are financially detrimental to the ability of a defined benefit scheme to meet its pension liabilities and where it may be appropriate to seek clearance.

(b)   **Type B** are events that do not affect a pension creditor (including commercial transactions at arm's length). Clearance is not necessary for these events.

(c)   **Type C** are events that might affect a pension creditor. All events that point towards the deterioration in the employer's covenant and which may be outside the control of the employer. Clearance is not available for these events if they do not also fall within Type A.

Type A events may include a change in the level of security that may be given to creditors with the consequence that the pension creditor may receive a reduced dividend in the event of an insolvency, for example, granting of fixed or floating charge. Another example given is a change or partial change in the group structure which will reduce the overall employer covenant, and could affect the ability of an employer to meet a *section 75* debt and lead to the Regulator imposing a financial support direction. For example, a change of employer or participating employer or change in parties connected with or associated with the employer. So share sales could potentially be caught.

Type B events are commercial transactions carried out at arm's length and include mergers and acquisitions such as:

(i)   sale and purchase of assets;

(ii)   sale and purchase of non-employer subsidiary;

(iii)   management buy-out or buy-in;

(iv)   privatisation or joint venture.

However, these events are only Type B events as long as they do not include a Type A event.

Type C events comprise events that point towards a deterioration in the employer's covenant and which may be inside or outside the control of the employer or its directions. The Guidance confirms that Type C events will include all Type A events, as any event which is financially detrimental to the ability of a defined benefit scheme to meet its liabilities will all point to a deterioration in the employer's covenant. Events which pass a Type A test may still fall into Type C. However, not all Type C events are notifiable or specified events, for example, the loss of a customer.

A clearance procedure is available under *PA 2004* so that the Regulator can provide confirmation as to whether or not a particular act or failure to act or set of circumstances which exists in relation to a person during the relevant period will lead to a contribution notice or FSD. The Regulator advocates contacting its office as soon as practicable when it becomes clear to the parties to a transaction that clearance may be required so that a quick determination can be issued and the Regulator can adhere to any timescales involved which are driving the transaction. Recent experience demonstrates that the Regulator is willing to be responsive and flexible in assisting the parties to reach a solution or structure for a transaction that meets as far as possible the needs of all parties, including the pension scheme.

The Regulator can be contacted at: clearance@thepensionsregulator.gov.uk.

Withdrawal arrangements

15.71 The Regulator issued Guidance in November 2005 on withdrawal arrangements. Where an employer ceases to participate in a defined benefit multi-employer occupational pension scheme, it may be liable to a debt on withdrawal from the scheme (as noted at 15.63 above). The amount of any debt due may be modified if the employer enters into a withdrawal arrangement approved by the Regulator. The Guidance is aimed at employers, trustees and advisers involved in defined benefit multi-employer occupational pension schemes who wish to enter into a withdrawal arrangement in relation to a cessation event arising on or after 2 September 2005. A cessation event is where it is intended that there will be no more active members in the scheme in relation to that employer and there is at least one other employer remaining in the scheme that employs active members. As noted at 15.63 above, this event will trigger a *section 75* debt at a buy-out level.

Status of a withdrawal arrangement and the guarantor

15.72 A withdrawal arrangement is a legally binding document between the withdrawing employer, the guarantor and the trustees which has been approved by the Regulator. The arrangement will set out the proposals for payment of a modified debt amount, usually to permit the withdrawing employer to pay a lesser amount on exit from a defined benefit multi-employer occupational pension scheme.

The arrangement will set out the lesser amount of the debt to be paid by the withdrawing employer (usually employer's share of the MFR debt) and confirm the amount to be paid by the guarantor which can be either:

- the difference between the unmodified withdrawal debt and the amount paid by the withdrawing employer; or

- the amount needed to secure the withdrawing employer's members' benefits in the event that:
  - the scheme commences wind-up;
  - there is no employer in the scheme that has not suffered a relevant event (i e an insolvency event; an application is made by the trustees to the PPF to assume responsibility for the scheme; or the trustees have received notice from the PPF under *section 129(5)* of *PA 2004*); or

–   the Regulator calls in the debt.

In practice this will be either a fixed amount or a floating liability.

The guarantor will generally be:

(*a*)   one of the remaining employers in the scheme;

(*b*)   someone connected with the withdrawing employer or remaining employers;

(*c*)   the withdrawing employer; or

(*d*)   the purchaser in a sale situation.

Statutory conditions

15.73   The withdrawal arrangement must meet a number of statutory conditions (contained in *Schedule 1A* to the *Occupational Pension Schemes (Employer Debt) Regulations 2005* (*SI 2005 No 678*) (as amended)) including:

- the trustees, the withdrawing employer and the guarantor (where it is not the withdrawing employer) must be parties;

- the parties must agree that the withdrawal arrangement is subject to the laws of England and Wales unless the scheme and/or the employer is based in Northern Ireland (in which case the laws of Northern Ireland apply);

- the withdrawing employer must agree to pay at least any MFR debt by a specified date;

- the guarantor must pay the outstanding debt if the scheme commences wind-up; there is no employer in the scheme which has not suffered a relevant event or the Regulator calls in the debt;

- if there is more than one guarantor, the arrangement must specify whether they are jointly and severally liable;

- the agreement must provide for the amount due to be paid by the guarantor(s) to be paid to the trustees unless the PPF has assumed responsibility for the scheme;

- either the withdrawing employer or the guarantor(s) should be liable for all the costs reasonably incurred by the trustees in connection with making the agreement and obtaining the Regulator's approval;

- the agreement must provide that it will remain in force until:

  –   the wind-up of the scheme is completed;

> – the Regulator issues a direction stipulating that the agreement is no longer required; or
>
> – the agreement is replaced with another agreement forming part of an approved withdrawal arrangement.

The intention is for each arrangement to be tailored to meet the circumstances involved. The Regulator can impose additional conditions which will usually be particular to each case and depend upon the financial strength of the guarantor. There is, however, one additional condition which the Regulator will impose on all arrangements submitted for approval and that is the guarantor's consent to the Regulator disclosing any notice of a notifiable event received from the guarantor(s) to the trustees and any other guarantor. This is to ensure that the trustees become aware of any notifiable events in the future in relation to the guarantor(s) that may cause concern regarding the financial security of the arrangement.

Before making the submission, all the parties concerned (the withdrawing employer, the trustees and the guarantor(s)) will have their own considerations and must agree between them the proposed withdrawal arrangement. For example, it will be difficult for the trustees to give up the prospect of an upfront funding injection on a buy-out basis without negotiating something extra in return, i e vendors may have to inject money into the scheme every time a company is sold. It is easy to see how the role of the trustees in transactions will become increasingly more important. Trustees are likely also to want to seek their own independent advice regarding the financial strength of the guarantor and its ability from time to time to meet the outstanding debt arising in relation to the withdrawing employer.

The application form is available on the Regulator's website (follow links to 'information for employers') and the Regulator can accept electronic applications although the security of the information cannot be guaranteed. The email address is: clearance@thepensionsregulator.gov.uk.

Parties' positions

15.74 The purchaser should be concerned about the risk that he may be entering into a transaction which may gives rise to a debt payable by him or by the company he is buying. Even if the purchaser can persuade the vendor to indemnify him against any such debt, there remains the possibility that a considerable period of time might pass before the actuarial calculations are complete and the debt is notified to the purchaser. There is a risk that, by this stage, the vendor may no longer be in a financial position to meet the indemnity. As well as an indemnity, therefore, the purchaser may ask the vendor to procure that the scheme will be valued, and the amount of any debt notified, within a set timescale.

None of this is likely to appeal to the vendor, especially if the scheme's funding is indeed weak. The prospect of an indemnity will be particularly unattractive if the vendor is promising a past service reserve transfer payment backed up by a shortfall clause (see 15.45 above). As for a commitment to procure an MFR (or other) valuation within a set timescale, this of course can only serve to increase the likelihood of the indemnity coming into operation. The vendor may require that the purchaser meet the costs of any such valuation, but this, like the surrounding matters, will ultimately be a matter for negotiation.

The possibility of an employer debt arising may, therefore, present major issues for the parties, and this highlights the need for early due diligence in relation to the scheme's funding position. It may, however, be possible to lessen the impact of the legislation by structuring the deal, for example, as an asset sale rather than a company sale, as illustrated in the following table:

	Potential size of debt	**Reason**
Company sale, no transitional period	Could be huge.	The purchaser acquires all the company's liabilities. The company may have participated in the vendor's scheme for years and be responsible for a huge proportion of the overall debt (calculated on a full buy-out basis). This will relate not only to the company's present employees, but also to pensioners and deferred pensioners formerly employed by it.
Company sale with transitional period	Larger still.	As above, except that the extra period of participation will increase any debt still further.
Asset sale, no transitional period	Nil (assuming the vendor of the assets continues to have some employees in the scheme following completion).	No employer will be ceasing to participate in the vendor's scheme.
Asset sale with transitional period	Smaller debt than for corresponding company sale (again, assuming the vendor of the assets continues to have some employees in the scheme following completion).	The purchaser will have participated in the vendor's scheme only for a short time following completion, and so be responsible for a (probably small) proportion of any overall deficit.

Member-nominated trustees

15.75   A commercial transaction of the sort considered in this chapter may cause the trustees to review the appropriateness of the member-nominated trustee arrangements (see chapter 3).

Public sector transfers

15.76   Bulk transfers from schemes such as the Principal Civil Service Pension Scheme and other public service pension schemes, of which the Government Actuary's Department is scheme actuary, have separate requirements which must be satisfied if a bulk transfer payment is to be made into a receiving scheme. These situations arise primarily when an outsourcing contract is entered into with a Government body or agency.

In order for the Government Actuary's Department to agree to the transfer of public service scheme benefits, the receiving scheme must satisfy prescribed criteria to its satisfaction. These criteria relate generally to the level of benefits to be provided and the balance of powers in the receiving scheme. The Government Actuary's Department will usually provide a standard pensions schedule setting out its requirements but its provisions can be negotiated to a limited extent, subject to the circumstances of a particular case. Some schemes may be required to make amendments to the scheme rules to satisfy the Government Actuary's Department's criteria. If the necessary criteria are satisfied, the Government Actuary's Department will issue either a 'certificate of broad comparability' or a 'passport'.

The distinction between the passport and the certificate of broad comparability is that the passport attaches to the receiving scheme and is valid for more than one transfer in, only ceasing to be of general application if the Government Actuary's Department's requirements change. A passport is more usually applied for when a new scheme is being established specifically to receive public service transfers. By contrast, a certificate of broad comparability will be required for all schemes without a passport on each occasion on which it is proposed that a transfer be made.

Of course, not all such outsourcing contracts will lead to transfers of benefits. The *Local Government Pension Scheme (Amendment etc) Regulations 1999 (SI 1999 No 3438)* provided a new method of addressing pensions on the transfer of employment in the context of local government outsourcing. This method is to admit the new employer to participate in the local government pension scheme. The new employer must enter into an admission agreement with the administering authority, and may also have to acquire an indemnity or bond (*regulation 5* of the *Local Government Pension Scheme Regulations 1997*

(*SI 1997 No 1612*)). The need for an indemnity or bond was previously an absolute requirement, but this changed under the *Local Government Pension Scheme* (*Amendment*) (*No 2*) *Regulations 2003* (*SI 2003 No 3004*). This substituted *regulation 5* with *regulations 5, 5A* and *5B* from 19 December 2003, but with effect from 1 January 2003. The new requirement is that where a new employer will provide services or assets in connection with the function of an existing 'Scheme employer' (the outsourcing council), as a result of the transfer of the service or assets by means of a contract or other arrangement, that 'Scheme employer' must:

> '... carry out an assessment, taking account of actuarial advice, of the level of risk arising on premature termination of the provision of the service or assets by reason of the insolvency, winding-up or liquidation of the transferee admission body.'

It is only 'where the level of risk identified by the assessment is such as to require it', that the prospective new employer is required to enter into an indemnity or bond. This means that where there are only a handful of employees transferring, for example, there may no longer be a need to go to the expense of providing an indemnity or bond. Where such a document is required, banks usually present their own 'standard' which is then considered by the outsourcing council's lawyers.

Negotiation of the admission agreement and indemnity or bond is usually a lengthy process and should be started as soon as the overall contract negotiations begin. Prospective new employers are increasingly seeking indemnities from an outsourcing council as to liabilities – past and future – in the local government pension scheme, including *Beckmann* type liabilities.

The requirement for the new contractor to provide either broadly comparable pension arrangements or admission to the local government pension scheme, is currently only contained in Government guidance which was published in June 1999 and updated in June 2004. The HM Treasury 'Guidance to Departments and Agencies: Staff Transfers from Central Government: A Fair Deal for Staff Pensions' dated June 1999 as annexed to the Cabinet Office 'Statement of Practice – Staff Transfers and the Public Sector' dated January 2000 ('Fair Deal') provides guidance on protecting all public service employees, including those transferring to a contractor under a Private Finance Initiative ('PFI') and Public-Private Partnership ('PPP') contracts.

The Fair Deal guidance essentially provides the public service employees with protection that is two pronged, covering past and future service rights. In respect of future service, the contractor must offer future service benefits which are 'broadly comparable' to the public service sector scheme they have left, which will be assessed by the Government Actuary's Department. The guidance explains that this means that there shall be 'no identifiable employees who will suffer material detriment overall'. If an individual will suffer, that individual must be awarded compensation (for example, a salary increase).

To protect past service, the contractor's scheme must be prepared to accept a bulk transfer, and 'day for day' transfer credits must be provided (or an equivalent basis as recommended by the Government Actuary's Department shall apply). The further guidance issued by HM Treasury and entitled 'The Fair Deal for Staff Pensions: Further Guidance – Fair Deal for Staff Pensions: Procurement of Bulk Transfer Agreements and Related Issues Guidance Note' dated June 2004 ('Fair Deal 2004') builds on the principles set out in the Fair Deal and clarifies the practical aspects of its application. One important point to note is that the Fair Deal and the subsequent Fair Deal 2004 guidance only apply to contracts let after the date of the Fair Deal. Therefore previous outsourcing contracts awarded prior to June 1999 will not be caught by the principles set out in the guidance on any subsequent re-let of those original contracts (although authorities may still wish to adopt such an approach voluntarily).

As a consequence of this guidance, the outsourcing process has been tightened up, but there could be some unwelcome side effects for contractors. Detailed pension information will have to be given by the contracting authority at the outset of the tendering procedure (this will be required before any shortlist of contractors is drawn up) and the transfer terms (i e the credits to be awarded in the contractor's scheme) will have to be settled at an early stage. This will have costs implications for the contracting authority. It is possible that delays will also occur further down the line. The Government Actuary's Department will be required to provide a full analysis of the terms of the transferring and receiving schemes, which must be made available to unions and employees. A reasonable period is to be allowed for discussion, and no contractual terms can be settled in that period.

The Government is, however, in the process of putting this on a statutory basis. *Sections 101* and *102* of the *Local Government Act 2003* provide that local authority transferees will be offered either continued membership of the local government pension scheme or membership of a broadly comparable scheme. However, the provisions are quite short and we will have to wait for appropriate directions to be issued pursuant to those sections to provide the necessary details.

All of the above applies to local authority employees transferring to a new employer as a result of an outsourcing contract. In addition, a Code of Practice on Workforce Matters in Local Authority Service Contracts contained in Annex D of the ODPM Circular 03/2003 deals with the terms and conditions and pensions of new joiners. The intention of the Code is to prevent the creation of a 'two tier' workforce and so requires contractors to provide new joiners with one of the following: membership of the local government pension scheme, membership of a good quality employer pension scheme – either being a defined benefit pension scheme or a money purchase pension scheme with matched employee and employer contributions up to 6 per cent – or a stakeholder pension scheme, under which the employer will match employee contributions up to 6 per cent. Further details regarding public sector transfers are to be found at 7.22 above.

Other types of scheme

Money purchase schemes

15.77 Where the vendor's scheme provides money purchase benefits, the issues are considerably simpler.

In the context of a money purchase occupational scheme, the warranties will focus far less on the sufficiency of the scheme's assets and more on the extent of the liability to contribute (and whether all the contributions due have been paid). There may still, however, be some defined risk benefits, and the purchaser should seek the necessary disclosures and warranty as to the insurance of these.

If the circumstances give rise to a transfer payment (see 15.20 above), the amount to be transferred will effectively be the sums in the transferring members' money purchase accounts, rather than involving complex valuation methods and assumptions.

If the purchaser is taking over the entire scheme (see 15.21 above), it will also require warranties to satisfy itself that the scheme complies with all relevant legal requirements. However, as illustrated by the table at 1.16 above, money purchase arrangements are less heavily regulated than defined benefit ones. Details of when a money purchase arrangements will be caught by the *Occupational Pension Schemes (Employer Debt) Regulations 2005 (SI 2005 No 678)* are set out at 15.64 above.

If the scheme is a personal pension arrangement, the purchaser will want to see the documentation setting out the contribution promise and information indicating the costs of those contributions. It will also need a warranty that all contributions due have been paid (and that there has been no proposal or announcement to pay higher contributions).

Small self-administered schemes

15.78 Most small self-administered schemes ('SSASs') are money purchase arrangements and so the same principles as mentioned in 15.77 above apply. These are less regulated than other types of scheme in many respects (see 13.34

above), although the purchaser should seek warranties that the investment and borrowing restrictions that apply to such schemes (see chapter 13) have been observed.

Often the company which the purchaser is buying will be the principal (or only) employer of the SSAS and the vendors will be the scheme members. The vendors (who in these circumstances will probably also be trustees of the SSAS) will wish to retain control over their scheme and so may, as a term of the sale agreement, require that the purchaser executes a deed of amendment transferring (so far as possible) the company's powers under the scheme rules in relation to the SSAS to the trustees. The purchaser may be happy to do this, as long as it is protected from any further liabilities in relation to the SSAS.

Unregistered schemes

15.79 The purchaser should seek to obtain as much information as it can about any unapproved/unregistered schemes that there may be.

Much of the legislation that applies to other schemes does not apply to unapproved/unregistered arrangements. This will to some extent lessen the level of warranty protection that the purchaser will require, although in assessing the costs of these arrangements it should be borne in mind that the early leaver legislation (see chapter 6) may apply (even to unfunded arrangements).

The key difference, however, between an unapproved/unregistered arrangement and any other type of scheme will, of course, be its tax treatment. This is considered in further detail in chapter 5.

Conclusion

15.80 This chapter is only an overview, but it should be sufficient to illustrate the complexity and the possible costs implications of pension arrangements in negotiations for the sale or purchase of a company or business. The potential impact of pensions issues for both the vendor and the purchaser should therefore never be underestimated, and the sooner these are addressed the better the chances of the deal progressing to a successful conclusion for both sides. This has never been more so than since the introduction of the Regulator's powers to issue contribution notices and FSDs by *PA 2004*, and the more onerous level of debt calculation on the withdrawal of a participating employer in a multi-employer defined benefit arrangement.

The introduction of the clearance procedure, however, can provide the parties to a transaction with greater certainty where the transaction involves a company with a defined benefit scheme. Clearance provides the parties with assurance

677

via the clearance statement that their proposed activities will not later be found to fall foul of the legislation. Similarly, withdrawal arrangements allow a withdrawing employer in a multi-employer scheme to pay a lesser debt but secure a guarantor who agrees to pay or secure a higher amount. Again, obtaining the Regulator's approval for such arrangements provides the parties with a level of comfort. It is intended that these measures address the concerns that were initially raised on the introduction of the new Regulator's powers and will ensure the continuance of merger and acquisition activity for employers with defined benefit arrangements.

Chapter 16

Pensions dispute resolution and litigation

Introduction

16.1   Whilst there has always been scope for disputes to arise over pension schemes, there has been a dramatic growth in this area since the early 1990s. The reasons for this include the increased regulation of pension schemes, the introduction of public bodies to police such schemes, the authority of the Office of the Pensions Ombudsman to adjudicate upon disputes, the introduction of internal dispute resolution procedures and increased public awareness.

The 1990s began with the high-profile *Maxwell* scandal and was followed by disputes over large surpluses in various privatised industries. However, the new millennium has witnessed a slump in the stock market causing large pension deficits, the high-profile *Equitable Life* case, the increasing cost of annuities, the closure of final salary pension schemes and the widely publicised 'pensions crisis'. These events have together served to increase public awareness about pension rights. This increased awareness has translated into an ever-increasing number of pensions-related complaints to both the Pension Ombudsman and TPAS. Pensions disputes are also affected by the new *Pensions Act 2004*, which has seen the replacement of OPRA with the new Pensions Regulator ('the Regulator'), with wider powers to regulate schemes. For example, with the introduction of the so-called 'moral hazard' provisions, the Regulator has new powers to seek contributions to underfunded pension schemes from entities other than the employer, and the actual or threatened exercise of such powers may give rise to a new area of disputes in the future.

As a consequence, the management and resolution of disputes has become an increasingly important factor for trustees in the administration of pension schemes. Trustees are now all too aware that their decisions may be subject to a complaint by an affected member. Similarly, employers, faced with increasing deficits in their pension schemes which they have to fund and which have implications for their balance sheets, are confronted with difficult decisions that impact on their employees.

In addition to the above more hostile types of disputes, less hostile litigation often arises in the context of the day-to-day administration of pension schemes. Trustees, in particular, can apply to court to resolve ambiguities or mistakes in pension scheme documents, and to seek approval of a proposed course of action which has certain consequences for the scheme.

The particular relationships of the parties involved in a pension scheme distinguish pensions disputes from normal commercial disputes. This chapter is not intended to be an exhaustive narrative of every type of dispute and procedure. Instead, it is intended to provide an overview of the principal forums for dispute resolution, and, in relation to litigation through the courts, to highlight some of the issues that may arise in pensions cases, including the use of alternative dispute resolution ('ADR') to settle disputes.

Non-court forums for dispute resolution

Internal dispute resolution procedure ('IDRP')

16.2   *Section 50* of *PA 1995* introduced a requirement for trustees of occupational pension schemes to implement a two-stage IDRP to deal with disputes by members and other beneficiaries about matters concerning the scheme. *Section 50*, together with the *Occupational Pension Schemes (Internal Dispute Resolution Procedures) Regulations 1996 (SI 1996 No 1270)*, set out the detail of who can make a complaint, the information it should contain and how it should be dealt with.

Section 273 of PA 2004 was due to make a number of key changes to how schemes will deal with dispute resolution from April 2006 by replacing the original *section 50* provisions with new *sections 50, 50A* and *50B*. However, whilst the policy intention was that there would no longer be a requirement for a two-stage dispute resolution procedure (although it was intended that schemes could retain one if they wished to do so) the DWP has since confirmed that the intended simplification and flexibility would not be achieved by the new provisions and has confirmed that they will therefore not be brought into force. IDRP is discussed in more detail in chapter 3.

IDRP should be capable of resolving the majority of the common complaints made by members and beneficiaries against the trustees and managers. It should be noted, however, that a complaint is exempted from the IDRP if proceedings have already been commenced in a court or other tribunal, or where the Pensions Ombudsman has already commenced an investigation. IDRP is also not the appropriate avenue for pursuing a complaint against an employer, as such complaints fall outside the scope of the procedure.

If the trustees do not implement any 'decision' made under the IDRP which requires implementation, the Pensions Ombudsman would be likely to determine that such failure constitutes 'maladministration' by the trustees, in the event that the member were to complain to him. Also, if the complainant is not satisfied with the 'decision' under the IDRP, the member may refer his complaint to TPAS (see below) and/or the Pensions Ombudsman (the Pensions Ombudsman will ordinarily require a complainant to have made full use of the IDRP before accepting a complaint for investigation).

Complaints to The Pensions Advisory Service ('TPAS')

16.3   TPAS (formerly known as OPAS) provides free advice and assistance to members of the public who have a complaint about their occupational or personal pension scheme and will seek to resolve a dispute by negotiation and correspondence between the parties. The success of this forum depends to a great extent on the willingness of the parties, as any suggested resolution proposed by TPAS is not directly enforceable. If TPAS cannot resolve the member's complaint, the complaint may then be submitted to the appropriate Ombudsman for resolution. The Pensions Ombudsman encourages individuals complaining to him to have consulted TPAS first. The contact details of TPAS can be found at 2.43 above.

Other forums

Financial Services Authority ('FSA') and Financial Ombudsman Service ('FOS')

16.4   Where a person has a complaint about the sale and marketing of a pension arrangement, the complaint may be investigated by the FSA (which regulates the industry) or the FOS (which settles disputes between consumers and financial institutions). If the complaint involves a financial product or service, the FOS requires the complaint to be submitted first to the firm involved to be considered under its internal complaints procedure. If the complainant is unhappy with the firm's final response to the complaint, or eight weeks have elapsed from the date the complaint was submitted without a final response from the firm, the complainant has six months in which to submit the complaint to the FOS. The FOS will first seek to resolve the complaint through an informal process of mediation. If that is unsuccessful, the FOS will conduct a full investigation into the complaint and issue a written determination which is binding on the firm (to a limit of £100,000).

Further information, the relevant forms and contact details can be found on the FOS website: www.financial-ombudsman.org.uk.

The Pensions Regulator

16.5 On 6 April 2005, the Regulator became the new regulatory body for work-based pension schemes in the UK, replacing the Occupational Pensions Regulatory Authority (known as 'Opra'). The Regulator regulates the compliance by trustees of occupational pension schemes with *PA 1995* and *PA 2004* and has a wide range of enforcement powers. A summary of those powers can be found at 2.12 above and the Regulator's contact details are give at 2.32 above. Details of the penalties the Regulator can impose are summarised in appendix I. In particular, where the Regulator considers that there has been a breach of the law it can require corrective action to be taken. Further, where it is believed that an employer is deliberately seeking to avoid its obligations to its pension scheme, the Regulator has powers to issue contribution notices, financial support directions and restoration orders for the purpose of restoring value to the pension scheme, thus reducing the exposure of the Pensions Protection Fund to an underfunded scheme. The exercise of these powers by the Regulator can potentially be challenged, giving rise to possible areas for disputes in the future.

Employment tribunals

16.6 Disputes concerning an employee's rights under an occupational pension scheme may also be dealt with during the course of employment tribunals. This is discussed in more detail in chapter 7.

Divorce proceedings

16.7 Disputes over pension benefits also arise in the context of divorce proceedings. This is dealt with in more detail in chapter 8.

Complaints to Pensions Ombudsman ('PO')

16.8 The role of the PO, his jurisdiction and a summary of the applicable procedure is set out in chapter 5 and at 2.44 to 2.46 above. The PO is not permitted to investigate or determine a complaint if proceedings have already been commenced in any court or employment tribunal in connection with matters to which the complaint relates, unless the proceedings have been discontinued without a settlement binding on the complainant. The court has the power to stay court proceedings concerning matters which are the subject of a complaint or dispute before the PO (*sections 146 and 148* of *PSA 1993*). The PO estimates that the average complaint will take about seven months to be determined by it. In November 2005, the PO issued a guide for trustees and employers on 'How to avoid the Pensions Ombudsman'. This guide can be downloaded from the PO's website at: www.pensions-ombudsman.org.uk/publications/. It provides a useful insight as to how the PO expects trustees and employers to fulfil their roles in relation to pension schemes.

Determination

16.9   A determination given by the PO is final and binding on the complainant and any person responsible for the management of the scheme to which the complaint relates (subject to being overturned, on appeal, by the court). The PO has the power to direct any person responsible for the management of the scheme to take, or refrain from taking, such steps as he may specify. Any determination of the PO is enforceable in a county court as if it were a judgment or order of that court (*section 151* of *PSA 1993*).

The PO's determination or direction must be in writing and state the grounds upon which it is made. A dissatisfied party may ask for the court's permission to appeal the determination on a point of law. The appeal is heard in the High Court (*section 151(4)* of *PSA 1993*) (see 16.12 below).

Human Rights Act 1998

16.10   The *Human Rights Act 1998* (*HRA 1998*) has been in force since October 2000. *Article 6(1)* of the *European Convention on Human Rights*, which *HRA 1998* incorporates into English law, provides that, in the determination of a person's civil rights and obligations, everyone is entitled to a fair and public hearing within a reasonable time by an independent and impartial tribunal established by law. Following doubts which were raised in connection with the office of the PO in this context, the PO obtained and published an opinion from counsel as to whether *Article 6(1)* applies to investigations by the PO and, if so, whether the PO's practice and procedure satisfy the principles set out in *Article 6(1)*. That opinion is available on the PO's website (www.pensions-ombudsman.org.uk). It concludes that *Article 6(1)* does apply and that the PO's practice and procedure in relation to the holding of oral hearings and otherwise are broadly compatible with *Article 6*. A party to a complaint to the PO can request an oral hearing, although this is not a common occurrence. However, particular criticism from legal commentators has been levied in the past at the role and influence of the PO's staff in investigating complaints and producing determinations, and it remains to be seen whether the PO's practice and procedure will be subject to a successful challenge in the High Court under *Article 6(1)*.

Court proceedings

Introduction

16.11 Litigation through the courts has, traditionally, been regarded as costly, time consuming and unpredictable. It is not surprising, therefore, that the PO and TPAS are attractive alternative forums in which beneficiaries of pension schemes may pursue their claims. However, court proceedings may be unavoidable in some circumstances, such as where a determination of the PO is appealed; where the trustees seek the court's directions on a pensions issue; or where the claimant has no other available forum in which to pursue the claim. Set out below is a summary of the most common types of applications that are made to the court in pensions disputes and a basic explanation of the various procedures under the *Civil Procedure Rules 1998 (SI 1998 No 3132)* ('the *CPR*'), which govern the procedure in the civil courts.

Types of application to court

Appeals from the PO

16.12 *Section 151* of *PSA 1993* provides a right of appeal to the High Court on a point of law arising out of a determination given by the PO. Any such appeal will be heard in the Chancery Division of the High Court. The procedure is set out in *Part 52* of the *CPR*, and the *Practice Direction on Appeals*. The party lodging the appeal – the 'appellant' – must file a notice of appeal (known as the 'appellant's notice') at the High Court within 28 days after the date of the PO's determination. A copy must also be served on the PO and the respondent (see *paragraph 17* of the *Practice Direction on Appeals*). The appellant's notice should be in a form prescribed by the *CPR* (Form N161) and set out the grounds for the appeal, the arguments in support of those grounds, the decision sought from the appeal court and any evidence in support of the appeal. It should be accompanied by a skeleton argument (a summary of a party's submissions) and a bundle of relevant documents.

The other parties to the appeal are referred to as 'respondents', and may include the PO as a respondent. A respondent can ask the appeal court to uphold the PO's determination for reasons different from or additional to those given by the PO, in which case that respondent must file a 'respondent's notice' within 14 days of being served with the appellant's notice. Like the appellant's notice, the respondent's notice should be in a prescribed form (Form N162), accompanied by a skeleton argument and bundle of relevant documents.

It is important to note that the time limits referred to above are strict and cannot be varied without the court's permission. This means that once the PO has issued a determination, the parties should take immediate steps to consider whether they wish to appeal and, if so, prepare the relevant documents. Both the appeal notice and the skeleton arguments should be prepared with care because a party will not be able to rely in the appeal on a matter not contained in the appeal notice without the permission of the court. An appeal does not operate as an automatic stay of the determination of the PO unless the court or the PO permits otherwise.

The appeal will be limited to a review of the PO's determination unless the court considers that, in the circumstances, it would be in the interests of justice to hold a rehearing. Oral evidence and evidence which was not before the PO are not allowed to be introduced in the appeal unless the court orders otherwise. The court has power to affirm, set aside or vary any determination made by the PO; refer any claim or issue back to the PO for determination; order a new hearing before the PO; and make orders for the payment of interest on any monies awarded and the parties' costs.

In practice, whilst an employer may have the resources to fund the costs of an appeal, an individual complainant may be reluctant to pursue an appeal given the costs of mounting the appeal and the risk of being ordered to pay the respondent's costs if the appeal is lost. In such circumstances, the potential appellant may consider applying for a prospective costs order (which is discussed in more detail at 16.36 below) before pursuing an appeal.

In certain appeals the PO may decide that he wishes to participate but, if he does, he will expose himself to a risk that, if he loses, the court may order him to pay the costs of the appeal (*Moore's (Wallisdown) Ltd v Pension Ombudsman [2002] 1 All ER 737*). For this reason, the PO has indicated a reluctance to participate in appeals, except where the issue is of wider public relevance. This approach was reflected in the 2003 case of *Legal & General Assurance Society Ltd v CCA Stationery Ltd [2003] EWHC 2989 (Ch), [2003] All ER (D) 233*, in which the court requested the PO's participation in the appeal but the PO declined because of the costs risk. The result was that the appeal hearing went ahead without the participation of the respondents.

The decision of the High Court may be appealed to the Court of Appeal. The court's permission is required and will only be granted if it is considered that the appeal would raise an important point of principle or practice, or there is some other compelling reason to hear it. The Court of Appeal's judgment may, with the court's permission, be appealed to the House of Lords.

It is relevant to note that recent attempts to seek judicial review of the PO's determinations, as an alternative to pursuing an appeal under the procedure explained above, have failed. In those cases, the court referred to the appeal procedure as being the more appropriate means of determining the issues.

Seeking directions from the court

16.13   The court has a wide jurisdiction to provide directions to trustees on matters relating to the administration of a pension scheme (see *CPR Part 64* and the *Practice Directions* to it). Applications to court for such directions usually concern issues arising out of the trustees' exercise of a discretion or a power under the pension scheme's trust deed or rules, or where the meaning of the scheme's trust deed or rules is unclear or ambiguous. For example, the trustees may seek the court's direction because:

(*a*)   they are uncertain whether or not a proposed course of action is within their powers;

(*b*)   they wish to seek the court's blessing to a proposed course of action which may have a significant impact on the scheme (for example, application for a *Beddoe* order – see 16.34 below); or

(*c*)   they wish to surrender the exercise of a discretion to the court because they are unable to arrive at a decision for some reason (for example, conflict of interest, deadlock).

Such applications are commonly referred to as 'construction' or 'directions' applications.

Where a question has arisen as to how the terms of a trust deed should be interpreted and the trustees have obtained a written opinion from a counsel of at least ten years' standing, in the absence of a dispute over the issue, the trustees may apply to the High Court (under *section 48* of the *Administration of Justice Act 1985*), without the need for a hearing, for an order authorising the trustees to take the proposed steps in reliance on the opinion. This abbreviated procedure has the potential of providing a relatively speedy and cost-efficient resolution of the issue. However, it is not appropriate where there may be a dispute over the proposed construction (for example, where the construction is not clear and is potentially favourable to one category of member over another). Where there is, or is likely to be, a dispute, a full application to court will be required.

These types of application are not usually of a particularly hostile nature (unless the employer and/or the beneficiaries take exception to what is proposed) and may be distinguished from proceedings in which the trustees' actions are being challenged by a third party, which are usually more hostile.

Directions applications are usually brought under the simplified *CPR Part 8* procedure (which is discussed in more detail in 16.21 below).

Claims by/against a third party

16.14   These are claims which involve the trustees and third parties, i e parties external to the trust. For example, they may include claims by trustees against their professional advisers for professional negligence or a claim by trustees against a former trustee for breach of trust. They are usually hostile in nature and are usually brought under the *CPR Part 7* procedure (which is discussed in more detail in 16.22 below).

Rectification

16.15   Where an error is discovered in the drafting of a pension scheme document, such that the document does not reflect accurately the true common intentions of the trustees and the employer, and that error cannot be resolved completely by other means (for example, by the proper construction of the document, or by the use of any applicable amendment power which does not offend *section 67* of *PA 1995*), the trustees may apply to the court to rectify the error. Basically, in order to succeed the trustees would have to provide credible evidence that the error did not reflect accurately the clear and common intentions of the trustees and employer when the wording in the document was drafted. They would have to prove that there is no other effective remedy available, that the mistake is of significant importance such that it justifies the court making an order for rectification and that in all the circumstances it is appropriate to grant rectification (for example, there are no legal bars to rectification).

Given the importance of documentary and oral evidence to a rectification application, it is usually made using the *Part 7* procedure (see 16.22 below), unless there is no dispute on the facts, in which case the *Part 8* procedure may be more appropriate (see 16.21 below). The trustees and the employer will both be parties to the application and a representative beneficiary (see 16.26 below), or more than one where appropriate, is usually appointed to represent the beneficiaries of the scheme. As a result of the evidential burden on trustees, rectification applications are usually not straightforward, particularly where another party objects to the proposed rectification. They are often made in conjunction with, and as an alternative to, an application for a declaration that the offending document can be properly construed to give effect to the parties' instructions, which, if successful, would mean that the trustees would no longer need to pursue the alternative rectification application.

Outline of procedure

Issues for consideration before commencing court proceedings

16.16   Before embarking on court proceedings, a claimant should consider, in particular, the following important factors:

(*a*)   Is the claim being brought within any relevant limitation period pre-scribed by law? If not, the claim may be time barred.

(*b*)   How will the costs of the proceedings be funded and paid? (Some relevant issues on costs are discussed in 16.30 below.)

(*c*)   Who will be the parties to the proceedings?

(*d*)   What remedy is sought and will it be an effective remedy?

(*e*)   What are the merits of the application?

The answers to these questions will assist a claimant in determining not only whether to commence proceedings in the civil courts, but also the strategy to be adopted in progressing the claim, including whether to pursue alternative dispute resolution methods ('ADR', for which see 16.38 below). The decision to commence court proceedings should not be taken lightly, because once com-menced, the claimant cannot unilaterally withdraw them without having to pay the other party's costs (unless the other party or the court agrees otherwise).

Trustees' obligations to disclose information to a beneficiary

16.17   Beneficiaries and trustees should be aware that the beneficiary may request disclosure by the trustees of certain 'trust documents', which the trustees may be legally obliged to disclose, without the need for litigation. This may assist a beneficiary's investigation into a matter. It is a common law principle that trustees are obliged to disclose 'trust documents' to beneficiaries who have a fixed (as opposed to discretionary) interest in a trust (including a pension scheme) (*O'Rourke v Darbishire [1920] AC 581, [1920] All ER Rep 1*). This obligation has been based on the principle that beneficiaries have the 'proprietary' right to the documents held by the trustees. Trust documents include the trust deed, rules, accounts and all documents relating to the trust, including minutes or trustee meetings. It may also extend to legal advice obtained by the trustees on behalf of the scheme, although not usually legal advice obtained in respect of the beneficiary's claim against the trustees or legal advice paid for by the trustees themselves rather than out of trust monies.

This disclosure obligation has not, however, extended to disclosing the trustees' deliberations on and reasons for exercising their discretionary powers under the scheme in a particular way. Therefore, trustees have not had to disclose any document evidencing their reasons and deliberations on that issue, unless there is evidence of improper conduct (*Re Londonderry's Settlement re Peat v Walsh [1964] 3 ALL ER 855; Wilson v Law Debenture Trust Corporation plc [1995] 2 All ER 337*). If the trustees fail to disclose the disclosable trust documents, they may be ordered by a court to pay the costs of any application that the beneficiary may make to the court to compel such disclosure.

However, this obligation has been affected by two recent decisions.

(*a*) In *Schmidt v Rosewood Trust Ltd [2003] UKPC 26, [2003] 3 ALL ER 76* the court appeared to move away from the 'proprietary right' as the underlying rationale of the obligation and, instead, asserted the court's inherent power to supervise the administration of trusts, and right to order disclosure of any trust documents if it is considered appropriate in all the circumstances. This potentially widens the scope of the disclosure obligation not only in terms of the range of documents that could be disclosable but also the type of beneficiary who may be entitled to disclosure. As a Privy Council decision, it is not binding on the English court or the PO, but nonetheless is of highly persuasive authority. It remains to be seen how this is further applied in practice by the court. However, the PO has already confirmed that he regards it as highly persuasive authority (see his determination in April 2005 in *Mr B Cameron [M00949]*).

(*b*) The PO indicated in a determination in 2002 (*Allen v TKM Group Pension Trust Ltd [2002] PLR 333*) that he considered it to be 'good administrative practice' for pension trustees to give reasons for their decisions and to make minutes of trustee meetings available to beneficiaries with a legitimate interest in the matter, even when exercising discretionary powers. Where he could see no good reason for trustees withholding disclosure of their reasons, he was prepared to determine that the trustees were guilty of maladministration. Given the above, trustees who receive a request for documents should consider it carefully, with appropriate advice, before deciding whether to reject it or the extent to which it should be complied with.

(See also a trustee's disclosure obligations pursuant to relevant pensions statutes and regulations at 3.22 above and appendix II.)

Pre-action protocols

16.18 The *CPR* set out steps that the court will expect the parties to undertake before proceedings are commenced. In particular, the court will expect all parties to have complied in substance with the terms of any applicable 'pre-action protocol' in the *CPR*. Whilst there is presently no specific protocol applicable to all types of pension disputes, there is a protocol which applies specifically to professional negligence claims (for example, a trustee's claim against his professional advisors for negligence).

Where there is no specific protocol that applies to the dispute in issue, the *Practice Direction on Protocols* (set out in the *CPR*) sets out a pre-action procedure that parties should seek to adhere to with the intention of avoiding litigation in so far as possible. The following procedure is specified, although this may be revised by the parties to suit their particular circumstances, provided that the revisions are reasonable:

(*a*)   Each party should act reasonably in exchanging information and documents relevant to the claim and generally in trying to avoid the necessity for the start of proceedings.

(*b*)   The claimant should write to the defendant setting out its claim. The letter should:

- give sufficient and concise details to enable the recipient to understand and investigate the claim without extensive further information;

- enclose copies of the essential documents which the claimant relies on;

- ask for a prompt acknowledgment of the letter, followed by a full written response within a reasonable stated period (for many claims, a normal reasonable period for a full response may be one month);

- state whether court proceedings will be issued if the full response is not received within the stated period;

- identify and ask for copies of any essential documents not in his possession which the claimant wishes to see;

- state (if it is so) that the claimant wishes to enter into mediation or another alternative method of dispute resolution; and

- draw attention to the court's powers to impose sanctions for failure to comply with this practice direction and, if the recipient is unlikely to be represented, enclose a copy of the *Practice Direction.*

(*c*)   The defendant should acknowledge the claimant's letter in writing within 21 days of receiving it and should state when the defendant will give a full written response. If this is longer than the period stated by the claimant, the defendant should give reasons why a longer period is needed.

(*d*)   The defendant's letter should, as appropriate, accept the claim in whole or in part and make proposals for settlement, or state that the claim is not accepted. If the claim is accepted in part only, the response should make clear which part is accepted and which part is not accepted.

(*e*)   If the defendant does not accept the claim, or part of it, the response should:

- give detailed reasons why the claim is not accepted, identifying which of the claimant's contentions are accepted and which are in dispute;

- enclose copies of the essential documents which the defendant relies upon;

- enclose copies of documents asked for by the claimant, or explain why they are not enclosed;

- identify and ask for copies of any further essential documents not in his possession which the defendant wishes to see; and

- state whether the defendant is prepared to enter into mediation or another alternative method of dispute resolution.

(*f*)   The claimant should provide requested documents within a reasonably short time or explain in writing why he is not doing so.

(*g*)   If the claim remains in dispute, the parties should promptly engage in appropriate negotiations with a view to settling the dispute and avoiding litigation.

It should be noted that any documents disclosed by either party in accordance with the above procedure, may not be used for any purpose other than resolving the dispute, unless the other party agrees. Further, if the dispute requires the assistance of an expert, the *Practice Direction* suggests that the parties should, wherever possible and to save expense, engage a single agreed expert (for example, if an actuary is required to provide a valuation). It should be noted that the court retains a power to refuse an expert's report sought by a party at this stage or refuse that party to claim the costs of an expert report in any subsequent proceedings.

It is important that a party follows this procedure, or any agreed revised procedure, as the court has an express power to apply costs and other sanctions in the event of a party's non-observance.

Whilst the above procedure provides for limited voluntary disclosure of documents, the *CPR* also provides a mechanism, in certain circumstances, for a potential claimant to apply to the court for an order obliging a potential defendant to anticipated proceedings to disclose documents before those proceedings are commenced (see *CPR 31.16*), although the party making the application will usually have to pay the other party's costs of the application and of complying with any order made.

Procedure in the civil court

16.19   Court procedure in civil cases is governed by the *CPR*. With the exception of appeals, court proceedings are initiated by the issue and service of a claim form (which replaces the 'writ' and 'originating summons'). There are two principal procedures under the *CPR* for issuing a claim (as opposed to an appeal) – the *Part 7* and *Part 8* procedures. They are discussed in more detail below. The *Part 7* procedure is the most commonly used procedure in claims involving third parties because such cases involve disputes of fact. The *Part 8* procedure is the standard procedure for directions applications by trustees.

Once proceedings have been commenced, the court will allocate the case to one of its three tracks:

(*a*)   *Small claims track*: This is for claims worth less than £5,000. It is designed to be an inexpensive and less formal, expedited procedure, in which the strict rules of evidence do not apply. Expert evidence is not allowed without the court's permission and the court allows a party, its lawyer or a lay representative to present its case at the hearing. The court may, if all parties agree, deal with the claim 'on paper' (i e without a hearing).

(*b*)   *Fast track*: This is for claims worth between £5,000 and £15,000. It involves an abbreviated but more formal procedure designed to allow for a trial within a reasonably short timescale, assuming a settlement cannot be reached.

(*c*)   *Multi-track*: This is for claims worth over £15,000. It is the most formal procedure of the three tracks, as a result of which cases usually take longer to be determined and are more costly.

Claims issued under the *Part 8* procedure are automatically allocated to the multi-track, whereas *Part 7* claims will be allocated to the appropriate track, according to the value of the claim.

Case management powers

16.20   In all proceedings, the court has wide case management powers. When exercising any power under, or interpreting any rule in, the *CPR*, the court must give effect to what is known as the 'overriding objective'. The overriding objective stipulates that the court must deal with cases justly (see *CPR Part 1* for a full definition). This includes dealing with the case expeditiously and fairly, and in ways which are proportionate to the amount of money involved; the importance and complexity of the case; and to the financial position of each party. The parties themselves are also required to help the court to further the overriding objective.

The court also has wide powers to penalise parties for their conduct in the proceedings by, for example, disallowing all or any part of their costs, or ordering them to pay another party's costs or, in more serious instances, by striking out their case. As a result, parties should aim to meet time deadlines imposed by the court and conduct themselves appropriately.

Part 8 procedure

16.21   The *Part 8* procedure is simpler and is designed to be more efficient than the *Part 7* procedure. The *Part 8* procedure should be employed where the court's decision is required on a question which is unlikely to involve a substantial dispute of fact or where a Practice Direction permits or requires its use for that type of proceedings. In pensions cases, a trustee's application for directions (see 16.13 above) is required to be brought under the *Part 8* procedure. Whilst third party claims (see 16.14 above) and claims for rectification (see 16.15 above) may also be brought under the *Part 8* procedure, such claims will often involve a substantial dispute of fact so the *Part 7* procedure is usually more appropriate. The court may, at any time, disapply the *Part 8* procedure to any proceedings brought under it. *Part 8* claims are automatically allocated to the multi-track.

An outline of the *Part 8* procedure is as follows:

(*a*)   *Issue and service of claim form*

   The *Part 8* claim form is in a prescribed form and should set out, among other things, the question(s) for determination by the court, the remedy sought and the legal basis for that remedy. Any evidence upon which the claimant wishes to rely at the hearing of the claim should accompany the claim form (set out either in the claim form or in a witness statement, but in both cases verified by a signed statement of truth).

(*b*)   *Acknowledgment of service*

   The defendant must acknowledge service of the claim form within 14 days by filing at court, and serving on all parties, the prescribed form or an appropriately worded letter. In acknowledging service, the defendant should state whether the claim is contested or whether a different remedy is sought. Unlike under the *Part 7* procedure, the defendant does not have to serve a defence. If the defendant disputes the court's jurisdiction to hear the claim, an appropriate application should be made within 14 days of acknowledging service. Failure to acknowledge service will result in the defendant not being able to take part in the hearing of the claim without the court's permission.

(*c*)   *Evidence*

   If the defendant wishes to rely on evidence at the hearing, that evidence, in the form of a witness statement with any relevant documents exhibited to it, should be filed and served at the same time as the acknowledgment of service. The claimant then has 14 days in which to serve any evidence in reply, unless an extension of time can be agreed with the defendant(s) or is ordered by the court.

(*d*)   *Case management directions*

The court may give case management directions when the claim form is issued. It is more usual, however, for the court to give directions after the defendant has acknowledged service or the time limit for acknowledging service has expired. The parties are encouraged to agree, so far as is possible, appropriate case management directions for the court's approval. The court may give such directions without a hearing or by calling a case management conference. Such directions may include the disclosure of documents (see 16.23 below), the exchange of further witness statements (see 16.24 below), the preparation and exchange of expert reports (see 16.25 below), and any other steps that may be necessary for the efficient management of the claim.

(*e*)   *Hearing of claim*

The hearing of the claim will take place in open court before a judge, unless the court permits it to be held in private. Written evidence may not be relied on by a party at the hearing unless it has been served in accordance with the rules or the court gives permission. At the hearing, each party's legal representatives make their oral submissions to the judge. The judge may require or allow a party to give oral evidence at the hearing and may require a witness's attendance for cross-examination.

(*f*)   *Judgment*

After hearing the parties' submissions, the judge will either hand down the judgment at the end of the hearing or may reserve judgment to a future date (in order to allow time for the judge to consider and draft the judgment).

In applications by trustees for directions in the administration of a pension scheme, the court's *Practice Direction* to *CPR Part 64B* provides additional guidelines, which include the following:

(i)   *Confidentiality*

If the confidentiality of the directions sought is important (such as in a *Beddoe* application – see 16.33 below), the claim form should only give a general description of the remedy sought, with a more detailed explanation set out in the trustee's witness statement.

(ii)   *Representative parties*

The trustees should consider carefully which beneficiaries should be 'representative parties' (see 16.26 below). It may not be necessary for a representative of each class of beneficiary in the pension scheme to be joined as a party to the proceedings because the trustees may be able to present the arguments for or against the application on behalf of some classes of beneficiary (although trustees will need to consider carefully whether it is prudent for them to pursue this course in the circumstances of the application). If the trustees are unable to decide which categories of beneficiaries to join as defendants (for example, where there are many members and categories of interest), the trustees may apply to issue the claim form without naming any defendants (under *CPR 8.2A*). At the same time, they may apply to the court for directions as to which persons to join as parties.

(iii)   *No defendants required*

If the trustees consider that the court may be able to give the directions sought without hearing from any other party, they may apply for permission for the claim form to be issued without naming any defendants (*CPR 8.2A*). However, in *Re Owens Corning Fibreglass (UK) Pensions Plan Ltd [2002] PLR 323* where a trustee applied for the court's approval of a compromise without informing the beneficiaries, the court indicated that, in most such cases, it would be desirable that potential beneficiaries, or their representatives (for example, their union representatives or the pensions committee) be informed about the proposed arrangement and of any related application to the court to allow them to make their views known. The court indicated that, but for overriding considerations specific to that case, as the beneficiaries had not been informed, it would have adjourned the hearing to allow the beneficiaries to be told of the proposed compromise.

(iv)   *Requirement for a hearing*

The court will always consider whether it can deal with the application on paper without the need for a hearing. If the trustees and/or the defendant(s) consider that a hearing is needed, they should state so, with reasons, in their evidence. If the court deals with the application on paper and refuses the application, the parties will be given an opportunity to request a hearing.

(v)   *Trustees' evidence*

The trustees' evidence, which is given by witness statement, should disclose fully any matters which are relevant to the application, failing which they may not be protected by the court's order. It should indicate the significance of the proposed course of action for the scheme; include a valuation of the trust assets (ie include the latest actuarial valuation, updated as may be appropriate); describe the membership profile; if a deficit on winding up is likely, it should describe the priority provisions and their likely effect; explain the significance of the proposed litigation or other course of action for the trust; and why the court's directions are required.

(vi)   *Consultation with beneficiaries*

The trustees' evidence should also describe what, if any, consultation there has been with beneficiaries, and the results of that consultation. As general guidance, unless the members are few in number, the court will not expect any particular steps by way of consultation with beneficiaries (including, where relevant, employers) or their representatives to have been carried out in preparation for the application. If no consultation has taken place, the court may direct that meetings of one or more classes of beneficiaries are held to consider the subject matter of the application, possibly as a preliminary to deciding whether a representative of a particular class ought to be joined as a defendant.

Part 7 procedure

16.22   The *Part 7* procedure is used if the *Part 8* procedure is inappropriate (for example, there is a substantial dispute of fact). The majority of third party claims (see 16.14 above) will therefore be brought under this procedure. The *Part 7* procedure usually requires more procedural steps prior to the trial than the *Part 8* procedure. An outline of the *Part 7* procedure is as follows:

(*a*)   *Claim form and particulars of claim*

The claimant issues and serves a claim form which sets out a basic summary of the claimant's claim. Unlike the *Part 8* procedure, the claimant's case is set out in a separate particulars of claim, which contains a detailed description of the claim and the facts on which the claimant relies.

(*b*)   *Acknowledgment of service*

Having been served with the claim form and particulars of claim, the defendant has 14 days to file an acknowledgment of service in the prescribed form, indicating whether it admits the claim, admits part of the claim but contests another part, or contests the entire claim. If the defendant fails to acknowledge service within the prescribed time limit and no extension of time has been agreed, judgment in default may be entered in the claimant's favour.

(*c*)   *Defence (and counterclaim if relevant)*

If the defendant contests all or part of the claim, unlike under the *Part 8* procedure, the defendant must prepare, file and serve a defence within 14 days after being served with the particulars of claim (if no acknowledgment of service has been filed) or 28 days after service of the particulars of claim (if an acknowledgment of service has been filed). If a defence is not filed within the prescribed time limit and no extension of time has been agreed, judgment in default may be entered in the claimant's favour. If the defendant wishes to make a counterclaim against the claimant, this should be served with the defence.

(*d*)   *Reply (and defence to counterclaim if relevant)*

If the claimant wants to allege facts to answer those alleged in the defence, the claimant may serve a reply. If the defendant has served a counterclaim, the claimant must, at the same time as serving the reply, serve a defence to the counterclaim, failing which judgment in default may be entered in the defendant's favour on the counterclaim.

(*e*)   *Case management directions*

The court will allocate the case to one of the three court tracks (see 16.19 above) and give case management directions. These typically involve the following (in chronological order):

(i)   disclosure and inspection of documents (see 16.23 below);

(ii)   exchange of witness statements (see 16.24 below); and

(iii)   exchange of expert reports (if necessary), followed by meetings of the experts in order to narrow the issues in dispute (see 16.25 below).

(*f*)   *Trial*

The trial of the claim takes place before a judge in open court, at which each party's advocate makes oral submissions, and the witnesses and experts give oral evidence and are cross-examined. At the conclusion of the trial the judge will hand down a written judgment and will make any appropriate costs orders.

Disclosure of documents

16.23   Disclosure in the context of court proceedings is the process by which each party discloses to the other parties to the claim relevant documents within that party's control and in respect of which privilege is not being claimed. The disclosure process aims to ensure that each party has sight of the material that is available to the other parties so that each party can prepare adequately before trial of the proceedings. Disclosure of documents is not always ordered under the *Part 8* procedure (see 16.21 above), whereas 'standard disclosure' is usually ordered under the *Part 7* procedure (see 16.22 above).

Standard disclosure requires a party to disclose those 'documents' on which it relies, as well as those which adversely affect its own case or another party's case or which support another party's case. The word 'documents' has a wide meaning and includes anything in which information of any description is recorded (for example, paper documents, computer files, film, video, photographs). It includes electronic documents, such as emails, databases, saved documents and other electronic communications, stored on a computer's hard drive or a server or a back-up system, or on other electronic devices and media. A party must conduct a reasonable search for, and disclose, documents within its control (i e where the party has or had a right to possess it, inspect it or take copies of it.) Disclosure usually takes the form of the parties exchanging a list of documents in a form prescribed in *CPR Part 31*. There are specific guidelines in relation to electronic documents (see *section 2A.1* of the *Practice Direction* to *CPR Part 31*).

A party is entitled to inspect and take copies of the documents disclosed by another party. However, a party giving disclosure may object to the inspection of certain documents on the grounds that they are legally privileged from inspection (an analysis of the various types of privilege that may be relied upon is outside the scope of the chapter). It should be noted that, as the duty to give disclosure continues to the end of the case, a party should take care when creating new documents in case they also need to be disclosed. A party who gives inadequate disclosure may be compelled by the court to give further disclosure. If a party fails to disclose a document, it may not rely on that document at the trial of the proceedings without the court's permission and, ultimately, if in breach of its obligations, a party may be held to be in contempt of court. (The rules of disclosure are set out in *CPR Part 31* and should be distinguished from trustees' obligations to disclose information to members under common law and under various pensions statutes and regulations, for which see 3.22 and 16.16 above and appendix II.)

Witness statements and affidavits

16.24 A fact which needs to be proved by the evidence of a witness must, as a general rule, be proved at the trial of the case by the oral evidence of that witness under oath. At any other hearing (i e before the trial) the fact may be proved by the written evidence of the witness (i e in a witness statement or affidavit). A witness statement is a written statement of a witness's evidence. It is signed by the witness and contains a statement that he believes the facts in it are true (a 'statement of truth'). If a witness makes a false statement without an honest belief in its truth, proceedings for contempt of court may be brought. Witness statements have largely replaced affidavits (a written sworn statement), although there may be occasions where an affidavit is still required. There are strict rules governing the form and content of witness statements and affidavits (see *CPR Part 32* and the *Practice Direction* to it).

Expert evidence

16.25 Expert evidence is frequently required in pension disputes to assist the court. For example, an expert actuary may be required to give an opinion on the valuation of the assets and liabilities of the pension fund or certain benefits under a pension scheme. The court has wide powers to control the use of expert witnesses in litigation because they are usually expensive and lengthen the proceedings. Expert evidence is restricted to that which is reasonably required to resolve the proceedings and a party may only call an expert with the permission of the court. In certain circumstances, the court may direct that expert evidence on an issue is to be given by a single expert, jointly instructed by both parties. The expert's overriding duty is to the court and not to the instructing or paying party. An expert will usually give his evidence in the form of a written report, which the parties exchange. Often the court will direct the parties' experts, following the exchange of reports, to meet in order to identify the technical issues in the proceedings and, where possible, reach agreement on those issues. An expert may be called to give oral evidence and be cross-examined at the trial of the action. (See *CPR Part 35* and the *Practice Direction – Experts and Assessors* for the rules and guidelines on the use of experts. In applications for directions, it is often the case that, where a party needs some statistical analysis carried out in relation to the scheme, to save costs, the parties agree to instruct the scheme actuary to carry out this work as, in effect, an expert (although this may not be appropriate in all cases, in which case the parties will need their own independent actuary expert).)

Representation orders

16.26 It is a basic rule under the *CPR* that, where the party making a claim is seeking a remedy to which another person is jointly entitled, every other person who is so jointly entitled to that remedy must be joined as a party to the proceedings, unless the court orders otherwise (*CPR 19.3*). There is no limit to the number of parties who may be joined to a claim (*CPR 19.1*). This rule is designed to prevent a multiplicity of proceedings for similar claims and is of particular relevance to litigation involving pension schemes (for example, trustees' applications for directions). Whereas the number of trustees of a pension scheme will be small, the number of beneficiaries under the scheme, who may be entitled jointly to a remedy, can be large – often amounting to hundreds, thousands and even tens of thousands. However, for each member or beneficiary of a scheme to be a named party to the litigation in accordance with the basic principle described above would give rise to a procedural and logistical burden which would seriously impair the efficient resolution of the litigation. That said, trustees require certainty that any order made by the court will be binding on all beneficiaries. The practical solution, therefore, is to appoint a party to represent the interests of other similarly interested parties. That party is known as a 'representative party' and may be appointed under two alternative provisions of the *CPR*:

(*a*) If more than one party has the same interest in a claim, the claim may be commenced, or the court may order the claim to be continued, by or against one or more of those parties as representatives of the other parties. Any judgment or order made by the court in the proceedings will bind all the persons represented in the claim (but may only be enforceable by or against a person who is not a party to the proceedings with the consent of the court) (see *CPR 19.6*).

(*b*) In claims concerning the assets of a pension scheme or the meaning of a document, the court may appoint, prior to or after the claim has commenced, a party to represent persons who are (i) unborn, or (ii) cannot be found, or (iii) cannot be easily ascertained. It may also appoint a party to represent a class of persons who have the same interest in a claim and either one or more members of that class fall within (i), (ii) or (iii) above, or if the court considers that the appointment would further the overriding objective of dealing with the claim justly (see 16.20 above) (see *CPR 19.7*). If a representative party has been appointed, the court must give its approval to any compromise of the proceedings, and will only do so where it considers that the compromise is for the benefit of all the represented persons. Any judgment or order made by the court will bind all represented persons unless the court orders otherwise, but can only be enforced by or against a person who is not a party to the claim with the court's consent.

Practical considerations

16.27   Given the frequently large membership of a pension scheme, representation orders provide a practical way for proceedings to be pursued in an efficient and timely manner, and provide certainty for the trustees that the judgment handed down will bind all affected beneficiaries. Where there is more than one distinct category of beneficiaries with a similar interest, it may be necessary to join more than one representative party. As each representative party will require legal representation, the court will usually seek to keep to a minimum the number of representative parties to minimise the costs as much as possible, particularly where the costs are being borne by the pension fund.

Trustees should therefore give proper consideration, at an early stage, as to who should be an appropriate representative party. A proposed representative party should not have a conflict of interest and should have sufficient mental capacity and availability to provide proper instructions to his legal representatives throughout the expected length of the proceedings. If the trustees in *Part 8* proceedings are undecided as to who or how many representative parties should be appointed or cannot find a willing volunteer, they may issue the claim form without naming the defendant(s) and seek the court's directions – (see also (iii) in 16.21 above).

It remains arguable whether a person whose interests are represented in proceedings by a representative party may challenge the representation order or challenge a settlement that has been approved by the court on the grounds that it is a breach of that person's right to a fair trial under *Article 6* of the *European Convention on Human Rights*. If a person objects to being represented in an action, a practical solution may be for that person to be joined as a party in his own right (although that person will run the risk that he will have to bear his own legal costs in the event that the court does not permit his costs to be paid from the pension fund). *Article 6* is likely to be of more relevance where a settlement is approved by the court and is binding on a person represented in the proceedings by a representative party, without that person having had a chance to state his own case. To reduce the risk of a successful challenge, trustees should consider giving proper notice of the proceedings to all the persons represented (in so far as they can be ascertained) before the compromise is put to the court for approval. Such notice should set out the terms of the proposed compromise, a beneficiary's right to object to the compromise and his right to be joined in as a separate party to the proceedings.

This approach was deemed 'desirable' by the court in *Re Owens Corning Fibreglass (UK) Pensions Plan Ltd [2002] ALL ER (D) 191*. In that case the court indicated that it would, but for other factors, have adjourned the application to allow the beneficiaries to be informed.

When applying for the court's approval of a settlement, it is common practice for each representative party to obtain a written legal opinion on the merits of the compromise, the purpose of which opinion is to assist the judge in his consideration of whether the settlement is for the benefit of all the persons represented.

Trustees representing beneficiaries' interests

16.28   Where proceedings are brought by or against trustees without joining any of the beneficiaries of the pension scheme, any judgment or order made in those proceedings will bind the beneficiaries, unless the court orders otherwise. The court may order otherwise if it considers that the trustees could not or did not in fact represent the interests of those persons in the proceedings (see *CPR 19.7A*). Trustees should therefore consider carefully whether they can and are properly representing the beneficiaries' interests in such proceedings, because if they cannot or are not, it may be necessary to appoint an additional representative party.

Group litigation

16.29   Where there are a number of individual claims by separate persons which all give rise to common or related issues of fact or law (for example, claims by individual members of a pension scheme against the trustees for a breach of trust that has caused each of them loss and which has arisen out of the same facts), the court may order each of the cases to be managed together under a group litigation order. This should be distinguished from a representation order, where each person represented has the same interest in the outcome of a claim. A group litigation order is a useful and efficient mechanism in circumstances where each of the claims is individually small, but collectively large. In principle, it allows for an efficient and cost-effective method of determining the claims. (The detailed provisions relating to group litigation orders can be found in *CPR 19.11* and the related *Practice Direction.*)

Costs in litigation

16.30   The issue of costs is central to the assessment of whether or not to pursue or defend a claim, what strategy to adopt, in which forum the matter should be pursued, settlement considerations, and whether alternative dispute resolution methods should be explored. It is also an important factor that the court considers when it exercises its case management powers.

General principles

16.31   The court has a broad discretion to award costs (*section 51* of the *Supreme Court Act 1981*). In deciding what costs order (if any) to make, the court will take into account all the circumstances, including the conduct of the parties before and during the litigation, whether a party was only partly successful and any offers of settlement (*CPR 44.3*). The court may penalise a party by denying it costs where it does not approve of that party's conduct or where the party has recovered a lesser amount than a previous offer of settlement which it rejected. Where the court orders a party to pay another party's costs, the amount of those costs will be assessed by the court, unless it can be agreed between the parties. The court may assess those costs summarily at the hearing itself, or conduct a separate detailed assessment of those costs after the hearing. In small claims track cases the court will only award limited costs and will assess those costs at the hearing. In fast-track cases the trial costs of the advocate that are awarded are also limited. In multi-track cases, there is no prescribed limit on the costs that can be recovered and the amount of those costs will be assessed by the court.

When ordering a party's costs to be assessed, the court will state the basis on which those costs will be assessed. There are two bases:

(*a*)   *Standard basis*: This is the usual basis ordered. On this basis the court will only allow costs which are proportionate to the matters in issue and will resolve any doubt which it may have over a specific cost incurred in favour of the paying party.

(*b*)   *Indemnity basis*: The court will resolve any doubt it may have over a specific cost incurred in the favour of the receiving party.

The receiving party can expect to recover more of its costs under the indemnity, rather than standard, basis. However, it is important for parties to appreciate that on neither basis is the receiving party ever likely to recover 100 per cent of its costs. Indeed, under the standard basis, the receiving party may recover as little as 60 per cent of its costs (or even less). This should be borne in mind at the outset of litigation and when considering offers of settlement.

The general rule followed by the court is that the winner's assessed costs are paid by the loser. In pensions cases involving third parties (see 16.14 above), this rule will usually apply. However, there are special rules that apply to trustees' costs and the costs of applications for directions brought in relation to the administration of a pension scheme. These are discussed below, in 16.32 onwards.

Solicitors are obliged to discuss with clients involved in litigation the possibility of purchasing an 'after-the-event' insurance policy to cover the potential liability to pay costs (his own and/or the other party's) in the event of an unsuccessful outcome. Such policies are yet to make a significant impact in the arena of pensions litigation, but are likely to be of most relevance in the future to claims against or by third parties.

Trustees' costs

16.32   Where a trustee is a party to proceedings in his capacity as trustee, as a general rule he is likely to be entitled to an indemnity out of the trust fund for his legal costs (which may include costs that the trustee is ordered to pay to another party) to the extent that they are not recovered from or paid by another person (*CPR 48.4*) and provided they are properly incurred. In such cases, those costs will be assessed on the indemnity basis. The court may order otherwise if it considers that the trustee has, in all the circumstances, acted improperly (see *section 50A* of the *Practice Direction* to *CPR 48.4*). By way of example, in *Mark Niebhur Todd v Judith Cobb Lady Barton & Others [2002] 2 WTLR 469*, the court disallowed a proportion of a trustee's costs which related to an application made by him which the court considered to be unnecessary.

Indemnity and power in trust deed

16.33   A pension scheme's trust deed may contain an indemnity clause which indemnifies the trustees against any costs and liabilities incurred in taking certain action for the benefit of the pension scheme. It may also give the trustees a power to agree to pay from the pension fund the costs of certain other parties to litigation. In the event that the trustees have, and exercise, such a power by agreeing to pay the costs of another party to the litigation (for example, in an application to court for directions), it is prudent for the trustees to enter into a formal agreement with that party stipulating what costs may be payable under that agreement and a mechanism for the trustees to control the level of costs incurred. The trustees' prior approval to large items of proposed expenditure (for example, expert witness fees, counsel's fees) should also prudently be sought by that party.

In applications to court concerning the administration of a pension scheme, if the trustees have and exercise properly a power to agree to pay the costs of another party to that application, the court will presume, when assessing the amounts of costs payable under that agreement, that (unless the agreement states otherwise) the costs have been reasonably incurred and are reasonable in amount (see *CPR 48.3*). In such a case, a prospective costs order (see 16.36 below) is not required and the trustees are entitled to recover out of the pension fund any costs of another party which they pay pursuant to such agreement (*paragraph 6.2* of the *Practice Direction* to *CPR 64*).

Beddoe orders

16.34 The proviso to the general rule entitling a trustee to an indemnity out of the trust fund for its costs (see 16.32 above) is that the costs must have been 'properly incurred'. If they are improperly incurred, a trustee may incur personal liability for those costs. To determine what costs are properly incurred, the court will examine all the circumstances of the case including whether the trustee obtained the court's directions before bringing or defending proceedings, acted in the interests of the scheme or some other interest or conducted himself unreasonably. If trustees propose to commence or defend proceedings against or by a third party, they are able to protect themselves from this risk of personal liability by applying at an early stage for the court's directions on their proposed course of action (this is known as a '*Beddoe*' application, following the Court of Appeal judgment in *Re Beddoe, Downes v Cottam [1893] 1 Ch 547*). If the court sanctions the proposed action, the trustees can proceed in the comfort that the court regards their action as being proper and reasonable.

A *Beddoe* application is treated as a directions application under *CPR 64* (see 16.13 above). The application must be made in separate proceedings under the *Part 8* procedure (see 16.21 above). The trustees should be the claimant and the beneficiaries of the pension scheme the defendants. In the event that a beneficiary is a party to both the main proceedings and the *Beddoe* application and has an interest which conflicts with that of the trustees, the trustees should exercise care not to disclose to that beneficiary privileged information (for example, the legal advice of the trustees' lawyer), and that beneficiary may be excluded from all or part of any hearing of that *Beddoe* application.

In a *Beddoe* application, the court is asked to express its view on whether the action proposed by the trustees is proper. To enable the court to express a considered view, the trustees' application should be supported by evidence (in the form of witness statements) giving full disclosure of, among other things, the proposed course of action and the strengths and weaknesses of the trustees' case. This means that the trustees must include in their evidence the advice of an appropriately qualified lawyer on the prospects of success, and other relevant matters to be taken into account, including a costs estimate for the proceedings, any known facts concerning the means of the opposing party to the proceedings, and a draft of any proposed statement of case (see the *Practice Directions* to *CPR 64* for a fuller description of what matters should be included in the evidence and for guidelines on trustee consultation with beneficiaries). If the trustees fail to reveal in full to the court the strengths and weaknesses of their case, they may expose themselves to personal liability, even if the court grants the *Beddoe* order sought.

Depending on the nature of the case, the *Beddoe* application will either be dealt with on paper, without the need for a hearing, or will be referred to a judge in which case a hearing will usually be necessary. If the court allows the trustees to pursue the litigation proposed, it may do so only up to a particular stage in the litigation, thereby requiring the trustees to make a further *Beddoe* application in order to proceed beyond that stage.

However, whilst the above process may afford trustees protection from personal liability for the costs they will incur, the court has become increasingly critical about the tendency of trustees to seek, at considerable cost to the pension scheme, *Beddoe* consent for steps which are clearly in the interests of the pension scheme. This concern is reflected in the court's *Practice Direction* which states as follows:

> 'There are cases in which it is likely to be so clear that the trustees ought to proceed as they wish that the costs of making the application, even on a simplified procedure without a hearing and perhaps without defendants, are not justified in comparison with the size of the fund or the matters at issue.'

> [*paragraph 7.2* of *Practice Direction B* to *CPR 64*]

Trustees should therefore consider carefully, with their legal advisers, the appropriateness of incurring the expense of making a *Beddoe* application. Equally, trustees should have regard to the uncertainties of litigation, even in the most apparently clear cut of cases, and the risk that if *Beddoe* consent is not sought prior to taking a step, the trustees may be held personally liable for their costs (unless they can prove to the satisfaction of the court that they were properly incurred). An assessment of the risk of proceeding without *Beddoe* protection must, therefore, be made by trustees with their legal advisers at the outset. One alternative to incurring the costs of a *Beddoe* application may be for the trustees to seek an indemnity from the employer, particularly if the employer is ultimately liable under the pension scheme's trust deed to make up any shortfall in the assets of the fund.

Beneficiaries' costs

16.35   The indemnity enjoyed by trustees (which is discussed in 16.32 above) is not shared by beneficiaries who are parties to proceedings. However, the court has traditionally sought to divide trust litigation into three categories when considering which party should pay the costs of those proceedings (following the decision in *Re Buckton, Buckton v Buckton [1907] 2 Ch 406*):

(*a*)   Proceedings brought by trustees for the court's guidance on the construction of the trust deed or a question arising in the course of the trust's administration. In such cases, the costs of all parties are usually treated as 'necessarily incurred for the benefit of the fund' and ordered to be paid out of the fund on an indemnity basis (such an application is usually brought under *CPR 64*).

(*b*)   Applications which are brought by someone other than the trustees, but which raise the types of issues as in (*a*) above and would have justified an application by the trustees. In this case, the costs are also usually treated as being 'necessarily incurred for the benefit of the fund' and ordered to be paid out of the fund on an indemnity basis (whilst such an application may be made under *CPR 64*, the *Practice Direction* to *CPR 64* only relates to applications made by trustees, and not other parties).

(*c*)   Proceedings in which a beneficiary is making a hostile claim against trustees or another beneficiary. The costs of such proceedings are usually treated in the same way as ordinary litigation and the winner's costs are usually paid by the loser, unless the winner has, in some way, conducted himself inappropriately in connection with the litigation or is only a partial winner or has failed to win more than a previous offer of settlement from the loser.

These are known as *Buckton* categories 1, 2 and 3 and the court still deems these general guidelines applicable, albeit that it now takes a more robust attitude towards costs (*D'Abo v Paget (No 2) [2000] WTLR 863*). There is a costs risk to both the trustees and the beneficiaries in the third category of claims, which is a principal reason why trustees generally seek *Beddoe* consent before pursuing or defending such proceedings, and why beneficiaries prefer to avoid such costs risk and pursue their complaints through the PO. It is often difficult, in practice, to assess whether a particular claim is a category 2 or 3 type claim, but given the costs consequences, it is important to reach a conclusion before embarking upon the litigation.

Prospective costs orders

16.36   Whilst the principles in *Buckton* provide a useful guide to what the likely costs order will be at the conclusion of the proceedings, a party may require greater comfort at the outset of the proceedings that its costs will be paid out of the fund no matter what the outcome of the proceedings. For example, a representative beneficiary may not wish to become a party in the proceedings if there is a risk that he will incur a personal liability for his, and other parties', costs of the proceedings. In applications to the court concerning the administration of a trust (i e under *CPR 64* – see 16.13 above), if the trustees do not have, or decide not to exercise, a power to agree to pay the costs of another party to the application, the trustees or the party concerned may apply to the court for an order that the costs of any party (including the trustees) shall be paid out of the assets of the pension scheme. These are known as 'prospective costs orders' (formerly as 'pre-emptive costs orders') and provide the applicant with the comfort that his costs of the proceedings will be paid, no matter what the outcome of the proceedings.

In *Buckton* category 1 and 2 cases (see 16.35 above) at the conclusion of the case the court will usually follow the general rule that the parties' costs (including those of any beneficiary) are paid out of the assets of the pension scheme. This makes the grant of a prospective costs order at an earlier stage in the case less problematic. A difficulty arises, however, in *Buckton* category 3 cases (hostile claims against the trustees). This is because in *Buckton* category 3 cases, the general rule is that the loser pays the winner's costs. This makes it difficult to make an assessment at any time prior to the full trial as to the likely outcome and therefore the likely costs order the court would make. In the leading case of *MacDonald v Horn [1995] 1 All ER 961* the court overcame this difficulty by deciding that an action by a member of a pension scheme to compel the trustees or others to account to the fund was analogous to what is known as a 'derivative action' by a minority shareholder on behalf of a company. In those circumstances a minority shareholder was entitled to a prospective costs order under the principle in *Wallersteiner v Moir (No 2) [1975] 1 ALL ER 849*. On this basis, the court held that a member of a pension scheme could also be entitled, by analogy, to a prospective costs order in those circumstances. When deciding whether to exercise its discretion to make such an order, the court has in each case a duty, under the *CPR*, to give effect to the overriding objective of dealing with cases justly. This includes ensuring, so far as possible, that the parties are on an equal footing and dealing with the case in a way which is proportionate to the financial position of each party. Such factors are particularly relevant in the pensions context, as the beneficiary who is a party to the case can often be a pensioner with limited financial resources.

Further guidance was given by the court in *Laws v National Grid [1998] PLR 295* where it considered that a prospective costs order should be made where the amount of money in issue is large, the matter in issue affects a large number of persons, the case involves difficult issues of law or fact, and the person applying for the order has substantial support from others in a similar position. In the subsequent case of *Chessels & ors v BT plc & ors [2002] PLR 141*, the court refused to grant a prospective costs order to a beneficiary to whom it had granted permission to appeal the court's judgment. The court followed the principle that prospective costs orders indemnifying a third party should only be made where the court is satisfied that no other orders can properly be made by the court which is to hear the substantive proceedings. The appeal in this case would, if successful, only benefit a relatively small number of beneficiaries of the scheme, was not for the benefit of the scheme as a whole, and was hostile litigation of the *Buckton* category 3 type in which the court usually awards the winner his costs. The court also reiterated the principle that the fact that the pension scheme had substantial assets, and was in surplus, was not relevant to whether or not it should grant the prospective costs order.

Applications for prospective costs orders can be made at any time during the proceedings but are usually made at the outset, or before a hearing. In the witness statement supporting the application the trustees and the applicant (if different) must give full disclosure of the relevant matters which show that the case is one which falls within the category of cases where a prospective costs order can properly be made. Ordinarily, the court will seek to deal with such an application on paper, without the need for an oral hearing, but if the trustees or any other party think a hearing should be held, they should set out their reasons in the evidence that they file at court. A model form of prospective costs order for straightforward cases is set out in the court's *Practice Direction* to *CPR 64*. It allows for a party's solicitor to request from the trustees monthly sums on account and for that party's costs to be subject to a detailed assessment by the court on the indemnity basis, unless agreed. It also indemnifies the party against any costs that it is ordered to pay to another party to the proceedings. When granting a prospective costs order the court may set a limit on the costs to be paid (as in *Re AXA Equity & Law Life Assurance Society plc (No 1) [2001] 2 BCLC 447*).

Alternative Dispute Resolution (ADR)

Introduction

16.37   Alternative dispute resolution ('ADR') is the generic phrase used to describe alternative means of resolving a dispute other than by a trial in court. The use of ADR has developed rapidly over the last twelve years and its importance is actively promoted by the courts. Under the *CPR*, the court is obliged when using its active case management powers to encourage parties to use an ADR procedure if it considers it appropriate and to facilitate the use of such procedure (*CPR 1.4(2)(e)*). Further, when trustees apply for *Beddoe* approval concerning actual or possible litigation, they are required to state, in the witness statement they prepare in support of their application, whether they have proposed or undertaken, or intend to propose, mediation by ADR, and if not why not (*paragraph 7.5* of the *Practice Direction* to *CPR Part 64B*).

In the case of *Halsey v Milton Keynes General NHS Trust [2004] EWCA Civ 576, [2004] ALL ER (D) 125*, the Court of Appeal provided some guidelines on the court's approach to ADR (mediation in particular) and to penalising parties who fail to agree to pursue ADR. In summary:

(*a*)   Although the court may encourage parties to seek to resolve a dispute through ADR in the strongest terms, it would not order parties to undertake ADR against their will.

(*b*)   As an exception to the general rule that the loser would be ordered to pay the winner's costs, the court may penalise a party, by making an alternative costs order, if that party has acted unreasonably in refusing to agree to ADR.

(*c*)   The burden is on the loser to show why the winner acted unreasonably.

(*d*)   In deciding whether a party had acted unreasonably in refusing to agree to ADR, the court will consider the following, non-exhaustive factors:

- Is the nature of the dispute suitable for ADR? Not every dispute is suitable for ADR, for example, a directions application concerning the construction of the pensions deed may be unsuitable for settlement.

- What are the merits of the case? A party, who reasonably believes that he has a strong case, may reasonably not wish to compromise his position through ADR.

- Have any other settlement methods been attempted before? A history of unsuccessful attempts at resolving the dispute may justify a decision not to agree to ADR.

- What are the likely costs of ADR? If the costs of ADR are likely to be disproportionately high, this may justify a party not agreeing to it.

- Will ADR cause unreasonable delay? Pursuing ADR will require the commencement or continuation of proceedings to be stayed which may cause unreasonable delay to the resolution of the dispute.

- Will ADR have a reasonable prospect of success? The more remote the prospect of ADR resulting in a settlement, the more reasonable a court is likely to regard a refusal by one party to agree to ADR.

(*e*)   All members of the legal profession should routinely consider with their clients whether their client's disputes are suitable for ADR.

These principles have been applied by the court in subsequent cases. For example, in *Daniels v Commissioner of Police for the Metropolis [2005] EWCA Civ 1312*, the Court of Appeal applied the *Halsey* decision and decided that where a defendant, particularly a public body, regularly faced unmeritorious claims which it chose to contest rather than settle, the court would be slow to view such conduct as being unreasonable. In *Re Midland Linen Services Ltd sub nom Chaudry v Yap & Ors [2004] EWHC 3380 (Ch)*, even though a party had offered mediation which was refused by the other party, the court viewed the refusal to mediate as not being unreasonable because it was questionable whether the party offering the mediation was sufficiently serious in pursuing it and, given the relationship between the parties, whether a mediation would have resulted in a resolution. These cases demonstrate that the court will consider the facts of each case in deciding whether there has been unreasonable conduct.

Types of ADR

16.38   There are different forms of ADR, but the principal ones are as follows:

(*a*)   *Mediation.* This is the most common form of ADR. It is a private, without prejudice process of negotiation between the parties, facilitated by an independent qualified mediator. It is non-binding so that a settlement can only be achieved if the parties agree. It is discussed in more detail below.

(*b*)   *Conciliation.* This is a more formal form of mediation, and often involves the use of a formal conciliation service (such as ACAS). The 'conciliator' will often take an active role (i e proffering his views) in the negotiations.

(*c*)   *Expert determination.* This is where the parties agree to refer a (usually) technical issue in dispute for a binding determination by an independent expert. For instance, a pension scheme's trust deed or rules may provide for an actuarial issue to be determined by an independent actuary, or the pensions schedule in a sale and purchase agreement may provide for expert determination in the case of disputes.

(*d*)   *Adjudication.* Like an expert determination, this usually involves the parties agreeing to submit the dispute for determination by a neutral third party (for example, a retired judge or experienced lawyer).

(*e*)   *Arbitration.* The process of arbitration takes place in a statutory frame-work which sets out various rules of conduct. It is common for commercial contracts to contain 'arbitration clauses' which require all disputes to be referred to arbitration. The arbitrator is usually a suitably qualified independent third party who determines the dispute, acting as a judge. The procedure can closely mirror that of court litigation. It is designed to be flexible and less procedural than court litigation. However, it is often regarded as being as time consuming and expensive as court proceedings.

Mediation

16.39   Mediation is the most common form of ADR adopted to settle disputes. Once the parties to a dispute have agreed to mediation, the next step is to appoint a mediator. The Centre for Early Dispute Resolution ('CEDR') and ADR Group are two of the most well known bodies that can assist parties in finding and appointing an appropriate mediator and setting up the mediation. They have lists of accredited and suitably experienced mediators. The Association of Pensions Lawyers also maintains a list of mediators with pensions experience (see its website: www.apl.org.uk).

The costs of the mediator(s) (there can be more than one if the parties wish) are usually borne equally by the parties. The costs of a mediation can be substantial as they may include the costs of the mediator, room hire and the costs of the parties' lawyers in preparing for and attending at the mediation. Before the mediation takes place, it is common for each party to exchange brief summaries of their case, if necessary accompanied by supporting documents. The mediation is usually attended by a senior person from each party who has the authority to negotiate and enter into a settlement agreement. The mediation often commences by each party giving an oral summary of its case to the other party in front of the mediator. The mediator may ask questions to clarify a point. Each party then retires to its own private room, and the mediator will visit each party in turn to discuss the structure of a possible settlement and the issues which each party should consider as part of the negotiations. Through this process of 'shuttle diplomacy' the mediator can gauge what possible terms of settlement may be agreeable to the parties and make appropriate suggestions to the parties to facilitate a settlement. As the process is without prejudice and non-binding, a settlement will only be achieved if both parties agree to it.

Practical considerations

16.40   Pension disputes between trustees and third parties are usually hostile, and in such cases, ADR may provide an efficient means of resolving the dispute, thereby avoiding the costs and risk of litigation. As stated above, trustees who seek a *Beddoe* order are required to tell the court whether a mediation has been or will be proposed. This means that trustees must factor into their consideration from the outset the potential for a mediation (or other appropriate form of ADR) as the court is likely to be interested. Further, trustees who have the benefit of a

Beddoe order (see 16.34 above), may wish or need to seek the court's approval of any settlement (although trustees have a power under *section 25* of the *Trustees Act 1925* to enter into a settlement), in which case this should be made clear to the other parties and may affect the choice of ADR method.

Claims against trustees by individual members may also be amenable to ADR, even if those disputes have been referred to the PO rather than the court.

Directions applications (see 16.13 above) are not always suitable for resolution by ADR. Some applications, by their nature, are not suitable to ADR (for example, where the trustees are requesting the court's approval of a proposed transaction or are surrendering their discretion to the court). Where ADR is possible, there are a number of practical issues which will require consideration, including the following:

(*a*)   Trustees will usually want to avoid negotiating with all the beneficiaries under the pension scheme, not only for logistical reasons but also the difficulty of reaching agreement with all of them. To facilitate negotiations trustees may, therefore, seek the appointment of a representative party with whom they may negotiate. This necessitates the commencement of proceedings prior to ADR being commenced.

(*b*)   Where a settlement is agreed, the trustees may seek the court's approval to that settlement (for example, if a *Beddoe* order has been granted or is sought, or where a representative party has been appointed). In any such application to the court, it is common practice for the trustees and/or the representative party to obtain and present to the court a legal opinion on whether the proposed settlement is in the interests of the members of the pension scheme (see 16.27 above). This means that the court will not examine the proposed settlement on a purely commercial basis, but will also consider to what extent the proposed terms reflect the legal merits of the members' case(s). Further, to produce a reasoned opinion, documents may have to be disclosed and exchanged, if disclosure has not already taken place.

Whilst such factors may provide practical hurdles to be overcome in order for ADR to lead to a successful resolution of the dispute, the advantages of ADR (notably, the potential for a relatively quick, private and less costly settlement of the dispute at an early stage) may justify its use as a means of resolving the dispute. Indeed, parties' solicitors are now expected by the court to consider, in every dispute, the appropriateness of ADR. In all cases, careful consideration should be given as to which form of ADR is most appropriate. If a party is considering rejecting an offer of ADR, it should first consider the guidelines given by the court in *Halsey. This may assist in an assessment of whether the rejection is likely to be considered unreasonable, as a refusal to agree to ADR could potentially expose that party to costs sanctions by the court.*

Chapter 17

Insolvency

Introduction

17.1   There are various types of corporate insolvency regimes ('regimes') under *IA 1986* (*IA 1986*) (as amended) supplemented by the *Insolvency Rules 1986* (*SI 1986 No 1925*) (*IR 1986*) (as amended) that may affect pension schemes. This chapter aims to be a general introduction to those regimes, and the relevant persons appointed under them to protect the interests of creditors. This chapter also details the effect of such regimes on pension schemes.

We have restricted our commentary in this chapter to the application of the regimes on and in relation to English formed and registered companies. However, it should be noted that entities that are not English formed and registered companies may also be able to become subject to a regime if they have a connection with England and Wales.

Consequences of corporate insolvency under English law – the regimes

Company voluntary arrangements ('CVAs')

17.2   Company voluntary arrangements ('CVAs'), under *IA 1986, ss 1 to7* and *Sch A1* and *IR 1986, Part 1*, are where a company enters into what is effectively a contract with its creditors for either a composition in satisfaction of its debts (an agreement that a debt is to be discharged by payment of a proportion of it), or a scheme of arrangement of its affairs (*IA 1986, s 1*). They are typically initiated by the directors of the company, but can also be initiated by a liquidator or administrator.

CVAs are initiated by the circulation of a proposal which is voted upon by creditors and members of the company. If approved (with or without modifications) the proposal (as modified) becomes the CVA; that is, the contract between the company and its creditors.

There are presently two broad types of CVA available. The original type of CVA is one where a proposal is put together without the benefit of any moratorium against creditor claims/actions. The provisions regulating this type of CVA are found in the main body of *IA 1986, ss 1* to *7*. The new type of CVA is one that does provide for a moratorium against creditor claims/actions while the proposal is being formulated and put out for approval. It is, however, only available to a 'small company' within the meaning of that term in *section 247* of the *Companies Act 1985* (*CA 1985*) (as amended), provided certain other prescribed criteria are also satisfied. This type of CVA was introduced into *IA 1986* by the *Insolvency Act 2000* (*IA 2000*). The provisions regulating it are to be found in *section 1A* of and *Schedule A1* to *IA 1986*.

The primary difference between the types of CVAs is that under the original type, the company has no protection from its creditors when formulating the proposal, but under the small company type, it does. That is, there is no bar on creditor action under the original type until and unless (typically) the proposal is approved.

The provisions regulating the content and procedure for approval and implementation of both types of CVA are broadly the same despite the fact that they are separately provided for in *IA 1986*.

Terms

17.3   The terms of either type of CVA (i e the terms of the 'contract') will depend entirely on what is proposed and accepted (creditors can propose modifications to the proposal put to them) by at least 75 per cent in value of the company's unsecured creditors. (Certain votes will not be taken into account, and/or may render invalid a resolution passed (*IR 1986, rr 1.19* and *1.54*).) For example, a resolution will be invalid if without taking into account the votes of connected creditors, the unconnected unsecured creditors have voted against the proposal. For the definition of 'connected' in this context, see *sections 249* and *435* of *IA 1986*. The terms will also depend on who are entitled to, and do, vote on the proposal, provided that (in general terms) a secured creditor (a creditor who has a valid right of recourse to the assets of the company, as opposed to only a right of action against the company – the latter is an unsecured creditor) or preferential creditor (a creditor whose claim is preferential as defined in *section 386* of and *Schedule 6* to *IA 1986*) cannot be affected by what is proposed without its express consent. This means that the general order of priority of payment of creditors on insolvency will typically not be affected by the CVA. That is, holders of fixed charge security are entitled to the net (less costs of/in connection with the sale) proceeds of sale of the fixed charge asset. Other assets are to be utilised to pay (in the following order): costs; preferential creditors; floating charge holders; and, only then, unsecured creditors. Except for secured creditors (where priority issues will be governed either by law, or if negotiated, by contract – typically, if there is more than one secured creditor, a deed of priority will have been entered into governing not only which creditor has priority to the assets, but also enforcement rights). Creditors in each category will rank *pari passu* (rateably) with each other if there are insufficient funds to pay them all in full.

Members (shareholders) of the company are also required to vote (approval by members is by more than one half in value of those voting, in person or by proxy, subject only to any express provision in the company's articles) on the proposal (and any proposed modifications).That said, the decision taken by the creditors will prevail, although an aggrieved member can challenge that decision by application to court within 28 days of the last meeting held.

If approved, the CVA binds all persons who:

(*a*)   were entitled to vote on the proposal whether or not they did so; or

(*b*)   would have been entitled to vote on it if they had had notice of the meeting at which the proposal was voted upon.

There is a right (among others) for creditors to challenge a decision taken in the meetings held to approve the proposal by application to court within a 28-day period, the starting date of which period depends on the circumstances. There are two grounds for such a challenge, being:

● the CVA unfairly prejudices the interests of a creditor; and/or

● there has been some material irregularity at or in relation to the meeting at which the proposal was voted upon.

The proposal will nominate a person to be the supervisor of the CVA if it is approved. A licensed insolvency practitioner ('IP') is typically nominated. To be qualified to act as an IP, an individual must be authorised so to act by a specified competent authority or by virtue of his membership to a specified professional body (*section 390* of *IA 1986* and properly bonded (insured). If an individual purports to act as an IP without being so qualified, he commits a criminal offence (*sections 388* to *389* of *IA 1986*. Authorisation and membership requires the individual to be generally fit and proper, to meet acceptable levels of education and to have sufficient practical experience in the field. An undischarged bankrupt or a person who has been subject to a disqualification order under the *Company Directors Disqualification Act 1986* is not qualified to act as an IP (*section 390(4)* of *IA 1986*). That said, since *IA 2000*, a supervisor can now (subject to certain restrictions) also be any individual who, although not an IP, is a member of a body recognised by the Secretary of State (*section 389A(1)* of *IA 1986*) and is satisfactorily bonded.

The extent of the supervisor's powers and obligations will be as prescribed in the CVA. In a CVA initiated by the directors of the company, it is typical for the company to continue trading as normal (with its own management), its obligations being simply to make contributions into the CVA from its trading ultimately to satisfy (or part satisfy) creditors' claims. In such a CVA, the supervisor's powers and obligations will typically be limited to monitoring the company's compliance with the CVA terms (defaulting it if the company is in breach), agreeing creditors' claims and making distributions in accordance with the CVA. It is presently rare for a supervisor's powers and obligations to extend to 'running' the company. This means the directors remain in office, although subject to any restriction imposed on them by the CVA. This can lead to some confusion for those dealing with the continuing company.

Typically, the terms of the CVA will prohibit action being taken against the company in connection with debt and liabilities bound by the CVA. However, action in respect of debt and liabilities outside of the CVA will not be prohibited. This means that if the company is continuing to trade, a creditor incurred by the company after the approval of the CVA will be entitled to take such steps as it deems appropriate against the company for that post-CVA debt, including steps to wind up the company.

What effect such steps (and indeed, any actions taken by the company post CVA) will have on the CVA and the funds realised in it will depend on the terms of the CVA. For instance, presentation of a winding-up petition could default the CVA, resulting in it being brought to an end. Typically now, CVAs will provide that funds realised in the CVA are held on trust for the CVA creditors meaning that even if it fails, the funds already realised can be paid to the CVA creditors and do not need to be shared with all of the company's creditors. In such a case of failure, however, the CVA creditors are not in principle prevented from also claiming in any liquidation of the company for the full amount of their debts, less the amount received in the CVA. (The interrelationship between CVAs and liquidation has been the subject of a number of cases and is a difficult area. Presently, the leading case is *Re NT Gallagher & Son Ltd, Shierson v Thompson [2002] 1 WLR 2380, [2002] 3 All ER 374*. Among other things, it confirms the basic principle that the terms of the CVA are key and should be respected. Also, even if the CVA terms do not expressly refer to a trust being created in respect of CVA funds, wording that in effect implies that to be the intention should be given effect to.)

What happens to the contracts of employees will depend upon the circumstances. It may be that the company seeks to terminate some employment contracts, leaving the employees with claims bound by the CVA. Alternatively, the company may decide that as it is continuing to trade, it wishes to retain its employees. How it does this will depend on circumstances.

The CVA will end when it states it will. A well-drawn CVA will contain clear and specific terms about how it will come to an end and in what circumstances, including what happens if the CVA terms are breached.

Liquidation

17.4   This is a regime that can either be initiated by the company voluntarily, or against the company by, among others, its creditors. It provides for the appointment of an IP to the company as a 'liquidator', who takes control of the company's assets, replacing, in effect, the directors, whose powers cease. It represents the beginning of the end for a company and, except in exceptional circumstances, its business, because once the liquidation ends, the company will be automatically dissolved (unless an appeal against dissolution is lodged). It will therefore cease to be a legal entity after the liquidation is completed.

Solvent liquidations

17.5   Solvent liquidations (members' voluntary liquidations ('MVL')) are used where, for example, a company was incorporated for a particular purpose which it has achieved and it is, therefore, no longer required. The aim of a MVL is to realise all remaining assets in the company and to settle all outstanding claims against it (with interest), with a view to realising whatever surplus there is in the company so that it can be distributed to the company's members.

The MVL process is initiated by the company's directors swearing a statutory declaration of solvency (under the threat of criminal liability if they do not do so reasonably) to the effect that they have made a full inquiry into the company's affairs and that having done so, they have formed the view that the company can pay all of its debts and liabilities, including contingent and prospective liabilities, in full within a period not exceeding twelve months. Once they have done this, they then call a meeting of the company's members to pass a special resolution (21 days' notice and a majority of 75 per cent in value of those voting, in person or by proxy) (*section 378* of *CA 1985*) to put the company into liquidation. The MVL takes effect from the time of the passing of this resolution. If the company is later found, by the liquidator appointed, to be insolvent, he has a duty to convert it into a creditors' voluntary liquidation ('CVL'), which is an insolvent liquidation. Unless the company turns out to be insolvent, creditors of companies that go into MVL should be paid in full for their debts.

Insolvent liquidations

17.6   Insolvent liquidations can be either voluntary (CVLs) or compulsory, the latter initiated through the court. These will usually occur where there is no prospect of the company being able to continue trading or of its business surviving in any form, and there is no option but to appoint a liquidator to collect in all the company's assets to distribute them fairly among the company's creditors in the order prescribed in *IA 1986*.

The general order of priority of payment of creditors on insolvency is that holders of fixed charge security are entitled to the net (less costs of/in connection with the sale) proceeds of sale of the fixed charge asset. Other assets are to be utilised to pay (in the following order): costs; preferential creditors; floating charge holders; and, only then, unsecured creditors, except in regards to secured creditors (where priority issues will be governed either by law, or if negotiated, by contract). Creditors in each category will rank *pari passu* with each other if there are insufficient funds to pay them all in full. The aim of an insolvent liquidation is to ensure a fair distribution to creditors of the company's remaining assets.

Like a MVL, a CVL commences when the members of the company resolve, by extraordinary resolution (75 per cent in value of those voting, in person or by proxy (*section 378* of *CA 1985,* and *IR 1986, r 4.67* contains detailed provisions about entitlement to vote)), to put it into liquidation. The liquidator will be the IP nominated by either the creditors or members.

A compulsory liquidation actually begins on the making of a winding-up order against the company, although after that happening, the liquidation is deemed to have commenced at the time of the presentation of the petition pursuant to which it is wound up (*section 129* of *IA 1986*).This, among other things, makes vulnerable actions taken by the company between presentation of the petition and the making of an order on that petition (*section 127* of *IA 1986*). If the company disposes of any of its property in that period, that disposition will be void unless it is authorised or ratified by the court. Even a payment by the company to a creditor during that period could be void on this basis. Generally, such a disposition will only be authorised or ratified if the disposition is likely to benefit all of the company's creditors, or at least not disadvantage them (*Re Gray's Inn Construction Co Ltd [1980] 1 WLR 711, [1980] 1 All ER 814*).

The first liquidator appointed to a company in a compulsory liquidation is typically the 'Official Receiver'. (The Secretary of State appoints a person to the office of Official Receiver and attaches him to the High Court of England and Wales, to carry out functions conferred upon him by *IA 1986* and by the Secretary of State.) The Official Receiver then has twelve weeks within which to investigate the company's affairs (*section 132* of *IA 1986* explains his duties) and to call meetings of, amongst others, the creditors of the company for the purpose of their choosing an IP to become the liquidator of the company in his place, or to give them notice that he will not be doing so, in which case he will continue as the liquidator (*section 136* of *IA 1986*). He will typically only call such meetings if there are assets in the company.

The company's business will typically cease on the company going into any form of liquidation. It will only ever continue after liquidation in exceptional circumstances (where it would be beneficial to the winding up). The liquidator's powers are very wide (*Schedule 4* to *IA 1986*), albeit not all of them can be actioned without the prior sanction of the creditors or the court.

Actions against the company and its property are prohibited without court leave in a compulsory liquidation (*section 130* of *IA 1986*).This means no actions already commenced against it can be proceeded with, and no new actions can be commenced unless the court gives its leave to that happening. The court will typically only give leave in cases where the normal process of making a claim in the liquidation is not seen as sufficient. The proving process (the process of making a claim in a liquidation is called 'proving' and the claim is called a 'proof' – the rules as to proofs can be found in *IR 1986, r 4, Chapter 9*) enables unsecured creditors to make their claim in the liquidation as fully as they wish to (providing such supporting evidence as they deem appropriate), which the liquidator considers in a quasi-judicial capacity. If the liquidator needs more information in order to reach a decision on the claim, he can ask for it. If the creditor is ultimately unhappy with the liquidator's decision on their proof (the liquidator can reject all or part of it), the creditor has a right to appeal by making an application to court within 21 days of receiving the liquidator's notice of the rejection. That is, an aggrieved creditor can have 'his day' in court if it is needed, but both parties can avoid the cost of litigation where it is not necessary. An unsecured creditor with a simple unsecured claim (for example, a simple debt claim) is unlikely to ever get leave to continue or commence proceedings, or indeed, for there to be any benefit to it seeking leave.

There is no such automatic prohibition on proceedings in a voluntary liquidation. That said, the liquidator may apply to court for a stay of any proceedings commenced for the same reasons as outlined above. A liquidator is likely to do so if proceedings for recovery of a simple debt claim are commenced.

The effect of liquidation on employment contracts is not prescribed in *IA 1986* (as it is in administration and receivership). As a consequence, there is some uncertainty as to what that effect is. It is generally accepted, although there is little firm authority on the point, that in a CVL and MVL, the employees' contracts typically terminate on liquidation, but not because of the liquidation, rather because the company's business has ceased and so their contracts are effectively repudiated. In a compulsory liquidation, on the other hand, it is thought that the employees' contracts automatically terminate because of the making of the winding-up order against the company. The reasoning for the distinction between the type of liquidation is not, however, clear.

Receivership

17.7   The method typically used by secured creditors to enforce their security is by appointing a receiver or manager over the assets secured in their favour.

In an enforcement context, a receiver is a person who is appointed by a creditor who holds security over a company's assets. The receiver's primary function is to utilise the powers given to him to deal with those assets, with the aim of satisfying the debt owed by the debtor to that secured creditor. A receivership appointment is not for the benefit of the company and its creditors as a whole, but rather for the benefit of the secured creditor alone. This means that the receiver owes only limited duties to the company and its creditors. The exact extent of those duties is not clear (there have been a number of cases on this point recently, which have called the extent into question). At the very least, it is presently clear that if the receiver realises any assets, he must get the best price reasonably obtainable for those assets in all the circumstances. (See, for instance, *Standard Chartered Bank v Walker [1982] 1 WLR 1410, [1982] 3 All ER 938*).

The receiver will not typically deal at all with the claims of the company's unsecured creditors. He would only do so if necessary, such as where the unsecured creditor is a crucial supplier to the company's business and so, to ensure continued supply, the receiver has to agree to pay some or all of the unsecured creditor's pre-receivership debt, as well as its new debt. This is what is typically referred to as a 'ransom payment'.

The types of receivership in this context are an administrative receivership and an ordinary receivership, often also referred to as 'fixed charge' or *Law of Property Act 1925 (LPA 1925)* receiverships (the *IA 1986* provisions which regulate these appointments are found in *sections 28 to 49* and *72* of *IA 1986* (including *sections 72A to 72H*); the *LPA 1925* provisions which regulate *LPA 1925* receiverships are found in *sections 99* to *109* of *LPA 1925*).

(*a*)   *Administrative receivers*: are those appointed by floating charge holders over all or substantially all of the assets of the company, which typically means that they are appointed over businesses. The *IA 1986* does not contain a right to appoint an administrative receiver. The floating charge must contain that right, otherwise no administrative receiver can be appointed. The appointee must be an IP.

(*b*)   *Ordinary or 'fixed charge' receivers*: are appointed over fixed charge assets – *LPA 1925* receivers being the type of receiver typically appointed by secured creditors where the only asset is land. *LPA 1925* receivers are the only type of receiver appointee that does not need to be an IP. *LPA 1925* contains a right to appoint a receiver where the security is a mortgage created by deed. Otherwise, a receiver can only be appointed if the security contains a right to appoint. (Most security these days contains a provision that provides that after the security becomes enforceable, the secured creditor can appoint a receiver over the secured assets.)

The ability to appoint an ordinary/*LPA 1925* receiver has not been affected by the recent legislative changes to *IA 1986* (introduced by the *Enterprise Act 2002*); only the ability to appoint an administrative receiver is affected (*IA 1986, s 72A*). Those changes mean that now unless the floating charge was created before 15 September 2003 or otherwise falls into the list of exceptions (*sections 72B* to *72H* of *IA 1986*), a floating charge holder, who prior to these changes would have had an unrestricted right to appoint an administrative receiver, no longer has that right.

Once a receiver is appointed, it is up to him to exercise his powers granted over the secured property as he deems appropriate to achieve the purpose for which the appointment has been made (i e to satisfy the debt for the person who appointed him). This is because the receiver is not the secured creditor's agent even though the secured creditor appoints him. (Under *IA 1986* and to a limited extent under *LPA 1925,* and in any event almost always also provided for in the security, the receiver is made the agent of the company over whose assets he is appointed. This agency lasts until the company goes into liquidation. So the company is liable in the normal course for the receiver's actions as the receiver's principal. Even after liquidation, the receiver does not become the secured creditor's agent, although his exact status after liquidation is not clear. What is clear, however, is that the secured creditor does not become liable for the receiver's actions simply because of the liquidation.)

Following appointment, the secured creditor is not involved in the enforcement process (although in practice, the receiver will typically report to the secured creditor along the way). The secured assets are usually managed and sold by the receiver in the company's name. The directors of the company remain in office notwithstanding the appointment, but they cannot exercise any powers over the assets over which the receiver is appointed.

What deductions must be made from any receivership realisations depends upon the nature of those realisations. Secured creditors are entitled to fixed charge realisations without any further deductions following deduction of the costs and expenses of the receivership where it is an *LPA 1925* receivership, or the costs and expenses incurred in connection with those fixed charge assets in an administrative receivership. Floating charge realisations are also available to meet preferential creditor claims, and for floating charges created after 15 September 2003, for payment of the 'prescribed part'. (The 'prescribed part' is a new concept introduced by the *Enterprise Act 2002*. It is a sum (presently up to a maximum of £600,000) of net (after deduction of the costs and preferential creditors) floating charge realisations that must be made available for unsecured creditors save in limited circumstances (mainly, in general terms, where the amount would be small and not cost-effective to distribute).)

The receiver is given powers to deal with the assets over which he is appointed. The powers given and where they can be found depend upon the type of appointment. They will often include a power to sell the assets. There are some restrictions to the exercise of that power, prohibiting a sale to the receiver and qualifying the right to sell to associated parties. An *LPA 1925* receiver will not have the power to sell, or indeed any powers other than to receive rent, and possibly insure, issue and accept lease surrenders, unless other powers are given to him in the security. The assets do not vest in the receiver, nor do they vest in the secured creditor, but the receiver is able to exercise those powers using the company's name, enabling him to pass title to the assets where necessary.

The receivership process does not prevent action being taken against the company by an aggrieved creditor. Indeed, such a creditor could issue a petition to wind up the company and it could go into liquidation, while still being in receivership. While a liquidation will affect the capacity in which the receiver acts (he will no longer act as the company's agent), it will not affect his powers over the secured assets.

If the secured assets are all the assets of the company and they are insufficient to pay in full the secured creditor's debt, then there is likely to be nothing left for the unsecured creditors. The unsecured creditors will then be reliant for some recovery on either:

(*a*)   the prescribed part (see above), if applicable; or

(*b*)   successful proceedings within the liquidation, in actions that do not form part of the company's assets.

(There are certain actions that only a liquidator can bring, which if successful will mean the recoveries go into the 'pot' available for unsecured creditors, and do not fall into the assets secured by the secured creditor's security.)

Ultimately, the level of any recovery will depend on the level of costs incurred, and of any unpaid preferential creditors.

Contracts of employment do not automatically terminate when a receiver is appointed. The receiver has 14 days' grace after appointment (*sections 37* and *44* of *IA 1986*) to decide whether or not to adopt any contract of employment. If he fails to take any steps in connection with any contract of employment within that period, he will (on the basis of current case law) be taken to have adopted it (see *Re Paramount Airways Ltd (No 3) [1994] BCC 172*). The liability that the receiver becomes subject to under the adopted contracts of employment depends on the nature of the receivership (see above). If the receiver decides not to adopt a contract of employment, the contract will be terminated and the employee will be an unsecured creditor of the company (albeit some parts of his claim may be a preferential debt).

Administration

17.8   Administration (see *sections 8* to *27* of *IA 1986* for old style administrations and *Schedule B1* to *IA 1986* for new style administrations) was introduced into *IA 1986*, as an alternative process to liquidation, where there is a chance of the company or its business surviving. It was based very loosely on *Chapter 11* of the *US Bankruptcy Code* and is presently the primary formal rescue process available in England. It has recently (since 15 September 2003) been substantially 'revamped' following the *Enterprise Act 2002*. Some of the changes are outlined below.

Administration involves the appointment of an IP to the company (called an administrator), whose purpose is to manage the company (effectively replacing the directors, who remain in office but neither they nor the company can exercise a management power without the administrator's consent) while putting together a proposal for the creditors to vote on which achieves the objectives for which the administrator is appointed. (In both old and new style administrations, the proposals will be approved if they are approved by a majority in value of those persons voting, in person or by proxy, and entitled to vote. Certain votes will not be taken into account, and/or may render invalid a resolution passed (see *IR 1986, Part 2*). For example, a resolution will be invalid if, without taking into account the votes of connected creditors, the unconnected unsecured creditors have voted against the proposal. For the definition of 'connected' in this context, see *sections 249* and *435* of *IA 1986*.) What that proposal is will depend entirely on the facts and circumstances. In both styles of administration, the proposal should be put to creditors within a short period after the administration is commenced (three months on the old style administrations (*IA 1986, s 23*), and ten weeks in the new style administration (*paragraph 51* of *Schedule B1* to *IA 1986*) – both periods can be extended), the intent being that the administration process should be creditor driven. That is, the ultimate fate of the company should be in the creditors' hands. The administrator may, however, before the proposals are put to the creditors, do such things as he thinks necessary and appropriate (including sell the company's business) if he is of the view that it is in the best interests of the company and its creditors to do so.

Until the recent legislative changes, administration was, in effect, an intermediate process in the sense that an administrator had virtually no powers to pay any of the company's creditors within the process. This meant that (unless the court's leave could be obtained to do otherwise, which was becoming increasingly common practice but recently disallowed in a 'typical' administration case) to pay realisations to creditors, administration would have to be exited into another formal insolvency process, such as liquidation. Administrators can now make distributions to secured and preferential creditors within the process, and with court leave, may also be able to make distributions to the company's unsecured creditors, effectively making it possible for administration to be a 'one stop shop'. The general order of priority of payment of creditors in an insolvency applies. See 17.6 above and the following in this section.

Until the recent legislative changes, there were also four aims the administrator could have been appointed to achieve, being (in summary):

(*a*)   the survival of the company; or

    (i)   the entering into by the company of a company voluntary arrangement; or

    (ii)   the entering into by the company of a scheme of arrangement with its creditors; or

(*b*)   getting a better realisation of the company's assets than would happen if the company is wound up immediately.

Administrations commenced before 15 September 2003 will have as their purpose(s) one or more of the above points. For administrations commenced on or after 15 September 2003, there is a sliding scale of objectives. The administrator must try to rescue the company as a going concern. There is no definition of 'rescue', making it extremely flexible as to what it might encompass. If the administrator concludes that the company cannot be rescued as a going concern or that the following objective would achieve a better result for all the creditors, his next objective is to get a better realisation of the company's assets than would be the case if the company had been immediately wound up instead of going into administration. Only if he concludes that this cannot be done and achieving the following objective will not 'unnecessarily harm' the interests of all creditors, the administrator's third objective is simply to sell the company's assets and distribute the realisations to the secured creditors and the creditors of the company who are preferential under *IA 1986*.

A key feature of the administration process under both the old style and new style administrations is that from initiation (except in one limited circumstance for new style administrations, when the moratorium will not commence until later) until either the application for administration is dismissed or the administration ends, there is a ring-fencing of the company from its creditors' claims and actions (including enforcement by secured creditors). This moratorium even prevents, in certain circumstances, a creditor trying to recover its own property from the company. Such claims can only be pursued with either the leave of the court, or (after the company is in administration) the administrator's consent. Consent/leave will only typically be given when there is some good reason to, such as because the prejudice being suffered by the creditor whose rights have been restricted by the moratorium outweighs the benefit the company/administration is getting. It is unlikely that a simple unsecured creditor would ever get consent/leave.

There are some limited exceptions to this ring-fencing in the initial period of the moratorium, which include that a secured creditor who can appoint an administrative receiver is still able to appoint one. If the secured creditor does so, administration cannot happen. This gives such floating charge holders some power, although this power has been severely curtailed by the recent restrictions on when such a receiver can be appointed. The intention of the moratorium is to give a company a breathing space and to give it time to enable something to be done.

That said and although the moratorium restricts the ability of secured creditors to enforce their security and gives, once the company goes into administration, the administrator rights (albeit with restriction in the case of fixed charge security) to deal with/dispose of the secured assets, the secured creditors' position in respect of those assets is in very general terms protected, primarily as regards fixed charge security where net proceeds of disposal must be paid to the secured creditor. Their position as a floating charge creditor is less satisfactory. This is because the floating charge realisations are first made available to meet the administration costs, expenses and liabilities and preferential creditors. In addition, for charges created after 15 September 2003, the prescribed part (see 17.7 above) needs to be considered.

Administrators have very wide powers (principally set out in *Schedule 1* to *IA 1986*), which include power to manage the business and to sell the company's assets. Administrators take control of the company. They act as agent of the company, however, so all actions are in the company's name.

Like administrative receivers, they have 14 days after appointment within which to decide what employment contracts, if any, they want to adopt, with the same consequences (*IA 1986, s 19* for old style administrations, and *paragraph 99* of *Schedule B1* for new style administrations).

In addition to those changes other significant changes are that:

- Administration is now available as an out of court process (previously, it was only available via an application to court).

- The time limits of steps within the administration, and the administration process as a whole, have been shortened/prescribed. For instance, there was no prescribed time within which an old style administration must end. A new style administration will, however, end automatically after a year, unless extended. Extensions can happen once with creditor consent but only if the court has not already extended it, and after that, consent must be by the court.

Notifying trustees of a pension scheme of the appointment of an insolvency practitioner

17.9   The IP must inform the trustees of a pension scheme that he has been appointed within one month of his appointment. Failure to do so may be subject to a civil penalty under the *Pensions Act 1995* (*PA 1995*). This is because every employer in relation to a pension scheme is under a duty to notify the pension scheme trustees within one month of the occurrence of an event relating to the employer which will be of material significance to the trustees or their advisors in the exercise of any of their functions under *section 47(9)(a)* of *PA 1995* and *regulation 6(1)(b)* of the *Occupational Pension Schemes* (*Scheme Administration*) *Regulations 1996* (*SI 1996 No 1715*). Under *section 10* of *PA 1995*, the Regulator can levy a civil penalty if there is failure by an employer to comply with the above information requirements. The maximum penalty is £50,000 for a company and £5,000 for an individual.

In such circumstances, the employer-nominated and member-nominated trustees of the pension scheme may want to resign as trustees of the pension scheme if they are no longer in employment. Those individual trustees that remain may be unwilling to act despite their continuing fiduciary duties to the pension scheme and its members. Under the provisions of *section 39* of the *Trustee Act 1925*, a resignation will be effective where it leaves the pension scheme with at least two persons to act as trustees or a trust corporation. However, the trust deed and rules governing the pension scheme may provide that the pension scheme has a minimum of one trustee. In the case of a corporate trustee the directors may resign their directorships leaving no directors of the corporate trustee in place. The consequences of leaving no directors should be set out in the memorandum and articles of association of the corporate trustee company.

Possible claims against the pension scheme by the insolvency practitioner

17.10   Administrators and liquidators have the power to make applications to the court, for certain transactions that the company has entered into prior to administration or liquidation, to be set aside. In the context of a pension scheme the most obvious vulnerability is under *section 239* of *IA 1986*, dealing with preferences. A preference is given if a company's actions at a time when it is unable to pay its debts (or as a consequence of which it becomes unable to pay its debts) puts a creditor, amongst others, into a better position in an insolvent liquidation than the creditor would have been if that action had not taken place and the administrator/liquidator can show that the company was influenced by a desire to put the creditor into such a better position.

This means that, at least in theory, an administrator/liquidator could make a claim in respect of contributions made into the scheme by the employer if he can show that the employer was influenced by a desire that the scheme was preferred. For example, the administrator/liquidator may argue that a preference occurred where benefit enhancements occurred or substantial contributions were made into the scheme when the company was in financial difficulties.

Independent trustee requirements

17.11 The statutory obligation on IPs to consider appointing independent trustees transferred to the Regulator with effect from 6 April 2005. In future IPs appointed to employers with relevant defined benefits schemes are obliged to report their appointment to the Regulator (as well as to the Pension Protection Fund ('PPF') and the trustees) and it is for the Regulator to consider whether the appointment of a statutory independent trustee is appropriate. Where any appointment is made, it must be a trustee taken from the register maintained by the Regulator.

Section 25(6) of *PA 1995* also requires that reasonable fees of the independent trustee be payable out of the pension scheme's funds regardless of any contrary provisions contained in the trust deed and rules governing the pension scheme. These are paid in priority to all other claims under the pension scheme.

Insolvency of the employer and the winding up of a pension scheme

17.12 When an employer becomes subject to a regime, the following are the typical considerations for the pension scheme trustees:

(*a*) Does the pension scheme have to go into winding up or is it advisable that it does?

(*b*) Are there unpaid contributions? If so, how do they rate in the insolvency? Can they be claimed from elsewhere?

(c) Is there a deficit? How is that deficit calculated and where does it rank in the insolvency?

(d)   What happens if there is a surplus in the pension scheme?

(e)   Can the IP have a claim against the pension scheme arising purely as
       s consequence of the insolvency?

These considerations are commented on below.

It is common for occupational pension schemes to include provisions that
require the scheme to be wound up (see chapter 12) in certain circumstances
involving the 'insolvency' of the employer or principal employer. In the case of
a CVL (see 17.6 above) the liquidation will be from the date of the passing of the
shareholders' resolution. In the case of a compulsory liquidation it will be from
the date of the passing of the order for the winding up of the company (*section
247(2) of IA 1986*). This date is also relevant as the 'applicable time' for the
purposes of the debt calculation under *section 75* of *PA 1995* (see 17.13 below).

Triggering events include:

- the appointment of an IP to the principal employer;

- the principal employer ceasing to trade;

- the winding up or liquidation of the principal employer; and

- a company goes from administration to winding up by way of a notice
  from the administrator.

Some schemes may simply refer to the company going into 'insolvency'.
Unless the context of the pension scheme would infer a meaning otherwise,
'insolvency' can probably be read wide enough to include all of the regimes,
particularly given *IA 1986, s 247*, but 'liquidation', on the other hand, has a
specific and narrower meaning and so would probably only be capable of being
read as when the employer goes into formal liquidation (see 17.4 to 17.6 above).
('Insolvency', in relation to a company, includes the approval of a voluntary
arrangement, or the appointment of an administrator or administrative receiver.
A company 'goes into liquidation' if it passes a resolution for voluntary winding
up or an order for its winding up is made by the court at a time when it has not
already gone into liquidation by passing such a resolution.)

Where the winding up of the scheme has not been triggered by the appointment
of an IP to the principal employer or the principal employer ceasing to trade it is
likely that the appointment of the IP will result in the termination of the
contracts of employment of all or most of the employees which may again
trigger the winding up of the scheme. The failure on the part of the principal
employer to pay contributions is also a triggering event. However, where the
triggering of the winding up has not occurred even as a result of these events, the
trustees may wish to use the power in the scheme rules to wind the scheme up or
continue the scheme as a closed scheme for the future.

A trustee claiming a debt under *section 75* of *PA 1995*, against the employer in a liquidation will be claiming as an unsecured creditor. In the event of the compulsory liquidation of the employer the trustees as unsecured creditors must lodge, with the liquidator, a claim for the deficit debt called 'proof of debt' or 'proof' (unless otherwise ordered by the court) in order for the trustees to seek recovery of the deficit or at least a share in what is available from the liquidation fund.

The trustees of a pension scheme can in certain circumstances enforce any debt or deficit in the pension scheme against the company (see *s 75* of the *PA 1995*). However, the liquidator, whether appointed by the creditors or the shareholders, can make an application to the court for an order to stay all actions against the company while it remains in voluntary liquidation. In view of the size of most pension scheme deficits, the liquidator is likely to proceed with such an application to prevent the trustees of a pension scheme from taking such action or proceeding with such claims.

The trustees governing the pension scheme may not be able to make a debt calculation under *section 75* of *PA 1995,* unless the trust deed and rules governing the pension scheme make provision for the triggering of the winding up of the scheme on the appointment of an IP or on the employer ceasing to trade.

Recent decisions indicate that administrators can also exercise the company's powers in relation to the scheme using their general powers (to do all things necessary to manage the affairs of the company) (*Polly Peck International plc (in administration) v Henry [1998] All ER (D) 647*).

There are also a number of cases which suggest that administrative receivers can exercise the company's powers in relation to the pension scheme on the basis that it forms part of the affairs of the company (*Simpson Curtis Pension Trustees Ltd v Readson Limited and others [1994] PLR 289, [1994] OPLR 231*).

The Pension Protection Fund

17.13   At its most basic level the PPF provides compensation to members of an eligible (see 17.14 below) defined benefits scheme, where the employer of that scheme has suffered a qualifying insolvency event (see 17.21 below) and the assets of the scheme are insufficient to meet the scheme's protected liabilities (see 17.23 below).

From even this simplistic statement it is obvious that entry into the PPF will be tightly regulated and controlled. For example, to enter the PPF:

(*a*)   the scheme must be 'eligible';

(*b*)   a 'qualifying insolvency event' must occur in relation to the employer; and

(*c*)   the assets of the scheme must be less than the protected liabilities.

It is possible to address each of these concepts in turn.

Eligible schemes

17.14   *PA 2004* itself, at *section 126*, does not specify many eligibility conditions. It merely comments that an eligible scheme is one which is not a defined contributions scheme and is not a scheme of a 'prescribed description'. However, these have since been supplemented by the voluminous *Pension Protection Fund (Entry Rules) Regulations 2005 (SI 2005 No 590)* ('the *Entry Rules*'). These set out a number of specific circumstances where a scheme will not be eligible.

Specific schemes

17.15   The list of excluded schemes is fairly predictable and can be found in *regulation 2* of the *Entry Rules*. Local government schemes and many other public sector schemes are excluded, often because they are backed up with a Crown guarantee. Non-approved schemes that are not statutory schemes also fall outside the PPF's remit, along with schemes that are administered outside the UK or are for employees outside the UK. Schemes which only provide death benefits or, in the case of a contracted-out centralised scheme, provide only lump sum benefits, are also excluded.

The number of members in a scheme can also be grounds for its exclusion from the PPF. A scheme with fewer than two members, or where there are less than twelve members and all are trustees making unanimous decisions (or it has a registered independent trustee), will not be able to enter the PPF.

A scheme which does not have an employer as at 6 April 2005 will also be ineligible.

However, after the beginning of an assessment period, if a scheme becomes unapproved, or as a result of members dying it ceases to have a sufficient number of members, it will still be eligible for the PPF as a result of the *Entry Rules*.

'Bradstock' agreements

17.16   The fact that entering into a Bradstock agreement (an agreement to compromise a debt due from an employer under *section 75 of PA 1995*) could prevent a scheme's entry into the PPF was well advertised prior to the PPF's introduction, but it is the *Entry Rules* again that set this out in detail (*regulation 2(2)* of the *Entry Rules*). The *Entry Rules* show that to enter into a Bradstock agreement, and still be eligible for the PPF, the scheme's assets before the beginning of the assessment period must be sufficient to meet the level of compensation that would be provided by the PPF (see 17.31 below). The scheme actuary will be required to provide a written estimate to the PPF of the assets and liabilities of the scheme, together with the effect that the Bradstock agreement would have on the value of those assets. [*Regulation 2(3)* of the *Entry Rules*].

Once the actuary has provided the Board with this statement, the PPF must decide whether to validate it through a validation notice. Only if the Board validates the actuary's statement will the scheme remain eligible for the PPF. It should be noted that the scheme will still come within the PPF if the agreement is one made between the PPF Board and the employer, or if the Bradstock agreement forms part of a wider compromise with the employer under *section 425* of the *Companies Act 1985*. [*Regulation 2* of the *Entry Rules*].

One issue that has emerged from this is that pre-April 2005 Bradstock agreements can still invalidate entry into the PPF. This is, of course, balanced by the fact that compromise agreements occur in relation to actual *section 75* debts which will most often have emerged from a scheme actually entering wind up. If wind up occurred pre-April 2005, the scheme will be ineligible for PPF protection in any event (see 17.17 below).

Date of winding up

17.17   If the scheme was being wound up prior to 6 April 2005 it will not be an eligible scheme for the PPF. [*Section 126(2) of PA 2004* and the *Pension Protection Fund (Eligible Schemes) Appointed Day Order 2005 (SI 2005 No 599)*].

Previous status of the scheme

17.18   It should be noted that even if a scheme is eligible at the requisite time, if it had not been eligible for a prior period the PPF need not assume responsibility for that scheme. If a scheme has not been eligible for the past three years from the date on which an assessment period begins (see 17.26 below), or was not eligible since the date of it inception, the PPF need not assume responsibility for it. Likewise, if the scheme was established to replace an existing non-eligible scheme within the last three years, it will not be taken into the PPF. [*Section 146* of *PA 2004* and *regulations 21* and *22* of the *Entry Rules*].

Qualifying insolvency events

Insolvency events

17.19   It is important to note that there are two separate tests when determining whether a qualifying insolvency event has occurred in relation to an employer. First, the employer must suffer an 'insolvency event', and then it must be considered to be a 'qualifying insolvency event'. *Section 121* of *PA 2004* lists the insolvency events. It sets out the particular events that must occur in relation to different types of corporate entity. In relation to companies, which will arguably be of most relevance, it is a fairly wide-ranging list and essentially seeks to catch most insolvency events except those that are solvent liquidations such as a members' voluntary liquidation. For the sake of completeness, in relation to a company, these are:

- the nominee in relation to a proposal for a voluntary arrangement under *Part I* of *IA 1986* submits a report to the court under *section 2* of *IA 1986* (procedure where nominee is not the liquidator or administrator) which states that in his opinion meetings of the company and its creditors should be summoned to consider the proposal;

- the directors of the company file (or in Scotland lodge) with the court documents and statements in accordance with *paragraph 7(1)* of *Schedule A1* to *IA 1986* (moratorium where directors propose voluntary arrangement);

- an administrative receiver within the meaning of *section 251* of *IA 1986* is appointed in relation to the company;

- the company enters administration within the meaning of *paragraph 1(2)(b)* of *Schedule B1* to *IA 1986*;

- a resolution is passed for a voluntary winding up of the company without a declaration of solvency under *section 89* of *IA 1986*;

- a meeting of creditors is held in relation to the company under *section 95* of *IA 1986* (creditors' meeting which has the effect of converting a members' voluntary winding up into a creditors' voluntary winding up); and

- an order for the winding up of the company is made by the court under *Part IV* or *V* of *IA 1986*. [*Section 121(3)* of *PA 2004*].

The *Entry Rules* also set out further events that will constitute an insolvency event in respect of a company:

- an administration order is made by the court in respect of the company by virtue of any enactment which applies *Part II* of *IA 1986* (administration orders) (with or without modification);

- a notice from an administrator under *paragraph 83(3)* of *Schedule B1* to *IA 1986* (moving from administration to creditors' voluntary liquidation) in relation to the company is registered by the registrar of companies;

- the company moves from administration to winding up pursuant to an order of the court under *r 2.132* of *IR 1986* (conversion of administration to winding up – power of court); or

- an administrator or liquidator of the company, being the nominee in relation to a proposal for a voluntary arrangement under *Part I* of *IA 1986* (company voluntary arrangements), summons meetings of the company and of its creditors, to consider the proposal, in accordance with *section 3(2)* of *IA 1986* (summoning of meetings. [*Regulation 5* of the *Entry Rules*].

The *Entry Rules* also assist in dealing with entities other than partnerships, companies and individuals, for example, building societies and friendly societies (*regulation 5* of the *Entry Rules*). Likewise, entities that cannot suffer an insolvency event, such as certain public bodies and charities that are not a body corporate, are dealt with in *regulation 7* of the *Entry Rules*. The mechanism for those entities essentially allows the trustees to make an application to the PPF to assume responsibility for the scheme, even though the employer cannot suffer the relevant insolvency event, by stating that the employer will not continue as a going concern. However, this is not a route for trustees generally to choose. It is specifically for those schemes which cannot suffer a relevant insolvency event and only schemes with public bodies or charities as an employer can take advantage of this (see 17.25 below).

Becoming a qualifying insolvency event

17.20   Any of these insolvency events in isolation will not trigger an assessment period (see 17.26 below), as the 'insolvency event' must be a 'qualifying insolvency event'. To be a 'qualifying' event, in accordance with *section 127(3)* of *PA 2004*, it must occur on or after the day appointed under *section 126(2)* (that date being 6 April 2005), and be the first insolvency event to occur in relation to the employer on or after that date.

Insolvency practitioner

17.21   An IP has a duty to give a notice to the Board of the PPF, the Pensions Regulator and the trustees or manager of an affected scheme if a qualifying insolvency event occurs in relation to that employer. It must give that notice within the 'notification period', which the *Entry Rules* set out as being within 14 days of the IP becoming aware of the qualifying insolvency event. [*Section 120 of PA 2004* and *regulation 4* of the *Entry Rules*].

The IP will then make a decision as to whether a 'scheme rescue' is possible. Where he believes it is not possible, he must confirm this with a 'scheme failure notice' or, alternatively, if a scheme rescue has occurred he must issue a 'withdrawal notice'. In looking at whether a scheme rescue is possible, the IP should turn to the *Entry Rules*. These show that a rescue occurs where the employer will continue as a going concern or where another company has taken on the pension liabilities. The *Entry Rules* also set out the required contents of these notices. [*Section 122* of *PA 2004* and *regulations 6* and *9* of the *Entry Rules*].

In order to become binding, the Board of the PPF must issue a determination notice. This determines whether the IP was required to give the notice and whether it complies with the requirements of the *Entry Rules*. Equally, the Board can issue the notice itself where the IP has failed to do so. [*Sections 123* and *125* of *PA 2004* and *regulation 13* of the *Entry Rules*].

Insolvency events and multi employer schemes

17.22 The *Pension Protection Fund (Multi Employer Scheme) (Modification) Regulations 2005 (SI 2005 No 441)* ('the *Multi Employer Regulations*') show how the PPF will be applied where the scheme is a multi employer scheme and employers are suffering qualifying insolvency events. Different types of scheme allow the PPF to act in different ways:

Broadly, according to the *Multi Employer Regulations*, there are two types of scheme:

(*a*)   *A segregated scheme.* This is where each segregated section has contributions payable allocated to that section only, and assets in that section can only be used within that particular section. Each segregated section can either have a single employer within it (a 'single employer section') or more than one employer in each section (a 'multi employer section').

(*b*)   *A non segregated scheme.* Here the contributions and assets are not allocated to different sections. It will be treated in the same way as a multi employer section in a segregated scheme.

A single employer section within a multi employer scheme is treated as a separate scheme for the purposes of the PPF. However, it is more complicated in multi employer sections and the PPF treatment will largely depend on whether a 'partial wind up' is required under the rules of the scheme in relation to each section:

(*a*)   *Requirement for partial wind up.* An employer's insolvency will result in a new segregated part being created within the previously non-segregated section for that specific employer. However, the PPF valuation should still take into account all of the assets of the whole section. [*Regulations 45* to *60* of the *Multi Employer Regulations*].

(*b*)   *No requirement for partial wind up.* The assessment period will not be triggered until all employers in the section are insolvent. [*Regulations 61* to *71* of the *Multi Employer Regulations*].

(*c*)   *Option available for partial wind up.* The PPF will act as if the partial wind up will occur, with the new segregated section within the section being formed. However, if the trustees do not trigger the wind up they must notify the PPF and IP who will then issue a scheme rescue notice. [*Regulations 72* to *73* of the *Multi Employer Regulations*].

Protected liabilities

17.23   *Schedule 7* to *PA 2004* highlights how compensation will be paid, and is set out later in this chapter (see 17.31 below). However, the amount of compensation payable needs to be separated from the concept of protected liabilities, of which compensation only forms a part. The PPF will look at the assets of the scheme in question to determine whether they will meet the 'protected liabilities' of the scheme (*section 131* of *PA 2004*). It will be this that goes towards ascertaining whether the PPF will assume responsibility of the scheme under *section 127* or *128* of *PA 2004* (see 17.29 below). The protected liabilities are made up of the cost of securing the PPF level of compensation together with the liabilities of the scheme which are not liabilities in respect of a member (i e third party debts) and the cost of winding up the scheme.

Applications to enter the PPF and assessment periods

Applications

17.24   There are two main routes through which applications are made to the PPF. These are either through notices from an IP acting in relation to the employer or, alternatively, an application from the trustees or Regulator but only in relation to certain scheme types.

Trustees and the Regulator

17.25   As mentioned at 17.19 above, a mechanism was included in *sections 128* and *129* of *PA 2004* and *regulation 7* of the *Entry Rules* to allow the trustees of a scheme or the Regulator to apply to the PPF where the employer is unlikely to continue as a going concern and certain prescribed requirements are met. This is designed to catch employers who cannot suffer insolvency events, and will therefore not have an IP appointed who can make the application listed in 17.28 below. The prescribed requirements, as listed in the *Entry Rules*, are that the employer is a 'public body' or charity. The *Entry Rules* show that the trustees should give such a notice within 28 days of becoming aware that the employer is unlikely to continue as a going concern. [*Regulation 8* of the *Entry Rules*].

It should be noted that this mechanism does not include overseas employers. Under the old *section 75* regime, an overseas employer could not always suffer an insolvency event, and, as a result, the debt calculations were set by reference to the date the scheme in question began winding up. It was initially thought that *sections 128* and *129* of *PA 2004* were inserted to allow schemes with overseas employers, who could not suffer an insolvency event, still to enjoy the benefit of the PPF. This was because those sections allowed for an application from the trustees where the employer would not be able to continue as a 'going concern' rather than suffering an insolvency event. Instead the *Entry Rules* clearly indicate that this is not what that section is intended to be used for. Instead it is anticipated that overseas employers, carrying on business in the UK, will have to be wound up under *section 225* of *IA 1986*, which in turn will trigger the insolvency event described in *section 121(3)(g)* of *PA 2004*.

Assessment periods

17.26   In addition to the application process described above is the concept of an 'assessment period' (*section 132* of *PA 2004*). Where a 'qualifying insolvency event' (see 17.19 above) occurs in relation to the employer of an eligible scheme (see 17.14 above) the assessment period will begin. It is during this period where the PPF will decide whether or not to assume responsibility for the scheme. The assessment period begins with the occurrence of the qualifying insolvency event and ends either:

(*a*)   when the Board ceases to be involved with the scheme (*section 149* of *PA 2004*);

(*b*)   when the trustees of managers receive a transfer notice under *section 160* of *PA 2004*; or

(*c*)   where, although no scheme rescue has occurred, there are sufficient assets to meet the protected liabilities of the scheme and the other conditions of *section 154(2)* of *PA 2004* have been met.

During the assessment period the PPF will try to assess whether the value of the scheme's assets are less than the scheme's protected liabilities (see above), which will be through an actuarial valuation instigated by the Board (*sec-*

tion 143 of *PA 2004*). They will also be looking at whether a scheme rescue can be effected, which the *Entry Rules* show to be the employer continuing as a going concern or another entity becoming responsible for the pension liabilities. During the assessment period a number of restrictions will apply to the scheme and these are dealt with in 17.29 below.

PPF admission

17.27 The PPF will take responsibility for the scheme at the end of an assessment period if the value of the assets are less than protected liabilities, a scheme failure notice has been issued and a withdrawal notice has not been issued between the insolvency event and issue of the scheme failure notice. [*Section 127* of *PA 2004*].

If the Board takes responsibility for the scheme it will issue a transfer notice which will transfer the obligations, liabilities and assets of the scheme to the PPF, resulting in compensation being paid. [*Section 160* of *PA 2004*].

However, if the assets were enough to meet the protected liabilities the trustees will have to wind up the scheme themselves (*section 154* of *PA 2004*). Equally the Board can cease to be involved with scheme during an assessment period, through the issue of a withdrawal notice, where a scheme rescue occurs or where it refuses to take responsibility for the scheme. [*Section 149* of *PA 2004*].

Appeals

17.28 There are provisions within *PA 2004* and the *Entry Rules* that would allow trustees or managers to appeal against the PPF's refusal to take on a scheme. For example, where the PPF does not take responsibility for a scheme under *section 127* or *128* of *PA 2004*, because the value of the assets was greater than the protected liabilities, the trustees or manager may apply for the PPF to reconsider and for the scheme to be taken on by the PPF after all (*section 151* of *PA 2004*). This application must be made in a form set out in *regulation 24* of the *Entry Rules* and within six months (*section 151(6)* of *PA 2004* and *regulation 24* of the *Entry Rules*). The intent is that the trustees get quotations from insurers to provide benefits at the level that the PPF would provide compensation at. If this is greater than the assets, together with the usual third party debts and winding-up costs, the PPF must assume responsibility after all. [*Section 151* of *PA 2004*].

Regulations have also been brought in to compel the PPF to review certain 'reviewable matters' on which it has made a decision (*Schedule 9* to and *section 206* of *PA 2004*). Reviewable matters include things such as making a determination, or issuing a notice under this part of the Act. As a result any determination made may be suspended while that matter is reviewed (*Schedule 9* to *PA 2004*). The Regulations dealing with this are the *Pension Protection Fund (Reviewable Matters) Regulations 2005 (SI 2005 No 600)*.

There is also to be a PPF Ombudsman (*section 213* of *PA 2004*). The PPF Ombudsman will be able to review decisions reconsidered by the PPF, and then determine what action the PPF should take. Once again, Regulations set out the mechanics of this (the *Pension Protection Fund (Multi-employer Schemes) (Modification) Regulations 2005 SI 2005 No 441*)). He will have many of the powers of the Pension Ombudsman, such as being able to hold oral hearings and compel the disclosure of documents.

Restrictions during the assessment period

17.29   During the assessment period, the Act allows for a number of restrictions to be imposed on the scheme and further powers made available to the PPF. These include:

- no new members of any class may be admitted to the scheme (*section 133(2)* of *PA 2004*);

- no further contributions, other than those due to be paid before the beginning of the assessment period or contributions from the employer relating to a *section 75, PA 1995* debt, will be paid towards the scheme during the assessment period (*section 133(2)* of *PA 2004* and *regulation 14* of the *Entry Rules*);

- benefits will not accrue during the assessment period (though this does not prevent any statutory increases in benefit or the accrual of defined contributions benefits to the extent that they are derived from income or capital gains arising from the investment of payments made in respect of the member) (*section 133(5)*, *(6)* and *(7)* of *PA 2004*);

- no transfers are to be made from the scheme or any discharge of other liabilities (other than pension credits), except in prescribed circumstances (*section 135(4)* of *PA 2004* and *regulation 16* of the *Entry Rules*);

- only the Regulator can begin winding up a scheme during the assessment period (*section 135(2)* and *(3)* of *PA 2004*);

- benefits payable to a member during the assessment period will reduce to the amount that would be paid by the PPF compensation. This same *section (138)* also contains a number of other restrictions available to the trustee, including the ability to curtail early leaver payments.

The PPF may also make certain directions in relation to the scheme, given to any relevant person (including the employer, the trustees or anyone else prescribed by regulation). The idea behind this would be to ensure that the scheme's protected liabilities do not exceed its assets (or if they do exceed the assets then any excess is kept to a minimum). This is so that the cost to the PPF is kept manageable. Such directions may concern:

- the investment of the scheme's assets (*section 134(2)* of *PA 2004*);

- the incurring of expenditure by the scheme (*section 134(2)* of *PA 2004*);

- the instigation or conduct of legal proceedings (*section 134(2)* of *PA 2004*);

- the right to any debt owed to the trustees transfers to the Board, though this must be subsequently paid to the trustees (*section 137* of *PA 2004*); and

- the PPF may make a loan to the trustees if they are not able to pay benefits as they fall due, though this will have to be repaid with interest at specified times (*section 139(2)* of *PA 2004*), though this is not a personal liability on the trustees.

Paying benefits during an assessment period

17.30 This will obviously be one of the key issues for trustees to consider during an assessment period. They (or their advisers) will need to undertake a review of the scheme rules to see where benefit adjustment should take place. The trustees will be asked to produce a project plan by the PPF to show how they will deal with this and other issues, which they will have to prepare in consultation with the Board of the PPF.

Payments made during an assessment period will be based on the scheme's 'admissible rules' (*paragraph 35* of *Schedule 7* to *PA 2004* and see also the *Pension Protection Fund (Compensation) Regulations 2005 (SI 2005 No 670)*). These are not the rules as they stand at that date, rather the PPF will ask the trustees to review them to determine which parts are admissible. For example, changes made three years before the assessment date and discretionary increases granted three years before the assessment date can be disregarded, along with any rule that operates by virtue of an insolvency event. They will be disregarded if they increase the scheme's overall liabilities.

The PPF will also be able to review ill-health awards made under the scheme prior to the beginning of the assessment period (*section 140* of *PA 2004* and also the *Pension Protection Fund (Reviewable Ill Health Pensions) Regulations 2005 (SI 2005 No 652)*).

Compensation

17.31 The compensation that will be paid will depend on the status of the member and the admissible rules (see 17.30 above) of the scheme (*Schedule 7* to *PA 2004*):

(1) Individuals who have already reached the scheme's normal retirement date, or are already in receipt of a survivor's pension or ill-health pension will be paid 100 per cent of their entitlement.

(2) Individuals who have not reached normal retirement date will be paid 90 per cent of their entitlement accrued up to immediately before the assessment period began. This will include those members who are still below the scheme's normal retirement date having taken early retirement.

For category 2, those limited to 90 per cent, there is an effective cap of £25,000 (for the year 2005/2006), while increases will be at the RPI, limited to 2.5 per cent, on pensions attributable to service after 6 April 1997 (*paragraph 28* of *Schedule 7* to *PA 2004*). It is important to note that the cap only applies to those individuals receiving compensation at the 90 per cent level. If entitled to receive 100 per cent, the member will indeed receive 100 per cent of his uncapped entitlement.

It is also worth noting that the *Pension Protection Fund (Pension Compensation Cap) Order 2005 (SI 2005 No 825)* shows that the cap this year (2006/2007) is £28,944.45. However, as the cap only applies to those who receive 90 per cent of their entitlement, they will only be able to receive 90 per cent of £28,944.45 which leads to the effective cap of £26,000. The cap will act on a sliding scale depending upon the member's age.

Compensation will be applied differently in respect of dependants where the member has died after the assessment period has begun. In many cases the dependant will only be able to receive 50 per cent of the member's compensation under the PPF. [*Schedule 7* to *PA 2004* and see also the *Pension Protection Fund (Compensation) Regulations 2005 (SI 2005 No 670)*].

Levies

17.32   One of the most controversial issues that emerged from the PPF was how it would be funded. The Government is not, despite public perception to the contrary, intending to guarantee the solvency of the PPF, and by extension the solvency of the schemes it seeks to support. Instead, it is to be funded in part by compulsory levies on all eligible schemes (see 17.14 above) with the balance of funding coming from the remaining assets of the schemes that the PPF takes on. Details are contained in chapter 2.

Financial assistance scheme

17.33   The Financial Assistance Scheme ('FAS') is to be established under *PA 2004* to assist members of schemes which commenced winding up before

6 April 2005 and thus cannot benefit from the PPF. The *Financial Assistance Scheme Regulations 2005* (*SI 2005 No 1986*) came into force on 1 September 2005 and provide:

- assistance for some members of defined benefits schemes commencing winding up between 1 January 1997 and 5 April 2005;

- the employer must be insolvent or become insolvent on or before 28 February 2006;

- assistance will be available only to those reaching the scheme's normal retirement age on or before 14 May 2007

- survivors' benefits attributable to members dying before the commencement of winding up are also covered, where the survivor will attain normal retirement age by 14 May 2007;

- members of defined benefits schemes where winding up has been completed will be included;

- assistance will be based on topping up the actual pension received to 80 per cent of the full pension capped at £12,000;

- initial payments of 60 per cent of the expected entitlement may be made to eligible members who have reached 65 but where winding up of the scheme has not been completed;

- payments to terminally ill eligible members under age 65 may be made with immediate effect;

- applications for assistance may be made by trustees, members or professional advisers from 1 September 2005.

For multi-employer schemes the following applies:

- in a sectionalised scheme the sole employer or principal employer or all employers of that section must have suffered an insolvency event;

- in a non-sectionalised scheme the sole employer, principal employer or all employers must have suffered an insolvency event.

The information which must be notified to the Secretary of State includes:

- name and registration number of scheme;

- name and address of employer;

- name and address of at least one trustee.

Surplus of scheme on employer insolvency

17.34   While it is an unlikely event in the light of the current financial circumstances that a surplus is found on the winding up of a pension scheme, if one becomes available the IP would request the return of the surplus to the employer so that there may be a further distribution to creditors.

Section 76 of the *PA 1995* provides that members must be notified prior to any repayment of surplus being made to an employer. Under *regulation 7* of the *Occupational Pension Schemes (Payments to Employers) Regulations 1996 (SI 1996 No 2156)* notices must be given to the members of the proposal to return the surplus to the employer. Any member dissatisfied with the proposal to return the surplus to the employer can make representations to the trustees or the employer or ultimately the Regulator. The surplus in the scheme can be returned to the employer, subject to a 35 per cent tax charge, provided that all the scheme liabilities have been discharged in full and the trust deed and rules which govern the pension scheme permit the return of surplus and subject to approval by APSS. In addition, if there is a power under the scheme to distribute any surplus assets to persons other than the employer, that power must be exercised or a decision taken not to exercise it. Pensions payment must be increased in accordance with *section 51* of *PA 1995* and members of the scheme must be given notice of any intention to pay any surplus of assets in the scheme to employers.

If the trust deed and rules governing the pension scheme are silent on the return of surplus to the employer or do not permit the return of surplus to the employer, any surplus must be used to augment members' benefits up to APSS maximum. In the unlikely event that any surplus remains after augmentation, it can be returned to the employer.

Penalties under the Pensions Act 1995, Pensions Act 2004 and other legislation

Types of penalty

General

The *Pensions Act 1995* (*PA 1995*) carries a number of sanctions for non-compliance, ranging from fines to, in extreme cases, imprisonment. Many failures to comply with the requirements of the *Pensions Act 2004* (*PA 2004*) give rise to penalties under other Acts and Regulations which contain sanctions, but these are usually confined to fines.

Civil penalties

The Regulator may require a person to pay a penalty in respect of an act or omission in contravention of various requirements of *PA 1995* and *PA 2004*. [*PA 1995, s 10*]. The maximum amount of the penalty varies from £5,000 in the case of an individual and £50,000 in any other case to £200 and £1,000 respectively. The time limit for payment is usually 28 days.

Where a penalty is recoverable from a corporate body, and the act or omission was done with the connivance or consent of an officer (or, in some cases, a managing shareholder) of the company, the Regulator may instead impose a penalty on that person.

Prohibition from acting as a trustee

The Regulator has the power to prohibit an individual from being a trustee (or director of a trustee company). The effect of a prohibition order is that the individual is removed as a trustee. [*PA 1995, s 3*]. The Regulator also has the power to suspend a trustee. [*PA 1995, s 4*]. The effect of the suspension order is to prohibit the trustee from exercising his functions in respect of the scheme(s) in question.

Criminal penalties

Certain transgressions carry criminal sanctions. Penalties for conviction of an offence are:

(*a*)   on summary conviction – a fine not exceeding the statutory maximum; and

(*b*)   on conviction on indictment – a fine or imprisonment or both.

Where an offence committed by a corporate body is proved to have been committed with the consent or connivance of an officer or purported officer of the company, that person is guilty of an offence and subject to the same punishment.

Appeals

The powers of the Regulator to impose penalties and prohibit trustees are 'reserved regulatory functions' exercisable by the Determinations Panel. [*PA 2004, s 10*]. Appeals against decisions of the Determinations Panel may be referred to the Pensions Regulator Tribunal. [*PA 2004, s 103*]. The Tribunal must determine any reference to it and then must remit the matter to the Determinations Panel with appropriate directions (which may include a direction to vary or revoke the original decision). A party to a determination of the Tribunal may, with permission, appeal to the court on a point of law.

Summary of penalties

A brief summary of the main transgressions for which penalties may be imposed is set out in the table below. This is not an exhaustive list.

Transgression	Penalty	Can be imposed on
Failure to comply with a direction of the Regulator to make payments to members, include a statement in the annual report and send a statement to members (*section 15* of *PA 1995*)	Civil penalty	Any trustee who fails to take all reasonable steps to secure compliance

Transgression	Penalty	Can be imposed on
Failure to make arrangements for member-nominated trustees or member-nominated directors or failure to implement arrangements or appropriate rules (*section 21* of *PA 1995*) (to be superseded by *s 241* of *PA 2004* from 6 April 2006)	Civil penalty and prohibition order	Any trustee who fails to take all reasonable steps to secure compliance
Failure to give notice to the Regulator that a trustee appointed under *section 23* of *PA 1995* is no longer an independent person (*section 25* of *PA 1995*, amended by *section 33* of *PA 2004*)	Civil penalty	Any trustee who without reasonable excuse fails to comply
Acting as an auditor or actuary whilst ineligible (*section 28* of *PA 1995*)	Criminal offence	Any actuary or auditor so acting
Purporting to act as a trustee whilst disqualified (*section 30* of *PA 1995*)	Criminal offence	Any person purporting to so act
Failure to give notice (required under *regulation 9* of the *Scheme Administration Regulations 1996* (*SI 1996/1715*)) of trustee meetings where decisions taken by majority (*section 32* of *PA 1995*)	Civil penalty and prohibition order	Any trustee who fails to take all reasonable steps to secure compliance
Failure to prepare or maintain a statement of investment principles or failure to obtain and consider advice before preparing the statement (*section 35* of *PA 1995*)	Civil penalty and prohibition order	Any trustee who fails to take all reasonable steps to secure compliance
Failure to obtain and consider proper advice before making an investment or failure to comply with the *Investment Regulations* (*section 36* of *PA 1995*)	Civil penalty and prohibition order*	Any trustee who fails to take all reasonable steps to secure compliance

Transgression	Penalty	Can be imposed on
Failure to comply with requirements in relation to the payment of surplus to an employer (*section 37* of *PA 1995*)	Civil penalty and prohibition order*	Any trustee who fails to take all reasonable steps to secure compliance
Non-trustee purporting to exercise a power in relation to the payment of surplus to the employer (*section 37* of *PA 1995*)	Civil penalty	Person purporting to exercise power
Investing in employer-related investments in excess of statutory limit (*section 40* of *PA 1995*)	Civil penalty and prohibition order*	Any trustee who fails to take reasonable steps to secure compliance
	Criminal offence	Any trustee or manager who agreed to make the investment
Placing reliance on the skill and judgment of legal or other specified professional advisers (as to which, see *regulation 2* of the *Scheme Administration Regulations 1996* (*SI 1996 No 1715*)) not appointed by the trustees (*section 47* of *PA 1995*)	Civil penalty and prohibition order*	Any trustee who does so
	Civil penalty	Any manager who does so
Failure to appoint a scheme auditor, scheme actuary or fund manager when required to do so or failure to comply with requirements prescribed regarding the appointment of professional advisers (*section 47* of *PA 1995*)	Civil penalty and prohibition order*	Any trustee who fails to take reasonable steps to secure compliance
	Civil penalty	Any manager who fails to take reasonable steps to secure compliance
Failure without reasonable excuse to obtain audited accounts or an auditor's contribution statement within seven months of end of scheme year (*Occupational Pensions Schemes* (*Requirement to Obtain Audited Accounts and a Statement from the Auditor*) *Regulations 1996* (*SI 1996 No 1975*))	Prohibition order	Any trustee failing to comply
	Civil penalty	Any trustee or manager failing without reasonable excuse to take all necessary steps to secure compliance

Transgression	Penalty	Can be imposed on
Failure to keep money in a separate account and failure to maintain adequate records relating to trustee meetings and certain transactions as required by regulations (see, in particular, the *Scheme Administration Regulations 1996 (SI 1996 No 1715)) (section 49 of PA 1995)*	Civil penalty and prohibition order*	Any trustee who fails to take all reasonable steps to secure compliance
Failure to keep adequate records, as required by regulations (*section 49 of PA 1995*)	Civil penalties	Any employer or prescribed person
Deducting contributions from employees' earnings and failing to pay them to the trustees within required time with no reasonable excuse for doing so (*section 49 of PA 1995*)	Civil penalty	Employer (unless it is required to pay a penalty under *section 3(7) of WRPA 1999* for failures in respect of stakeholder schemes)
Failure to give notice to the Regulator and the member of the failure of the employer to pay deductions from the employee's earnings to the trustees within the prescribed time (*section 49 of PA 1995*)	Civil penalty and prohibition order*	Any trustee who fails to take all reasonable steps to secure compliance
	Civil penalty	Any manager who fails to take all reasonable steps to secure compliance
Being knowingly concerned in the fraudulent evasion of the obligation to pay deductions from employees' earnings to the trustees within the prescribed time (*section 49 of PA 1995*)	Criminal offence	Any person
Failure to comply with the statutory requirements to keep written records of any determinations or decisions in relation to the winding up of the scheme (*section 49A of PA 1995*)	Civil penalty and prohibition order*	Any trustee who fails to take all such steps as are reasonable to secure compliance
	Civil penalty	Any manager who fails to take all such steps as are reasonable to secure compliance

Transgression	Penalty	Can be imposed on
Failure to make and/or implement arrangements for the resolution of disputes (*section 50* of *PA 1995*)	Civil penalty	Any trustee or manager who fails to take all reasonable steps to secure compliance
Failure to obtain actuarial valuations or certificates when required to do so and failure to make them available to the employer within seven days of their receiving it (*section 57* of *PA 1995*) (to be repealed by *section 320* of *PA 2004* from 30 December 2005)	Civil penalty and prohibition order	Any trustee who fails to take all reasonable steps to secure compliance
	Civil penalty	Any manager who fails to take all reasonable steps to secure compliance
Failure to prepare a schedule of contributions in accordance with statutory requirements (*section 58* of *PA 1995*) (to be repealed by *section 320* of *PA 2004* from 30 December 2005)	Civil penalty and prohibition order	Any trustee who fails to take all reasonable steps to secure compliance
	Civil penalty	Any manager who fails to take all reasonable steps to secure compliance
Failure to give notice to the Regulator and to members, or failure to prepare a report, when contributions are not made or the MFR is not met (*sections 59* and *60* of *PA 1995*) (to be repealed by *section 320* of *PA 2004* from 30 December 2005)	Civil penalty and prohibition order	Any trustee who fails to take all reasonable steps to secure compliance
	Civil penalty	Any manager who fails to take all reasonable steps to secure compliance
Failure to comply with statutory scheme modification requirements (*section 67* of *PA 1995*, inserted by *section 251* of *PA 2004* from 6 April 2006)	Civil penalty	Trustee or any other person failing to comply with requirements
Failure to comply with the statutory order on a winding up (*section 73B* of *PA 1995*)	Civil penalty	Any trustee or manager who fails to take all reasonable steps to secure compliance

Transgression	Penalty	Can be imposed on
Exercising a power to distribute excess assets on a winding up to an employer without having complied with the statutory requirements (*sections 76* and *77* of *PA 1995*)	Civil penalty and prohibition order*	Any trustee who fails to take all reasonable steps to secure compliance
	Civil penalty	Any person other than the trustees who purports to exercise the power (under *section 76* of *PA 1995* only)
Failure to prepare a schedule of payments for a defined contributions scheme (*section 87* of *PA 1995*)	Civil penalty and prohibition order*	Any trustee who fails to take all reasonable steps to secure compliance
	Civil penalty	Any manager who fails to take all reasonable steps to secure compliance
Failure to make payments to a defined contributions scheme in accordance with the schedule of payments (*section 88* of *PA 1995*)	Civil penalty	Employer
Failure to notify the Regulator and members within the required time where payments have not been made in accordance with the schedule of payments (*section 88* of *PA 1995*)	Civil penalty and prohibition order*	Any trustee who fails to take all reasonable steps to secure compliance
	Civil penalty	Any manager who fails to take all reasonable steps to secure compliance
Failure to provide a statement of guaranteed cash equivalent when required to do so or failure to comply with a transfer notice given by an eligible member (*section 153* of *PA 1995*/*sections 93A, 99* and *101* of *PSA 1993*) (includes statements/transfers in respect of pension credit benefits)	Civil penalty	Any trustee or manager who fails to take all reasonable steps to secure compliance
Failure to disclose documentation and information when required to do so (*Disclosure Regulations* made under *section 41* of *PA 1995*)	Civil penalty and prohibition order*	Any trustee who has failed to take all reasonable steps to secure compliance
	Civil penalty	Any manager who has failed to take all reasonable steps to secure compliance

749

Transgression	Penalty	Can be imposed on
Failure to obtain actuarial certification or failure to comply with consent requirements before modifying the scheme to the detriment of member's accrued rights (regulations made under *section 67 of PA 1995*) (*section 67* is to be amended on 6 April 2006 by *section 262 of PA 2004*)	Civil penalty	Any person who fails to comply
Failure to issue appropriate notice within one month following determination to defer winding up of scheme or as to when liabilities are to be determined (*Winding-up Regulations 1996 (SI 1996 No 3126)* made under *section 38 of PA 1995*)	Civil penalty	Any person who fails to comply
Failure to make a report regarding a scheme's winding up where required to do so (*section 72A of PA 1995*)	Civil penalty	Any trustee or manager who has failed to take all reasonable steps to secure compliance
Failure to comply with a direction given by the Regulator to facilitate winding up (*section 72C of PA 1995*)	Civil penalty	Any trustee who fails, without reasonable excuse, to take all reasonable steps to secure compliance with the direction
	Civil penalty	Any manager or other person to whom a direction is given who fails, without reasonable excuse, to take all reasonable steps to secure compliance
Failure to comply with an improvement notice issued by the Regulator (*section 13 of PA 2004*)	Civil penalty	Any trustee or manager who fails to take all reasonable steps to ensure compliance
Failure to comply with a third party notice issued by the Regulator (*section 14 of PA 2004*)	Civil penalty	Any person to whom a third party notice is issued who fails without reasonable excuse to comply

Transgression	Penalty	Can be imposed on
Failure to comply with a pensions liberation restraining order issued by the Regulator (*section 20* of *PA 2004*)	Civil penalty	Any deposit taker who fails without reasonable excuse to comply
Failure to comply with a pensions liberation repatriation order issued by the Regulator (*section 21* of *PA 2004*)	Civil penalty	Any deposit taker who fails without reasonable excuse to comply
Failure to comply with the terms of a freezing order issued by the Regulator (*section 24* of *PA 2004*)	Civil penalty	Any trustee or manager who fails to take all reasonable steps to comply
	Civil penalty	Any employer who without reasonable excuse fails to repay contributions required
Failure to comply with a winding-up order or a freezing order issued by the Regulator (*section 28* of *PA 2004*)	Civil penalty	Any trustee or manager who fails to take all reasonable steps to secure compliance
Failure to comply with directions where the Regulator revokes a freezing order (*section 30* of *PA 2004*)	Civil penalty	Any trustee or manager who fails to take all reasonable steps to secure compliance
Failure to comply with a requirement from the Regulator to make a contribution on the revocation of a freezing order (*section 30* of *PA 2004*)	Civil penalty	Any employer who fails without reasonable excuse to secure compliance
	Civil penalty	Any trustee or manager who fails to take all reasonable steps to report the failure of the employer to pay
Failure to comply with a notification order issued by the Regulator in relation to a freezing order (*section 31* of *PA 2004*)	Civil penalty	Any trustee or manager who has failed to take all reasonable steps to secure compliance
Failure to comply with a direction from the Regulator to suspend recovery of a *section 75* debt (*sections 41 and 50* of *PA 2004*)	Civil penalty	Any trustee or manager who has failed to take all reasonable steps to secure compliance

Transgression	Penalty	Can be imposed on
Failure to provide the Regulator with information in relation to the register (*section 62* of *PA 2004*)	Civil penalty	Any trustee or manager who has failed to take all reasonable steps to secure compliance
Failure to provide a scheme return to the Regulator (*section 64* of *PA 2004*)	Civil penalty	Any trustee or manager who has failed to take all reasonable steps to secure compliance
Failure to notify the Regulator of 'notifiable events' (*section 69* of *PA 2004*)	Civil penalty	Any trustee or manager who has failed to take all reasonable steps to secure compliance
	Civil penalty	Any prescribed person (employer) who without reasonable excuse has failed to comply
Failure to report breaches of law to the Regulator (*section 70* of *PA 2004*)	Civil penalty	Any person on whom an obligation is imposed who without reasonable excuse fails to comply
Failure to comply with a report notice issued by the Regulator (*section 71* of *PA 2004*)	Civil penalty	Any trustee or manager who has failed to take all reasonable steps to secure compliance
	Civil penalty	Any other person issued with a report notice who without reasonable excuse has failed to comply
Failure to provide information or produce a document when required under *section 72* of *PA 2004* (*section 77(1)* of *PA 2004*)	Criminal offence	Any person who without reasonable excuse neglects or refuses to comply
Delaying or obstructing an inspector exercising any power under *section 73, 74* or *75* of *PA 2004,* neglecting or refusing to produce any document under *section 75* of *PA 2004* or neglecting or refusing to answer questions or provide information when required by the Regulator (*section 77(2)* of *PA 2004*)	Criminal offence	Any person who without reasonable excuse fails to comply

Transgression	Penalty	Can be imposed on
Intentionally and without reasonable excuse altering, suppressing, concealing or destroying a document required by the Regulator (*section 77(5)* of *PA 2004*)	Criminal offence	Any person who is required to produce the document
Providing false or misleading information to the Regulator (*section 80* of *PA 2004*)	Criminal offence	Any person who knowingly or recklessly provides the Regulator with false information
Disclosing restricted information received from the Regulator (*section 82* of *PA 2004*)	Criminal offence	Any person who discloses information without authority
Failure to comply with statutory requirements during an assessment period (*section 133* of *PA 2004*)	Civil penalty	Any trustee or manager who has failed to take all reasonable steps to secure compliance
Failure to comply with directions of the PPF Board during an assessment period (*section 134* of *PA 2004*)	Civil penalty	Any trustee or manager who has failed to take all reasonable steps to secure compliance
Failure to comply with statutory restrictions on winding up during an assessment period (*section 135* of *PA 2004*)	Civil penalty	Any trustee or manager who has failed to take all reasonable steps to secure compliance
Payment of benefits at PPF level during an assessment period (*section 138* of *PA 2004*)	Civil penalty	Any trustee or manager who has failed to take all reasonable steps to secure compliance
Deciding applications for ill-health pensions within six months of the assessment date (*section 140* of *PA 2004*)	Civil penalty	Any trustee or manager who has failed to take all reasonable steps to secure compliance
Failing to comply with directions of the PPF Board to wind up the scheme (*section 154* of *PA 2004*)	Civil penalty	Any trustee or manager who has failed to take all reasonable steps to secure compliance

Transgression	Penalty	Can be imposed on
Failure to provide information or produce a document when required under *section 191* of *PA 2004* (*section 193(1)* of *PA 2004*)	Criminal offence	Any person who without reasonable excuse neglects or refuses to comply
Delaying or obstructing a person appointed by the PPF Board exercising any power under *section 192* of *PA 2004,* neglecting or refusing to produce any document under *section 192* of *PA 2004* or neglecting or refusing to answer questions or provide information when required (*section 193(2)* of *PA 2004*)	Criminal offence	Any person who without reasonable excuse fails to comply
Intentionally and without reasonable excuse altering, suppressing, concealing or destroying a document required by the Board of the PPF (*section 193(6)* of *PA 2004*)	Criminal offence	Any person who is required to produce the document
Providing false or misleading information to the Board of the PPF (*section 195* of *PA 2004*)	Criminal offence	Any person who knowingly or recklessly provides the Board of the PPF with false information
Disclosing restricted information received from the Board of the PPF (*section 197* of *PA 2004*)	Criminal offence	Any person who discloses information without authority
Failing to comply with directions of the Regulator in relation to backdating the winding up of a scheme (*section 219* of *PA 2004*)	Civil penalty	Any trustee or manager who has failed to take all reasonable steps to secure compliance
Failure to prepare and review statement of funding principles (*section 223* of *PA 2004*) (from 30 December 2005)	Civil penalty	Any trustee or manager who has failed to take all reasonable steps to secure compliance

Transgression	Penalty	Can be imposed on
Failure to obtain, receive and make available to the employer, an actuarial valuation or report (*section 224* of *PA 2004*) (from 30 December 2004)	Civil penalty	Any trustee or manager who has failed to take all reasonable steps to secure compliance
Failure to report to the Regulator when no certificate of technical provisions can be given (*section 225* of *PA 2004*) (from 30 December 2004)	Civil penalty	An actuary who fails without reasonable excuse to comply
Failure to comply with the requirements in relation to a recovery plan (*section 226* of *PA 2004*) (from 30 December 2004)	Civil penalty	Any trustee or manager who has failed to take all reasonable steps to secure compliance
Failure to comply with the requirements in relation to a schedule of contributions (*section 227* of *PA 2004*) (from 30 December 2004)	Civil penalty	Any trustee or manager who has failed to take all reasonable steps to secure compliance
Failure to report to the Regulator when the schedule of contributions cannot be certified (*section 227* of *PA 2004*) (from 30 December 2004)	Civil penalty	An actuary who fails without reasonable excuse to comply
Failure to report failure to pay contributions where reasonable grounds to believe it may be of material significance to the Regulator (*section 228* of *PA 2004*) (from 30 December 2005)	Civil penalty	Any trustee or manager who has failed to take all reasonable steps to secure compliance
Failure without reasonable excuse to pay contributions in accordance with the schedule of contributions or debt arising (*section 228* of *PA 2004*) (from 30 December 2005)	Civil penalty	An employer

Transgression	Penalty	Can be imposed on
Failing to secure the agreement of the employer where required (*section 229 of PA 2004*) (from 30 December 2005)	Civil penalty	Any trustee or manager who has failed to take all reasonable steps to secure compliance
Failure to report failure to agree to the Regulator (*section 229 of PA 2004*) (from 30 December 2005)	Civil penalty	Any trustee or manager who has failed to take all reasonable steps to secure compliance
Failing to obtain the advice of the actuary where required (*section 230 of PA 2004*) (from 30 December 2005)	Civil penalty	Any trustee or manager who has failed to take all reasonable steps to secure compliance
Accepting a funding payment if the scheme is not established under trust or does not have written benefit rules (*section 252 of PA 2004*)	Civil penalty	Any trustee or manager of a UK-based pension scheme who has failed to take all reasonable steps to ensure no funding payment was accepted
A UK-based occupational pension scheme has activities which are not 'retirement based' (*section 255 of PA 2004*)	Civil penalty	Any trustee or manager who has failed to take all reasonable steps to secure that all activities are retirement based
No amount may be paid out of scheme assets for the purpose of reimbursing any trustee or manager in relation to fines or civil penalties imposed under *PA 1995, PA 2004* or *PSA 1993* (*section 256 of PA 2004*)	Civil penalty	Any trustee or manager who has failed to take all reasonable steps to secure compliance
Accepting or permitting reimbursement for fines or civil penalties imposed under *PA 1995, PA 2004* or *PSA 1993* (*section 256 of PA 2004*)	Criminal offence	Any trustee who, knowing or having reasonable grounds to believe he has been reimbursed, fails to take all reasonable steps to secure that he is not reimbursed
	Civil penalty	Any trustee who fails to take all reasonable steps to secure that reimbursement is not made

Transgression	Penalty	Can be imposed on
Failure to secure that the conditions for registration of a stakeholders' scheme are fulfilled while the scheme is registered (*section 2* of *WRPA 1999*)	Civil penalty	Any trustee or prescribed person who fails to take all reasonable steps to secure compliance
Failure to comply with duty to facilitate access to stakeholders' pension scheme (*section 3* of *WRPA 1999*)	Civil penalty	Employer
Failure to discharge liability in respect of a pension credit within the implementation period (*section 33* of *WRPA 1999*)	Civil penalty (see *regulation 5* of *SI 2000 No 1053*)	Any trustee or manager who has failed to take all reasonable steps to ensure that liability in respect of the credit is discharged before the end of the implementation period
Failure to notify the Regulator of a failure to discharge liability for a pension credit within the implementation period (*section 33* of *WRPA 1999*)	Civil penalty (see *reg 5* of *SI 2000 No 1053*)	Any trustee or manager who has failed to take all reasonable steps to ensure the obligation is performed
Failure to notify the Regulator of the failure to comply with the transfer notice in respect of a pension credit benefit (*section 33* of *WRPA 1999*)	Civil penalty	Any trustee or manager who has failed to take all reasonable steps to ensure that the obligation is performed
Failure to provide a statement of entitlement to members when applied for by a member (*section 93A* of *PSA 1993*)	Civil penalty	Any trustee or manager who has failed to take all such steps as are reasonable to secure compliance
Failure to carry out what a member of the scheme requires within six months of the necessary date as regards the exercise of the option conferred by *section 95* of *PSA 1993* (*section 99* of *PSA 1993*)	Civil penalty	Any trustee or manager who has failed to take all such steps as are reasonable to ensure it was so done

Transgression	Penalty	Can be imposed on
Failure to notify a member of his right to a cash transfer sum within a reasonable period (*section 101AC of PA 2004*) (coming into force 6 April 2006)	Civil penalty	Any trustee or manager who has failed to take all such steps as are reasonable to secure compliance
Failure to carry out early leaver's request for a cash transfer sum (*section 101AG of PA 2004*) (coming into force 6 April 2006)	Civil penalty	Any trustee or manager who has failed to take all such steps as are reasonable to secure compliance
Failure on application of an eligible member of a salary related occupational pension scheme, to provide him with a written statement of the amount of cash equivalent of his pension credit benefit under the scheme (*section 101H of PSA 1993*) (coming into force 6 April 2006)	Civil penalty	Any trustee or manager who has failed to take all such steps as are reasonable to secure that the obligation was performed
Failure to notify the Regulator of the failure to comply with transfer notice before the end of the period for compliance (*section 101J of PSA 1993*) (coming into force 6 April 2006)	Civil penalty	Any trustee or manager who has failed to take all steps as are reasonable to ensure that the notice was complied with before the end of the period for compliance
Failure to prepare/maintain a record for direct payment arrangements regarding contributions to personal pension schemes or to send a copy of the record to the trustees or managers (*section 111A of PSA 1993*)	Civil penalty	Employer (unless it is required to pay a penalty under *section 3(7) of WRPA 1999* for failures in respect of stakeholder pensions)

Transgression	Penalty	Can be imposed on
Failure to notify the Regulator and/or the employee where contributions shown on the record of the direct payment arrangements had not been paid before the due date or failure to provide information to employee at specified intervals (*section 111A* of *PSA 1993*)	Prohibition order*	Any trustee who has failed to take all reasonable steps to secure compliance
Failure to pay the contribution payable under direct payment arrangements to the trustee/managers of the scheme on or before its due date (*section 111A* of *PSA 1993*)	Civil penalty	Employer
Failure to provide information regarding transfer of accrued rights without consent (*regulation 27B* of the *Occupational Pension Schemes* (*Preservation* of *Benefit*) *Regulations 1991* (*SI 1991 No 167*))	Civil penalty	Any person who fails without reasonable excuse to comply
Failure to comply with any requirement of the *Disclosure Regulations* (*SI 1996 No 1655*)	Civil penalty	Any person who fails without reasonable excuse to comply
Failure to provide specified information regarding pension sharing (*regulation 9* of the *Pensions on Divorce etc* (*Provision* of *Information*) *Regulations 2000* (*SI 2000 No 1048*))	Civil penalty	Any trustee or manager who fails without reasonable excuse to comply
False statements on application for approval or in order to secure tax relief (*sections 605A, 619, 653* and *658* of *ICTA 1988*) (to be repealed 6 April 2006)	*Civil penalty*	*Any person making such statements either fraudulently or negligently* (*section 605A* of *ICTA 1988*) *or knowingly* (*otherwise*)

Transgression	Penalty	Can be imposed on
Failure to provide information to the APSS when required to do so, or failure to keep books, documents and other records as required (sections 605 and 651A of ICTA 1988) (to be repealed 6 April 2006)	*Civil penalty*	*Any person failing to comply*
Failure to provide scheme return (*section 257* of *FA 2004*)	Civil penalty	Scheme administrator
Failure to provide information required by regulations (*section 258* of *FA 2004*)	Civil penalty	Person who fails to comply
Failure to comply with notice to provide documents or particulars (*section 259* of *FA 2004*)	Civil penalty	Person who fails to comply
Failure to make an accounting return (*section 260* of *FA 2004*)	Civil penalty and scheme sanction charge	A scheme administrator failing to make a return
Providing false or fraudulent information in relation to enhanced lifetime allowance or failing to provide information (*sections 261* and *262* of *FA 2004*)	Civil penalty	The individual member
Failure to notify APSS of relevant benefit accrual in relation to enhanced protection of lifetime allowance (*section 263* of *FA 2004*)	Civil penalty	The individual member
Fraudulently or negligently making a false statement (*section 264* of *FA 2004*)	Civil penalty	Person making the statement
Winding up wholly or mainly to facilitate the payment of lump sums (*section 265* of *FA 2004*)	Civil penalty	Scheme administrator

Transgression	Penalty	Can be imposed on
Transferring sums to insured schemes unless payment is made to the scheme administrator or relevant insurance company (*section 266* of *FA 2004*)	Civil penalty	Scheme administrator
Carrying on a regulated activity while unauthorised, or outside the exempt regime (*section 23* of *FSMA 2000*)	Criminal offence	Any person acting in the course of business
Communicating an invitation or inducement to engage in investment activity (*section 25* of *FSMA 2000*)	Criminal offence	Any person acting in the course of business
An unfit and improper individual carrying out functions in relation to a regulated activity for an authorised person (*section 56* of *FSMA 2000*)	Prohibition order	Any person who is deemed to be unfit and improper by the FSA
Failure to comply with a statement of principle issued by the FSA (*section 66* of *FSMA 2000*)	Civil penalty or statement of misconduct	Any approved person issued with a statement of principle
Knowing concern in a contravention, by a relevant authorised person, of a requirement imposed on that authorised person by, or under, *FSMA 2000* (*section 66* of *FSMA 2000*)	Civil penalty or statement of misconduct	Any approved person
Engaging in, or by act or omission encouraging or requiring another to engage in, market abuse (*section 123* of *FSMA 2000*)	Civil penalty or statement indicating engagement in market abuse	Any person or persons privy to unpublished price sensitive information
Failure to notify the FSA of a step which would result in the acquiring of control over, additional kind of control or an increase in the relevant kind of control over, a UK authorised person (*section 178* of *FSMA 2000*)	Criminal offence (punishable by fine only) (see *section 191* of *FSMA 2000*)	Any person under a duty to notify

Transgression	Penalty	Can be imposed on
Failure to notify the FSA of a step which would result in ceasing to have control over, or reducing relevant control over, a UK authorised person (*section 190* of *FSMA 2000*)	Criminal offence (punishable by fine only) (see *section 191* of *FSMA 2000*)	Any person under a duty to notify
Failure to abide by a notice of objection issued by the FSA (*section 191* of *FSMA 2000*)	Criminal offence	Any person subject to a notice of objection
Contravention of a requirement relating to authorised persons under *FSMA 2000* (*sections 205* and *206* of *FSMA 2000*)	Civil penalty or statement of contravention issued by the FSA	Any authorised person
Communicating an invitation or inducement to participate in an unauthorised collective investment scheme (*section 241* of *FSMA 2000*)	Civil action by a private person	Any authorised person
Disclosure or use of confidential information by, or obtained from, a primary recipient without the relevant consent (*section 352* of *FSMA 2000*)	Criminal offence	Any person who is in possession of confidential information
On application to the FSA or the Secretary of State there is a reasonable likelihood, possibility or actual case of a relevant requirement under the Act being contravened (*section 380* of *FSMA 2000*)	Injunction	Any person
Accruing profit or causing loss as a result of a contravention or knowing involvement in a contravention of a relevant requirement (*section 382* of *FSMA 2000*)	Restitution order	Any person

Transgression	Penalty	Can be imposed on
Making a statement, promise or forecast which is known to be misleading, false or deceptive in a material particular (*section 397* of *FSMA 2000*)	Criminal offence	Any person
Dishonestly concealing any material facts whether in connection with a statement, promise or forecast made by the offender or otherwise (*section 397* of *FSMA 2000*)	Criminal offence	Any person
Recklessly making (dishonestly or otherwise) a statement, promise or forecast which is misleading, false or deceptive in a material particular (*section 397* of *FSMA 2000*)	Criminal offence	Any person
Knowingly or recklessly giving the FSA information which is false or misleading in a material particular in purported compliance with any requirement imposed by or under the *Act* (*section 398* of *FSMA 2000*)	Criminal offence (punishable by fine only)	Any person

Human Rights Act 1998 implications of the Regulator's powers

As a public authority, it is unlawful for the Regulator to act in a way that is incompatible with rights under the *European Convention on Human Rights*.

The *Convention* Article of primary relevance for the Regulator is *Article 6(1)*, which lays down certain requirements in relation to the determination of a person's civil rights and obligations and in relation to criminal charges. Extra requirements are laid down in relation to criminal procedures in *Article 6(2)* and (*3*). How might these apply to the Regulator's activities?

Prohibition orders

There is some debate over whether the imposition of a prohibition order would be subject to the requirements of *Article 6(1)*. It would be more likely to be the case where a professional trustee is the subject of the prohibition order. *PA 2004* removes many of the circumstances when prohibition orders may be made.

* The asterisks in the table refer to where prohibition orders may be removed, but at the date of writing, such prohibition orders are still in place.

Fines

The imposition of fines under *section 10* of *PA 1995* certainly involves the determination of a person's civil rights and obligations and, it has been suggested, could be regarded in the nature of a criminal penalty. If the fines are to be regarded as criminal penalties, then the absence of the availability of legal aid is of concern as this is required under *Article 6* for the purposes of criminal proceedings.

In addition, there is currently no right to a public hearing in relation to the imposition of a penalty under *section 10*. The *European Convention on Human Rights* case law suggests that it is sufficient that the opportunity is given to the person in question. However, it may be difficult for the Regulator to deny a hearing if a person requests it.

Finally, there are some question marks over whether the Regulator is sufficiently impartial to comply with *Article 6(1)*, particularly if the fines imposed can be categorised as criminal penalties. Any problems that arise in this regard can be overcome, provided that there is an adequate appeals procedure. In the case of the Regulator, decisions on imposing penalties are subject to review by the Pensions Regulator Tribunal and an appeal from the Tribunal to the court is available with permission on a point of law.

Summary of the application of the Occupational Pension Schemes (Disclosure of Information) Regulations 1996 (SI 1996 No 1655) (the 'Disclosure Regulations') to approved schemes, and other requirements to disclose information

NOTE: The *Disclosure Regulations* are due to be replaced in April 2006 by the *Occupational Pension Schemes (Disclosure of Information) Regulations 2006* – at the time of going to press these have been published in draft form only and are referred to in notes at the end of Appendix II.

To be disclosed	Disclosure to	Form of disclosure	When
CONSTITUTION OF THE SCHEME (*Regulation 3*,[1] *Disclosure Regulations*) (all schemes)			
The contents of: • the trust deed or other document constituting the scheme; • the rules (if not in above document); • any documents amending, supplementing or superseding any of the above; • a document setting out the names and addresses of participating employers, if not in the above documents. Reference to (or text of) relevant provisions of Acts or statutory instruments set out or referred to in the above documents. English translation if necessary.	• Members, prospective members and their spouses or civil partners. • Beneficiaries. • Recognised trade unions. *Only information relevant to an individual need be disclosed to him or to his trade union.*	• Copy for inspection, free of charge at a place which is reasonable; or • Personal copy at a reasonable charge (i e cost of copying, postage & packaging) or, if publicly available, notice of where a copy may be obtained from.	On request, within two months[2] of the request being made.
BASIC INFORMATION ABOUT THE SCHEME (*Regulation 4* and *Schedule 1*,[3] *Disclosure Regulations*) (all schemes)			
Membership			
Categories of people who are eligible to be members and whether they are admitted: • only on their own application; or • automatically unless they request not to be admitted; or • subject to the consent of their employer.	• Members, prospective members and their spouses or civil partners. • Beneficiaries. • Recognised trade unions. [4]	No specified form but must include a written statement that further information is available, giving address to which inquiries should be sent.	As of course, to every prospective member or, if not practicable to do so, within two months[5] of his becoming a member.

To be disclosed	Disclosure to	Form of disclosure	When
The conditions of eligibility for membership. The period of notice (if any) which a member must give to terminate his pensionable service.[6] Whether and on what conditions (if any) a member may re-enter pensionable service before normal pension age.[7] **Contributions** How employers' contributions are determined. How members' normal contributions are determined. What arrangements are made for members to pay additional voluntary contributions.[9]	*Only information relevant to an individual need be disclosed to him or to his trade union.*		To the extent that any information has not been given to a person who was a member or pensioner on 5 April 1997, it must be given to that person by 5 April 1998 (or, in the case of a deferred member, within two months of him becoming a pensioner, if later).[8] Otherwise, on request, (unless the same information was provided in the twelve months prior to the request being made), as soon as practicable and in any event, within two months[10] of the date of receipt of request.

To be disclosed	Disclosure to	Form of disclosure	When
Scheme details			
Whether the scheme is a tax-approved scheme and, if not, whether an application for tax-approval has been made.[11]			Details of material changes must be drawn to attention of members and beneficiaries (but not excluded persons) before the change if practicable, but in any event, within three months[12] after the change.[13]
Which of the relevant employments are, and which are not, contracted-out.			
Whether the scheme is contracted-out for these employments by virtue of the *Pension Schemes Act 1993 (PSA 1993)*[14] or by being one to which regulations made under *section 149* of the *Pensions Act 1995 (PA 1995)* apply (mixed benefit contracted-out schemes).			
The short title of the enactment (if any) which provides for:			
• the setting up of the scheme;[15] and			
• the determination of the rate or amount of the benefits.[16]			

To be disclosed	Disclosure to	Form of disclosure	When
Benefits			
Normal pension age under the scheme (except simplified defined contribution schemes).[17]			
What benefits are payable and how they are calculated (including how pensionable earnings are defined and the rate at which benefits accrue and including, in a contracted-out money purchase or hybrid scheme, that the amount of assets allocated for the provision of protected rights benefits are increased, how they are increased and why that method is used).[18]			
The conditions on which benefits are paid.			
Whether and, if so, when and on what conditions, survivors' benefits are payable.			
Which benefits, if any, are payable only at some person's discretion.			
Whether there is a power under the scheme to increase pensions after they have become payable, and, if so, who may exercise it, and to what extent it is discretionary.			

To be disclosed	Disclosure to	Form of disclosure	When
Where the scheme is a hybrid scheme for contracting-out purposes, the circumstances in which the nature of a member's accrued rights may alter and a statement that the trustees will notify the member if his rights are affected.[19]			
Administration			
What arrangements are made, and in what circumstances, for estimates or statements of a guaranteed cash equivalent, for the refund of contributions and the preservation or transfer of the accrued rights of early leavers.			
Whether, and the circumstances in which, the trustees will accept cash equivalents and provide transfer credits and whether this is discretionary.			
If applicable, a statement to the effect that the trustees have directed that any cash equivalent shall not take into account discretionary benefits.			

To be disclosed	Disclosure to	Form of disclosure	When
A statement summarising the way in which transfer values are calculated. A statement that an annual report is available on request (except public sector schemes). *[Whether information about the scheme has been given to the Registrar of Occupational and Personal Pension Schemes].*[20] A statement that the following information is available on request: • Unless the scheme is exempt, what procedures it has for the internal resolution of disputes, including the address and job title of the person to be contacted. • A statement that the Pensions Regulator is available to assist in connection with queries and unresolved disputes and the address at which it may be contacted. • A statement that the Pensions Ombudsman may investigate and determine any complaint or dispute of fact or law in relation to an occupational pension scheme and the address at which he may be contacted.			

To be disclosed	Disclosure to	Form of disclosure	When
• A statement that the Pensions Regulator is able to intervene in the running of schemes where trustees, employers or other professional advisers have failed in their duties, and in certain other circumstances, and the address at which it may be contacted. • The address to which inquiries about the scheme generally or about an individual's entitlement to benefit should be sent. • The address to which inquiries about the scheme generally or, about an individual's entitlement to the benefit should be sent.			

To be disclosed	Disclosure to	Form of disclosure	When
INFORMATION TO BE MADE AVAILABLE TO INDIVIDUALS *(Regulation 5 and Schedule 2, Disclosure Regulations)* (all schemes)			
Pensions (all schemes)			
The amount of benefit which is payable and if a benefit is payable periodically: <ul><li>the conditions (if any) subject to which payment will be continued; and</li><li>the provisions (if any) under which the amount payable may be altered.</li></ul> The rights and options (if any) available on the death of a member or beneficiary, and the procedures for exercising them.	Any person to whom a benefit has become, or is about to become, payable.	Information plus written statement that further information is available, giving address to which inquiries should be sent.	As of course, before or within one month (two months where the person is retiring before normal pension age) after the date on which benefit becomes payable.[21]
If the amount of benefit is to be altered (other than under a provision already notified to the person concerned): <ul><li>the amount of benefit which is payable to the person; and</li><li>the rights and options (if any) available on the person's death and the procedures for exercising them.</li></ul>	Any person in receipt of a benefit.	Information plus written statement that further information is available, giving address to which inquiries should be sent.	As of course, before or within one month after the later of the date of the decision to make the alteration and the effective date of the alteration.[22]

773

To be disclosed	Disclosure to	Form of disclosure	When
Active members, deferred members and pension credit members: all schemes except money purchase schemes	Any member.	Information plus written statement that further information is available, giving the address to which inquiries should be sent.	On request (unless within twelve months of information being given following a similar request), as soon as practicable, and in any event within two months of the request.[24]
• in the case of an active member:			
– [24]the amounts of the member's and his survivors' benefits which would be payable (ignoring future salary increases) from normal pension age or death if his pensionable service were to terminate either (at the trustees' discretion) within one month of the date on which the information is given or on his normal pension age; and[25]			
– [26]the amount of any death in service benefits which would be payable if he died within one month of the date on which the information is given, with details of how those benefits are calculated (except simplified deferred contributions schemes).			
[27]• In the case of a deferred member, the date pensionable service ceased and the amounts of his own and his survivors' benefits payable from normal pension age or death.[28]			

To be disclosed	Disclosure to	Form of disclosure	When
• In either case the information must include: – date on which the member's pensionable service commenced; – the accrual rate or formula for calculating the member's own benefits and any survivors' benefits; – the amount of the member's pensionable remuneration on the relevant date (i e for an active member the date when the information is given or a date within a month thereof and for a deferred member, the date pensionable service ceased); and – details of how any deduction from benefits is calculated. • In the case of a pension credit member, the amounts of his own benefits and of any survivors' benefits payable from normal pension age or death. The information in respect of a pension credit member must include:			

To be disclosed	Disclosure to	Form of disclosure	When
– the method or formula for calculating the member's own benefits and any survivors' benefits; and – details of how any deduction from benefits is calculated. [29]**All members: money purchase schemes** In the case of a scheme which provides money purchase benefits (excluding stakeholder schemes): • the amount of contributions (before the making of any deductions) credited to the member during the preceding scheme year and, where the scheme is contracted-out, the contributions attributable to: – the minimum payments required to be made in respect of the member by his employer during the preceding year; – any rebate payments made by the DWP; – the age-related payments (if any) made by the DWP; and	Each member who is eligible for money purchase benefits (except excluded persons).	Information plus written statement that further information is available, giving address to which inquiries should be sent.	As of course, within twelve months of the end of each scheme year.[30]

776

To be disclosed	Disclosure to	Form of disclosure	When
– the date of birth used in determining the appropriate age-related percentage and name and address of whom to contact should the date of birth be incorrect. • in the case of a simplified defined contribution scheme,[31] the amount or fraction of contributions applied to insure death benefits; • the value of: – the member's protected rights as at a specified date; – the member's accrued rights (other than protected rights) at the same or another specified date; and – the cash equivalent of the member's rights, if different. • in the case of a pension credit member: – his safeguarded rights under the scheme as at a specified date; and – his accrued rights other than his safeguarded rights under the scheme at the same or another specified date; and			

To be disclosed	Disclosure to	Form of disclosure	When
– his cash equivalent if different. ● an illustration of the amount of the pension which would be likely to accrue to a member, or be capable of being secured by him at retirement in respect of his money purchase benefits that may arise under the scheme. The following statements must accompany the illustration: – that the information is provided only for the purposes of illustration; – that its provision is required by law; – how to obtain further information from the trustees that the information has been prepared by reference to the assumptions; – that certain general assumptions have been made about the nature of the investments and their likely performance; – that the amount referred to is expressed in today's prices;			

To be disclosed	Disclosure to	Form of disclosure	When
– that the actual amount of any pension under the scheme will depend on considerations which may differ from the assumptions made for the purpose of providing the illustration; – specifying any assumptions made in relation to future contributions to the scheme; – of the assumptions; – of the member's retirement date; and – of the illustration date used for the purpose of calculating the amount referred to in the illustration. **Hybrid schemes** Where a hybrid scheme is contracted-out and under the rules of the scheme an earner's service is contracted-out, employment will cease to qualify him for benefits under one part of the scheme but begin to qualify him for benefits under another part of the scheme: ● the date he begins to qualify for different benefits; and	Each member who ceases to qualify under one part of the scheme and begins to qualify for benefits under the other part of the scheme.	Information plus written statement that further information is available, giving address to which inquiries should be sent.	Within two months[32] after the date on which his service begins to qualify him for different benefits.

To be disclosed	Disclosure to	Form of disclosure	When
• the basis on which his rights accrued after that date will be contracted-out.			
Money purchase schemes			
Where a scheme is, or has been a money purchase scheme or provides money purchase benefits, the options available to the member within the scheme rules.	Each member and pension credit member who is eligible for money purchase benefits.	Information plus written statement that further information is available, giving address to which inquiries should be sent.	As of course, at least six months prior to normal pension age or date of retirement (or within seven days if less than six months until retirement).[33]
Money purchase schemes ceasing to contract out			
Where a scheme ceases to be a contracted-out money purchase scheme:	Each member who has ceased to be contracted-out.	Information plus written statement that further information is available, giving address to which inquiries should be sent.	In respect of the notification that the scheme has ceased to be contracted-out, as soon as practicable but in any event within one month[34] of the scheme ceasing to contract out.
In the case of a member other than a pension credit member: • the amount of contributions (before any deductions) credited to the member during the immediately preceding scheme year including contributions attributable to:			

To be disclosed	Disclosure to	Form of disclosure	When
– the minimum payments required to be made in respect of the member by his employer during the preceding year; – any rebate payments made by the DWP; – the age-related payments (if any) made by the DWP; and – the date of birth used in determining the appropriate age-related percentage and the name of whom to contact and their address should the date of birth be incorrect. In the case of a simplified defined contribution scheme, the amount or fraction of contributions applied to insure death benefits ● the value of: – the member's protected rights as at a specified date; – the member's accrued rights (excluding protected rights) as at the same or another specified date; – the cash equivalent of the member's rights, if different;			In respect of the other information, as soon as practicable and in any event within four months[35] of the scheme ceasing to contract out.

To be disclosed	Disclosure to	Form of disclosure	When
● the date on which the scheme ceased to be such a scheme; ● the options available in respect of protected rights; and Where a scheme ceases to be a contracted-out money purchase scheme: ● if the scheme is not able to meet its liabilities in full, an account of the amount by which accrued rights, safeguarded rights and protected rights have been reduced, and of the action taken by the scheme, or which is open to the member to take, to restore their value. In the case of a pension credit member: ● the value of the pension credit member's safeguarded rights under the scheme as at a specified date; and ● the value of the pension credit member's accrued rights (other than his safeguarded rights under the scheme at the same or another specified date); and ● his cash equivalent if different.			

To be disclosed	Disclosure to	Form of disclosure	When
Contingent beneficiaries (all schemes) Where a member or beneficiary has died: ● the rights and options (if any) available to the contingent beneficiary, and the procedures for exercising them; and ● the provisions under which any contingent pension may or will be increased, and the extent to which such increases are discretionary or a statement that there are no such provisions.	Any contingent beneficiary who is at least 18 and whose address is known to the trustees. Personal representative of the deceased or any person entitled to act on behalf of the contingent beneficiary.	Information plus written statement that further information is available, giving address to which inquiries should be sent.	As of course, as soon as practicable and in any event within two months[36] of trustees receiving notification of the death. On request (unless within three years of information being given to same person in same capacity), as soon as practicable and in any event within two months[37] of request being made.
Transfers (all schemes) Whether the member or prospective member is entitled to acquire transfer credits in exchange for a cash equivalent or other transfer payment provided by another scheme, and if so, a statement of those transfer credits.	Any member or prospective member.	Information plus written statement that further information is available, giving address to which inquiries should be sent.	On request (unless within twelve months of information being given following a similar request) within two months[38] of request.

To be disclosed	Disclosure to	Form of disclosure	When
Winding-up (all schemes)			
Where, after 5 April 1997,[39] trustees have commenced winding-up the scheme or a section of a multi-employer scheme which is to be treated as a separate scheme: ● notification of name and address of a person to whom further inquiries about the scheme can be made; ● notification of the winding-up and the reasons for it and the name and address of a person to whom any further inquiries about the scheme should be sent; ● notification of whether death benefits will continue to be payable; ● if the independent trustee requirements apply, notification that at least one of the trustees is required to be an independent person;	All members, all persons entitled to a pension credit and beneficiaries (except excluded persons) (but only active members in relation to the second point).	Information plus written statement that further information is available, giving address to which inquiries should be sent.	As of course, as soon as practicable and in any event within one month[40] of the winding-up trigger. In addition, in the case of the final point, at least once in every successive 12 month period until the completion of the winding-up.

784

To be disclosed	Disclosure to	Form of disclosure	When
• what action is being taken to establish the scheme's liabilities and to recover any assets; when it is anticipated final details will be known; and (where the trustees have sufficient information) an indication of the extent to which, the actuarial value of accrued rights are likely to be reduced.			
Where, before 6 April 1997, trustees have commenced winding-up the scheme or a section of a multi-employer scheme which is to be treated as a separate scheme: • what action is being taken to establish the scheme's liabilities and to recover any assets; • when it is anticipated final details will be known; and • (when the trustees have sufficient information) an indication of the extent to which the actuarial value of accrued rights is likely to be reduced.[41]	All members and beneficiaries (except excluded persons).[42]	Information plus written statement that further information is available giving address to which inquiries should be sent.	At least once in every successive twelve-month period beginning with the date of commencement of the winding-up and ending with the date of the completion of the winding-up.[43]

785

To be disclosed	Disclosure to	Form of disclosure	When
Where trustees are engaged in winding-up the scheme or a section of a multi-employer scheme which is to be treated as a separate scheme: ● the amount of benefit which is payable to the person; ● if a benefit is payable periodically: – the provisions (if any) under which the amount payable may be altered; – the conditions (if any) subject to which payment will be continued; ● (except in the case of money purchase schemes) if the member is not entitled to payment of benefits an estimate of amount of the member's own benefits and of his survivors' benefits which are expected to be payable from normal pension age or death; ● notification of: – whether, and if so by how much, the benefits are reduced because of insufficient scheme resources;	Every beneficiary and every member who is entitled to payment of benefits (except excluded persons).[44]	Information plus written statement that further information is available, giving address to which inquiries should be sent.	As soon as practicable and in any event within three months the trustees having discharged their liabilities.[45]

To be disclosed	Disclosure to	Form of disclosure	When
– who has or will become liable to pay benefits after scheme is wound up. Where a report has been made by the trustees or managers of the scheme to the Regulator under *section 72A of PA 1995* a copy of the report must contain the following: • name of scheme; • date on which winding-up commenced; • scheme registration number; • statement as to the nature of the benefits provided by the scheme; • statement as to whether an independent trustee has been appointed; • name and address of scheme actuary (if relevant); • name and address of any third party administrator; • estimate of when winding-up will be completed;	Any member or beneficiary who requests a copy.	Written report.	Within two months[46] of the request.

787

To be disclosed	Disclosure to	Form of disclosure	When
• statement as to what steps have been taken in the winding-up, what steps remain and when each step is estimated to be completed; • a statement as to whether any particular difficulties are hindering the winding-up.			
Stakeholder pensions			
Where stakeholder scheme is removed from the register of such schemes: • notification of that fact and of the fact that it is required to commence winding-up under the rules.	Every member (except excluded persons).	Information plus written statement that further information is available giving address to which inquiries should be sent.	Within two weeks[47] of being notified of the removal from the register.
Scheme funding			
[48]Where the scheme is one to which *Part 3 of the Pensions Act 2004 (PA 2004)* applies and a valuation under *section 224* has been obtained: • summary funding statement.	All members and beneficiaries (except excluded persons)		Within a reasonable period after the date by which the trustees are required to ensure that the valuation or report is received by them.

To be disclosed	Disclosure to	Form of disclosure	When
AVAILABILITY AND CONTENT OF ANNUAL REPORT (*Regulation 6 and Schedule 3,*[49] *Disclosure Regulations*) (*all schemes except certain public sector schemes* (*Regulation 6(2)*))			
A document which contains: <ul><li>the audited accounts and the auditor's statement required under *section 41 of PA 1995*[50] for the scheme year to which the document relates;</li><li>the latest actuarial statement given under *section 41 of PA 1995*;[51]</li><li>the latest annual certificate obtained in accordance with the *Occupational Pension Schemes (Minimum Funding Requirement and Actuarial Valuations) Regulations 1996 (SI 1996 No 1536)*;</li><li>the names of the persons, including the directors of any sole trustee company, who were trustees during the relevant year;</li><li>the provisions of the scheme (or articles of association in the case of a sole trustee company) in relation to appointing and removing trustees (or directors of the sole trustee company);</li></ul>	<ul><li>Members and prospective members and their spouses or civil partners.</li><li>Beneficiaries.</li><li>Recognised trade unions.[52]</li></ul>	<ul><li>Personal copy of latest report/information free of charge (on first request) plus written statement that further information is available, giving address to which inquiries should be sent;</li><li>Copies of reports/information for previous five years available: – for inspection (free of charge) at a place that is reasonable; or – personal copy (at a reasonable charge), plus written statement that further information is available, giving address to which inquiries should be sent.</li></ul>	To be available within seven months of end of each scheme year which ends after 6 April 1997 and to be provided within two months of request.[53]

To be disclosed	Disclosure to	Form of disclosure	When
• the names of the professional advisers and others who have acted for the trustees during the year, with an indication of any change since the previous year; • the address to which inquiries about the scheme generally or about an individual's entitlement to benefit should be sent; • the number of active, deferred and pensioner members and beneficiaries as at any one date during the scheme year; • except in a money purchase scheme, the percentage increases made during the year to pensions in payment and deferred pensions and a statement of the extent to which they are discretionary (if variable for different individuals, state the maximum, minimum and average); • (except in the case of insured money purchase scheme) a statement, where applicable, explaining:			

790

To be disclosed	Disclosure to	Form of disclosure	When
– why any cash equivalents paid during the year were not calculated and verified in accordance with legislative requirements; – why cash equivalents paid during the year were less than the amount for which legislation provides and when full values were or will be available; and – whether, and if so how, discretionary benefits are included in the calculation of transfer values; • a statement as to whether the accounts have been prepared and audited in accordance with *section 41* of *PA 1995* (unless exempt), and if not, the reasons why not, and a statement as to how the situation has been or is likely to be resolved; • details of who has managed the investments during the year and the extent of any delegation by the trustees;			

791

To be disclosed	Disclosure to	Form of disclosure	When
• confirmation of whether the trustees have produced a statement of investment principles in accordance with *section 35* of *PA 1995* (unless exempt), advising that a copy is available on request; • a statement as to the trustees' policy on the custody of the scheme's assets (except in relation to a wholly insured scheme); • unless exempt from the requirement to produce a statement of investment principles, an investment report containing: – a statement by the trustees, or fund manager, providing details of any investments which were not made in accordance with the statement of investment principles, giving the reasons why and explaining what action, if any, has been or will be taken to resolve the position;			

792

To be disclosed	Disclosure to	Form of disclosure	When
– a review of the investment performance during the year and a period of between three and five years ending with the year, including an assessment of the nature, disposition, marketability, security and valuation of the scheme's assets; ● a copy of any statement made on the resignation or removal of the auditor or actuary; ● where the scheme has employer-related investments a statement: – as to a percentage of the scheme's resources so invested; – if that percentage exceeds 5%, as to the percentage of the scheme's resources which are not subject to the statutory restrictions; and – if the statutory restriction on employer-related investments is exceeded, the steps taken (or to be taken) to secure compliance, and when those steps will be taken.			

To be disclosed	Disclosure to	Form of disclosure	When
NB Reference to reports/information in relation to a scheme year ending before 6 April 1997 are deemed to include references to copies of documents made available under regulation 9 of the Occupational Pension Schemes (Disclosure of Information) Regulations 1986 (SI 1986 No 1046).[54]			

AVAILABILITY OF ACTUARIAL VALUATION, SCHEDULE OF CONTRIBUTIONS, PAYMENT SCHEDULE AND STATEMENT OF INVESTMENT PRINCIPLES (*Regulation 7, Disclosure Regulations*) (**Public service schemes are exempt**)

To be disclosed	Disclosure to	Form of disclosure	When
Latest actuarial valuation required under: • *section 41(1)* and *(2)(c)* of *PA 1995;* • *section 57(1)(a)* of *PA 1995,* if appropriate.[55] Schedule of contributions or payment schedule required under *section 58*[56] or *87* of *PA 1995,* if appropriate.[57] Latest statement of principles governing decisions about investment required under *section 35* of *PA 1995*.	• Members, prospective members and their spouses or civil partners. • Beneficiaries. • Recognised trade unions.	• Copy for inspection, free of charge at a place which is reasonable. • Personal copy at reasonable charge. Document must be accompanied by a written statement that further information is available, giving address to which inquiries should be sent.	On request, within two months[58] of the request being made.

To be disclosed	Disclosure to	Form of disclosure	When
LIMITED DISCLOSURE IN RELATION TO UNAPPROVED SCHEMES (*Regulation 8 and Schedule 1,*[59] *Disclosure Regulations*) (all schemes other than public sector schemes[60])			
• What benefits are payable under the scheme and how they are calculated (including how pensionable earnings are defined and the rate at which benefits accrue). • What arrangements are made and in what circumstances for estimates of cash equivalents, statements of entitlement to guaranteed cash equivalents, refunds to contributions and preservation or transfer of accrued rights in relation to early leavers.[61] [• *Whether information about the scheme has been given to the Registrar of Occupational and Personal Pension Schemes.*[62]] • What procedures the scheme has for the internal resolution of disputes and the address and job title of the person to be contacted in order to have recourse to these.	• Members. • Prospective members. • Recognised trade unions. *Only information relevant to an individual need be disclosed to his trade union.*	Written statement that further information is available, giving address to which inquiries should be sent.	As of course, to every prospective member and, where not practical, to a person within two months of his becoming a member.[63]

795

To be disclosed	Disclosure to	Form of disclosure	When
● A statement that the Occupational Pensions Advisory Service is available at any time to assist members and beneficiaries of the scheme in connection with pension queries and the resolution of disputes and the address at which OPAS may be contacted. ● A statement that the Pensions Ombudsman may investigate and determine any complaint of fact or law in relation to an occupational pension scheme and the address at which he may be contacted. ● A statement that the Regulator is able to intervene in the running of schemes where trustees, employers or professional advisers have failed in their duties and the address at which it may be contacted. ● The address to which inquiries about the scheme generally or about an individual's entitlement to benefit should be sent. ● A statement as to which of the benefits are and which are not funded and, where benefits are funded, the manner in which they are secured.			

To be disclosed	Disclosure to	Form of disclosure	When
• A statement that the provisions of *PA 1995* are not applicable to the scheme (subject to certain exceptions).			
INFORMATION TO BE FURNISHED TO EARLY LEAVERS (*Regulation 27A of the Occupational Pension Schemes (Preservation of Benefit) Regulations 1991*) (*SI 1991 No 167*) (all schemes)			
Any information relating to the rights and options available to a member whose pensionable service terminates before he attains normal pension age.	Any member or prospective member.	To be furnished in writing.	As soon as practicable and, in any event, within two months of the request being made (unless within twelve months of information being given following a similar request).
	Any deferred member.	To be furnished in writing.	As of course, as soon as practicable and, in any event, within two months of notification of termination of pensionable service.
Information whether a refund of contributions is, or would be, available in any circumstances together with an estimate of the amount of the refund and an explanation of the method of calculation.	Any person who has paid contributions to the scheme (which have not already been refunded).	To be furnished in writing.	As soon as practicable and, in any event, within two months after request (unless he has already been told that there will be no refund or the request is within twelve months of information being given following a similar request).

797

To be disclosed	Disclosure to	Form of disclosure	When
TRANSFER OF MEMBER'S ACCRUED RIGHTS WITHOUT CONSENT (*Regulation 12(4B)* **of the** *Occupational Pension Schemes* (*Preservation of Benefit*) *Regulations 1991*) (*SI 1991 No 167*) (**all schemes**)			
Information about the proposed transfer and details of the value of the rights to be transferred including rights in respect of death in service benefits and survivors' benefits.	Those members being transferred.	In writing.	Not less than one month before the proposed transfer is due to take place.
CASH EQUIVALENTS AND TRANSFER VALUES (*Regulation 11* **and** *Schedule 1* **of the** *Occupational Pension Schemes* (*Transfer Values*) *Regulations 1996* (*SI 1996 No 1847*)) (**all schemes**)			
The 'Schedule 1 Information', ie: Whether a cash equivalent is available or would be available if pensionable service were to terminate and, if so: ● an estimate of the amount and date used for basis of calculation; ● the accrued rights to which it relates; ● whether any part of the estimated part of the cash equivalent is attributable to additional benefits awarded at the discretion of the trustees or which will be awarded if their established custom continues unaltered;	Active members of any scheme. Deferred members of a money purchase scheme.	To be provided by the trustees in writing.	As soon as practicable and, in any event, within three months of the member's request (such request not being one made less than twelve months since the last occasion when the information was provided).

To be disclosed	Disclosure to	Form of disclosure	When
● if appropriate, a *Regulation 8(2)* statement indicating that calculation of the estimated cash equivalent does not take account of discretionary benefits and a statement that the trustees must get the actuary's written report (which must be available to the member) before including such liabilities.			
● Notification of any reduction of the member's cash equivalent including: – the reasons for and the amount of the reduction; – an estimate of the date (if any) by which an unreduced cash equivalent will be available; – a statement of the member's right to obtain further estimates; – a statement explaining that the member has a further three months from the date on which the member was informed of the reduction to make an application to take the cash equivalent as reduced.			

799

To be disclosed	Disclosure to	Form of disclosure	When
Whether any transfer value is available or would be so available if the member's pensionable service were to terminate and if so: • an estimate of its amount; • the accrued rights to which it relates; • whether any part of the estimated amount of the transfer value is attributable to additional benefits (wholly or only to part) which have been or will be awarded at the discretion of the trustees; – if the estimated amount of the transfer value has been reduced to an amount which is less than it otherwise would be because of an actuary's opinion that the scheme's assets are insufficient to meet its liabilities in full, then a statement of that fact and an explanation and an estimate of the date (if any) by which it will be possible to make available a transfer value the amount of which is not so reduced, and a statement of the member's rights to obtain further estimates.			

To be disclosed	Disclosure to	Form of disclosure	When
A copy of the actuary's written report (where the trustees of a scheme have directed that discretionary benefits will not be included in the calculation of cash equivalents).	Any active or deferred member of any scheme.	A copy of the written report to be sent to the member.	Within one month of that member's request.
The statement of entitlement to a guaranteed cash equivalent shall be accompanied by: ● 'Schedule 1 Information' in relation to any cash equivalent of or transfer value in relation to the member's money purchase benefits (if any) under the scheme calculated by reference to the guarantee date; ● A statement as to: – where the trustees have given a direction indicating that the cash equivalent does not take account of discretionary benefits, indication that the trustees have been obliged to obtain the actuary's written report (of which the member can request a copy) before excluding such benefits from the calculation of the cash equivalent;	An active or deferred member whose membership has terminated at least one year before normal retirement age.	Statement/report in writing.	Within a period of ten working days after the 'guarantee date' (which must be within a period of three months beginning with the date of the member's application).

801

To be disclosed	Disclosure to	Form of disclosure	When
– whether, for what reasons and by what amount the member's cash equivalent has been reduced as well as the paragraph of *regulation 8* which has been relied upon, together with an estimate of the date by which it will be possible to make available a guaranteed cash equivalent which is not so reduced; – the terms and effect of *regulation 6(3)* (no right to make an application for a guaranteed statement of entitlement within twelve months of the last application); – an explanation of the member's right to take the guaranteed cash equivalent and the need for that member to submit a written application to do so within three months beginning on the guarantee date; – an explanation that in exceptional circumstances the guaranteed cash equivalent may be reduced and that member will be so informed if that is the case.			

To be disclosed	Disclosure to	Form of disclosure	When
● Notification of any member's reduction or increase in guaranteed cash equivalent under *regulation 9* including: – the reasons for and the amount of the reduction/increase; – *[an estimate of the date (if any) by which an unreduced guaranteed cash equivalent will be available;]* – indication of the paragraph of *regulation 9* which has been relied upon; – a statement explaining that the member has a further three months from the date on which the member was informed of the reduction/increase to make a written application to take the guaranteed cash equivalent as reduced/increase].	Relevant member.	In writing.	Within ten days of reduction/increase (excluding weekends, Christmas Day, New Year's Day and Good Friday).

803

To be disclosed	Disclosure to	Form of disclosure	When
WINDING-UP (*Regulation 11 of the Occupational Pension Schemes (Winding Up) Regulations 1996 (SI 1996 No 3126) (all schemes)*			
Details of any determination made: • to defer winding-up the scheme; • as to the time when the priorities into which the liability in respect of any person falls under *section 73(4)* of *PA 1995* is fixed; or • as to the time when the amounts or descriptions of liabilities of the scheme are to be determined for the purposes of any rule of the scheme setting out the scheme's winding-up priorities.	The members of the scheme. Any other person whose entitlement to payment of a pension or any other benefit under the scheme has arisen.	In writing.	Within one month of the date that the determination is made.
MODIFICATION ON WINDING-UP (*Section 71A of PA 1995 and regulation 8 of the Occupational Pension Schemes (Winding Up Notices and Reports etc) Regulations 2002 (SI 2002 No 459)*)			
Where the trustees or managers make an application to the Pensions Regulator to modify the scheme in accordance with *section 71A of PA 1995*, a notice setting out: For all recipients: (a) the modification requested; (b) the effects, if any, which the modification would or might have:	Members for whom they have a current address. The insolvency practitioner (if the modification would reduce the value of the assets which might otherwise be distributed to the employer on the winding-up) or, as the case may be, the official receivers.	In writing.	Before the trustees or manager make the application to the Pensions Regulator.

To be disclosed	Disclosure to	Form of disclosure	When
(i) on benefits under the scheme that are in payment at the time of the application, and (ii) on benefits under it which are or may be payable at a later time; (c) the reason for requesting the modification. For the insolvency practitioner: (d) the date of the notice; (e) whether any previous application has been made to the court or to the Pensions Regulator for an order to make the modification requested by the application or any similar modification (only to be included in notice to insolvency practitioner).			
BASIC INFORMATION ABOUT PENSIONS AND DIVORCE (*Regulation 2 of the Pensions on Divorce etc (Provision of Information) Regulations 2000 (SI 2000 No 1048)*)			
• A valuation of pension rights or benefits accrued under the member's pension arrangement not available to the spouse or civil partner of the member.	Member. Member's spouse or civil partner. Court.		• On request within three months beginning with the date the trustees receive the request or order for the provision of information; or

To be disclosed	Disclosure to	Form of disclosure	When
• A statement that on the member's request or pursuant to a court order a valuation of pension rights or benefits will be provided to the member or the court.			• Within six weeks if the member has notified the trustees on the date of the request or order that the information is needed in connection with proceedings commenced under any of the provisions referred to in *section 23(1)(a) of WRPA 1999;* or
• A statement summarising the way in which the valuation is calculated.			• Within such shorter period as the court may specify; or
• The pension benefits which are included in the valuation. • Whether the trustees offer membership to a person entitled to a pension credit and, if so, the types of benefit available. • Whether the trustees intend to discharge their liability for a pension credit other than by offering membership. • A schedule of charges which will apply.			• If the request does not include a request for a valuation or if the member's spouse or civil partner requests the information under *regulation 2(3) of the Pensions on Divorce etc (Provision of Information) Regulations 2000,* within one month of the date of receipt of the request or court order.

To be disclosed	Disclosure to	Form of disclosure	When
• Any other information relevant to any power relating to matters specified in *section 23(1)(a)* of the *Welfare Reform and Pensions Act 1999 (WRPA 1999)* and which is not specified in *Schedule 1 or 2* to the *Occupational Pension Schemes (Disclosure of Information) Regulations 1996 (SI 1996 No 1655)* or *Schedule 1 or 2* of the *Personal Pension Schemes (Disclosure of Information) Regulations 1987 (SI 1987 No 1110)* (available to the court only). At the same time as providing the information set out above, the trustees may supply information specified in *regulation 4 of the Pensions on Divorce etc (Provision of Information) Regulations 2000 (SI 2000 No 1048)*.			

To be disclosed	Disclosure to	Form of disclosure	When
DIVORCE (*Regulation 4 of the Pensions on Divorce etc (Provision of Information) Regulations 2000 (SI 2000 No 1048)) (all schemes*)			
● The full name of the pension arrangement and address to which any order or provision should be sent. ● In the case of an occupational pension scheme whether the scheme is winding-up and, if so, the date of commencement of the winding-up and the name and address of the trustees who are dealing with the winding-up. ● In the case of an occupational pension scheme whether a cash equivalent of the member's rights would be reduced if calculated on the date the trustees received notification that a pension sharing order or provision may be made. ● Whether the person responsible for the pension arrangement is aware of the member's rights being subject to any of the following and, if so, to specify which: – any order or provision specified in *section 28(1) of WRPA 1999;*	To the member or the court.		Within 21 days of the date when the trustees received notification that a Pension Sharing Order or provision may be made or if later a date set by the court or, if the court has specified a date which is more than 21 days, by that date.

To be disclosed	Disclosure to	Form of disclosure	When
– an order under *section 23* of the *Matrimonial Causes Act 1973* (so far as it includes provision made by virtue of *section 25B* or *25C* of that Act);			
– an order under *section 12A(2) or (3)* of the *Family Law (Scotland) Act 1985* which relates to benefits or future benefits to which the member is entitled under the pension arrangement;			
– an order under *article 25* of the *Matrimonial Causes (Northern Ireland) Order 1978* so far as it includes provision made by virtue of *article 27B* or *27C* of that order;			
– a forfeiture order;			
– a bankruptcy order;			
– An order of sequestration on a member's estate or the making of an appointment on his estate of a judicial factor under *section 41* of the *Solicitors (Scotland) Act 1980*.			

809

To be disclosed	Disclosure to	Form of disclosure	When
● Whether the member's rights under the pension arrangement include any rights which are not shareable.			
● If not provided previously, whether the trustees require any charges to be paid and, if so, whether prior to the commencement of the implementation period those are required to be paid in full, or the proportion which is required.			
● Whether the trustees may levy additional charges and, if so, the scale which is likely to be charged.			
● Whether the member is a trustee of the pension arrangement.			
● Whether the trustees may request information about the member's state of health if a pension sharing order or provision were made.			
● Whether the trustees require information in addition to that specified in *regulation 5* of the *Pensions on Divorce etc (Provision of Information) Regulations 2000* in order to implement the pension sharing order or provision.			

PROVISION OF INFORMATION AFTER THE DEATH OF THE PERSON ENTITLED TO THE PENSION CREDIT
(*Regulation 6 of the Pensions on Divorce etc (Provision of Information) Regulations 2000 (SI 2000 No 1048)*)

To be disclosed	Disclosure to	Form of disclosure	When
Where the person entitled to the pension credit dies before the trustees have discharged their liability, the trustees must notify relevant persons: • how the trustees intend to discharge their liability; • whether the trustees intend to recover charges and, if so, a schedule of those charges; • a list of any further information required in order to discharge the order.	Any person whom the trustees consider should be notified.	In writing.	Within 21 days of receipt of the notification of death.

811

To be disclosed	Disclosure to	Form of disclosure	When
PROVISION OF INFORMATION AFTER RECEIVING A PENSION SHARING ORDER (*Regulation 7 of the Pensions on Divorce etc* (*Provision of Information*) *Regulations 2000* (*SI 2000 No 1048*))			
On receipt of a pension sharing order or a provision: ● a notice of charges; ● a list of information relating to the transferor or the transferee or (where *regulation 6(1) of the Pensions on Divorce etc* (*Provision of Information*) *Regulations 2000* applies a person other than the person entitled to the pension credit, which has been requested already, which the trustees need or which remains outstanding; ● a notice of implementation; or ● a statement of why the trustees are unable to implement the pension sharing order or agreement.	The transferor or transferee or where *regulation 6(1) of the Pensions on Divorce etc* (*Provision of Information*) *Regulations 2000* applies to the person other than the person entitled to the pension credit (referred to in *regulation 6 of the Pension Sharing* (*Implementation and Discharge of Liability*) *Regulations* (*SI 2000 No 1053*).	In writing.	Within 21 days of receipt of the pension sharing order or provision or, in the case of a notice of implementation, the later of the days specified in *section 34(1)(a) and (b)* of *WRPA 1999.*

To be disclosed	Disclosure to	Form of disclosure	When
PROVISION OF INFORMATION AFTER IIMPLEMENTATION OF AN ORDER (*Regulation 8* of the *Pensions on Divorce etc* (*Provision of Information*) *Regulations 2000* (*SI 2000 No 1048*))			
Notice of discharge of liability including: (*where the transferor's pension is not in payment*) • the value of the transferor's accrued rights on a cash equivalent basis; • the value of the pension debit; • the amount deducted by way of charges; • the value of the transferor's rights after the deductions of the pension debit and charges; • the transfer day; **OR** (*where the transferor's pension is in payment*) • the value of the transferor's benefits on a cash equivalent basis; • the value of the pension debit; • the amount of the pension which was in payment before the pension credit liability was discharged;	Transferor or transferee or the person entitled to the pension credit by virtue of *regulation 6* of the *Pension Sharing* (*Implementation and Discharge of Liability*) *Regulations* (*SI 2000 No 1053*).		Within 21 days of the date of discharge of the pension credit.

813

To be disclosed	Disclosure to	Form of disclosure	When
● the amount of pension payable following the deduction of the pension debit; ● the transfer day; ● the amount of any unpaid charges; ● how those charges will be recovered; **OR** *(in the case of a transferee whose pension is not in payment and who will become a member)* ● the value of the pension credit; ● the amount deducted by way of charges; ● the value of the pension credit after deduction of charges; ● the transfer day; ● any periodical charges to be made including when and how those charges will be recovered;			

814

To be disclosed	Disclosure to	Form of disclosure	When
• information concerning membership of the pension arrangement which is relevant to the transferee; **OR** *(in the case of the transferee who is transferring his pension credit rights out of the pension arrangement from which those rights were derived)* • the value of the pension credit; • the amount of any charges deducted; • the value of the pension credit after the deduction; • the transfer day; • details of the pension arrangement including its name, address, reference number, telephone number and where available the business facsimile number and e-mail address to which the pension credit has been transferred: **OR** *(in the case of a transferee who has reached normal benefit age on the transfer day and whose pension credit liability has been discharged)* • the amount of pension credit benefit to be paid to the transferee;			

To be disclosed	Disclosure to	Form of disclosure	When
• the date when the pension credit benefit is to be paid to the transferee; • the transfer date; • details of any unpaid charges and how those charges will be recovered; **OR** *(in the case of a person entitled to the pension credit by virtue of regulation 6 of the Pension Sharing (Implementation and Discharge of Liability) Regulations (SI 2000 No 1053))* • the value of the pension credit rights; • any amount deducted by way of charges; • the value of the pension credit after deduction of charges; • the transfer day; • details of any unpaid charges, including how and when those charges will be recovered.			

To be disclosed	Disclosure to	Form of disclosure	When
PROVISION OF INFORMATION AFTER RECEPT OF AN EARMARKING ORDER (*Regulation 10 of the Pensions on Divorce etc* (*Provision of Information*) *Regulations 2000* (*SI 2000 No 1048*)) (*all schemes*)			
• If a member's pension is not in payment, a list of circumstances in respect of any changes which the member or spouse or civil partner must notify to the trustees. • (except in Scotland) If the order is made in respect of a member whose pension is in payment the notice will include: – the value of the pension rights or benefit of the member; – the amount of the member's pension after implementation of the order; – the first date when a pension pursuant to the order is to be made; – a list of the circumstances which the member and spouse or civil partner must notify to the trustees; – (to member only) the amount of the member's pension currently in payment and the amount of the member's pension after the order has been implerrented.	• Member. • Spouse or civil partner.	Notice in writing.	Within 21 days of receipt of the order.

817

Appendix II

To be disclosed	Disclosure to	Form of disclosure	When
• In any event: – the amount of any charges not yet paid by the member or spouse or civil partner in respect of the provision of information and how those charges will be recovered including the date when payment is required in whole or in part, the sums payable by the member and spouse or civil partner respectively and whether the sum will be deducted from payments of pension to the member or from payments for the spouse or civil partner.			

To be disclosed	Disclosure to	Form of disclosure	When
INFORMATION ABOUT PENSIONS AND DIVORCE AND DISSOLUTION OF A CIVIL PARTNERSHIP: VALUATION OF PENSION BENEFITS (*Regulation 3 of the Pensions on Divorce etc* (*Provision of Information*) *Regulations 2000* (*SI 2000 No 1048*))			
Information set out in *regulation 11* and *Schedule 1* to the *Occupational Pension Schemes* (*Transfer Values*) *Regulations 1996* (*SI 1996 No 1847*).	Any member.	In writing.	[*Within ten working days after the 'valuation date' elected by the trustees and upon the request of the member as petitioner or respondent in proceedings for divorce, nullity of marriage or judicial separation or dissolution of the civil partnership or upon request by the court.*]
DISCLOSURE OF INFORMATION TO MEMBERS (*Regulation 18 of the Stakeholder Pension Schemes Regulations 2000* (*SI 2000 No 1403*)) (all schemes)			
For as far as that information relates to that statement year or to the part of that statement year beginning with the first day of that statement year (whether or not that day is earlier than the day on which he becomes a member) and ending with the time at which he so ceases:	Member for all or part of a statement year.	In writing.	Within three months of the end of that statement year or where he ceases during that statement year to be a member, or from the time he ceases to be a member to within three months of the end of that statement year.

To be disclosed	Disclosure to	Form of disclosure	When
• the value of the member's rights under the scheme on the day before the first day of the statement year, being an amount which is not less than the cash equivalent of those rights on that date; • the value of the member's rights on the last day of the statement year, being an amount which is not less than the cash equivalent of those rights on that day or where he ceases during the statement year to be a member, at the time immediately prior to the time at which he so ceases, being an amount which is not less than the cash equivalent of those rights at the time immediately prior to the time at which he so ceases (and the amount of the value that is attributable to investment gains or losses made or sustained); • the amount of each contribution made by or on behalf of the member and the date on which it was received; • the amount of each contribution made by any employer and the date on which it was received;			

To be disclosed	Disclosure to	Form of disclosure	When
● except where contributions referred to in sub-paragraphs (d) and (e) are increased by the trustees or manager in anticipation of a payment to the scheme by the Inland Revenue by way of tax relief in respect of the member, the amount of each such payment by the Inland Revenue and the date on which it was received; ● the amount of each payment to the scheme by way of minimum contributions in respect of the member and the date on which it was received; ● the amount of each payment made to the scheme by way of minimum payments in respect of the member and the date on which it was received; ● the amount of each payment made to the scheme under *section 42A(3)* of *PSA 1993* in respect of the member and the date on which it was received; ● the amount of any transfer payment made to the scheme in respect of the member, the name of the scheme or arrangement from which the payment was made and the date on which it was made;			

To be disclosed	Disclosure to	Form of disclosure	When
• any amount credited to the member's account in respect of a credit within the meaning of *section 29* (pension sharing: creation of pension debits and credits); • any reduction under *section 31* (pension sharing: reduction of benefit), or any enactment in force in Northern Ireland corresponding to that section, in the benefits or future benefits to which the member is entitled under the scheme; • any contributions refunded under the provisions of *Chapter IV* of *Part XIV* of the *Income and Corporation Taxes Act 1988* (pension schemes, social security benefits, life annuities etc); • any amount paid to the member in accordance with *section 634A* of the *Income and Corporation Taxes Act 1988* (income withdrawals by member) or *section 636A* of that Act (income withdrawal after death of member);			

To be disclosed	Disclosure to	Form of disclosure	When
● any other amount deducted from the member's account, the nature of the deduction and the date on which it was made; ● the total amount of any part of any of the contributions and payments which has not been credited to the member's account and the manner in which that amount has been used; ● the member's date of birth used in determining the appropriate age-related percentage for the purposes of *section 42A of PSA 1993* and the name and address of whom to contact should that date be incorrect; ● where the whole or any part of the member's rights under the scheme is represented by rights in a with-profits fund; ● the principles adopted in allocating rights under that fund, including the extent of any smoothing of investment returns and the levels of any guarantees, and			

To be disclosed	Disclosure to	Form of disclosure	When
• in relation to any reduction relating to the reduction of members' rights, the rate, expressed as an annual percentage rate, at which, and the period in relation to which, deductions giving rise to that reduction were made, or where such deductions were made in relation to different periods at different rates; • each rate, expressed as an annual percentage rate, at which those deductions were made; and • the period in relation to which they were made at that rate.			
DISCLOSURE REQUIREMENTS AND PENALTIES *(Regulation 13 of the Occupational Pension Schemes (Independent Trustee) Regulations 2005 (SI 2005 No 703))*			
The trustee and the independent trustee must provide: • their name and address; • the scale of fees chargeable; • details of amounts charged to the scheme by the trustees in the past twelve months.	Every member and or relevant trade union (in relation to the first point, as of course, within a reasonable period of appointment). Every member, prospective member or relevant trade union (in relation to all three points).	In writing.	As of course, within a reasonable period of appointment. On request (unless the same information was provided to the same person or trade union in the twelve months prior to the request being made).

To be disclosed	Disclosure to	Form of disclosure	When
NOTIFICATION OF RIGHT TO CASH TRANSFER SUM OR CONTRIBUTION REFUND *(section 264 of PA 2004, inserting section 101AC into PSA 1993)*			
Information adequate to explain the nature of the right acquired by him and how he may exercise the right and such other information as may be prescribed. The statement must specify, in particular in relation to the cash transfer sum to which the member acquires a right, its amount and the permitted ways in which the member can use it, the amount of the contribution refund to which the member so acquires a right, and the last day on which the member may exercise the right.	A member whose pensionable service has terminated.	A statement in writing.	Within a reasonable period after the termination.

825

To be disclosed	Disclosure to	Form of disclosure	When
INFORMATION AND CONSULTATION OF EMPLOYEES (*Information and Consultation of Employees Regulations 2004* (*SI 2004 No 3426*))			
Provision of information on decisions likely to lead to substantial changes in work organisation or in contractual relations, e g introduction of, or a change to, compulsory retirement age or changes to an occupational pension scheme but only where there was a contractual right to participate in the scheme.	Employees in organisations with 150 or more from 6 April 2005, with 100 or more from 6 April 2007 and with 50 or more from 6 April 2008.	Ensure that the method and content of the consultation are appropriate. Consult on the basis of the information supplied to the information and consultation representatives and in such a way as to enable the information and consultation representatives to meet the employer at the relevant level of management depending on the subject under discussion and to obtain a reasoned response from the employer to any such opinion. The employer must notify the information and consultation representatives in writing that it is complying with its duty under the legislation.	Either in line with any existing information or consultation agreements, or a negotiated information and consultation agreements or, in default, with appropriate timing. Must be given at such time, in such fashion and with such content as are appropriate to enable, in particular, the information and consultation representatives to conduct an adequate study and, where necessary, to prepare for consultation.

To be disclosed	Disclosure to	Form of disclosure	When
DRAFT REGULATIONS – CONSULTATION BY EMPLOYERS REQUIREMENT (*Occupation and Personal Pension Schemes* (*Consultation by Employers*) *Regulations 2006*)			
For employers with occupational pension schemes, the changes caught by the consultation requirement include: • increasing the normal retirement age; • closing to new members; • stopping accrual of all benefits; • removing an employer's liability to make contributions; • introducing member contributions or increasing them by at least 2%; • changing any final salary benefits to money purchase benefits; • reducing the rate of future accrual of final salary benefits; • Reducing any other future accruals in a final salary scheme; • reducing employer contributions for money purchase benefits by at least 2% or to below 3%. For employers with personal pension schemes, the changes which are caught include: • ceasing employer contributions to a scheme which are payable under direct payment arrangements; • reducing employer contributions by 2% or to a rate of less than 3%; • increasing member contributions by more than 2%.	The employer must embark on a consultation process with one or more of the following: • a trade union representative recognised for collective bargaining purposes; • an elected information and consultation representative (elected under the *Information and Consultation of Employees Regulations 2004 (SI 2004 No 3426)*; or • representatives elected under the pension consultation requirement specifically in relation to the proposed pension changes; • affected members of the pension scheme (which includes employees who are not yet members of the scheme but who are or will become eligible to join). The employer must consult directly with the employee where there are no employee representatives or there is an agreement in place for direct consultation.	Consultation but employer must provide written information about the proposed changes.	At least two months before the change takes effect.

827

To be disclosed	Disclosure to	Form of disclosure	When
	All employees affected by the proposed changes must be consulted except those in: ● public service pension schemes; ● small occupational pension schemes, i e a scheme with fewer than twelve members where all the members are trustees of the scheme and either the rules of the scheme provide that all decisions are made only by the trustees who are members of the scheme by unanimous agreement or the scheme has a trustee who is independent in relation to the scheme for the purposes of *section 23* of *PA 1995* and is registered in the register maintained by the Authority in accordance with regulations; ● an occupational pension scheme with fewer than two members; and		

To be disclosed	Disclosure to	Form of disclosure	When
	• an occupational pension scheme which is an employer-financed retirement benefits scheme. • In employment where the employer has a maximum of 150 employees from 6 April 2006, 100 from 6 April 2007 and 50 from 6 April 2008.		

Notes to Appendix II

[1]   In the *Draft Occupational Pension Schemes* (*Disclosure of Information*) *Regulations 2006* (the '*Draft 2006 Regulations*') the 'Constitution of the Scheme' is also dealt with in *Schedule 1*.

[2]   *Draft 2006 Regulations*. This period will become 'a reasonable period'. The Pensions Regulator consulted on the meaning of 'a reasonable period' in its Code of Practice 'Reasonable periods for the purposes of The Occupational Pension Schemes (Disclosure of Information) Regulations 2006'. The consultation period ended on 2 December 2005.

[3]   The *Draft 2006 Regulations* change this to *Schedule 2* with reference also to *Schedule 3*.

[4]   The *Draft 2006 Regulations* insert 'Member representative organisations'.

[5]   *Draft 2006 Regulations*; *see* n 2 above.

[6]   The *Draft 2006 Regulations* remove this.

[7]   The *Draft 2006 Regulations* remove this and insert that the Scheme's normal pension age should be provided.

[8]   The *Draft 2006 Regulations* remove this reference.

[9]   The *Draft 2006 Regulations* remove this reference.

[10]   *Draft 2006 Regulations*; see n 2 above.

[11]   *Draft 2006 Regulations*.

[12]   *Draft 2006 Regulations*; see n 2 above.

[13]   The *Draft 2006 Regulations* insert that in the case of a trust scheme, the information is to be provided on request to any members' organisation (unless the same information was provided in the twelve months prior to the request being made), as soon as practicable and in any event within a reasonable period of the request being made.

[14]   *Draft 2006 Regulations*.

[15]   *Draft 2006 Regulations*.

[16]   *Draft 2006 Regulations*.

[17]   The *Draft 2006 Regulations* remove '(except simplified defined contribution schemes)'.

[18]   The *Draft 2006 Regulations* remove the text from 'and including' why that method is used)'.

[19]   *Draft 2006 Regulations*: under Benefits no reference is made to the conditions on which benefits are paid.

[20]   *Draft 2006 Regulations*: under Administration, the first six points are removed.

[21]   *Draft 2006 Regulations*; see n 2 above.

[22]   *Draft 2006 Regulations*; see n 2 above.

[23]   The *Draft 2006 Regulations* insert the normal pension age under the scheme.

24 In the *Draft 2006 Regulations* this becomes as of course, annually in relation to any period prior to 6 April 2007 within a reasonable period following the end of each scheme year and for pension credit members on or after 6 April 2007 upon request within a reasonable period from the date the request is received.

25 The *Draft 2006 Regulations* remove 'either (at the trustees' pension age' and places it with 'on his attaining normal pension age, calculated without regard to possible increases in salary'.

26 The *Draft 2006 Regulations* insert 'except in the case of employer-financed retirement benefits'.

27 The *Draft 2006 Regulations* insert that if the trustees so decide, the amounts of his own benefits and of his survivors' benefits which would be payable from normal pension age or death of his pensionable service were to terminate within one month from the date on which information is provided to him.

28 *Draft 2006 Regulations*; and adds the normal pension age under the scheme.

29 The *Draft 2006 Regulations* insert normal benefit age under the scheme.

30 *Draft 2006 Regulations*; see n 2 above.

31 *Draft 2006 Regulations*: 'simplified defined contribution scheme' is changed to 'employer-financed retirement benefits'.

32 *Draft 2006 Regulations*; see n 2 above.

33 *Draft 2006 Regulations*; see n 2 above.

34 *Draft 2006 Regulations*; see n 2 above.

35 *Draft 2006 Regulations*; see n 2 above.

36 *Draft 2006 Regulations*; see n 2 above.

37 *Draft 2006 Regulations*; see n 2 above, further 'as soon as practicable' is removed.

38 *Draft 2006 Regulations*; see n 2 above.

39 In the *Draft 2006 Regulations* reference to this date does not appear.

40 *Draft 2006 Regulations*; see n 2 above, further 'as soon as practicable' is removed.

41 In the *Draft 2006 Regulations* no reference is made to circumstances prior to 6 April 1997.

42 In the *Draft 2006 Regulations* references to 'except excluded persons' have been removed.

43 *Draft 2006 Regulations*; see n 2 above, the reasonable period being from the end of the scheme year.

44 In the *Draft 2006 Regulations* references to 'except excluded persons' have been removed.

45 *Draft 2006 Regulations*; see n 2 above, further 'as soon as practicable is removed'.

46 *Draft 2006 Regulations*; see n 2 above.

47 *Draft 2006 Regulations*; see n 2 above.

48   In the *Draft 2006 Regulations* where the scheme is one to which *Part 3* of
      PA 2004 applies by 22 September 2006:
      - annual funding statement;
      - if no valuation under *section 224* of *PA 2004:*
        - a summary of the funding position of the scheme; and
        - a statement of which options are available to a member on
          request;
      - and within a reasonable period following receipt of request:
        - a statement of funding principles;
        - actuarial valuation of report;
        - a recovery plan; and
        - actuary's certificate.

49   *Draft 2006 Regulations*, becomes *Schedule 4 [however the Draft 2006
      Regulations refer to Schedules 3 and 5, whereas it is Schedule 4 which, in
      fact, deals with information to be included in the annual report].*

50   *Draft 2006 Regulations*, reference to *section 41* of *PA 1995* is removed.

51   *Draft 2006 Regulations*, reference to *section 41* of *PA 1995* is removed.

52   The *Draft 2006 Regulations* insert 'member representative organisa-
      tions'.

53   *Draft 2006 Regulations*; see n 2 above.

54   In the *Draft 2006 Regulations* this section is removed.

55   In the *Draft 2006 Regulations* this is now replaced with 'where the
      scheme is not exempt from the requirement to produce such a valuation'.

56   In the *Draft 2006 Regulations* this is removed.

57   In the *Draft 2006 Regulations* reference to *section 227* of *PA 2004* is
      inserted.

58   *Draft 2006 Regulations*; see n 2 above.

59   In the *Draft 2006 Regulations Schedule 1* is replaced by *Schedule 2,
      sections 9–14 [although the Draft 2006 Regulations only have sec-
      tions 9–11]* and *Schedule 3, sections 15–19.*

60   *Draft 2006 Regulations*; see n 2 above.

61   The *Draft 2006 Regulations* remove this section.

62   In the *Draft 2006 Regulations* there is no reference.

63   *Draft 2006 Regulations*; see n 2 above.

Index

[all references are to paragraph number]